The Method
and
Message of Matthew

Augustine Stock, O.S.B.

A Michael Glazier Book
THE LITURGICAL PRESS
Collegeville, Minnesota

A Michael Glazier Book published by The Liturgical Press

Cover design by David Manahan, O.S.B. *Illustration:* St. Matthew, from the Gospel Book of Ebbo, Bibliothèque Municipale, Épernay.

1   2   3   4   5   6   7   8   9

Library of Congress Cataloging-in-Publication Data

Stock, Augustine.
    The method and message of Matthew / by Augustine Stock.
        p.   cm.
    "A Michael Glazier book."
    Includes bibliographical references and index.
    ISBN 0-8146-5022-8
    1. Bible.   N.T.   Matthew—Criticism, interpretation, etc.
    I. Title.
    BS2575.2.S79   1994
    226.2'077—dc20   93-19236
                                                            CIP

Contents

Abbreviations

Introduction

(1) Narrative Criticism

The dominant mode of biblical studies for more than a century has been the historical-critical method. Through a variety of approaches (source, form, redaction) this method seeks to reconstruct the life and thought of biblical times through an objective, scientific analysis of biblical material. This analysis is meant to shed light upon significant periods in the transmission of the Gospels: the period of the historical Jesus, the period of oral tradition in the early Church, and the period of the final shaping of the Gospels by the evangelists. The accomplishments of historical criticism have been great and are of permanent value. But among historical critics (and others) the conviction arose that something was being left unsaid. It fell to Hans Frei to lay his finger on the trouble. In his *The Eclipse of Biblical Narrative* (1974), Frei asserted that the historical approaches failed to take seriously the narrative character of the Gospels. He emphasized that the gospels "are stories about Jesus, not compilations of miscellaneous data concerning him. They are intended to be read from beginning to end, not dissected and examined to determine the relative value of individual passages. In focusing on the documentary status of these books, the historical-critical method attempted to interpret not the stories themselves but the historical circumstances behind them" (2).

Other questions arose out of this rediscovery. If the Gospels are stories, should they not first be comprehended on their own terms before they are treated as evidence of something else? And if the evangelists are authors, then must they not be studied as other authors are studied? It was out of such questions that Biblical Literary Criticism (Narrative Criticism if it is concerned with stories) arose.

Biblical Narrative Criticism borrows some concepts from secular literary scholarship, such as story and discourse, implied author and implied reader. These concepts will be touched on briefly here and then applied

1

in this work. A fuller explanation can be found in M. Powell, *What Is Narrative Criticism?* (1990).

Much can be learned from noting the major differences between literary criticism and historical criticism:

1. Literary criticism focuses on the finished form of the text. It is not the objective of literary-critical analysis to set forth the process through which a text has come into being but to study the text that now exists. Literary criticism does not deny the findings regarding the development of the text made by source, form, and redaction criticism, but it does ignore them. "Ultimately, it makes no difference for a literary interpretation whether certain portions of the text once existed elsewhere in some other form. The goal of literary criticism is to interpret the current text, in its finished form" (Powell, 7).

2. Literary criticism emphasizes the unity of the text as a whole. Literary analysis does not dissect the text but strives to discern the connecting threads that hold it together. The Gospels are viewed as coherent narratives, and individual passages are interpreted in terms of their contribution to the story as a whole.

3. Literary criticism views the text as an end in itself, while historical criticism treats the text as a means to an end. This end is a reconstruction of something to which the text attests. Historical criticism regards the text as a *window* through which the critic hopes to learn something about another time and place. The immediate goal of a literary study, on the other hand, is to understand the narrative itself—the story that is told and the manner in which it is told. So literary criticism, in contrast, regards the text as a *mirror*; the critic is set upon looking at the text, not through it, and whatever insight is obtained will be found in the encounter of the reader with the text itself.

Literary criticism deals with the *poetic function* of a text. Literary critics are able to appreciate the story of a narrative apart from consideration of the extent to which it reflects reality. Historical criticism, on the other hand, deals with the *referential function* of a text and evaluates everything in terms of historicity.

The objection most frequently made against the use of literary (narrative) criticism in biblical studies is that the method is somehow antihistorical and so undermines the historical grounding of Christian faith. Actually, nothing in the assumptions or presuppositions of narrative criticism calls into question the legitimacy of historical investigation. There is no reason why a text that is examined with regard to its poetic function cannot also be examined by a different method that concentrates on its referential function. "Although the two methods cannot be used simultaneously, they can be used side by side in a supplementary fashion. They might even be viewed as necessary complements, each providing information that is beneficial to the exercise of the other" (Powell, 98).

"By using such methods as source criticism, form criticism, and redaction criticism, scholars have been able to learn about the life and teaching of Jesus of Nazareth and to gain insight into the interests and concerns of the community that produced Matthew's Gospel. In the 1980s, however, the interests of scholarship expanded to include inquiry into the function of Matthew's Gospel as literature." So writes Mark Allan Powell in the fall 1992 issue of *Interpretation*. This issue is the first in a new series on the Gospels—the first since 1975. The number also includes articles by the two other authors most frequently quoted in this book—Jack Dean Kingsbury and David R. Bauer. Powell's article, "Toward a Narrative-Critical Understanding of Matthew," is preceded by this superscription: "A scant decade ago, virtually anyone studying Matthew's Gospel approached it from the standpoint of redaction-critical method. Today, students of Matthew increasingly approach it from the standpoint of narrative-critical method," *Interpretation* 46 (October, 1992) 341.

(2) Parts of Narrative

If Matthew's Gospel is a narrative and Matthew is an author, there is no reason why he cannot be studied in the same way that secular literary criticism studies an author and his work. As narrative (the story of Jesus' life with beginning, middle, and end), Matthew can be studied employing the standard concepts used in narrative theory: story and discourse, real and implied author, narrator and narratee, real and implied reader.

If the "story" of a narrative such as Matthew is "what" is told (the life of Jesus from conception and birth to death and resurrection), the "discourse" is "how" this story is told, the means the author uses in order to put the story across. Each narrative has two parts: a story, the content or chain of events and a discourse, the expression, by which the content is communicated. The story is the *what* in a narrative that is depicted, discourse the *how*. This kind of distinction has been recognized since Aristotle's *Poetics* (cf. Chatman, *Story and Discourse,* 19).

Discourse selects which story elements to incorporate in the narrative and in what order. We can call these two features, common to all narratives, *selection* and *order*. *Selection* is the capacity of any discourse to choose which events and objects actually to state and which only to imply. *Order* refers to the order of the appearance of the events in the work itself. A narrative is a communication, and so presupposes two parties, a sender and a receiver. Each party involves three different personages. On the sending end are the real author, the implied author, and the narrator (if any); on the receiving end, the real audience (listener, reader, viewer), the implied audience, and the narratee.

"The 'real author' of Matthew is the historical person who created this narrative, the one scholars call the first evangelist. In the act of creating this narrative, the first evangelist also created a literary version of himself, a second self, which the reader comes to know through the process of reading the narrative. This second self is the 'implied author'" (J. Kingsbury, *Matthew as Story,* 31).

The phrase "literary version" also appears in Chatman's treatment of the "implied author." The real author creates an implied version of himself as he writes. This entity is "implied," that is, reconstructed by the reader from the narrative. He is not the narrator, but rather the principle that invented the narrator, along with everything else in the narrative. Unlike the narrator, the implied author can *tell* us nothing; he, or better, *it* has no voice, no direct means of communicating. It instructs us silently, through the design of the whole. "We can grasp the notion of implied author most clearly by comparing different narratives written by the same real author but presupposing different implied authors" (Chatman, 148). For example, Henry Fielding was the real author of *Tom Jones, Joseph Andrews* and *Amelia*, but in those three novels he created three clearly different implied authors.

Just as there are three different personages on the sending end of a narrative, so there are three different personages on the receiving end: the real reader, the implied reader, and the narratee. The "real reader" denotes any flesh-and-blood person who has actually heard it or read it, or hears or reads it today. This person may be the Christian of the first century for whom the gospel was originally written or anyone in the twentieth century who takes it to hand. By contrast the term "implied reader" denotes no flesh-and-blood person of any century. It refers rather to an imaginary person who is to be envisaged as responding to Matthew's story at every point with whatever emotion, understanding, or knowledge the text ideally calls for. The implied reader is that imaginary person in whom the intention of the text is to be thought of as always reaching its fulfillment. The implied author is counterpart of the implied reader—not the flesh-and-bones you or I sitting in our living rooms reading the book, but the audience presupposed by the narrative itself. Like the implied author, the implied reader is always present. In one way or another the author imparts to the implied reader the desired audience stance, which *Weltanschauung* to adopt. In so doing, he informs the real reader how to perform as implied reader.

Kingsbury uses these concepts to explain an important aspect of Matthew's Gospel, a phenomenon which we shall call "speaking past." Having fixed the position of the implied author and implied reader in the world of Matthew's narrative, Kingsbury then shows that Jesus at times "speaks past" his contemporary audience and addresses the implied reader directly, in his or her position.

Matthew's narrative world serves as an "index" to Matthew's community (cf. Powell, 97–98). This community of Christians for which Matthew's story was originally written, is best referred to as the "intended readers" of Matthew. The index provides us with an idea about what kind of people they were and what the conditions—social, economic, and religious—in which they lived were (cf. *Story*, 147).

A clue to the place in history of the Matthean community comes from Matthew himself, as implied author. This comes in the form of brief phrases where Matthew breaks the bounds of the story he is telling of Jesus' life and ministry in order to address the implied reader directly. Examples are: "Let the reader understand," 24:15; "to this day." 27:8; and "to this day," 28:15. "Temporally, these passages locate the implied reader at a point after the resurrection but short of the Parousia" (*Story*, 147). This is the time of the messianic woes. From this vantage point, the implied reader oversees the story of the life and ministry of Jesus of Nazareth as Matthew conveys it through his voice as narrator, and he or she can comprehend the whole of this story.

This insight is especially important for understanding the discourses of Jesus. Consider, for example, the missionary discourse in 9:35–10:42. In 10:5-6, Jesus enjoins a mission restricted to Israel. He tells the disciples: "Go nowhere among the Gentiles, and enter no town of the Samaritans, but go rather to the lost sheep of the house of Israel." For the implied reader, this injunction comes as no surprise, because it dovetails neatly with the story of Jesus' ministry to Israel as recounted thus far (4:17, 23; 9:35-36). In 10:17-18, however, Jesus suddenly speaks of a mission that includes Gentiles. He tells the disciples about persecutions that will befall them and that include not only a mission to Israel, but also a mission aimed at Gentiles. "Beware of them, for . . . you will be dragged before governors and kings because of me, as a testimony to them and the Gentiles." For the implied reader, this sudden reference in chapter 10 to a Gentile mission comes unexpectedly.

Still, from another perspective, the movement in the text of chapter 10 is understandable. The perspective in question is the temporal position of the implied reader beyond the resurrection. The movement is from an exclusive mission to Israel (vv. 5–6) to a mission that also includes Gentiles (v. 18). This movement merely parallels the movement within the wider story of Jesus. This movement portrays Jesus, on the one hand, as being sent only to the lost sheep of the house of Israel (15:24) but, on the other hand, as initiating a universal mission to the Gentiles immediately after his resurrection (28:18-20). "From his or her peculiar vantage point beyond the resurrection, the implied reader is fully able to comprehend and to relate to each other, the particularism of 10:5-6 concerning Israel and the universalism of 10:18 concerning the Gentiles" (*Story*, 39). The same saying that causes surprise for the implied reader when he or she approaches it in terms of the flow of Matthew's story is comprehensible and causes no surprise when he or she views it in terms of a special position in the time following the resurrection.

There are other instances in the discourses where Jesus "speaks past" his stipulated audience. The expression "on my account" (5:11) envisages a time when Jesus is no longer physically present; in 6:16-18 fasting is cited as fundamental to proper piety, while 9:14-15 relates that prior to his death Jesus absolves his disciples of any necessity to fast; while 7:15-23 presupposes a situation in which "Christians" who are false prophets are active.

This is one of the curious features of Jesus' great speeches—that they contain sayings that seem to have no relevance for the characters to whom they are addressed, the crowds and the disciples. Time and again, Jesus touches on matters that are alien to the immediate situation of the crowds or the disciples. This peculiar phenomenon—that Jesus speaks past his stipulated audience at places in his speeches—compels one to ask whether Jesus is not to be construed as addressing some person(s) other than simply the crowds or the disciples in the story. From a literary-critical standpoint, he is addressing the implied reader(s).

(3) Structure of Matthew's Gospel

When Matthew's Gospel is read as a narrative (story), narrative critics maintain, a threefold structure emerges. J. Kingsbury, D. Bauer, and M. Powell set up this threefold structure in opposition to the fivefold structure that was followed almost universally at mid-century. B. W. Bacon (*Studies in Matthew*, 1930) was responsible for the basic outline that countless others adopted. His position is that the first Gospel contains five "books" which culminate in discourses of Jesus and are supplemented by preamble (chs. 1-2) and epilogue (chs. 26-28).

In opposition to this fivefold structure Kingsbury, for example, sets a threefold structure. His position is that Matthew is not a collection of discourses but a narrative, the story of Jesus life, with beginning, middle, and end, with the divisions occurring at 4:17 and 16:21. Thus Kingsbury writes: "Contrary to what many scholars have claimed over the years, the great speeches of Jesus do not constitute the climactic feature of Matthew's Gospel nor do they stand apart from the rest of the story being told. On the contrary, each speech can be seen to be appropriately situated within the story's plot" (*Story*, 113). Kingsbury was not the first to advocate a topical outline in three parts with 1:1; 4:17; and 16:21 marking the beginning of each part. N. Neirynck (*ETL* 64 [1988] 21) traces this way of dividing Matthew's gospel back to the nineteenth-century scholar Theodor Keim. Keim's book, *The History of Jesus of Nazara* was first published in German in 1867 and translated into English as early as 1873.

Writing in 1989, Kingsbury (quoting Neirynck) lists eight writers who have incorporated this theory into their writings, extending from W. G. Kuemmel in 1975 to S. Freyne in 1988 (*Structure*, xvi). To these should be added the works of D. Bauer (1988) and M. Powell (1990). The criticism of the fivefold division coming from narrative critics centers upon these points:

1. They find it inappropriate to designate the infancy narratives of Matthew as a "preamble," and the passion and resurrection narratives as an "epilogue." To do this is to place these narratives, two of the main elements in the Gospel, outside the main structure of the Gospel. It is also to overlook both the climactic nature of the cross and resurrection in the Gospel-story and the fact that Matthew is not without a concept of history, as is shown by the genealogy of chapter 1.

2. That there are actually *five* great discourses and hence a Pentateuchal pattern is open to question. Owing to the complete change of setting between chapter 23 and chapters 24–25, to be consistent one can speak of six great discourses or of a "Matthean Hexateuch." Indeed, the logia-character of chapter 11 has prompted A. Farrer (pp. 177–197) to suggest that the first Gospel in reality contains seven great discourses (cf. *Structure*, 4–5).

3. Other Pentateuchal patterns alleged by Bacon are open to question. The fivefold stereotyped formula "And when Jesus finished . . ." found at the end of discourses (chs. 7, 11, 13, 19, 26) does not, as we shall see, serve a structural function. Bacon's division of each of the "books" of Matthew into a narrative section and a discourse section allegedly in accordance with the Pentateuch does not stand. A glance at Genesis, Leviticus, and Numbers shows that they do not admit of any neat division between narrative and legal materials. And as far as the "new Moses" typology is concerned, while Matthew may in instances have permitted this to color his Gospel, it is not so dominant a trait as to render Bacon's proposal credible. An even more extensive criticism of the fivefold structure will be found in Bauer, pp. 32–35.

In rejecting the fivefold division narrative, critics also reject the structural function assigned to the stereotyped formula "Now when Jesus had finished (*kai egeneto hote etelesen ho Iēsous* (7:28; 11:1; 13:53; 19:1; 26,1) in Bacon's outline. The formula cannot be pressed thematically, and neither literarily nor theologically is there sufficient cause for regarding it as the principle by which the Gospel is to be organized into five parts with prologue and epilogue.

Yet the formula does have functions within the narrative. It serves to signal the termination of five discourses. With its emphasis on finishing, the formula necessarily points in each case to the discourse preceding it. It calls attention to Jesus, the Messiah, whose words have the status of divine revelation; and it points beyond itself to Matthew's concept of the history of salvation. Both directly and indirectly the fivefold formula imparts a sense of *historical movement*. Directly, by making reference to Jesus as "finishing" any given discourse; and indirectly, by preparing for or modifying clauses that record that Jesus "come down from the mountain" (8:1) or "went on from there" (11:1) or "left that place" (13:53; 19:1) or "spoke" anew to the disciples (26:1). Ultimately this emphasis on historical movement is seen to form part of Matthew's concept of the history of salvation.

It is the position of Kingsbury and like-minded critics, that Matthew's narrative, the story of the life of Jesus, unfolds in three broad segments. To signal the beginning of Part II and Part III, Matthew employs a formulaic phrase: "From that time on Jesus began to preach (to show his disciples . . ." 4:17; 16:21). Each time this formula occurs, it introduces a new phase in the ministry of Jesus. Each of the verses in which the formula is embedded stands apart from its context and sounds the theme that Matthew subsequently develops in Parts II and III.

Hence, if one construes these verses, and 1:1 as well, as "headings" and presses them thematically, this broad outline of Matthew's story emerges: (I) The Figure of Jesus Messiah (1:1–4:16); (II) The Ministry of Jesus Messiah to Israel and Israel's Repudiation of Jesus (4:17–16:20); and (III) The Journey of Jesus Messiah to Jerusalem and his Suffering, Death, and Resurrection (16:21–28:20). This outline suggests that Matthew tells the story of the life of Jesus first by presenting him to the implied reader and then by describing, respectively, his public ministry to Israel and his journey to Jerusalem where he suffers, dies, and is raised.

Each of the three main parts has a culminating scene. In all of them Jesus is portrayed as the Messiah, the Son of God. Thus, in Part I, the culminating scene is Jesus' baptism in the Jordan. There God himself declares that Jesus is his unique son (3:13-17). In Part II, at Caesarea Philippi, Peter declares on behalf of the disciples that Jesus is the Messiah, the Son of the living God (16:16-20). In Part III, the exalted Jesus, on the mountain in Galilee, refers to himself as "the Son"—"Go therefore and make disciples of all nations baptizing them in the name of the Father and of the Son and of the Holy Spirit'' (28:19).

Strung along these sections of narrative are various core elements which serve as signposts. These elements are: (1) Five *discourses*, which are found in chapters 5-7, 10, 13, 18, and 24, called respectively, the Sermon on the Mount (5-7), the Missionary Discourse (10), the Parable Discourse (13), the Ecclesiological Discourse (18), and the Eschatological Discourse (24); (2) *Summary Statements*, concentrated in the first half of Part II; (3) lastly, three *Passion Predictions*, all Part III.

4) The Sacred Canopy

In his *Matthew's Gospel and Formative Judaism* (1990), J. Andrew Overman illuminates several aspects of Matthew's Gospel by bringing it into conjunction with Peter L. Berger's sociological theory of religion. One such aspect is the concept of "On earth as it is in heaven" (cf. Berger's *The Sacred Canopy. The Elements of a Sociological Theory of Religion*).

The Matthean community understands itself as the reflection of the kingdom which is in heaven. Its reality has become closely identified with the ultimate reality of the kingdom of heaven. There is a parallel between the behavior and the will of the Matthean community and the will of God in the kingdom of heaven. The social structure and cosmic structure have developed along the lines of "microcosm" and "macrocosm." The community understands itself as living out the order, structures, and values of the sacred cosmos (cf. Overman, 31).

Such is the "Sacred Canopy." But what line of thought led Berger to this conclusion? Berger begins his text with the assertion that every human society is an enterprise of world-building and that religion occupies a distinctive place in this enterprise (cf. p. 3). Accordingly, his first chapter is entitled: "Religion and World-Construction" and his second "Religion and World-maintenance." *Homo sapiens*, says Berger, occupies a peculiar position in the animal kingdom. Unlike other higher mammals, who are born as essentially completed organisms, man is curiously "unfinished" at birth. Essential steps in the process of "finishing" man's development which take place in the fetal period for the other higher mammals, occur in the first year after birth in the case of man (4).

The "unfinished" character of the human organism at birth is closely related to the unspecialized character of its instinctual structure. The non-human animal enters the world with highly specialized and firmly directed drives. As a result, it lives in a world that is more or less completely determined by its instinctual structure. By contrast, man's instinctual structure at birth is both underspecialized and undirected toward a specific environment.

The world into which the human is born is not simply given, prefabricated; he or she must *make* a world through culture. The fundamental purpose of culture is to provide structures which humans lack biologically. These humanly-produced structures can never have the stability that marks the structures of the animal world. Culture must be continuously produced and reproduced. "While it is necessary that worlds be built, it is quite difficult to keep them going" (Berger, 6.)

The difficulty of keeping a world going manifests itself psychologically in the difficulty of keeping this world subjectively plausible. The world is built up by conversation with significant others and is maintained as subjective reality by the same sort of conversation. Religion is the human enterprise by which a sacred cosmos is established and maintained.

> Religion legitimates social institutions by bestowing upon them an ultimately valid ontological status, that is, by locating them within a sacred and cosmic frame of reference. The historical constructions of human activity are viewed from a vantage point that, in its own self-definition, transcends both history and man. This can be done in different ways. Probably the most ancient form of this legitimation is the conception of the institutional order as directly reflecting or manifesting the divine structure of the cosmos, that is, the conception of the relationship between society and cosmos as one between microcosm and macrocosm. Everything "here below" has its analogue "up above." By participating in the institutional order men, *ipso facto*, participate in the divine cosmos. The kinship structure, for example, extends beyond the human realm, with all being (including the being of the gods) conceived of in the structures of kinship as given in the society.
>
> *The Sacred Canopy*, 34.

(5) Sectarian Language and Procedures

Any contemporary reader of Matthew's Gospel is sure to be surprised, if not shocked, by the abundance of vituperative inflammatory language found there. There is one whole chapter of "Woes" ("Woe to you scribes and Pharisees, hypocrites,!" ch. 23). Also, an extensive section of chapter 5 is given over to Antitheses ("You have heard . . . but I say to you"), while a drumbeat of vituperation against the Jewish leaders runs throughout the Gospel.

Jesus is the protagonist of Matthew's story, and the religious leaders, as his principal opponents in the human realm, are the antagonists. Except for Jesus himself, they are the ones in Matthew's story who most influence the development of the plot. Although they go by many names—Pharisees, Sadducees, chief priests, leaders, scribes, and Herodians—they form a united front against Jesus and hence can be treated as a single character. These people are "flat" and not "round" characters because Matthew presents their traits as offshoots of one "root trait," namely, "evilness." "Accordingly, the picture the reader gets of the religious leaders in Matthew's story is not historically objective but wholly negative and polemical" (*Story*, 115). The religious leaders are a "brood of vipers"—lawless hypocrites who shed innocent blood.

Is there any explanation for this use of vituperative language? This is the problem that J. Andrew Overman deals with in his *Matthew's Gospel and Formative Judaism, The Social World of the Matthean Community.* Overman's principal source is Peter L. Berger's *The Sacred Canopy. Elements of a Sociological Theory of Religion* (cf. *Current Biography*, 1983).

Quoting Max Weber, Overman appeals to sociological necessity to explain the vituperative language:

> Matthew's community, like any other, was confronted with the task of explaining the experiences and convictions of the community to ensuing members as well as developing structures and procedures that would help protect it from alien forces and beliefs. . . .
>
> The nature and shape of a community owe much to the social forces and dynamics which surround that community. It is the problems and issues of day-to-day life in any given community that more than anything else provoke and shape its social development and transformation. The roles, patterns of behavior, and the institutions emerging within a community will to a large degree be in response to the questions and struggles the community must regularly face. Such is the case with Matthew's community.
>
> Overman, 1.

The factor which most profoundly influenced the development of Matthew's community was the competition with so-called formative Judaism—a group which, like the Matthean community, was involved in a process of social construction and definition. Both communities were in the process of *becoming*.

Christianity and Judaism, it has been said, are "fraternal twins." These movements share the same historical matrix and often defined themselves in opposition to one another. If that is true of Christianity and Judaism generally, it is all the more true where Matthew's Gospel and formative Judaism are concerned. In Matthew's Gospel we encounter a Jewish community, which claims to follow Jesus the Messiah, discovering that they are now different from the dominant form of Judaism in their setting. The defensive posture of the Gospel and strident attacks on the Jewish authorities, represented in Matthew by "the scribes and Pharisees," express the emotions of a family "falling apart."

The term *sectarian* describes "a group which is, or perceives itself to be, a minority in relation to the group it understands to be the 'parent body.' The sect is a minority in that it is subject to, and usually persecuted by, the group in power. The dissenting group is in opposition to the parent body and tends to claim more or less to be what the dominant body claims to be" (Overman, 8). This is best exemplified by the the period 165–100 B.C. in Jewish history—the time of the Hasmoneans from Judas Macabbaeus to the revolt against Alexander Jannaeus, which led to the intervention of Rome. This was a period of fragmentation and factionalism—the Judaism of this period was sectarian in nature.

The three sects of this period of Jewish history were: the Dead Sea community (Qumran), the Sadducees, and the Pharisees. The later two groups took turns being "parent body" and "sect" depending on which body enjoyed the favor of the Hasmonean rulers. The Dead Sea community, on the other hand, in a self-imposed exile, denounced the Jerusalem leadership in the bitterest of terms and anticipated its vindication by God through a holy war. The community's faithfulness would be rewarded, and the apostasy of the majority of Israel, the priests and religious leadership in particular, would be punished.

1 Enoch, a document which dates from approximately the same period as the Qumran writings, is interesting because of the characteristics it shares with Matthew's Gospel. Those who are in power are corrupt and faithless and will soon be judged. The author describes them as "sinners," who commit idolatry, blaspheme, and curse. They oppress the righteous and just; they bear false witness in order to persecute the righteous; they coerce the righteous with their power and pervert the law for their own evil purposes.

A community that finds itself cast in the role of *sect* usually tries to imitate the methods that led to the parent body's success. Thus we find Matthew replicating the teaching office of the Jewish *rabbi* in his version of the Christian disciple. Or the sect can react with *vituperation*, bitterly denouncing the parent body; this is what gives rise to the "language of sectarianism."

The struggle between the sectarian communities and those in power was cast in stark terms. The members of the community were righteous, just, faithful to God, and sure to be vindicated by God. Those in the parent group, on the other hand, were corrupt lawbreakers who were far from God, oppressed God's people, and would have no share in the world to come. The attitudes and actions of those in power are frequently described as hypocritical, self-serving, and deceptive.

The use of inflammatory language is usually indicative of a speaker who belongs to a minority group. The sectarian communities of this period felt persecuted. They did not possess political power. They believed that those in power, the parent body, were corrupt and false leaders. The highly charged language employed by these communities reveals the frustration and anger they felt toward those in power. This language highlights the caustic setting and the sectarian background out of which both formative Judaism and Matthean Judaism came. Matthew freely adopts this language and employs it in his struggle to legitimate the position of his community in the face of the influence of formative Judaism.

Most of this hostility was directed against the Jewish leaders and a number of the symbols used to express this hostility also appear in Matthew's Gospel. Three of these are: the keys of the temple, tearing of the temple veil, and the shedding of innocent blood. According to circumstances, the Jewish leaders could be the priests in the Jerusalem temple (Qumran), leaders of the Hasmonean empire (1 Enoch), or people allied with the Romans or local leaders who had gained power (Matthew).

Thus, the *keys of the temple* become a symbol in the post-70 A.D. period for the failure of the priests and religious leaders to be faithful and to execute their duties properly. In the lamentation over the destruction of the temple in 2 Baruch (Syriac Apocalypse of Baruch) 10:18, the priests are ordered to take the keys of the sanctuary and to cast them up to heaven, "because behold, we have been found to be false stewards." The priests ask God to "guard your house yourself." In Matthew's Gospel, after Peter makes his confession, Jesus says to him, "I will give you the keys of the kingdom of heaven" (16:19). This text is intimately bound up with our next topic, the sacred canopy. For Jesus goes on to say: "And whatever you bind on earth shall be bound in heaven, and whatever you loose on earth shall be loosed in heaven."

A second symbol of hostility toward Jewish leaders was the *tearing of the temple veil*. This symbol expresses the conviction common in the sectarian documents that Jerusalem is a corrupt and sinful place, which springs out of hostility toward the Jewish leadership. "The tearing of the temple veil" is described in Testament of Levi 10:3 to draw attention to the shameful behavior of the priests behind the veil. They profane the priesthood, defile the altars of the sanctuary, set aside the law, and nullify the words of the prophets with their perversity. The Jewish leaders, specifically those associated with the temple, were viewed in many circles in the post-70 period as corrupt and faithless. The leaders "twist the law for their own purposes, they are hypocrites who . . . have profaned the sanctuary and the offerings with their lawless acts. They break their oaths and contracts and no longer act on God's behalf. The worst possible fate is wished upon these false leaders" (Overman, 22). In Matthew's Gospel, the death of Jesus on the cross is followed by the assertion: "And behold, the curtain of the temple as torn in two, from top to bottom" (27:51).

A third symbol of hostility toward the Jewish leaders was the *Shedding of innocent blood*. 2 Baruch 64:2 connects the wickedness of Manasseh ("he killed the righteous and shed innocent blood") with the action of the Jewish leaders. The sectarians have been oppressed by those in control. They interpret their rejection and persecution in terms of Israel's prophetic history and the fabled persecution of the righteous at the hands of corrupt leaders. These sectarian communities claim an association with the prophets of old, who were by this time widely recognized as righteous persons and agents of God who were unjustly persecuted by corrupt leaders. In developing this theme these communities have begun to align themselves with some of the heroic underdogs of Israel's history. At the same time the Jewish leaders are being associated with some of the storied villains of the same history.

The Matthean community fits easily into this world and reflects much of the same hostility toward the Jewish leadership. It is within this milieu and context that Matthew's Gospel must be read and understood. Matthew had to contend with opponents from without, the Jewish leaders and those who had gained authority in this community. But there are also parts of his Gospel which make it clear that he had to contend with opponents from within. Avoiding or resolving conflict within the community emerges as a pronounced theme of the Sermon on the Mount (cf. 7:1-5). The members of the Matthean community are "peacemakers" (5:9). They are not to insult each other (5:22) but are to be reconciled to one another (5:24). They are to offer the left cheek to those who slap them on the right (5:39) and to love friends and enemies alike (5:43-44). All this suggests a situation of tension and struggle within the community.

Matthew applies the term *anomia* to anyone who deviates from the will of God or fails to produce "good fruit" (see 7:17; 12:33; 21:43). For this reason, both the enthusiastic prophets of 7:15-17 and the scribes and Pharisees can be called *anomia* (7:23; 23:38). These groups could not be more different in terms of makeup and practice; however, they both receive the epithet "lawless" because of their corruption of the law and the will of God. "Lawless," then, does not refer to a specific group within the Matthean community which is creating tension; it is the preferred Matthean term for anyone who does not accurately understand God's law and will or corrupts it. This is a term—more importantly, a sentiment—Matthew shares with other sectarian groups in the late first century. Matthew's use of this term tells us much more about him and his community than it does about the people or group that is causing dissension.

Bibliography

Achtemeier, P., ed. *Harper's Bible Dictionary.* (San Francisco: Harper & Row, 1985).

Bacon, B. W. *Studies in Matthew.* (London: Constable, 1930).

Beare, F. *The Gospel according to Matthew.* (New York: Harper & Row, 1981).

Berger, P. L. *The Sacred Canopy, The Elements of a Sociological Theory of Religion.* (Garden City: Doubleday, 1969).

Brown, R. *The Birth of the Messiah.* (Garden City: Doubleday, 1977).

Chatman, E. *Story and Discourse: Narrative Structure in Fiction and Film.* (Ithaca: Cornell University Press, 1978).

Daube, D. *The New Testament and Rabbinic Judaism.* (New York: Arno Press, 1956).

Davies, W. D. and Allison, D. *The Gospel according to Saint Matthew.* International Critical Comentary. (Edinburgh: T & T Clark, Vol. 1, 1988; Vol. 2, 1991).

Derrett, J.D.M. *Law in the New Testament.* (New York: Fernhill House, 1970).

Farrer, A. *St Matthew and St Mark.* (London: Dacre, 1954).

Fenton, J. *The Gospel of St Matthew.* Pelican Gospel Commentaries. (Baltimore: Penguin Books, 1863).

Frei, H. *The Eclipse of Biblical Narrative.* (New Haven: Yale Uiversity Press, 1974).

Garland, E. *The Intention of Matthew 23.* (Leiden: Brill, 1979).

Gerhardsson, B. *Memory and Manuscript. Oral Tradition and Written Transmission in Rabbinic Judaism and Early Christianity.* (Lund: Gleerup, l961).

_____. *The Origins of the Gospel Traditions.* (Philadelhia; Fortress, 1979).

_____. *The Testing of God's Son (Matt 4:1811 and Par).* (Lund: Gleerup, 1966).

Gnilka, J. *Das Matthaus-evangelium.* HTKNT. (Freiburg: Herder, Vol. 1. 1986; Vol. 2, 1988).

Goulder, J. *Midrash and Lection in Matthew.* (Naperville, Ill.: Allenson, l974).

Guelich, R. *The Sermon on the Mount.* (Waco: Word Books, 1982).

Gundry, R. *Matthew, A Commentary on his Literary and Theological Art.* (Grand Rapids: Eerdmans, 1982).

Heil, J.P. *The Death and Resurrection of Jesus.* (Minneapolis: Fortress 1991).

_____. *Jesus Walking on the Sea.* Analecta Biblica 87. (Rome: Biblical Institute Press, 1981).

Hill, D. *The Gospel of Matthew.* New Century Bible Commentary. (Grand Rapids: Eerdmans, 1972).

Jeremias, J. *The Parables of Jesus.* (New York: Scribner, 1972).

Keim, T. *The History of Jesus of Nazara.* (London: Williams and Norgate, 1876).

Kingsbury, J. *Matthew.* Proclamation Commentaries. (Philadelphia: Fortress, 1986).

_____. *Matthew as Story.* (Philadelphia: Fortress, 1988).

_____. *Matthew: Structure, Christology, Kingdom.* (Philadeliphia: Fortress, 1989).

_____. *The Parables of Jesus in Matthew 13, A Study in Redaction-Criticism.* (London and St. Louis: SPCK and Clayton Publishing House, 1969).

Limbeck, J. *Mathaus-Evangelium.* (Stuttgart: Katholisches Bibelwerk, 1986).

Louw, J. and Nida, E., *Greek-English Lexicon of the New Testament.* Two vols. (New York: United Bible Society, 1988).

Luz, U. *Das Evangelium nach Matthaus.* EKK. (Zurich/Neukirchen-Vluyn: Benziger/Neukirchener, Vol. 1, l985; Vol. 2, 1990).

_____. *Matthew 1-7, A Commentary.* (Minneapolis: Augsburg, 1989).

Overman, J. *Matthew's Gospel and Formative Judaism. The Social World of the Matthean Community.* (Minneapolis: Fortress, 1990).

Powell, M. *What Is Narrative Criticism?* (Minneapolis: Fortress, 1990).

Saldarini, A. *Pharisees, Scribes and Sadducees in Palestinian Society.* (Wilmington: Michael Glazier, 1988).

Sand, A. *Das Evangelium nach Matthaus.* (Regensburg: Pustet, 1986).

Schweizer, E. *The Good News according to Matthew.* (Atlanta: John Knox, 1975).

Senior, D. *The Passion of Jesus in the Gospel of Matthew.* (Wilmington: Michael Glazier, 1985).

Stendahl, K. *The School of St. Matthew.* (Philadelphia: Fortress, 1968).

Stock, A. *The Way in the Wilderness.* (Collegeville: The Liturgical Press, 1968).

Thompson, W. *Matthew's Advice to a Divided Community: Mt. 17, 22—18, 35.* AnBib 44. (Rome: Biblical Institute Press, 1970).

Zerwick, M. and Grosvenor, M. *A Grammatical Analysis of the New Testament.* (Rome: Biblical Institute Press, 1981).

Part I:
The Figure of Jesus Messiah (1:1–4:16)

Matthew's Gospel falls into three broad segments (cf. Introduction, pp. 6–9). In the first (1:1–4:16), Jesus Messiah Son of God is presented to the implied reader; in the second (4:17–16:20), his public ministry is described; in the third (16:21–28:20), his journey to Jerusalem, his passion, death, and resurrection. Each segment climaxes in an affirmation that Jesus Messiah is the Son of God. "The structural features that point to Jesus as the Son of God . . . indicate that christology is the central concern of Matthew's gospel" (Bauer, 145).

The first segment, which presents the Figure of Jesus, climaxes in the baptism scene, when the voice from heaven declares: "This is my beloved Son" (3:17). In this segment, the genealogy and the infancy narrative are followed in chapter 3 by the public ministry of John the Baptist. Because of the difference between these two elements, chapters 1–2 have often been seen as standing apart from the rest of the Gospel and have been construed as its prologue. The commentary on 1:1–4:16 will show that Chapters 1–2 and Chapters 3–4 deserve to be regarded as a single unit, the first broad segment of the Gospel.

THE PREHISTORY, 1:1–2:23

The prehistory of the Gospel of Matthew concentrates on the person of Jesus Messiah. By means of the genealogy, chapter 1 informs the reader that Jesus is indeed to be the Messiah. He is the "Son of Abraham," for God has directed the whole of Israelite history to the end that it might issue climactically in him (vv. 11–17). He is the "Son of David," for Joseph son of David gives him his name, adopting him (1:1, 16, 20, 25). But above all, he is the "Son of God," for he is conceived "by (ek) the Holy Spirit"

(1:18, 20). Through the prophet, God himself says that Jesus will be called "Emmanuel" (1:23), a name that attests that his origin is in God and that in him God dwells with his own.

Chapter 2 continues to treat of the person of Jesus; it asserts that the messianic King who will shepherd the people of God is in reality the Son of God. From verse 7 on, Matthew consistently designates Jesus as "the child" (*to paidion*). But in verse 15, he breaks this pattern and in this way explains how he would further define this term. "The child" Jesus is in fact "my Son," the Son of God. Like Moses, he escapes death at the hands of an evil sovereign and finds refuge in a foreign land. Upon the death of his adversary, he returns to his homeland.

Both Matthew and Luke devote—independently of each other—the first two chapters of their Gospels to describing and commenting on "happenings," which seek to explain the "beginning" of Jesus—his origin, his coming to be. These are not childhood "happenings" in the usual sense, so Luke has placed the genealogy of Jesus in the context of Jesus' baptism (3:23-38). The independence of the two evangelists is evident from factual differences and especially from the length of their respective narratives. Without prologue, Luke's infancy narrative has 128 verses, Matthew's 48 verses. Inserted hymns (Magnificat 1:46-55; Benedictus 1:68-79; Gloria in excelsis 2:14; Nunc dimittis 2:29-32) account for Luke's greater length.

In addition to the differences in length and explanation of origin between the two Gospels, it is important to note that Matthew and Luke report very different events. None of the scenes related by Matthew are found in Luke (and vice versa) and even the genealogies are at odds. There are also noticeable differences regarding the literary characters. While Luke, for the most part, narrates in a friendly tone, the picture sketched by Matthew is a darker one. From the start, Jesus is the persecuted one and the Messiah not received by the leaders of Israel. Even the magi pericope cannot dispel this impression, serving as it does as the background against which the negative elements take on an even sharper contour. The idea that Luke wrote his infancy narrative from the standpoint of Mary, while Matthew wrote his from the standpoint of Joseph can hardly be sustained. The child is in the middle in both traditions. Joseph and Mary were chosen by both evangelists to be the persons with whose "help" the theological conception connected with the child can be expressed. Both genealogies are genealogies of Jesus, running through the person of Joseph. Everything that is said about Joseph has meaning only insofar as it involves Mary's child.

But, despite the differences cited, we must not overlook the points that the two accounts have in common. Jesus was born in the time of Herod;

Bethlehem in Judea is designated as his birthplace; his mother is named Mary; Joseph is Mary's husband but not the father of Jesus; the family established a home in Galilee. These few biographical details have their origin in a pre-synoptic tradition. But Matthew did not write to confirm this historical substratum, but to further the theological goal he had set for himself and his community.

Genealogy: Jesus Messiah, Son of David, Son of Abraham
1:1-17

In prefixing a genealogy to his work, Matthew's purpose was to assert that God had guided history so that it might culminate in the birth of "Jesus," who is "Messiah," "Son of David," and "Son of Abraham." This is an initial evaluative point of view concerning Jesus' identity which Matthew advances in his role as narrator. The "narrator" is the voice, or invisible speaker, the reader hears as he or she moves through the story, the one who tells the reader the story. It is the narrator, for example, who intones the first words, "The book of the genealogy of Jesus Christ, the Son of David, the Son of Abraham."

By making the reader the recipient of inside information, Matthew places him or her in the privileged position of being better informed than the characters in the story. The reader knows far in advance of any human character that Jesus is Israel's Davidic Messiah, God's Son. The genealogy is an example of narrative commentary.

> **1** An account of the genealogy of Jesus the Messiah, the son of David, the son of Abraham. **2** Abraham was the father of Isaac, and Isaac the father of Jacob, and Jacob the father of Judah and his brothers, **3** and Judah the father of Perez and Zerah by Tamar, and Perez the father of Hezron, and Hezron the father of Aram, **4** and Aram the father of Aminadab, and Aminadab the father of Nahson, and Nahson the father of Salmon, **5** and Salmon the father of Boaz by Rahab, and Boaz the father of Obed by Ruth, and Obed the father of Jesse, **6** and Jesse the father of King David.
>
> And David was the father of Solomon by the wife of Uriah, **7** and Solomon the father of Rehoboam, and Rehoboam the father of Abijah, and Abijah the father of Asaph, **8** and Asaph the father of Jehoshaphat, and Jehoshaphat the father of Joram, and Joram the father of Uzziah, **9** and Uzziah the father of Jotham, and Jotham the father of Ahaz, and Ahaz the father of Hezekiah, **10** and Hezekiah the father of Amos, and

Amos the father of Josiah, **11** and Josiah the father of Jechoniah and his brothers, at the time of the deportation to Babylon.

12 And after the deportation to Babylon: Jechoniah was the father of Salathiel, and Salathiel the father of Zerubbabel, **13** and Zerubbabel the father of Abiud, and Abiud the father of Eliakim, and Eliakim the father of Azor, **14** and Azor the father of Zadok, and Zadok the father of Achim, and Achim the father of Eliud, **15** and Eliud the father of Eleazar, and Eleazar the father of Mathan, and Mathan the father of Jacob, **16** and Jacob the father of Joseph the husband of Mary, of whom Jesus was born, who is called the Messiah.

17 So all the generations from Abraham to David are fourteen generations; and from David to the deportation to Babylon, fourteen generations; and from the deportation to Babylon to the Messiah, fourteen generations.

Ancient Semitic genealogies served different purposes and only rarely and to a limited degree did they afford a list of strictly biological ancestry. This does not necessarily make them inaccurate, since the intention of those who preserved them was not strictly biological. This is seen most clearly in the fact that an individual could be accorded two or more different genealogies according to the purpose for which they were drawn up—to prove identity as a member of the tribe, to undergird status, to structure history into epochs. There are some two dozen genealogical lists in the Old Testament and two in the New Testament.

In his genealogy, Matthew makes a statement about Jesus' identity. Jesus is the Messiah because he is the Anointed One, Israel's long-awaited King (vv. 17; 2:2, 4). He is the Son of David because Joseph adopts him into the line of David (vv. 16, 18–25) and he fulfills the eschatological expectations associated with David. He is the Son of Abraham because in him the entire history of Israel attained its culmination and the Gentiles, too, find blessing (v. 17). The genealogy asserts God's direct control of Israel's history and sets forth in the listing of Jesus' forebears an initial evaluative point of view concerning his identity.

Verse 1: "An account of the genealogy (*Biblos geneseos* LN 33.38; 10.24) of Jesus the Messiah." In using this expression, Matthew echoes such Old Testament passages as Genesis 2:4 and 5:1 (LXX). The closest of these in wording to verse 1 is that of Genesis 5:1: "This is the list of the descendants (*biblos geneseos*) of Adam," a formula that introduces the Noah story, as Matthew's formula introduces the Jesus story. These passages are introductions to genealogies which bear witness to God's governance of human history. Taken in conjunction with the interpretive clues provided by verse 17, the message of the genealogy is clear—the whole of Israel's history has been guided by God so that the promises made to Abraham and king David have been fulfilled in the coming of the heir of Abraham and David, namely, the Messiah. Jesus is "the Messiah," "the son of David," and "the son of Abraham." While Jesus is preeminently "Son of God," Matthew makes no mention of this here, perhaps because the genealogy begins not with God and Adam (Luke 3:38), but with Abraham.

Genesis gives us the leitmotif of the passage: the related verbal form is used throughout the list, and the noun "generation," appears in the summary statement at the end (v. 17). The reuse of *genesis* in verse 18 shows that Matthew is thinking here of the birth of Jesus. Matthew rules out using the term *genesis* to cover the whole Gospel, which would then have to be understood as "the book of the origins of Jesus Christ" (cf. *Structure,* 10).

Verse 1 does not belong to the genealogy or the infancy narratives alone, nor is it the title to the entire Gospel. Rather, it serves as a superscription for the first broad segment of the Gospel, 1:1–4:16 (cf. Bauer, 73–78). Like the other two superscriptions, it is particularized and reaches a climax in the segment as a whole. "Messiah," "the son of David," and "the son of Abraham" are all taken up in the narrative materials.

While the genealogy in Genesis 5 leads from Adam to Noah (the genealogy of Adam is a genealogy of his descendants), the genealogy of Jesus is a genealogy of his ancestors. "In Christian salvific history there can be no genealogy of Jesus' descendants because history has reached its goal in Jesus" (R. Brown, *Birth*, 67).

"The genealogy of *Jesus*." "Jesus" is the personal name of the protagonist of Matthew's story. Although Joseph is the one who gives Jesus his name (v. 25), he does so on instructions from the angel of the Lord (v. 20). Ultimately, therefore, God himself is the source of Jesus' name. "Jesus" denotes that "God [is] salvation," and the angel touches on this as he tells Joseph that Jesus "will *save* his people from their sins" (v. 21). Accordingly, the force of the name "Jesus" is that in the one so called, God is active to save.

"Jesus" occurs no fewer than 150 times in Matthew's story, yet human characters never make use of it in direct address to Jesus. "Jesus" is the name Matthew as narrator reserves for his own use. This forges the closest possible association between himself as narrator and Jesus. Matthew's evaluative point of view coincides with that of Jesus, and both he and Jesus will reliably advocate God's evaluative point of view.

"Genealogy of Jesus *the Messiah*." Here the Greek term *christos* ("Anointed One," "Christ," "Messiah") is both a personal name ("Jesus *Christ*") and a title ("Jesus [who is] "Messiah"). "Among the major titles ascribed to Jesus in Matthew's story *christos* is the most general. This explains why one must always look to the context, immediate or wider, in order to know how to construe it" (*Story*, 46). In 1:1, *christos* is interpreted in terms of "the son of David" and "the son of Abraham;" elsewhere it is interpreted in terms of the "Coming One," "King of the Jews," and "Son of God." In Matthew's Gospel, *christos* summarily characterizes Jesus as God's Anointed, the King and Shepherd of Israel (2:2, 4, 6).

"Jesus . . . the *son of David*." Matthew goes to some lengths to show not only "that" but also "how" Jesus can legitimately be designated as the "Son of David" (cf. v. 16). The title Son of David has a special relationship to healing (cf. 9:27; *Matthew*, 58-60); "Jesus . . . the *son of Abraham*"—both because it is in him that the entire history of Israel, which had its beginning in Abraham, attains its goal (v. 17) and because he is the one through whom God will extend his blessing of salvation to the nations (8:11; 28:18-20). If his genealogy had gone back to Adam and God, Matthew might well have introduced the title Son of God here.

As in the case of "the Messiah," and "the son of David," the title "the son of Abraham" in verse 1 is also expanded throughout 1:1-4:16. This reference to "the son of Abraham" anticipates the universalism of the Gospel. Abraham and David are singled out in the genealogy because they received promises of progeny in the Old Testament. One of the functions of the Gentile women in this genealogy from Abraham is to point to the universalism which would come in Christ, "the son of Abraham." Matthew's proclivity for bracketing the Gospel with common themes at the beginning and end suggests that "the son of Abraham" corresponds to the universal missionary charge of 28:18-20.

Verses 2-6a: "Abraham was the father of . . . David." The formula "A begot B: B begot C" is a standard one in Old Testament genealogies (cf. Ruth 4:18-22 and 1 Chr 2:10-15), the Old Testament genealogies which are closest to the first, pre-Davidic section of Matthew's record. In this first section of the genealogy, there are fourteen names and thus implicitly fourteen generations. This set the pattern for Matthew's entire Gospel.

Matthew made some changes in his source, especially by adding the names of the women, Tamar, Rahab, and Ruth (cf. v. 17). In his Gospel, Jesus' ministry has a particularly Jewish aura (concentration on Israel, attitude toward the Law, unexplained Jewish terms). This unmistakable Jewishness favors the thesis that Matthew wrote with a sizable Jewish-Christian audience in mind. At the same time, the attitude he takes toward the mission to the nations shows that he also wrote with a view to intended Gentile readers. In Matthew there are no traces of the fierce controversy surrounding the Gentile mission which are so prominent in Paul. The presence of four non-Israelite women in Jesus' genealogy ("Tamar,"

"Rahab," "Ruth," and "the wife of Uriah" [Bathsheba]; 1:3, 5-6) also points in this direction, as does the adoration of the Magi, and Jesus' settlement in the "Galilee of the Gentiles." The element of scandal is also important in connection with the four women (cf. v. 16).

Verses 6b–11: "David . . . deportation (LN 85.83) to Babylon." The second section of the genealogy covering the monarchical period was a popular genealogy of the Royal House of David, containing the names of the kings who ruled in Judah. This list was dependent on Old Testament information, but its circulation in a popular, rather than an archival context is suggested by its errors and omissions, probably stemming from confusing similarities in the Greek forms of the royal names. In this section Matthew adds the name of "Uriah's wife."

Verses 12–16: "Deportation (LN 85,83) to Babylon . . . Christ." The third section of the genealogy adds the names from some generations of the descendants of Zerubbabel, i.e., the post-exilic Davidic scions. Matthew noticed that in the shortened monarchical section there were again fourteen generations, while in the post-exilic section a pattern of fourteen names emerged if one added Joseph and Jesus. Matthew advances a 3 x 14 pattern as the key to God's plan of salvation. In this third section Matthew adds Mary's name to the list of women.

Verse 16: "The husband of Mary, of whom (*ex hēs*) Jesus was born." In recounting this final link of the genealogy, Matthew permits it to be "broken." Instead of stating, in line with the pattern he has established, ". . . and Jacob fathered Joseph, and Joseph fathered Jesus," he states, ". . . and Jacob fathered *Joseph the husband of Mary, of whom* (fem.) *Jesus was born*" (1:16). The problem Matthew thus incorporates into the genealogy is this: How can Jesus legitimately be designated "the son of David" (v. 1) when Joseph, son of David (v. 20), is not his father and Mary, his mother, is not said to be from the line of David? Matthew's answer to this problem is found in the account of Jesus' birth (1:18-25). Jesus can legitimately be designated "the son of David" because Joseph, son of David, obeys the instructions he receives from the angel of the Lord and gives Jesus his name (1:20-21, 25). In other words, Jesus, born of Mary but not fathered by Joseph, is legitimately "the son of David" because Joseph, son of David, adopts him into his line.

Tamar, Rahab, Ruth, Bathsheba, Mary—Matthew added the names of these women as examples of how God uses the unexpected to triumph over human obstacles and intervenes on behalf of his planned Messiah. It is the combination of the scandalous or irregular union with divine intervention through the woman that best explains Matthew's choice of examples. The element of scandal is important. The women foreshadow the role of Mary, the wife of Joseph. In the eyes of men, her pregnancy was a scandal since she had not lived with her husband (v. 18); yet the child was actually begotten through God's Holy Spirit, so that God had intervened to bring the messianic heritage to fulfillment. It was also of interest to Matthew that the four Old Testament women were Gentiles, or associated with Gentiles. This foreshadows the role of the Messiah who would bring Gentiles into God's plan of salvation.

While God's declaration of Jesus as his Son in 3:17 constitutes the climax of the first part of Matthew's story, there are indications prior to the baptism that Jesus is God's Son. So in 1:16 of the genealogy, Matthew casts the verb "to be born [begotten]" in the passive voice (the "divine passive") to alert the reader to the fact that Jesus is born [begotten] by an act of God.

Verse 17: "Fourteen generations"—Matthew expresses awe at the providential plan whereby the genealogy of the Messiah can be divided into three sections of fourteen generations each and that each section matches a major portion of salvation history. In the first section we are shown how the divine selective process produced the Davidic line. Jesus is Abraham's son not through the older Ishmael, but through Isaac; Jesus is Isaac's son not through the firstborn Esau, but through Jacob. In the second section Matthew lists the kings of the Davidic line who reigned in Jerusalem. This line concludes with Jechoniah who, despite the Exile, begot an heir and thus enabled the Davidic line to survive. The last section connects the end of the monarchy with the appearance of the final anointed king, the Messiah (Christ) Jesus.

Matthew has a penchant for numerical arrangements, with a special fondness for threes and sevens: seven petitions in the Lord's Prayer (6:9-13), seven parables in chapter 13, seven woes in chapter 23. He seems to use the number seven in order to indicate completeness or sufficiency. The three series of fourteen names in the genealogy may indicate that the number seven has been doubled each time.

The Birth: Virginally Conceived, Yet Son of David, 1:18-25

The Gospel story Matthew narrates is of the life and ministry of Jesus of Nazareth (1:18–28:20). Matthew first surveys in the genealogy the history of Israel (1:1-17), and then tells the story of the life of Jesus from conception and birth to death and resurrection.

The genealogy ended with a broken link (cf. v. 16). Now Matthew not only tells us that Jesus is son of David, but also tells us how that came about. Joseph is the source of Jesus' Davidic descent, but Mary's pregnancy is through the Holy Spirit. Davidic descent is transferred not through natural paternity, but through legal paternity. Genealogy and narrative fit together smoothly. Matthew's two ways of telling us about the *genesis* of Jesus, by a numerically structured genealogy followed by a narrative, may be compared to the two accounts in Genesis 1 and Genesis 2: the first is the numerical pattern of the creation of six days, and the second is the narrative account.

As to origin and pedigree, Jesus is miraculously conceived by the Spirit and adopted into the line of David (1:18-25).

> **18** Now the birth of Jesus the Messiah took place in this way. When his mother Mary had been engaged to Joseph, but before they lived together, she was found to be with child from the Holy Spirit. **19** Her husband Joseph, being a righteous man and unwilling to expose her to public disgrace, planned to dismiss her quietly. **20** But just when he had resolved to do this, an angel of the Lord appeared to him in a dream and said, "Joseph, son of David, do not be afraid to take Mary as your wife, for the child conceived in her is from the Holy Spirit. **21** She will bear a son, and you are to name him Jesus, for he will save his people from their sins." All this took place to fulfill what had been spoken by the Lord through the prophet:
> **23** "Look, the virgin shall conceive and bear a son, and they shall name him Emmanuel,"
> which means, "God is with us." **24** When Joseph awoke from sleep, he did as the angel of the Lord commanded him, he took her as his wife, **25** but had no marital relations with her until she had borne a son; and he named him Jesus.

Verse 18: "Now the birth (*hē genesis* LN 23.46)"—sends us back to verse 1, "The account of the genealogy (*Biblos geneseos)*. The genealogy has told the reader that Jesus is "the son of David" and "the son of Abraham." Matthew leaves the "son of Abraham" motif and its Gentile background until the story of the Magi in chapter 2, and concentrates first on Jesus as son of David. In so doing, he moves to a motif of divine sonship.

"Betrothed (*mnēsteutheisēs*) to Joseph." Matthew avoids the usual verbs for marrying as well as the related noun *gamos*. It may have been as difficult in Greek to find the exact word to cover the appropriate stage in the Jewish matrimonial procedure as it is for us in English. This procedure was spelled out in later rabbinic documents. It consisted of two steps: a formal exchange of consent before witnesses, and the subsequent taking of the bride to the groom's family home. While the term marriage is sometimes used to designate the second step, in terms of legal implications it would be more properly applied to the first step. The betrothal, usually entered into when the girl was between twelve and thirteen years old, constituted a legally ratified marriage in our terms. The girl was henceforth the man's wife (cf. *gyne*, vv. 20, 24), and any infringement on his martial rights could be punished as adultery.

"Before they lived together (*prin hē synelthein autous*)." The wife continued to live at her own family home, usually for about a year. Then the second step took place—the formal transferral or taking of the bride to the husband's family home where he assumed her support. "Of the Holy Spirit (*ek pneumatos agiou*)." C. E. B. Cranfield points out that the arguments for accepting the historicity of the virgin birth are weighty (*Scot Journ Theol* 41 (2, 1988) 177–189).

The Holy Spirit is not the male element in a union with Mary, supplying the husband's role in begetting. The word for "spirit" is not male (feminine in Hebrew; neuter in Greek); also the manner of begetting is implicitly creative rather than sexual. The Holy Spirit is the agency of God's creative power, not a male partner in a marriage between a deity and woman. A new outpouring of the Spirit was expected at the beginning of the age of fulfillment, as is demonstrated also by the appearance of John the Baptist. The relationship of the Holy Spirit to Jesus' divine sonship was articulated first in reference to his resurrection, and then retrojected to the beginning of his ministry (baptism). "Thus, an articulation of this relationship in reference to Jesus' conception came after considerable Christian reflection upon the Spirit of God" (R. Brown, *Birth*, 125).

Verse 19: "Being a righteous (*dikaios* LN 88.12) man"—in a double sense: Joseph wishes to show loyalty and kindness to Mary, yet he must satisfy the requirement of the Law not to countenance adultery. He seeks to satisfy both desires (as far as possible) by giving Mary the prescribed document of divorce privately. Everything would come to light eventually, but he would not have had an active part in its revelation.

Verse 20: "Joseph, son of David"—Matthew uses the title "son (LN 10.30) of David" for Jesus more frequently than the other evangelists. John never uses it; Mark and Luke use it four times, while Matthew uses it a total of ten times. Verse 20 is the only instance in the New Testament of the title being applied to someone other than Jesus. "Is of the Holy Spirit"—(cf. v. 18). Having drawn attention to Joseph as the source of Jesus' Davidic descent, Matthew takes pains to stress that this descent was not communicated through normal sexual relations between husband and wife. He goes to great lengths to make the point. He tells the reader ahead of time (v. 18) that Mary's pregnancy is through the Holy Spirit. He refuses to allow the reader to misunderstand Mary's situation the way Joseph does in verse 19. In so doing, he violates the normal pattern of angelic revelation whereby the reader learns of God's action through the words addressed to the visionary. Now Joseph learns from the angel that the child is through the agency of the Holy Spirit.

By addressing Joseph as "son of David" and commanding him to give Jesus his name and to adopt him, the angel affirms that Jesus is "the son of David." Moreover, he declares that Jesus has been conceived by the Holy Spirit, a claim made by Matthew himself in 1:18. Thus, the angel is a reliable character: his testimony agrees with that of Matthew.

Verse 21: "You are to name him Jesus." By legal paternity Jesus can legitimately be designated "the son of David" (1:1), even though Joseph, son of David, is not his father. Although Joseph is the one who gives Jesus his name (1:25), he does so on instructions from the angel of the Lord.

Davidic descendance is to be transferred not through natural, but through legal paternity. The two steps in the legal paternity are dictated by the angel and carried out by Joseph exactly. The first step is to take Mary into his home; thereby he assumes public responsibility for the mother and the child who is to be born. The second and more important step is to name the child, by which Joseph acknowledges him as his own. In this matter Jewish law is clear. Sometimes it is difficult to determine who begot a child biologically. Since normally a man will not acknowledge and support a child unless it is his own, the law prefers to base paternity on the man's acknowledgment. The *Mishnah* states the principle: "If a man says, 'This is my son,' he is to be believed" (*Baba Bathra* 8:6). Westerners must adjust themselves to the seriousness with which legal paternity was taken among Semites. One translation (Syriac Sinaiticus) does not hesitate to say that Joseph begot Jesus and that Mary gave birth to a son *to Joseph*, yet the virginal conception is not denied and Mary is firmly described as a virgin. The seeming contradiction disappears when we realize that the translator accepted legal paternity as real paternity.

"Jesus, for he will save his people." Joseph's key role is to act as the child's father by giving it the name God has already chosen, the common but significant name Jesus, a later form of the biblical Joshua. Originally it meant "Yahweh helps." but by the first century AD the popular explanation of the name was "Yahweh saves." The angel, in true Genesis style, makes a pun on the popular meaning by declaring that Jesus will *save* his people from their sins (cf. Ps 130:8). The Jews were "expecting a national liberator like David, but Jesus the Davidic liberator will grant his people a spiritual liberation in an almost priestly fashion. The liberation Jesus offers will not be acceptable to most of the people of Israel. The people who actually accept Jesus' saving act, *his* people, will be the group Jesus calls '*my* church' (Matt 16:18)" (Meier, 7-8). The cross of Jesus in Matthew's story serves not as the symbol of his destruction, but as the means whereby God accomplishes the salvation of all humankind, Jew and Gentile alike.

Verse 22: "To fulfill (LN 13.106) what the Lord had spoken." This is the first of about twelve "reflection citations" or "formula quotations" which Matthew added to his narrative, commenting on his "life" of Jesus. Each quotation shows that, in Jesus' life, God is carefully ordering history towards the fulfillment of his prophetic word.

Within the context of Matthew's story, particular times and places are significant, Thus, the conception, birth, and naming of Jesus mark the end of the time of prophecy and the beginning of the "time of fulfillment." The age of fulfillment, or the "time of Jesus (earthly—exalted)," runs from Jesus' birth (1:16, 22-23) to his return in majesty and splendor at the consummation (25:31-46). "Within this epoch, Matthew differentiates among several periods through his use of the expressions 'the Kingdom of Heaven is at hand' and 'the Gospel of the Kingdom.' In particular, Matthew employs these expressions to divide the 'time of Jesus (earthly—exalted . . .)' into the ministries to Israel of John (3:1-2), of Jesus (4:17), of the pre-Easter disciples (10:7), and the ministry to the nations of the post-Easter disciples or Church (15:14; 26:13)" (*Story*, 41).

Verse 23: "Look, a virgin (*parthenos* LN 9.39) shall conceive." In this citation of Isaiah 7:14, Matthew reworks the original text to underline the eschatological fulfillment in Christ. Isaiah spoke of a young woman (*alma*) who would conceive; Matthew adopts the standard Greek translation, "a virgin shall conceive." "Shall be called (LN 33.131) Emmanuel"—the first member of an *inclusio* that helps tie Matthew's Gospel together. It is Jesus, "God-with-us" in person, who concludes Matthew's gospel by promising his church: "Lo, *I am with you* always, to the close of the age." It is precisely by removing sin from his people that *Jesus* ("he shall save from sin") removes the distance separating God from humanity and makes God present among his people. Thus he makes good the promise of his throne-name, Emmanuel.

"Emmanuel (*Emmanouel*) . . . God with us." It will require all the rest of Matthew's Gospel to bring out all that this affirmation means to the evangelist. This is the first half of an *inclusio* which expresses the central, fundamental thought of Matthew's Gospel. The inclusion consists of 1:23 and 28:20, with 18:20 serving as a connecting link. In 1:23 Matthew quotes Isaiah as saying that in Jesus "Emmanuel . . . God [is] with us." In chapter 28 the Risen Jesus comes to the disciples in Galilee and gives them their Great Commission—they are "to make disciples of all nations. . . . And remember, I am with you always" (v. 20). Between the two parts of the inclusion, Jesus declares that where two or three are gathered in his name, "I am among them" (18:20). Our reading of Matthew's Gospel, lying between those two enclosing passages, can fill them with content, making it clear that the central, fundamental message of Matthew's Gospel is that: "*in the person of Jesus Messiah, his Son, God has drawn near to abide to the end of time with his people, the church, thus inaugurating the eschatological age of salvation*" (*Story*, 42).

At the same time "Emmanuel . . . God with us" introduces us to the fact that "being with Jesus" takes on special significance in Matthew. Jesus grants the privilege of his company only to his own. Before the resurrection these are his disciples; after the resurrection, they are his church" (cf. 2:11).

It might seem that the formula citations, taken from the prophets sacred to the Jews, were meant to prove to the Synagogue that God had foretold the career of Jesus. But if this were the case, one would expect more of these citations in the passion narrative. This was the "stumbling-block to the Jews." It seems more likely that the formula citations had a didactic purpose, informing the Christian readers and giving support to their faith. Five out of fourteen citation are found in the infancy narrative. Matthew seems to have regarded the infancy as a section of Jesus' life still relatively unexplored in reference to the Old Testament.

Verse 25: "Until (*heōs hou*) she had borne a son." In Greek and Semitic such a negation often has no implication at all about what happened after the limit of the "until" was reached. "*Until (the time when)* but not excluding continuation of action beyond the time indicated; author only concerned here to indicate virginal conception" (M. Zerwick, *ad loc*). Matthew uses the "son of David" title more often than the other evangelists (cf. v. 20). He confines it to the earthly career of Jesus, a sign that it does not capture the mystery revealed through the resurrection. Nor does "son of David" capture the mystery of the earthly Jesus. It is chiefly given to Jesus by outsiders when they come to recognize him as the Messiah because of his miracles, but it is never used by Jesus himself or by his close disciples. It never signifies an intimate penetration of Jesus' identity. "Son of David" is a correct but inadequate title for the Jesus of the Matthean ministry. The adequate answer to the question, "What do you think of the Messiah—whose son is he?" is not "son of David" but "Son of God."

Magi: Homage to the King of the Universe, 2:1-12

The first part of chapter 2 depicts a positive response to Jesus' coming. It centers on Bethlehem with the Magi foiling Herod. Matthew's presentation of Jesus as son of David and Emmanuel was in part inspired by controversy with Jews who did not believe in Jesus—Jews who denied his divine origin because they knew of his humble human family and may have questioned his legitimacy. The geographical theme of chapter 2 seems to have been aimed at the same group. Jesus' opponents mocked the fact that he was from Nazareth in Galilee, an obscure locale that lent little support to either Davidic or divine origin. In verses 1-12 Matthew shows that Jesus did meet the strictest Jewish expectations about the Messiah: as a true son of David, he was born in Bethlehem, the ancestral Davidic home.

After Jesus' birth, Herod the Great threatens his life (ch. 2). If Jesus is the protagonist of Matthew's story, the Jewish leaders are the antagonists. In his conflict with Jesus, Herod is the precursor of both Pilate and the leaders of the Jews. Matthew introduces the religious leaders to the reader in the first part of his story (1:1–4:16) in three segments, the first of which is found in chapter 2. Here, Herod the Great figures prominently. When asked by the Magi where the King of the Jews has been born, Herod and all Jerusalem become frightened at hearing news of such a birth (2:1-3). Moreover, to discover the whereabouts of the Messiah-King, Herod assembles "all the chief priests and scribes of the people" and makes inquiry of them (2:4). In replying to Herod, they announce that the place of the Messiah's birth is Bethlehem, and to prove it they cite Scripture (2:5-6).

> 2 In the time of King Herod, after Jesus was born in Bethlehem of Judea, wise men from the East came to Jerusalem, asking, "Where is the child who has been born king of the Jews? For we observed his star at its rising, and have come to pay him homage." 3 When King Herod heard this, he was frightened, and all Jerusalem with him; 4 and calling together all the chief priests and scribes of the people, he inquired of them where the Messiah was to be born. 5 They told him, "In Bethlehem of Judea; for so it has been written by the prophet:
> 6 'And you, Bethlehem, in the land of Judah,
>   are by no means least among the rulers of Judah;
>   for from you shall come a ruler
>   who is to shepherd my people Israel.' "
> 7 Then Herod secretly called for the wise men and learned from them the exact time when the star had appeared. 8 Then he sent them to Beth-

lehem, saying, "Go and search diligently for the child; and when you have found him, bring me word so that I may also go and pay him homage." **9** When they had heard the king, they set out; and there, ahead of them, went the star that they had seen at its rising, until it stopped over the place where the child was. **10** When they saw that the star had stopped, they were overwhelmed with joy. **11** On entering the house, they saw the child with Mary his mother; and they knelt down and paid him homage. Then, opening their treasure chests, they offered him gifts of gold, frankincense, and myrrh. **12** And having been warned in a dream not to return to Herod, they left for their own country by another road.

The universalistic character of "the son of Abraham" suggests that the reference to the coming of the wise men points to Jesus as the Son of Abraham who draws Gentiles to his worship.

Verse 1: "*Wise men (magoi) from the East*"—As depicted by Matthew the Magi are wholly admirable; they represent the best of pagan lore and religious perceptivity which has come to seek Jesus through revelation in nature. "Magi *from the East (apo anatolōn)*. The phrase *apo anatolōn* occurs in the Balaam story (LXX of Num 23:7) which is part of the background of Matthew's Magi story. The pagan magus Balaam receives from the God of Israel an authentic prophetic spirit; so too the Matthean Magi receive a further revelation from the Jewish Scriptures.

The episode centering on Balaam in Numbers 22-24 has for its setting the plot of Balak the Transjordanian king of Moab, who feared the Israelites who were being led by Moses out of Egypt, and sought to destroy them. To this end, King Balak summoned a famous seer named Balaam to put a curse upon Israel. He was a curious figure: obviously a non-Israelite, an occult visionary, and a practitioner of enchantment (23:23). Philo calls him a *magos* (*Vita Moysis* I L; no. 276). Like all magi, Balaam is thought of as both good and evil (cf. Num 25), and this negative element is known in the New Testament (Rev 2:14). But in Numbers 22–24 itself, Balaam is seen in a positive way, for he prophesied good for Israel. Like Philo, Matthew was of the conviction that Balaam was filled with an authentic prophetic spirit. Like the Magi, and indeed in the same phraseology, Balaam comes "from the East" accompanied by two servants. Thus a party of three is constituted, even as Christian tradition came to settle on three Magi. And when he came, he foiled the hostile plans of King Balak by delivering oracles that foretold the future greatness of Israel and the rise of its royal ruler. In other words, the wicked king sought to use the foreign magus to destroy his enemy, but the magus actually honored his enemy. Obviously this is very close to the story of Herod and the Magi.

Verse 2: "King of the Jews"—this is the evaluative point of view of the Magi concerning Jesus' identity. And because the Magi have come to offer Jesus sincere worship (2:2, 11), Matthew intimates that the implied reader should also accept this title as correctly applying to Jesus. Later, Matthew will show that Jesus is indeed the King of the Jews, but not one who foments rebellion against Rome or restores national splendor to Israel. "Observed his star"—Matthew's age would not have been surprised by the claim that a star rose to herald the birth of the King of the Jews and subsequently guided magi-astrologers in their quest to find him. Virgil reports that a star guided Aeneas to the place where Rome should be founded (*Aeneid* II 694), and Josephus speaks of a star that stood over Jerusalem at the time of the fall of the city (*War* VI v. 3; no. 289). The births of both Alexander of Macedon and Caesar Augustus were said to have been presaged by the appearance of a star. "Come to worship him (*proskyneo*, LN 53.56)"—a favorite verb of Matthew; the Magi come to worship the king by prostration, which indicates an activity properly rendered only to God or Jesus.

Verse 3: "Herod . . . was frightened." In contrast to the Magi, Herod the Great and all Jerusalem react with fear to the news that the Messiah, the King of the Jews, has been born. Here Herod is prototypical of other human characters with whom Jesus will come into conflict (Pilate and the Jewish leaders). As the Messiah, the King of the Jews, Jesus looms in Herod's eyes as a threat to assume the throne of Israel; according to Herod's evaluative point of view, Jesus is an insurrectionist. Pilate will think the same (27:11-14).

Verse 4: To discover the whereabouts of the Messiah-King, Herod assembles "all the chief priests and scribes of the people" and makes inquiry of them. This is the initial appearance of the religious leaders, the antagonists of Matthew's story. Two things stand out here. The leaders make their debut as allies of Herod. Like Herod, they react with fright and not joy to the news of the Messiah's birth. Even in searching scripture, they do Herod's bidding. The manner in which the leaders "read" scripture shows that although they are well-versed in it, the truth of it escapes them. "Scripture tells them that the one born in Bethlehem is Israel's end-time King. The irony, however, is that when they later confront this King, they will charge him with making common cause with Satan (9:34; 12:24) and repudiate him as being a fraud, or a false messiah (27:63)" (*Story*, 116). Herod presents himself in Matthew's story as the "precursor" of the religious leaders. The same character traits (spiritually blind, fearful, conspiratorial, guileful) that Herod exhibits in chapter 2, the leaders will exhibit later in the story (cf. Introduction, Sectarian Language, pp. 10–15).

Verse 5: "They told him." Some have questioned whether this is truly a formula citation (cf. 1:22), since it lacks the usual formula: "(All) this was to fulfill what the Lord had spoken by the prophet," and the citation is presented as part of the direct speech of the chief priests and scribes. The latter could scarcely be quoted using the fulfillment formula, and by making the citation part of their direct speech Matthew underlines their obduracy. Even though they can read the Scriptures correctly, they do not choose to believe.

"Written by the prophet"—Micah 5:2. The coming of Gentiles from the East begins to illustrate the theme that Jesus is the son of Abraham by whom "all the nations of the earth gain blessing for themselves" (Gen 22:18). In 1:1 the "son of Abraham" theme stands side by side with the "son of David" theme. So it is appropriate that Matthew should continue the son of David motif here by a formula citation. The quotation from Micah states that from Bethlehem will come one who is to be a ruler in Israel; the next line in Micah even uses birth terminology: "when she who is in labor has brought forth." Since Bethlehem was David's place of origin, Micah was speaking of a Davidic king.

Verse 6: "Who is to shepherd my people Israel"—the Davidic implication is made explicit by the addition of 2 Samuel 5:2. This line was spoken to David when, as King of Judah, he was being asked by the tribes of Israel to extend his sovereignty over them as well. The passage has a shepherd motif, which protects against an interpretation of Micah that would support an absolute ruler and offer backing for a tyrant like Herod.

Verse 7: "When the star had appeared"—Herod needs to know this so that he can gauge the age of the child. This points ahead to the slaughter of the Innocents. The original christological moment (i.e. the moment when Jesus' identity was revealed) was the resurrection, which produced a twofold reaction. Some believed it and paid homage; others rejected it. "In short, the christological revelation was followed by proclamation and by the twofold reaction of acceptance/homage and rejection/persecution" (R. Brown, *Birth*, p. 181). When this faith was retrojected to the beginning of the ministry, and then to the birth, the same pattern of acceptance/homage and rejection/persecution was also retrojected.

Verse 8: "That I may also go and pay him homage"—Matthew often rails against the sin of hypocrisy. Here we meet it for the first time and in an especially repellant form.

Verse 11: "Child with Mary"—"Except for Mary his mother (2:11), toll-collectors and sinners (9:11), the list of those who are 'with Jesus' or of whom it is said that Jesus is 'with them' includes only Peter (26:69, 71), one of Jesus' followers (26:51), Peter and the two sons of Zebedee, and the twelve or eleven disciples'' (*Story*, 131). "Gifts of gold, and frankincense, and myrrh"—In the ancient world, one never visited a god or king without gifts. The Magi offer gold (Ps 72:10-15), frankincense (Isa 60:6, LN 6.212) and myrrh (LN 6.208), another type of aromatic gum, like frankincense. The three *gifts* later gave rise to the idea of three *magi*, who still later became *kings* with specific names.

The Magi regard Jesus as the King of the Jews and worship him as such. Conversely, Herod the Great and, later, Pilate take "King of the Jews" to mean that Jesus is an insurrectionist (2:6, 13; 27:37). Because the Magi have come to offer Jesus their sincere worship (2:2, 11), Matthew urges the reader to accept this title, too, as correctly applying to Jesus. The role of the Magi again underlines Matthew's Gentile bias (cf. 1:5).

Verse 12: "Warned in a dream"—the regular form of revelation in the infancy narrative, prevents the Magi from being Herod's accomplices. God guides the course of history to save his Son and his people.

Jesus, God's unique Son, enters the Exodus Pattern, 2:13-18

The second part of chapter 2 depicts a negative response to Jesus' coming. Herod's reaction to the birth of the King of the Jews is to seek to kill the child, an attempt that is foiled by God's guidance of Joseph through an angel. As a result, Jesus enters into the Exodus pattern, which will bring him out of Egypt, through the waters of the Jordan, and out into the trials of Wilderness.

> **13** Now after they had left, an angel of the Lord appeared to Joseph in a dream and said, "Get up, take the child and his mother, and flee to Egypt, and remain there until I tell you; for Herod is about to search for the child, to destroy him." **14** Then Joseph got up, took the child and his mother by night, and went to Egypt, **15** and remained there until the death of Herod. This was to fulfill what had been spoken by the Lord through the prophet, "Out of Egypt I have called my son."
> **16** When Herod saw that he had been tricked by the wise men, he was infuriated, and he sent and killed all the children in and around Bethlehem who were two years old or under, according to the time that he had learned from the wise men. **17** Then was fulfilled what had been spoken through the prophet Jeremiah:
> **18** "A voice was heard in Ramah
>   wailing and loud lamentation,
> Rachel weeping for her children;
>   she refused to be consoled,
>   because they are no more."

Verse 13: "Flee to Egypt." The story of a narrative is made up not only of "characters" and "events," but also of "settings." A "setting" is the place or time or social circumstances in which a character acts. In some instances, a setting simply makes action possible, in other instances the setting may be highly charged with meaning (cf. 27:45).

Within the context of Matthew's story, particular times and places can be significant. "Bethlehem" is the lowly town in which prophecy dictates that the royal Messiah shall be born (2:4-6). "Egypt" is the land of refuge, just as Jacob/Israel, who was God's Son, found refuge in Egypt and was later called out, so Jesus son of God finds refuge in Egypt and is later called out (2:13-15).

Paradoxically, the Egypt tradition has two aspects: it is both the traditional Old Testament place of refuge and a place of persecution. Here we see that the child is saved by flight *to Egypt*. Jesus relives not only the Exodus of Israel from Egypt, but also (and first) the departure of Israel from Canaan into Egypt. This detail is partially explained by the fact that the main figure in the flight to Egypt is Jesus' legal father Joseph, who plays the role of Joseph the patriarch bringing Jacob/Israel down to Egypt. But it was not persecution that caused Jacob/Israel to go to Egypt under Joseph's guidance. Therefore, a comparison is also made between Laban the Aramean who sought to destroy Jacob and his family, and the Pharaoh who sought to destroy the Hebrew male children. "Laban's usual designation, 'the Aramaean', was regarded by the Rabbis as referring not only to his origin but also to his character as 'the deceiver', *rammay*; and there are numerous descriptions of him stressing the same characteristic. Herod was 'a fox' " (Daube, 190-91). An ancient Passover Haggadah draws together two separate biblical events pertaining to Jacob/Israel: his difficulties with Laban (Gen 31) and his subsequent migration to Egypt during the famine (Gen 46). Thus, in sequence we have an attempt against Jacob and his family by Laban the Aramean, a flight to Egypt as directed by God in a dream, and a later return of Israel under Moses.

"To destroy him (*apolesai*)"—the same verb *apollymi* appears in the passion narrative, 27:20: "Now the chief priests and the elders persuaded the people to ask for Barabbas and to have Jesus killed." The manner in which Herod reacts to the perceived threat posed by the infant Jesus anticipates the manner in which the religious leaders will later respond to the adult Jesus. In Matthew's story, Herod is the precursor of the religious leaders, and his opposition to Jesus foreshadows theirs. In immediately obeying the command from God and the other commands that follow, Joseph's righteousness (1:19) casts Herod's wickedness in ever sharper relief.

Verse 14: "Departed (*anechōresen*) to Egypt"—in Exodus, we read that after Moses had killed the Egyptian whom he had seen beating a Hebrew, the Pharaoh heard of it and sought to kill him. "But Moses fled (*anechō-resen* in the LXX) from Pharaoh, and stayed in the land of Midian" (2:15). Herod's power would not reach to Egypt, which had been under Roman control since 20 B.C. It was a classic land of refuge for those fleeing from tyranny in Palestine. When King Solomon sought to put him to death, Jeroboam "promptly fled to Egypt" (1 Kgs 11:40, a passage with close verbal similarity to Matt 2:14). Similar flights are recorded; the prophet Uriah, son of Semaiah (Jer 6:21 [LXX] 33:21); the high priest Onias IV (Josephus, *Ant.* XII ix 7:#387).

So the child Jesus is saved by flight *to Egypt*. "Jesus relives not only the Exodus of Israel from Egypt but also (and first) the departure of Israel from Canaan into Egypt. This detail is to some extent explained by the fact that the main figure in the flight to Egypt is Jesus' legal father Joseph, who plays the role of Joseph the patriarch bringing Jacob/Israel down to Egypt under Joseph's guidance (R. Brown, *Birth*, 216).

Anachōrein is characteristic of Matthew's style and thought; for similar passages, in which Jesus departs from one place to another because of unbelief, see 2:22; 4:12; 12:15; 14:13; 15:21. In later Christian times it became the technical term for monaticism—i.e. withdrawal from the world—hence "anchorite."

Verse 15: "I have called my son." In this verse, Matthew directs a comment to the reader which provides him or her with inside information not available to the characters in the story. Matthew places the reader in the privileged position of being better informed than the characters in the story. Through narrative comments as are found in 1:1 and 2:15, the reader knows far in advance of any human character that Jesus is Israel's Davidic Messiah, God's Son. Through these comments, Matthew is also urging the reader to appropriate as "true" his understanding of Jesus.

"Through the prophet"—Hosea 11:1. Matthew's formula citation here is not foreign to the historical setting of the basic story to which it has been appended. Originally, the Hosea passage referred to the Exodus of *Israel* from Egypt, but Matthew sees that the filial relationship of God's people is now summed up in Jesus, who relives the history of that people. If the whole people was God's "son," how much more is that title applicable to him who "will save his people from their sins" (1:21). In 1:1 Matthew himself designated Jesus as "son of David, son of Abraham," titles that he expounded in his account of the birth and the visit of the Magi, respectively. But the designation of Jesus as God's "Son" is left to God speaking through the prophet; for divine sonship is a matter revealed by the Father in heaven and does not come from a human source (16:16-17).

Verse 16: "Had been tricked (*enepaichthē*)"—this verb also appears in the passion account. The verb *empaizein* has a tone of mockery or ridicule. It is used for the mockery of Jesus as king during the passion narrative (27:29, 31, 41).

Verse 17: "Then was fulfilled"—Matthew pointedly does not introduce this formula quotation with the usual "in order that. . . ." He narrates the fact of fulfillment, but shrinks from saying that this is God's direct intention. "Sin is directly willed by man, though God's wisdom can encompass even man's sin and insert it into the divine plan for salvation. Interestingly, Matthew avoids the phrase "in order that" in only one other formula quotation: the suicide of Judas (27:9)" (Meier, 14).

"Through the prophet Jeremiah"—31:15. Rachel, the wife of Jacob/Israel, is imagined to be weeping at Ramah, five miles north of Jerusalem. Ramah was both the place of her death and also the place where, centuries later, the Israelites were gathered for the march into the Babylonian exile. Later tradition placed Rachel's tomb on the road to Bethlehem, and this tradition may have influenced Matthew's choice of this Old Testament text. As Jesus, the new Israel, goes into exile, Rachel bewails her slaughtered children of a later age.

The massacre of the male children in Bethlehem faithfully echoes Pharaoh's slaughter of the male infants of the Hebrews. But Matthew works to connect this event in Egypt with another tragedy, the Exile to Assyria and Babylon. The persecution in Egypt and the Exile where the two greatest trials to which God's people had been subjected; the Exodus and the return from Exile were the two greatest manifestations of Yahweh's protective power. Matthew's ingenuity lies not so much in connecting these two events, as in relating them to what happened at Bethlehem. Jesus. who is to save God's people (1:21), relives both great past moments of divine salvation. The three formula citations of chapter 2, by mentioning *Bethlehem*, the city of David, *Egypt*, the land of the Exodus, and *Ramah*, the mourning-place of the Exile, offer a succinct history of Israel. Just as Jesus sums up the history of the people named in his genealogy, so also does his early career by geographical allusion.

Divine Guidance to Israel, to Galilee, to Nazareth, 2:19-23

Matthew's tradition presupposed that Joseph and Mary came from Bethlehem: there was no need to explain how Jesus came to be born there. But everyone knew that Jesus grew up at Nazareth and was called a Nazarene. Now Matthew explains how this came about.

Joseph's righteousness (1:19) contrasts sharply with Herod's wickedness. After Herod's death, the angel of the Lord again comes to Joseph in a dream and orders him to return to Israel (2:19-21). Then, warned by God through still another dream, Joseph settles in Nazareth (2:22-23).

> **19** When Herod died, an angel of the Lord suddenly appeared in a dream to Joseph in Egypt and said, **20** "Get up, take the child and his mother, and go to the land of Israel, for those who were seeking the child's life are dead." **21** Then Joseph got up, took the child and his mother, and went to the land of Israel. **22** But when he heard that Archelaus was ruling over Judea in place of his father Herod, he was afraid to go there. And after being warned in a dream, he went away to the district of Galilee. **23** There he made his home in a town called Nazareth, so that what had been spoken through the prophets might be fulfilled, "He will be called a Nazorean."

Verse 20: "Go to the land of Israel"—a free quotation from the Lord's instruction to Moses: "Go back to Egypt; for all those who were seeking your life are dead" (Exod 4:19). Three geographical indications, each a phrase governed by *eis* and each more specific, form the backbone of this scene, guiding the Exodus and the return of Joseph with the child. The purpose of the directive to go "to the land of Israel" is easily detected: Jesus, reliving Israel's experience under Moses after the escape from the Pharaoh, is to go to the Promised Land of God's people.

Verse 22: "But when he heard." Verses 22-23 are narrative comment. Here, Matthew directs private comments to the reader which are not communicated to any human character within the story (2:15). As omniscient narrator, Matthew is privy to what characters sense, what they may hear (2:22; 4:12) or see (3:16; 9:11) on several occasions.

"Notice the contrast between the Old Testament and the New: in Exodus, the king of Egypt is the enemy of Israel, here, a king of Jerusalem is the enemy. In Exodus, Moses flees for safety out of Egypt and then returns; here, Jesus is taken into Egypt for safety and then returns. In the Old Testament, Egypt and Pharaoh are the symbols for unbelief and hardness of heart; in the New Testament, Jerusalem and Herod fulfil this role" (J. Fenton, *ad loc*; cf. A. Stock, *Way in the Wilderness*, 25–27).

"To the district of Galilee"—the divine purpose that Matthew finds here is probably related to the motif explicated in connection with the beginning of Jesus' preaching in Galilee. Galilee is the land of the Gentiles, and Jesus goes there in order that the people who sit in darkness and death may see the light (4:14-16). By combining the reference to Israel with the

Galilee of the Gentiles, Matthew has Jesus divinely directed to the two groups that make up the Matthean community: Jew and Gentile.

Verse 23: "A town called Nazareth." Jesus' move to Galilee represents a stage in the completion of his preliminary travels; the reference to a "town" also tells us something about the social background of Matthew's community (cf. 4:12-13).

The divine purpose in relation to the third geographical direction needs no angelic vision or dream to be articulated. "What was spoken by the prophets"—this is the most difficult formula citation in Matthew since it is not indisputably related to an identifiable Old Testament text. "Called a Nazorean"—the birth of the Messiah at Bethlehem was predicted by the prophet Micah (v. 5); and so was the fact that Nazareth, not Bethlehem, should serve as his home. Accordingly, as the formula citations in the account of the Birth and Flight to Egypt (vv. 1-18) gave us three names (Bethlehem, Egypt, and Ramah) evocative of great moments of Old Testament history, so the removal to Nazareth also gives us three names (Israel, Galilee, and Nazareth) anticipatory of the career of Jesus and the membership of his Church. The infancy narrative ends in the place from which Jesus will go forth to begin his mission.

"Called a *Nazarene* (*Nazōraios*)." This name evokes more than the name of a place. Three derivations have been supported by scholars, but these are not mutually exclusive. Rather, they reflect the allusive wealth of the term. Some have said that *nazoraios* is derived from Nazareth. Philologists have questioned the correctness of such a derivation, but it is certainly one that Matthew accepted.

It has also been said that Nazareth is providentially the home of the child Jesus because it gives him a Gentile designation, "Nazorean," which reminds us that he is a Nazirite (*Nazir*)—a select holy one set aside to God's service from his mother's womb, like Samson (Judg 13:5, 7) and Samuel (1 Sam 1:11). Still others have argued that the Gentile designation "Nazorean" also reminds us that Jesus is the messianic "branch" (*nēser*)—the blossom from the Davidic root predicted in Isaiah 1:2, as part of Isaiah's description of Emmanuel. According to this last interpretation, Matthew brings together with ingenious symmetry Isaian themes in his first and last formula citations in the infancy narrative: "Shall name him Immanuel" (Isa 7:14, cf. v. 23), and "He will be called a Nazorean" (the *nēser* (branch) of Isaiah 11:1, cf. v. 2:23). The first citation concerned the conception, birth, and identity of the prophesied child; the last citation concerns his mission and destiny. The annunciation of the birth of the child (1:18-25) closed with Joseph calling the child *Jesus*; the aftermath of the birth of the child (2:1-23) closes with Joseph bringing the child to Nazareth so that all may call him a *Nazorean*. We now have Jesus' full identity. He is the son of David, the Son of Abraham, the Son of God, who will also be known as Jesus the Nazorean.

The fact that the *Nazarene* citation is ascribed to "the prophets" in general is justified in the view that, though the prophetic voices have a different timbre, it is the one God who has spoken through them—a God who planned for the birth and career of his son in intricate detail. If Matthew could recognize this intricate plan, it was because he was a scribe well versed in the Law and the Prophets—a "scribe trained for the kingdom of heaven . . . who brings out of his treasure what is new and what is old" (13:52).

Biblical derivations and etymologies are rarely accurate by scientific criteria; they are often the product of analogy rather than of phonology. The fact that one derivation is possible does not mean that all others are automatically excluded. The biblical attitude is often a "both . . . and," rather than an "either . . . or." Christian expositors may have been attracted by the wealth of possible allusions in the term Nazorean when applied to Jesus.

John the Baptist, 3:1-12

In the first of the three broad segments into which the Gospel of Matthew falls (cf. p. 1A1), the genealogy and the infancy narratives (chs. 1–2) are followed in chapter 3 by the public ministry of John the Baptist. Because of the break in time between the years of Jesus' infancy (1:1–2:23) and the appearance of John and Jesus as adults (3:1–4:16), chapters 1–2 are often seen as a separate prologue to the rest of the Gospel. However, there are reasons why the whole section (1:1–4:16) should be regarded as the first larger section of the Gospel. Among them are: the climactic statement regarding the identity of Jesus does not occur until the baptism (3:13-17); Jesus' travels prior to the public ministry do not end until he takes up residence in Capernaum (4:12-14); the connecting particle *de* stands in 3:1, connecting chapters 3–4 to chapter 1–2; all the events in this section are preliminary to Jesus' ministry to Israel; and the whole section is unified by the motif of the divine sonship of Jesus Messiah (cf. *Story*, 43–45). "Although it is true that a significant lapse of time exists between 2.23 and 3.1, this does not outweigh the consideration that the whole of 1.1–4.16 has to do with events preceding the public ministry of Jesus" (Bauer, 83).

To prepare for the ministry of Jesus, John the Baptist undertakes his ministry to Israel (3:1-12). As the forerunner of Jesus, he typifies in his person and work the person and work of Jesus. The division in Israel that

John occasions foreshadows the division Jesus, too, will at first encounter: the favorable response of the people will contrast with the obduracy of the religious leaders.

> **3:1** In those days John the Baptist appeared in the wilderness of Judea; proclaiming, **2** "Repent, for the kingdom of heaven has come near." **3** This is the one of whom the prophet Isaiah spoke when he said,
>
> "The voice of one crying out in the
>   wilderness:
> Prepare the way of the Lord,
>   make his paths straight."
>
> **4** Now John wore clothing of camel's hair with a leather belt around his waist, and his food was locusts and wild honey. **5** Then the people of Jerusalem and all Judea were going out to him, and all the region along the Jordan, **6** and they were baptized by him in the river Jordan, confessing their sins.
>
> **7** But when he saw many Pharisees and Sadducees coming for baptism, he said to them, "You brood of vipers! Who warned you to flee from the wrath to come? **8** Bear fruit worthy of repentance. **9** Do not presume to say to yourselves, 'We have Abraham as our ancestor'; for I tell you, God is able from these stones to raise up children to Abraham. **10** Even now the ax is lying at the root of the tree; every tree therefore that does not bear good fruit is cut down and thrown into the fire. **11** "I baptize you with water for repentance, but one who is more powerful than I is coming after me; I am not worthy to carry his sandals. He will baptize you with the Holy Spirit and fire. **12** His winnowing fork is in his hand, and he will clear his threshing floor and will gather his wheat into the granary; but the chaff he will burn with unquenchable fire."

Verse 1: "In those days (*En de tais hēmerais*). The presence in the Greek text at 3:11 of the particle *de* ("now," "then") attests to the unity of 1:1–4:16. This particle frequently appears in the opening line of a pericope in order to connect that pericope with preceding narrative. By employing *de* at 3:1, Matthew shows that the interpreter is not to posit a fundamental break in the text between chapters 2 and 3 but is to regard the materials of the two chapters as belonging together.

"When John the Baptist appeared (*paraginetai*)." John's appearance is described very succinctly. *Paraginetai* both connects back to 2:1 (the wise men *paregenonto*) and forward to verse 13, where Jesus' appearance will be described in the same terms. The time phrase "in those days" also indicates that Matthew sees no break between the infancy history and the

appearance of the Baptist which is to be thought of as coming a generation later; it embraces both. In this key section Matthew also introduces
the basic theological themes of the Gospel. "In those days" seems to be
based on the time of Mark 1:9 ("In those days *Jesus* came"), which shows
how close Matthew considers John and Jesus to be. "In those days" also
indicates both that Matthew views the past time of Jesus as something
sacred, finished, and unique, and that the period of eschatological revelation is dawning.

The Baptist appears "in the wilderness of Judea." Thereby Matthew
not only gives a historical detail,but also make a theological observation—
the Baptist has been sent to Israel; all Jerusalem, Judea, and the Jordan
districts go out to him in the wilderness. In the desert of Judea, where
the Qumran community also awaited eschatological deliverance, John
preaches primarily repentance.

The setting "wilderness" (cf. 4:1; 15:29) is a place of end-time expectation, where John the Baptist prepares Israel for the coming of its Messiah (3:1-12). It will also show itself to be a place of testing, where Satan
tempts Jesus to break faith with God (4:1-4) and the place where Jesus
will have the disciples realize that they already possess the authority to
feed the hungry crowds (14:16; 15:33)."

Verse 2: "Repent (*metanoeite*, LN 41; 50-52). The Baptist's mission is
to "restore all things" (17:11). To accomplish this, he proclaims repentance to Israel. At the heart of this summons lies the notion that Israel
has lost its way. What is required is that Israel turn from evil, place its
trust in God, and obey him. Urgency is also of the essence, for God has
already set in motion the events that will end in judgment. Indeed, the
Coming One is soon to appear. Here, Matthew makes John proclaim the
very words that Jesus will later pronounce in 4:17.

While the ministry of John precedes that of Jesus, the term "forerunner" connotes more than mere temporal precedence. As Jesus' forerunner, John foreshadows in his person and work the person and work
of Jesus. Both John and Jesus are the agents of God sent by God (11:10;
10:40). Both belong to the time of fulfillment (3:3; 1:23). Both have the
same message to proclaim (3:2; 4:17). John is the forerunner who readies
Israel for the imminent arrival of Jesus. In spite of these similarities, John's
conception of Jesus' ministry, though correct, is insufficient. According
to John's evaluative point of view, Jesus' arrival on the scene of history
portends the end-time judgment—Jesus will appear in order to carry out
the final judgment. John does not reckon with the possibility of a delay
between the opening of the age of salvation and its consummation.

"The kingdom of heaven has come near." Matthew marks off two
epochs in the history of salvation: the age of prophecy, or the "time of

Israel (Old Testament)" and the eschatological age of fulfillment, which is the "time of Jesus (earthly—exalted)."

The age of fulfillment, or the "time of Jesus (earthly—exalted)," runs from Jesus' birth (1:16, 22-23) to his return in majesty and splendor at the consummation (25:31-46). Within this epoch, Matthew differentiates among several periods through his use of the expressions "the Kingdom of Heaven has come near" and "the Gospel of the Kingdom." In particular, Matthew employs these expressions to divide the "time of Jesus (earthly—exalted)" into the ministries to Israel of John (3:1-2), of Jesus (4:17), and of the pre-Easter disciples (10:7) and the ministry to the nations of the post-Easter disciples, or Church (24:14; 26:13).

Verse 3: "One of whom the prophet." The Baptist's coming was foretold in the Old Testament. Matthew's introductory formula resembles those of the fulfillment formulae and so helps to fix the Baptist at the side of Jesus, who is the subject of all fulfillment formulae. "Wilderness" is a catchword in the context. Taken in connection with the "wilderness of Judea" of verse 1, it is to be understood as a reference to the sending of the Baptist to Israel.

Verse 4: "Camel's hair, a leather belt." Matthew has taken over the description of the food and clothing of the Baptist almost unchanged from Mark. Since he explicitly identifies John with Elijah (11:4; 17:12), he intends the leather belt to be understood in the first place as an allusion to Elijah's clothing (2 Kings 1:8). Naturally, the verse also presents John as an ascetic. Even if originally nothing more than the food and clothing of Bedouin was understood, the description of John would have indicated that he was an ascetic. As an ascetic (11:18), John stands in contrast to Jesus as a time-conditioned figure. The description hardly has a parenetic undertone. Isaiah 40:3 was a key text for the desert community of Qumran as well. Qumran prepared the way of the Lord in the desert by study and punctilious observance of the Law.

Verse 5: "Jerusalem . . . Judea . . . region about the Jordan." The crowds in Israel listened to John's proclamation. Like Mark, Matthew lends prominence to the Baptist's success. Unlike the identification of all Jerusalem with the wicked Herod (2:3), here a distinction is made between the people who come to John in crowds, confess their sins and are baptized, and the hardened leaders of the people, the Pharisees and the Sadducees (v. 7). The meaning of the differentiation remains unclear for the moment, yet the content and the formulation make it clear that it is Jews who are repenting.

Verse 6: "Confessing their sins." Submitting to John's baptism, the crowds confess their sins and show themselves to be a repentant people ready for the arrival of the Coming One and the final judgment (3:6, 11-12). Matthew notes that the baptized confessed their sins; but he pointedly omits Mark's designation of the baptism itself as being "for the forgiveness of sins" (1:4). Matthew instead has the phrase joined to the consecration of the wine at the Last Supper (26:28). "For Matthew, forgiveness of sins is possible only through Jesus the Savior (1:21), whose atoning death (20:28) is appropriated by believers in the eucharist" (J. Meier, 24). At the outset, the prospects that Jesus will attain his goal seem bright, for John the Baptist readies the crowds to receive Jesus, the Coming One.

Verses 7a: "Many Pharisees and Sadducees." Five times Matthew makes reference to "the Pharisees and Sadducees" as a single group, despite the fact that, in the days of Jesus, the Pharisees and the Sadducees constituted two distinct "parties" with sharply contrasting views and theologies. The Pharisees had a progressive program. They wanted to adapt the law of Moses to later times and changing demands. The Sadducees, a wealthy, conservative party, advocated a rigorous application of the law of Moses to the life of the nation. They also espoused a political and religious policy, including cooperation with the Romans, which was aimed at preserving the status quo.

That Matthew treats the two parties as one group follows from the fact that he did not approach his materials from a historical-biographical point of view as conceived by the modern mind. Matthew's procedure is literarily and theologically motivated. He has both John the Baptist and Jesus call the "Pharisees and Sadducees" a "brood of vipers." Matthew was not concerned to distinguish historically, in terms of the days of Jesus, between particular factions of the leaders of Israel within his Gospel-story. They are presented as representatives of a monolithic front implacably opposed to Jesus.

According to this view, Matthew's "characterization of the Jewish leaders is a literary and theological device for identifying the Christian community in contrast to Judaism and explaining the rejection of Jesus by Judaism. . . . In Matthew's narrative the leaders form a united front against Jesus and need not be precisely distinguished from one another in themselves or by specific function in the community" (A. Saldarini, *Pharisees, Scribes and Sadducees*, 158; but see C. Kazmierski *Biblica* 68(1, '87) 28).

Matthew's joining Pharisees and Sadducees exemplifies a recurring phenomenon in his Gospel: "speaking past" the supposed audience contemporary with Jesus, and "speaking to" the implied reader situated between resurrection and parousia. This happens most frequently in the discourses.

Verse 7b: "Brood of vipers." This is the first major appearance of the religious leaders in Matthew's story. The attitude that John, the forerunner of Jesus, assumes toward the leaders predicts the attitude that Jesus will assume toward them. The first words John directs at them are the epithet with which he denounces them, namely, "brood of vipers," that is, as persons who are "evil" at the very core of their being (cf. 12:34; 23:33). It is because they are evil that they are, as John says, ripe for eschatological judgment (cf. Introduction, Sectarian Language, p. 12). "The leaders are never called evil in Mark (or in Luke), but they are explicitly identified as such several times in Matthew (9:4; 12:34, 39, 45; 16:4; 22:18). In addition, reliable characters in Matthew's story, such as Jesus and John the Baptist, describe them with such epithets as 'brood of vipers' (3:7; 12:34; 23:32) and 'child of hell' (23:15), which clearly depict them as evil" (Powell, 62).

Both John and Jesus enter into conflict with Israel: in the case of the crowds, a favorable reception ultimately gives way to repudiation; in the case of the leaders, the opposition is implacable from the outset (3:7-10; 9:3).

Verse 9: "We have Abraham as our father." John warns the leaders not to suppose that appeal to Abraham as father can serve as a substitute for repentance or enable them to persevere in the approaching judgment. "John the Baptist makes explicit reference to sonship to Abraham (3.9) when he warns the Pharisees and Sadducees not to presume to say 'We have Abraham as our father,' since God was able to raise up children to Abraham from stones (another probable anticipation of universalism)" (Bauer, 77).

Verse 10: "Ax is laid to the root." John's conception of Jesus' ministry, thought correct, is insufficient (cf. v. 2). John the Baptist thinks of Jesus as the Coming One, that is, the Messiah, who is to carry out *at once* the final judgment. According to John's evaluative point of view, Jesus is the Coming One whose arrival on the scene of history portends the end-time judgment. This evaluative point of view explains why John later sends disciples to Jesus to ask whether he is in fact the Coming One or whether they are to await another (11:2-3).

The leaders must reflect in their lives the fruit that only repenatance can produce. That John's preaching elicits no such repentance in the religious leaders is something that they themselves will later acknowledge (21:25) and Jesus will confirm. According to C. Kazmierski (cf. v. 6), the New Testament Baptist traditions grew out of the rejection faced by early Christian charismatic preachers in Palestine.

Verse 11: "With the Holy Spirit and with fire." LN 53.49., fnt. 6 notes: "In Matthew 3.11 'fire' is generally regarded as a reference to the experience of Pentecost, but it is possible to understand 'fire' in this context as referring to judgment.''

Verse 12: "His winnowing fork (LN 6.6)" "The theme of the final separation of the good and the bad is a favorite of Matthew's, and it is graphically portrayed here by a farmer using a 'winnowing fork' to separate the edible wheat from the inedible chaff. Chaff was indeed used for heating, but the eschatological reality peeps through the parable when the fire is called 'unquenchable' " (Meier, *ad loc.*).

The Baptism: God declares Jesus to be his unique Son, 3:13-17

The first segment of the topical outline according to which the contents of Matthew are arranged (cf. p. 8) culminates in the baptism scene, when the voice from heaven declares: "This is my Son, the Beloved" (3:17).

By juxtaposing the baptismal pericope with the pericope on the ministry of John, Matthew leads the reader to understand that the "Coming One" of whom John prophesies is Jesus, the Son of God whom God empowers with his Spirit (3:11, 13-17).

> **13** Then Jesus came from Galilee to John at the Jordan, to be baptized by him. **14** John would have prevented him, saying, "I need to be baptized by you, and do you come to me?" **15** But Jesus answered him, "Let it be so now; for it is proper for us in this way to fulfill all righteousness." Then he consented. **16** And when Jesus had been baptized, just as he came up from the water, suddenly the heavens were opened to him and he saw the Spirit of God descending like a dove and alighting on him. **17** And a voice from heaven said, "This is my Son, the Beloved, with whom I am well pleased."

God, participating as "actor" in the story, empowers Jesus for messianic ministry and solemnly declares "who Jesus is." Apart from the introduction (3:13), the unit falls neatly into two sections: the dialogue between John and Jesus (3:14-15), and the two revelatory events that follow (3:16-17).

13-14: "To be baptized"—Once Jesus makes his appearance in the story as an adult, Matthew as narrator "accompanies" him, with few exceptions, from baptism to death (3:13–26:56). No sooner has John foretold the imminent arrival of the Coming One than Jesus appears at the Jordan River to be baptized by John. John would prevent this, objecting that he has need to be baptized by Jesus.

Verse 15: "Let it be so." Jesus overrules John, asserting that it is fitting for them "to *fulfill* all righteousness (*plerōsai pasan dikaiosynen*)." Matthew reserves the verb "to fulfill (*pleroō*)" to Jesus alone; for the actions of the disciples Matthew uses, e.g., "to *do (poieō)* the will of God" or "*observe (tereō)* the commandments." "To fulfill all *righteousness*"—that is, God would have them be wholly obedient and do all that he requires of them. The reason Jesus insists on being baptized at the Jordan is that it is God's will that John should baptize him and that he should submit to such baptism. Although Jesus does not undergo baptism because he, like Israel, has need to repent of sin, in being baptized by John, he volunarily identifies himself with sinful humankind (cf. 1:21; 26:28).

"Let it be so now." These are the first words of Jesus recorded in Matthew. In Mark and Luke the encounter between John the Baptist and Jesus transpires without a word from Jesus. Why did Matthew depart so noticeably from his source? Rivalry between the followers of John and the followers of Jesus has been suggested, but there is no evidence that this rivalry lasted for any time. And while the sinlessness of Jesus was an important theological consideration for Paul (cf. 2 Cor 5:21), this is not the case with Matthew.

M. Limbeck considers a third solution the most likely. "For it is overarchingly important *how* we humans fulfill God's will, i.e. *our* righteousness (cf. 5:20: 'Unless your righteousness exceeds that of the scribes and Pharisees, you will never enter the kingdom of heaven'). *How* that must happen, Jesus himself illustrates at the beginning of Matthew through his submission under John. Only by acting in such a way that the Greater defers to the Smaller can we fulfill God's will. 'Thus it is fitting *for us* to fulfil all righteousness'" (*ad loc*).

Matthew does not describe the baptism of Jesus itself. The focus is on the two revelatory events that follow.

Verse 16: "The heavens were opened." Only Jesus sees the Spirit descend upon him and only he hears the voice from heaven. Later developments in Matthew's story confirm this. Had the crowds heard the voice from heaven, it is inexplicable why at least some of them did not accept Jesus as the Son of God. And had John heard the voice from heaven, it is odd that that he should later send his disciples to question Jesus about his role (11:2-3).

At first Jesus and John stood alone in private conversation (vv. 14-15). Now Jesus steps unaccompanied into God's presence. Only Jesus himself sees the Spirit descend and only he, along with such transcendental beings as Satan (4:3, 6), hears the voice from heaven.

The purpose of the opening of the heavens is both to permit the Spirit to descend and to signal that divine revelation is about to take place (Ezek

1:1). "He saw the Spirit of God descending"—which denotes the divine act whereby God empowers him to accomplish the messianic ministry he is shortly to begin (4:17). But this empowerment is not Jesus' initial endowment with the spirit, for he was conceived by the Spirit. Rather, it specifies the way in which Jesus is the Mightier One John had said he would be. This empowerment also explains the "authority" with which Jesus discharges his public ministry (7:29). Empowered by God's Spirit, Jesus speaks as the mouthpiece of God and acts as God's instrument. The "opening of the heavens" at Jesus' baptism is linked in a most remarkable way with the "tearing of the temple curtain" at the moment of Jesus' death, cf. 27:51.

Verse 17: "A voice from heaven"—the second revelatory event is one of sound; the voice from heaven is the voice of God. "This is my Son, the Beloved." The words God speaks reflect three Old Testament contexts: (1) Isaiah 42:1, where the Servant in whom God delights is the one God has "chosen" for ministry; (2) Genesis 22:2, where Abraham's beloved son Isaac is declared to be his "only" son; (3) Psalm 2, where God is described as solemnly addressing the words "You are my son" (v. 7) to the king-designate from the house of David, his anointed ("messiah"), who assumes the throne of Judah on the day of his coronation. These emphases combine in verse 17 to form a solemn affirmation in which God declares that Jesus, the Anointed One (Messiah-King) from the line of David, is his only Son, whom he has chosen for eschatological ministry. This is God's own evaluative point of view which the implied reader can recognize as the normative understanding of Jesus.

This declaration from heaven and empowerment of Jesus with the Spirit bring the entire first part of Matthew's story (1:1–4:16) to its climax. Although there were earlier indications that Jesus is the Son of God, here this truth, uttered by God as "actor," assumes the form of an event that occurs within the story itself. "In this part, Matthew presents Jesus to the reader. The evaluative point of view concerning Jesus' identity which Matthew sets forth is that Jesus, the Messiah-King from the line of David and of Abraham, is uniquely the Son of God. The crucial element in this evaluative point of view—that Jesus is the Son of God" (*Story*, 54).

Thus the first of the three main parts of the topical outline of Matthew's Gospel culminates in Jesus' baptism. Here Jesus is portrayed as the Messiah, the Son of God. The same is true of the culminating scenes of the other two main parts. Thus at Caesarea Philippi, Peter declares on behalf of the disciples that Jesus is the Messiah, the son of the living God (16:13-20). And at the Great Commission, the exalted Jesus, to whom God has entrusted all authority in heaven and on earth, refers to himself as 'the Son' (28:16-20), which is but one indication that he stands before his disciples and commissions them in his capacity as the resurrected Messiah, the Son of God. This special stress on Son-of-God Christology in the three main parts of the topical outline singles out Jesus Messiah, the Son of God, as the "place" where God encounters people with his eschatological rule.

The same conclusion follows from other key scenes. Thus at the transfiguration, Jesus is suddenly transfigured before Peter, James, and John, and from a cloud that overshadows them a voice exclaims, "This is my son, the Beloved, with whom I am well pleased; listen to him!" (17:1-5). As at the baptism, the voice is God's, Matthew confirming the validity of Peter's recent confession (cf. 17:5 with 16:16). Finally, as Jesus hung dead on the cross the Roman centurion said, "Truly this man was God's Son!" (27:54). This confession serves at once to call attention to the circumstance that his earthly ministry is now at an end and to vindicate the claim to divine sonship he had raised at his trial.

Thus Matthew's "book" begins with a series of affirmations from reliable witnesses regarding the person of Jesus: from Matthew himself (1:1); from an angel (1:18-25); from the wise men (2:2); from John the Baptist (3:11).

"The next and last testimony to Jesus in this succession of reliable witnesses comes directly from God himself; in 3.17 the heavenly voice declares, 'This is my beloved son'" (Bauer, 80).

The Testing of the Son of God, 4:1-11

By this point in Matthew's story, Jesus stands before the reader preeminently as the Son of God who has been empowered with the Spirit of God. Now the Spirit leads Jesus into the desert to engage the devil, or Satan, in conflict in the place of his abode. Three times Satan tests Jesus' obedience to God, hoping to entice Jesus to break faith with God, his Father, and thus disavow his divine sonship. In testing Jesus, Satan cunningly adopts God's evaluative point of view, according to which Jesus is his Son.

Satan's testing of Jesus is patterned after the testing Israel faced in its desert wanderings from Egypt to Canaan (Deut 6:10-19; 8:1-10). Israel, too, was designated by God as "his son" (Exod 4:22-23). But while Israel's history was one of failure, repentance, and restoration, Jesus remains unshaken in his fidelity.

> **4:1** Then Jesus was led up by the Spirit into the wilderness to be tempted by the devil. **2** He fasted forty days and forty nights, and afterwards he was famished. **3** The tempter came and said to him, "If you are the

Son of God, command these stones to become loaves of bread.'' **4** But
he answered, "It is written,

'One does not live by bread alone,
but by every word that comes from the
mouth of God.' ''

5 Then the devil took him to the holy city and placed him on the pinnacle of the temple, saying to him, "If you are the Son of God, throw
yourself down; for it is written,

'He will command his angels concerning you,'
and 'On their hands they will bear you up,
so that you will not dash
your foot against a stone.' ''

7 Jesus said to him, "Again it is written, 'Do not put the Lord your
God to the test.' ''

8 Again, the devil took him to a very high mountain and showed him
all the kingdoms of the world and their splendor; **9** and he said to him,
"All these I will give you, if you will fall down and worship me." **10**
Jesus said to him, "Away with you Satan! for it is written,

'Worship the Lord your God,
and serve only him.' ''

11 Then the devil left him, and suddenly
angels came and waited on him.

A narrative like Matthew's Gospel contains "events", "characters",
and "settings." "Events" are the string of incidents, or actions, which
stretch the length of the story. They comprise the "plot," or flow, of a
story, and the element of conflict is central to the plot of Matthew. Jesus
is the royal Son of God, in whom God's end-time Rule is a present, albeit
hidden, reality. Jesus is thus the supreme agent of God. The conflicts in
which he becomes embroiled are with Satan, demons, the forces of nature and of illness, civil authorities (such as Herod and Pilate), Gentiles
(including Roman soldiers), Israel, and, above all, Israel's religious leaders.
In the pericope on Jesus' confrontation with Satan, the groundwork is
laid for a later point in the story at which the reader will recognize that
the religious leaders, in their confrontations with Jesus, show that they
have affinity with Satan.

Verse 1: "To be tempted by the devil." Approaching Jesus three times,
Satan urges him to place concern for self above allegiance to God. In the
first test, Satan suggests that Jesus miraculously still his hunger. But were
Jesus to do so, he would be forcing, solely for his own benefit, a change
in the circumstances into which God has brought him.

Verse 2: "Fasted forty days (LN 67.93)"—Matthew adds forty nights to the forty days in order to conform to Moses' fasting forty days and forty nights according to Deuteronomy 9:9-18, the section of Deuteronomy that will provide Jesus' answer to the Devil in verse 4.

Verse 3: "And the tempter came (*proselthōn*). In the LXX and Hellenistic literature the Greek word *proserchesthai* carries cult connotations. The term is used of those who approach God or bring sacrifices to an altar, or of those who approach someone of cultic importance either to make a request or to render some form of sacral service (cf. J. Edwards, *JBL* 106/1[1987] 65-74; *NTA* 31[3, '87] #1050). In Matthew *proserchesthai* occurs in a similar fashion, except that its cultic connotations are transferred to Jesus. With but few exceptions Jesus is the object of this verb in Matthew and, as is also true in Hebrews, *proserchesthai* denotes his unique, messianic character.

Matthew shows a striking preference for the term: of the approximately nincty occurrences in the New Testament, Matthew accounts for fifty-two and in nearly three-fourths of Matthew's uses, Jesus is the object of the verb. In ten instances, those who approach Jesus come with intent to test or trap him (the religious leaders, the devil (v. 3), Judas (26:49), Roman soldiers (26:50), and false witnesses). Even in these adversarial approaches, Matthew demonstrates that Jesus' opponents come to him because he has authority and that in every instance the authority of Jesus is vindicated.

"If you are the Son of God." "Phraseological point of view" concerns the "speech," or "diction," that typifies and distinguishes Matthew as narrator or any given character. Here, we see that the words "If you are the Son of God" are first associated in Matthew's story with Satan, who utters them in order to test Jesus (4:3, 6). Later, therefore, when Jesus hangs upon the cross and the passersby shout at him. ". . . if you are the Son of God, come down from the cross" (27:40), the reader recognizes from the phraseology of the passersby that they, like Satan previously, are testing Jesus and that they consequently have aligned themselves with Satan.

Verse 5: "Then the devil took him." In the second test (vv. 5-7), Satan suggests that Jesus cast himself down from the pinnacle of the temple. But were Jesus to do so, he would make himself guilty of endeavoring to coerce God into serving him by wondrously preserving his life from destruction.

Verse 6: "Throw yourself down . . . commanded his angels." Two associations are important here. On the cross Jesus again forgoes calling upon God's angels for help and remains faithful to scripture (26:53-54). A short time later another meaningful scene follows: Jesus refuses compliance to the scribes who call out: "If you are the Son of God," (27:40) and demand that he come down from the cross. The second temptation points forward to the obedience of the Son of God in his life and above all during his passion.

Verse 8: "Again the devil." In the third test (vv. 8-10), Satan suggests that Jesus, to secure control over the nations of the world, fall down and worship him. But were Jesus to do so, he would be placing lust for the wealth of the world above fealty to God.

"To a very high mountain (*horos hypselon lian)*"—*hypselon* anticipates the description of the Mount of Transfiguration (17:1). "Above all, the added phrase carries forward the parallel between Jesus and Moses: Jesus views all the kingdoms of the world from a mountain just as Moses viewed not only all the land of Canaan (Deut 34:1-4), but also 'the west and north and south and east' (Deut 3:27), from Mount Pisgah, or Nebo. Again the portrayal of Jesus in terms of that man of law, Moses, strikes against antinominism in the church" (Grundry, *ad loc*).

The baptism and temptation passages, therefore, aim to show that when Jesus steps up from the waters of Jordan, he is the first born of the new Israel, "Israel after the spirit," the herald of the new covenant whose members will have God's spirit in their breast and his law written in their heart.

Verse 10: "Away with you (LN 15.52) . . . Satan." This phrase reappears in 16:23: Peter who would keep the Son of God (LN 12.34) back from suffering is repelled with these words. Jesus then speaks about suffering and self-sacrifice among his disciples. Right afterwards he again ascends a high mountain with some disciples (17:1) where the second divine proclamation of the Son of God takes place in the Transfiguration. But most important are the manifold echoes in the concluding pericope of Matthew: after Jesus, as the obedient Son, had foregone the divine manifestation of power, had suffered, and had died on the cross, there finally comes, again on a mountain (28:16), the proclamation of his authority not only over the kingdom of the world, but over heaven and earth (28:18). The earthly Jesus' foregoing of power points forward to the omnipotence of the Risen One.

Verse 11: "Devil left . . . angels came (*proselthon*)." Just as Satan, defeated by Jesus in debate, withdraws from him, so the Jewish leaders, defeated in debate, withdraw from Jesus in the temple (22:46). And although Satan, the transcendent fountainhead of evil, continues to vie with Jesus Son of God in this age for the allegiance of humans, at the consummation he and his angels will be utterly vanquished.

Although the temptation scene makes no mention of the religious leaders of Israel, it lays the groundwork for a later point in the story at which the reader will recognize that the religious leaders, in their confrontations with Jesus, show that they have affinity with Satan. John the Baptist's encounter with the religious leaders anticipates Jesus later encounters with them because John is Jesus' forerunner. Jesus' encounter with Satan likewise anticipates Jesus' later encounters with the leaders because Satan is the Evil One with whom they have affinity. As Satan puts Jesus to the test three times (4:1-10), the religious leaders will also repeatedly put Jesus to the test. And as Jesus has the last word, so that Satan leaves the scene, so in debate with the leaders, Jesus will again have the last word (22:46–23:1). If Jesus ultimately bests Satan in conflict, he will also ultimately best the leaders in conflict.

The baptismal scene establishes that Jesus is preeminently the Son of God who has been empowered with the Spirit of God. So identified, Jesus is led by the Spirit into the wilderness to engage Satan in conflict in the place of his abode. Three times Satan puts Jesus to the test. The substance of each test has to do with Jesus' obedience to God. Satan's intent in each test is to entice Jesus to break faith with God, his Father, and thus to disavow his divine sonship. In testing Jesus, Satan cunningly adopts God's evaluative point of view, according to which Jesus is his Son (4:3, 6).

Satan's testing of Jesus is antitypical to the testing Israel faced in its desert wanderings from Egypt to Canaan (Deut. 6:10-19; 8:1-10). Israel, too, was designated by God as "his son" (Ex 4:22-23), but when Israel son of God was put to the test, it failed.

The first main division of Matthew (1:1–4:16) prepares the reader for the rest of the gospel by presenting directly the nature and identity of Jesus. By a series of reliable witnesses Jesus is identified as "Christ," "Son of David," "Son of Abraham," and "king." These designations are elaborated throughout the rest of the Gospel. Yet while Jesus fulfills expectations associated with these titles, he is presented above all as "Son of God." "The primary nature of this christological category is indicated by the fact that this division comes to a climax in the declaration from God that Jesus is, in fact, his Son (3.17)" (Bauer, 143).

Move to Capernaum, 4:12-16

On hearing news that John the Baptist has been "delivered up" and taken into custody, Jesus returns to Galilee. His move from Nazareth to Capernaum completes his preliminary travels. This is one of the signs of the unity of Part I. All is now right for Jesus to embark on his ministry to Israel.

12 Now when Jesus heard that John had been arrested, he withdrew to Galilee. 13 He left Nazareth and made his home in Capernaum by the sea, in the territory of Zebulun and Naphtali, 14 so that what had been spoken through the prophet Isaiah might be fulfilled:
15 "Land of Nabulun, land of Naphtali,
　　on the road by the sea,
　　　across the Jordan,
　　　Galilee of the
　　　Gentiles—
16 the people who sat in darkness
　　have seen a great light,
　and for those who sat in the region and
　　shadow of death
　　light has dawned."

Verse 12: "Now when Jesus heard (*Akousas de hoti*)." Some writers discern a major structural break between 4:11 and 4:12, maintaining that the settlement of Jesus in Galilee marks the beginning of his public ministry. But the "Now (*de*)" links 4:12 to the preceding and the absence of Jesus' name in 4:12 (in the Greek) forces the reader back to infer the subject from 4:10. Moreover, the mention of John the Baptist points back to chapter 3. Matthew 1:1–4:16 thus stands as a unified whole, providing the background for the rest of the Gospel.

As omniscient narrator, Matthew is privy to what characters sense, what they may hear (2:22) or see (3:16; 9:11) on this or that occasion. "That John had been arrested (*paredothē*)." After the Baptist's arrest Jesus withdraws into Galilee. The verb *paradidomi*, so prominent in the passion account, is used here to underline the parallel between Jesus and John in proclamation and fate. Jesus goes to Galilee for the sole reason that it accords with the divine plan that he should work in the "Galilee of the Gentiles."

Verse 13: "Made his home (*katokesen*) in Capernaum." One of the things that argues for the unity of 1:1–4:16 is the fact that Jesus' travels prior to his public ministry do not end until he takes up residence in Capernaum. It is to make this point that Matthew shapes the passage 4:12-14 in such a way that it takes up flawlessly on the previous passage 2:22-27. Taking up on his previous notation that Joseph "went and *made his home (katōkesen)*" in a city called Nazareth" (2:23), Matthew documents with a formula quotation the circumstance that Jesus "left Nazareth and went and *made his home (katōkesen)* in Capernaum." The two passages are also linked by fulfillment formulas. Later Capernaum is designated as "his own town" (9:1), and it may be that the "house" there is to be thought of as belonging to Jesus or Peter.

Verse 15: "Galilee of the Gentiles" ties together the four preceding geographical details. This is what Matthew is primarily interested in. It is clear that by this he does not mean that Galilee had been settled by Gentiles or that Jesus' ministry is carried out entirely or partially among Gentiles. This is precisely the point that Matthew makes clear in his Gospel—that Jesus was the Messiah of Israel, worked in Israel's synagogues, and forbade his disciples to undertake a mission outside Israel. And historically Galilee was the heartland of Israel even after 70. The label "Galilee of the Gentiles" therefore has a fictive character. With the Old Testament designation Matthew anticipates on a second level what Jesus' coming had set afoot in salvation history—the movement of salvation to Gentiles. For also in Galilee the Risen Lord will give the disciples the command to make disciples of all Gentiles (28:16-20).

Under the future perspective of salvation coming to the Gentiles precisely in conformity with God's plan, Jesus begins his proclamation in verse 17. Matthew refers to a perspective that applies to all of Jesus' activity in Israelite Galilee. The fulfillment citations in 2:23 and 12:17-21 also refer to this hidden perspective. It is important for Matthew that the salvation for the Gentiles is a biblical, prophetic perspective. The Gentiles coming to salvation as the *basileia* means its withdrawal from Israel (21:43). Our citation is an expression of the fundamental polemical tension which, writing in a time after the separation of Christian community and synagogue and the destruction of Jerusalem, Matthew traces back to Israel's scriptures.

Originally Isaiah 8:23–9:1 was concerned with the birth of a Davidic heir as a sign of the approaching liberation of three provinces occupied by the Assyrians: Dor, Megiddo, and Gilead. Matthew's interpretation of the passage does not reflect the original meaning and could not do so. Like all early Christian interpretation and the interpretation of the prophets among the Qumran sectarians, the meaning of Old Testament prophecies unfold themselves to Matthew in the light of the present, which was understood as the special time of God's salvation activity. A distinction can be made between the original meaning of a passage and a later actualization.

Matthew 1:1–4:16 (Part I) thus stands as a unified whole, providing the background for 4:17–28:20 (Parts II and III). "It prepares the reader for all that follows (a) by presenting the true and proper understanding of the person of Jesus, (b) by setting forth in stark contrast the two essential reactions to the person of Jesus, and (c) by anticipating the rejection of Jesus by the Jews and the consequent universal appeal of the Gospel" (Bauer, 84).

Part II:
The Ministry of Jesus Messiah to Israel and Israel's Repudiation of Jesus (4:17–16:20)

Matthew's Gospel falls into three broad segments. In the first (1:1–4:6), Jesus Messiah, Son of God, is presented to the reader: in the second (4:17–16:20), his public ministry is described; in the third (16:21–28:20), his journey to Jerusalem, his passion, death, and resurrection. Each segment culminates in an affirmation that Jesus Messiah is the Son of God (cf. introduction, p. 8). The first segment had its general heading (superscription) in 1:1, which is particularized in the rest of the segment and brought to a climax at 3:17. The same pattern is followed (superscription, particularization, and climax) in the other two segments of Matthew. The other two superscriptions are 4:17 and 16:21.

These two verses are similar and very distinctive: "From that time Jesus began to proclaim. . . ." 4:17: "From that time on Jesus began to show. . . ." 16:21. While "From that time on" appears at two other places in the Gospels "The phrase in 4:17 and 16:21 is utterly distinctive; in the other two passages it is neither linked with Jesus, nor does it contain any reference to 'begin' " (Bauer, 85).

At 4:17 and 16:21 "From that time on Jesus [Christ] began to. . . . signals the beginning of a new phase in the life and ministry of Jesus. In addition, each of the verses in which the formula is embedded stands apart from its context and sounds the theme that Matthew subsequently develops throughout the following segment. The formula signals the beginning of the second and third segments of the Gospel of Matthew.

The second segment of the topical outline (4:17–16:20), according to which the contents of Matthew are arranged (cf. p. 8) culminates in the Caesarea Philippi scene when, in response to Jesus' question, Peter replies: "You are the Christ, the Son of the living God" (16:16). This segment falls into two parts: the first (A) devoted to Jesus' preaching,

4:17–11:1; the second (B) to his repudiation, 11:2–16:20. Interspersed in this first part are three *summary passages*.

A. THE MINISTRY OF JESUS TO ISRAEL, 4:17—11:1

Jesus launches his ministry by proclaiming, "Repent, for the Kingdom of Heaven is at hand!" (4:17). Jesus, like John the Baptist before him (3:2), looks on Israel as a people that has lost its way.

Jesus' next act is to call four fishermen to become his disciples, thus surrounding himself with eye- and ear-witnesses (4:18-22). He ascends a mountain and there programmatically teaches the will of God (Sermon on the Mount, 5:1–7:19). Descending from the mountain, he wanders in the area of Capernaum and travels across the Sea of Galilee and back (8:1-9:34). While so doing, he performs ten mighty acts of deliverance and educates his followers in the nature and cost of discipleship. At the height of his activity, he commissions the Twelve to a ministry of their own in Israel, one of preaching and healing though not of teaching (9:35-10:42). The interspersed *summary passages* describe Jesus as discharging throughout the whole of Galilee a ministry of teaching, preaching, and healing whereby he proffers salvation to Israel.

The element of conflict does not dominate the plot of 4:17–11:1. However, the reader at first encounters intimations of conflict between Jesus and the religious leaders through sayings of Jesus and of Matthew as narrator which cast the religious leaders in a negative light. Jesus predicts persecution for the disciples at the hands of Israel (5:11-12), and declares that the righteousness of the scribes and Pharisees is insufficient for gaining entrance into the Kingdom of Heaven (5:20). Matthew remarks that while Jesus taught "as one having authority," the scribes did not (7:28-29). Jesus' opponents will be cast into the darkness outside, while Gentiles will sit at table in the future Kingdom.

Controversies between Jesus and the religious leaders flare up in chapter 9, yet these controversies are still "preliminary": they are not so acutely confrontational as subsequent conflicts. Jesus is not directly attacked; these conflicts do not have to do with the Mosaic law as such, and they do not incite the religious leaders to make the decision to kill Jesus.

B. ISRAEL'S REPUDIATION OF JESUS, 11:2–16:20

As a result of Jesus' widespread activity of teaching, preaching, and healing, his fame spreads, but this is no indication that Israel has accepted him. John the Baptist, perplexed because Jesus has not carried out the final judgment as he had anticipated (3:10-12), questions whether Jesus is, in fact, the Coming One. The Jewish crowds reject both John and Jesus (11:16-19). The cities of Chorazin, Bethsaida, and Capernaum refuse to be moved to repentance (11:20-24).

The religious leaders clash with Jesus and the level of tension increases perceptibly. The leaders (Pharisees) charge the disciples with breaking the law by plucking grain on the sabbath. The leaders not only engage Jesus himself in debate, but even level charges against him for an action they anticipate he is about to take (12:9-12). For the first time, Matthew remarks to the reader that "the Pharisees went out and took counsel against him, how to destroy him" (12:14).

Aware that the danger he faces has become mortal, Jesus temporarily withdraws (12:15). The leaders next demand of Jesus that he perform a sign so as to prove to them that he is not the agent of Satan but the agent of God (12:38-45). At last, like the others in Israel, even the family of Jesus deserts him, which leaves the disciples as the only ones who still adhere to him (12:46-50).

Repudiated by all segments of Israel, Jesus responds by declaring that Israel has become hard of heart (13:1, 3-15). He gives public demonstration of this by addressing the crowds in parables, in speech they cannot comprehend. When the people of Nazareth hear him teach in the synagogue they take offense. Even more ominously, news reaches Jesus that Herod Antipas has beheaded John the Baptist (14:1-13). Once again Jesus withdraws, embarking on a series of journeys to deserted places, back and forth across the sea, and into Gentile lands. The notion that Jesus, sensing mortal danger, takes evasive action serves the motif that Israel has repudiated him (11:2–16:2).

Jesus' First Proclamation and First Disciples, 4:17-22

The second part of Matthew's story (4:17–16:20) falls into two sections. In the first section (4:17-11:1), Jesus discharges his ministry to Israel of teaching, preaching, and healing, thereby offering it salvation (4:17). The conflict between Jesus and the religious leaders that suddenly flares up (ch. 9) prepares the reader for the more intense conflict soon to follow, in the second section of part two.

John and Jesus both belong to the time of fulfillment (3:3; 4:23) and they have the same message to proclaim (3:2; 4:17). Indeed, a glance back to 3:2 shows that John the Baptist and Jesus begin their public ministry with the very same message, word for word.

> **17** From that time Jesus began to proclaim, "Repent, for the king-
> dom of heaven has come near."
> **18** As he walked by the Sea of Galilee, he saw two brothers, Simon,
> who is called Peter, and Andrew his brother, casting a net into the sea—
> for they were fishermen. **19** And he said to them, "Follow me, and I
> will make you fish for people." **20** Immediately they left their nets and
> followed him. **21** As he went from there, he saw two other brothers, James
> son of Zebedee and his brother John, in the boat with their father Zebe-
> dee, mending their nets, and he called them. **22** Immediately they left
> the boat and their father, and followed him.

Verse 17: "From that time Jesus began (*Apo tote ērxato ho
Iesous.* . . .)." This formula, at 4:17 and 16:21, signals the beginning
of the second and third segments of the topical outline. Each time the
formula occurs it introduces a new phase in the ministry of Jesus; it plays
a dynamic role, guiding the reader through Matthew's story. Specifically,
the double use of this formula calls the reader's attention to the turn of
the story from its beginning phase (1:1–4:16) to its middle phase
(4:17–16:20), and from its middle phase to its end phase (16:21–28:20).
   Jesus "began *to proclaim (keryssein)*" LN 33.256–261. The same verb,
"to preach or proclaim (*keryssein*)" designates the activity of John the
Baptist and Jesus at the start of their ministries; both call for repentance
and proclaim the nearness of the Kingdom. In Jesus' person and work,
God's eschatological rule has become a present reality—this is the Kingdom. It is God's activity in Jesus Messiah, the Son of God. Both John
and Jesus "proclaim" and after them it is extended to the disciples, and
the post-Easter Church.
   "Repent, for the kingdom of heaven has come near (*metanoeite, ēggiken gar he basileia tōn ouranōn*)." The term "the kingdom" is simply
an abbreviation of the fuller idiom "the kingdom of heaven." Matthew
prefers this to "the kingdom of God," yet the two expressions are synonymous. The purpose of the expression "the kingdom of heaven" is to
assert the truth that "God rules, reigns"; the "rule of God" and "the
reign of God," mean the same.
   "Has come near (*ēggiken*)." John the Baptist, Jesus, and the disciples
all announce that "the kingdom of heaven is at hand (*ēggiken*)." This
verb denotes a "coming near," an "approaching," that is both spatial
or temporal in character. "Spatially" the kingdom has drawn near because God in the person of his Son even now resides with those who live
in the sphere of his rule. The will of the Father is not hidden but known
on earth, and the disciples of Jesus respond to it with lives that reflect
the greater righteousness. Temporally, too, the kingdom of heaven has

drawn near; the kingdom has both a present and a future aspect. While it belongs to the future, in the person of Jesus Son of God it has come upon the present so as radically to qualify it. The present is to be viewed in the light of the future and seen as moving toward the consummation and Jesus' parousia.

The theme of 4:17, namely, that Jesus publicly presents himself to Israel, announcing the kingdom of heaven and consequently calling Israel to repentance, provides the framework for 4:17–16:20. First (4:17–11:1), Jesus goes about Galilee teaching, preaching the Gospel of the kingdom, and healing. But Jesus' proclamation of the kingdom and call to repentance meet with rejection by Israel as a whole. In response to this lack of acceptance, Jesus moves away from those who are on the outside and toward his disciples, the only group that accepts his ministry. The theme of Jesus' proclamation of the kingdom and call to repentance (4:17) is expanded (particularized) throughout the following segment: proclamation of the kingdom of God leading to rejection by Israel as a whole, but acceptance by the disciples.

Verse 18: "Simon, who is called Peter." Jesus' next act is to call four fishermen to become his disciples, thus surrounding himself with eye- and ear-witnesses. In calling disciples, Jesus creates a new community described as a brotherhood of the sons of God and of the disciples of Jesus. The purpose of this new community is to engage in missionary activity. The initiative lies squarely with Jesus in the callings, and the pattern that governs the calling of each pair of brothers is the same: Jesus sees, Jesus summons, and at once those summoned leave behind everything—nets, boat, and father—in order to follow him (4:18-20, 21-22).

Unlike Mark 3:16 here Peter is introduced as one already known to the community as by that name. As the first apostle (10:2) he is the first named in the synoptic lists, as distinct from John 1:40-42. Peter is his nickname, not his name of office. The order in which the disciples are called is important: Peter is cited as being first (4:18). Later at 10:2, Matthew makes specific mention of this: "These are the names of the twelve apostles: first, Simon, also known as Peter. . . ." Matthew in his story pointedly ascribes some kind of primacy to Peter.

Verse 19-20: "Follow me." Jesus calls them away from their work and declares that he will make them fishers of men. Because of the parable of the Fishnet in Matthew, this experience clearly applies to mission activity (cf. 13:47). The brothers straightway leave their nets and follow Jesus. The word *akoloutheo*, so important for Matthew, appears here for the first time. The particle *eutheos* and the leaving of the nets, which were not even drawn up on shore, express the radical obedience of the two.

Verses 21–22: "Two other brothers." In the second episode the hired men of Zebedee are omitted, not because Matthew refuses to attribute relative wealth to the family, and also not because he wished to convey the painfulness of the break with the father, who is left alone, but because they are superfluous and would disturb the symmetry of the two vocation accounts. On the other hand, he has deliberately stressed the word "immediately," in order to emphasize (as in v. 20) that the two who are called heed Jesus in radical obedience. The exactly parallel final phrases *ha de eutheōs aphentes . . . ēkolouthesan autō* in verse 20 and verse 22 show what is important for Matthew. (For "to follow," *akoloutheō*, cf. 4:25; 8:1.)

In each of the segments the superscription (heading) is expanded upon. This is one of the four structural elements that Bauer finds in Matthew (57). Another is "repetition of comparison." The relationship between Jesus and the expectations for the disciples in Matthew is essentially that of comparison. Matthew sets the expectations for, or the role of, the disciples and the person of Jesus side by side in terms of their relation to God, manner of living, and mission. What Jesus says and does is compared to the expectations for the disciples. The clearest analogy is that of their respective ministries: the geographical sphere is the same; they perform the same acts of ministry; and they share the same kinds of persecutions. Matthew also compares Jesus and the expectations for the disciples in terms of ethical behavior, or manner of living. "Further, Matthew points to the essential comparison between Jesus and the role of the disciples by his use of filial language: even as Jesus is the Son of God so the disciples are sons of God" (Bauer, 138).

First Summary Passage, 4:23-25

In Part 1 of his story Matthew presents Jesus to the implied reader. Part 2 (4:17–16:20) falls into two phases: in the first Matthew tells of Jesus' ministry to Israel (4:17–11:1) and in the second, of Israel's repudiation of him (11:2—16:20).

Jesus' ministry to Israel (4:17–11:1) is one of teaching, preaching, and healing. To bring this home to the implied reader, Matthew punctuates the narrative with summary passages. These passages alert the reader to the direction that the plot of the Gospel-story is taking. Two sets of three summary passages each dominate the greater part of the Gospel. In 4:17–16:20, the passages are 4:23; 9:35; and 11:1, which describe Jesus as discharging his ministry of teaching, preaching, and healing (4:17–11:1). Israel, however, responds to Jesus' ministry by repudiating him (11:2–16:20) and taking counsel on how to destroy him (12:14). This, in turn, sets the tone for the three summary passages that govern the final third of the Gospel: the passion predictions (16:21; 17:22-23; 20:17-19). These predictions repeatedly remind the reader that the Gospel-story is moving inexorably toward the cross and resurrection.

> 23 Jesus went throughout Galilee, teaching in their synagogues and proclaiming the good news of the kingdom and curing every disease and every sickness among the people. 24 So his fame spread throughout all Syria, and they brought to him all the sick, those who were afflicted with various diseases and pains, demoniacs, epileptics, and paralytics, and he cured them. 25 And great crowds followed him from Galilee, the Decapolis, Jerusalem, Judea, and from beyond the Jordan.

Matthew composes a comprehensive summary before he gives particular examples of Jesus' teaching and healing activity. Through the numerous passages that appear more than once, an impression of the typical is created. The pieces from the preaching and healing activity of Jesus following in chapters 5–9 are particular examples. It is not Matthew's intention to give a full historical-biographical account of events. Rather, he begins with an overall picture which he then concretizes with particular examples in what follows.

Verse 23: "Went throughout Galilee." Following the tradition (cf. Mark 6:6), Matthew has Jesus move about in Galilee. He applies the introductory phrase to everything that follows, up to the equally significant turning point in 19:1 ("he left Galilee"). The composition shows that Matthew presents Jesus as in the vicinity of his dwelling place, Capernaum (8:5, 29; 9:1).

"*Teaching* in their synagogues." By citing teaching (*didaskein*) ahead of preaching and healing in the summary passages (4:23; 9:35; 11:1), Matthew gives it the position of stress and invites the implied reader to attach special importance to it. But while the verb "to teach" (*didasko*) has the position of stress, showing that Matthew attaches special importance to it, Matthew would not call Jesus the "Teacher." "Teacher" is a title of human respect not a title of majesty. Only outsiders and enemies do this. The disciples consistently address Jesus as "Lord."

Jesus' teaching "*in their synagogues*" has two aspects: Jesus reaches out to Israel and teaches as the Teacher of Israel in the synagogue, even as his miracles are for the Chosen People. At the same time the stressed "*their* synagogue" makes it clear that Matthew and his community have places of their own outside these synagogues. That "preaching" and "teaching" do not mean two distinct things will become clear only from the Gospel of Matthew as a whole. Matthew has already suggested the content of the preaching in 3:2 and 4:17: it is a matter of repentance in view of approaching justice. Chapters 5–7 will unfold what Matthew understands by "teaching."

"Proclaiming *the good news of the kingdom* (*to euaggelion tēs basileias*) (cf. 4:23; 9:35; 24:14; 26:13). Matthew does not distinguish between the message *of* Jesus to Israel and the post-Easter message of the Church *about* Jesus. He designates both as "the [this] good news of the kingdom." In 4:23 and 9:35 Matthew describes Jesus Messiah as going around all Galilee proclaiming to Israel "the good news of the kingdom." In 24:14 and 26:13 he records that what the disciples, or Church, of Jesus will proclaim in all the inhabited world is "this good news of the kingdom."

In Matthew's thought "the [this] good news of the kingdom" is christological in coloration. In 4:23 and 9:35 it refers to the message that specifically Jesus Messiah, the Son of God, proclaims. "The good news of the kingdom" is the news about the kingdom, which saves or condemns, which is revealed in and through Jesus Messiah, the Son of God, and is announced first to Israel and then to the Gentiles to the effect that in him the eschatological Rule of God has drawn near to humankind.

"Healing every disease and every infirmity." Along with teaching and preaching, "healing," too, is singled out in the summary passages as being typical of Jesus' ministry to Israel (4:23; 9:35). Jesus heals, just as he preaches and teaches, in his capacity as the Messiah, Son of God (4:17, 23–25). Still, Jesus Son of God is at the same time the servant of God (12:18), and the Greek verb *therapeuein* can mean to "serve" as well as to "heal" (cf. 8:16).

The miracles Jesus performs are divided into two groups: (1) therapeutic miracles (miracles of healing), in which the sick are returned to health or the possessed are freed of demons (cf. esp. chs. 8–9); and (2) nontherapeutic miracles, which have to do with exercising power over the forces of nature. In the summary passages only therapeutic miracles are involved. This has the effect of highlighting their prominence as a part of Jesus' ministry. "Moreover, it is also these miracles that create the stir in public astonishment among the crowds but disapprobation among the leaders (9:34; 12:24). In short, an essential mark of the therapeutic miracles is that they picture Jesus as being active in the full view of Israel" (*Story*, 69–70).

The miracles Jesus performs are termed "deeds of power" (*dynameis*, plural of *dynamis*). *Dynamis* is associated with God (22:29) and can even be used, as Jesus does in the words of the psalmist, as a metaphor for God (26:64). Contrariwise, "power" in the sense of *dynamis* is not something that is predicated to Satan, demons, or the opponents of Jesus. Jesus and the disciples, in turn, are never reported as doing "wonders" (*terata*,

24:24), and the "sign" (*semeion*) is characterized as a miraculous feat that the religious leaders demand of Jesus as they tempt him to prove he is not in collusion with Satan (12:24, 38; 16:1). God, the source of "power," has empowered his Son Jesus with the Spirit; in consequence of this, the miracles Jesus performs are "deeds of power" and not false "signs and wonders."

Verse 24: "Fame spread throughout all Syria." Here "Syria" (only here in Matthew) does not mean the Roman province, but the districts surrounding Galilee seen from a Jewish viewpoint. While the districts mentioned in the next verse refer to "biblical" districts, Jesus' fame, and his alone, already passes beyond the limits of Israel.

Here with the three catchwords "demoniacs, epileptics (sleep walkers) and the paralytics," Matthew also anticipates afflictions of which he will later (8:28-34; 9:1-8; 17:14-21) cite examples. With respect to the Sermon on the Mount, it is important that a summary presentation of Jesus' healing activity has already been given: Matthew places Jesus' teaching in the first place, and therefore chapters 5-7 before 8 and 9. But the teaching Jesus is none other than the Son of God, who with his helping power accompanies men and women—also the community—so that the crowds can follow him. Verse 23f. thereby hints at a dimension of the "indicative" of salvation otherwise so often missing in Matthew.

Verse 25: "Great crowds followed him." That crowds follow him belongs to the picture of Jesus' activity. What "followership" is the reader knows from 4:21; through the following of the crowds Matthew indicates that the discipleship history (4:18-22) is to be understood as typical. The crowds and the disciples who follow in verses 18-22 are not to be understood as two absolutely distinct circles. Matthew's purpose is to indicate in this way that discipleship will be broadened. He also uses the crowds for purposes of composition, to convey his understanding of the Sermon on the Mount, where the crowds together with the disciples become the hearers (cf. at 5:1 f.), for what is said then also applies to the crowds called to discipleship.

THE SERMON ON THE MOUNT, CHAPTERS 5-7

The Sermon on the Mount has always loomed large in the Gospels. Situated toward the beginning of the First Gospel, it came to be called the Charter of the Kingdom of God. Then there are scholars such as Benjamin Bacon (1920), who said that the Sermon dominates the whole of Matthew's Gospel in the sense that from it one gains insight into the structure of the Gospel and into its nature and purpose.

The method that Bacon used (and other scholars for fifty years after him) was redaction criticism. In this perspective, the Gospel of Matthew is regarded as an amalgamation of traditions and a revision of Mark. As compared with Mark, the most striking feature of Matthew is the presence of the great discourses. As the first and greatest of these, the Sermon on the Mount came to be accepted as the climactic feature of Matthew.

Recently another approach has come into use, literary criticism, which approaches a Gospel not as an amalgam, but as a unified narrative made up of story and discourse (cf. Introduction). Integral to the story are the events which make up the plot, and in the case of Matthew, the driving force of the plot is seen in the element of conflict, which in Matthew, climaxes not in the Sermon on the Mount, but in the Passion.

What role, then, do the Sermon on the Mount and the other discourses play in Matthew? We have just seen that in his summary passages Matthew places "teaching" ahead of "preaching" and "healing" (cf. 4:23). Matthew also characterizes the Sermon as "teaching" (5:2; 7:28). The Sermon is the example par excellence of this facet of Jesus' activity, yet it is not the climax of Matthew.

And in what capacity does Jesus deliver the Sermon on the Mount? Some interpreters press the parallels between Sinai and the mount of the Sermon and take Jesus to be a "second Moses" or "Lawgiver." The corollary of the thesis that Matthew culminates in the discourses is that Jesus is made out to be the "Teacher." Yet it is very clear that "teacher" remains for Matthew no more than a term of human respect. Conceived and empowered by the Holy Spirit, Jesus enjoys a unique filial relationship, by virtue of which he speaks and acts with the authority of God. Jesus delivers the Sermon as the "Son of God" and the crowds are astonished at his teaching, "for he taught them as one having authority" (7:29). Indeed, in the sermon Jesus speaks as the resurrected and exalted Son of God, instructing the faithful in the Greater Righteousness. This explains why the Sermon on the Mount has such an exalted ethic.

And to whom does Jesus deliver the Sermon? Jesus presents none of his great speeches to the religious leaders, for there is never a time in Matthew's story when their ears are not deaf to his teaching. At first sight the setting of the Sermon (5:1-2) would seem to indicate that it was the "crowds" and the first "disciples" whom Jesus has just called (4:18-22) who received Jesus' teaching atop the mountain, but the contents of the Sermon argue against this. The crowds are outsiders, while "passages like 5:11-12 and 7:15-23, which speak of enduring persecution on account of Jesus or tell of followers of Jesus who prophesy, cast out demons, and perform many miracles in his name but are in reality workers of lawlessness, simply have no place in the picture the narrator paints of the disciples during the earthly ministry of Jesus" (J. Kingsbury, "The Place, Structure, and Meaning of the Sermon on the Mount within Matthew," *Interpretation* 41(2, '87) 131–43, 135). Nor can it be said that the first-century Christians who comprised the membership of Matthew's Church are the recipients of Matthew's Gospel. These first-century Christians are not living within the "world of the story" Matthew is narrating but apart from it, in the real world. The persons indicated by the contents of the Sermon on the Mount as being its recipients are the "implied reader" (or the "implied readers") of Matthew's Gospel.

The implied reader is the one who is silently and invisibly present throughout Matthew's story. He/she has a position within the world of Matthew's story, past the resurrection, but short of the Parousia. This insight is of great importance, especially for understanding the great discourses of Jesus (chs. 5-7; 10; 13; 18; [23]; 24-25). In his great speeches Jesus periodically "speaks past" his story-audience of crowds or disciples, and addresses the implied reader(s) directly (cf. 5:11-12; 7:15-23).

If Jesus' great speeches are "heard" from the vantage point of the intended reader, one sees at once that the implied reader is able to relate to all those matters Jesus raises in his speeches which envisage a time or situation strikingly different from the one in which the crowds or disciples in the story find themselves. The very sayings in Jesus' speeches that are so ill-suited to address the immediate situation of the crowds or the pre-Easter disciples prove to be well-suited indeed to address the situation of the implied reader.

This phenomenon of having Jesus "speak past" his story-audience is only one of the rhetorical devices that Matthew, as implied author, utilizes in order to insure that the great speeches of Jesus will relate directly to the implied reader.   Other linguistic devices or modes that Matthew uses to turn Jesus' great speeches into a direct word of address to the implied reader are: the imperative mood, the pronoun "you" (whether singular or plural), "timeless expressions," and parables. Indeed, the tone of Jesus' speeches is virtually that of a homily being addressed to the implied reader.

The theme of the Sermon on he Mount is: The Greater Righteousness—the quality of life which is indicative of disciples who make up the Church. It is the behavior that comports itself with living in the sphere of God's kingdom (5:20; 6:33).

While the kingdom may perhaps be described accurately as a gift from God, "righteousness (*dikaiosyne*)" emerges in the Gospel as the demand placed upon humans and the response expected from members of the Matthean community. "When Matthew speaks of righteousness within the

Sermon on the Mount, he is referring to the behavior and actions expected of those within the community'' (Overman, 92).

The Sermon spells out in concrete fashion the specific contents of the behavior and attitudes expected from the community member. Matthew's Gospel constitutes ''community-forming literature'' and nowhere is the community-forming activity more evident than in chapters 5–7. ''This section of the Gospel has as its primary focus the ordering of relationships and behavior within the community. The personal traits and characteristics of the members are made explicit. There is significant material in this portion of the Gospel which is devoted to the subject of maintaining relationships and resolving disputes within the community. Matthew 5-7 amounts to something like a constitution for the community, which instructs and guides the members'' (A. Overman, 94–95).

Jesus instructs disciples: ''Be perfect, therefore, as your heavenly Father is perfect'' (5:48). What ''being perfect'' means here is not being flawless but ''being wholehearted.'' In Jesus' teaching to do God's will is, at its core, to exercise love (22:34-40, the Greatest and First Commandment). Loving as God loves is of the essence of the ''greater righteousness.'' And Matthew most assuredly holds up Jesus' teaching in the Sermon as an ethic disciples are to live. For disciples who live in the sphere where God rules through the risen Jesus, doing the greater righteousness is the normal order of things.

The Sermon on the Mount is structured as follows:
Ascent of the Mountain, 5:1-2
1st Part: Those who practice the Greater Righteousness, 3-16
2nd Part: Greater Righteousness before Neighbor, 17-48
3rd Part: Greater Righteousness before God, 6:1-18
Almsgiving, Prayer, Fasting
4th Part: Greater Righteousness in other areas, 19–7:12
5th Part: Injunctions (Conclusion), 13-27.

Preamble to the Sermon, 5:1-2

There is never a time in Matthew's story when the ears of the religious leaders are not deaf to Jesus' teaching. So Jesus presents none of his great speeches to them. At first sight, the setting of the Sermon on the Mount would seems to indicate that it was the ''crowds'' and the first ''disciples'' whom Jesus has just called (4:18-22) who received Jesus' teaching atop the mountain, but the contents indicate that the ''implied reader(s)'' are the recipients of Matthew's Sermon on the Mount.

1 When Jesus saw the crowds, he went up the mountain; and after he sat down, his disciples came to him. **2** Then he began to speak, and taught them, saying:

Matthew keeps his discourses well integrated into the narrative. D. Bauer says three factors are important here: (1) the formula which is repeated at the end of the discourses is a link rather than a conclusion—"they do not function to separate, but rather to connect, the discourses with what follows" (Bauer, 129); (2) lack of clear, decisive beginnings to the discourses indicates that they are also integrated into the material that precedes; and (3) this "is indicated also by an examination of the contexts of each of the discourses. The Sermon on the Mount (chs. 5–7) is placed in the context of the proclamation of Jesus that the kingdom of heaven is at hand (4.17), a theme emphasized in the sermon itself (for instance, 5.10; 6.10). The calling of the disciples (4.23-25) and the mention of the crowds which followed Jesus (4.23-25) prepare for the sermon by providing its audience (5.12; 7.28). In terms of the material that follows . . . the sermon is joined to chapters 8–9 by means of the inclusion of 4:23 and 9:35" (Bauer, 130).

Verse 1: "*He* went up." In the Sermon the focus is on the words, or teaching, of Jesus, bringing the Law and the Prophets to fulfillment (v. 17). Hence, a primary way in which the Law and the Prophets (viewed ethically as the norm of human behavior) receive their final revelation is in the teaching of Jesus.

"Went *up the mountain (anebē eis to oros)*"—neither a mountain range nor some individual mount which can be located. The mountain in Matthew is the special place of divine action and revelation, a fitting place for the discourses to begin. "He sat down"—the ancient posture of teachers, a sign of their dignity and authority. Jesus sits down as was customary with a teacher in a synagogue service.

Associations with Moses' ascent of Sinai (Exod 19:3, 12; 24:15, 18; 34:1-2, 4) are connected with Matthew's formulation; the conclusion of the Sermon also reflects these texts. But this does this mean that Matthew wishes to set Jesus antithetically over against Moses and the law of the second Moses as the invalidation of the first. Israel's basic history is clearly reflected. Now God will again speak to Israel through Jesus in a fundamental way as formerly he had spoken on Mount Sinai.

For the concept Setting, cf. 4:1. As a setting, *mountain* is a site of end-time revelation. Here God declares Jesus to be his unique son (Transfiguration, 9:7), and here Jesus Son of God, unlike Israel son of God of old, resists temptation and keeps faith with God (4:8-10). Here Jesus also performs such end-time acts as teaching the will of God (Sermon, 5:1-2); foretelling the events that will lead up to the close of the age (Eschatological Discourse, 24:3); and, following his resurrection, commissioning his disciples to their end-time ministry (28:16).

Verse 2: "Then he began to speak". lit. "he opened his mouth (*anoigō to stoma autou*. While there may be an allusion to Mount Sinai and the giving of the Law, Jesus is not the new Moses here. He is the one who speaks revelation and gives Law on the mount; he speaks in the place of God while the disciples who come up to receive Jesus' instruction stand in the place of Moses and his close companions, while the crowds at a distance might represent Israel of old. The Biblical expression *anoigo to stoma autou* both heightens the solemnity of Jesus' action and strengthens the Biblical character of the scene. The Son of God will now, for the first time, after his summary statements in 3:15 and 4:17, proclaim the Gospel to Israel.

1st Part of the Sermon on the Mount, 5:3-16
Those Who Practice the Greater Rightousness

The Beatitudes, 5:3-12

The Greater Righteousness is the theme of the Sermon on the Mount. In the Introduction (5:3-16), Jesus specifies the types of persons disciples are who practice the greater righteousness. The introduction falls into two parts: the Beatitudes (5:3-12), and Jesus' words on salt and light (5:13-16).

In pronouncing the Beatitudes, the Matthean Jesus confers end-time "blessings" upon disciples who are characterized by what they are (e.g., the poor) or do (e.g., the peacemakers). These blessings assure disciples of the vindication and reward of God's consummated kingdom. If the ethic of the Sermon is exalted, this is because it is the resurrected and exalted Jesus who is instructing his own in the ideals of the Kingdom. Yet Matthew holds up Jesus' teaching in the Sermon as an ethic disciples are to live. Disciples have been called by Jesus to enter the sphere of God's eschatological kingdom. The ethic of the Sermon describes life in this sphere. Disciples are called upon to be "perfect." This does not mean that they are to be flawless, but that they are to be "wholehearted." They are to love God with heart, soul, and mind and to love the neighbor as the self.

3 "Blessed are the poor in spirit, for theirs is the kingdom of heaven.
4 "Blessed are those who mourn, for they will be comforted.
5 "Blessed are the meek, for they will inherit the earth.

6 "Blessed are those who hunger and thirst for righteousness, for they will be filled.

7 "Blessed are the merciful, for they will receive mercy.

8 "Blessed are the pure in heart, for they will see God.

9 "Blessed are the peacemakers, for they will be called children of God.

10 "Blessed are those who are persecuted for righteousness' sake, for theirs is the kingdom of heaven.

11 "Blessed are you when people revile you and persecute you and utter all kinds of evil against you falsely on my account. 12 Rejoice and be glad, for your reward is great in heaven, for in the same way they persecuted the prophets who were before you.

Verse 3: "Blessed (*makarioi*) are the poor in spirit (*hoi ptōchoi tō pneumati*," LN 88.57). "The poor in spirit" are disciples who are not only economically deprived, but who also stand before God with no illusions of self-righteousness or self-sufficiency. There are reasons to believe that Luke's Beatitudes, with their more direct reference to socio-economic circumstances (e.g., "Blessed are you poor"), are more nearly original than are Matthew's, which appear to represent a later, "spiritualizing" tendency on the part of early Christians (e.g., "Blessed are the poor in spirit").

In fact, there are reasons to believe that Matthew's community is rather well-off. In Mark disciples going on mission are commanded to take no "copper coin," (6:8), while in Matthew they are to take neither "gold, nor silver, nor copper coin" (10:9). In Luke Jesus tells a parable about "minas" (19:11-27) but in Matthew, about "talents" (25:15-28), one of the latter being worth approximately fifty times one of the former. In the parable of the great supper in Luke, the householder says: "Go out at once into the streets and lanes of the town and bring in the poor, the crippled, the blind, and the lame" (14:21). The Matthean Jesus makes no such explicit reference to the disenfranchised but merely says: "Go therefore to the main streets, and invite everyone you find to the wedding banquet" (22:9). In Mark (15:43) and Luke (23:50-51), Joseph of Arimathea is a member of the council who is looking for the Kingdom of God, but in Matthew he is a "rich man . . . who was also a disciple of Jesus" (27:57). The intended readers of Matthew's Gospel were also well accustomed to dealing in a wide range of money.

While "blessed" (*makarios*) portrays the present in the light of the future and hence attests to the tension between the two in Matthew's understanding of the rule of God, it nevertheless bears strong witness to the Kingdom as a present reality. It expresses the unique religious joy that follows for those who share in the salvation God bestows upon all who live in the sphere of his sovereignty. Matthew uses a wide variety of word-pictures to characterize the future Kingdom as the perfect realization of hope. The future Kingdom is a realm that the righteous will "enter." What this means is evident from parallel passages that tell of "entering life," "entering the joy of the Lord," "inheriting eternal life." The bliss that the righteous will experience in the future Kingdom is described in figurative language that refers to Jesus as the eschatological "bridegroom," and to the consummated Kingdom as a "wedding celebration" or as banquet, and to the righteous as perfected ones who "shine as the sun." In turn, Matthew exhorts the members of his community to see that their lives in the present are being shaped by God's future promises.

Verse 4: "Those who mourn (*penthountes*) . . . comforted (*paraklēthē-sontai*)." "*Those who mourn*" points in the same direction as the previous beatitude; taken together, verses 3 and 4 are an allusion to Isaiah 61:1-2. "To comfort all who mourn" is one of the promises of the anticipated messianic salvation. In the LXX, the verb *mourn* is used both for mourning in behalf of the dead and for the sins of others. "It is a common verb in biblical Greek and cannot be confined to the idea of mourning for sin. According to Matthew, one hates sin and forsakes it; one does not mourn it. In the present context the idea is best interpreted as a contrast between the 'mourning' of the present age and the 'comfort' of the coming age" (NS 113).

Verse 5: "The meek (*praeis*) . . . inherit the earth (*klēronomēsousin tēn gēn*)." The "meek" are disciples who are lowly and powerless, whose only hope is God. In the same way that verses 3–4 are based on Isaiah 61, so verse 5 finds its background in Psalm 37:11. As the psalm indicates, the metaphor was taken over from the possession of Canaan by the Israelites. The *meek* of this verse and the *poor* of verse 3 are the same people viewed from a different perspective. In fact, in the language of Jesus the word could hardly be distinguished from *poor*. The promise of possessing the land was originally limited to the land of Canaan (cf. Gen 17:8), but then was extended to include the entire earth, over which God would someday rule. In essence, then, this is simply another expression for the Kingdom of Heaven of verse 3.

Verse 6: "Who hunger and thirst for righteousness (*hoi peinōntes kai dipsōntes ten dikaiosynēn* . . . they shall be satisfied (*chortasthēsontai*)." Jesus predicates "righteousness (*dikaiosynē*)" to both God and humans. The righteousness of God is his justice, which will issue at the consummation of the age in salvation or condemnation for humans (5:6). The "greater righteousness" to which Jesus refers envisages human conduct, but a human conduct that contrasts sharply with that of the scribes and Pharisees (5:20). The greater righteousness is doing the will of God, including the law (5:17), as Jesus teaches this. One does God's will when one is perfect, or wholehearted, in one's devotion to God (5:48), and one is such when one loves God with heart, soul, and mind and the neighbor as self (22:37-40). At the center of the greater righteousness, then, is undivided fealty toward God and selfless love of the neighbor.

Those who hunger and thirst for rightousness are disciples who yearn for the final salvation that only God can effect. Hungering and thirsting are figures for longing after God, both in the Old Testament and the New Testament. The meaning of the figure is to seek something with all one's heart, to desire it above all else. The parallel passage in Luke reads "Blessed are you that hunger now, for you shall be satisfied" (6:1). But Matthew moves from a literal, physical hunger to that of hungering after *righteousness*. Some translations reflect the meaning "as the desire to do right."

Verse 7: "The merciful (*eleemones*) . . . obtain mercy (*eleethesontai*)." These are disciples who eschew judgment and forgive. This beatitude is best interpreted in light of a passage such as the fifth petition of the Lord's Prayer. For Matthew, the point is that a person who does not show mercy cannot count on God's mercy.

Verse 8: "Pure in heart (*katharoi tē kardia*) . . . see God (*ton theon opsontai*)." "The pure in heart" are disciples who are undivided in their allegiance to God. In this context the *heart* represents more than the seat of emotions; it refers to one's innermost being, that which shapes a person's life. The purity referred to means singleness of motive and of devotion, as opposed to a divided motive.

Verse 9: "The peacemakers (*eirēnopioi*) . . . called sons of God (*huioi theou klēthēsontai*)." These are disciples who work for the wholeness and well-being that God wills for a broken world. Both the non-Biblical Jewish literature and the Biblical writings themselves support the idea that the peace spoken of is that which is established among people. "They shall be called children of God" translates a Greek passive structure which presupposes that God is the actor. Through Jesus, disciples know God as Father in prayer, cf. 5:45; 6:9, 14-15; 7:7-11; 18:19.

Verse 10: "Persecuted (*dediōgmenoi*) for righteousness' sake." These are disciples who incur tribulation because they serve God. "Theirs is the kingdom of heaven" occurs in both the first and the eighth beatitudes. This signals the beginning and the end of a section, as it is an example of a literary device known as "incluosion," found elsewhere in Matthew. The differences between the form of these beatitudes and the form of the last one, verses 11–12, are quite clear. "*Are persecuted*" translates a perfect participle in Greek, which suggests that as Matthew writes, the Church of his day is suffering persecution. Only Philips and NEB take seriously the perfect tense—"who have suffered persecution." Reference to "persecution" at this point makes sense if we bear in mind that these words are addressed to the implied reader in his position between resurrection and parousia. This is an example of "speaking past."

Verse 11–12b: "Persecuted the prophets." The *Shedding of innocent blood* was one of the symbols used in sectarian language during the post-70 period to express hostility toward the Jewish leaders (cf. Overman, 22–23; Introduction, p. 14). The shedding of innocent blood "once again reflects the social location of these sectarian communities. They, the righteous, have been oppressed by those in control. They have interpreted the rejection and persecution they experience in terms of Israel's prophetic history and the fabled persecution of righteous men at the hands of corrupt leaders. These sectarian communities claim an association with the prophets of old, who were by this time widely recognized as righteous men and agents of God who were unjustly persecuted by corrupt leaders. In developing this theme these communities have begun to align themselves with some of the heroic underdogs of Israel's history. At the same time the Jewish leaders are being associated with some of the storied villains of the same history" (23).

What Jesus promises the disciples in all these beatitudes is fundamentally the same benefit, the eschatological salvation that attends God's kingdom. The exalted tone of the Sermon does not mean that Matthew is impossibly idealistic and completely unrealistic. His Gospel taken as a whole shows that he is fully aware of the reality of sin and of little faith. Disciples must pray for the forgiveness of their sins. Yet Matthew refuses to make the reality of sin and of little faith the determining factor in his ethic. Instead, the determining factor for him is the reality of God's eschatological kingdom which is present even now in the earthly and risen Jesus Son of God. While disciples will, to be sure, have to contend with sin and little faith, they are nonetheless summoned to be the kind of person Jesus describes in the Sermon on the Mount—the kind of person who loves God perfectly and the neighbor as the self.

The beatitudes describe in ideal terms the traits and characteristics of the members of the community. The members are to be humble and intent on pursuing acts of mercy . Righteousness should be their goal; they should be pure in heart and people eager to "make peace" (*eirenopoioi*). "Like the prophets of ancient Israel, the Matthean community will be persecuted for their commitment to righteousness and the will of God. This, however, they are told, is cause for joy, because of the great reward which is theirs in heaven" (Overman, 95).

Salt of the Earth and Light of the World, 5:13-16

Jesus pronounced his beatitudes upon disciples who together form the new community of God's eschatological people, i.e., the Church. In 5:13-16, Jesus affirms that this community is called to be the "salt of the earth" and the "light of the world." As it pursues the life of the greater rightousness, this community summons others to glorify God, that is, to live in the sphere of his eschatological rule by themselves becoming disciples of Jesus.

> **13** "You are the salt of the earth; but if salt has lost its taste, how can its saltiness be restored? It is no longer good for anything, but is thrown out and trampled under foot.
>
> **14** "You are the light of the world. A city built on a hill cannot be hid. **15** No one after lighting a lamp puts it under the bushel basket, but on the lampstand, and it gives light to all in the house. **16** In the same way, let your light shine before others, so that they may see your good works and give glory to your Father in heaven.

Verse 13: "You are (*Hymeis este*)." The pronoun is placed up front for maximum emphasis and connects with the "you" plurals of verses 11-12. The community as a whole is addressed, not just the apostles or the narrator. And the thought of verses 11-12 is also taken up—it is a persecuted community that is addressed. "Just you, you who will be reviled and persecuted, are the salt of the earth." Verses 13-16 point out what its missionary duty is to the persecuted community.

"You are the *salt of the earth (to halas tēs gēs)*." "Salt of the earth" is a defamiliarizing metaphor. Because its meaning is not immediately apparent, the reader is left wondering. That "earth (*gē*)" refers to the world and not to the ground emerges in verse 14 ("you are the light of the world") and was suggested already by verse 5 ("they shall inherit the earth"). Both sayings are to be understood in the sense of Matthean universalism. While the sense in which Matthew takes the salt metaphor is not apparent, the meaning closest at hand lies in the daily use of salt as seasoning. Through the use of *artyo* this meaning is definite for Mark (9:49) and Luke (14:34). And the idea of seasoning fits in best in Matthew also. If it has lost its taste (*mōranthē*), literally, it has "become foolish." Because of chemical impurities, salt from the Dead Sea could decompose and lose its taste; the salt could leach out, leaving behind the impurities (LN 5.25, "what was often sold as salt was highly adulterated and the sodium chloride could leach out in humid weather"). "No longer good for anything"—the weight of the saying lies upon the warning. "Is thrown out" and "trodden under foot" awakens associations with judgment terminology. What is demanded is first suggested indirectly through the metaphor "salt of the earth:" salt is not salt for itself but seasoning for food. So the disciples are not for themselves but for the earth (world). What Matthew means exactly he will bring out in verse 16, which also ties our verse together.

According to S. Hellestam, "Cooking salt (sodium chloride = NaC) could be derived from seawater in an evaporation process. But if the process were continued too long with the same batch of water, magnesium salt, which is more soluble than NaCl, would then also crystallize. Though this salt looks like NaCl, it is bitter and good only for use on roadways for weed and dust control, i.e. 'To be trodden underfoot' (Matt 5:13)." Cf. *NTA* 35(2, '91) #624, abstract by B. Pearson.

Verse 14: "Light of the world (to ph*ōs tou kosmou*)." This verse also begins with a metaphor, of which the hyperbolic character is even more pronounced than that of verse 13. "You, the small persecuted group of disciples, are the light of the world." The metaphor is clarified by verses 15-16. But Matthew first introduces the image of the "city on a hill," which does not fit in well with the idea of "works." The lack of a definite article shows that Matthew did not have in mind the Holy City of Jerusalem on Mount Zion, but simply a city on a hill. All metaphorical or allegorical applications are to be avoided; the only point is that the city is visible from afar.

Verse 15: "Light to all in the house"—corresponding to the "city on the hill" we have the "light on a stand" (LN 6.105), which no one would put under a bushel because its purpose is to give light. This partially clarifies the meaning of the metaphor "light of the world": Matthew has in mind the holiness which causes the Light to shine into the world.

"Light" is an open metaphor whose meaning is determined by the context. In Judaism we encounter it in a number of usages: Israel, the just individual, the teacher, the Torah, the servant of God or Jerusalem can be characterized as light (of the world). The manifold uses forbid our understanding the saying to be a polemic against some particular Jewish self-understanding of Israel. The reader of Matthew will think back to 4:16, where Isaiah spoke of light seen by the people sitting in darkness. Seen in this connection the application of the metaphor to the disciples corresponds to the sending of Christ himself. Beyond that, the meaning of the parable still remains hidden. The imperative of verse 16 will first make its meaning clear: the community, the light of the world, must let the light shine, otherwise it is just as absurd as an oil lamp under a bushel. With verse 16 it becomes clear why Matthew introduced a universal aspect: the light on the lampstand gives light to everyone in the house.

Verse 16: "Let your light shine (*houtōs lampsatō to phōs hymon*)." This is the universal key to our pericope. The perspective slides from the designated persons to their works. The linguistic sign for this is the switch from *lampei* to *lampsato* (vv. 14–16). For Matthew, this does not mean the introduction of a new category, because for him the human is constituted by his works and lives in them. The disciples, viz., the Christians, are the light of the world when they let their works shine forth, just as salt is only salt when it seasons. The indicative, "you are the light of the world" is therefore at the same time a demand—the works need to be actualized.

"That they may see your good works (*ta kala erga*)." "Matthew thinks of the indicative and the imperative differently from Paul. The condition of salvation, granted by God ('salt,' 'light'), is at the same time an exhortation to action. Matthew speaks without embarrassment of good works, without meaning self-justification by works. There are only a few texts in the New Testament where the honor of God is so clearly the goal of Christian conduct. At the same time, God is here for the first time in the Gospel of Matthew designated as 'your Father in heaven.' Presumably, this expression was not surprising for the readers because it became customary in the synagogue at that time, and was the designation for God which was familiar to the community from its own worship services. Nevertheless, it deserves our attention, for the designation of God as 'Father' plays an extraordinarily important role in the Sermon on the Mount. It determines the center, i.e., that part where Matthew unfolds the relationship to the Father as the 'inside' of the Christian way to perfection (6:8f., 14f.; cf. 6:1,4,6,18). Thus our passage points to this center, particularly the dimension of prayer. A 'signal' which points to the relationship to God, so central to the practice of the Sermon on the Mount, flashes like a beacon in verse 16" (Luz, 253).

2nd Part of the Sermon on the Mount, 5:17-48
Greater Righteousness before Neighbor

Having spoken in the Beatitudes of *those who practice* the Greater Righteousness (vv. 5-16) Jesus asserts that, salvation-historically, he has come not to annul the law or the prophets, but to fulfill them—that is to say, to bring them to completion. How does Jesus do this? By being who he is (the Messiah Son of God) and through what he both says and does. In the Sermon on the Mount, the focus is on the words or teaching of Jesus. Hence, as far as the law and the prophets (as functioning ethically as a norm of human behavior) are concerned, a primary way in which this norm receives its final revelation is in the teaching of Jesus.

17 "Do not think that I have come to abolish the law or the prophets; I have come not to abolish but to fulfill. **18** For truly I tell you, until heaven and earth pass away, not one letter, not one stroke of a letter, will pass from the law until all is accomplished. **19** Therefore, whoever breaks one of the least of these commandments and teaches others to do the same, will be called least in the kingdom of heaven; but whoever does them and teaches them will be called great in the kingdom of heaven. **20** For I tell you, unless your righteousness exceeds that of the scribes and Pharisees, you will never enter the kingdom of heaven.

Verse 17: "Abolish the law." In the passage 5:17-20, Jesus no longer speaks of law and prophets but solely of the law. The law is, as was mentioned, the law of Moses. But again, it is the law of Moses as it is being taught by Jesus. In the final analysis, therefore, what Jesus says about the law applied to it as something being authoritatively reinterpreted by his teaching. It is not the Mosaic law, in and of itself, that has normative and abiding character for disciples, but the Mosaic law as it has passed through the filter of Jesus' teaching. In the Greater Righteousness is doing the will of God, including the law (5:17), as Jesus teaches this.

Verse 18: "Will pass from the law." Until heaven and earth pass away at the consummation of the age, the law will retain its validity so that all the things of the law might be done (5:18). The completion of all the things of the law will come to light in Jesus' teaching of love, as that which lies at the heart of the whole of the law (and the prophets) (22:37-40). With this in mind, not even the most insignificant commandment is to be broken by a disciple's actions or teaching (5:19).

"The attitude Jesus takes toward the Mosaic law and the tradition of the elders is yet another factor suggesting that the first evangelist wrote for a strong Jewish-Christian constituency. Although the law retains its validity until the consummation of the age only as interpreted by Jesus, it is nonetheless not set aside (5:17-20)" (*Story*, 150).

Verse 19: "Called least . . . called greatest." Disciples are pledged higher and lower degrees of eschatological reward. At the same time they are warned, on the one hand, against breaking even the most insignificant of the commandments and, on the other, urged to observe all of them. Indeed, so serious is the breaking and keeping of commandments that it will affect a disciple's "ranking" in the consummated Kingdom of Heaven. With this in mind, not even the most insignificant commandment is to be broken, by what a disciple does or by what a disciple teaches.

Verse 20: "For (*gar*) I tell you." *Gar* connects the verse with the sayings in verses 17-19; but the comparative expressed by "greater" points already to the antitheses which illustrate the "more" of what Jesus commands. The "righteousness" which is demanded of Jesus' disciples (cf.

3:15, 5:6-10) should surpass that of the scribes and Pharisees. Matthew uses this double expression often (seven times); it expresses opposition to post-70 Judaism led by the Pharisaic scribes (the Woes, ch. 23). In Jesus' time there were also Sadducean scribes; but already then the "Brotherhood" of the Pharisees with their teachers was very influential. The expression "enter the kingdom of heaven," here for the first time in Matthew, is found already in Mark (9:47; Matthew took up the expression in a strengthened form (21:31). Originally an image for entrance into the promised land, then also into the Temple (Torah liturgies, cf. 5:8), now it is transferred to participation in the Kingdom of God. The expression places the antithesis in the perspective of the Kingdom of God.

"Unless your righteousness exceeds." The righteousness the disciples are to evince in their lives is a conduct that shows itself to be superior to ("greater than") that which typifies the scribes and Pharisees. He similarly enjoins disciples to practice the greater righteousness "now" on pain of otherwise not entering the consummated Kingdom of Heaven "then." On balance, Jesus Son of God asserts in 5:17-20 that in his coming, whereby God's kingdom has become a present though hidden reality, he accomplishes the fulfillment of the law, giving it abiding validity, and that to do the law (or will of God), is to do the greater righteousness, at the heart of which, (it will be brought home to us), is love toward God and neighbor.

"The mission of Jesus consists exactly in his establishing of the Torah through his obedience, up to the last and least commandment. Jesus is not servant but Lord of the Torah but he exercises his lordship in such a way that he lets the Torah remain valid without restrictions" (Luz, 269).

Antitheses, 5:21-48

The basic principle of the Greater Righteousness just enunciated in verse 20 is now illustrated and developed as distinctive injunctions in six so-called antitheses. These authoritative sayings of Jesus appear as variations of the formula, "You have heard that it was said to the men of old . . . but I say to you. . . ." As the antitheses prescribe, the disciple is not only not to kill but not even to become enraged; not merely to comply with the law in obtaining a divorce but not to divorce at all; not merely to obey the law and not swear falsely but not to swear at all; not merely to adhere to the law in securing retribution but to offer no resistance at all to one who would harm or exploit the disciple; and not merely to love the neighbor while hating the enemy but not to hate the enemy at all, and instead to love him.

Through parallel formulation in verse 21 and verse 33 (in the latter with "again") Matthew sets up two series of three antitheses, as he elsewhere shows a preference for the number three (cf. Intro. 2). Commentators on the antitheses divide themselves into two camps. Some hold that Jesus in the antitheses only deepens, intensifies, or radicalizes the intention of the law of Moses, while others contend that, in certain of the antitheses, Jesus radicalizes the intention of the law of Moses to such a degree that he abrogates it. The third and sixth antitheses are commonly regarded as falling into the latter category.

The introductory formula may be longer or shorter in length. Always intended, however, is the formula in its entirely, which reads: 'You have heard that it was said to the people of old. . . .'' (5:21, 33). As is apparent, this formula divides itself into three parts. The first part ("You have heard") reminds disciples of the traditional custom (e.g., in the Jewish synagogue) of hearing the law read and expounded in services of worship. The second part ("it was said") features the use of the "divine passive" and is a periphrasis for "God said." The third part ("to the people of old") envisages the Israelites at Sinai who received the law but includes as well the generations subsequent to them who have also received it. In its totality, therefore, the formula introducing each thesis reminds the disciples that it has been taught them that God, at Sinai, delivered Israel his law.

In stark contrast to this introductory formula stands the formula with which Jesus introduces each of his antitheses. It reads: 'But I say to you. . . .' (cf., e.g., 5:22). The force of this formula is unparalleled, for Jesus, in uttering it, is in effect pitting his word against the word God spoke at Sinai. Therefore, the astonishing thing about the antitheses is that in them Jesus Son of God dares to place his word and his authority above those of Moses.

The antitheses "demonstrate how the Son of God fulfills in complete sovereignty God's word of law and prophets in putting his word over against Moses. Matthew had indicated this already through the localizing of Jesus' first proclamation of the Gospel 'on the mountain.' Now 5:17-48 make clear that this does not mean that a second Moses abolished the Torah of the first Moses. Instead, Jesus' proclamation of the will of God is the 'door' to the Old Testament" (Luz, 279).

The First Antithesis, 5:21-26. Jesus commands that disciples are not only not to kill, but not even to become enraged. Scholars seem to agree that the first and second antitheses, on murder and on adultery, merely intensify commands of Moses.

> **21** "You have heard that it was said to those of ancient times, 'You shall not murder' and 'whoever murders shall be liable to judgment.'

22 But I say to you that if you are angry with a brother or sister, you will be liable to judgment; and if you insult a brother or sister, you will be liable to the council; and if you say 'You fool,' you will be liable to the hell of fire. 23 So when you are offering your gift at the altar, if you remember that your brother or sister has something against you, 24 leave your gift there before the altar and go; first be reconciled to your brother or sister, and then come and offer your gift. 25 Come to terms quickly with your accuser while you are on the way to court with him, or your accuser may hand you over to the judge, and the judge to the guard, and you will be thrown into prison. 26 Truly I tell you, you will never get out until you have paid the last penny.

Verses 21: "To those of ancient times (*archaiois*)"—the old Israel that received the Sinai revelation (the Decalogue). Jesus will spiritualize the prohibition of killing (Exod 20:13; 21:12; Deut 5:17) and make it a prohibition of anger. "Liable to judgment (*enochos estai tē krisei*)"—*krisis* can be connected with the Old Testament punishing judgment against murder. *Enochos* is in Greek a legal term meaning "to be subject to."

Verse 22: "But I say to you." The phenomenon of having Jesus "speak past" his story-audience is only one of rhetorical devices that Matthew as implied author utilizes in order to insure that the great speeches of Jesus will relate directly to the implied reader.

The very structure Matthew has given the speeches enhances their capacity to serve as an immediate address to the implied reader. They are all comparatively lengthy, which means that the implied reader, in hearing them, is exposed to long stretches of uninterrupted direct discourse. Thereby Jesus draws the implied reader to his side and schools him or her in his evaluative point of view on the ethical and eschatological issues which are of the utmost importance within the world of Matthew's story.

Matthew also makes effective use of such linguistic devices as the imperative mood, the pronoun "You" (whether singular or plural), "timeless expressions," and parables so as to turn Jesus' great speeches into a direct address to the implied reader. Jesus is enabled to address the implied reader in a very personal and immediate way: indeed, the tone of Jesus speeches is virtually that of a homily being addressed to the implied reader.

"But I say to you," found in all the antitheses, cannot be explained simply as a set-phrase in Rabbinical exposition of the Scriptures. Rather, it brings Jesus' teaching "in power" to expression (cf. 7:29). Jesus expressly places his conception of the divine will over against the wording of the Decalogue. Anger is something to be avoided already in Judaism as leading to murder. This attitude was even a distinctive mark of the Jew (Billerbeck I, 276–282). Contentwise, Jesus has not said anything very new.

The beginnings of this "absolute" prohibition of *orge* are found in the Old Testament; anger is dangerous because it does mischief and has evil consequences, and is thus to be avoided and placated (cf. Prov 6:34; 15:1; 16:14; 19:19; 27:4). Hence, the longsuffering person is praised as the true sage (Prov 14:29; 15:18; 16:32), while the angry person is condemned as a fool (Prov 14:17, 29). This exclusively negative judgment of anger found in Proverbs perhaps explains why the New Testament assessment of human anger is so severe. The antithesis angry person/wise person is picked up in the Epistle of James (1:19-20), which is close to the Old Testament Wisdom literature, and in Romans one reads that to refrain from anger is to give place to God (12:19).

But Jesus brings out in a stronger form what the Torah had not expressly commanded and legally formulates the obligation for the salvation community, which must understand itself as a brotherhood ("brother," v. 22). What "judgment" means here remains unspecified, but will become clear in what follows. Judgment can hardly be taken to mean local law; the gradation leads on to high council (highest Jewish law) and to divine judgment (hell fire).

The "Council" just makes visible the seriousness of the guilt. For Jesus, divine judgment stands behind all anger, derogatory speech, all violations of brotherhood (cf. 6:14-15; 18:35; 25:41)—this is what Matthew wants to say, despite the presentation in steps, which is peculiar to him.

Verses 23-24. Anger is inflamed by insults, slanders, and hatred. So this saying passes on to positive demands that disciples seek reconciliation with opponents. Originally the saying was within the bonds of the Tradition (cf. "So"), therefore entirely within the Jewish horizon, as the image of bringing an offering shows. It is the same whether it is a question of a sin or a peace offering; the offerer seeks peace with God; but—that is the meaning of the saying—without reconciliation with the brother, community with God is impossible. We are not to ask about the other's guilt; it is sufficient that "your brother has something *against you*." The love commandment must take precedence over cultic routine (12:7; Mark 12:33-34).

Verses 25-26. What was originally an eschatological parable (Luke 12:57-59) Matthew here turns into a warning, to come to an understanding with the process server. The situation is grave, because a guilty verdict and imprisonment threaten an unspecified burden of guilt. In this urgency ("quickly"), there is a step beyond the cultic picture of verses 23-24. Behind the imprisonment there stands the thought of the divine judgment (cf. 18:35). As before, the basic demand is for reconciliation with one's neighbor, in accordance with the primacy of love.

"The framing of the series of Anitheses through the first and sixth anitheses makes clear that Matthew sees the center of the Old Testament in love. Love is the fulfillment, not the abolition of law and prophets (5:17). The love commandment does not abolish the 'least commandments' (5:18f.) but relativizes them from case to case. In this sense, law and prophets 'Hang' on the love commandment (22:40)'' (Luz 279).

The Second Antithesis, 5:27-30. Jesus commands the disciple not only not to commit adultery, but even to lust. The first and second antitheses, on murder and adultery, merely intensify commands of Moses.

> **27** You have heard that it was said, 'You shall not commit adultery.' **28** But I say to you that everyone who looks at a woman with lust has already committed adultery with her in his heart. **29** If your right eye causes you to sin, tear it out and throw it away; it is better for you to lose one of your members than for your whole body to be thrown into hell. **30** And if your right hand causes you to sin, cut it off and throw it away; it is better for you to lose one of your members than for your whole body to go into hell.

Verses 27-28: "Looks at a woman with lust." The introduction is shorter than in the first hypothesis. The prohibition of adultery is again taken from the Decalogue (Exod 20:14; Deut 5:18). Over against this, Jesus places the prohibition of lust after a married woman (whose marriage the lusting man violates "in his heart"). This is surprising, because lust after another's wife was already forbidden in Deuteronomy 5:21. The Old Testament law already prohibited lustful glances (Job 31:1); and not a few rabbis prohibited these no less strongly than Jesus did. Thus, as with anger Jesus does not demand anything new as to content. In the framework of the other antitheses, it is a question of overcoming legal thinking concerning God's demand which searches the heart; here, the divine judgment (Hell, vv. 29-30) also threatens those who sin in secret.

Verses 29-30: "Tear it out." This is hyperbole, corresponding to Jesus' highly colored, vigorous figurative speech (cf. 7:3). Those guilty of sexual excesses are threatened with being sent to the place of punishment. But hell (Gehenna, borrowed from the grim Valley of Hinnom in Jerusalem), (LN 1.21) should no more be interpreted in a material way than was the fire (3:12; 5:22). The images show the seriousness of the situation of decision in God's eyes. Unexpressed is the entrance into God's Kingdom assured to those who hold out in temptation (Mark 9:47).

> On the basis of the kingdom of God, the integrity of the woman and/or the sanctity of God-ordained marriage is so important for Jesus that already the lustful look of a man at a married woman amounts to the act

of adultery. That means on the one hand that the act of adultery, in the sense of the Old Testament-Jewish law, is displaced to the background. In the light of the kingdom of God Jesus is not interested in it. Such adulteries are not worth considering in any case if the sanctity of a marriage is already destroyed through a lustful look. On the other hand, this demand of Jesus, which is expressed as a sentence of absolutely binding law, again avoids making an unfulfillable demand on humans only if it is heard together with the presupposition corresponding to it. With Jesus this presupposition is the arrival of the kingdom of God, in the anticipation of which a partial integration of the disadvantaged woman takes place; with Matthew it is the community standing under the support of the exalted Lord in which precisely the 'little ones' have a special weight'' (Luz, 296–7).

The Third Antithesis, 5:31-32. Because of its relationship with adultery (vv. 27-30), Matthew takes up a traditional saying of Jesus on divorce and fashions it into an antithesis. In so doing he sets Jesus' decision in formal opposition to a Scripture saying (Deut 24:1), which he later characterizes as a concession of Moses (19:8). As in no other antithesis, a sovereign decision of Jesus is placed above Scripture and allowed to stand in opposition to it. "It would seem that the Matthean Jesus, in the fifth antithesis for sure, and very likely in the third and fourth antitheses as well, does abrogate part of the Mosaic law in the interest of promulgating more stringent injunctions'' (*Matthew*, 87).

> **31** "It was also said, 'Whoever divorces his wife, let him give her a certificate of divorce.' **32** But I say to you that anyone who divorces his wife, except on the ground of unchastity, causes her to commit adultery; and whoever marries a divorced woman commits adultery.

Verse 31: "Whoever divorces"—the introduction is even shorter than in verse 27 (without "you have heard"). The citation is taken from Deuteronomy 24:1, but significantly shortened. The provision that the husband who divorces his wife because he has discovered "some indecency" in her must give her a certificate of divorce (LN 33.41) was intended as a provision to protect the wife. Once the certificate was given, the husband could not reclaim the wife. The unspecific meaning of the "some indecency" clause led to a lax divorce practice.

Verse 32a: "Except on the ground of unchastity (*parektos logou porneias*)." Some commentators point out that for Jewish thought it was a man's sacred duty to divorce an adulterous wife. The intention was to fulfill the divine will precisely by doing so. They understand the "exception clause" as a provision making it possible for an injured husband to maintain his membership in a Jewish Christian community. While the phrase *"parektos logou parneias"* may have been used in this connection, this meaning does not fit the context of the Sermon on the Mount. There the exalted Jesus is expounding the ethical ideal to members of the Kingdom. A good obtained at the cost of a divorce does not fit in well with such a context.

One traditional interpretation is that advocated, for example, by the translators of the NRSV. As they construe it, the expression *parektos logou parneias* means "except on the ground of unchastity." The contention of this interpretation is that the Matthean Jesus, though he forbids divorce in principle, nevertheless sanctions it in the event that a spouse commits adultery. Against this interpretation stand at least two objections: (1) Since Matthew, in referring to "adultery," uses the Greek word *moicheia*, it is unlikely that *porneia* is to be understood as a mere synonym of *moicheia* (cf. 15:19); and (2) one can also question whether the Matthean Jesus, in sanctioning divorce by reason of unchastity, can truly be said to radicalize the Mosaic commandment on divorce (Deut 24:1).

A second interpretation understands the exceptive clause to mean "Notwithstanding the word about immorality" (found in Deuteronomy 24:1). The idea here is that the Matthean Jesus most assuredly does radicalize the command of Moses, for he forbids divorce altogether.

"The third interpretation of the exceptive clause would render 5:32 as follows: 'But I say to you that whoever divorces his wife, except on the grounds of an incestuous marriage, makes her an adulteress.' This rendering of 5:32 portrays the Matthean Jesus as flatly forbidding divorce in every case except one: Should, for example, a Gentile couple join the church, whose marriage would (on the basis of a passage like Leviticus 18:6-18) have to be adjudged to be incestuous, that couple would be required to divorce (cf. also Acts 15:20, 29)" (J. Kingsbury, *Int* 41 [1987], 139).

"But only in the event two people (e.g., gentiles joining the church) have, in violation of Leviticus 18:6-18, entered into what must be judged to be an 'incestuous marriage.' So understood, the third antithesis does not provide a 'loophole' for easy divorce (namely, adultery), but, on the contrary, is thoroughly radical in its prohibition of divorce" (J. Kingsbury, *Matthew*, 86–87).

Verse 32b: "Makes her an adultress." The guilt falls on the man who dismisses his wife. Thereby, it is assumed that the dismissed woman is driven to marry another man through the divorce. But Jesus holds every divorce of a wife as forbidden and also regards the first marriage as still valid. The rigid Essene community demands (according to Gen 1:27) that a man "not take two wives in his lifetime" (CD 4:21, cf. for the king 11 Q Temple 57:17-19). With no dependence on Qumran and not out of the same legal perspective, Jesus pushes through to God's original will.

The Fourth Antithesis, 5:33-37. Here Jesus revokes the permission the law grants, as well as the obligation it in some instances enjoins, to make use of vows and oaths. The thrust of this antithesis is that vows and oaths are wrong because they infringe upon the majesty of God: he who is holy and ever truthful is made the guarantor of the alleged truth of sinful human beings. Here again an abrogation of part of the Mosaic law in the interest of promulgating more stringent injunctions seems likely.

> 33 "Again, you have heard that it was said to those of ancient times, 'You shall not swear falsely, but carry out the vows you have made to the Lord.' 34 But I say to you, Do not swear at all, either by heaven, for it is the throne of God, 35 or by the earth, for it is his footstool or by Jerusalem, for it is the city of the great King. 36 And do not swear by your head, for you cannot make one hair white or black. 37 Let your word be 'Yes, Yes' or 'No, No'; anything more than this comes from the evil one.

The second group of antitheses ("again") begins with the same larger introductory formula as verse 1. The development is not unified and betrays a growth of the text in the tradition. The three prohibitions involving God (vv. 34b-35) are followed by the prohibition of swearing by one's own head (v. 36). After the prohibition comes the strict command to truthful speech without oath (v. 37). The Scripture citation has fallen out of the motivation (vv. 34bc-35), the only instance of this in the whole series.

Verse 33: "Shall not swear falsely." A formal prohibition of perjury is not found in the Decalogue, but Leviticus 19:12 demands that God's name be kept holy. The second sentence ("but shall perform") which concerns the fulfillment of a promise given to God (vows), is freely formulated on the basis of various Old Testament texts (Deut 23:22-24; Num 30:3; Ps 50:14). The vow reaches far back into Israel's history and was bound up with Yahweh's call ('so truly as Yahweh lives'). The religious meaning of vows and oaths is also shown by the fact that Yahweh himself swears—on himself (Gen 22:16; Exod 22:11; Amos 6:8; 8:7). This religious horizon must be kept in mind in considering Jesus' injunction.

Verses 34-35: "Do not swear . . . by heaven." Jesus' word is clear and emphatic. The background shows an exalted concept of God as the Lord of heaven and earth (Isa 66:1; cf. Ps 11:4; 103:19). Despite Matthew's "omniscience" and "omnipresence" as narrator (cf. Introduction, p. 5), there is one area in which he does not exercise these powers. This has to do with the way he deals with God. Unlike in the case of other characters, Matthew never permits the reader to imagine that he has "immediate access" either to heaven, God's abode (5:34-35; 23:22), or to his "mind" (cf. *Story*, 32), The swearing by Jerusalem (or according to the Greek proposition: in the prayer direction 'to Jerusalem') is otherwise unknown. "The city of the great king" (Ps 48:2) shows the belief of Israel in the dwelling and throne of God on Zion-Jerusalem (Ps 78:68). Paradoxically, Jerusalem "the holy city" and the "city of the great King" (5:35), will prove to be the city of repudiation and of death for Jesus, the place where his enemies are at home.

Verse 36: "Do not swear by your head." This motive is of a different nature. Oaths by one's own head, frequent also outside Israel, show the inability of mortals to change anything by an oath. Hair color is cited to picture this, but with length of life within the scope of reference. Such oaths, often combined with oaths on oneself (cf. 26:74) were meant to strengthen a statement. The line sinks from "holy oath" (especially vows) to reinforcing merely human statements.

Verse 37: " 'Yes, Yes,' or 'No, No.' " The command to abide by simply yes and no fits smoothly with the above. The doubling bespeaks the unconditioned truthfulness that is called for (cf. James 5:12, a text that is formulated more succinctly and closer to the original). That Matthew 5:37a has the same meaning is shown by the addition 37b, which traces everything back to evil or evil men (cf. 6:13 in the masculine; 13:19-38; John 8:44). James 5:12 warns of God's judgment. Paul says of Christ Jesus, that he was not "Yes and no," that in him there was only a "Yes" (2 Cor 1:19). The prohibition of oaths creates great difficulties. Criticism of oaths on a number of grounds is found in Hellenism, also in Hellenistic Judaism (Philo, *On the Decalogue,* 92–95). The rabbis wished to protect the Divine Name through circumscriptions and restrictions (cf. Matt 23:16-22). Lightminded, superfluous oaths were all too common. But Jesus' sweeping prohibition of swearing cannot be limited to such misuse; they were only the occasion. The antithesis is just as sharply formulated as the prohibition of divorce. Yet the prohibition of swearing was not received in the same way; the interpretation history is confused. Paul repeatedly calls on God to witness (1 Thess 2:5; 2 Cor 1:23; Rom 1:9; Phil 1:8). The ancient Church took the prohibition earnestly (even for the oath of allegiance); since the early Middle Ages the Church has used oaths—down to the present. Jesus' absolute command is explained by his proclamation of the Kingdom of God: where God with his truth and goodness holds sway, those who belong to his community must deal with one another in the same way. Earthly relationships (also before law) drop out of the field of vision; only God's new ordinance is valid, however difficult it is to fulfill in the world. Again, the basic problem of the Sermon on the Mount.

"As with other categorical demands of Jesus, this one also is somewhat unrealistic. Jesus does not consider what an absolute prohibition of oaths would involve, namely, consequences of a very problematic kind. Jesus considers this as little as he does with his demand to renounce force or with his prohibition of divorce. The will of God has priority over everything else. In this radicality one may see a sign of the eschatological kingdom of God to which Jesus knew himself bound, although the text does not speak explicitly of it" (U. Luz, 316).

We can hardly say for sure how Matthew himself has interpreted the text. Through his concluding "what is more is of evil" he points out that he wants to understand the prohibition and the command of Jesus literally. He makes Jesus keep his own command: when the high priest "adjures" Jesus to confess himself as Son of God, which is to be understood most likely as an exhortation to an oath, Jesus does not answer with an oath but with *sy eipas* ("you have said so"), which leaves the responsibility for the statement with the high priest without contesting its truth (26:63).

The Fifth Antithesis, 5:38-42. Those scholars who take the position that Jesus in certain of the antitheses so radicalizes the law of Moses that he abrogates it, all appear to agree that such is the case in the fifth antithesis. For whereas the Mosaic law regulates retribution but also makes provisions for it, Jesus forbids it altogether.

> **38** "You have heard that it was said, 'An eye for an eye and a tooth for a tooth.' But I say to you. Do not resist an evildoer. But if anyone strikes you on the right cheek, turn the other also; **39** and if any one wants to sue you and take your coat, give your cloak as well; **40** and if anyone forces you to go one mile, go also the second mile. **41** Give to everyone who begs from you, and do not refuse anyone who wants to borrow from you.

This antithesis is fashioned from warnings which in Luke are connected with the love of enemies (6:29-30). Matthew constructed them into an antithesis which likewise functions as an introduction to the commandment of love of enemies. Still, it is an important antithesis for Matthew and so, like the first (anger) and the fourth (oaths) it is given both a negative and a positive formulation. For verse 42 goes beyond the examples in

31b-41 through the injunctions to giving and loaning, in which elements of the Lukan text (6:30-35) are used. Since no motivation for the demanded behavior is given, the meaning of this antithesis is especially difficult and has given rise to the most widely different interpretations which have far-reaching consequences for practical behavior.

Verses 38-39a: "Do not resist." Again, the shorter introductory formula is used (as in vv. 27 and 43). It introduces a principle which in Exodus 21:24; Leviticus 24:20 and Deuteronomy 19:21 is formulated as the right of equal retaliation (so-called *jus talionis*). Matthew uses this legal outlook which was meant to prevent an excessive retribution, as a lead-up to the saying transmitted from Jesus. Matthew sees what is new in the affirmation "do not resist an evildoer."

Verses 39b-41: "If any one strikes." The three instances (in Luke the third, v. 41 is lacking) all lie on the same line: no resistance to any evil that anyone suffers, but on the contrary a yielding and a going beyond what is demanded. In the first instance an actual attack is envisaged, which likewise involves a serious insult. The blow on the *right* cheek ("right" is lacking in Luke), which could be executed by a right-handed only with a back hand blow, which perhaps inflicts an especially serious insult.

Verse 40: "Coat (*chitona*) . . . cloak (*himation*) (LN 6.172, 176)." In the second example, seizure of clothing for debt the order indicated (coat-cloak) stands out; but in the Orient the cloak was especially important for protection against the night cold and a pledged cloak had to be returned to a poor person before sunset (Exod 22:25; Deut 24:13). Luke, who has the opposite order (6:29), has a robbery in mind.

Verse 41: "If anyone forces you (*se*)." The third example arises from forced labor and socage which, in Palestine at that time, was usually demanded by the Roman soldiery (cf. 27:32). The example uses the familiar form of address (like 5:23, 25), but is not to be limited to the interpersonal realm; it speaks to the disciple community in its relationship to an evil environment based on force. It is difficult to specify what such behavior was meant to accomplish: shaming, changing the minds of others, overcoming power by powerlessness (this as a "weapon" against rule by force) as Paul, among others, demands, to overcome evil by good (Rom 12:17-21)—likewise a first commentary on the words of the Sermon on the Mount.

Verse 42: "Give to everyone." The positive commandment to give to the one who asks and not to refuse the one who would borrow is meant just as radically, and even sharpened in Luke: "Do not ask them again" (6:30). This too contradicts ordinary conventions and behavior. Such love of neighbor already embodies something of love of enemies, with which Luke connects it.

This antithesis is understandable only in the context of the message of the kingdom of God, which on the basis of the goal picture of the future dispensation of salvation, makes demands on the present dispensation. In earthly reality, these demands can be realized only with difficulty, if at all. Therefrom can and should follow ever new impulses to actions (cf. Paul on lawsuits, 1 Cor 6:7). Matthew has in mind especially the life of the community (cf. 5:23) and its conduct in a persecution situation (cf. also 1 Peter 2:20-23; 3:14; 5:9).

If it is the case that Jesus here so radicalizes the Mosaic law that he abrogates part of it, how does abrogation of parts of the Mosaic law harmonize with the words of Jesus in 5:7-18, where he announces that he has "not come to abolish the law or the prophets . . . but to fulfill them," and that "till heaven and earth pass away, not an iota [yod], not a dot [stroke], will pass from the law?"

The answer, it appears, is that Matthew, as 11:13 indicates, sees the law and the prophets, the entire Old Testament, as "prophesying," as pointing forward, to the events that mark the eschatological age of salvation. At the center of these events, of course, is Jesus Messiah, the Son of God. With his coming, in what he says and does, the law and the prophets attain to their "fulfillment" (5:17). The law that remains in force as long as heaven and earth shall last (5:18) is the law precisely as Jesus delivers it to his disciples and Church. It is, properly understood, the messianic law. For none other than Jesus Messiah is the one who teaches the "way of God" with absolute truth and authority and hence, stands above Moses.

U. Luz finds the following thrusts of the text to be especially important: (1) To forgo the use of force is a "contrasting sign" of the kingdom of God or a part of a new way of righteousness which has been opened up by Jesus. On this basis, any realization of our text will have to make clear that "use of force" belongs to the unredeemed world which urgently is in need of salvation and therefore of the signs of renunciation of force. (2) Renunciation of force is understood by Jesus and by Matthew as an expression of love. "The juxtaposition of renunciation of force and commandment of love in Jesus and Matthew is a reminder to Christian love of its origin from the kingdom of God and the radicality which is derived from it. It is able to preserve love from being *only* a secular aid to survival" (337).

The Sixth Antithesis, 5:43-48. A majority of interpreters hold that the sixth antithesis, on love of one's enemy (5:43-48), is also intended simply to intensify a command of Moses (cf. Lev 19:18).

43 "You have heard that it was said, 'You shall love your neighbor and hate your enemy.' **44** But I say to you, Love your enemies and pray for those who persecute you. **45** so that you may be children of your Father in heaven; for he makes his sun rise on the evil and on the good, and sends rain on the righteous and on the unrighteous. **46** For if you love those who love you, what reward do you have? Do not even the tax collectors do the same? **47** And if you greet only your brothers and sisters, what more are you doing than others? Do not even the Gentiles do the same? **48** Be perfect therefore, as our heavenly Father is perfect.

Verse 43: "Love . . . hate." The Scripture citation (Lev 19:18) takes in only the first part, and taken alone cannot constitute an antithesis, because Matthew takes it up positively in the Great Commandment (22:39). So he adds by way of contrast "and hate your enemy." That is found nowhere in the Old Testament, not even in rabbinical texts (at most: to hate evildoers). The antithesis can hardly be blamed entirely on the Qumran community ("to love all sons of light . . . but to hate all sons of darkness" 1QS 1:9). In Matthew's view it characterizes Judaism as a whole. Judaism no where attains the broadness of Jesus' command.

Verse 44: "Love your enemies." The fourfold Lukan form of the commandment draws Matthew into a compound sentence, in which the demand to pray for the "persecutor" (Luke "for those who abuse you") stands out. Matthew is thinking of the tribulations of his community (cf. 5:10).

Verse 45: "Your Father who is in heaven"—cf. Introduction, the Sacred Canopy). The motif is reminiscent of the promise to the peacemaker (5:9). The future reward (Luke 6:35) is more involved than the present likeness to God's behavior, although the imitation of God will be spoken of in what follows. The wisdom motif of the blessing of God the Creator (Ps 145:9; Job 5:10-11, Wisdom 11:23; Sir 18:11) is taken up, but only in support of the all-embracing love of enemies. Similar sayings are found in Stoic philosophy, as part of the world reason pervading the cosmos (Seneca, *De benef.* IV, 26, 1; Mark Aurel, *In sem.* IX, 11), and love of enemies is to be found in other religious systems of thought. The Biblical theology goes deeper. For it the imitation of God is basically incomprehensible, but the motif begins to appear in Judaism (cf. v. 48). Through Jesus, disciples know God as Father in prayer (cf. 5:9; 18:19).

"*Chiasm* has to do with a repetition of elements in an inverted order: 'a, b, b, a' (e.g., the elements evil/good/righteous/unrighteous in Matt 5:45)" (Powell, 33).

Verses 46-47: "Love those who love you." These verses apply more clearly to love of enemies, which does not stop short at natural love (v.

46) or fraternal solidarity (v. 47). They bring into view Jesus' new "greater" righteousness (5:20), which goes beyond ordinary measure. Ordinary behavior is demonstrated by the tax collector, a despised profession, and the Gentiles, the non-Jews, whom the members of Israel looked down upon. In the Jewish-Christian communities these Jewish attitudes were still alive (18:17), although Jesus himself adopted a different attitude toward the two groups.

Verse 48: "Be perfect." In the Holiness Command it is said: "You shall be holy; for I the Lord your God am holy" (Lev 19:2, cf. 11:44). Such a demand springing from God's being was seen in Judaism as an all-embracing "imitation of God," however unattainable and paradoxical it may be. For it, Matthew uses the expression "perfect," which in the Biblical understanding designates the complete fulfillment of God's will (Gen 6:9; Deut 18:13), unblemished observance of the Law (so especially at Qumran). For Matthew, the perfection actualizes itself in the following of Jesus (19:21). Thereby the "fulfilling" of the Law (5:17) in the (Jewish)Christian understanding becomes clearer: the divine commandments are agreed to, but according to Jesus' interpretation, which overcomes a legalist understanding and uncovers their true meaning. Perfection is not (as in the Greek understanding) the highest grade of the practice of the virtues, but the comprehensive commitment to the way pointed out by Jesus, to arrive in the Kingdom of God. The love of enemies required of all Christians is an expression of Jesus' maximum demands and is fulfillable. According to the conception of the early Church, it is made possible through God's mercy (Luke 6:36) and the power of the Holy Spirit (Rom 8:2-4). It is not feeling or illusion but perseverance in behavior and action, in all areas; in personal encounters as in the social realm, between the Christian community and the world about it, and in the common life of the people.

The love of enemies commandment is both the climax and the heightening of all the demands made in all the antitheses. The demand that we surpass all previous righteousness (5:20) resounds again (v. 47). God, in whose name Jesus proclaims with authority ('But I say to you'), as the allusions to the divine law also show (vv. 22, 26, 29 f.), now comes to the fore as the heavenly Father (5:16) as exemplar, enticing and promising. The comprehensive culminating warning (v. 48), formulated by Matthew connects not only with verse 45, but also closes the entire antitheses series. The buildup is smoother than that of Luke (6:27, 33-36): it is double-membered throughout. The antithesis (v. 43) is followed immediately by an upward look to the Father in heaven with the two wisdom motifs of sunshine and rain (v. 45) and the resulting impulses—to surpass run-of-the mill behavior (tax collectors and Gentiles) (v. 46), followed by the closing warning (v. 48). While Luke is closer to the original in the ordering, following Q, Matthew is closer to the original in some formulations. He fashioned the antithesis himself, changing "merciful" of Luke 6:36 to "perfect" (v. 48).

> Jesus, Matthew, and the critics of the command of the love of enemies are in agreement on the fact that this command is not a "natural" demand. How could it be? Jesus had formulated it in a mottolike contrast to "natural" behavior. It is not the tactic of a fighter, not the generosity of a victor, not the resignation of a defeated one, and also not the solitariness of a sage. Rather Jesus has made his demand under the completely "unnatural" presupposition that the kingdom of God is breaking in and that the human being should be in harmony with it. Therefore it must not be understood, as has often been done in the history of interpretation, as the acme of the "natural" human love. Matthew has not advocated it because it is reasonable or natural or promises success but because the one who makes it is as the risen Lord with his community all the days to the close of the age. Thus the question is not directly whether it is tactically or psychically realistic but whether the experience of grace which is presupposed in it is so strong that the human being can become free for such a love (Luz, 351).

Part III of the Sermon on the Mount, 6:1-16
Greater Righteousness before God
(For Structure of the Sermon, cf. p. 67)

The third part of the Sermon (6:1-18) constitutes its center, both formally and materially. Formally, the third part stands at the center of a five-part structure. And the third part itself contains three parts: it treats of almsgiving, prayer, and fasting. At the center of the middle part, on prayer, is the Lord's Prayer. Formally, therefore, the Lord's Prayer can be seen to lie at the very heart of the Sermon on the Mount.

Materially, too, the third part constitutes the center of the Sermon on the Mount. Following on the introduction and the section devoted to practicing the greater righteousness toward the *neighbor*, Jesus concerns himself with the fundamental issue of practicing the greater righteousness before *God* (6:1-18). In the Lord's Prayer, the centerpiece of the Sermon, Jesus highlights the essential element on which all such practice is predicated: that disciples know God as "Father" (6:9).

> **6:1** "Beware of practicing your piety (*dikaiousynēn*) before others in order to be seen by them; for then you have no reward from your Father in heaven.

Verse 1a: "Beware" (*prosechete*, LN 27.59). Practicing your piety—here "piety" (*dikaiousynē*) "serves as a summary term for almsgiving, prayer, and fasting, which were for Judaism the three most important expressions of one's religious duties" (NS, p. 163).

It quickly develops that Jesus has the Jewish leaders in mind. In the first half of the second part of Matthew (4:17–11:1), the reader is led to anticipate conflict, and then take note as conflict finally erupts. To lead the reader to anticipate conflict, sayings of Jesus occur casting the religious leaders in a negative light. We have already seen Jesus predicting persecution for the disciples at the hands of Israel (5:11-12; 23:29-36), and he declares that the righteousness of the scribes and Pharisees is insufficient for gaining entrance into the Kingdom of Heaven (5:2). Now Jesus enjoins the disciples to practice their piety, not after the manner of the hypocrites in the synagogues whose aim is to win public acclaim for themselves, but in true worship of God. Evidence that the leaders do not love God is adduced from their practice of piety; as they give alms, pray, and fast, they act not in worship of God but ostentatiously, out of eagerness to be seen by people.

Jesus contrasts "to be seen by others" (6:1) with "in secret" (6:4, 6, 18). The contrast is not between "public and private" per se, as though Jesus were denying legitimacy to all public expression of charitable activity, prayer, and fasting. "To be seen by men" expresses intent, and the contrast Jesus draws is between "ostentation" and "proper motivation." The hypocrites who practice their acts of piety ostentatiously do so in order to win public acclaim for themselves. Such acclaim is all the reward they shall receive (6:2, 5, 16). Disciples are to practice their acts of piety "in secret," that is, out of heartfelt devotion to God. Eternal reward at the latter day is promised such practice (6:4, 6, 17-18). Verse 1b: "Your Father in heaven," cf. 5:45.

The Greater Righteousness before God: On Almsgiving, 6:2-4

This passage has been called a Jewish-Christian *didache*, since it so closely resembles the early Christian writing of the same name. It is a "Church catechism" containing rules of piety. The sanctified life is righteousness, and part and parcel of it are almsgiving, prayer, and fasting.

> 2 "So whenever you give alms, do not sound a trumpet before you, as the hypocrites do in the synagogues and in the streets, so that they may be praised by others. Truly I tell you, they have received their reward. 3 But when you give alms, do not let your left hand know what your right hand is doing, 4 so that your alms may be done in secret; and your Father who sees in secret will reward you."

Verse 2: "Whenever you give alms" (*poies eleemosynen* LN 57.111, 112). Almsgiving was an expression of Jewish piety that was also of central importance in the Christian community. Besides the general meaning of "compassion," in the Jewish context this also had the special meaning of "good deeds," "charitable acts." At the time of early Christianity the Synagogue did not yet have a service for the care of the poor, organized on the community level, which later became its distinctive glory. The distribution of poor relief was entrusted to individual discretion, which meant that there was all the more emphasis on giving.

As a consequence, charitable giving became a matter for rivalry. Sometimes it was misused and afforded opportunity for self-seeking public exhibitionism, as Jewish sources bear witness.

The trumpet sounding (LN 6.90) may be an ironic characterization, but fasts undertaken and contributions in the synagogue could attract public notice. One who made an especially large contribution could be especially honored and could, for example, sit next to the rabbi.

The text denounces such possibilities as hypocrisy. *Hypokrites* (LN 88.228) is a neutral word in Greek usage, meaning "actor." Transferred into the ethical realm, in both Greek and Jewish usage it takes on a negative sense and designates a person who is or does something other than what he says. Unlike Matthew 23, it is not the actions of the Jewish adversaries that is attacked but their motivation; they are reproached because they give the promised alms not for the love of neighbor, viz. for God's sake, but for their own sake. With the honor that has been accorded them they have already obtained their reward. In the background stands the rabbinic concept of God's equalizing justice: to each individual, and especially to the pagans and the evildoers, the reward for good deeds will be paid on earth and the punishment in the afterlife, while the just often suffer on earth and therefore will be rewarded in the afterlife. The hypocrites are not identified with any particular group, but remain an anonymous negative type. Apparently Matthew has the scribes and Pharisees primarily in mind.

Verse 3: "But when you give alms." The text formulates the opposite position in an exaggerated and hyperbolic manner: The left hand should not know what the right hand is doing (LN 28.74). This sprightly saying becomes a word picture and is not to be pressed. The thought is not that "even the almsgiver himself does not know that he is practicing charity." The ideal concept of "wholly unknowing, wholly unreflective" charitable activity is foreign to the text. The picture is only: no one, not even the most intimate, need know anything about your alms.

Verse 4: "And your Father who sees in secret" (LN 28.71). Charitable activity takes place for God alone, who—again a Jewish concept—will manifest hidden deeds in the last judgment and will reward and punish. The perspective is that of eschatological judgment according to deeds, as with Paul in Romans 2:16, 28-29. Those who do good deeds will receive their reward from God. It is not the aim of the text simply to inculcate a more skillful way of thinking or a more subtle life style, which would be a quasi-religious form of self glorification. Rather it uses the reference to the reward which is really given by God to expose human self-glorification as the secret goal of good deeds.

Matthew not only describes the guilt of Jesus' adversaries in general terms, he analyzes and expands upon their moral failures throughout the course of his narrative. The religious opponents are most often referred to as "hypocrites." Indeed the term "hypocrite" is used by Matthew almost exclusively to refer to the opponents of Jesus. Moreover, the contexts surrounding this term in chapter 6 point to the type of activities which characterize the religious "elite." "Here hypocrisy is understood as a dichotomy between act and motive. Although the acts are ostensibly directed toward God, the motives center on appearances before humans 'that they may be praised by people' (6.13, 5, 16)" (Bauer, 68).

Greater Righteousness before God: On Prayer, 6:5-15

In the Sermon on the Mount Jesus instructs his followers in doing the "greater" righteousness (5:20). The possession of *dikaiosynē* is presupposed for entry into the kingdom. While the kingdom is a gift from God, "righteousness (*dikaiosynē*) emerges in the Gospel as the demand placed upon humans and the response expected from members of the Matthean community. . . . When Matthew speaks of righteousness within the Sermon on the Mount he is referring to the behavior and actions expected of those within the community" (Overman, 92–93).

The disciples' acts of piety (almsgiving, prayer, and fasting) are to be performed in worship of God and not for public show (6:11). As an example of how his disciples should pray, Jesus recites the Lord's Prayer, which is devoid of the "empty phrases" and "many words' that characterize the prayers of the Gentiles (6:7). The Lord's Prayer is a model that the disciples are to approximate in formulating their own prayers.

> 5 "And whenever you pray, do not be like the hypocrites; for they love to stand and pray in the synagogues and at the street corners, so that they may be seen by others. Truly I tell you, they have received their reward. 6 But whenever you pray, go into your room and shut the door and pray to your Father who is in secret, and your Father who sees in secret will reward you.

7 "When you are praying, do not heap up empty phrases as the Gentiles do; for they think that they will be heard because of their many words. 8 Do not be like them, for your Father knows what you need before you ask him.

9 "Pray then in this way:
Our Father in heaven,
 hallowed be your name.
10 Your kingdom come,
 Your will be done,
 on earth as it is in heaven.
11 Give us this day our daily bread.
12 And forgive us our debts,
 as we also have forgiven our debtors.
13 And do not bring us to the time of trial,
 but rescue us from the evil one.
14 For if you forgive others their trespasses,
 your heavenly Father will also forgive you;
15 but if you do not forgive others,
 neither will our Father forgive your trespasses.

Verse 5: "They have received their reward." The second strophe deals with right-ordered prayer. In Judaism the synagogue was the preferred place of prayer. But since it was not understood as a holy place, in principle one could pray anywhere. The text presupposes regular prayer, morning, noon, and evening. The times of prayer were not fixed exactly, as in Islam, for example; prayer was only specified within a certain time period. So it could just happen that some were often to be seen praying on busy street corners (*gōniais*, LN 79.107). Loud, effusive prayer in the synagogue service may be aimed at.

Verse 6: "Go into your room (*tameion*, LN 7.28)." Again the positive instruction in a dramatic, graphic form. A *tameion* is properly the storeroom, found even in the houses of Palestinian farmers. In a wider sense it can designate an out-of-the-way room, one not visible from the street. It is not the purpose of the precept simply to prescribe a certain place for prayer. To this extent the early Christian saying is correct: "It is not the place (*topos*) that does the harm, but the kind (*propos*) and the goal (*skopos*)."

This cultic *didachē* springs from the concept of the hidden God who dwells "in heaven" (6:1), who is "in secret" (6:6, 18), and who "sees in secret" (6:4), and who is a God who rewards and punishes. The righteousness (*dikaiosynē*) demanded of humans is recognized as the condition of redemption. But reward for good deeds can be bestowed only once. Therefore the devout person who is in need of reward to bring about redemption in the last judgment (6:1b: "from your Father in heaven") must avoid the anticipation of reward in this life (6:1a: "before others") under all circumstances. In accordance with the concept of the imitation of God, cultic acts must take place "in secret."

The Our Father. The Lord's Prayer divides itself into four parts. The "address" (v. 9b) shows that the prayer is directed to God as Father. The "your petitions" (vv.9c-10) focus on God and the advent of his kingdom as a consummated reality. The "we petitions" (vv. 11-13) focus on the suppliants and their physical and spiritual needs.

Verse 7: "Do not heap up empty phrases (*me battalogēsete*, LN 33.87). As an example of how his disciples should pray, Jesus recites the Lord's Prayer, which is devoid of the "empty phrases" and "many words" that characterize the prayers of the Gentiles. The Lord's Prayer is a model that the disciples are to approximate in formulating their own prayers.

If the verse is only a warning to short prayer, it accords with many Jewish and many Hellenistic sayings. But it does more. As verse 7b shows already, the wordy prayer is not rejected simply because it is wordy, but as a means of winning God's hearing.

Verse 8: "For your Father (*ho pater hymōn*) knows." Long prayers are not necessary because God knows what we need before we pray, and so removes the need for lengthy prayer (NS, 172).

The Address. Verse 9b: "Our Father (*'abba'*) who art in heaven." This "address" shows that the prayer is directed to God as Father. "In its original form, the Lord's Prayer probably comes from the earthly Jesus himself. One indication of this is that the version in Luke essentially reappears in Matthew. Another is the Jewish and Aramaic character of the prayer" (J. Kingsbury, *Harper's Dictionary*). First, in form and content, the Lord's Prayer parallels Jewish prayers (the Kaddish and the Eighteen Benedictions) apparently in use, in their oldest forms, in the synagogue worship of Jesus' time. Secondly, behind the Greek word for "Father" is the Aramaic *abba*, and behind the Greek for "debts" and "sins" is *choba*.

Choba means "debt" or, in a religious context, "sin" or "guilt"; thus, in Aramaic, forgiveness of "debts" (Matt 6:12) is the same as forgiveness of "sins" (Luke 11:4). *Abba* is the definite form of the Aramaic word "father" (lit. 'the father'), properly translated as "my father" or "our father." Used by Jesus (and early Christians) to address God (Mark 14:36; cf. Rom 8:15; Gal 4:6), the word suggests familial intimacy. Many scholars find indications of such use in ancient Judaism, but others argue that it originated with Jesus. Jesus himself addressed God as *abba* (cf. Mark

14:36), thus establishing a custom that was continued even by Greek-speaking Christians (Gal 4:6; Rom 8:15).

The form stems from family speech and was used as an address form by small and grown children to their father and as a respectful address to old men. In the time after Jesus it had entirely replaced the usual form of address 'abi ("my father") and 'aba (status emphaticus). From the Jewish prayers many forms of address of God as Father are found, but not 'abba'. The choice of this form of address is therefore striking.

J. Jeremias saw in this choice a trace of the *ipsissima vox* of Jesus and an expression of the unique relationship of the Son, Jesus, to his Father. Even if his thesis is not tenable as applying exclusively to Jesus, it must still be asked whether Jesus did not use 'abba' as an expression of an understanding of God, imbued with the thought of God's nearness and love, special to Jesus yet valid for everyman.

As the Greek New Testament texts which retain the Aramaic divine address 'abba' (Rom 8:15; Gal 4:6) in visibly liturgically influenced texts (Mark 14:36) show, the Christian community saw something special in Jesus' manner of addressing his Father. The distinctive use of 'abba' to address God in the *Diatessaron* and in the old Syrian translations point in this direction. In the Our Father, the break in the rhythm—'abba' standing alone clashes with the two beat rhythm and demands a pause after it—shows what weight lies upon this form of address. It is in accord with Jesus' proclamation of God's nearness through his love to the poor, sinners, and outcasts: it also accords with Jesus' important father parables (Luke 11:11-13; 15:11-32) and the strong emphasis on the certainty that prayer will be heard (Matt 6:7-8, Father; Luke 11:5-13, Father; 18:1-8).

Beginning with the reverent, yet intimate 'abba', the *Our Father* begins with a salvation statement: it is the prayer of the children of God. God beckons us, that we should believe, and as true children pray to him as our true father.

"Our Father *in heaven*." The words, "in heaven," found only in Matthew, characterize God as the heavenly Father of the disciples in contradistinction to their earthly fathers. More importantly, "heaven" is also seen as that indeterminate place from which God exercises his rule and, through Jesus, effects his purposes on earth.

The You Petitions, 9c–10b. The "You" petitions of the Lord's Prayer focus on God and implore God to act so as to achieve his purposes in the world. *Hallowed be your name,* v. 9c: this first petition is further explicated by the second (coming of God's Kingdom, 10a) and the third, found only in Matthew (doing God's will 10b). God's "name" is synonymous with God himself; the first petition invokes God to make his holiness manifest to the world by ushering in the final day of salvation.

Verses 10a, b, c. To concretize this, the disciples pray, "Your kingdom come" 10a and, "Your will be done on earth as it is in heaven" 10b. Here, God is called upon, as part and parcel of his nation, and (in Matthew), to exercise his will here on earth with as much freedom from opposition as he presently exercises it in the sphere of his heavenly abode.

"Your kingdom come," 10a. God's Kingdom which comes is frequently the object of Jewish prayers; indeed it is striking how often the future kingdom is the object of rabbis' prayers, since otherwise the present aspect of God's rule stands in the foreground. As compared with the Jewish parallels, Jesus' way of speaking about the coming of God's kingdom is striking. Jesus understands it as something dynamic and powerful. The lapidary briefness of the petition is also striking. In the Jewish Eighteen Benedictions, the eleventh and twelfth beraka speak of the return of the Judge and the destruction of Rome; the Kaddish prayer prays that God's Kingdom come with haste. The Lord's Prayer lacks such accents and this fits Jesus. He gives no graphic description of God's Kingdom, does not fix it in time, and allows its political and national dimensions to fade into the background. The open formulation is perhaps also typical of Jesus. It imposes no particular understanding of the Kingdom on the one who prays. This prayer is entirely free of doubt in its eschatological dimension, although the interpretation history of the Church has taken a different direction.

"Your will be done," 10b. Matthew 6:33 helps us to understand how God and his creatures work together: "Seek first his kingdom *and his righteousness.*" Act according to the Kingdom, and practice the justice corresponding to it. Even more important is the Gethsemane scene, 26:42, when Jesus prays that "your will be done," he prays not only that God do what he wills, but also for the strength to actively apply this will of God to himself. So our petition aims at an active disposition of men and women. But it is not just a simple imperative but it lays at God's feet the activity of humans in the form of a petition. In the realm of Old Testament-Jewish thinking, the will of the active God is always understood as a demand for an active partner. It is not a question of a surrender to an inscrutable fate to be accepted in faith. An alternative between God's activity and human activity seems impossible. While the Kingdom is a gift from God, righteousness in Matthew is the demand placed upon humans and the response expected from members of the Community.

"On earth as it is in heaven" verse 10c (cf. 5:45).

The "We" Petitions, verses 11-13. The 'we' petitions focus on the physical and spiritual needs of the disciples.

Verse 11: "Our daily bread" (*ton arton hemon epiousin*), LN 67.183, 206. The petition for bread is a request for the necessities of life. Traditionally translated (in Matthew), "Give us this day our daily bread," it is more accurately rendered, "Give us today our bread for tomorrow." The NRSV gives "our bread for tomorrow" as an alternate reading. At the basis of this petition is the notion that the disciples pray for the necessities of life that they require "today" in view of the fact that "tomorrow" God's splendid Kingdom will come.

The fourth petition of the Our Father belongs to a social situation of need, in which food for the coming day was not simply to be taken for granted. Semiologically, "Bread," as the most important food item can stand pars pro toto for "food" in general, but cannot be extended to any and every life-necessity. We might think of the situation of a day laborer who does not yet know whether he can find work on the following day, by which he and his family can live. "Bread for tomorrow" also entails a limitation: it is a matter of survival, not of riches. "Today" is by no means superfluous, but reveals the urgency of the petition. From the Ninth Beraka of the Schemone, where from the perspective of the peasant the fruit of the year is prayed for, there is a characteristic distinction.

12: "Forgive us . . . as we also have forgiven." The petition for the forgiveness of debts, or sins, is an appeal that God, as father of the disciples, will graciously forgive them their sins and so enable them to forgive one another. While the Jewish parallels have the fewest concrete details comparable to the Bread petition, in the Forgiveness petition, we are again involved with a central theme of Jewish prayer. The most striking thing about it is the addition. In fact the thought that divine forgiveness is bound up with human forgiveness is widespread in Judaism, but there is, in my opinion, no case where human actions are taken up in this way into a central prayer text. What in our exposition has been implicit up to this point, here becomes crystal clear: prayer and human actions are not mutually exclusive. On the contrary, prayer is a speaking of the active human person with God.

Verse 13: "Do not bring us to the time of trial." The *NRSV* gives "us into temptation" as an alternate reading. The final petition is a plea that God so guide the disciples through life that their relationship to him as Father may never come into jeopardy and that they may be preserved from Satanic evil of every kind.

"But deliver us from the evil one." The *NRSV* gives "from evil" as an alternate reading.

Verses 14-15. In this logion, Matthew takes up the Forgiveness petition of the *Our Father* and gives it a paraenetic formulation. Both the conditional formulation and also the "negative" verse 15 (lacking in Mark 11:25) make it clear that human forgiveness is the condition for divine forgiveness. So the evangelist stresses precisely those places where the Old Testament was most directly concerned with human activity. As distinct from the introductory logion of the *Our Father* (v. 7-8), which stresses God's nearness, this concluding logion stresses the connection between prayer and action. Matthew makes it clear that prayer too is Christian practice, which 6:19–7:27 will deal with again. Contentwise, the Forgiveness command corresponds to the center of his ethic, the Love command. Through prayer disciples know God as Father (cf. 5:9; 7:7-11; 18:19).

Greater Righteousness before God: On Fasting, 6:16-18

Again, Jesus cites "fasting" as one of the three fundamentals of proper piety and enjoins his hearers to the true practice of it (i.e., without ostentation).

> 16 "And whenever you fast, do not look dismal, like the hypocrites, for they disfigure their faces so as to show others that they are fasting. Truly I tell you, they have received their reward. 17 But when you fast, put oil on your head and wash your face. 18 so that your fasting may be seen not by others but by our Father who is in secret; and your Father who sees in secret will reward you.

Verse 16: "And whenever you fast." The intended readers of Matthew appear to have been people of Jewish and of Gentile background. This is suggested by the contents of the Gospel, which presuppose knowledge of Jewish thought, history, and traditions on the one hand, and openness toward Gentiles on the other. Features suggesting that Matthew wrote for a sizable Jewish-Christian constituency are numerous. Many of the key terms in the Gospel are thoroughly Jewish in tone. Just so, the sanctified life of the disciple is known as "righteousness" (*dikaiosyne*), and part and parcel of it are almsgiving, prayer, and fasting.

The passage on fasting presents a somewhat exaggerated portrait of the opposite type, the hypocrite (LN 88.228). In the background are such practices as wearing sackcloth, non-use of body oil, and the sprinkling of the head with ashes, customs which were used in public fast only in extreme situations, e.g., draught. If a person practiced private fasting in so extreme a manner, he could get the reputation of a holy person. True devotion calls for individual fasts as an expression of sorrow, penance, and humility for the strengthening of prayer.

Verse 17-18: "Put oil on your head"— the text advises the contrary— when fasting anoint the head and wash the face. This does not seem to be an exaggeration, as in the foregoing. Washing of the face, frequent baths and anointings were recommended by the rabbis. These were much more the object of daily hygiene. So the command could also be meant realistically: when you fast, conduct yourself in such a way that no one will take note of this fact.

Although the four disciples already called (4:18) are plainly identified as hearers of Jesus, one learns only three chapters later (9:14-15) that, prior to his death, Jesus absolves his disciples of any necessity to fast. Here again Jesus utters words in the Sermon on the Mount which have little import for the immediate situation of his pre-Easter disciples (cf. Introduction, Speaking Past).

4th Part of the Sermon on the Mount, 6:19–7:12
Greater Righteousness in Other Areas

In the fourth part of the Sermon on the Mount (6:19–7:12), Jesus deals with the practice of the greater righteousness in areas of life he has not already touched on. The imperatives (negative and positive) Jesus employs mark the subunits: "Do not store up" (6:19-24); "Do not be anxious" (6:25-34); "Judge not" (7:1-5); "Do not give" (7:6); and "Ask . . . seek . . . knock" (7:7-11). The Golden Rule (7:12) serves as both the conclusion and culmination of this fourth part.

In each of these subunits, a climactic utterance of Jesus occurs which captures the unit's intention. The result is a series of sayings which includes many of the most familiar and thought-provoking to be found in the Gospels: "No one can serve two masters" (6:24); "With the judgment you make you will be judged" (7:2); "Do not throw your pearls before swine" (7:6); "Every one who asks receives" (7:8).

The Two Masters, 6:19-24

This section (6:19–7:12) corresponds exactly in length to the Antitheses. Matthew obviously intended this and viewed the section as a unit.

While more attention is given to questions of community life than is the case in the Antitheses, it is not easy to give it a heading that will sum up its content. The section is unified formally through four negative prohibitions in the second person plural as introduction to new sections (vv. 19, 25; 7:1, 6):

> **19** "Do not store up for yourselves treasures on earth, where moth and rust consume and where thieves break in and steal **20** but store up for yourselves treasures in heaven, where neither moth nor rust consumes and where thieves do not break in and steal. **21** For where your treasure is, there your heart will be also.

> **22** "The eye is the lamp of the body. So, if your eye is healthy, your whole body will be full of light; **23** but if your eye is unhealthy, your whole body will be full of darkness. If then the light in you is darkness, how great is the darkness!
>
> **24** No one can serve two masters; for a slave will either hate the one and love the other, or be devoted to the one and despise the other. You cannot serve God and wealth."

Verses 19: "Moth and rust consume" (*sēs kai brōsis aphanizei*). The appeal is to a long-range prudence: laying up treasure does not pay. "In the NT the Greek term *sēs* is used only in reference to the larvae of moths" (LN 4.49). The moth—already almost the symbolic creature for earthly destruction—will consume the stores of clothing. In the Orient, clothing was for women an understandable expression of wealth; the rich selection in textiles reminds us of this. "Though in Mt 6.19 *brosis* has been generally understood to mean corrosion, it might actually refer to a type of insect, as it does in the Septuagint of Mal 3:11" LN 2.62. Apparently, the reference is to a particular eating insect (the Eater), e.g., the woodworm. This would bespeak destruction of chests containing various types of goods.

Verse 20: "Thieves do not break in. The "breaking in" of the thief does not apply solely to buried money (frequent in Palestine), or the criminal breaking in of underground passages, or the breaking in of houses with mud walls. The word *dioryssō* (LN 19,41) had long since become the term for "burglary." Positively, the storing up (*thesaurizō*, LN 65.10) of heavenly treasure is by alms, prayer, and fasting.

Verse 21: "Where your treasure is." A sharpening of the warning follows here. Although there is no direct Jewish parallel to this sentence, it is Jewish in thought; *kardia* is a person's center; the "treasure" makes it clear where a person stands in his center and what is most important to him. So verse 21 radicalizes the warning of verses 19-20: in the matter of wealth, a person's essence is at stake.

Verse 22-23: "No one can serve." It is possible that here "serve" has the sense of "to be a slave" (cf., LN 34.27). This helps to make it clear that it is an either/or proposition.

Verses 22-23 are metaphorical; the text "does not speak of the bodily eye." In Jewish thought "eye" is often a metaphor; character and the moral quality of a person is mirrored in the eye. Often the comparison is that of the "bad" and the "good" eye, by which is meant the miserliness and calculation, generosity and honesty. The Jewish-Christian reader of Matthew's Gospel would have thought of this comparison in reading 6:19-21..

Our text does not deal with the *essence* of man but with his *actions*, which make him full of light or darkness. The "light in you" of verse 23c, means the same as "the lamp of the body" of verse 22a, but now formulated even more sharply: "that which should be light in you." The meaning of verse 23c, d, is: if your obedience, especially your generosity, does not conform with your actions, the darkness is total. Verses 22-23 do not lead the reader away from human actions to an inner level nor do they lead away from the question of possessions. The relationship to possession remains central; in the handling of money the total person is at stake and it becomes a matter of light and darkness.

Verse 24. "God and wealth." *Mamōna* "(an Aramaic word); wealth and riches, with a strongly negative connotation—'worldly wealth, riches' " LN 57.4. The struggles of parents to provide their children with the necessities of life are not aimed at.

Confronted with this stark alternative, the reader will be guided and sustained if he or she can bring it together with the basic law of love that Jesus will later proclaim—the love of God with all the heart, soul, and mind (Matt 22:37). In worst-case scenarios such love can call for clear-cut, painful decisions. When push comes to shove, no other love can be put on the same level as the love of God. The one master (love of God) must be placed before any other.

In our pericope this is said explicitly only at the end: verse 24d brings God into play for the first and only time. Thus the high point is reached. After it was stressed in verses 21 and 23 that in the relationship to possessions the whole person (human existence) is at stake, things are advanced another step. Even right worship is involved.

In difficult passages such as this it is also useful to recall the situation in the Sermon on the Mount—that it is the Risen Jesus who is proclaiming the law of the eschatological Kingdom (cf. p. 68).

"Do Not Worry," 6:25-34

> 25 "Therefore I tell you, do not worry about your life, what you will eat or what you will drink, or about your body, what you will wear. Is not life more than food, and the body more than clothing? 26 Look at the birds of the air; they neither sow nor reap nor gather into barns, and yet your heavenly Father feeds them. Are you not of more value than they? 27 And can any of you by worrying add a single hour to your span of life? 28 And why do you worry about clothing? Consider the lilies of the field, how they grow; they neither toil nor spin, 29 yet I tell you,

even Solomon in all his glory was not clothed like one of these. **30** But if God so clothes the grass of the field, which is alive today and tomorrow is thrown into the oven, will he not much more clothe you—you of little faith? **31** Therefore do not worry, saying, 'What will we eat?' or 'What will we drink?' or 'What will we wear?' **32** For it is the Gentiles who strive for all these things; and indeed your heavenly Father knows that you need all these things. **33** But strive first for the kingdom of God and his righteousness, and all these things will be given to you as well. **34** So do not worry about tomorrow, for tomorrow will bring worries of its own. Today's trouble is enough for today.''

Verse 25: "Therefore I tell you." The introductory formula is neither prophetic nor simply a strengthening of the authority of a wisdom teacher. It is deliberate "Jesus language," teaching of Jesus. Behind the following words stands the authority of the Lord Jesus. "Do not *worry*" (*mē merimnāte*)—"the term *mermina* may refer to either unnecessary worry or legitimate concern" LN 25.224. "Anxious about your *life*" (*tē psychē*); *psyche* is not "soul", since it eats and drinks, but (Semitically) "life."

Verse 26: "Birds of the air" (*tou ouranou*). *Ouranos is the "space above the earth, including the vault arching high over the earth from one horizon to another, as well as the sun, moon, and stars—'sky.'"* LN 1.5. "*Birds* of the air"—the Greek expression simply designates wild birds in contrast with domestic fowl, such as chickens.

"Neither sows nor reaps." From the realm of birds the text leaps into the human realm: they neither sow nor reap. This is to name two characteristic works of the male. Does this mean unlike you, the birds neither sow nor reap: how much more will God care for you, since you do work? But God does not care more for humans than for birds and lilies because humans work, but because he is their Father. The non-working birds are not a model for humans but a witness of God's providence. Matthew is not saying that those addressed should not work. "*Of more value than they*"—The rhetorical question has a form in Greek which requires the answer "Yes." It might be rendered as an exclamation: "Are you not worth much more than all birds!"

Verse 27: "Span of life (*helikia*)." *NRSV* gives an alternate reading: "add one cubit to your height." LN 87.151: "*Helikia* may also denote height (see 81.4). If one understands *helikia* in Matthew 6.27 as time, then obviously some adjustment needs to be made in the meaning of *mechys* 'cubit' (81.25)."

Verse 28: "Lilies of the field (*krina tou agrou*)" may be any one of several types of flowers, usually uncultivated—"wild flower." LN 3.32:

"Though traditionally *krinon* has been regarded as a type of lily, scholars have suggested several other possible references, including an anemone, a poppy, a gladiolus, and a rather inconspicuous type of daisy."

Verse 29: Solomon is proverbial for the splendiferous king.

Verse 30: "Thrown into the oven (*klibanon*)—"a dome-like structure made of clay, in which wood and dried grass were burned, and then after being heated, was used for baking bread—'over.' " LN 7. 74.

"You of little faith (*oligopistoi*)." The direct address "indicates that specific people are addressed. People with deficient faith . . ., according to old rabbinical traditions are, e.g., those Israelites who wanted to gather manna and quail on the sabbath in the wilderness. For Matthew, this traditional expression became important; it characterizes the situation of the community as standing between unbelief and faith which can be helped again in its doubt by the power of Jesus (8:26; 14:32)" Luz, *ad loc.*

Verse 32: "Your heavenly Father knows." Especially important for Matthew is the allusion back to his framing of the Our Father: "Your heavenly Father knows what you need before you ask him" (6:8). The following verses are to be understood in the light of the faith of the praying community whose Heavenly Father knows what they need even before they pray. This is above all to be considered for the interpretation of "kingdom" and "righteousness."

Verse 33: "Seek first his kingdom and his righteousness." "Kingdom" is, as elsewhere in Matthew, the coming reign of God, which the community hopes to enter through judgment. "Righteousness." according to U. Luz:

> Means the activity of righteousness which humans are to perform, i.e., that action which agrees with God and his kingdom. Through the insertion of "righteousness" Matthew wanted to clarify that the seeking of the kingdom is not a passive waiting, not an only internal religious attitude, but a tangible practice of righteousness as the Sermon on the Mount unfolds it. The relationship of righteousness and kingdom of God is, in the sense of 5:20, the relation of human practice and promised reward. "His rightousness is that we are taught to act rightly; his kingdom that we know what is the reward which is established for work and patience." Nevertheless, it does not mean works-righteousness, for what is demanded of the community is an acting toward the heavenly Father who knows their needs and listens to them before they ask. The juxtaposition of *basileia* and *dikaiosyne* thus corresponds to the juxtaposition of the second and third petition of the Lord's Prayer, except that here the task of the person, there the asked for action of God for and through

the person stands in the foreground. Human acting includes the action
of God: God will create his kingdom and, already now, simultaneously
as an additional gift, grant his disciples food and clothing (cf. Mark 10:30;
1 Tim 4:8), p. 407.

Verse 34: "Enough for the day"—secondary interpretation of our text
in wisdom style. Understood optimistically, the verse may open up the
possibility to live for today. But the pessimistic interpretation is more likely.
All planning is in vain; it is enough to bear the burden of the day. The
appearance of the verse here shows how, in early Christianity, the hope
of the Kingdom of God by no means determined life throughout, but eschatological hope and pessimistic realism could stand immediately side
by side.

Matthew 7:1-5

Jesus continues to deal with the practice of the greater righteousness
in areas of life he has not already touched on. In 7:1-5 we come to the
third prohibition which marks a subunit (cf. *supra,* p. 105). Here, Jesus
forbids disciples to judge others, on pain that "with the judgment you
pronounce you will be judged" (7:2).

> **1** "Do not judge, so that you may not be judged. **2** For with the judg-
> ment you make you will be judged, and the measure you give will be
> the measure you get. **3** Why do you see the speck in your neighbor's eye,
> but do not notice the log in your own eye? **4** Or how can you say to your
> neighbor, 'Let me take the speck out of your eye,' while the log is in
> your own eye? **5** You hypocrite, first take the log out of your own eye,
> and then you will see clearly to take the speck out of your neighbor's eye.

Verse 1: "Do not judge . . . not be judged." Matthew makes effective
use of various linguistic devices to turn Jesus' great speeches into a direct
word of address to the implied reader. As a consequence, the tone of Jesus'
speeches is virtually that of a homily being addressed to the implied reader.
As the oldest part the composition, verse 1 could almost be interpreted
standing alone. *Krinō* has a very wide field of meaning; the text gives no
indication of a more restricted meaning. So it seems best to use a general
translation, "to judge," "to be active as a judge," "to pronounce." Luke
carries the common *krino* further through the special *katadikazō* ("to condemn"). "That you be not judged" refers to the eschatological equivalent: lest God judge you in the same way in his judgment. Wisdom
warnings of this kind are directed primarily to individuals; but the wisdom dimension is exceeded through the eschatological addition. In Q this

saying comes immediately after the basic passage about love of enemies, which was meant in a universal and basic sense and goes beyond personal emnities. In Jesus we encounter not only an entirely judgment-free community with outcasts like sinners and publicans, but also with a notable indifference regarding the law then holding sway in Israel, shown, e.g., in the story of the woman taken in adultery (John 7:53–8:11), or indirectly in the fact that Jesus was not greatly concerned about the halaka. All of this indicates that the validity of our sentence should not be restricted to the personal domain. Like the love of enemies, it must be understood in the context of Jesus' eschatology. The Kingdom of God is coming; therefore there must in principle be an end to the judgment of human beings by others.

Verse 2: "Judgment you make . . . will be judged." This saying makes reference to a principle that was widespread in business, in everyday life, in law, and in anticipation of the Last Judgment: measure for measure. Verse 2 brings out what this means for God's judgment. Since we all will have to face God's judgment, the measure (LN 57.92) with which we measure others will finally be laid on us. These (perhaps secondary) explanations do not mean generally a narrowing of the warning: in your judgments think of God's judgments. The idea can also be: if God in judgment uses the principle "measure for measure," then all people are such "debtors" that they should forgo judging at all. A story that illustrates this and recommends boundless forgiveness is Matthew's Jesus' story of the unmerciful servant (18:23-35).

Verses 3-4: "The speck (LN 3.66) . . . the log (LN 7.78)." The warning to think first about the log in one's own eye is—like the warning to forgo the use of force in Matthew 5:39-41—an exemplary illustration of the basic principle of 7:1. The verses by no means want to limit the principle of not judging *only* to the admonition to see the log in one's own eye before dealing with a neighbor. Rather, it is a specific example in the area of interpersonal relations. The sharpness of the verse lies not in the fact that the ego of the judging individual is put in a new light. It lies much more in that the one judging is made into one judged. The force of the metaphor is impressive. The hyperboles of the speck and the log are blows struck at the heart of the person who allegedly knows bad and good. He is brought into question; he is startled. The direct address with "you" (singular) strengthens the effect. On the basis of verses 1-2, you know the judgment which threatens your "log." The repeated expression *adelphos* ("brother") strengthens the effect in the Christian community: the fellow human, whose failing we so willingly expose, is a fellow Christian. The metaphor heightens the grotesqueness; while it can indeed happen that someone could get a speck in his eye, a log in one's own eye exceeds the dimensions of the credible. The hearer is asked whether he should not regard his own sins in just this way. That the log sticks in the eye is likewise deliberate strengthening: Whoever has a log in his eye is completely blind and therefore cannot accurately judge about a speck in a brother's eye.

Verse 5. "You hypocrite, first take the log out." The "hypocrite" lives in a contradiction, since he undertakes putting his brother on the right path but does not eliminate his own imperfection. His behavior is that of the blind guide who wants to lead another blind person, so that both come to a fall. By contrast, Jesus demands that one first eliminate one's own fault, then undertake the attempt to correct that of a brother or sister. While Matthew knows the need for disciplinary procedures within the Church (18:15-18), the supreme rule must always be mercy and forgiveness. Disciples are called to exercise not judgment, but fraternal correction. This demands that disciples be conscious that the one to be corrected is a brother or sister and that their own fault (the log) may be greater than his or hers and require attention first. "Self-righteous superiority dooms fraternal correction to failure; only self-correction makes fraternal correction credible and effective" (Meier, 69).

"What is Holy!" (7:6)

Jesus continues to deal with the practice of the greater righteousness in areas of life he has not already touched on. The third prohibition marks the third subunit (cf. *supra,* p. 105). In a prohibition, whose meaning is much disputed, Jesus warns disciples against giving what is sacred and precious to persons who are undeserving.

> 6 "Do not give what is holy to dogs; and do not throw your pearls before swine, or they will trample them underfoot and turn and maul you."

"I propose not to interpret the logion at all in its Matthean context. Matthew was a conservative author; he took it over from his tradition because it stood in his copy of Q" (Luz, *ad loc*).

In a chiastic framework, we are warned not to give food offered in sacrifice ("what is holy") to dogs, lest they attack (literally, "maul") us, and not to give pearls to swine, lest they trample them. The original meaning is puzzling. In any case, something especially valuable and holy is set over against unclean animals. Presumably, it is a question of a profane, proverbial expression with the meaning: you should not turn over something precious to someone who does not know how to appreciate it; otherwise you yourself will suffer.

Since our logion was never really anchored in the Matthean context it had, to a high degree, the same fate that we can observe elsewhere: the saying was freed from its context and made to work as a detached saying. Many usages were possible, to the protection of the Gospel, of the perfect law, the churchly communion, the heavenly wisdom, baptism, the Lord's Supper, against the pagans, the false teachers, the scoffers, the immoral children of the world or the ordinary believers. Especially influential was the use for the establishment of the arcanum discipline at the Lord's Supper, which the Didache 9:5 speaks of, corresponding to the later liturgical principle: the holy for the holy.

"Ask, Seek, Knock" 7:7-11

Jesus concludes the series which deals with the practice of the greater righteousness in areas of life not previously touched on. After three prohibitions which mark subunits (cf. *supra,* p. 105), Jesus suddenly shifts from the negative to the positive and exhorts disciples to constant and fervent prayer ("Ask . . . seek . . . knock").

> **7** "Ask, and it will be given you; search, and you will find; knock, and the door will be opened for you. **8** For everyone who asks receives, and everyone who searches finds, and for everyone who knocks, the door will be opened. **9** Is there anyone among you who, if your child asks for bread, will give a stone? **10** Or if the child asks for a fish, will give a snake? **11** If you then, who are evil, know how to give good gifts to your children, how much more will your father in heaven give good things to those who ask him!

Verse 7. "Ask, search, knock." The text begins with an admonition to ask. It is threefold, which heightens the urgency. All three verbs *aiteō, zeteō* and *krouō* have a religious dimension in Judaeo-Christian usage: one prays to or seeks God, one knocks on the "gates of mercy." In Greek, the three imperatives are present imperatives and may carry the force of "keep on asking, seeking, knocking." The imagery of knocking on a door has associations in Judaism with the study of the Law and its interpretation and with prayers for God's mercy. To *seek* means to look for, to try to find a particular thing. It is not God we are to seek in this verse, but rather we are to look to him for what we want. Thus it could be rendered "seek what you are looking for" or "seek from God what you are looking for."

The two passive structures (*will be given . . . you will find*) presuppose God as the subject: "God will give you . . . God will let you find." The last clause may be rendered accordingly: "knock, and God will open the door for you." But this teaching is not intended to make prayer into a magical ritual, nor is it to suggest that one can coerce God into acting. The real emphasis is upon the certainty that God will answer the prayer, and that it is a prayer that *every one* can pray.

Verse 8: "Every one who asks." The basis for the petition lies in the certainty that God hears the one who prays. As compared with verse 7, the accent has shifted in verse 8; now it lies each time on the second verb. The Greek translator chooses the present for two of the verbs, to make it clear that the promise of answer to prayer is not valid exclusively for the eschaton. The text is formulated as openly as possible: *every one* who prays, receives. Any limitation, e.g., to designated groups of petitions, runs counter go the direction of the text.

"The comparisons (*bread* with *stone* and *fish* with *serpent*) were used for perhaps two reasons: (1) bread and fish were the foods that would be most common near the Sea of Galilee, and (2) bread is shaped somewhat like a stone, and a fish has scales and other features similar to those of a snake. One commentator, in fact, notes that a certain species of fish (*barbut*) even has the appearance of a snake. Though most translations retain the question form of the Greek text, it is obvious that in many languages a statement would be more effective: 'No father would give his son a stone when he asks for bread. . . .' This can also be rendered 'Surely none of you who is a father would give' or 'No father would give his son a stone . . . would he?' " (NS, 207).

Verses 9-10: "Bread, fish: stone, serpent." The promise of answer to prayer is explained by two illustrations taken from everyday life. Bread and fish belong to the basic foods of the Jews. The association of bread and stone are traditionally close; outwardly they look somewhat alike. To some extent the same applies for serpent and fish. Both pictures involve the opposition: "useless—useful," not, as in Luke, the opposition "dangerous—useful." Jesus' absolute formulation of the certainty of answer is not unheard of for the believing Jews of his time. As distinct from the even more emphatic formulation in 6:7-8, there are many Jewish parallels to our text. The function of the two images does not consist in illustrating something unknown or in alienating people's expectations. By pointing out and sharpening a well-known Jewish article of belief, they have a rhetorical function. They are intended—by means of the introduction to the parables "what man of you,"—to draw the hearer in and impress him. The stylistic tool of repetition strengthens the effect.

Verse 11: The parables work with the principle of evidence. But it is not simply lifted to the theological level but heightened through the "how much more *posō mallon*": God's love is much more certain than the love of an earthly father. Only faith can speak in these terms; the "rational access" to faith-inspired "certainty" is surpassed by faith. Already the choice of illustration—the Father—was made under the presupposition Jesus' faith in his heavenly Father. The conception of God is not projected simply in such a way that a human experience with an earthly father is projected onto God. Instead, the one who is founded on faith in the heavenly Father, can, in—admittedly ambiguous—experience of the love of earthly fathers, recognize helpful pointers to the heavenly Father. Faith in God stands at the beginning of this parable and is not the result. The reference to the wickedness of men is a rhetorical device which tends to intensify the certainty of faith. "To give good things," is formulated so generally that any limitation of the promise (e.g. *only* good gifts) contradicts the scope of the text. As in 6:7-8, so goes it here also; the point is to give courage to "childlike" prayer. The certainty of the answer does not make the prayer superfluous, but possible.

"*Who are evil*" is not intended to be a philosophical statement regarding human nature; the comparison is between God and the human race, all of whom are sinful. The phrase *who are evil* may be expressed 'Even though you are sinful (or, bad),; you know how to. . . .'

"*How much more* introduces an argument 'from the lesser to the greater' (see 6:30 for this same form of argument): human fathers are evil, but they still give good things to their children; our Father in heaven is good, and so he is much more ready to give good things to those who ask him" NS, p. 207.

Exegesis can only partially answer our question on the basis the history of interpretation. The certainty of *Jesus'* answer belongs most likely with his hope for the coming of the Kingdom of God, a hope unbroken until his death.

"In a superficial sense it failed. Was it blind to reality? In any case, Jesus submitted to his death out of the power of this hope. For Matthew answer to prayer means the presence of the Lord Jesus Christ with his community until the close of the age (Matt. 28:20). He makes this clear by his entire story of Jesus: God has led the Lord, who is present with his community, through suffering and dying to resurrection" Luz, *ad loc.*

For Matthew, Christian faith in prayer in no way means that the heavenly Father spares his community all suffering and in a superficial sense answers all prayers. But nowhere is that reflected explicitly. Rather, he shows in another connection how well thought out his prayer theology really is. For him, faith in prayer is not a substitute for proper human activity, but has its place alongside of it. Deliberately, at the end of the main part of the Sermon on the Mount, he speaks once again, as at its center (6:6-15) of prayer to the Father. Just as deliberately he will later on speak of the presence of the Lord Jesus with the one who takes the risk of faith and keeps the commandments (cf. 14:28-31; 28:19-20). Faith in prayer means the joining of an active Christian life in prayer to a loving Father. This shows how little Matthew's understanding of righteousness has in common with work righteousness in the Pauline sense.

The Golden Rule in the Sermon on the Mount, 7:12

Jesus ends this part of the Sermon on the Mount with the Golden Rule, which reminds the disciples of what he has stressed earlier: Doing the greater righteousness is always, finally, an exercise in love. That "love" is the deepest intention of the will of God as taught by Jesus is also apparent from other passages in Matthew's story. In the verse that concludes the antitheses in the Sermon on the Mount, Jesus mandates that disciples be "perfect" (*teleios*), that is, give demonstration of their love of God by rendering to God wholehearted devotion (5:48; Deut 18:13). At the end of the Sermon on the Mount, Jesus enjoins love of neighbor by citing the Golden Rule.

> 12 "In everything do to others as you would have them do to you; this is the law and the prophets.

Matthew is striving to give the reader a comprehensive maxim for ethical behavior. The need for such is of long standing (cf. Mark 12:28, par Matt 22:36), which is understandable for catechetical instruction. In the earlier texts, love of God and neighbor is offered as the action principle; here it is the Golden Rule (LN 41.7). For Matthew the two must be seen in close union, because both the love-of-God-and-neighbor and the Golden Rule are characterized as the summa of the Law and Prophets and the kernel of the Scriptures as interpreted by Jesus. The connection is also factually necessary because the Golden Rule cannot stand alone. It presupposes a standard of behavior.

The Golden Rule is found universally; it was not indigenous to Judaism. Most of the non-Christian examples formulate the Golden Rule negatively, but positive formulations also occur. The combination of the Golden Rule with the commandment of love of neighbor (Lev 19:18) occurs already in Jewish thinking (Hillel).

One should not see great significance in the fact that the Golden Rule is formulated positively in the synoptic tradition and negatively by Hillel.

The positive formulation demands that the person addressed take the initiative, while the negative version may end with mere passivity. But the context of the content is much more decisive than the positive or negative formulation. Thus, to interpret Matthew 7:12 does not mean to ask for the meaning of the text in itself. Rather, we have to ask what meaning the positively formulated Golden Rule receives in the context of the Matthean Sermon on the Mount, and, conversely, what direction of interpretation it indicates for the Matthean Sermon on the Mount.

The Golden Rule cannot be directly a normative ethical basic principle; it has no normative character. The Golden Rule must already presuppose a standard of behavior. For it does not contain the principle of duties to oneself, nor of the duties of benevolence to others. Many a one would gladly consent that others should not benefit him, provided only that he might be excused from showing benevolence to them.

Therefore, in the history of interpretation of Matthew 7:1, the command of love of neighbor was put as a preceding clause before the Golden Rule from the very beginning. What meaning does the Matthean Sermon on the Mount give to the Golden Rule? Through Matthew's addition "for this is the law and the prophets," it is lifted out and made a foundational sentence. Matthew points back to 5:17, where Jesus spoke of fulfilling the law and prophets through his life and teaching. It is in harmony with Matthean thinking (22:40), to remember first of all love in connection with the fulfilling of the law.

The idea of the love commandment, which has such great significance in the main part of the Sermon on the Mount through the first and last antitheses, through the petition for forgiveness in the Lord's Prayer, moves into the foreground. It is the most central "preamble" of the Golden Rule of Matthew.

"That means that the Golden Rule is radicalized by the Sermon on the Mount. Everything, without exception, which is demanded by love and the commandments of Jesus you should do for other people. *Panta* receives its meaning on the context of Matthean perfectionism. The higher righteousness and the command of perfection of the one who teaches his disciples to keep 'all which I have commanded you' (28:20) is the subject. On the basis of the Matthean 'preamble' the positive formulation of the Golden Rule becomes important, maintaining that Christian practice is to be initiative, not reactive, behavior. The Christian is to be the first one to begin loving, in agreement with Jesus' commands, e.g., in 5:38-48" (U. Luz, *ad loc*).

In turn, the Golden Rule interprets the Sermon on the Mount. With its comprehensive formulation, it recalls that the individual directions of the Sermon are living examples of perfection, which are to be integrated and extended in the whole of life. It excludes the thought that only the commandments mentioned there are meant. The Sermon on the Mount is a summa of Christian righteousness which is intended comprehensively to determine the entire life of Christians.

5th Part of the Sermon on the Mount
Concluding Injunctions, 7:13-27
(For Structure of the Sermon, cf. p. 67)

In the fifth part of the Sermon on the Mount (7:13-27), Jesus concludes his teaching. The point he emphasizes to his disciples is unmistakable: It is not only the hearing of his words, but also the doing of them that counts. Disciples who both hear and do are like the "wise man who built his house on rock" (7:24). They, unlike the false prophets who will prove themselves to have been workers of lawlessness, will at the latter day "enter the kingdom of heaven," for they shall have done "the will of my Father who is in heaven" (7:15-16, 20-23).

This conclusion of the Sermon is best divided into three sections: The two ways (7:13-14), the warning against the false prophets (7:15-23), and the parable of building a house (7:24-27). In form, the first and the second pericope are connected by the key words "enter *eiserchomai*" (13 [2 times], 21), and "many *polloi*" (13, 22); the second and third pericopes are connected through the key word "do *poieo*" (altogether nine times). In this way, essential tendencies of the section already are indicated: it is the concluding admonition to the community for Christian praxis. It has a fundamental character: all three sections are defined by antithetical contrasts (broad/narrow way or gate; good/bad fruit; doers of the will of God/doers of lawlessness; house on rocky/sandy foundation). All are concerned with the final judgment. The negative aspect, the warning of the catastrophe, predominates. The conclusion of the Sermon on the Mount corresponds to the conclusion of typical Matthean speeches, which end with a look to the judgment that the community will face.

Gates Narrow and Wide, 7:13-14

The motif of the two gates is relatively rare in Jewish texts, but the contrast of the two ways is a topic of preaching which can be documented in many Jewish texts.

> **13** Enter through the narrow gate; for the gate is wide and the road is easy that leads to destruction, and there are many who take it. **14** For

the gate is narrow and the road is hard that leads to life, and there are few who find it.

Verse 13: "Through the narrow gate (*pyle*)." *Pyle* is the gate of a city or a temple, in distinction from *thyra*, door. One should not think of the ancient city gate with the great main gate and the more narrow side door; the two Matthean gates lead to different destinations. The image of the gate suggests various possibilities of association; the gates of the heavenly city, etc. But it was unusual to speak of the narrow gate. Therefore the imperative of verse 13a has to be supported. The reasoning starts with the negative side. The broad way, leading to destruction, belongs to the wide gate. Here, Matthew stands close to the Jewish usage.

Verse 14: "The road is hard *hodos tethlimmene*" cf. LN 22.21. The hard road stands opposite the broad way. Not simply a narrow, crowded way—only few go on the way which leads to life. Therefore, it is better with *tethlimmenos* to think of the "woes *thlipseis*" which Matthew mentions variously for the time before the eschaton. Already 5:10-12, he spoke of the persecutions which hit the community. Thus the way to life is full of afflictions. "Narrow (*stenos*)" is metaphorical. The thought of the "distress" experienced in suffering may be included. Thus the way to life means suffering for the sake of the faith. "Life (*zoe*)," like "destruction (*apoleia*)," is an eschatological term. The evangelist uses the verb "enter (*eiserchomai*)" as in the sayings of the entering into the Kingdom of Heaven.

Concerning the relationship of gate and way, the gate is not conceived as the entry gate to the way. Instead, the gate is at the end of the way, for one enters through the gate into life, i.e., into the Kingdom of God in the eschaton. Matthew takes up again his model of the Christian faith as a way to perfection which is to be practiced actively by the community (5:20, 48), at whose end the entry into the *basileia* is promised (cf. Luke 13:24). The difficult way, which with afflictions is a passage for the few to the narrow gate, is the way of righteousness.

The "many" are Christians, members of the community. Thus Matthew again applied to the community a motif which up to now has been used in a different manner (*Did.* 1:2-5:2). The community is on the way to the gate of life. It constantly faces the choice of the two ways. Being a Christian, being baptized, does not mean a tranquil certainty of salvation but the constant challenge of the decision between the broad way and the difficult way.

A focal point in the history of interpretation of verses 13-14 is the Christological understanding of them. They lend themselves to being read in a Johannine sense. "Christ is the gate of life: Whoever enters through

me, enters into life.'' Then a "play" could arise with the "way": the righteous are on the narrow way of suffering. But Christ, who is "the way,''
helps on the "way," offering healing medicines and healing the wounded,
although looking like one of the wounded. "He is our example, our example to bear everything patiently." Thus the way becomes the way of
discipleship; allegorically interpreted, "Christ is the narrow gate, the devil
the broad.''

Prophets Who are Workers of Lawlessness, 7:15-23

In 7:15-23, Jesus predicts repudiation at the latter day for certain disciples who, although they prophesy, exorcise demons, and perform miracles in his name, are nevertheless condemned as workers of lawlessness.
Clearly, neither the crowds nor the four disciples we have met so far have
known any situation in which Christians who are false prophets are active.

This is one of those passages in the discourses of Jesus that occasions
surprise for the implied reader in light of the flow of Matthew's story—
because they do not "fit" the earthly ministry of Jesus and are so clearly
"out of place." Yet this and similar passages are perfectly intelligible when
viewed from the perspective of the intended reader's position between
resurrection and parousia.

> 15 "Beware of false prophets, who come to you in sheep's clothing
> but inwardly are ravenous wolves. 16 You will know them by their fruits.
> Are grapes gathered from thorns, or figs from thistles? 17 In the same
> way, every good tree bears good fruit, but the bad tree bears bad fruit.
> 18 A good tree cannot bear bad fruit, nor can a bad tree bear good fruit.
> 19 Every tree that does not bear good fruit is cut down and thrown into
> the fire. 20 Thus you will know them by their fruits.
> 21 "Not everyone who says to me, 'Lord, Lord,' will enter the king-
> dom of heaven, but only the one who does the will of my Father in heaven.
> 22 On that day many will say to me, 'Lord, Lord, did we not prophesy
> in your name, and cast out demons in your name, and do many deeds
> of power in your name?' 23 Then I will declare to them, 'I never knew
> you; go away from me, you evildoers.' "

Verse 15: "Beware of false prophets." The warning against pseudoprophets begins without preparation. The community obviously knows
who is meant. The external and the internal aspects of these persons are
in disharmony. The sheep's clothing in which they camouflage themselves
is probably not the typical garment of the prophets, but a metaphor: since
peaceful and defenseless sheep are the classical opposite to rapacious

wolves, their dressing in sheep's clothing means that they only pretend to be peaceful and defenseless.

Verse 16a: "Know them by their fruits." Matthew gives the community a rule according to which they can recognize these apparently harmless prophets: by their fruit. "Fruit" is a metaphor which is common everywhere, but especially in the Old Testament, which may denote on the one hand the consequences of deeds, and on the other hand the deed itself (as "fruit" of people, cf. LN 42.13). In our passage, not the consequences of the activity of the false prophets in the congregations, but their deeds are meant.

Verse 16b: "Thorns . . . thistles." In context, the question has the rhetorical function of moving the pseudoprophets close to the thorns and thistles and thus, of devaluing them.

Verses 17-18: While it is a true parable in the Q, Matthew suggests a metaphorical understanding: "Good" and "bad" clearly are ethically colored expressions, so that the mention of the "bad" fruit is striking and makes the reader think right away of deeds of people.

Verse 19-20: "Thrown into the fire." Here the metaphor is shifted. The trees which do not bring good fruit are burned. The false prophets face God's annihilating judgment. Matthew formulates it with the words of John the Baptist of 3:10, and thus emphasizes once more that the proclamation of judgment by Jesus and by John are the same.

Verse 21: "Lord, Lord:" A new beginning with a broader perspective. Now the final judgment is spoken of directly. Jesus speaks here as the judge of the world. The doubled *kyrie* is especially expressive and imploring. "Lord" is, in Matthew, the address of the disciples, not of outsiders, to Jesus, and especially the address to the world judge, the Son of Man. Thus Matthew is thinking of the community. Not all its members will enter the kingdom of heaven. The address to the judge of the world as "Lord" is theologically correct, but nothing is decided by the correct address. The redactional logion of "entering into the kingdom of heaven," (v. 21) recalls 5:20 where the community was confronted with the demand for higher righteousness. This is what Matthew is thinking of when he speaks of "doing of the will of my Father" as a condition for salvation.

Verses 22-23: "I never knew you." The false prophets who are to be burned in the judgment like unfruitful trees are the scribes and Pharisees. In retrospect, it becomes significant that Matthew had not spoken of an excommunication of the pseudoprophets in verses 15-20 (cf. 7:1f). This is in agreement with his understanding of community. The community is not to anticipate the divine judgment and not to separate the weeds from the wheat (13:36-43), (cf. 22:11-14). Therefore, Matthew restricts himself to giving his community a "rule of recognition" and the admonition to keep to the way of righteousness. The judgment on the false prophets will be executed by the judge of the world himself. On that great day of judgment, many—the word recalls the broad way of 7:13—will appeal to their having prophesied in Jesus' name. Many have done miracles in Jesus' name. Matthew does not turn against prophecy and miracles. The judge of the world holds against the charismatics only that they do not satisfy the criterion of the works. Solemnly he testifies to them that they do not belong to him.

"Matthew would remind us that the ethical 'criterion' is not simply a general one but the norm of the commands of Jesus (28:2). This norm is for him a clear point of orientation for all Christians. It remains more important that Matthew does not want to render judgments with the aid of a standard, for that would mean to anticipate the judgment of God (cf. 7:1-5). In the frame of his ecclesiology of the church as a *corpus permixtum* (mixed body), it is not primarily the issue that the community with a criterion separates weeds from the wheat before the right time, but rather that the righteousness of the genuine disciples of Jesus is greater than that of the false prophets. The criterion of works is primarily a criterion of *acting*, not of *judging*. One must not change it into a criterion by which then again (problematical) theological judgments could be rendered. The issue is that one acts personally" (Luz, 449-50).

In our passage reference is made to prophets who were, it seems, active within the community. These prophets were "enthusiasts," for it is said that in the name of Christ they have prophesied, cast out demons, and performed many miracles (7:22). Their works, however, are castigated as contravening their profession of the name of Christ (7:16-20). The result is that they are condemned in words of Jesus as "workers of lawlessness" whom the exalted Jesus will banish from his presence at the latter day (7:23). "The point is: Is one to infer from such reference to false prophets as active within the community that, conversely, legitimate Christian prophets, too, are to be thought of as having engaged in ministry not only as missionaries beyond the community but also as preachers of the Gospel of the Kingdom within the community? One can only conjecture" (*Story*, 157).

Internalizing Jesus' Speeches, 7:24-27

Matthew concludes his Sermon on the Mount—as the Sayings Source concluded the Sermon on the Plain—with a double parable. Like the end of the holiness code (Lev 26), the readers are once more placed before a stark alternative (rock or sand). As in the discourse on the community (18:23-35) and in the eschatological discourse (24:45-25:46), it is an eschatological parable which puts before the readers the two possibilities.

> **24** "Everyone then who hears these words of mine and acts on them will be like a wise man who built his house on rock. **25** The rain fell, the floods came, and the winds blew and beat on that house, but it did not fall, because it had been founded on rock. **26** And everyone who hears these words of mine and does not act on them will be like a foolish man who built his house on sand. **27** The rain fell, and the floods came, and the winds blew and beat against that house, and it fell—and great was its fall!"

In his great speeches, Jesus directly addresses not only the crowds or the pre-Easter disciples but also, and above all, the implied reader—a post-Easter disciple of Jesus who is at home in the time between the resurrection and the Parousia. "Like all disciples, the implied reader, too, is summoned 'to be like his teacher' (10:25; 16:24). To this end, he or she is summoned to hear and to internalize Jesus' speeches (cf., e.g., 7:24-27)" (*Story*, 111).

Verse 24. "Every one then who." Now the meaning of the address as a whole will be summarized. First comes the positive example. Not just the hearing of this word is important, doing is the decisive thing. Hearing and doing are often joined also in Deuteronomy. So God speaks to Moses: "Assemble the people . . . so that they may hear and learn to fear the Lord your God and to observe diligently all the words of this law" (31:12). The conclusion of Deuteronomy can therefore serve as a comparison, because here too the people are confronted with a choice, to choose between life and happiness, or unhappiness and death (3:15). The appeal back to Moses stresses that the word of Christ has replaced the Law. This word can save, but its neglect brings damnation.

It is to be noted that the introductory formula is in the future tense (*homoiothetai*). "Through this future tense [Matthew] indicates that it is not an inner-worldly connection of acting-destiny, but that the last judgment is meant. The enduring of the work of the housebuilder who has built on the rock and the catastrophe for the one who has built on sand will become clear in the last judgment, which will reveal the truth of the parable" (Luz, 453).

Verse 25. "Beat on that house." The reliability of the foundation of the house becomes evident when it is threatened by the forces of nature. In Israel this is in the rainy season (October/November), which brings possible danger through floods and storms. Rivers can become torrents.

In the transmission of the text a number of different verbs were used; "Beat upon" (*prosepesan*) is a comprehensive verb which can refer to both flood waters and storms. And what picture should be drawn from this most extreme of threats? Surely, the end time judgment, but perhaps also the end-time trials are involved (cf. Mt 24). The unusual picture recommends this broader interpretation.

Verses 26-27. The negative example presents a contrasting picture. The fool erects his house in a different place. Thoughtlessness and foolishness bring him to choose sand for the site of his house. The inevitable happens. In Job 1:19 we have another sketch of the collapse of a house in a storm, and in Ezekiel 13:11 of a wall in a cloudburst, storm, and hail. In both cases, the inhabitants are buried under the ruins. Matthew limits himself to the statement: "and great was its fall." *Ptosis* in Greek, like the English word "ruin," serves both for the collapse of the house and in a transferred sense (cf. Luke 2:34).

The message of the parable is: As a person who builds his house on rock survives the storm, so every person who trusts in the teaching of Jesus survives the trial of the end-time. But to trust Jesus' teaching also means to do it. Whoever does not observe it comes to judgment. Wisdom and foolishness become words which mark the quality of life of a person. Jesus' word is firm and outlasts the catastrophe (cf. 24:35). The wise person recognizes the worth of the word, and exerts himself to allow it to take form in his life. The much discussed grace problem in Matthew's Gospel is thereby given an orientation. It is the word of Christ that saves men, not the doing; but his prevenient word saves a person only then when he does it.

Matthew has maintained the fulfilling of God's law by Jesus (cf, 5:17-20) and demanded the "doing" of the greater righteousness by the community. "Everything depends on the praxis. This does not mean that Christology is dissolved in ethics, for Jesus is the one who has fulfilled law and prophets in his mission and grants the community the possibility of going the way of righteousness" (Luz, 454). Christ opens the way into life for those who *do* righteousness; he helps those, but only those. Christ gives his grace to the doers of the word. Any ethics of intention which is not willing to be measured by its fruit comes to ruin in view of this conclusion of the Sermon on the Mount. To be a Christian means the praxis of the commands of Jesus. *In* this practice, there is the experience of grace and prayer. This is what the Sermon on the Mount proclaims from the Beatitudes to the conclusion.

Formal Ending of First Discourse, 7:28–8:1

The concluding formula links back to the opening scene of the Sermon on the Mount (4:25-26), with the following crowds and the mountain. Therefore it seems best to join 8:1 to the concluding remarks. The formal conclusion, "Now when Jesus had finished. . . ." ties the Sermon on the Mount to the other four which are likewise ended in this way; (11:1; 13:53; 19:1) and to 26:1 ("Now when Jesus had finished saying"). Thus the discourses are joined to an overall complex. This structure shows the importance that Matthew attributed to the discourses. Our text also has a transition function. The authority that Jesus shows in his teaching will be substantiated by the authority of his miracles described in the next section (9:6, 8).

> **28** Now when Jesus had finished saying these things, the crowds were astounded at his teaching, **29** for he taught them as one having authority, and not as their scribes. **8:1** When Jesus had come down from the mountain, great crowds followed him.

In consequence of the unique relationship that exists between Jesus Messiah, the Son of God, and God his Father, the Father entrusts the Son with divine authority (*exousia*). As a result, what the Son says and does is said and done on the authority of God. God himself is fully active in the messianic ministry of his Son. Matthew never tires of making this point. Often he does so obliquely, but in select passages he does so explicitly. In the Sermon on the Mount it is as one invested with divine authority that the Matthean Jesus declares: "You have heard . . . but I say to you." And now at the conclusion of the sermon, Matthew writes that the crowds were astounded at his teaching, because he taught as one having authority.

Verse 28: "When Jesus had finished." Matthew turns back to the narrative in which he has embedded the entire Sermon on the Mount. He brings out more clearly than in 5:1 that the crowd also heard the Sermon on the Mount. It is a speech to the disciples in the sense that the life of the disciples is to shine (5:16) in the world, and thus to confront the nations with the commands of Jesus which apply also to them (cf. 28:20). The crowd is addressed as potential disciples. The Sermon on the Mount, as the salvific command of Jesus, is at the same time a missionary preaching.

When Matthew describes the ending of the Sermon with words of Deuteronomy, which there sketch the end of Moses' address, he recalls that it is addressed to the People of God. Whoever accepts these words of Jesus is God's People, enrolled as part of it. The reaction of the people is that they are "astonished (*exeplessonto*)" at his teaching. This reaction, which implies puzzlement, is not the proper reaction to the hearing of the word and not at all identical with faith. In 13:54 the same verb is used to express an explicitly unbelieving reaction (cf. 19:25; 22:33).

Verse 29: "As one having authority." In describing the teaching activity of the Messiah Son of God, Matthew emphasizes one aspect in particular: that Jesus makes known the will of God in terms of its original intention. The Son of God is the mouthpiece of God in a direct and immediate fashion. Here Matthew affirms that Jesus teaches with an authority not found among the scribes, and depicts the crowds as being astonished by it. Jesus teaches in a way that makes him the supreme interpreter of the law. His word is more radical than that of Moses and can even stand above it. In disputes between Jesus and the Israelite leaders over matters of law, Matthew, in comparison for instance with Mark, prefers to address the fact that Jesus speaks the mind not merely of Moses but, more importantly, of God.

8:1. As Jesus went up the mountain, so he comes back again. The story of Moses also calls this to mind. He, from the mountain of Sinai, descended to the people (Ex 19:14, 25; 34:29). Again Jesus is accompanied by the great crowds. Also here, in the following of the masses is the beginning of the possibility to win full attachment to him.

The people are astonished because Jesus teaches with *eousia*. This authority shows first of all in his teaching; it will later be shown in his deeds, in what follows, and in 10:1 it is transferred to the disciples. On the basis of 28:18 it is anticipation of the universal authority which is given to the one who is exalted above heaven and earth. Thus, for the believer, there shines in the Sermon on the Mount a glimpse of the glory and power of the heavenly Lord. The church's interpretation therefore has rightly recalled the sovereign "But I say to you" of the Antitheses and the Christological sentence about the "fulfillment" of law and prophets.

THE MIRACLE CHAPTERS, 8–9

After three chapters devoted to word (Chs 5–7, the Sermon on the Mount), the Miracle Chapters (8–9) have often been characterized as providing deed by way of contrast. But on closer examination, these chapters are seen to be theologically rich as well.

Appropriating the contents from Mark and Q, Matthew has rearranged them to form four subsections: (I) themes of Christology, 8:1-17; (II) discipleship, 8:18-34; (III) questions pertaining to the separation of Jesus and his followers from Israel—the problem of the rejection of Israel, 9:1-17;

and (IV) faith, 9:18-34. Although chapters 8–9 are commonly called "The Miracle Chapters," not all the incidents involve miracles in the strict sense. Subdivision I contains three miracles and a summary.

Here Jesus is presented as the Messiah, the Son of God, present in the midst of Israel, carrying out a ministry of healing, and gathering disciples. These chapters set forth for the members of Matthew's church the cost and commitment of discipleship and ways in which they are distinct from contemporary Israel. They invite these Christians, as persons of faith, to approach the exalted Son of God, to offer to him their petitions for help.

The broad significance of the miracle story is that it portrays Jesus as bringing the gracious, saving power of God's eschatological rule to bear upon the ills of people and the disturbances in nature. In these chapters, Matthew has gathered together a series of ten miracle stories, edited them so as to place the accent on the direct speech between Jesus and his partners in dialogue, and embedded them in a framework that has to do mainly with the theme of "following" Jesus. For Matthew's church, Jesus is the exalted Son of God and no longer the earthly Son of God. Just as the earthly Son of God performed mighty acts of power with divine authority, so the exalted Son of God, who resides in the midst of his Church, can perform mighty acts of power.

Chapters 8–9 function not only as a major part of the Gospel-story Matthew narrates, but also as a form of theological address directed to the members of his community. But this meant that such past acts as the miracles of Jesus had to be made to serve as theological addresses to the people of Matthew's church. We can see how Matthew accomplished this by observing how Matthew has redacted the miracle-stories he has taken into his Gospel.

Aside from Jesus, other notable figures in the first century (*magoi*, Jewish and Hellenistic exorcists) reputedly possessed miraculous power. And the miracle-stories attributed to Jesus exhibit the same overall structure as those attributed to such figures. The basic features are introduction, exposition, center, and conclusion. Still, in his redaction of miracle-stories Matthew has enhanced the element of direct speech to the point where the dialogue between Jesus and the suppliant(s) has become the focus of attention. Hence, the basic features of Matthean miracle-stories are, respectively, the introduction, the request for help or healing, the reply of Jesus, and the conclusion. In general, the traits characterizing the form of Matthean miracle-stories are: a) introductions and conclusions are marked by stereotyped speech, and there is little breadth of description; b) secondary characters and actions receive little attention; c) the outstanding feature is the dialogue between Jesus and the suppliant(s); d) the catchword is frequently employed as a literary device to lend greater coherence to the unit; and e) the element of 'faith' plays a prominent role in the story. Taken together, these formal traits indicate that as far as Matthew's editing of miracle-stories is concerned, the emphasis is on the personal encounter, mediated as much or more by the dialogue as by the miraculous deed, between Jesus and the suppliant(s).

Verse 1 recalls 4:25, for both read that "great crowds followed him." By the same token, 8:16, which is the chief summary-passage in chapters 8–9, picks up in chiastic sequence of 4:24. In 4:24, Matthew records that "they brought to him all the sick . . . [and] demoniacs"; and in 8:16 Matthew states that "they brought to him many who were possessed with demons . . . and [he] cured all who were sick." In addition, references in both 4:24-25 and chapters 8–9 to "diseases," to great suffering, to "paralytics" and to the fact that word of Jesus spread throughout a whole area or region also directly relate chapters 8–9 to the summary-passage 4:24-25.

Chapters 8–9 constitute Matthew's extended commentary on the summary-passage 4:24-25. In 4:24-25, Matthew speaks of Jesus' ministry of healing and of his being followed by great crowds from all Israel and the Decapolis. In regard to the latter point, the concept of "following" Jesus is expressed in both 4:24-25 and chapters 8–9 by the verb *akolouthein*, which Matthew sometimes uses literally, in which case it means "coming or going after a person in time, place, or sequence," and sometimes metaphorically, or religiously, in which case it connotes "coming or going after a person as his disciple."

"In other words, with the aid of the verb *akolouthein* Matthew depicts Jesus in chapters 8–9 as being in the midst of Israel (8:1, 10), carrying out a ministry of healing and, at the same time, gathering disciples (cf. 8:18-20, 21-22; 9:9 [10-14]) and therefore dealing with matters that pertain to discipleship. Significantly, each of the four subsections comprising chapters 8–9 can be found to contribute in some substantial way to this general picture. It is, consequently, this picture of Jesus that governs the manner in which Matthew has developed chapters 8–9 as a major section of his Gospel" ("Miracle Chapters," 568.)

(I) Christology 1: Cleansing of a Leper, 8:1-4

After presenting Jesus in the first main part as the Messiah, the Son of God, Matthew depicts him in the second main part (4:17–16:20) as discharging his public ministry to Israel. Empowered for messianic ministry by the Holy Spirit (3:16), Jesus teaches with authority (*exousia*, 7:28-29), and performs mighty acts. It is in his capacity as the Son of God that Jesus Messiah both delivers the Sermon on the Mount in chapters 5–7 and undertakes in chapters 8–9 his ministry of healing.

In the first of the four subsections of the Miracle Chapters, verses 1-17, Jesus reveals himself, through his healing activity in and around Capernaum, to be the one who, in fulfillment of Old Testament prophecy, "takes" his people's sicknesses and "bears" their diseases.

> **1** When Jesus had come down from the mountain, great crowds followed him; **2** and there was a leper who had come to him and knelt before him, saying, "Lord, if you choose, you can make me clean." **3** He stretched out his hand and touched him, saying, "I do choose. Be made clean." Immediately his leprosy was cleansed. **4** And Jesus said to him, "See that you say nothing to anyone; but go, show yourself to the priest, and offer the gift that Moses commanded, as a testimony to them.

Verse 1: "Great crowds followed him (*ēkolouthēsan autō ocloi polloi*)" "To follow (*akoloutheō*)" is an important word in Matthew's vocabulary. In some passages it has a literal sense, but in others it can connote discipleship. This is the case when the idea of *cost* and *commitment* are joined to it. In verse 1, Matthew portrays the crowd(s) as following Jesus in the purely literal sense of the word. This is also the case even when he heals their sick, as in 12:15; 14:13-14; and 19:2. In all of these narrative passages Matthew employs the verb *akolouthein* to make Jesus the focal point of public attention, in this way marking him as a person of great respect, and to describe especially his healing activity as taking place in the broad view of Israel. At the same time, since the twin elements of cost and commitment do not color the use of *akolkouthein* in these passages, it can be seen not to mean "accompaniment as one's disciple."

Verse 2: "Lord (*kyrie*), if you choose." In Matthew's editing of miracle-stories the emphasis is as much on the personal encounter mediated by the dialogue between Jesus and the suppliant(s) as by the miraculous deed. In this encounter, Jesus stands out as a figure of exalted station and divine authority, while others are regularly portrayed as coming to him. They, in need, call upon him as "*kyrie*" ("Lord"), i.e., as one who wields divine power (8:2, 6, 8, 21, 25).

Conversely, in the encounter with Jesus the suppliants are described as persons of "faith," i.e., as "believers" who ardently desire, and actively grasp after, the help of God. This picture of the suppliants is subtly projected in all of a variety of ways: they address Jesus as *kyrie*; their request for help often takes the form of a "prayer-like" petition; the capacity to "believe" (*pisteuein*) is directly predicated to them; and it is said of them that, in approaching Jesus, they "kneel down" before him or "worship" him (*proskynein*) or "implore" him (*parakalein*) and, in order to reach him, are undaunted by obstacles placed in their way. The fact that the response of Jesus is at times described in terms that closely correspond to the request made of him is another feature that shows the suppliants to be persons of faith.

Verse 3: "Be made clean." Jesus, for his part, mercifully hears the petitioners' appeal for help or healing, and, with the touch of his hand (8:3, 15; 9:29; 20:34) or by taking hold of them, or from a distance with a word or command that cleanses leprosy (8:3), expels a demon (17:18), rebukes wind and sea (8:26), or dispels fear (14:27), he "saves" them or "heals" them.

The description of the cure itself is strikingly short; expressions of feeling (as found in Mark) are not to be found in Matthew. Matthew "reduces the miracle stories as a whole to about 55% of their compass in Mark, while shortening the narratives that display Jesus as the Christ by only about 10% and the narratives associated with controversies by 20% on the average" (Schweizer, *ad loc*). The healing happens in word alone, unaccompanied by therapeutic gesture. "I will"—in the synoptic tradition Jesus speaks only four times of his own will. Hence these instances have a special weight: they stand in texts in which the omnipotence, as it manifests itself in Jesus' will, needs to be brought out.

Verse 4: "Say nothing to anyone." Here Matthew allows to stand the command to silence that has come down to him from the tradition, while he elsewhere eliminates it. Here it functions as a Scripture proof. By this action Jesus shows that he is the *Servant of the Lord* (*ebed Yahweh*)—one who chooses not to draw attention to himself. The first three miracle accounts of Chapter 8 close with the fulfillment citation from Isaiah 53:4, 11: "He took our infirmities and bore our diseases" (8:17). The second command is a confirmation of 5:17: Jesus did not come "to abolish the law and the prophets, but to fulfil them." Thus the close of this miracle account is connected with the Sermon on the Mount and the mighty work interprets Jesus' mighty word.

By placing the personal encounter and the dialogue between Jesus and the suppliants at the center of his miracle-stories, Matthew provides the key to a proper understanding of their paradigmatic function. For Matthew, the mystery of Jesus' divine sonship is that in him God has drawn near to dwell with his people to the end of the age, thus inaugurating the eschatological time of salvation. For God to draw near in the person of his Son, however, is for his Kingdom, or Rule, to draw near. Hence, in the presence of Jesus, whether as the earthly Son of God before Easter (1:23; 11:27) or as the exalted Son of God following Easter (18:20; 28:18-20), the Kingdom of Heaven, or the Rule of God, is a present, thought not yet consummated, reality (8:29; 12:28).

(I) Christology 2: The Centurion's Servant, 8:5-13

We encounter universalism already in Part I of Matthew's account of the ministry of Jesus. A hint that the mission of the disciples will lead to the evangelization of the Gentiles appears in the first words Jesus speaks to the disciples: "I will make you fish for people" (4:19). Jesus' first discourse contains similar indications; Jesus tells his disciples that they are the salt of the earth and the light of the world (5:13-14).

This universalism is found not only in the Sermon on the Mount but also in the account of Jesus' mighty works in chapters 8-9. The second healing recorded in Matthew is that of the centurion's servant (8:5-13). "Jesus 'marvels' at the centurion and contrasts this faith with the relative unbelief encountered in Israel (8.10). This contrast in turn leads to a crucial passage in which Jesus declared that many Gentiles will share the eschatological banquet with Abraham, Isaac, and Jacob, while the 'sons of the kingdom' (that is, the Jews) will be expelled into outer darkness (8.11-12)" (Bauer, 122).

> 5 When he entered Capernaum, a centurion came to him, appealing to him 6 and saying, "Lord, my servant is lying at home paralyzed, in terrible distress." 7 And he said to him, "I will come and cure him." 8 The centurion answered, "Lord, I am not worthy to have you come under my roof but only speak the word, and my servant will be healed. 9 For I also am a man under authority, with soldiers under me; and I say to one, 'Go,' and he goes, and to another, 'Come,' and he comes, and to my slave, 'Do this,' and he does it." 10 When Jesus heard him, he was amazed, and said to those who followed him, "Truly, I tell you, in Israel in no one have I found such faith. 11 I tell you, many will come from east and west and eat with Abraham and Isaac and Jacob in the kingdom of heaven, 12 while the heirs of the kingdom will be thrown into the outer darkness, where there will be weeping and gnashing of teeth." 13 And to the centurion Jesus said, "Go; let it be done for according to your faith." And the servant was healed in that hour.

In addition to this account, a similar narrative is to be found in Matthew 15:21-28 (healing of the daughter of a Canaanite woman). A comparison of the two accounts reveals the following agreements: the subject is in both cases a Gentile person whose servant (daughter) is ill; both come to Jesus to ask a healing; both expressly acknowledge their faith (8:8-10; 15:27-28a); in both cases Jesus gives the assurance of help, which is straightway realized. In both cases Jesus heals at a distance, solely by the power of his word, and the pericope closure is almost identical in the two narratives.

Verse 5: "He entered Capernaum." After locating Jesus in Capernaum before the Sermon on the Mount (cf. 4:13), Matthew reestablishes Jesus' connection with that key city at the conclusion of the Sermon. Later Capernaum is designated as "his own town" (9:1), and it may be that the "house" there is to be thought of as belonging to Jesus or Peter.

"A *centurion* came" (cf. LN 55.16). The centurion is one of the "minor characters" who dot the pages of Matthew's story, who appear briefly in a scene and then vanish. Most of these persons do not so much as bear a name, passing before the reader merely as the "Magi" (2:1-12), "a leper" (8:2), "a centurion" (8:5).

Almost without exception, these persons are "stock" characters, that is to say, they possess one trait only. But unlike the disciples, the religious leaders, and the crowds, they cannot be treated as through they were all alike. The particular trait of any one or group of these persons is what determines to what extent the reader approves or disapproves of that person or group. The principal way the reader discovers "what kinds of persons" the minor characters are is by observing them as they serve as "foils" for other characters in the story, that is, as contrasts to other characters. The "Magi" (2:1) and the "centurion" serve as foils for Israel: the faith of these Gentiles contrasts with the unbelief of Israel.

Verse 6: "And saying, "Lord."" Matthew anticipates the title "Lord" from verse 8; it stands entirely in the service of Matthew's theology (cf. already v. 2): Jesus is one who has power, he is a *Kyrios* with authority. "At home *paralyzed*" (cf. LN 23.170-173; 78.24). The illness is mentioned in Matthew's summary-statement, 4:23-26. It was one of worst illnesses of the time, physically and psychologically.

Verse 7: "And he said (*Kai legei*)." To be noted in Jesus' answer is the introduction in the present historical, which underlines the importance of the following saying. There follows a saying of Jesus in which his authority is stressed. "I come and I shall heal him;" the "I" emphatically placed at the beginning stresses Jesus' authority once more (cf. Gundry, 142).

Verses 8-9: Faced with Jesus' willingness to come into his house, the centurion cites his unworthiness and appeals to Jesus' powerful (and healing) word. The centurion's unworthiness stands in contrast to Jesus' authority. Jesus' authority lies in his powerful word. The centurion himself is a subordinate but at the same time one who can give orders. He is ready to submit himself to this authority for the sake of his servant's health.

Verses 10-11: "Found such faith." Jesus' amazement at such an expression of faith and at the centurion's readiness to entrust himself to his healing word, permits him to make a declaration to those following him ("those who followed" are the "great crowds" mentioned in verse 1). With the affirmation formula found so often in Matthew, Jesus states that nowhere else had he found such faith. For the first time in Matthew we have here a reference to *pistis* (elsewhere only in 9:2, 22, 29; 15:28; 17:20; 21:21; 23:23). All references to "faith" are found in connection with miracle stories (with the exception of 23:23, where *pistis* corresponds to the Hebrew *'aemaet*). But the relationship of faith and miracle is such that it does not become understandable without the influence of Jesus' message. The faith expressed in the request to Jesus precedes the cure: it is the condition for the miracle to happen. There is nothing analogous to this understanding of miracle and faith in the non-Christian world; it has its ultimate ground in Jesus' work. Matthew has retained this tradition of miracle interpretation in his Gospel.

The Gentile world puts Israel to shame precisely because the Israelites would not recognize in Jesus the Kyrios endowed with divine authority. Again with a solemn introduction (now without "Amen," cf. 10b), Jesus draws from just such experiences the salvation-history consequence: Israel, insofar as it did not see and acknowledge the *exousia* (might, power) of the Messiah and Kyrios Jesus, is shut out from the Kingdom of Heaven, while the Gentiles become the true heirs of Abraham, Isaac, and Jacob. Matthew concentrates the logion from the saying tradition (cf. Luke 13:28-29) upon the same thought. In place of a national, religious, and cultic claim that ignores and distorts the true revelation of God in Jesus, there enters the faith of all those who acknowledge God showing mercy to all.

Verse 12: "Heirs of the Kingdom." As often in the Gospel of Matthew a judgment saying becomes a crisis word. The all too confident sons of the Kingdom (LN 11.13) will be excluded from the Kingdom; they will be thrown into the outer darkness (22:13; 25:30; LN 1.23). The redactional phrase "weep and gnash their teeth" (cf. also 13:42, 50; 22:13; 24:51: 25:30) expresses how Matthew wants the crisis word to be taken seriously.

Verse 13: Matthew resumes the course of the healing pericope. In direct address, the centurion is instructed to "go" (cf. 8:4) (to his servant); and this with the assurance that it will be done for him as he has believed (for "be done" [*genetheto*] cf. 6:10; 9:29; 15:28; 26:42). "In that hour" (10:19; 18:1; 26:55; LN 67.1) the servant is healed (*iaomaij = heal*, make healthy [so already v. 8]), in practically the same sense as the more usual *theapeuein* means to make healthy, free from an illness.

Jesus' declaration here, after the second of a series of ten miracle reports, is an important stage in his growing conflict with the Jewish leaders. Before the outbreak of open conflict between Jesus and the religious leaders, Matthew leads the reader to anticipate such conflict. Jesus (or Matthew as narrator) utters statements about the religious leaders which are negative or suggestive of conflict. In the Sermon on the Mount, Jesus predicts persecution for the disciples after the manner of the Old Testament prophets (5:1-12), declares that the righteousness of the scribes and Pharisees falls short of what is necessary for gaining entrance into the Kingdom of Heaven (5:20), and castigates the "hypocrites" in the synagogues for performing their act of piety not in worship of God, but so as to win public acclaim for themselves (6:1-18). After the Sermon, Matthew bluntly tells the reader that the scribes are "without authority" in their teaching (7:28-29). Now, "implored by a centurion to heal his slave, Jesus asserts in view of the centurion's faith that whereas the 'sons of the Kingdom' will be cast into the outer darkness, Gentiles will share in the bliss of the future Kingdom with Abraham, Isaac, and Jacob (8:10-12)" (*Story*, 118).

And as conflict increases, so does universalism. The universalism encountered in Part I is found also in Part II, Matthew's account of the ministry of Jesus. A hint that the mission of the disciples will lead to the evangelization of the Gentiles appears in the first words Jesus speaks to the disciples: "I will make you fish for people" (4:19). Jesus tells his disciples that they are the "salt of the *earth*" and the "light of the *world*" (5:13-14). This universalism is found also in the account of Jesus' mighty works in chapters 8-9. The second healing is that of the centurion's servant (8:5-13). Here Jesus "was amazed" at the faith of the centurion and contrasts this faith with the relative unbelief encountered in Israel (8:10). "This contrast in turn leads to a crucial passage in which Jesus declares that many Gentiles will share the eschatological banquet with Abraham, Isaac, and Jacob, while the 'sons of the Kingdom' (that is, the Jews) will be expelled into outer darkness (8:11-1)" (Bauer, 122).

(I) Christology 3: Peter's Mother-in-Law, 8:14-15

14 When Jesus entered Peter's house, he saw his mother-in-law lying in bed with a fever; **15** he touched her hand, and the fever left her, and she got up and began to serve him.

In Mark and Luke the account of the healing of Simon's mother-in-law is joined to Jesus' preaching in the synagogue at Capernaum: Matthew, on the other hand, inserts the pericope into his comprehensive presentation of Jesus' healing activity, where it forms the third of the ten "miracles" in chapters 8–9. Like Mark and Luke, Matthew joins a Summary Statement (8:16-17) to the healing collection. The literary linking of a fever victim and an attached Summary Statement is found also in Acts (28:8-9).

Matthew's account is strikingly succinct in comparison with that of the other two versions; it gives the impression of a report from some remove: participants remain unmentioned. On the other hand, Jesus' name appears explicitly at the beginning, for he is the subject of the principal verb in the account. The mother-in-law of Peter (Matthew names Simon by his community name) "got up," and waited on Jesus herself. The structure of Matthew's account reveals his intention, as it clearly appears in most calling accounts: healing is a call to discipleship (cf. 8:14-15 with 9:9); "serve" and "follow" are synonymous concepts.

Verse 14: "Entered Peter's house (*eis tēn oikian Petrou*)." Countering the opinions of Schweizer, Theissen, and Betz, J. D. Kingsbury takes this verse as indicating that Matthew's community was domiciled. "Matthew, taking up on his previous notation that Joseph 'went and "dwelt" (*katōkēsen*) in a city called Nazareth' (2:23), documents with a formula quotation the circumstance that Jesus 'left Nazareth and went and "dwelt" (*katōkēsen*) in Capernaum . . .' (4:13-16). Indeed, Capernaum is designated as 'his own town' (9:1), and it may be that the 'house' there is to be thought of as belonging to Jesus (cf. 9:10, 28; 12:46 and 13:1; 13:36; 17:25); if not, is that of Peter, who is also depicted as being 'married' (8:14/Mark 1:29-30). . . . Socio-economic and socio-cultural factors, as reflected in the first Gospel, further challenge the notion that the community of Matthew constituted in large part a band of wanderers who had literally turned their backs on house and belongings. Indeed, there is good reason to believe that the Matthaean community was a 'city church' that was materially well off" *"Akotouthein,"* 66.

The scene is set in the house of "Peter." From the start Matthew presents Simon as "Peter" (4:18), as the first of the twelve (10:2). That Jesus gives the nickname Peter to the disciple Simon is no longer of special meaning for Matthew. The post-Easter Church's Peter (16:18) is, for Matthew, "Peter" from the beginning. The emphasis that Peter's mother-in-law "was lying," stands in contrast to the "and she got up" in verse 15. (For the verb "to have a fever," cf. LN 23.159). The verb is lacking in the LXX; it is found only in Mark 1:30 and here (Luke uses the substantive [fever]). In Luke the healing has more the character of an exorcism; Jesus "rebuked the fever."

For the community Peter is the witness of the Jesus tradition. Familiar stories and recollections are no longer meaningful for the community. A traditional narrative of a miraculous event is therefore stripped by Matthew of its personal and wondrous characters and presented to the community, and precisely in its catechetical aspect, to show that the meeting with Jesus is still a call to service, to discipleship.

Verse 15: The healing gesture is the "touching the hand" of the sick woman (cf. 8:3; 9:20, 21, 29; 14:36; 17:7; 20:34), i.e. the healing and blessing touch by which the illness is overcome. The rising up [a Hebraism] and serving express readiness for discipleship. But discipleship means to enter into the service of the One whom Matthew indicates by the personal pronoun in the singular (*autō*).

(I) 4: Summary Statement, 8:16-17

The threefold pre-Synoptic tradition had already referred to Jesus' activity in so-called Summary Statements: Mark 1:32-34; Luke 4:40-41. Acting alone, Matthew has already inserted a Summary Statement, 4:23-25, placing it as a summary at the end of his account of Jesus' first week in Galilee. Mark's first Summary Statement (after the healing of Simon's mother-in-law, 1:29-30), in Matthew likewise stands after this healing narrative, but as a summary statement in a strongly shortened form inserted into the miracle sequence (chs. 8-9). For this reason Kingsbury does not include it in the Summary Statements that he sees as strung out along the first half of Part II. In Matthew this summary concludes the first three of the ten miracle accounts; at the same time it serves as a transition to the following account.

> 16 That evening they brought to him many who were possessed with demons; and he cast out the spirits with a word, and cured all who were sick. 17 This was to fulfill what had been spoken through the prophet Isaiah, "He took our infirmities and bore our diseases."

Verse 16: "Many who were possessed." In Matthew the stress is on the demoniacs, who are brought to Jesus (so already 4:24). A person "possessed with demons" (in the New Testament thirteen times, exclusively in the four Gospels, seven times in Matthew) is a person in an afflicted state, in a declining condition, for which there is no explanation, or that can be explained only through the indwelling of an (evil) demon. Unexplainable illness, physical and psychological, were attributed to the working of demons. Therefore a cure consisted in a "throwing out," in an expulsion of the evil demons. The inexplicable bodily demonic influences are expressed in the tendency to speak of *pneumata*: of the supersensible powers who by their psychic power influence humans negatively. Yet Jesus is not just an exorcist, a conjurer with magic powers. He heals with the "word"; he drives out the demons with his powerful word and so cures all illnesses. This "word" belongs in the context of the Discourses (7:28; 19:1; 26:1): Jesus' proclaiming word is at the same time also an effective power word. That Jesus cures "all," corresponds to Matthew's conception that Jesus' salvation works should be seen as unlimited both spatially and chronologically, but above all sociologically.

Jesus heals, just as he preaches and teaches, in his capacity as the Messiah, Son of God. Still, Jesus Son of God is at the same time the servant of God: "Here is my servant, whom I have chosen" (12:18). Indeed the Greek verb *therapeuein* can mean to "serve" as well as to "heal." It is to cast Jesus' activity of healing in the mold of "serving," that Matthew informs the reader in a formula quotation that Jesus, through healing, fulfills the words of the Servant Song of Isaiah: "Surely he has borne our infirmities and carried our diseases" (Isa 53:4). "In healing, Jesus Son of God assumes the role of the servant of God and ministers to Israel by restoring persons to health or freeing them from their afflictions (11:5). Through serving in this fashion, Jesus 'saves' (9:22)" (*Story*, 68).

Verse 17: "Took our infirmities and bore our diseases." Although these words are those of the fourth servant song (Isa 53:4) it is significant that Matthew nowhere in chapters 8–9 specifically refers to Jesus as the "Servant of God" (*pais theou*). The reason is that he applies these words of Isaiah to Jesus Messiah, not as the servant *per se*, but as the Son of God (*huios tou theou*). This understanding of Jesus is rooted in the first main part of the Gospel (1:1-4; 6), where Matthew's chief concern is to present Jesus Messiah as the Son of God.

Having presented Jesus in the first main part of the Gospel as the Messiah, the Son of God, Matthew depicts him in the second main part (4:17–16:20) as discharging his public ministry to Israel. It is in his capacity as the Son of God that Jesus Messiah both delivers the Sermon on the Mount in chapters 5–7 and undertakes, in chapters 8–9, his ministry of healing. A telling argument against the position that Jesus Messiah is to be seen in chapters 8–9 as the Servant of God is the fact that it cannot be demonstrated that Matthew develops a Servant-christology. Only once does the term "Servant" (*pais*) occur in Matthew in a quotation of Isaiah 42:1-4 in 12:18-21 (cf. "Miracle Chapters," 564-65).

The summary is supported by a fulfillment formula. What Jesus does (as helping and healing Messiah) is fulfillment of what the Prophet Isaiah had said (53:4) about the Suffering Servant. Jesus himself is not the Suffering Servant (cf. 12:18-21). He does not take the infirmities and diseases "on himself"; rather he is the Messiah, the Son called by God (cf. 1:1–4:16, where Matthew presents the Messiah Jesus as God's Son), who heals all illnesses. Precisely there lies the meaning of the fulfillment citation: that there is One, who knows about the infirmities and diseases of men and does something about it; he assures healing and restoration of health (*therapeuo* indicates the healing process, even more the working, the effect of Jesus' healing action).

Matthew has related three "healings" (8:1-4, 5-13, 14-15) to his community to tell them that the proclamation of the Kingdom of Heaven makes clean—in every respect. Now Matthew feels obligated to add a Scripture interpretation that refutes every objection: what happens is not against Scripture, not detached from the Scripture tradition, but is always the fulfillment of the salvation pronounced in the Scriptures. Isaiah is the witness: he speaks of a Suffering Servant, still unclear and directed to the future, but it is foreseen that this one would lead in the time of salvation. Matthew now says to his community that this future is now present: the one working in his powerful word is the foreseen Messiah for all.

(II) Discipleship 1: A Scribe and a Disciple, 8:18-34

Subdivision I of chapters 8–9 (vv. 1-17) contained three miracles in the strict sense and a summary. Subdivision II (vv. 18-34) will be concerned with discipleship. Here Jesus makes known, through his interaction with his disciples and others, the cost and commitment of discipleship.

> **18** When Jesus saw great crowds around him, he gave orders to go over to the other side. **19** A scribe then approached and said, "Teacher, I will follow you wherever you go." **20** And Jesus said to him, "Foxes have holes and birds of the air have nests; but the Son of Man has nowhere to lay his head." **21** Another of his disciples said to him, "Lord, first let me go and bury my father." **22** But Jesus said to him, "Follow me, and let the dead bury their own dead."

It is significant that precisely a "scribe" and a "disciple" are involved here. Indications are that the scribe remained a scribe, and did not become a disciple, For his part the disciple receives a sharp reminder as to what discipleship can entail. The passage consists of an introduction (v. 18) and two contrasting scenes. In the first scene (vv. 19-20), a scribe approaches Jesus and offers to become his disciple. In the second scene (vv. 21-22) a disciple asks to postpone the demands of discipleship.

Verse 18: "Jesus gave orders (*ekeleusen apelthein*)." This brings out very strongly that what happens, happens at Jesus' initiative. Again the crowds are present, and again Jesus "sees" the need to impart an important message to the throng.

Verse 19: "Teacher (*Didaskale*). This form of address, taken together with Jesus' use of the title "Son of Man," indicate that the scribe's offer to become a disciple was not accepted. The scribe addresses Jesus as "teacher" and Jesus refers to himself in his reply as "the Son of Man." "Teacher" is not the term of address employed by those in Matthew's story who approach Jesus in "faith." These persons call on Jesus as "Lord." "Teacher" is the term of human respect that is used, for example, by the opponents of Jesus.

"I will follow (*akolouthēso*) you." Matthew uses the verb "to follow" in both an ordinary sense ("to come after") and in a metaphorical sense ("to follow as a disciple"). The latter seems to be the case here, since the scribe is aware of the cost and the commitment of following as a disciple.

Verse 20: "Son of Man." "The Son of Man" is the term by which Jesus refers to himself in public or with a view to the public, especially his opponents. "In sum, the use of the two terms 'teacher' and 'the son of man' in the scene of 8:19-20 has the effect of highlighting the distance that exists between Jesus and the scribe: they are not of one mind and one will. Jesus turns the scribe away" (*Story*, 134). If the sub-units 8:19-20 and 8:21-22 are in fact antithetical to each other, it becomes clear that Matthew did not think of the scribe as a disciple of Jesus and did regard Jesus' reply to him as refusing his offer.

Pericopes that portray the call of true disciples have a definite pattern, which places the initiative squarely with Jesus. Jesus sees, Jesus summons, and those who are summoned follow him. This pattern is fractured in our passage. The scribe arrogates to himself the authority to make of himself a disciple of Jesus. He believes that he can measure up to the demands of discipleship. But Jesus counters that the life of discipleship is so rigorous that no one, apart from his enabling call, is capable of embarking upon this life and sustaining it.

Verses 21-22: "First let me go." The second scene concerns a man described as already being a disciple of Jesus. His use of the term "Lord" and not "teacher" and Jesus' use of the pronoun "me" and not "Son of Man" are also proof of this. Earlier, Jesus had ordered the disciples to board a boat and set sail for the other side of the sea (8:18). With a view to Jesus' command, this disciple makes his request. He desires to suspend for a time his commitment to follow Jesus. Moreover, his request is exceedingly well-founded: he has the sacred trust to go and look after the burial of his father (cf. Gen 50:5-6). Jesus' response is swift and sharp. The commitment of discipleship brooks no suspension. No obligation exists that can be permitted to take precedence over it.

The insertion of the discipleship scene interprets the three preceding healing accounts: the cleansing does not have its goal in itself, but is the condition that one so cleansed must be ready for discipleship, for service.

The healing and cleansing word of Jesus is—so the community experiences—a word with authority, so also is the power to call into discipleship. But the two discipleship scenes give rise to a new thought: the demand will suffer no delay. For the one who speaks there is, in reality, the Son of Man. His call must be answered straightway, without delay, without hesitation.

(II) Discipleship 2: Stilling of the Storm, 8:23-27

The preceding passage (vv. 18-22) illustrated that the life of discipleship cannot be undertaken apart from the enabling call of Jesus but, once entered upon, brooks no suspension. Now it will be shown that the life of discipleship is also a life always open to attacks of "little faith."

> 23 And when he got into the boat, his disciples followed him. 24 A wind arose on the sea, so great that the boat was being swamped by the waves; but he was asleep. 25 And they went and woke him up, saying, "Lord, save us! We are perishing!" 26 And he said to them, "Why are you afraid, you of little faith?" Then he got up and rebuked the winds and the sea; and there was a dead calm. 27 They were amazed saying, "What sort of man is this, that even the winds and sea obey him?"

Verse 23: "His disciples followed him." Having ordered the disciples to the other side of the sea (8:18), Jesus now boards the boat and the disciples follow him in. Placing the Master before the disciples is again stressed. This already indicates that the pericope will be a "story about Jesus and his disciples" and must be understood as such.

Verse 24: "A wind (*seismos*) arose." *Seismos* refers to "a violent action of the surface of a body of water as the result of high waves caused by a strong wind" (LN 14.22, 25). Though the term obviously implies the strong action of the wind, the focus is upon the violent motion caused by the waves.

Verse 25: "Lord, save us!" The disciples approach the sleeping Jesus and awaken him. They wanted to call his attention to the situation (fear or anxiety are not directly mentioned). They address him as "Lord" (which in Matthew always means a reverent acknowledgement by the disciples). They request only: "Save! (*soson*)." Because the imperative here stands without object, many manuscripts incorrectly supply "[Save] us!"). The absolute imperative of the verb *sozein* in conjunction with the solemn "Kyrie" signals a situation of transcendent petition: "Lord, save (not) just now, but always! (Kyrie, sōson!)."

D. Bauer pays particular attention to the relationship between the narrative and the discourses in Matthew, and demonstrates that they are not sealed in separate compartments. The discourses are integrated into the narrative framework, and there is no alternation between narrative and discourse material. There is much "discourse" in the so-called narrative sections, and narrative elements within the great discourses. The narrative material frequently contains *paraenetic* value for the post-Easter Church. "Bornkamm and Held . . . for instance, have demonstrated this *paraenesis* in the narrative material in their studies on the boat scenes at 8.23-27 and 14.22-33" (Bauer, 131).

Verse 26: "You of little faith (*oligopistoi*)." Matthew's interest does not lie in the power over the forces of nature (so Mark and Luke), but in the relationship of the Kyrios to the disciples. The situation is therefore set for the decisive question: "Why are you afraid?" And connected with the question is the reproach: "You of little faith" (cf. above at 6:30). The disciples are not unbelievers (only the mass of the people are so designated) (17:17). Rather, they are fearful, shaky in the faith, apt to fall away in situations of crisis (14:31; 16:8). "Little faith" does not mean the fundamental denial of faith, but a lack of trust and the assurance of faith.

"The miracles Jesus performs in Matthew's story divide themselves rather neatly into two groups: (*a*) therapeutic miracles (miracles of healing), in which the sick are returned to health or the possessed are freed of demons (cf. esp. chaps. 8-9); and (*b*) nontherapeutic miracles, which have to do with exercising power over the forces of nature. In the summary passages devoted to Jesus' healing, it is exclusively the therapeutic miracles to which Matthew makes reference" (*Story*, 69–70). For therapeutic miracles, cf. 4:24.

As a group, the therapeutic miracles are remarkably uniform in structure, the nontherapeutic miracles less so. "Here the focus is on Jesus and the disciples, and the characteristic features that Jesus reveals, in the midst of situations in which the disciples exhibit 'little faith,' his awesome authority. Then, too, the way in which Jesus reveals his authority is by exercising power over the forces of nature" (*Story*, 70). Here, he calms wind and wave. J. Heil has shown that this sea-rescue epiphany and the later sea-walking epiphany should be viewed together (cf. 14:22-33).

Two contrasting themes dominate this episode: the phenomenon of "little faith," and Jesus' fidelity to his wavering disciples. "Little faith" manifests itself as a "crisis of trust" which can thwart the disciples' ability to carry out the task, or mission, Jesus has given them. While Jesus expresses surprise that the disciples should be so weak, he still expects them to obey his command. But Jesus does not abandon his disciples at such times but stands ever ready with his saving power to sustain them so that they can in fact discharge the mission he has entrusted to them.

(II) Discipleship 3, In Gadara 8:28-34

This account is also found, in an expanded form, in Mark and Luke. Matthew shortened the existing text by two-thirds, thereby forming an actual and logical presentation. At the core of the narrative is the story of how Jesus sends the demons into the swine, which hurl themselves mindlessly into the water. The inhabitants of the district then ask Jesus to leave their neighborhood.

> **28** When he came to the other side, to the country of the Gadarenes, two demoniacs coming out of the tombs met him, so fierce that no one could pass that way. **29** Suddenly they shouted, "What have you to do with us, Son of God? Have you come here to torment us before the time?" **30** Now a large herd of swine was feeding at some distance from them. **31** The demons begged him, "If you cast us out, send us into the herd of swine." **32** And he said to them, "Go." So they came out and entered the swine; and suddenly, the whole herd rushed down the steep bank into the sea and perished in the water. **33** The swineherds ran off, and on going into the town, they told the whole story about what had happened to the demoniacs. **34** Then the whole town came out to meet Jesus; and when they saw him, they begged him to leave their neighborhood.

Verse 28: "Two demoniacs." The importance of Jesus' meeting with the demoniacs is underlined by the fact that the disciples are not involved: "he" (alone) faces the demoniacs. Matthew has two demoniacs instead of one: the more strongly the situation of need is presented, the more clearly can Matthew present Jesus as helper and savior. The demoniacs are "fierce" (*chalepos*, LN 20.2). According to the custom of the time they were driven out of the community and confined to the graveyards. Their fierceness is not described, but their conduct was such that the townspeople could not pass their way.

Verse 29: "Son of God." The sudden shout makes the use of the absolute "Son of God" all the more startling and impressive. Matthew's Christological perspective is made abundantly clear. Jesus is the Son of God come to torment (*basanisai*, LN 38113) the demons before the time, i.e., "to hand them over to judgment before the definitive inbreaking of the Kingdom of God" (Held, *Matthew* 164). Already in the meeting with

Jesus it is clear that the powers harmful to humans are sentenced to power-lessness and given over to destruction.

Verse 30: "Now a herd (*agele*, LN 4.8) of swine (*choiron*, LN 4.36) was feeding (*boskomenē*, LN 23.9)." The mention of the herd of swine (verse 30) does not follow from the logical sequence, but functions rather as a parenesis, which places the destruction event on a mythological basis, but at the same time "characterizes the pagan milieu" . . .; that the swine are placed at some distance mirrors the Jewish background of the Mat-thean redaction and takes its addressees into consideration. The condi-tion of the demons (Matthew does not speak of "unclean spirits"), which also embodies the unsaved situation of the pagans, is hopeless (in Mat-thew there is no mention of any resistance). They see a last chance for survival, if they can gain possession of the swine.

Verse 32: "Go." Jesus' "mastering word" is not an exorcism formula in the proper sense. It stands absolute, as at 4:10 where Jesus deals out a rebuff to Satan—"Begone, away with you!" The concession afforded the demons is in reality the expression of an impending disaster: the pos-sibility of flight afforded means, in reality, for their final destruction. The demons will be banished to their proper place (corresponding to the Jew-ish world picture), and thus stripped of their demonic power. That "they perished in the water" is not only a clarification of their rushing down the steep bank but but also an affirmation that they disappeared into the abyss, the prison of the evil spirits. Matthew's overall concern is the total conquest of the demonic powers through Jesus, the Son of God.

Verses 33-34: "Then the whole town." The stress on the universal ("whole") is an important motive for Matthew; so "the whole town" came out to meet Jesus. But the meeting does not lead to recognition of the help given and of his authority but to denial. The request that he leave the district says that the pagans (still) are not ready to acknowledge that the time (v. 29) has come. They still do not grasp the meaning of the time, because they do not "understand" who Jesus really is. As the swine herds had fled in dismay, so also the inhabitants of the city do not become masters over their demon angst.

Again the evangelist succeeds in presenting Jesus to his community as the powerful Son of God. Before the backdrop of a traditional exorcism narrative, Matthew portrays Jesus as exorcist, but one who, in an un-paralleled degree, is the vanquisher of all diabolic powers. His activity is a sign: God works salvation and well-being by banishing evil from the world. And God brings this well-being for all, even though the pagans do not yet recognize that the time of well-being is already present, be-cause they are not yet capable of recognizing Jesus as one sent by God to bring well-being to all. That this happens "now," already "before the time," is a warning to the community. They must not, like the pagans, relinquish the field to demon belief and demon angst Jesus' exorcising action is to be understood in the sense that already "now" the destruction of unclean and unholy demonic powers is happening. It would be a mistake to think that we must wait for the end-time for this to happen.

If Jesus is the protagonist of Matthew's story, then the *religious leaders*, as his principal opponents in the human realm, are the antagonists. In the Part I of his story (1:1–4:16), Matthew introduces the religious leaders to the readers. In chapter 2 Herod the Great is associated with them; seeking to kill Jesus, he assembles "all the chief priests and scribes of the people" and makes inquiry of them (2:4). Seeing the Pharisees and Sadducees coming out to him, John the Baptist denounces them as a "brood of vipers" (3:7). John's attitude toward the leaders anticipates that of Jesus. In the Temptation scene (ch. 4), Jesus' encounter with Satan anticipates his later encounter with the leaders.

Part II of Matthew's story (4:17–16:20) falls into two sections. In the first section (4:17–11:1), the conflict between Jesus and the religious leaders suddenly flares up (ch. 9), which prepares the reader for the more intense conflict soon to follow, in the second section of part two.

With the onset of chapter 9, the anticipated conflict between Jesus and the religious leaders finally materializes, yet this conflict remains preliminary to the more intense conflict to come.

1) This conflict does not become so virulent that it incites the religious leaders to mobilize themselves against Jesus; the leaders do not yet conspire to destroy Jesus (cf. 12:14). In chapter 9, Jesus' conflict with the leaders is not yet to the death.

2) None of the issues that provoke the religious leaders to attack Jesus touches on Mosaic law as such. It is a mark of the enormous importance Matthew attaches to Mosaic law that he does not state that the religious leaders take counsel on how to do away with Jesus until the conflict between Jesus and them has shifted to focus on a precept of Mosaic law (12:2, 10, 14).

3) The conflict is not so acutely confrontational as later conflict: Jesus is not directly challenged for something he does. In point of fact, it is following Jesus' healing on the sabbath that Matthew recounts for the first time that the Pharisees go out and take counsel against him, how to destroy him (12:9-14).

Pharisees, Sadducees, chief priests, elders, scribes, and Herodians—all these form a united front against Jesus. They are treated as a single character, and a "flat" character as well. All the traits attributed to them are offshoots of one "root trait," evilness. Accordingly, the picture the reader gets of the religious leaders in Matthew's story is not historically objective, but wholly negative and polemical.

(III) 1. Forgiveness of Sins, 9:1-8

In the third subsection of chapters 8–9, Jesus, in Capernaum, engages in debate with the leaders of the Jews and with the disciples of John, showing thereby that he and his followers constitute a group that stands apart from contemporary Israel.

> **1** And after getting into a boat he crossed the sea and came to his own town. **2** And just then some people were carrying a paralyzed man lying on a bed. When Jesus saw their faith he said to the paralytic, "Take heart, son, your sins are forgiven." **3** Then some of the scribes said to themselves, "This man is blaspheming." **4** But Jesus, perceiving their thoughts, said, "Why do you think evil in your hearts? **5** For which is easier, to say, 'Your sins are forgiven,' or to say, 'Stand up and walk'? **6** But so that you may know that the Son of Man has authority on earth to forgive sins"—he then said to the paralytic—"Stand up, take your bed and go to your home." **7** And he stood up and went home. **8** When the crowds saw it, they were filled with awe, and they glorified God, who had given such authority to human beings.

In Matthew's version this pericope contains two traditional pieces, which were also handed on by Mark and Luke as a literary unit: a healing account (9:1-2, 7-8), into which the controversy about forgiveness of sins is inserted (9:3-6). Since Matthew has taken the healing account into the large miracle sequence of his Gospel and had it follow the narrative of the healing of the two possessed of Gadara, in verse 1 (redactional) he must establish the connection of the two accounts set in different places. As so often, Matthew here has sharply abbreviated the miracle narrative: secondary figures and circumstances fall away. This shortening serves to stress Jesus' words and the Christological affirmation, and the affirmation about forgiveness of sins comes more sharply into focus.

As Mark and Luke also witness, the speech about authority to forgive sins was inserted secondarily into the miracle narrative. The insertion serves to clarify the question, viz., by what authority Jesus, the Son of Man, can declare a forgiveness of sins which is also valid in heaven.

The addition of the word of encouragement, "Take heart!" is, on the one hand, Jesus' answer to the trusting faith (of the bearers) and of the paralytic, and, on the other, is the link with the "controversy speech." This draws attention to the authority of the Son of Man. The "chorus closure" (v. 8) underlines—in an almost stereotyped fashion—the fear of the crowd, who glorify God who had given such authority to men. Once again, Matthew takes up the theme of the "authority," and so underlines in the "chorus closure" his Christological objective.

With the onset of chapter 9, the anticipated conflict between Jesus and the religious leaders finally materializes, yet it still remains for the more intense conflict to come. The religious leaders do not yet mobilize against Jesus, none of the issues touch on Mosaic law as such, and Jesus himself is not directly challenged for something he does.

Verse 1: "Came to his own town"—(regarding the role of Galilee and Capernaum, cf. 4:12-13). The reference to Capernaum, a literary linking, is necessary at this point because of the insertion of the healing pericope.

Verse 2: "They brought (*prospheron*). Here the generally favorable attitude of the "crowds" toward Jesus is clearly in evidence (cf. 9:23). The paralytic (LN 23.171) lies on a "bed" (*klinē*, bed or stretcher for the sick, LN 6.106). The faith that Jesus notices is primarily that of the bearers, but indirectly also that of the paralytic. The injunction to "take heart" is an appeal to the faith of the paralytic.

The words "Your sins are forgiven" could awaken courage, especially in the light of the Jewish conception according to which illness and sin are viewed as closely connected (cf. John 9:2). "Take heart" anticipates the story of Jesus' walking on the water during a storm on the Sea of Galilee (14:27). Matthew has this story in mind because shortly before, he recorded a similar one about Jesus' calming of the sea (8:24-27). "Sins" (plural) are the failures that can be forgiven only by God (cf. the theological passive). Since the forgiveness of sins is attributed to Jesus, the theological intention is clearly expressed: with Jesus, the messianic salvation-time has opened, in which God will forgive all sins.

Verse 3: "Then some of the scribes." "Then" marks a new start but at the same time connects the "controversy" with the forgiveness expressed in verse 2c. Some of the scribes (it is not said to which party they belonged) are displeased by the word of forgiveness, but do not express this outwardly: Whoever speaks thus is a blasphemer (also the absolutely used *blasphemein* means "blasphemes God": Matt 26:65a; John 10:36; cf. 2 Macc. 10:34; 12:14).

In his account of Jesus' ministry, Matthew depicted Jesus as becoming successively involved with three major groups, each of which functions as a character in his story: the *disciples* (4:18-22); *crowds*, together with the disciples (4:25, 5:1-2); and the religious *leaders* (9:2-13). Later, Matthew depicts Jesus' involvement with each of these same three groups as being successively terminated in a reverse order to the initial one, that is to say, in an order that is chiastic in nature (cf. 22:46).

Verse 4: "Knowing their thoughts" (LN 30.1). Verse 4a stresses that Jesus "knows, sees" their thoughts which are expressions of unbelief and doubt (in contrast to the faith in verse 2). Verse 4b [5a] gives Jesus' answer, which makes the false thoughts of the scribes manifest. Matthew's "why" sharpens Jesus' leading question and the hardness is further underlined by "evil (things)."

Verse 5: "For which is easier." The "For" of the second question binds the two questions tightly together: the second question gives the reason why the "thoughts" are evil. The question "Which is easier?" is to be understood from the viewpoint of the skeptics, who demand a visible confirmation of an invisible process. For the skeptical, it is easier to say the uncontrollable word of forgiveness; harder to pronounce a healing word, whose effectiveness can be straightway checked. Although Jesus had rejected all demands for signs, here he gives in to the unspoken demand for a "proof" of the authority given him by God, by using the argument "from light to heavy (*a minore ad maius*)" in a sovereign and paradoxical way, to demonstrate his authority as the Son of Man. The healing is the prerequisite for the forgiveness of sins; so it serves primarily for the awakening of faith and thereby the better "understanding" of his person: Jesus is not a wonder worker who must display himself, but the Son who forgives sins.

Verse 6a: "May know that the Son of Man." As Jesus clothed the act of forgiveness in the theological passive, so now he uses only the third person for self-identification. For the second time in the Gospel of Matthew, we encounter the expression "the Son of Man" (in 8:20 the expression had the generic and so the original meaning). Here, the self-identification comes to the fore: "I" (possibly with the overtone: "I as man.") God has authorized this man, Jesus, (in his name) to forgive sins (v. 8).

Verse 6b: "Then he said to the paralytic"—connects back to verse 2, and continues the narrative of the healing after the insertion (cf. the typical Matthew "then"—ninety times as compared with six times for Mark and fifteen times for Luke [without Acts]). The present ("he says" *legei*) indicates that the following word of Jesus is an important statement. In the three imperatives the paralytic is told what he should do: stand up, take up his bed, and go home.

Verse 8: "When the crowd saw it (*idontes de oc.*)." The chorus closure, distinguished from the healing narrative by *de*, registers the crowd's reaction. In accordance with Jewish tradition (Exod 15:1, 11; Lev 10:3), they glorify God because he had given "such authority" to human beings. This reaction of those present (chosen and formulated by Matthew) speaks of power given "to human beings," not—as we might expect—to Jesus alone. Here Matthew includes the disciples (cf. 6:14-15; John 20:23), and anticipates a community tradition that he will develop more clearly in chapter 18 (cf. 16:19; 18:18 [John 20:23]). God alone forgives sins; Jesus receives a share in this authority. His healings and forgiveness indicate that the community also forgives, and make this authority believable through miracles. God is glorified not because those present have "seen" a miracle, but because they have seen the power to forgive sins.

The scribes, Jesus' bitterest opponents, mark down Jesus' word of forgiveness to the paralytic as a blasphemous appropriation of a right that belongs only to God. But in the community as well, this doubt and complaint are expressed again and again in the question: Which is easier, which is harder? The double pericope attributes the veiled or open objection of blasphemy to the doubters who do not recognize Jesus' authority and will not join in praising God.

The miracle story (and especially the "controversy") defends Jesus' authority. Therein lies the redactor's Christological objective. By shortening the forgiving word to the paralytic at the beginning of the text (v. 2), Matthew brings the reaction of the scribes, who think "evil," into sharp focus (v. 4). They doubt the reality of the forgiveness—the power of the Son of Man and the "power of human beings" (v. 8), of the Christian community, to forgive. Forgiveness, as liberation from sin, is already to Matthew a "fruit" of the life and death of Jesus (1:21; 26:28). In the community, forgiveness should go up to seventy times seventy. This is clearly the "harder." But the "easier" is also imposed on the community. The community, which has received gratuitously should also give gratuitously (10:8): it must be concerned about the health of the entire person (10:8), so of human beings in their illnesses, anxieties, and needs.

(III) 2. The Calling of Matthew, 9:9-13

Jesus, in Capernaum, continues to engage in debate with the leaders of the Jews and with the disciples of John, showing thereby that he and his followers constitute a group that stands apart from contemporary Israel. As Jesus Son of God calls disciples to live in the sphere of God's end-time Rule, he forms a new community (16:18; 21:43). In its ranks are not only the so-called upright, but also the despised and the outcast (9:9). As described by Jesus, the ministry of the disciples to Israel foreshadows in many respects their later ministry to the nations (10:5b-42).

9 As Jesus was walking along, he saw a man called Matthew sitting at the tax booth; and he said to him, "Follow me." And he got up and followed him.

10 And as he sat at dinner in the house, behold, many tax collectors and sinners came and were sitting with him and his disciples. 11 When the Pharisees saw this, they said to his disciples, "Why does your teacher eat with tax collectors and sinners?" 12 But when he heard this, he said, "Those who are well have no need of a physician, but those who are sick. 13 Go and learn what this means, 'I desire mercy, not sacrifice.' For I have come to call not the righteous but sinners."

Verse 9: "Sitting at the tax booth." Matthew's call illustrates yet another aspect of discipleship—the broad spectrum of those whom Jesus summons to follow him. The pattern of the pericope reveals that the call of Matthew is the call of a true disciple: Jesus sees, Jesus summons, and the one summoned follows after Jesus. Peter and Andrew, James and John, were fishermen called to become his disciples, persons who were considered as upright citizens. Matthew, a toll-collector, is looked upon by Jewish society as no better than a robber, and one whose testimony would not be honored in a court of law. Nevertheless, Jesus makes him one of the Twelve (10:3).

"Follow me." Matthew employs "to follow" (*akolouthein*) in both a literal and a metaphorical manner. Two factors help to determine which of the two meanings is intended. First, "personal commitment"—Jesus is pictured as issuing a direct summons to follow him (cf. 4:19, 21; 9:9), or as addressing his words about following him to those who are his disciples already (cf. 19:27-28). Secondly, the factor of "cost"— there is some notation to the effect that walking in the company of Jesus entails personal sacrifice.

Verses 10-11: "Why does your teacher eat." In the label "your teacher" a negative undertone can be sensed, which contains the unexpressed reproach that Jesus is a "false" teacher, a false rabbi, because he shares table companionship with the unclean.

Directly or indirectly, the issue of authority underlies all the controversies Jesus has with the religious leaders. The religious leaders attempt to impugn the authority of Jesus, either by disputing his right to act as he does (here to forgive sins and to have table fellowship with toll-collectors and sinners), or to release his disciples temporarily from the obligation to fast (9:14-17).

Verses 12: "Those who are well." A wisdom saying with fundamental meaning opens Jesus' answer. Daily, universal experience shows that doctors are there for the sick and weak, not for the healthy and strong. The content of the saying cannot be misunderstood: Jesus is the healing doctor. But the Pharisees still have learning to do (*manthanō*, here—as in 11:39—absolute LN 27.15); they must still learn the real sense of the Scripture and translate God's mercy into human mercy. (As in Hosea 6:6, so in Matthew 9:13, we must think of mercy among men, above all mercy toward sinful men, cf. also 12:7).

Verse 13: "Go and learn." Matthew analyzes the nature and severity of the disobedience and guilt of Jesus' opponents, indicating the basis of their wrongdoing. They fail to understand the eschatological significance of the ministry of Jesus. But "Matthew goes further. He links the failure of the opponents to fulfill the will of God with their inability to determine what that will is. As opposed to Jesus, who is the true interpreter of the mind and will of God, they do not know the will of God. Jesus teaches the will of God as one with authority, 'not as their scribes' (7.29). Jesus orders them to 'Go and learn what this means, "I will have mercy and not sacrifice"' (9.13; 12.2), thus pointing to their "ignorant state" (Bauer, 71).

"*Go and learn*" (cf. 10:7; 11:4) underlines the earnestness of the imperative, which then comes to expression with special clarity in the contrast of (owed) mercy and (unowed) sacrifice (sacrificial victims are meant). The negatively formulated "Elthon-speech" ("I came not") at the close of the pericope entails an authority claim that goes far beyond the prophetic consciousness of mission, and expresses a Christological belief of the community. He, who pushes mercy to the fore in this way, is the one whom God calls Son. His proclamation of *hesed* (love, kindliness, unshakable devotion, proof of mercy)—one of the richest concepts in the Hebrew ethical and religious vocabulary (cf. LN 88.76)—is an expression of God's will, which does not exclude sinners, but integrates them into the eschatological gathering movement.

"*Mercy, not sacrifice*." Hosea 6:6 is important for Matthew. He is the only Gospel writer to quote it and he does so twice. Here the passage is used in response to an accusation from the Pharisees. It is directed against Matthew's opponents with respect to the law. Matthew applies this verse in a manner that summarizes his community's view and interpretation of certain laws. More than once the Matthean community must have had to answer for what appeared to be a lax disposition toward he law. "For our purposes it is important to see the way in which Matthew has transformed his tradition in order to show that Jesus and his disciples do not break the law" (Overman, 81-82). While Mark is apt to say that the law no longer counts, Matthew insists from first to last that he and his community do observe the law.

In this pericope Matthew does not speak of "some" Pharisees but of *the* Pharisees. Against the standpoint sketched in this pericope the community of Matthew's Gospel had to evaluate itself. The standpoint of a religious and moral way of life represented by the questioners contradicts the opening and the openness begun by Jesus and continued in the community. And the reproach framed against Jesus is even sharpened in the Jewish complaint against the community. The community defends itself against it by appealing to the example of their teacher. The pericope provides the community not only "apologetic material" for emerging controversy but also has a parenetic character: since the community itself, as a sinful community, was called to discipleship, its principal duty must be to receive and welcome all weak and sinful people and to refuse mercy to none of them. The community itself is in an unending learning process.

(III) 3. Fasting, 9:14-17

In chapter 9, the conflict between Jesus and the religious leaders that the reader has been led to anticipate, suddenly materializes. This conflict, however, is carefully orchestrated. Fierce as it is, this conflict is still preliminary to the more intense conflict to come. The conflict does not become so intense that it causes the religious leaders to mobilize against Jesus; none of the issues touch on Mosaic law as such; Jesus is not directly challenged for something he does. On the contrary, the various charges brought against him or the disciples are all "indirect" in character. Some scribes, watching Jesus forgive a paralytic his sins, declare "within themselves" that Jesus is guilty of committing blasphemy (9:3-4). Then the Pharisees, in seeing Jesus sit at table with toll-collectors and sinners, approach the disciples and complain to them about Jesus (9:10-11); the disciples of John, siding on one occasion with the Pharisees, take exception to the fact that Jesus' disciples are not observing the custom of fasting and question Jesus about this.

> **14** Then the disciples of John came to him, saying. "Why do we and the Pharisees fast often but your disciples do not fast?" **15** And Jesus said to them, "The wedding guests cannot mourn as long as the bridegroom is with them, can they? The days will come when the bridegroom is taken away from them, and then they will fast. **16** No one sews a piece of unshrunk cloth on an old cloak, for the patch pulls away from the cloak, and a worse tear is made.
> **17** Neither is new wine put into old wineskins; otherwise the skins burst, and the wine is spilled, and the skins are destroyed; but new wine is put into fresh wineskins, and so both are preserved."

The pericope on fasting consists of two parts: (a) the controversy proper (v. 14-15), and (b) the two sayings (J. Meier, "parables") (vv. 16-17). Originally the sayings were handed on independently and later joined to the fasting pericope.

Verse 14: "Your disciples do not fast" (LN 53.65). Matthew's "Then" binds the fasting passage closely to the preceding passage. For John's disciples fasting was a form of asceticism, a kind of penance (cf. Zech 7:1-3; 8:18-19), as it will be expressly attributed to the Baptist (11:18-19). That Jesus and his disciples did not adopt this practice brings them into disfavor with the "Pious" and "True Believers."

Verse 15a: "Bridegroom is with them." Jesus' answer comes in the form of a counterquestion: If it is fitting that a wedding be a feast, can the guest (*hyioi tou nymphōnos,* LN 11.7) behave as if they were at a funeral? In Jesus' mouth the saying was possibly: "Can the wedding guests fast during the wedding?"

Verse 15b: "Bridegroom is taken away" (LN 15.177). The logion which points to the future mirrors the situation of the community: the bridegroom is Jesus who was taken away by his death. The time of the community then beginning is no longer festival time, but time of waiting in which the practice of fasting has its legitimate place (the text gives no indication that we should think of Friday as a fast day). But this fast is not an adoption of the ascetically oriented fast of John's disciples, it is a new, Christologically oriented fast (as preparation for the Bridegroom's return).

At the very beginning of the Gospel, the genealogy (1::1-17) shows that Jesus stands as the climax to the history of salvation. That Jesus is the climax of salvation history stands behind Matthew's understanding of Jesus' fulfillment of the Old Testament. Here, this notion is expressed in form of the New Wine.

Verses 16-17: "Unshrunk cloth (LN 48.8) . . . new wine." The added double-logion of new patch and old garment (LN 15.157) and of new wine in old wineskins fits the fasting pericope without a seam; from the beginning it was understood as a logion consisting of two similarly structured wisdom sayings which express human experience proverbially. No one who is wise and experienced acts so foolishly that he does harm to himself; and the clarifying addition in verse 17c ("But . . .") underlines the experience sentence. The theological message therein expressed is: In Jesus' preaching the New (and that is the Kingdom of God in the final analysis) has taken its beginning and leaves no more room for the Old, unless it furthers sharing in the Kingdom of God.

The community must keep two things in mind regarding the inbreaking Kingdom of God:

1. The Kingdom of God has a festival character which excluded all asceticism, penance, and mourning; it was characterized only by joy. During the earthly lifetime of the Messiah this festival time broke in, so that every fasting practice was excluded. In the time "between," between Jesus' work and the definitive inbreaking of God's Kingdom, lies the period of waiting. In the time of waiting, fasting *is* in place again, which fixes the gaze on the Coming One and prepares for the future.

2. The community stands before the question: What in the traditional can be given up, what cannot be given up, at any price to be retained New? Two wisdom rules give the answer in penetrating pictures. Given to the community by Jesus, they represent decisive maxims. Now the community knows "that in Jesus something fundamentally new has dawned" (Schweizer 227). Jesus' preaching of the Kingdom of God therefore has a tradition-critical function. Where the New comes, there appears the Old and its retentiveness, its "fragility," and outmodedness. The New cannot be mixed with the Old, for it shows its power and its dangerousness toward the Old.

(IV) Faith 1: A Healing within a Raising, 9:18-26

In the fourth subsection of chapters 8–9, Jesus performs additional healings in Capernaum, and, through his encounter with the suppliants, the essence of faith is disclosed. So again, in chapters 8–9, Jesus is presented as discharging in Israel a ministry of healing and, gathering or refusing followers along the way, as addressing himself to questions concerning discipleship.

> **18** While he was saying these things to them, suddenly a leader came in and knelt before him, saying, "My daughter has just died; but come and lay your hand on her, and she will live." **19** And Jesus got up and followed him, with his disciples. **20** Then suddenly a woman who had suffered from hemorrhages for twelve years came up behind him and touched the fringe of his cloak; **21** for she said to herself, "If I only touch his cloak, I will get well." **22** Jesus turned, and seeing her he said, "Take heart, daughter; your faith has made you well." And instantly the woman was made well. **23** When Jesus came to the leader's house, and saw the flute players and the crowd making a commotion, **24** he said, "Go away; for the girl is not dead but sleeping." And they laughed at him. **25** But when the crowd had been put outside, he went in and took her by the hand, and the girl got up. **26** And the report of this spread throughout that district.

This raising and healing account, which is in all three synoptics (cf. Mark 5:21; Luke 8:40-56), continues the miracle accounts after Matthew has inserted three controversy speeches. The connection of the two accounts must have been realized on the pre-literary level. In its present form the pericope has two parts:

a) The account of the raising of the ruler's daughter (9:18, 19, 23-26);

b) The account of the healing of the bleeding woman (9:20-22). Of all the miracle accounts this is the one that Matthew shortened in the most drastic way. All vivid scenes and expansive motifs are—in comparison with Mark and Luke—eliminated. As is his practice, Matthew shrinks the circle of persons to the one who brings and the one who needs healing: the crowd is not mentioned. Again the healing *word* stands at the center (the woman is not healed by touch but by word): "Your faith has made you well."

Verse 18: "Knelt before him." Matthew links the pericope closely with the preceding controversies (about: forgiveness of sins, table companionship, and fasting), (9:3-6a, 9-13, 14-17). Matthew omits the name of the ruler (Mark and Luke: Jairus). Acting in behalf of his sick daughter the ruler comes and shows Jesus the *poskynesis* ("knelt"), which expresses both petition and reverent acknowledgement (cf. LN 17.21). *Proskyneō* is one of Matthew's favorite words (cf. 8:2; 9:18; 14:33; 15:25; 20:20): here the word expresses the trusting reverence of a person who recognizes God's action in Jesus. By the use of this verb Matthew allows to shine forth, from behind the earthly Jesus, the glory of the Christ raised to the right hand of God and thereby, God's power. In Matthew the daughter (Mark has the diminutive, "little daughter") has just died; the ruler trusts that she "will live" if Jesus lays his hands on her. The contrast Death/Life characterizes Matthew's raising narrative.

Verse 19: "Jesus got up" connects back to the publican meal: Jesus rises from table and follows the ruler. "With his disciples" is possibly a relic from the preceding pericope. There they were involved in the action in an essential way; but they are not mentioned in what follows; Jesus acts alone ("He follows": v. 19; he "came to the house": v. 23).

"And followed him"—"A review of the verb *akolouthein* shows that Matthew can in fact use it simply to signify accompaniment in the literal sense of the word. The passage 9:19 provides an excellent example of this, for here Matthew records that 'Jesus followed him [the ruler].' Now if Matthew had regarded *akolouthein* exclusively as a *terminus technicus* connoting discipleship, obviously he could not have written these words, for he would thereby have made Jesus the disciple of the ruler" ("Akolouthein," p. 57).

Verses 20-21: Through the "then suddenly" Matthew connects the healing story with the raising narrative. The woman's illness is presented with a minimum of words (three): "A hemorrhage for twelve years"; further details (see Mark and Luke) go unmentioned. LN 8.64 mentions that "it may be important to use a special term for blood, since this passage is a reference to the hemorrhaging of menstruation." That the woman is neither repulsed nor rebuked, but is accepted and healed because of her faith makes it clear that here too, an element of Jewish blood-awe is overcome (cf. Lev 15:19-33). The atoning and apotrophic blood rites of Judaism lose their relevance in the New Testament, which follows the prophetic tradition. There is no magical thinking at the basis of the woman's faith, but the trusting certainty that only a word (8:8) or a touch (8:15) would suffice to be healed by Jesus (note the *sōzein* = save; cf. especially 14:36).

Verse 22: "Your faith has made you well." Again, Matthew does not give the details of the healing. Instead he mentions Jesus again by name and the fact that he turns to her, sees her, and speaks to her. The "take heart" (found already in 9:2) underlines the fact that the woman's faith is not the consequence but the condition for the healing from bodily ill. In the man Jesus, the eschatological Savior and so the Healer has come. The assertion that the healing did indeed take place (cf. 8:13; 15:28; 17:18) certifies that healing and saving follow from faith in Jesus.

Verses 23-24: The narrative resumes its path interrupted in verse 19 and reports what happens in the leader's house. The flute players (cf. Jos*Bell* 3.9.5 #437; bKetub. IV. 4): "even the poorest in Israel use not fewer than two fluteplayers and a wailing woman"). Jesus tells the lamenting crowd to leave (*anachoreō*: withdraw) ten times in Matthew. The girl is (only) sleeping. The raising account reaches a climax in the riddle word with the contrast dead/sleeping. It is greeted with non-understanding laughter, for understanding for the deeper meaning of the sleep (unto resurrection) is lacking. This throws the theme of faith into the foreground.

Verses 25-26: In a few words Matthew reports what Jesus—left alone with the girl—does; he went in and took her by the hand. The girl arose (the translation "and the girl was awakened" is also possible). The report of this went "throughout the district" (*ge* is properly the earth—overtones of universality). In Jesus has come the dispenser of new life and the message goes forth "to all lands."

The raising story sees the community in conjunction with Jesus' resurrection. It is a sign that the salvation time, which means victory over death and saving for life, has broken in, but this can be effected only by faith. The inserted healing story brings out the fact that courage is part of faith.

For only readiness to risk makes the right faith possible. The meeting with Jesus that is effected in faith makes clear the decisive importance of personal decision, and at the same time makes possible the recognition, the insight, as to who Jesus really is. Not only in Matthew's community, but also "in all lands" the message spreads: in Jesus, God's salvation comes to all.

(IV) Faith 2: A Son of David Healing, 9:27-31

Whether extolled by the crowds or denounced by the leaders, Jesus' healings still do not move Israel to repentance and to recognition of him as its Messiah (11:20-24, 25). On this score, the healing ministry that Jesus carried out specifically as the Son of David assumes significance.

> **27** And as Jesus went on from there, two blind men followed him, crying aloud, "Have mercy on us, Son of David." **28** When he entered the house, the blind men came to him, and Jesus said to them, "Do you believe that I am able to do this?" They said to him, "Yes, Lord." **29** Then he touched their eyes and said "According to your faith be it done to you." **30** And their eyes were opened. And Jesus sternly ordered them, "See that no one knows of this." **31** But they went away and spread the news about him throughout all the district.

The principal source for 9:27-31 is the narrative about the healing of the blind man of Jericho (20:29-34); yet the first evangelist has radically edited the Jericho event, taking some traits from the pericope of the cleansing of the leper (8:1-4) and working them in ("be able," "touch," "cleansed [opened]," "command to silence"). It is also meaningful that in both healing accounts Matthew speaks of two blind men, while in the Jericho pericope both parallel texts speak of only one.

Verse 27: "Son of David." The cry for mercy stands emphatically at the beginning, the petition taking the form of an outcry (*krazō*, cf. LN 33.83) to the "Son of David" (cf. also 15:22; 17:15; 20:30,31). The address "Son of David" is a Jewish term for the Messiah. In times of defeat Israel had attached specific future expectations to the person of David; the promises to David were recalled and a David Redivivus was proclaimed (Isa 11:1-3; Hos 3:5; Jer 30:9). Even more meaningful was the expectation of a "Son of David" with a messianic function; this is most clearly worked out in Matthew (cf. LN 10.30) and is met there in connection with the salvation activity of the earthly Jesus.

Those who appeal to, or hail, Jesus as the Son of David are blind men, a Gentile woman (15:22), and children (21:15). These are minor characters in Matthew's story, disenfranchised and without power in Jewish society. "For them to approach or acclaim Jesus as Israel's Davidic Messiah is for them to 'see' and to 'confess' the truth with which the crowds only toy and which the religious leaders will not even so much as entertain. Accordingly discernible in Jesus' healing as the Son of David is a polemical strain: such healing underlines the guilt that is Israel's for repudiating its Messiah" (*Story*, 69) (cf. 1:1, 16; 22:42-46).

Verse 28: "Do you believe?" The dialogue between Jesus and the blind men leads to an explicit expression of their belief; the belief motif is found already in 8:10, 13; 9:2, 22. The terse answer, "Yes, Lord" acknowledging Jesus' lordship, is the presupposition of his action with authority.

Verse 29: "Then he touched." Only now is the healing gesture mentioned, which will be completed and elucidated through the decisive healing word. The word brings healing because of the faith of the blind men (cf. 8:13): corresponding to their faith, God's power works in them opening their eyes.

Verses 30-31: "Sternly charged them." In Old Testament expressions (2 Kgs 6:20; Isa 35:5; 42:7), Matthew speaks of "opening" of the eyes. The eyes of a blind person were thought of as being closed and needing to be opened (Matthew uses "to open" eleven times, including three times of opening of the mouth and three times of eyes). The use of *embrimaomai* is striking (LN 33.322). Seldom used in classical Greek, it means to shout with rage, to shout at, to scold (in the New Testament it is found only five times). In the context of the present pericope, the verb refers to a stirring of the spirit, bound with a feeling of annoyance. This is understandable only when we take into consideration that in old times blindness was regarded as the work of an evil spirit; so Jesus' annoyance is directed against a presumed demon. "The command to silence in the miracle account no longer has any Christological implication as in Mark. It is intended to suggest that there were many who sought help from Jesus" (J. Gnilka I 345). In any case it was unsuccessful: the healed men spreads Jesus' fame. In connection with a miracle narrative the command to silence was intended to prevent a great to-do being made about Jesus' person; only the selfless service to the suffering should be expressed by the miracle account.

The community knows that Jesus is "David's Son" and that as such he is Messiah for all. He concerns himself with Israel (8:10), with tax collectors and sinners (9:10-11), and with the sick especially; the healing of the two blind men is an impressive example of this concern for those in need.

In all this Jesus draws his disciples to faith. And it is for the same purpose that the healing miracles are related to the Christian community—to establish faith in the disciple community, i.e. the readiness to accept the proclamation that in Jesus, the God-chosen Salvation-Bringer has come, to believe this proclamation, to acknowledge it, and to shape their lives (individually and as a community) by this conviction. The responsibility of the disciples toward this proclamation is great; in that land (and again this means in all lands) Jesus' call has resounded; to heed it and to hold it fast is the duty imposed upon the community in a special way (cf. 28:20a).

(IV) Faith 3: Collusion with Satan, 9:32-34

The crowds are amazed but the Pharisees object—the conflict between Jesus and the religious leaders, which the reader has been led the anticipate, suddenly materializes. The account of the healing of a dumb demoniac (the last in the chapters 8–9 miracle sequence) is closely connected with the preceding narrative. As Jesus was leaving the place where the two blind men were healed, a dumb man is brought to him.

> **32** After they had gone away, behold, a demoniac who was mute was brought to him. **33** And when the demon had been cast out, the one who had been mute spoke; and the crowds were amazed and said, "Never has anything like this been seen in Israel." **34** But the Pharisees said, "By the ruler of the demons he casts out the demons."

Verse 33: "The crowds were amazed." The "crowds" in Matthew have a character of their own. Although they are without faith in Jesus and see in him only a prophet, in being generally well-disposed toward him they contrast sharply with their leaders. If the crowds are not disciples of Jesus, neither are they his inveterate enemies. While the scribes regard it as blasphemy that Jesus forgives the sins of the paralytic, the crowds witness the absolution and healing of the man, are awe-struck by this, and glorify God (9:2-8). Following an exorcism by Jesus, the crowds are amazed and say, "Never was anything like this seen in Israel."

Verse 34: "But the Pharisees said." Entirely in contrast to the reaction of the crowds, the Pharisees render an entirely negative judgment: Jesus is in contact with the prince of demons; the latter gives Jesus the power to drive out demons. The slander functions as a character assassination; it was calculated to cause people to regard Jesus as dangerous, possibly insane, someone to be avoided. Matthew points out the gulf between the folk (*ochloi*) and the leaders of the folk (*Pharisaioi*). While this is a personal attack on Jesus, the hostility still remains preliminary. The Pharisees cast their aspersions either to themselves alone or merely in the hearing of fellow conspirators.

The overcoming of demons (and unclean spirits), but even more the overcoming of the fear of demons, was one of Jesus' most pressing tasks. The driving out of demons was always accompanied by the relief from the bodily and psychic afflictions which, it was commonly said, were caused by them. Matthew's community could still fall back into *demonangst*, not yet having found full trust in the Vanquisher of all malevolent powers. For the community could fall into the doubt, as expressed by the Pharisees' judgment.

Second Summary Statement, 9:35-38

In the summary passages, Matthew deftly alerts the reader to the direction that the plot of the Gospel-story will take. In the first half of Part II these are 4:23; 9:35; and 11:11. They describe Jesus as discharging throughout the whole of Galilee a ministry of teaching, preaching, and healing whereby he proffers salvation to Israel (4:17-11:1).

The conclusion of verse 35 repeats almost *verbatim* the words of 4:23, making a change only from "all Galilee" to "all the cities and villages." This "inclusio" binds together the two great intervening sections—the Sermon on the Mount, and the catena of miracle stories. "It must be recalled that in ancient manuscripts there was nothing akin to our 'chapters' or other divisions (or even to mark the end of a word or of a sentence). If a writer wanted to indicate to the reader how he intended his material to be organized, he had no other means than the incorporation of such signals into his text" (Beare, p. 237).

> **35** Then Jesus went about all the cities and villages, teaching in their synagogues and preaching the good news of the kingdom, and curing every disease and every sickness. **36** When he saw the crowds, he had compassion for them, because they were harassed and helpless, like sheep without a shepherd. **37** Then he said to his disciples, "The harvest is plentiful, but the laborers are few. **38** Therefore pray the Lord of the harvest to send out laborers into his harvest."

Verse 35: "Teaching, preaching, curing." The Summary Statement is the real conclusion of chapters 8-9 (Jesus is once more expressly named). Verse 35 looks back, forming an inclusion with the first Summary Statement, 4:23, while verses 36-38 look forward to the Missionary Discourse (ch. 10).

Verse 36: "He had compassion for them." Despite his tendency to avoid references to Jesus' emotions, Matthew stresses the sense of compassion Jesus feels for the crowds of ordinary Jews, dejected because they lack true leaders. "They look like frightened sheep who simply fall helpless and exhausted to the ground (cf. Num 27:17; 1 Kings 22:17; Zech 10:2). Mark 6:34 mentions a similar sight, which moves Jesus to teach and feed the crowd of five thousand" (Meier, *ad loc*).

Verses 37: "The harvest is plentiful." The sight moves Jesus to think of the need for a mission by his disciples. Jesus himself is the true shepherd of Israel (2:6), but he desires his disciples to act as shepherds of his people in his place and after his manner (cf. 18:10-14). Despite everything, Jesus foresees a great harvest (Hos 6:11; Joel 3:13). The mission of his disciples, bringing the good news to others and gathering believers into his community, is part of the eschatological event. That is why Matthew will insert part of Mark's apocalyptic discourse into the missionary discourse of chapter 10. But the demands of this eschatological ingathering are great, while the laborers in the field, the missionaries bringing people into salvation, are few.

Verse 38: "Pray the Lord of the harvest." Jesus produces no miracle or magic solution to solve this problem. Like the whole unfolding of the eschatological drama, this problem lies in the hands of the Father, the Lord of the harvest. The disciples impart him in prayer to send out more laborers on mission. In this vision, prayer itself becomes missionary and eschatological.

The second Summary Statement (as closure of chs. 8-9) and the reference to the sad situation of the people (as introduction to the Mission Discourse) present to the community a Jesus whose sense of mission impels him to prepare for the approaching harvest. Jesus' compassion for the crowds is therefore not just an expression of human compassion, but an expression of pity for a misled and abandoned people that wanders about helpless and lost. This Jesus is an example for the community that demands imitation. The imperative ("Pray the Lord," v. 38) is first injunction for prayers, but then also a warning word, to be concerned about the critically necessary co-workers for the impending harvest time.

Understanding the Discourses
Implied Reader's Vantage Point beyond the Resurrection
Cf. 7:15; 13:38

The implied reader not only is present throughout Matthew to hear the whole story but also has a position of his or her own, which lies between the resurrection and the Parousia. This insight is significant, especially for understanding the discourses of Jesus (chs. 5–7, 10; 13; 18; [23]; 24–25). In the Missionary Discourse, for example, Jesus enjoins the disciples, "Go nowhere among the Gentiles, and enter no town of the Samaritans, but go rather to the lost sheep of the house of Israel" (10:5–6). For the implied reader, this injunction occasions no surprise, because it accords with the story of Jesus' ministry to Israel as recounted up to that point. In 10:17-18, however, Jesus declares: "Beware of them . . . you will be dragged before governors and kings for my sake, to bear testimony before them and the Gentiles." This prediction of persecutions envisages not solely a mission to Israel, but also a mission aimed at Gentiles. For the implied reader, this sudden reference to a Gentile mission comes unexpectedly. The flow of Matthew's story has not prepared the reader for this.

From the temporal position of the implied reader beyond the resurrection, the movement from an exclusive mission to Israel (vv. 5–6) to a mission that includes Gentiles as well (v. 18) parallels the movement within the wider story of Jesus. Jesus, on the one hand, was sent only to the lost sheep of the house of Israel (15:24), but, on the other hand, he initiated a universal mission to the Gentiles immediately after his resurrection (28:18-20). From his or her vantage point beyond the resurrection, the implied reader can relate to each other, both a mission limited to Israel and a universal mission which includes Gentiles. "Consequently, the same saying or event that occasions surprise for the implied reader when he or she approaches it in terms of the flow of Matthew's story is comprehensible and occasions no surprise when he or she views it in terms of a special position in the time following the resurrection." (*Story*, 39). And there are other passages in the discourses which seem "out of place" with respect to the earthly ministry of Jesus, but which become intelligible when viewed from the perspective of a position in the time of the risen Jesus and of the universal mission.

In chapter 10, Jesus summons the disciples and delivers to them his Missionary Discourse. By the end of this discourse, the reader can sense that the trend of Matthew's story is toward irreconcilable conflict between Jesus and the religious leaders. In ominous words, Jesus describes the bitter conflict the disciples will face as they go out to preach and heal in Israel (10:16-39). On hearing this, the reader no longer doubts that the time is fast approaching when the religious leaders will confront Jesus personally and attack him directly. And the reader also knows that Matthew is speaking past Jesus' contemporaries and addressing the members of his community and Christians of every age who will read his story.

Mission A: Calling of the Twelve, 10:1-4

Up to this point the focus has been on Jesus calling of disciples. But with chapter 10 the disciples' mission to Israel becomes the topic. To indicate that the circle of the twelve disciples is now complete and that the disciples are to be "fishers of men" in Israel, Matthew recites the names of the Twelve and terms them "apostles" ("Ones who are sent" 10:2-4). The mission Jesus gives them is plainly an extension of his own and he endows them with the authority on which they are to act (10:1).

Matthew uses the term "to follow" in both an ordinary sense ("to come after") and in a metaphorical sense. The latter is the case when "cost" and "commitment" is entailed. Disciples called earlier in the Gospel (Peter and Andrew, James and John [4:20, 22] and Matthew [9:9]) were called in this sense. Now Matthew gives his list of the disciples of Jesus and he cites the names of all five of the above (vv. 2-3). Moreover, in 19:27-29 he has Jesus confirm the fact that those whose "vocation" it is to "follow" him do so as his closest companions, who have forsaken all and will have their share in his future glory. Without doubt therefore, *akolouthein* in the first Gospel can connote accompaniment in the extended sense of discipleship.

> **1** Then Jesus summoned his twelve disciples and gave them authority over unclean spirits, to cast them out, and to cure every disease and every sickness. **2** These are the names of the twelve apostles: first, Simon known as Peter, and his brother Andrew; James the son of Zebedee, and his brother John; **3** Philip and Bartholomew; Thomas and Matthew the tax collector; James the son of Alphaeus, and Thaddaeus; **4** Simon the Cananaean, and Judas Iscariot, who betrayed him.

Verse 1: "To cast out . . . to cure." In the two summary passages we have had so far (4:23; 9:35), Jesus is described as discharging a ministry of teaching, preaching, and healing. It is striking that for the moment, the authority to teach and preach is withheld from the disciples.

Verses 2-3. "Names of the twelve apostles." The twelve disciples are now called "twelve apostles"; but it is Matthew himself who introduces this term, not Jesus (differently Luke 6:13 and Mark 3:14b). "Matthew calls the twelve 'apostles' *on* his own part—i.e., without saying that Jesus named them 'apostles'—and simply lists their personal names. This change stems from his omitting their appointment. . . . The center of gravity shifts, then, from the appointment of the twelve to their being sent (v. 5a)" (Gundry *ad loc*). Matthew is not interested in the "title," but in the person whom he lists in the nominative, and in their assigned task ("send": v. 5).

Simon's importance is stressed in two ways: he stands as "first" (*protos*) in the list, which expresses a rank, and he is the one who is called Peter (cf. 4:18), i.e., who is known as Peter. Andrew is named in the second place (so also Luke; Mark mentions him in the fourth place) and called Peter's brother, which expresses the close connection between Simon and Andrew (*adelphos* hardly expresses the strongly fraternal nature of the Church). That Jesus gave the nickname Boanerges (Sons of Thunder) to James and John is unknown to Matthew and Luke. As already in 4:18-22, Simon Peter, Andrew, James, and John form a special quartet (their names are connected by an "and"); they had special importance in the community. "Peter is called 'first' (*protos*) among the disciples in Matthew 10:2, and he is the first called to be a follower of Jesus in 4:18. There are occasions when it is clear that Peter is simply the spokesperson for the disciples or their representative. . . . Peter, however, is not simply one of the disciples; he is not portrayed as an equal within the story. Peter emerges as a leader or, as Matthew says, 'first' among the followers of Jesus" (Overman, 137).

In the rest of the list Matthew gives the names in pairs; possibly this expresses that they were sent out in pairs (cf. Mark 6:7), which corresponds to the Old Testament principle that only the witness of two or three was valid (cf. 18:16 [special to Matthew]). In dependency on 9:9, Matthew receives the nickname "the tax collector," but unlike Mark and Luke—he is placed after Thomas. Judas is (in a participle construction) presented as the "Hander Over" (the Betrayer, *paradous*); his role in Jesus' trial is already referred to here. It is the label that adheres to him even beyond death (27:3-10) and in the community as an insistent warning uttered with every mention of the name (cf. 26:[14]15, 25; 27:3).

Verse 4: "Judas Iscariot (*Iskariotes*)." According to some scholars no Jewish nationalist party existed in Jesus' time; accordingly, Iscariot would mean simply one zealous for national independence. "Therefore, one might speak of Simon as 'Simon the patriot'" (LN 25.77). Matthew's listing of the names (in the nominative) gives the impression of a catechism ordering for easy memorization. Yet there is another redactional objective: the twelve disciples named in verse 1 represent the (new) community of Matthew's Gospel. In them (and their authority), the work of the group of twelve known in the community by name continues. The community must no longer have had detailed knowledge about most of the persons named, and the twelve disciples must not have acted as a closed group, as one might conclude from the list. So the structure of the pericope must have been shaped by the desire to represent Matthew's community as the legitimate heir of the Jewish twelve tribes community, endowed with apostolic authority.

On the other hand, the list of twelve formed by Matthew contains a reference to rank. Simon/Peter is the first (*protos* here does not have temporal meaning but refers to rank); with three other disciples he forms a quartet which has a special, community constituting function. In this carefully structured form of the list an "office structure," already partially established in Matthew's community, is justified.

Mission B: Sent to the Lost Sheep of Israel, 10:5b-42

Until Easter, the disciples in Matthew's Gospel also share in Jesus' concentration on Israel. To stress this, the first evangelist devotes the whole of the section 9:35-10:42 to their projected mission to Israel, which goes beyond anything one finds in either Mark or Luke.

> 5 These twelve Jesus sent out with the following instruction, "Go nowhere among the Gentiles and enter no town of the Samaritans, 6 but go rather to the lost sheep of the house of Israel. 7 As you go, proclaim the gospel saying, 'The kingdom of heaven has come near.' 8 Cure the sick, raise the dead, cleanse lepers, cast out demons. You received without payment, give without payment. 9 Take no gold, or silver, or copper in your belts, 10 no bag for your journey, or two tunics, or sandals, or a staff; for the laborers deserve their food. 11 And whatever town or village you enter, find out who in it is worthy, and stay there until you leave. 12 As you enter the house, greet it. 13 If the house is worthy, let your peace come upon it; but if it is not worthy, let our peace return to you. 14 If any one will not welcome you or listen to your words, shake off the dust from your feet as you leave that house or town. 15 Truly, I tell you, it shall be more tolerable for the land of Sodom and Gomorrah on the day of judgment than for that town.

Verse 5a: "These twelve Jesus sent out." The demonstrative pronoun "These" refers back to verses 1-2; the "twelve" is the abbreviated expression for the "twelve disciples" of verses 1 and 2. Only now is it said that the twelve are "sent": the title "apostle" (i.e., the Sent One) from verse 2 is only now taken up with respect to its functional meaning and its content fulfilled. The sending consists of a basic commission (the verb means "to order, instruct") on which Jesus' "mission rules" are based.

Verses 5b-6: "Lost sheep of the house of Israel." Two (negative) imperatives express what the twelve must definitely avoid (v. 5b); a third imperative (v. 6) states what is to be done; the vocabulary betrays Matthew's hand. Galilee consisted—except for the south—of mostly heathen districts; in the south lay Samaria, which was to be avoided by reason of cultic and theological differences. The activity of the twelve was to be confined to Galilee and seems to correspond to Jesus' activity (cf. 4:14-16; see further 15:24). Verse 6 confirms this interpretation: the lost sheep of the house of Israel must first be sought out. The sheep are the people (cf. 2 Sam 24:17), more precisely the People of God (Ps 74:1), who constitute the House of God (cf. Lev 10:6; Amos 5:25; Jer 31:33). So Matthew deliberately points to a continuity between Jesus' mission and that of his community.

The emphasis on the exclusivity of Jesus' mission and that of his disciples is found only in Matthew's special material (10:5b, 6; 10:23; 15:24). While in 10:5b-6 the *mallon* ("rather") hints at the possibility of a (later) revision of the mission task (by reason of the context this applies also to 10:23), in 15:24 the command is absolute. Matthew therefore has retained the expression of Jesus' mission preserved in the earlier tradition —a mission only to the house of Israel. This retention is not an indication of Matthew's fidelity toward the Jesus' tradition, but corresponds to his conviction that "Israel" has not lost her "primacy," so also in the *heilsgeschichlich* phase opened by Jesus, she is the first partner to be addressed in the ingathering movement.

Verses 7-8: "Preach, heal, raise." Thus far, Jesus has been calling Israel, through his ministry of teaching, preaching, and healing, to repentance and to entrance into the sphere of God's end-time Rule. In extension of his ministry, Jesus now commissions the disciples to a ministry in Israel of their own (9:35–10:42). Except for the activity of teaching, which Jesus reserves for himself, the disciples are to do exactly as he has done. Like him, they are to restrict their activity to Israel: "Go nowhere among the Gentiles . . . but go rather to the lost sheep of the house of Israel" (v. 6; 15:24). Like him, they are to summon Israel to the Kingdom by proclaiming, "The Kingdom of Heaven has come near" (10:7; 4:17). And like him, they are to "Cure every disease and every sickness" among the people (10:1; 8:35; 4:23). The content of the mission task, is, first the proclamation of the Kingdom of Heaven, which has drawn near, and secondly the conquest of sickness, need, and death. The disciples' preaching corresponds to Jesus' preaching (cf. 4:17). In addition to the threepart "topical outline with superscription" that D. Bauer holds in common with J. Kingsbury, Bauer sees the Gospel of Matthew as constructed according to four major structural elements, the first of which is "repetition of comparison" (57). "The relationship between Jesus and the expectations for the disciples in Matthew is essentially that of comparison. Matthew sets the expectations for, or the role of, the disciples and the person of

Jesus side by side in terms of their relation to God, manner of living, and mission."

Verses 9-10: "Take (*ktēsēsthe*) no gold." (*Ktaomai*, acquire, get). "Jesus made the prohibition for the sake of a speedy mission through Galilee: the disciples were to depend entirely on hospitality in order to accomplish their mission quickly" (Gundry, *ad loc*). The added concrete instructions are details concerning the subsistence of Wander Missionaries, who are entirely dependent on the hospitality of others. That Matthew—unlike Mark and Luke—speaks of "acquiring, earning," need not refer absolutely to the town mission as opposed to country mission. The concern is rather that the mission should be carried out without any delay. Whether Matthew's formulation points to the conduct of false prophets who enrich themselves by their office cannot be determined with certainty; the concluding observation "The laborers deserve their food" (added only by Matthew [cf. also 1 Cor 9:14; 1 Tim 5:18]) is to be taken in a general sense. It merely says: "Hospitality must not be refused to the missionaries." Matthew replaces the original "wages" (so Luke 10:7) with "food," since he forbids earning one's keep.

Verse 11: "Who is worthy (*axios*)." Before the missionary enters a town, he is to test its worthiness, i.e., investigate (*exetazo*: ascertain, found only in Matt 2:8; 10:11 John 21:12), who is worthy in the city. The "worthy" in the proverb of verse 10 serves as the key word to add to other thoughts about worthiness; but this consists in recognizing the wandering missionary, accepting him, and supporting him in his missionary activity, which is devoted to the proclamation of the Kingdom of God. He should remain in that city until the time comes for him to preach elsewhere.

Verses 12-13: "Salute it (*aspasasthe autēn*). The missionary brings Peace, which—as the Luke formulation shows—comes to expression already at his entrance greeting (the Greek verb for "greet" corresponds to Hebrew, "to offer peace": Exod 18:7; Judg 18:15; cf. LN 33.20).

The Matthew "and if—but if it is not" makes it possible to represent, in a pregnant speech form, what happens when worthiness/unworthiness is found. In the one case, the peace will come upon the inhabitants of the house, in the other case it will not (*epistrepho*: turn around, cf. 12:44; 13:15; 24:18). Peace was not just a friendly wish, but had, as it were, an objective existence (cf. Isa 45:23; 55:11; Zech 5:3-4). Matthew uses the concept "peace" only in the Mission Discourse (v. 13 [twice], v. 34 [twice]); the thought he has already touched upon in the Sermon on the Mount: (5:23-26; 6:12, 14-15; cf. also 18:21-22); the peace spoken of here brings salvation and reconciliation with God.

Verse 14: "Shake off the dust." This verse deals with the situation where God's greeting is not received and where the word is not heard, i.e., accepted. Unlike Mark and Luke, Matthew speaks directly of the man who refuses; thereby the personal relation becomes clearer (cf. v. 40, 41). The addition "listen to your words" is theologically especially relevant (cf. at 7:24-26, 28, the plural "words" are also found in 12:37 [twice]; 19:1; [24:35]; 26:1); they give special weight to the content of the disciples' message ("the kingdom of God has come near": v. 7), and stress the parallel and continuity between Jesus and his disciples. Matthew frequently stresses Jesus' "words" (cf. Gundry 189). In a gesture of dismissal, dust which (in unfriendly places) had stuck to the feet of wandering missionaries, is ostentatiously shaken off, expressing separation and a negative judgment. Matthew has eliminated the phrase "as a witness against them" which (according to Mark 6:11 and Luke 9:5) originally stood in the threefold tradition. Matthew reserves the expression as a positive saying in connection with the proclamation of the Gospel: (8:4; 10:18; 24:14).

Verses 15-16: Matthew ends the judgment on those who refuse the message with a word of warning. They are threatened with a worse fate for judgment day than is the land of Sodom and Gomorrah. Gomorrah is added here; the two towns are often named together in the Old Testament, but only the inhabitants of Sodom criminally violated the law of hospitality. *Anektoteros* is met in the New Testament only in the neuter comparative.

In conclusion and transition, Matthew uses a saying the first half of which, in Luke, opens the sending out of the seventy(two). The saying deals with the hard lot of the messengers, which will be more fully described in verses 17-25. Their lot characterizes the situation of Matthew's community. The disciples of this community are sent like sheep among wolves to carry out their task. "I" stands emphatically at the beginning preceded by "Truly," stressing the meaning of the sending. Jesus' full authority stands behind this saying. While previously the sheep image was for the shepherdless people of Israel (9:36; 10:6), now the Christian missionaries are so designated; they are threatened by wolf-like enemies who reject the missionaries. "Thus a certain solidarity exists between the persecuted missionaries and the harried people; both suffer from the same source" (Gundry, *ad loc*).

The concluding wisdom saying has no parallel in the synoptic tradition (but see EvThom 396). As in 7:24, wisdom is demanded of the disciples, who stand in obedience to Jesus' instruction: serpents' wisdom (cf. Gen 3:1) must be united with doves' innocence (cf. Hos 7:11). The two are required not only by the wolflike harassers but also because of Jesus' authority represented by the "I" at the beginning of the verse.

The mission instructions that Matthew presents here are also instructions for his community. It is their task to go like Jesus to lost sheep of Israel and tell them that the Kingdom of God has come near. The problem of "the time of the coming" has not arisen in the community. They understand themselves as the disciple group chosen by the (earthly) Jesus which must guard and fulfill "all the words" of Jesus. The word of the nearness of the Kingdom of God which Jesus had proclaimed has lost nothing of its validity and urgency. The Kingdom of Heaven is near also for Matthew's community: it calls for decision "now." The guarantee for this nearness is the Lord's presence in the community, and his "words" entrusted to the community. The glimpse of the future (Judgment Day) in no way dissolves the nearness, but underlines it still more. How near the Kingdom of God is becomes clear above all through the difficulties and obstacles that are placed in the way of the wandering missionaries of Matthew's community. The confrontation with recusant persons has begun, and this is a clear sign that the Kingdom of God has drawn near. This nearness is reflected in the duty, which brooks no neglect, to push the Christian mission activity, which is primarily directed to Israel.

Matthew introduces Jesus' missionary discourse with the narrative comment: "These twelve Jesus *sent out*, with the following instructions" (10:5a). Yet Matthew never reports that the disciples actually embark upon, or return from, this ministry. Matthew makes no mention of the disciples' departure or return because the disciples are obligated to continue missionary work aimed at Israel until Jesus' Parousia at the end of the age (10:23). He leads the reader to assume that the disciples did undertake a ministry to Israel, yet spares himself the need to take note of any return of the disciples. This arrangement leaves an aura of unresolved tension surrounding the missionary discourse but Matthew achieved what is crucial for him: the continuance to the end of the age of the disciples' mission to Israel. "The actual sending out occurs at verse 5, so that the discourse can proceed unimpeded by further narrative and can expand its horizons to an apocalyptic future. Indeed, the discourse later becomes so general and future-oriented that neither the mission nor the return of the twelve is narrated after the discourse (contrast Mk 6:12-13. 30; Lk 9:6,10)" (Meier, 106).

Mission C: On Responding to Persecution, 10:16-25

Some of the material in the discourses has specifically to do with the period of Jesus' earthly ministry. Such is the case for the commands to restrictive proclamation in chapter 10 (vv. 5-6, 23). "These few references within the great discourses do not, however, contradict our claim that the focus of these discourses is clearly upon the post-Easter church (see, for example, 10.16-42, and observe that Matthew nowhere mentions that the twelve actually went out on a missionary journey during Jesus' earthly existence)'' (Bauer, 37).

> **16** See, I am sending you out like sheep into the midst of wolves; so be wise as serpents and innocent as doves. **17** Beware of them; for they will hand you over to councils, and flog you in their synagogues. **18** and you will be dragged before governors and kings because of me, as a testimony to them and the Gentiles. **19** When they deliver you over, do not worry about how you are to speak or what you are to say; for what you are to say will be given to you at that time; **20** for it is not you who speak, but the Spirit of your Father speaking through you. **21** Brother will betray brother to death, and a father his child, and children will rise against parents and have them put to death; **22** and you will be hated by all for my name. But the one who endures to the end will be saved. **23** When they persecute you in one town, flee to the next; for truly, I tell you, you will not have gone through all the towns of Israel, before the Son of Man comes.
>
> **24** A disciple is not above his teacher, nor slave above his master; **25** it is enough for the disciple to be like the teacher, and the slave like his master. If they have called the master of the house Beelzebul, how much more will they malign those of his household!

The more general instructions in 10:1-16 take on a clearer outline in the following instructions. Here Matthew reworked the existing material, filled it out, and reinterpreted it. The developments may be summed up under the heading ''Betrayal and Persecution.''

Verse 17: ''Beware (*prosechete,* LN 27.59). ''Matthew first used this injunction in the Sermon on the Mount (6:1; 7:15), now in the Mission Discourse, and he will use it for the third time in chapter 16. The addressees are always the disciples. Very generally Matthew says: Beware of them. He chooses this formulation in preparation for verses 32-33.

''They will hand you over (*paradōsousin*).'' The disciples must beware of men who will deliver them to judgment and flog them. Since the terminology corresponds to Jesus' passion (cf. 20:19), Jesus' fate is referred to as a warning. While according to 20:19, Jesus is betrayed to Jews and then handed over to the Gentiles for scourging, here only Jews are in question: non-understanding or malicious men will do the bidding of Jewish authorities; they will be scourged in Jewish synagogues.

''Up to councils (*synedria*)'' (cf. LN 11.79).

Verse 18: "As a testimony (*martyrion*)." Even the intra-Jewish boundaries are exceeded; missionaries will also be led before (Gentile) governors and kings—for Jesus' sake: as a witness to them. *Martyrion* means witness, testimony; in this case, the Christian witness of the persecuted disciples on trial. According to Matthew it must—corresponding to his universal, supranational tendency—be brought also before the Gentiles.

Here the phenomenon of "speaking past" is very evident. Jesus warns the disciples that they will be dragged before governors and kings. The anomaly of these words is that they presuppose a mission on the part of the disciples among Gentiles within a speech in which Jesus sends them solely to Israel. As those being readied for an exclusive mission to Israel, the disciples are unprepared at this point in the story to entertain the notion of a mission among Gentiles.

Verses 19-20: "The Spirit of your Father speaking." When the handing over takes place the disciples should not be anxious (*merimnaō*, LN 25.225) about what to say in their defense. They are to concentrate on what is existentially most important—saying the right thing at the right time. Here it is not—as elsewhere—a matter of care for material security, but of inner concern whether one will say the right thing at the right time. This will be given to them—a comfort and an assurance. Because then the Spirit of the Father will be speaking. In Matthew—as in the synoptics generally—little is said about the spirit; this is the only place where a promise of the Spirit is mentioned. It is not said that the Spirit will be "visibly present" with the disciples; it will only be shown in the working of the Spirit in that hour.

Verse 21: "Brother will betray (*paradōsei*) brother." The saying about the fate of the missionaries is taken up again (a *de* separates the sayings of v. 20 and 21). The division about Jesus reaches into the family and extends to taking of life.

Verse 22: "For my name." The missionaries too will be drawn into the situation of hatred; actually the hatred is directed against Jesus' name (as often the "name" is an alternate concept for "Jesus," direct speech requires the personal pronoun (cf. at 5:11; 10:18). In dependence on Daniel 12:12-13, salvation is promised to him who endures.

Verse 23: "When they persecute (*diōkōsin*) you." In persecution situations the itinerant prophets are commanded to flee to the next town. The verb (*diōko*) means properly to charge before law; but already in the LXX, the thought of [religious] persecution was connected with the word. To fulfill the mission injunction they must save their lives through flight, if necessary.

With the typical Matthean solemn declaration ("for I tell you" cf. 5:18), the disciples' missionary activity is interpreted theologically. The disciples will not have completed their work before the Son of Man comes. In their flight from persecution situations, the disciples will always find another refuge town in Israel, before the Son of Man comes. You will not complete the missionary work (in the towns of Israel) before the Parousia shall come.

In their fulfillment of the missionary task the disciples will always find a place of refuge before the Parousia of the Son of Man happens. Jesus' injunction ("flee to another [town")]) is valid until the Son of Man comes (Sabourin, *BTB* 7(1977) 5-11, 6-8).

Verses 24-25: These two verses form a unit by reason of content and are only loosely connected with the foregoing. In Luke (6:40), the saying has it that when fully taught, a disciple will be like his/her teacher. To clarify the picture of the disciple/teacher relationship Matthew has sharpened and filled it out by means of the servant/master relationship: disciple and servant must be satisfied to become like their teacher and master. In their mission activity it will go no better for them than it did for their master. If the master of the house is slandered as Beelzebul, the prince of demons, the household members will experience the same. From the slanderous reproach of a demonic cooperation they are no more immune than their Master. Beelzebul, a parody of the Hebrew *Baal Sebub* (i.e., Lord of the Flies), was a heathen god; for the believers in Yahweh the heathen gods are demons, whose names offer opportunity for distortion.

Matthew draws the community directly into the mission discourse which was originally directed only to Jesus' disciples. The warning regarding the persecution fate and the injunction in the persecution situation to conduct themselves rightly, i.e., in accordance with Jesus' will, also applies to them. The community must be aware that in the fulfillment of their task—to proclaim the message of Jesus (of the Kingdom of Heaven)—they do not stand over the Teacher but, like him, must experience the fate of persecuted and harassed messengers of God.

A consequence is that the community lives in anxiety that in the decisive hour it might be speechless before the prosecuting officials, not knowing what to say, what would be right and proper, what significant and convincing. This concern is removed from them through the assurance that at such times the Spirit of the Father will guide the response and bring forth what is fitting through the disciples.

Basically important—and the community is told this very clearly—is the fact that the preaching belongs to all the towns of Israel, and to all the peoples. As earlier, it was emphasized that they dare not allow themselves to be delayed by anything, so now it is enjoined upon the community to flee from persecution. Neither capitulation nor rash heroics in the face of persecution is the proper attitude, but the conviction that an assignment must be carried out at all cost. It shall not be fulfilled before the Son of Man comes; his Parousia will happen only then, when the missionary commission has been completely fulfilled (and even if this is through flight from town to town).

Mission D: Fearless Confession, 10:26-31

Matthew continues the instruction of the disciples with a demand for fearless confession. He took the text from the sayings tradition (cf. Luke 12:2-9); Mark (4:22) also provides the first verse; it is an apocalyptic saying that has been passed on in various forms (cf. also Luke 8:17 and EvThom 5).

> **26** "So have no fear of them; for nothing is covered up that will not be uncovered, or secret that will not become known. **27** What I say to you in the dark tell in the light; and what you hear whispered, proclaim upon the housetops. **28** Do not fear those who kill the body but cannot kill the soul; rather fear him who can destroy both soul and body in hell. **29** Are not two sparrows sold for a penny? Yet not one of them will fall to the ground apart from our Father. **30** Even the hairs of your head are all counted. **31** So do not be afraid; you are of more value than many sparrows.

The pericope has a clear structure. The threefold "Fear not!," the first of which Matthew places emphatically up front (almost as a statement of theme), tie the elements of the instruction together. As compared with Luke's version, Matthew's is shorter, tighter, and thereby more insistent: all parts diverting from the main line of thought, as found in Luke's version (which is the oldest), Matthew has eliminated: consequently, the didactic/catechetical objective stands forth clearly.

Verse 26: "Have no fear." By placing a "Fear not!" at the head of the first saying Matthew turns the following general logion into a direct parenesis. Moreover the pronoun ("of them") provides a connection with the preceding; the antecedent are those who call both the master of the house and the members of the household Beelzebul.

The demand follows the grounds for the action ("So"): everything covered and hidden will be made known. The saying is drawn from the apocalyptic tradition (aethHen 51:3; syrBar 54:1-3; cf. already Deut 29:29), which justifies the confidence that the disciples must have that everything that is now covered and hidden will sometime be uncovered. The theological passive suggests that it is God who will bring about the uncovering. In the later Gospel of Thomas, on the basis of the *ginosko*, the "to know" of Matthew's and Luke's text, the saying is developed gnostically. The *enlightened* shall know what is before their eyes; what is hidden from them will be make known.

Verse 27: "Dark/light . . . whispered/housetops" (LN 24.64). Again there follows an injunction with a parallel structure. With antithetic images, Jesus demands that the disciples should proclaim visibly and audibly, in public, what they heard in secret. The present tense bespeaks the logion's original *Sitz im Leben*—the instruction of the disciples. The short, repeated "what," includes, as in verse 26 (also twice), everything that Jesus told and entrusted to his disciples. Clearly, this disciple instruction draws upon the Sermon on the Mount, 5:13-16.

Verse 28: "Soul and body in hell." While in verse 26a the opponents are cited only by a personal pronoun, they are more accurately designated by their malevolent activity: they kill the body, i.e., they are in a position to kill the earthly body (*apokteino*; the prefix strengthens the negative meaning of the verb). The saying does not propose a bodyless surviving soul but makes clear that God, also the other side of death, can preserve the life of the whole person (*psychē* means not the soul in the Graeco-Hellenistic sense, but the life power of the person (cf. LN pp. ix, x); the *psychē* together with the *soma* (LN 8.1) forms the whole person. We must fear much more those who are able to destroy the whole person (life and body) definitively (in hell) (*geenna* = place of the fire hell, cf. at 5:22, 29-30; the concept is met also in 18:9 and twice in 23:15, 33). Matthew's habitual "rather," (three times in the Mission Discourse) underlines the distinction between human and divine power: man is capable of much, but everything that really counts is in God's power alone.

Verses 29-30: Two word pictures interpret the foregoing word of warning. Sparrows could be an object of commerce: "Sparrows were sold for food" (LN 4.46, Gundry *ad loc*). But they brought so little that they were worth "next to nothing." For two sparrows (Luke: five), a person can hardly get one (Lk: two) "as, *assarion*" (a small Roman copper coin, the sixteenth part of a silver denarius, about the wage for a day's work). Still, despite their little worth they are under the observation and care of "our Father" (Luke: before God), none is forgotten or overlooked (cf. Amos 3:5: "Does a bird fall in a snare on the earth, when there is no trap for it?"). The second picture speaks of the many hairs of his head, which are numbered ("by God" in Luke; "our Father" in Matthew) (cf. 1 Sam 14:45; 2 Sam 14:11; Acts 27:34); the picture is not only stronger and more expressive—through the personal pronoun the disciples are drawn directly into the imagery.

Verse 31. "Therefore . . ." The third "Fear not!" rounds out and concludes the parenesis; the comparison with the sparrows (but not that with the hair) is taken up once more and even more concretely. The disciples (the "you" is again brought to the fore) are worth much more than the worthless sparrows (for *diapherō*, cf. 6:26; the verb is found a third time in 12:12). They need have no fear on account of their persecutors and opponents, for God, the Father, protects them.

The community is threatened, fear is widespread. Through the threefold "Fear not!" anxiety should be banished through a word of power, i.e., power of imperative reassurance. Through the assurance that all will eventually come to light, that only one can really destroy a person's life, and that the disciples are worth more than sparrows and hairs of the head, fear is banished. The verbal demand is strongly depicted and insistently presented in powerful pictures. The community's mission has the assistance of God's help: it may be that for the sake of the confession the earthly person may be destroyed; even so, the certainty remains that God, the Lord of "eternal life," will stand by the fearless confessor.

Mission E: Acknowledgement of Jesus, 10:32-33

In content, verses 32 and 33 belong to the foregoing passage (so also in Luke); but because they advance a new theological thought, it is right to treat them separately (in Luke the separation from the foregoing is made clearer by the inserted "But I say to you"). For one thing, the question about the consequences of Christological acknowledgment/non-acknowledgement is dealt with; for another, through the generalizing "every one," the theme of the Mission Discourse is given a character of general validity.

> **32** Everyone who acknowledges me before others, I also will acknowledge before my Father who is in heaven; **33** but whoever denies me before others, I also will deny before my Father who is in heaven.

"Acknowledges . . . denies." The repeated "acknowledge/deny" is central. *Homologeō*, i.e., acknowledge (extol), is found four times in Matthew (10:23; 10:32 [twice]; 14:7, cf. LN 33.274). The construction *homologein en* is un-Greek; a Semitism lies behind it. The structure (a double saying in antithetic parallelism in the conditional mood) also betrays its Semitic origin. The saying, addressed to the disciples but above and beyond them to all, is the expression of Jesus' sovereignty and authority. He makes both promise and warning clear—that the position taken toward him will decide eternal salvation or damnation. He who acknowledges Jesus now, shall be recognized as belonging to him in the final judgment; he who denies him now (*arnĕomai* = reject, rebel, LN 33.277), will hear the word of refusal and definitive separation in the judgment.

Matthew has retained the original intention of the double saying in the sense of an instruction for the disciples. Only one who realizes discipleship in public confession can be a disciple. At the same time, Matthew applies the logion to the salvation of his community; he interprets "to acknowledge" in terms of the confession that his missionaries must impart within the structure of their missionary activity. This community catechesis of the first evangelist finds its clearest expression in Revelation 3:5: "I will confess your name before my Father and before his angels."

Mission F: Not Peace but a Sword, 10:34-39

Matthew has united two thoughts in this pericope about the burdens of discipleship. On the one hand, he repeats the theme often heard since verse 17—that the call to discipleship is bound up with suffering (vv. 34-36). On the other, he speaks of the demanding conditions of discipleship (vv. 37-39). The second theme will be taken up once more in 16:24-28.

According to Luke's witness, the units were originally unconnected and were first brought into the present order by Matthew. He brought them together not only on account of the keyword "father and mother," but because of the common theme. The parallel sayings "contain references to father, mother, son, and daughter and play on the theme of Jesus upsetting family loyalties. Their similarities to the foregoing sayings brought them to Matthew's mind" (Gundry, *ad loc*).

> **34** "Do not think that I have come to bring peace to the earth; I have not come to bring peace, but a sword.
> **35** For I have come to set a man against his father.
>   and a daughter against her mother,
>   and a daughter-in-law against her mother-in-law;
> **36** and one's foes will be members of one's own household.
> **37** Whoever loves father or mother more than me is not worthy of me; and whoever loves son or daughter more than me is not worthy of me; **38** and whoever does not take up his cross and follow me is not worthy of me. **39** Those who find their life will lose it, and those who lose their life for my sake will find it.

Verse 34: "Do not think." With these negative imperative (cf. 5:17), Matthew provides a redactional introduction to the saying about the purpose of Jesus' coming. The so-called *elthon*-sayings (cf. 5:17; 9:13; 10:34; 10:35, LN 15.89) stress that Jesus' mission exceeds every human expectation. In the "peace"-logion (cf. already 10:12-13) Jesus tells the disciples that the goal of his coming to humans ("earth," as in 5:13, stands for "humankind") is not peace (so in Isa 8:23–9:6; 11:6-9), but "a sword." "Sword" (*Machaira* = sword in a general sense, which e.g., the soldiers (and also one of Jesus' disciples) use at the time of Jesus' arrest (26:47), stands for hardship, lack of peace (LN 39.25). Using vivid images (cf. Rev 6:11), Jesus refers to the afflicting power that manifests itself in time of persecution.

Verses 35-36: "To set a man against." A saying from Micah 7:6 illustrates the turmoil that threatens: Jesus came to set at loggerheads (*dichazo* only here in the New Testament), i.e., to embroil in discord and strife. The character of the warning that the word had already in Micah is retained: the crisis that arises with Jesus' coming tears apart even the closest bonds of human community. The replacement of "son" (so Micah 7:6 and Luke 12:53) with "man" corresponds to Matthew's generalizing tendency, which becomes especially clear in verse 36 ("man" here is inserted by Matthew into the Micah citation). The disciples will not be able to be certain even about members of their own household (cf. v. 25).

Verse 37: "Whoever loves . . . more than me." The fact of total conflict deflects the question to "love" (*phileo* appears five times in Matthew); in connection with a person as object it appears only here (LN 2.33). The logion "insures love of Jesus against all limitations through love of relations" (Stahlin, *phileō* in *TWNT* IX 17, 129). The twofold scope (children to parents; parents to children), the closest personal bond between humans, is set in relation to Jesus: "more than me" states both times that love of Jesus must be given the preference, because by it "worthiness" is measured (cf. v. 10:11 and 13): the worth of the disciples is guaranteed not through the bond of blood but only through the decision for Jesus.

Verse 38: In the negative mode, Matthew adds the words of Jesus about taking up one's cross (LN 24, 83) to concentrate the condition of discipleship on its innermost kernel. The connection with "and" makes clear the closeness of the bond (in the sense of an interpreting and deepening unity). Jesus demands readiness for following involving suffering (not to martyrdom, even less to allowing oneself to be crucified as a freedom fighter). The logion acquires its meaning from Jesus' death: the disciples must bear the burden of following as a person carries the stake of a cross. For a third time, Jesus places lack of readiness for attachment to him under the verdict of unworthiness.

A review of the verb "to follow" shows that Matthew can, in fact, use it simply to signify accompaniment in the literal sense of the word. By the same token, there are other passages in which it is equally clear that Matthew utilizes "to follow" precisely in order to point out that those who accompany Jesus do so as his disciples. In those cases where it is not apparent which meaning is intended, two factors become important: personal commitment and cost. "In 10:38 and 16:24, Jesus teaches the disciples that following him means taking up one's cross and losing one's life" ("Akolouthein," 57).

Verse 39: "Those who find their life (*psychē*)." In Jesus' words *psyche*, which is met in four different forms in the gospel tradition (Mark 8:35 par. Matt 16:25 and Luke 9:24; Matt 11:39 par., Luke 17:33 and John 12:25), means the proper life of the human (as distinct from the merely physical and temporary). The contrast between "find" and "lose" (cf. 23:113) determines the meaning of the logion. "For (Jesus') sake" (cf. 5:11 10:18; 16:25) affords the disciples the distinction between the two lives: without Jesus the attained (earthly) life in reality is lost; in union with Jesus the earthly life can indeed be lost but in exchange, the true life, promised by Jesus and the only valid life before God, is won.

Through the joining of two related sayings on discipleship, Matthew succeeds in placing before the eyes of his community with special insistence the consequences of discipleship. The hearers must recognize that the Master has in truth come to cast a sword into the world, and above all into the community. This saying and the related consequences may have produced a shock, when one recalls how family ties and duties were taken so seriously in the Jewish milieu. But—and herein Matthew remains true to Jesus' demand in his instruction to his community—discipleship means "to take up the cross," to lose this life to win the future life. One might almost expect those other sayings of Matthew to be joined to the text: "Who can take it, let him take it," and "He who has ears to hear let him hear."

The connection of verse 34a and verse 35b refers to a situation in which the community has experienced discipleship as threat. So the question arises all the more insistently: if Jesus is the Messiah, the Peace Bringer (cf. Luke 1:79; John 12:27; Eph 2:17), why does such hardship and danger threaten the community? Here again, the community is referred to the Scriptures; the prophet Micah gives the explanation why there must be such suffering. They belong to the eschatological woes, as symbolized by the sword (cf. Isa 34:5; 66:16; Ezek 21). The turn of the age begins with Jesus' coming and the beginning of the King's Reign, which Jesus proclaims.

Mission G: Reception of the Disciples, 10:40-42

Matthew concludes the Missionary Discourse with the ending found in Q (with borrowings from Mark and John). By carefully arranging the sayings, Matthew creates the order: apostles ("you"), prophets, righteous persons (an eminent member of the Church), little ones (ordinary members of the Church). This may reflect the structure of Matthew's Church.

> **40** "Whoever welcomes you welcomes me, and whoever welcomes me welcomes the one who sent me. **41** Whoever welcomes a prophet in the name of a prophet will receive a prophet's reward; and whoever welcomes a righteous person will receive the reward of the righteous; **42** and whoever gives even a cup of cold water to one of these little ones in the name of a disciple—truly I tell you, none of these will lose their reward."

Verse 40: "The one who sent (*aposteilanta*) me." The dynamic relation of the apostles to Jesus reflects the dynamic relation of Jesus to the Father. To offer hospitality and a receptive ear to the earthly envoys of Jesus is to receive *the* earthly envoy of the Father, and ultimately, the Father himself. The apostle-concept is well expressed by rabbinic statements about a *shaliah*, a messenger empowered to act for his sender. The *shaliah* of a person is as the person himself.

Verse 41: "Prophet . . . righteous person." Similar rewards await those hospitable to prophets and the righteous because of their dignity. The rewards due such holy persons will be shared by those who shared their goods with them. Here, Jesus speaks of the eventuality that the missionary-disciples he sends out may be received as a "prophet" or "righteous person" or "little one." But it was not until just prior to Jesus' missionary speech to them that the disciples had even been constituted as a group (10:2-4). So one may ask how they can be thought to recognize themselves in the above designations and to apply them to themselves. This is another circumstance which can be attributed to "speaking past"—it reflects the situation in the Church community rather than the community of disciples in Jesus' time.

In principle, the entire Christian community of Matthew's time regarded itself "as standing in the tradition of the OT prophets and the twelve disciples of Jesus (5:12; 13:17). It appears, however, that there were also certain Christians in the community who were specifically thought of as being "prophets." They seem to have been itinerant missionaries who proclaimed the Gospel of the Kingdom to Jews but especially to Gentiles" (*Story*, 156.

Another identifiable group is those who functioned as "teachers." The "righteous person" (*dikaios*; 10:41) was a teacher of righteousness, while the "rabbi" (*hrabbi*; 23:8), the "scribe" (*grammateus*; 23:34), and the "wise person" (*sophos*; 23:34) were those expert in matters pertaining to the scripture and the law. "Christian teachers, too, served as missionaries to the Jews, perhaps conversing or debating with them about the meaning of the scriptures, the law, and the traditions in light of the coming of Jesus Messiah" (*Story*, 157).

Verse 42: "One of these little ones (*mikroi*)." The "little ones" are almost without connection with the foregoing (so the twice-used participle construction is replaced by a finite verb). The "little ones" are the general group of disciples (cf. 18:10, 14), who—as such—possess neither power or position. Through the connection with verses 40, 41 (note the connecting "And"), the prophets' "office" and the assignment to proclaim righteousness are transferred to all community members. In the fulfillment of the assignment they are exhorted always to show helpfulness to others. And whoever extends the smallest love service to these itinerant preachers will receive his reward (so that of a disciple). The presence of the assurance formula precisely in the last verse of the mission discourse constitutes an emphatic closure (cf. v. 15 and 23), which underlines the importance of thoroughgoing following, above all through the renewed emphasis on the concept "disciple."

The disciple is a prophet, a righteous one, and a teacher invested with authority. As such, Jesus' mission mandate drives him out "unprotected" to all. The only thing he can count on is readiness of others to afford him help because he comes as fully authorized in the threefold fashion just named. The uncertainty and basic defenselessness of the disciples loses something of its harshness because he can trust that there will always be persons who recognize God's action in the disciples activity, and, trusting in the guaranteed reward promise, give the Christian missionary what is sufficient to provide for the necessities of life.

Above all, the harshness of Jesus' demands are made bearable by the fact that the community knows that they were made for the sake of eschatological salvation and are supported by words of encouragement and comfort. Hence, all demands are part of the general obligation to take up the cross. Missionary mandate and carrying one's cross are inseparably bound together.

Third Summary Statement, 11:1

Matthew 11:1 serves a number of purposes: 1) It is the stereotyped conclusion of the Second (Mission) Discourse; 2) It is the third (and last) Summary Statement; 3) It marks the beginning of a new stage of heightened hostility between Jesus and the Jewish leaders.

> **11:1** Now when Jesus had finished instructing his twelve disciples, he went on from there to teach and proclaim his message in their cities.

Verse 1a: "Jesus had finished instructing (*diatassōn*)." This phrase is important for three reasons. First, verse 1 is the stereotyped conclusion of a discourse. Five times throughout Matthew's story the streotyped formula appears: "And it happened when Jesus finished these words [these parables; instructing his twelve disciples] . . ." (7:28; 11:1; 13:53; 19:1; 26:1). Each time this formula occurs, it calls attention to the termination of a speech Jesus has delivered (cf. 7:28).

The changes from the discourse conclusion in 7:28 are important. There it only says that Jesus "had ended these words," now the saying has it: "Jesus had finished instructing his twelve disciples." The thought of the mission is not taken up again: the emphasis on guidance and/or instruction dominates (*Diatasso*, "to order, command," LN 33.325) is found only here in Matthew. He understands the Mission Discourse as an order; as a command to which one owes obedience. As such, it is clearly distinguished from Jesus' teaching and proclamation (v. 1b). Every word of Jesus to the disciples in Matthew's Gospel is empowerment and obligates the leaders of the community as the successors of the twelve. Regarding the "twelve disciples" (cf. 10:1); the conjunction between 10:1 and 11:1 forms an inclusio. Secondly, verse 11:1 is the last of the three Summary Statements which are strung out along the first half of Part II of Matthew's Gospel. Thirdly, verse 11:1 marks the beginning of a new stage of heightened hostility between Jesus and the Jewish leaders. With the onset of chapter 9, the anticipated conflict between Jesus and the religious leaders finally materialized. But fierce as it was, this conflict is preliminary to the more intense conflict to come.

Verse 1b: "He went on from there." The redactional introduction to the following section states that Jesus continues to wander (what is meant by "from there" is not made clear in either 9:35 or 10:1) and to teach and preach "in their cities." This is a formal transition (cf. 12:9; 13:54) and has primarily a literary function.

D. Bauer views the transition from the first to the second part of Part II of the topical outline in terms of causation and effect—as movement from the proclamation to the response to the proclamation. "The two major sections within 4.17-16.20 are determined by the structural phenomenon of causation. 4.17-11.1 is the cause: Jesus presents himself to Israel by means of teaching, preaching, and healing (4.23-9.35) and by means of sending out his disciples to perform eschatological ministry to Israel analogous to his own (9.35-11.1). 11.2-16.20 is the effect: the response, both positive and negative, to the proclamation of Jesus to Israel'' (Bauer, 88).

Repudiation 1: John in Prison, 11:2-6

The more intense conflict that Part II has been building up to erupts in 11:2-16:20–the latter half of the second part of the Matthew's story. Attention now shifts from Jesus' ministry of teaching, preaching, and healing to Israel's response to him, which is that of repudiation. Three features stand out from now on: (a) Debate becomes increasingly confrontational; (b) Debate centers on Mosaic law itself (12:1-8, 9-13); and (c) the religious leaders are incited to conspire to take Jesus' life (12:14).

> **2** When John heard in prison what the Messiah was doing, he sent word by his disciples **3** and said to him, "Are you the one who is to come, or are we to wait for another?" **4** Jesus answered them, "Go and tell John what you hear and see: **5** the blind receive their sight, the lame walk, the lepers are cleansed, the deaf hear, the dead are raised, and the poor have good news brought to them. **6** And blessed is anyone who takes no offense at me."

Following D. Bauer's schema, with 11:2 we move from the area of causation to that of effects—responses to Jesus' proclamation. Matthew begins his catalogue of responses in 11:2-16:2 by reintroducing the person of John the Baptist (cf. 4:1). "The proclamation of John regarding the coming one in chapter 3 was full of apocalyptic fire, but included no predictions of such deeds of healing as Matthew records in chapters 8–9. This disappointment in his expectation led John to uncertainty regarding the messianic mission of Jesus. The question from John implied not rejection, but doubt'' (Bauer, 92).

Verses 2-3: "The one who is to come." According to 4:12 Jesus had heard that "John had been arrested." "What the Messiah was doing" are the mighty works of chapters 8–9. John is the one really asking. The emphatic "you" characterizes the aim of the question, which consists not in the alternative "you or I," but in "you or another." At the same time John recedes into the background—through the formula "he who is to come" the question is directed to the "identity of Jesus with the end-time Judge," "the one who comes after me" points to the apocalyptic tradition. While a clear-cut eschatological salvation form cannot be affirmed, the text lies close to the interpretation, that the Coming One is the "apocalyptic Judge of the Parousia."

Verse 4: "What you hear and see." The verb with prefix (*ap + aggello* = report, announce) indicates a deeper meaning: Jesus has important information for the questioning John. The addition "hear" and "see" shows that not just a "Messiah of deeds" is involved but a Messiah whose revelation embraces word and deed. In the first part of Jesus' answer, which represents the high point of the pericope, clear references to the prophet Isaiah are visible (cf. Isa 29:18-19; 35:5-6; 42:18; 26:19; 61:1), and here Matthew and Luke agree almost word for word. On the other hand Matthew has strongly shortened the introduction, while at the same time adding: "when (he) heard in prison about the deeds of the Christ" to explain the sending of the two disciples.

Verses 5-6: The second part of the answer consists of a recounting of the salvation signs (v. 5) and a beatitude (v. 6). In the mighty works now happening, the Old Testament salvation prophecies are fulfilled (the citation amalgam consists of six members arranged in parallel, all bound together in a series by "and"). Jesus' salvation acts correspond to the signs of the end-time prophets, and especially those of the prophet Isaiah and their interpretation in Judaism. "Lame, *chōlos*" (LN 23.175). The reference "to lepers cleansed" has no precedent in Isaiah (nor in other prophets). The pre-Matthean tradition relied not only on Old Testament miracles but also referred to Jesus' special activity, which culminated in the Gospel proclamation. "Hear, *akouō*" (LN 24.58). The beatitude (v. 6) must originally have been passed on separately; early on it was bound up with the prophet word in verse 5 with the connecting "and." The "taking offense" refers to Jesus, who (now) works miracles that properly could be expected only from the prophets of the end time.

The Baptist's question is the community's question; the uncertainty expressed therein is the uncertainty of Matthew's community. It too is not free of doubt about the Jesus tradition, to which it must hold fast. In a twofold fashion the pericope seems to free the community of its doubting uncertainty: the tradition about Jesus is in reality a tradition about the Christ (v. 2), the Messiah sent by God—that is a positive message. Even more meaningful is the prophetic saying with its attached beatitude. There is even a first warning connected therewith: "For Matthew, the beatitude makes John's example a dangerous example not to be followed by Christians who find themselves in similar straits" (Gundry, *ad loc*). A first demand for faith is here placed before the community; it has eschatological relevance regarding the mission mandate to Israel, to which Matthew's community has been called.

Repudiation 2: Like John, Like Jesus 11:7-15

The encounter with the disciples of John leads to Jesus' denunciation of "this generation." This generation has rejected the message of John, which portends the rejection of Jesus as well, since John is the forerunner and herald of the Messiah (11:9-15).

> **7** As they went away, Jesus began to speak to the crowds about John: "What did you go out into the wilderness to look at? A reed shaken by the wind? **8** What then did you go out to see? Someone dressed in soft robes? Look, those who wear soft robes are in royal palaces. **9** What then did you go out to see? A prophet? Yes, I tell you, and more than a prophet. **10** This is the one about whom it is written.
>
> "See, I send my messenger ahead of you, who shall prepare your way before thee." **11** Truly, I tell you, among those born of women no one has risen greater than John the Baptist; yet the least in the kingdom of heaven is greater than he. **12** From the days of John the Baptist until now the kingdom of heaven has suffered violence, and the violent take it by force. **13** For all the prophets and the law prophesied until John came; **14** and if you are willing to accept it, he is Elijah who is to come. **15** Let anyone with ears listen!

The account of Jesus' witness to the Baptist has a parallel in Luke 7:24-28 and 16:16. The high point of Jesus' saying is the double citation Exodus 23:20; Malachi 3:1; four separate logia can be distinguished in Jesus' witness; a) verses 7b–10: Jesus corrects a false representation of John's person; b) verse 11: the meaning of John (now with the title "the Prophet") with respect to the Kingdom of Heaven; c) verses 12-13 (cf. also the separate tradition in Luke): the so-called Sturmer speech; d) verses 14-15 (special to Matthew): the relationship between John and Elijah.

Verses 7a: The disciples sent by John (they are indicated by the demonstrative pronoun) follow Jesus' instruction (v. 4); Jesus is—as already in verse 4—indicated by name here. Now he speaks of John, i.e., concerning who John really is. The addressees are the crowds.

Verses 7b-9: "More than a prophet." Through three rhetorical questions Jesus draws attention to John; the first two are denied, the third agreed to. The composition is artfully built up (three questions in parallel structure, of which the second and the third are longer than the first). The "wilderness," in which John preached (3:1[3]), is less a geographical than a theological concept: the wilderness is the place of revelation. Whoever goes into the wilderness does so not out of ordinary carefree interest (one sees a reed on all the rivers and seas; cf. Job 40:21; Ps 68:30; Isa

19:6; 35:7); it would also be absurd to wish to see a weakling, a sybarite in the wasteland. Rather, the crowds go out (this last generation before the approaching end) to see a prophet. In the "Yes" (i.e., certainly), Jesus affirms that the people's desire is fulfilled: they indeed saw a prophet. Yet immediately through the "I tell you" the crowds are corrected and informed more precisely: John was more than a prophet and must not be seen solely in the context of Old Testament prophetic tradition.

Verse 10: "I send my messenger." What the "and more" consisted in is expressed through a double citation (a combination of Malachi 3:1 with Exodus 23:20). For emphasis, it is formulated as God's address to Jesus and as spoken about John. Although the text referred to a precursor in a general way, now John is understood concretely as the end-time prophet, who then—by reason of the context—will be pointed out as the Elijah Returned.

Verse 11: "No one greater." The verse is a commentary on verse 10. The redactional introduction shows that the logion is an insertion into the present context in the form of commentary. It has a double objective: the concept of the Baptist advanced by John's disciples is first accepted by Jesus (acknowledged), but then subordinated to the recognition of the superiority of the least in the kingdom of heaven. Among those "born of women" (cf. Job 14:1; 15:14; 25:4; Gal 4:4) no one has arisen who was greater than John; this is undisputed. But measured by the kingdom of heaven, John not only has no advantage over any members of the kingdom but is inferior to them. So the logion expresses that no one greater than John has risen among normal mortals, yet even the least among those who have acquired a new existence in the now in-breaking kingdom (and all the more naturally Jesus himself) is superior to even these great ones.

Verses 12-13: The so-called *Sturmersprache* (*biastēs* = man of violence, Sturmer) one of the most difficult logion of the synoptic tradition (cf. J. Gnilka, *ad loc*). The three decisive terms are: "has suffered violence," "the violent," "take by force" (translation possibilities Schrank, *biazomai* TWNT I 609–13). The meaning of the saying in verse 12 is determined by *harpazo*: this has a negative connotation—an armed robbery. The negative connotation is strengthened when one notes that *biastēs* means "a violator, rapist"—one who seeks his ends by violence. Therefore the verse speaks of a violent seizing, and not of a struggle or murder, (LN 20.9, 10, 11). The addressees of the logion were originally religious groups of Judaism in Jesus' time; one first thinks of the Zealots who sought to attain their national and religious goals by force of arms. It is the context which shows that the Sturmerspruch is directed to the adherents of the

Baptist movement who, inspired by John, set out to win the Kingdom through penance, asceticism, and prayer.

This is confirmed by the time indication in verse 12a ("from the days of John" is to be understood in the inclusive sense), through which the logion mirrors the conflict between Jesus' disciples and those of the Baptist. Verse 13 stands in some tension with verse 12, which can only be explained by the fact that two logia were originally handed on separately. In the post-Easter situation, competition between Jesus' disciples and adherents of the Baptist was no longer a threat; Matthew's community was the legal guardian of the Baptist tradition. So seen, the explanation ("For") in verse 13 is clear: Law and Prophets as the whole of the revelation of God preserved in the Torah and legitimately interpreted by the prophets (not "the Old Testament as a whole"), is dissolved through the time of the *basileia*. Salvation awaits only the members of the Kingdom of God. Between stands John with a positive function at the end of the Old Testament salvation dispensation, and at the same time at the beginning of the inbreaking of God's reign, but beneath those who share in the Kingdom of God.

P. Papone suggests that *biazetai* ought to be translated intransitively ("Presses to come") rather than passively ("suffer violence"). "The uses of *biazo* in the Septuagint suggest that notions of insistence, pressure, and force were more important than violence. . . . The *biastai* in 11:12b refer to those who oppose the coming of God's kingdom and block access to it" (cf. *NTA* 35 [2, '91] #626), abstract by D. Harrington.

Verses 14-15: "If you are willing to accept it." Redactionally, Matthew adds an interpretation to Jesus' witness. He interprets Malachi 3:1 (cf. v. 10) from Malachi 3:23 and applies it to Elijah. He understands John, who is mentioned in Malachi 3:1, as Elijah. The "if you are willing to accept it" appeals to John's readiness to serve as the precursor of the messianic time. Because the Baptist does not correspond to the Jewish expectation of a Elijah Redivivus, the will of the hearer is appealed to: the warning in verse 15 makes it clear that it will not be left to the hearer's discretion whether or not he accepts the truth about John.

The question "Jesus or John" played an important role in the pre-Easter and immediate post-Easter tradition. The logia brought together in our pericope still mirror the conflict about this question. But in the time of the evangelist and his community, this discussion had lost its weight and had become a question about the relationship between Jesus and John. Against the background of a changed situation the community experiences who John really was—false concepts are corrected, the true one underscored and made credible by a Scripture "proof." John's greatness can be freely stressed, his subordination brings out Jesus' special excellence.

In relation to the kingdom of God John is less than every member of the *basileia*. This is the "measure" for the community; where one errs against the intention of the *basileia*, the sharing in the Kingdom of Heaven remains intact. The implicit warning to Matthew's community is expressed in terms of the Baptist, who is the Elijah returned (the end-time prophet): the conversion preaching of John had proclaimed and dramatized the end-time, which the community understands as the last time of waiting. The alternative at first reduced to two persons "Jesus or John" is transformed into the basic message: "John, Jesus, and the Kingdom of Heaven."

Repudiation 3: Children in the Marketplaces, 11:16-19

"This generation's" rejection of the message of John portends the rejection of Jesus as well, since John is the forerunner and herald of the Messiah (11:9-15). The people are stubborn and inclined not to believe; they have rejected John because of his asceticism, while they have rejected Jesus because of his lack of asceticism (11:16-19).

> **16** "But to what will I compare this generation? It is like children sitting in the marketplaces and calling to one another, playmates,
> **17**   'We played the flute for you,
>   and you did not dance;
>   we wailed, and you did not mourn.'
> **18** For John came neither eating nor drinking, and they say, 'He has a demon'; **19** the Son of Man came eating and drinking, and they say 'Look, a glutton and a drunkard, a friend of tax collectors and sinners!' Yet wisdom is vindicated by her deeds."

Verses 16-17: "Did not dance . . . did not mourn." With "But" Matthew indicates that he understands the parable as a contrast to the cooperation (v. 14) and the attention (v. 15) of his hearers: "this generation" is stiff-necked. This characterization always stands alone in Matthew, without "men of" (cf. 12:39, 41, 42, 45; 16:4; 17:17; 23:36; 24:34). In Q it is directed, in dependence on Jewish apocalyptic, against Israel as the last generation before the end. "This generation" always has a negative sense in Matthew (cf. 16:4: "evil and adulterous generation"). The parable compares the addressees to children (LN 9.42) who want to play wedding and funeral in the marketplace, but cannot bring it off because of willful lack of cooperation. "John proffered the way of asceticism, Jesus the way of freedom, but the people refused to take either" (Schweizer, *ad hoc*).

Verses 18-19ab: "John . . . the Son of Man." Originally the explanation was not part of the image. As a consequence, it is not possible to make a clear-cut application to John and Jesus respectively. Yet the overall point comes across. This generation—like willful children at play—has a false conception of John and Jesus. False expectation leads this generation to false conclusions: the ascetic is judged a demoniac, the world-enjoying Son of Man as a glutton and drunkard. The use of the title "Son of Man" for the earthly Jesus corresponds to the post-Easter conviction of the community, that the might and dignity of the apocalyptic Son of Man belonged already to the earthly Jesus.

Verse 19c: The saying about vindication does not stem from Jewish tradition but is formed *ad hoc* as interpretation of the foregoing. The "deeds of wisdom" are the works of John and the Son of Man (cf. the "deeds of Christ" in v. 2). And as all (true) wisdom receives its vindication out of its works, so will John and the Son of Man, who are understood in a special way as God's wisdom, be justified by their works, i.e., shown to be correct. The predicate ("vindicate") is to be understood as standing in contrast to the slander about John and Jesus.

Matthew's community too, sees itself confronted with the adherents of "this generation"; the danger of false ideas and expectations threatens not just the latter, but members of the community as well. And this presents the danger of false behavior as well as false judgments and evaluation. The example of the playing children is a stern warning not to judge the conduct of John and Jesus, who is seen as the Son of Man, inadequately and so, negatively. The evidence of the works made it possible for the community to come to a correct understanding. In contrast to "this generation," the community must be another generation, a generation of the new aeon, which accepts and realizes its new order of worth, new system of values.

In Jesus' presentation of the kingdom of God, the emphasis thus far has been on the kingdom as a present reality. But the kingdom is also both a hidden reality and a reality yet to be consummated. The circumstance that the kingdom is a hidden reality is attested to by the reaction Jesus' activity elicits from the crowd and the religious leaders. "Some judge John to have a demon. Although the crowds follow Jesus (4:25) and even acclaim him for his ministry of word and deed, they do not perceive him to be the bearer of God's kingdom. On the contrary, they see in him only a prophet, and he in turn censures them as 'this [evil] generation' that repudiates both him and John the Baptist, his forerunner (11:16-19)" (*Structure*, 62).

Repudiation 4: Unrepentant Cities, 11:20-24

Jesus' accusations against "this generation" intensify with the woes of 11.20-24. His mighty works have borne witness, but the stubbornness of the people has robbed them of their witnessing power. Jesus' call to repentance has fallen on deaf ears (11:20-21); (cf. 4:17). Indeed, the hardness of their hearts has kept the people from understanding the true meaning of the events. The guilt of the people and the depth of their stubbornness are indicated by the contrast between their rebellion and that of the most notorious Gentile cities; their guilt and punishment far surpass that of Tyre and Sidon, or even Sodom (11.22-24).

> **20** Then he began to reproach the cities in which most of his deeds of power had been done, because they did not repent. **21** "Woe to you, Chorazin! Woe to you, Bethsaida! For if the deeds of power done in you had been done in Tyre and Sidon, they would have repented long ago in sackcloth and ashes. **22** But I tell you, on the day of judgment it will be more tolerable for Tyre and Sidon than for you. **23** And you, Capernaum,
> Will you be exalted to heaven?
> No, you will be brought down to Hades. For if the deeds of power done in you had been done in Sodom, it would have remained until this day. **24** But I tell you that on the day of judgment it will be more tolerable for the land of Sodom than for you.' "

Verse 20: "Most of his mighty deeds of power" (*dynameis*). The miracles Jesus performs are termed "deeds of power" (*dynameis*, plural of *dynamis*). "Power" is associated with God (22:29) and can even be used as a metaphor for "God" (26:64). On the contrary, "power" in the sense of *dynamis* is not something that is predicated to Satan, demons, or the opponents of Jesus. False prophets may perform deeds of power, but these are miraculous, but lawless, works, and those who perform them will be condemned by him at the latter day (7:21-23). Otherwise, false messiahs and false prophets perform "signs and wonders" (24:24). Jesus and the disciples, in turn, are never reported as doing "wonders" (*trerata*) and the "sign" (*semeion*) is characterized as a miraculous feat that the religious leaders demand of Jesus as they tempt him to prove he is not in collusion with Satan (12:24, 38; 16:1). "The logic of Matthew's world of thought is plain as regards Jesus' miracles: God, the source of 'power,' has empowered his Son Jesus with the Spirit; in consequence of this, the miracles Jesus performs are 'deeds of power' and not false 'signs and wonders' " (*Story,* 69).

Verses 21-22: "They would have repented." In the Old Testament, Tyre and Sidon are representative heathen cities (cf. Isa 23; Jer 25:22; 27:3; 47:4). These are compared to Chorazin and Bethsaida (LN 1.fn 15)—like Capernaum in verse 23—representing the entire geographical district in which Jesus' mighty works took place. The double woe (one attached to each of the cities) underlines the sharpness of the criticism: in their recusant behavior they "surpass" even the impenitence for which the prophets already reproached these cities. If the mighty works had happened in them that had happened in Chorazin and Bethsaida, they would have repented in sackcloth (LN 6.164) and ashes (Est 4:3; Isa 58:5; Jer 6:26; Dan 9:3; Jonah 3:5-6), i.e. they would have reversed direction. Therefore (one can so interpret v. 22a) the heathen cities of the Old Testament will fare better than others when judgment day comes (cf. 10:15; [11:24]; 12:36).

Verses 23-24: "Tolerable (*anektos* LN 25.172) on the day of judgment." The first woe is followed by a second, applied to Capernaum (cf. 4:13; 8:5; 9:1; 17:24), which is compared to the Old Testament Sodom. It is announced to the inhabitants of this district, with reference to Isaiah 14:13-15, that its pride will end in a great fall (LN 15.108) (the Isaiah text is connected with a taunt song against the king of Babel). The image of Hades as "counterplace" of heaven is not to be understood in the sense of a place of punishment; the unbridgeable contrast of "highest of the high" and "deepest abyss" should be stressed much more. Verse 23b repeats verse 21b, but with the (historically oriented) variant: Sodom would not have been destroyed (Gen 13:10; 19:24-28; Deut 29:23; Isa 13:19; Amos 4:11), but would have remained intact down to the present time, when Jesus' mighty works take place and as signs of divine revelation demonstrating the inbreaking of the kingdom of God. The second threat speech (v. 24) ends like the first with the reference to the eschatological judgment day; already at 10:15 Matthew had joined it to the Mission Discourse (cf. v. 22).

It is characteristic of Matthew that again and again he inserts the thought of the judgment into the overall story line. The connection is often very loose, and the reader (hearer) must make an effort to grasp the meaning of the briskly inserted judgment discourse. This pericope especially shows that Matthew was at pains to present the time of the community as the time of testing and decision. The community, here settled in the districts of Chorazin, Bethsaida and Capernaum, knows Israel's history, knows the fate of Israel's unrepentant cities. The evangelist uses this knowledge to lend to Jesus' repentance preaching and his call to conversion the sharpness required. The knowledge then leads irresistibly to a comparison. Yet the comparison turns out unfavorably for the inhabitants of the cities where

Jesus had been active; the community is warned not to ignore so unheedingly Jesus' revelation works, as they had done.

Repudiation 5: Father and Son, 11:25-30

In the section 11:2–16:20, the disciples are characterized, in the main, by being contrasted with Israel: while Israel is darkened and without understanding, the disciples are "enlightened." Thus, what the Father conceals from the wise in Israel, he reveals through Jesus to "infants," that is, to the disciples (11:25-27). Whereas all segments of Israel repudiate Jesus, the disciples become his new family called to do the will of his heavenly Father (chs. 11-12).

In addition to the threefold topical outline (which he shares with J. Kingsbury), D. Bauer sees Matthew's Gospel as constructed according to four major structural elements. The first of these is repetition of comparison (cf. *supra,* p. 165). The second is repetition of contrast. "One of the clearest structural patterns in Matthew's Gospel is the recurring contrast between Jesus and his opponents, especially the religious leaders. Other minor recurring contrasts likewise appear, such as the dichotomy between those who approach Jesus in faith and those who approach him without faith, and the differences Matthew emphasizes between the disciples and their opponents. Moreover, we have indicated that there is also an element of contrast between Jesus and his disciples." (Bauer, 65).

> 25 At that time Jesus said, "I thank you, Father, Lord of heaven and earth, because you have hidden these things from the wise and intelligent and revealed them to infants; 26 Yea, Father, for such was your gracious will. 27 All things have been handed over to me by my Father; and no one knows the Son except the Father, and no one knows the Father except the Son and any one to whom the Son chooses to reveal him. 28 Come to me, all you who are weary and are carrying heavy burdens, and I will give you rest. 29 Take my yoke upon you, and learn from me; for I am gentle and humble in heart, and you will find rest for your souls. 30 For my yoke is easy, and my burden is light."

Verse 25: "Revealed them to infants (*nepios*, Bertram *TWNT* IV 921-22)." Although the fame of Jesus has spread and the crowds throng to him, they repudiate him. In private prayer, Jesus attributes his repudiation to the will of God himself: it has pleased God to hide his revelation from Israel. He has made it known, to "infants," to Jesus' disciples. Within the surrounding context of chapters 11-12, this hiding and making known corresponds to the fact that whereas all Israel turns away from

Jesus, the disciples continue to adhere to him. Against the backdrop of Israel's repudiation of Jesus, the disciples stand out as the recipients of divine revelation.

Verse 26: "Your gracious will" (*eudokia*) (cf. Schrenk, *TWNT* II 742-51, par. 747). This repeats in more succinct terms the thought of verse 25: God has so willed it, it conforms to the *eudokia*, God's free decision.

Verse 27: "Handed over to me by my Father." Matthew imbues the title "my son," Son of God, with a quality the others do not possess in like measure. It attests to the unique filial relationship that exists between God and Jesus. Jesus is conceived by God's spirit (1:18, 20) and empowered by God's Spirit (3:16) so that he is Emmanuel, "God with us." Jesus is the one in whom God reveals himself to humankind (11:27); and who is God's supreme agent of salvation.

In thus claiming for himself the identity of Messiah Son of God, Jesus is at the same time claiming for himself divine authority (8:16-17; 11:27). Only by revelation from the Father is knowledge of his divine sonship possible (16:17). In perceiving Jesus to be the Son of God, the disciples perceive that God is uniquely present and at work in Jesus.

The logion is found in a similar form also in John 3:35, but there reversed. The "Father-Son" relationship characterizes the two sayings: the Father has "delivered"—the Son "knows." The strengthened form of "give" ("handed over," i.e., to place over a power area, endow with full power) expresses that Jesus is endowed with authority by the Father (cf. 28:18). The verb *ginoskein* goes back to the Hebrew *iada*, which means an existential, not an intellectual knowledge (LN 28.2). The Father's knowing of the Son happens in his election; the Son's knowing of the Father consists in the latter's entrusting his entire existence to the Father. The Son reveals this close community between the Father and the Son to others (*apokalypto* is found in Matthew only at 10:26; 11:25, 27; 16:17). It has the meaning: to uncover something hidden, make known, reveal. This lies within the Son's free decision; his authority is bound up with this "revelation," i.e., the proclamation of the Secret (the community of life between the Father and the Son) (cf. 10:26).

Verses 28-30: "Handed over to me by my Father." These three verses form a closed literary unit and are carefully structured. The structure corresponds to the literary form of wisdom literature (cf. Sir 1:26, 30), for which Matthew shows throughout a certain preference (12:33; 18:19-20; 26:41). In content, the logion consists of two injunctions and two promises. The linking through "rest" (once substantive, once verb) shows that the two injunctions also correspond; whoever would come to Jesus must take on Jesus' yoke; whoever takes it on is already underway to Jesus. Sirach

51:23-27 already spoke of the yoke of wisdom, yet the meaning in Matthew, despite the connection to Sirach 51, is different. The yoke that the disciple should assume is easy (LN 22.38), is a light burden. Accordingly, the yoke is the image for Jesus' gentleness and humility: Jesus' demands are heavy, but as postures of the heart they are lighter than the former religious demands.

Chapter 11 comes to a climax in this passage, where Jesus gives one reason for his rejection by the greatest part of Israel. It is due to the will of God, who has withheld his revelation from Israel. Here, too, Matthew presents a contrast between the "infants" (that is the disciples), who enjoy the revelation from above, and the "wise and understanding" (that is, "this generation") who reject Jesus.

Conflict 1: In the Grainfields, 12:1-8

Foreshadowed in Part I, conflict burst into the open in chapter 9 and now crystallizes into irreconcilable hostility chapter 12. As the Jewish leaders see it, Jesus threatens the overthrow of law and tradition and the destruction of the nation (12:1-14). Almost always at issue in these debates is the correct interpretation of, or the proper adherence to, the Mosaic law or the Pharisaic tradition of the elders. Here, the debate centers upon alleged violations of the sabbath law (12:1-8).

> **12:1** At that time Jesus went through the grainfields on the sabbath; his disciples were hungry, and they begin to pluck heads of grain and to eat. **2** When the Pharisees saw it, they said to him, "Look, your disciples are doing what is not lawful to do on the sabbath." **3** He said to them, "Have you not read what David did when he and his companions were hungry? **4** He entered the house of God and ate the bread of the Presence, which it was not lawful for him or his companions to eat; but only for the priests? **5** Or have you not read in the law that on the sabbath the priests in the temple break the sabbath and yet are guiltless? **6** I tell you, something greater than the temple is here. **7** But if you had known what this means, 'I desire mercy, and not sacrifice,' you would not have condemned the guiltless. **8** For the Son of Man is lord of the sabbath."

In the first debate, the Pharisees confront Jesus, but the charge they raise is against the disciples: in plucking, or "reaping," grain to eat, the disciples have "worked," and this the Pharisees adjudge to be unlawful.

Verse 1: "The disciples were hungry." Matthew, in contrast to Mark and Luke, explains that the disciples were hungry and for this reason, plucked grain while passing through the field and began to eat, though it was the Sabbath. Luke and Mark offer no explanation for the disciples' actions. Matthew adds the point about the disciples' hunger to make a clearer and more cogent connection between the actions of the disciples and that of David in the Temple, which is the analogy used by all three evangelists.

Verse 2: "Not lawful to do on the sabbath." Unlike earlier conflicts, the Mosaic law itself, or, more particularly, violation of the command to rest on the sabbath, is the issue that sparks controversy.

Verse 3: "What David did." In the two debates that follow there is progression as one moves from the first debate (vv. 1-8) to the second (vv. 9-14), in terms of how acutely confrontational each is. In the first debate, the Pharisees confront Jesus, but the charge they raise is against the disciples: in plucking, or "reaping," grain to eat, the disciples have "worked," and this the Pharisees judge to be unlawful (vv. 1-2). In the second debate, the Pharisees again confront Jesus, but this time, and indeed for the first time in Matthew's story, the accusation they make in the question they raise concerns an act of Jesus himself. In the case of both charges, Jesus rebuts the Pharisees by asserting that meeting human need in these instances is not only not unlawful but is necessitated by God's will that mercy be shown or good be done (vv. 3-8).

Verse 5: "The priests in the temple." Both the disciples in Matthew and David in the Temple were hungry and therefore at work on the Sabbath. Matthew reiterates the point by describing the actions of the priests on the Sabbath who "break the sabbath" yet are "guiltless."

Verse 6: "Something greater than the temple"—cf. 9:13.

Verse 7: "I desire mercy." Following the claim that the priests who do work in the Temple on the Sabbath are guiltless, Matthew adds a citation from Hosea which explains the scriptural foundation for Jesus' understanding and the behavior of his followers. The disciples of Jesus are guiltless and have not violated the law. The problem is that the Pharisees do not understand the law properly. This is made explicit by the application of Hosea 6:6 in this context by Matthew.

> Jesus and his disciples do not break the law. They break with the Pharisees over interpretation of the law, but not with regard to its validity or importance. The law and its application, in Matthew's view, are to be understood primarily in terms of Jesus' demand for compassion. It is this "core value" that guides the application of the sabbath laws. This is emphasized by Matthew in 12:9-14, which continues with the same theme. In this passage Jesus goes on to heal a man with a withered hand

on the Sabbath. Verse 12 provides a summary for the whole section starting in 12:1. That is, it is lawful to do good on the sabbath. Those people
in the Matthean community who are being accused of breaking the sabbath law are really not doing so. Their detractors fail to understand what
the Lord really requires, as expressed in Hos. 6:6. Overman, 60.

This passage from Hosea, "I desire compassion and not sacrifice," is
important for Matthew. He is the only Gospel writer to cite this prophetic
verse, and he does so twice (cf. 9:13).

Matthew transformed his tradition in order to show that Jesus and his
disciples do not break the law. What is at stake is the *interpretation* of
the law. Here, Matthew stands in contrast to Mark. In his version of the
same Sabbath controversy, Mark makes no attempt to absolve Jesus or
the disciples of any guilt. The priests in the temple are not "guiltless;"
they broke the law. But this is not a problem for Mark. In his mind these
laws are no longer an issue for the faithful. Mark puts the issue to rest
with a sweeping statement: "The Sabbath was made for humankind, and
not humankind for the Sabbath" (2:27). This is far too radical a view
of the law for Matthew. His community still maintains the validity and
application of the law for their life. E. Schweizer is right in saying that
the Matthean community still practiced Sabbath observance. The disciples
did break the law, but this law is no longer in force.   Matthew's treatment of the conflict story "In the Grainfields" takes seriously the accusation made by the Pharisees. He shows that his community's view of the
Sabbath laws is consistent with the Law and the Prophets. The beliefs
and behavior of his community are not erroneous or a radical break with
Israel's laws and traditions. "The followers of Jesus are 'guiltless' (cf.
Matt. 12:7). Matthew asserts that his community is lawful and, indeed,
possesses the true interpretation of the law" (Overman, 82).

Hostility 2: A Cure on the Sabbath, 12:9-14

In the second debate, the Pharisees again confront Jesus, but this time,
and indeed for the first time in Matthew's story, the accusation they make
concerns an act Jesus himself intends to perform: if Jesus heals a man
on the sabbath who is not in danger of dying, he will have broken the
command of Moses that enjoins rest (12:10).

> 9 He left that place and entered their synagogue. 10 A man was there
> with a withered hand. And they asked him, "Is it lawful to cure on the
> sabbath?" so that they might accuse him. 11 He said to them, "Suppose
> one of you has only one sheep and it falls into a pit on the sabbath; will

you not lay hold of it and lift it out? **12** How much more valuable is a human being than a sheep! So it is lawful to do good on the sabbath.'' **13** Then he said to the man, ''Stretch out your hand.'' He stretched it out, and it was restored, as sound as the other. **14** But the Pharisees went out and conspired against him, how to destroy him.

The text structure of this healing story is, in principle, identical in the three synoptics (cf. Mark 3:1-6 and Luke 6:6-11); but in details there are decisive differences. In Matthew the action is put into the background; as happens so often, the speech (Jesus' words) stands at the key junctures of the story. Typical motifs of a miracle story are lacking (e.g. scenic preparation, ecstatic excitement), as well as connecting and clarifying elements of the narrator (the evangelist), e.g. the outcries and silences of opponents. Jesus' word and healing action, which should also determine the community's behavior (''is it lawful to cure on the sabbath''), are pointed out as legitimate and authorized actions.

Verse 9: ''Entered *their* synagogue.'' The increasing distance between Church and synagogue is clearly visible in Matthew. That Jesus met the Pharisees (in the synagogue), is first stated expressly in verse 14, but could also follow from the preceding incident.

Verse 10: ''Man with a withered hand (*cheira echōn xēran*) Some think, ''degenerative atrophy,'' some an ''injured hand.'' It is idle to try to make a precise diagnosis; it must remain hypothetical. The (still not named) Pharisees ask him if a cure of the sick is allowed on the sabbath: ''In Matthew the Pharisees do not merely wait to see what Jesus will do. They deliberately egg him on to break the Sabbath in order that they may accuse him'' (Gundry *ad loc*). The question provokes a cure, to which then a complaint should follow (*kategoreo* = complain, charge—a juridical technical term, which is always used of Jesus in the synoptics [cf. also 27:12]). The question form ''is it lawful. . . .'' corresponds to the answer in verse 12b (cf. also Luke 14:3). The rabbinical interpretation permitted medical help on a sabbath, if life was directly threatened (cf. *m. Toma* 8:6; *Mek. Exod* 22:2; 23:13; the healing of a hand did not fall among the special cases).

Verses 11-12: ''Do good on the sabbath.'' Jesus' answer follows in a figure of speech (the subject matter explains the allusions to Luke 14:5b [a son or an ox falls into a well], yet the descriptive saying is more precise in Matthew: a sheep [the only] falls into a pit. The parable of the Lost Sheep (18:12-14) has an influence on the present Sabbath discussion. For no one is the obligation of sabbath rest a ground not to lay hold of the one and only sheep fallen into a pit and to lift it out) (the twofold activity in the saving underlines the activity in opposition to the cited inactivity). Applied to the sick man that means: because he is worth more (cf. 6:26; 10:31) than a sheep (again the rabbinic conclusion *a fortiori*), it is permitted to "do him good on the sabbath." *Kallos poiein* (Mark and Luke have *agathon poiein, agathopoiein*) replaces the *therapeuein* in verse 10, and "lifts the whole problem to a higher sphere." Every healing and helping activity is now designated as a "good deed" basically as permitted on the sabbath (cf. 5:16; the phrase "to do good" is found already in the LXX [Lev 5:4; 1 Kgs 8:18; 2 Ch 6:8; Zech 8:15; Jer 4:22]).

Verse 13: The healing gesture confirms the healing affirmation. The restoration (cf. Ex 4:7; [Lev 13:16]; Luke 5:13) of the sick hand through a "stretching out" (twice) to the condition of the other (healthy) member is a demonstration of the basic affirmation that, on the sabbath it is permitted to do good.

Verse 14: The reaction of the Pharisees who are present is negative: they "conspired" (*symboulion elabon*) (the phrase is found only in Matthew (22:15; 27:1, 7; 28:12) to destroy him.

To understand the plot of a narrative, it is important to recognize elements of causality that link events to each other. All four Gospels have plots that are basically *episodic*. The stories consist of brief incidents or episodes that are reported one right after another. In many cases, these episodes may be understood and appreciated apart from the rest of the narrative. Yet a literary reading will expect to find causal links between them, links that may be explicitly stated or simply implied. Here the narrator does not say that the Pharisees conspired against Jesus, how to destroy him, on account of what has just happened in the synagogue but the reader is meant to infer such a causal link. "Thus, the importance of this passage in Matthew's Gospel is not limited to what insight it offers concerning the relative ethical value of Sabbath laws and deeds of mercy. It is important for an understanding of the narrative as a whole because it provides the immediate motivation for the introduction of the plot to kill Jesus, which will be a major concern in the story from this point on" (Powell, 41).

This controversy has this in common with the preceding one that Jesus interprets the Torah not according to formal casuistic, but according to its ethical aspects: according to the will of God, as Jesus experiences and proclaims it, the human stands over all creation. Help to the sick—and of these there were many both within and without Matthew's community—is not suspended by the sabbath ordinance. But this means the end of the absolute validity of the Law and the end of Judaism. If Judaism is to remain what it is, Jesus must be expelled. The reaction of the Jewish leaders is—from the Jewish viewpoint—consistent: whoever rejects God, the Lord of the Sabbath and makes himself the Lord of the Sabbath, without being authorized to do so, is guilty, and must be punished by death; involved is a sin against God's very own authority (cf. Exod 31:14-15; Num 15:32-36).

The two conflict stories just considered help to define the conflict between Jesus and the religious leaders. The leaders are opposed to Jesus because they perceive him as posing a threat to the authority and sanctity of the law particularly (in this case) the sabbath law. "This marks a new development in the conflict between Jesus and the leaders. Up to now, their opposition to him has not been defined in terms of a threat to the law. It is noteworthy, that in this same episode the leaders' threat to Jesus' life is brought into the narrative for the first time" (Powell, 43).

Hostility 3: Command to Silence, 12:15-21

15 When Jesus became aware of this, he departed. Many crowds followed him, and he cured all of them, **16** and he ordered them not to make him known. **17** This was to fulfill what had been spoken through the prophet Isaiah.

18 "Here is my servant, whom I have chosen, my beloved with whom my soul is well pleased.

I will put my Spirit upon him, and he will proclaim justice to the Gentiles.

19 He will not wrangle or cry aloud, nor will anyone hear his voice in the streets.

20 He will not break a bruised reed or quench a smoldering wick until he brings justice to victory.

21 And in his name the Gentiles will hope."

Substantially this pericope is Matthew's redaction. Only verses 15-16 have a distant parallel in Mark 3:7, 10, 12; Matthew took it from the tradition to form the necessary basis for the fulfillment citation. The opportunity was afforded by the emerging controversy between leaders and people in the preceding pericope. The crowd also follows him and Jesus healed them all. But the time has finally come to command the silence which was enjoined by a prophet's word (Isa 42:14).

Verse 15: "When Jesus became aware of this." In just one sentence Matthew sums up Mark's more lengthy report (3:7, 10, 12) (cf. the related Summary Statement 4:23-25). Jesus became aware that his opponents had determined to kill him; accordingly he decided to depart (place not indicated). Yet the crowds follow him seeking cure, which Jesus grants generally to "all."

Verse 16: "And ordered (*epetimēsen*) them." The command to silence (cf. 8:14 par. 9:30) is the precondition for the understanding of the fulfillment quote. "Ordered" appears six times in Matthew with a variety of meanings; here it includes an authoritative word of command; those healed must not make him known, i.e., publicize him.

Verses 17-21: "Here is my servant (*ho pais mou*": LN 25. 45). Although Jesus does not play the role of Suffering Servant (cf. 8:17), Matthew sees in this behavior of Jesus the fulfillment of a saying of the prophet Isaiah (the Targum already related the text to the Messiah, cf. Gundry, *ad hoc*). The (longest) citation in Matthew contains two important Christological sayings: Jesus is the "Servant (of God)"; and he is the "beloved (Servant)." The saying about the "Beloved" is found neither in the Hebrew Text nor the LXX; so the redactional addition stresses the evangelist's special theological intention. Already in 3:17 Jesus was referred to as the "beloved (Son)." Here "servant" does not refer to the Suffering Servant; rather "servant" is to be understood in the sense of "son" (as in 3:17). He does not wrangle or cry aloud, nor does anyone hear his voice. So in the silence of the "servant" lies the connecting point of the citation with the context. The point of the Matthew saying to is be seen in the two concepts *krisis* ("justice" LN 56.25) and *ethne* ("Gentiles") (vv. 18 and 21). The use of the concept "Gentiles" in the closing sentence of this citation especially expresses Matthew's conception that Jesus is the Messiah of all peoples (28:19).

This saying of Matthew's lies between the citation of Isaiah 42:1-4 (vv. 18-21) and the citation of Isaiah 29:18-19 (cf. Isa 35:5-6; 42:18; 26:19; 61:1 in 11:5) and is illustrated by these citations. The two citations are introduced to present to the community, against the background of the prophetic tradition, the person of the Messiah, his work (11:5) as well as his closeness to God and his behavior in the performance of his messianic salvation task. His mercy toward all men is the overwhelming experience of his contemporaries, even if every appeal to publicity regarding this is to be foregone.

For the community, the command to silence is still valid only in the sense that when it makes Jesus the Servant known—and the community is obligated to do this—it must keep to the interpretation of Jesus' salvation activity by the prophet Isaiah: the Elect is the fulfillment of the hope of all peoples; he leads them to victory even though through judgment. But he does not do this with loud outcries, not harshly and recklessly, but as one who is filled with God's merciful and sanctifying Spirit.

Hostility 4: Son of David, Prophet, Son of Man, 12:22-32

The religious opponents are on the attack in chapter 12. They first accuse the disciples (12:1) and then Jesus himself (12:9-13) of breaking the law. Finally, they plot to destroy Jesus (12:14). Indeed, they accuse Jesus directly of casting out demons by the prince of demons (12:24). In response, Jesus indicates that not only are their lives at cross-purposes with his own, but that they are even in danger of blaspheming against the Holy Spirit (12:32). The Christological titles Son of David and Son of Man figure prominently here.

> 22 Then they brought to him a demoniac who was blind and mute; and he cured him, so that the one who had been mute could speak and see. 23 All the crowds were amazed and said, "Can this be the Son of David?" 24 But when the Pharisees heard it, they said, "It is only by Beelzebul, the ruler of the demons, that this fellow casts out the demons." 25 He knew what they were thinking and said to them, "Every kingdom divided against itself is laid waste, and no city or house divided against itself will stand. 26 If Satan casts out Satan, he is divided against himself; how then will his kingdom stand? 27 If I cast out demons by Beelzebul, by whom do your own exorcists cast them out? Therefore they will be your judges. 28 But if it is by the Spirit of God that I cast out demons, then the kingdom of God has come to you. 29 Or how can one enter a strong man's house and plunder his property, without first tying up the strong man? Then indeed the house can be plundered. 30 Whoever is not with me is against me, and whoever does not gather with me scatters. 31 Therefore I tell you, people will be forgiven for every sin and blasphemy, but blasphemy against the Spirit will not be forgiven. 32 Whoever speaks a word aginst the Son of Man will be forgiven, but whoever speaks against the Holy Spirit will not be forgiven, either in this age or in the age to come.

Verse 23: "Can this be the Son of David (*Meti houtos estin*)." The crowds were amicable but without faith in Jesus. They raise the question of whether he is the Son of David (cf. 9:27). But the grammatical form in which they put their question anticipates a negative answer. And when asked who this Jesus is whom they have hailed as the Son of David, they reply that he is the prophet from Nazareth (21:11). And in Matthew's story this is a misguided conception, for Jesus is in reality the Messiah Son of God (3:17; 16:16).

Verses 25-26: "He knew what they were thinking." As in 9:4, Jesus knows the Pharisees' thoughts. *Enthymēsis* in the New Testament has the quality of superstition, evil and foolish. In graphic debate style Jesus begins to refute the false opinion: every divided kingdom (*kata* with genitive sharpens the saying) is laid waste (lit. "made into a wasteland") and every city (*polis* has a similarity to *basileia*) or (every) house similarly divided, will not stand. Then the image of the split political unity is transferred to Satan's Kingdom: in every exorcism—according to the complaint of the Pharisees—one Satan expels another (*ekballō*, technical term for exorcism activity); but then how will (Satan's) kingdom stand?

Verse 28: "The kingdom of God has come to you." How does Matthew conceive of God as having drawn near? God comes near in the person of Jesus who is the Messiah Son of God. In words drawn from the Old Testament, Matthew puts it this way at 1:23: in the son (conceived by the Spirit) and born of the virgin, God has at last come near to dwell with people. And here Jesus himself declares: "But if by the Spirit of God I cast out demons, then the Kingdom of God has come upon you!"

Verses 31-32: The two verses are a doublet of the same logion, which was originally passed on in a variety of forms. "Therefore" joins the double saying with the foregoing, especially with verse 28. "Every sin and blasphemy" (LN 33.400-401) will be forgiven (by God, cf. the divine passive); but the "blasphemy against the spirit" remains excluded. The saying possibly goes back to Jesus' original statement that God's forgiveness did not exclude even blasphemy. Through the addition of "blasphemy of the spirit," the logion took on a Christological component: a rejection of the eschatological Spirit of God, which was manifested in Jesus' action (v. 28), can not be forgiven. A word against the Son of Man finds God's forgiveness, but not speech against God's Spirit: neither now nor in the future (LN 67.143) is there forgiveness for such blasphemy. To speak against Jesus as the worldly Son of Man out of lack of understanding (cf. Acts 3:17) can at times be forgiven; but to speak against Jesus as the bearer and revealer of God's spirit "who is regularly manifested in the works of the community" cannot be forgiven.

1. This whole section is dominated by the logion that the Kingdom of God has broken in. The healings and the eschatological theophany are signs that cannot be ignored. The might and majesty of God, which has come to humans in Jesus, shows that Satan's dominance has been broken.

2. Therewith the time of the Spirit has begun, concerning which the prophet Joel had said already that it would be poured out on "all flesh"; the "in those days and at that time" refer to the End Time (cf. 4:1; also Acts 2:17: "in the last days"), that will bring salvation for Israel. Since this time of the Spirit is the last time for the community, it is at the same time the time of crisis; a decision against the Spirit is definitive and therefore, unforgiveable.

3. In the fact that the Spirit of God makes possible and establishes unity, the opposite of emnity, an important topic comes to the fore. The community has been liberated from satanic dominance, which destroys peace and unity, and this through Jesus, the spirit-full Son of Man. As Son of Man he may also at times trigger uncertainty and doubt among the disciples of Matthew's community; this should not be, but it would be forgiveable. Against the bearer and bringer of God's Spirit the community should not be guilty of any blasphemy; for such a sin would never be forgiven.

Hostility 5: Good Tree, Bad Tree, 12:33-37

In relation to himself, Jesus possesses "integrity." The operative principle in this connection is the affirmation that "the tree is known by its fruit" (7:16, 20; 12:33). When Jesus is judged by this principle, no discrepancy is found between what he says and what he does. In relation to the religious leaders, Jesus is "confrontational." In Jesus' view, the religious leaders are evil, "a brood of vipers" (12:34), and they take after the one with whom they have affinity, the devil or the "Evil One" (13:38-39).

> 33 "Either make the tree good, and its fruit good; or make the tree bad, and its fruit bad; for the tree is known by its fruit. 34 You brood of vipers! How can you speak good, when you are evil? For out of the abundance of the heart the mouth speaks. 35 The good person brings good things out of a good treasure, and the evil person brings evil things out of an evil treasure. 36 I tell you, on the day of judgment you will have to give an account for every careless word you utter; 37 for by your words you will be justified, and by your words you will be condemned."

The contrast between Jesus and his opponents appeared clearly in the pericope regarding the baptism of John (3.1-17). This pericope presented a programmatic contrast between Jesus and the Pharisees and Sadducees. John addressed these persons as a "brood of vipers" (3:7), a term which Jesus now also uses of them. In Matthew, this phrase points to the imminent judgment that awaits the Pharisees because of the great guilt they have incurred.

Verse 33: "Good tree, bad tree." The addressees are the Pharisees (cf. 12:24) in a figure of speech. (J. Meier speaks of a parable.) In antithetic parallel, the alternative is presented: the tree is either good, the fruit is also good, or it is bad (*sapros* = foul, rotten; then, useless, harmful).

Decisive in the figure of speech is the thought: the quality of the tree determines the quality of the fruit.

Verse 34: "Brood of vipers." The attitude that John the Baptist assumes toward the leaders is predictive of the attitude that Jesus will assume toward them. Seeing the Pharisees and Sadducees coming out to him, John attacks them. He denounces them as a "brood of vipers," that is, as persons who are "evil" at the very center of their being (3:9; 12:34).

Verse 35: A second image interprets verse 34: the heart is like a (treasure) chest (LN 7.32) full of treasure. The saying, originally handed on in isolation (with a general meaning) is applied to human speech. A good person brings forth good words out of good treasure (literally: "throws [them] out): the bad, on the contrary, bad words, because his treasure is full of bad things (*poneros*—one of Matthew's favorite words [26 times]).

Verses 36-37: With an authoritative word ("I tell you"), the first image, the explanation, and the second image are placed in the context of judgment day. The logion takes on the character of a threat: every "careless word" (LN 30.44; 72.21) must be accounted for (*rhema* is every [single] word that a person speaks). The transition to the second person singular (v. 37) strengthens the impact of the threat; a person will be either justified or condemned according to the spoken word. With *dikaioo* (as already in 11:19) means that a man will be shown as just on account of his good speech. *Katadikazo* means: to declare against someone to decide, so to judge. Harmful and evil (sinful) talk brings judgment.

In 12:32 the community was instructed about what consequences would follow if anyone spoke against the Son of Man and against the Holy Spirit. This provided the key words (speak, word, speech) needed to make a statement about the connection between the heart of person and speech. The Pharisees provide a negative example. But while they were upbraided (v. 34a) and then warned about judgment day (v. 36a), the community must answer for its words on judgment day. The rabbis also knew a similar thought: "Even the words in which there is no sin, will be written on men's heavenly tablet."

Hostility 6: The Sign of Jonah, 12:38-42

As a sign that the situation is not likely to improve, Jesus and the religious leaders continue to clash in fierce debate. They demand of him a sign to prove that he acts on the authority of God and not of Satan, and he again assails them, for being both evil and faithless to God. They are "malicious," charging Jesus with blasphemy for forgiving sins (9:3-4), demanding of him a sign, and repeatedly putting him to the test in ways that, ironically, place them in the service of Satan, the fountainhead of all temptation.

> **38** Then some of the scribes and Pharisees said to him, "Teacher, we wish to see a sign from you." **39** But he answered them, "An evil and adulterous generation asks for a sign; but no sign shall be given to it except the sign of the prophet Jonah. **40** For just as Jonah was three days and three nights in the belly of the sea monster, so for three days and three nights the Son of Man will be in the heart of the earth. **41** The people of Nineveh will rise up at the judgment with this generation and condemn it because they repented at the proclamation of Jonah, and see, something greater than Jonah is here! **42** The queen of the South will rise up at the judgment with this generation and condemn it, because she came from the ends of the earth to listen to the wisdom of Solomon, and see, something greater than Solomon is here."

Verse 38: "To see a sign (*semeion*) from you" (Cf. LN 33.477). Jesus' miracles are called "mighty works" (*dynameis*). Jesus and the disciples are never reported as doing "wonders" (*terata*), and the "sign" (*semeion*) is characterized as a miraculous feat that the religious leaders demand of Jesus as they tempt him to prove he is not in collusion with Satan (12:24, 38; 16:1). The sign Jesus does give them, a word prophesying his death and resurrection (12:39-40; 27:63), is not what they have in mind. When the death and resurrection occur, the leaders refuse to acknowledge them (27:62-64).

Verses 39: "No sign . . . except." Jesus does give them a sign, but one they cannot immediately test, namely, the announcement of his death and resurrection.

Verse 40: "The Son of Man will be." The designation the "Son of Man" is a "public" designation in the sense that it is primarily with an eye to "outsiders" or the "world," Jews and Gentiles and especially opponents, that Jesus calls himself the Son of Man. "In the suffering Son-of-man sayings, it is to some of the scribes and Pharisees (12:38, 40) or to the religious leaders (20:18), of Gentile opponents (20:19), and of the rulers of the Gentiles (20:25, 28) that Jesus speaks of himself as the Son of man" (*Story*, 101).

In Matthew, the religious leaders hold to a human point of view because they are incapable of receiving revelation from God. "Incredibly, even news of Jesus' resurrection (the 'sign of John,' 12:40) fails to have any effect on them (28:11-15). This characterization is in keeping with a theme developed throughout Matthew, namely, that 'understanding' is something that must be given by God" (Powell, 61).

Verses 41-42: "Nineveh . . . the queen of the South." The book of Jonah does not call Jonah a "prophet" as Matthew does (v. 39c). Jonah's preaching met with success, so that in the judgment, the inhabitants of Nineveh will come forward as plaintiffs against "this generation"; for "this generation" had not acknowledged that "more" than Jonah and Solomon was here. The second example fills out—from a different historical connection—the first. It too stresses the prophetic character of the sign: Solomon's wisdom was "heard." The "more" over against the prophet Jonah and King Solomon consists in the fact Jesus speaks as the one with whose word "the almighty grace of the Kingdom of God comes to all."

Thematically, both the Jonah sign and the attached double speech about the men from Nineveh and the queen of the South serves as a warning. The request for a wonder sign, which before the unbelieving Jews should show Jesus as the designated and awaited eschatological prophet, is refused. For it is the request of an evil generation, which does not acknowledge the inbreaking *Basileia*. For this "last generation"—but also Matthew's community—a special faith sign is refused; it is referred solely to Jesus' death, his salvation acts, and his proclamation of the Gospel, and thereby placed in the situation of eschatological decision (cf. at 11:2-6).

Like the evangelist, the community should see in the "wonder" of Jonah a prophecy about the fate of the Son of Man. To this intention also corresponds the exact parallel of the three days and three nights. Matthew—as often—is at pains to stress the content exactitude of the fulfillment of the prophecy. Also for the Matthean community, the reliability of the Scripture is the guarantee of the credibility of the Gospel of the Suffering Son of Man.

Hostility 7: Seven Other Evil Spirits, 12:43-45

Dualism pervades Matthew's story. In Matthew's world of thought, the one who is "good" is God himself (19:17), and the one who is the "Evil One" is the devil (13:19, 38-39). As the supreme agent of God, Jesus raises up in the world "sons of the Kingdom" (13:38), whereas the devil raises up "sons of the Evil One" (13:38-39). The notion that "evilness" is the root trait of the religious leaders harmonizes with this dualism. As persons who are evil, the leaders have affinity with the devil (12:34). They "think evil in their hearts" (9:3-4), and Jesus discerns this (9:4; 22:18). On two occasions Jesus excoriates them as "an evil and adulterous generation," that is, as a generation that does the devil's will and is faithless to God (12:39; 16:4). Opposed as they are to him, Jesus foresees that they will be no less opposed to the post-Easter missionaries (23:33-36).

43 "When the unclean spirit has gone out of a person, he wanders through waterless regions looking for a resting place, but it finds none. **44** Then it says, 'I will return to my house from which I came.' And when it comes it finds it empty, swept and put in order. **45** Then it goes and brings along him seven other spirits more evil than itself, and they enter and live there; and the last state of that person is worse than the first. So shall it be also with this evil generation."

Verse 43: "The unclean spirit" is a frequent Semitic modifier of "demon" (Schweizer, *pneuma TWNT* VI 396), whose stopping places are unclean places. If it is driven out of a person (behind the "gone out" stands a previous exorcism), he wanders through waterless places, the desert (LN 1.86), which was regarded as the favorite stopping place for demons. He seeks rest (LN 27.87) but finds no resting place.

Verse 44: In a "small monologue" the musings of the unclean spirit are revealed: he desires to return. And he finds "his house" not only standing empty (LN 59.43) (literally: unused), but swept and cleaned (cf. the paradox "cleaned" for the "unclean)."

Verse 45: The house is inviting and the spirit gets the idea of inviting seven other spirits; they are (even) worse than it is. The point lies in verse 45b: for this person (v. 43) things will end up worse than they were before (LN 61.13). With the interpretation "So" (*houtos* is one of Matthew's favorite words), he understands the image as a simile for "this generation."

This passage contains a clear warning regarding Jewish exorcisms. These help only temporarily and superficially, since they ignore the inbreaking Kingdom of God, present in Jesus' exorcisms and those of his messengers. In the exorcisms of Jesus and those of his disciples the first manifestations of the definitive destruction of all powers inimical to salvation become visible. But since the old aeon (the time of the unclean spirits) and the new aeon (the time of the Spirit of God) even now exist together and beside each other (in the sense of an antagonistic co-existence), openness to God's saving power is the most pressing duty for the disciples.

"These opponents are capable of such sins because they are in collusion with Satan. . . . In all the Gospels, and especially Matthew, there are only two positions: the right, which is the way of God; and the wrong, which is the way of the devil. There is ultimately no middle ground. Throughout the Gospel, these opponents are related to Satan even as Jesus is related to God" (Bauer 69).

Hostility 8: Family Ties No Exception, 12:46-50

Within the context of chapters 11-12, the hiding of divine revelation and making it known (11:25) correspond to the fact that whereas all Israel turns away from Jesus, the disciples continue to adhere to him. Jesus summons both crowds and leaders to turn about and to live in the sphere of God's Rule by becoming his followers and, through him, sons of God (5:45; 13:38), brothers of himself and of one another. But even the family of Jesus deserts him, which leaves the disciples as the only ones who still adhere to him (12:46-50).

> **46** While he was still speaking to the crowds, his mother and his brothers were standing outside wanting to speak to him. **47** Someone told him, "Look, your mother and your brothers are standing outside wanting to speak to you." **48** But to the one who had told him this, Jesus replied, "Who is my mother, and who are my brothers?" **49** And pointing to his disciples, he said, "Here are my mother and my brothers! **50** For whoever does the will of my Father in heaven is my brother and sister and mother."

Verse 46: Jesus speaks to the crowds (in a house), while his relations (his mother and his brothers, LN 10.49) stand outside (83.20) and seek to speak with him. No reasons are given for this arrangement. Unlike Mark (3:31-32), the scene has no negative accent: in Mark *zeteō*, "seek," verse 32, expresses a negative intention. In Matthew, on the contrary, a "wanting to" is involved—they "exerted themselves." His relations wished to speak to him straightway, even with the crowd in the way.

Verse 48: "Who is my mother?" Jesus' answer is directed only to the bearers of the message (unlike Mark and Luke); thereby it loses something of its weight. Yet it does not say simply that Jesus now has no time for his relatives, nor is it simply a question of an interruption of Jesus' discourse. The question, "Who is . . ." has an explanatory character, telling how the answer is to be taken.

Verses 49-50: Jesus points to the disciples, not to separate these from the crowds (v. 46), but to underline the saying which follows and to designate the crowds in the widest sense as his mother and his brothers. Jesus' (true) brothers, and sisters, and mother is every one who does the will of the Father in heaven (cf. 6:10; 7:21; 18:14; 21:31; 26:42). In the in-breaking salvation aeon all who do the Father's will constitute Jesus' family; for it is the Father who calls together the new community.

Matthew uses the appearance of the relatives to tell the community who Jesus' true brother, sister, and mother are. Repeatedly the community must learn that only the doing of the God's will determines the right relationship to Jesus. Whether Jesus' relatives knowingly are placed on the "side of non-understanding," can hardly be determined. That the mother is not named by name says at most, that she played no special role in the Jesus tradition. Only the intended contrast is important— to take up the one and only decisive connection with Jesus is possible only for the person who does God's will. This is the *conditio sine qua non* of Christian brotherhood, discipleship, and Christian house and family community.

PARABLE CHAPTER

This, the third of five discourses, works together with Matthew's overall plan for his Gospel. It falls into two parts (vv. 1-35, vv. 36-52) which have similar structures. Each begins with verses which give the setting, in each case there is an "excursus" (vv. 10-23, vv. 36b-43) and a number of parables. The first half has four (Sower, Tares, Mustard Seed, Leaven); the second has three (Hidden Treasure, Pearl, Net). The crowds are present at the first half but not at the second half. Only the disciples are present there. B. Gerhardsson contends that Matthew shaped his parable chapter after the pattern of the *shema* (cf. "The Parable of the Sower and its Interpretation" *NTS* 14 [1968], pp. 165–93; "The Seven Parables in Matthew XIII," *NTS* 19 [1972], pp. 16–37).

Jesus responds to the rejection of "this generation" by turning away from the crowds and turning toward his disciples. In the first discourse (chs. 5-7), the crowds were present at the beginning and at the end; here they are present at the beginning, but not at the end. In 13:2 their presence is stressed, but at 13:36 Matthew reports that Jesus left the crowds and went into the house, and his disciples came to him. This change in locale and audience represents a change of focus in the ministry of Jesus.

Jesus speaks to the crowds in parables because the secrets of the kingdom of heaven have not been granted to them (13:11). They are dull of hearing, and in them the dire prophecy from Isaiah is fulfilled (19:14-5). In stark contrast to them, the disciples have eyes that see and ears that hear (13:36). To the disciples, God has given the mysteries of the kingdom (13:11).

After the parable of the Sower, the parables of the tract of seven parables begin with the phrase "The kingdom of heaven is like . . ." The kingdom of heaven refers to God's kingly rule as a present and future reality. God has always been the ruler of the world and, in a special sense, of Israel. In Jesus, God has manifested his rule eschatologically, and, through Jesus, in the Twelve as well. And God continues to exercise his rule in the Church, and, at the Parousia of Jesus, the Son of Man, God will manifest his rule in all its fullness and glory before the whole human race. The kingdom of heaven, therefore, denotes no less than God's total salvation for humankind as revealed in Jesus. So the term kingdom of heaven can denote the message Matthew's Church proclaims, the doctrine it teaches, the hope it cherishes, and the life it is to lead.

Introduction to the Tract of Seven Parables, 13:1-3a

Matthew's "tract of seven parables" falls into two main sections: 1) Jesus instructs the crowd (*ho ochlos*) in public, speaking enigmatically in parables (*en parabolais*), verses 1-35; 2) Jesus instructs his disciples (*hoi mathetai*) privately at home, giving them an unveiled glimpse into the secrets of the Kingdom of Heaven, verses 36-52.

> 1 That same day Jesus went out of the house and sat beside the sea.
> 2 Such great crowds gathered around him that he got into a boat and sat there while the whole crowd stood on the beach. 3 And he told them many things in parables, saying:

Verse 1: "Jesus went out of the house (*exelthōn ho Iesous tēs oikias*)." Matthew has clearly marked this division in the framework of the chapter. In the introduction (vv. 1-3a) he writes that Jesus *went out of the house* (where he lived and where he met and talked with his friends) and sat down beside the sea. Since great crowds gathered round him, he then went and sat in a boat and taught *the people* (*ho ochlos*) who stood on the beach. In verses 34-35, Matthew summarizes this section by remarking that Jesus spoke all these parables to the people and, moreover, did not speak to them except in parables and, having quoted a passage from the prophets, continues in verse 36: "Then he left the crowds and went [*back*] *into the house*. And *his disciples* approached him saying . . ." At the end of the section of teaching which then follows, Matthew again makes clear that Jesus was saying this to his disciples (vv. 51-52). Here the "house" functions as a teaching center for the chosen group of disciples that Jesus has around him.

"And sat (*ekathēto*) beside the sea." Jesus again sits, as he had at the beginning of the Sermon on the Mount (5:1), in the posture proper to a teacher. Matthew uses the verb *kathemai* (to teach twice in vv. 1-3a alone). The twin verbs *kathemai-kathizo* often possess a connotation that marks the person who is "seated" as worthy of special honour or reverence. This explains why the Old Testament frequently pictures God as sitting upon a throne, an image with which Matthew, too, is familiar (5:34). Matthew describes Jesus as sitting when he assumes the role of teacher (5:1; 24.3), judge (19:28; 25:31), or ruler (20:21; 26.64).

Indeed, the express pattern Matthew is following in his use of *kathemai* in our text is apocalyptic, an example of which we find in the book of Revelation (7:9-12). Here God is pictured as sitting (*kathemai*) upon his throne with a great crowd (*ochlos*) of worshippers standing (*histemai*) before him, the very sequence that Matthew, by means of redaction, has carefully reproduced: Jesus *sits* while the *crowd stands* on the shore. It would seem, then, that Matthew's intention in verse 2 is to fashion a setting that will, in itself, attribute honor to Jesus and underline, not merely a rabbinic, but even a divine dignity.

Verse 2: "Such great crowds." To understand the "parable chapter" of Matthew in its entirety, we must realize that the tension is not between Jesus and the Pharisees or between church and synagogue; the contrasted groups are the spiritually inert crowds (*ho ochlos*) and the inquiring disciples (*hoi mathetai*). "The problem under review is not why some go to church and others to the synagogue, but why so few of the people are spiritually alive, and so reveal themselves to be true children of the heavenly kingdom" (B. Gerhardsson, "Parable of the Sower," 173).

"Got into a boat and sat there." Does Matthew understand the boat here in the extended sense of the Church? This is possible. If so, then Matthew, in having Jesus address the crowds from the boat, is emphasizing the fact that since the resurrection, the word of Jesus comes to all from the Church.

But it is to be noted that Jesus does not enter the boat to cross to the other side following his discourse in parables. In fact, Matthew makes no further reference to the boat in chapter 13. Furthermore, Matthew appears to conceive of Jesus as sitting alone in the boat, whereas in those pericopes in which the boat does symbolize the Church, the presence of Jesus and the disciples in it together is vividly dramatized (cf. 8:23-7; 14:22-33).

Apparently Matthew is here making use of [the boat] in much the same way as he makes use of the mountain in 5:1 and 15:29-32a. In these two passages, Jesus is described as sitting on the mountain with the disciples and crowds assembled before him. So here, our text describes Jesus as sitting in the boat with the crowds standing before him on the shore. "Hence, the function of the boat in 13.2 is to provide Jesus with a place where he may be seated, which is a sign of honour,; and to set him apart from the crowd, thereby emphasizing that he is the focal point of attention" (*Parables*, 24).

Verse 3: "He told (*elalēsen*) them." The fact that Jesus "tells" rather than "teaches" or "proclaims" is highly significant. It fits in with Matthew's basic ground plan. There are Jews in the "crowds" who hear the parables, and after 11:1 Jesus never "teaches" or "proclaims" the Gospel of the Kingdom to Jews. By systematically employing the term *laleo* (to "speak", vv. 3, 10, 13, 33, 34a-b), Matthew both provides 13:1-35 with a coherent structure and eliminates direct references to teaching or proclaiming. *Didaskō* denotes for Matthew the function whereby the "law and the prophets" are interpreted in terms of their fulfillment in Jesus. *Kēryssō* denotes the function whereby the Gospel of the Kingdom (4:23; 9:35) is proclaimed (10:27; 24:14; 26:13).

Neither to "teach" nor to "proclaim," would be appropriate in the context of chapter 13, because *within the ground plan of* Matthew's Gospel, teaching and preaching cease, as far as the Jews are concerned, after the conflict-discourses of chapter 12. So it is that following 11.1, preaching is mentioned only in connection with the Church's universal missionary assignment (24:14; 26:13). As for teaching, even though the word itself occurs in several instances where Jesus is engaged in discussion with Jews, it is never used positively in the sense that Matthew provides us with an elaboration of the message of Jesus (cf. 5:2; 7:28f), nor does it ever appear in a situation where the Jews seem receptive to him.

Verse 3: "Many things in parables (*parabolais*)." Matthew does not observe the distinction between parable and allegory; his are allegorized parables. Nor can it be shown that Matthew has developed a theory of parable. "Matthew has incorporated a double tradition into his book regarding their perspicuity, and therefore the nature, of the parables of Jesus" (*Parables*, 49).

In chapter 13, Matthew argues that while the disciples (i.e., his Church) can comprehend the parables of Jesus, the Jews cannot, for they stand before them as before riddles. At the same time, Matthew records elsewhere in his Gospel that the Jews are able to master parables of Jesus. Following the narration of the parables of the Two Sons (21:28-32) and of the Wicked Husbandmen (21:33-46), Matthew reports that "when the chief priests and the Pharisees heard his *parables*, they realized that he was speaking about them" (21:45).

But since we find two traditions in the first Gospel with respect to the intelligibility of the parables of Jesus, we conclude that Matthew does not reduce his views on this matter to any unified concept. Yet this is something we should certainly expect were Matthew's remarks concerning parables subject to a fixed theory of parables.

Matthew's use of the parable is governed, not by an abstract theory or dogmatic principles, but by eminently pragmatic interests. Matthew takes the parables of Jesus, spoken in a totally different context and subsequently exposed to the influences of both an oral and a written tradition, and applies them to the circumstances of his own day so that they speak for the needs of his Church. In this way, Jesus once more brings God's kingly rule to bear on the life-situations of a later generation. "Matthew's pragmatism in relation to parables further reflects itself in the way he makes each parable totally subservient to the context into which he inserts it" (*Parables*, 50).

The Parable of the Sower, 13:3b-9

After Jesus had told the parable of the Sower, the disciples asked him "about the parables." According to Mark's Gospel, Jesus replied: "Do you not understand this parable? Then how will you understand all the parables?" (4:13). The saying does not mean that the Sower is the most easily understood of all that Jesus told. It indicates rather that the Sower is *fundamental*. For one thing, it is found in all three synoptics. That it is fundamental is "further indicated by the fact that the parable serves to introduce a section about Jesus' preaching in parables and and that the conversation which ensues is concerned with two questions, the significance of Jesus' use of parables as a whole, and the meaning of this parable in particular" (B. Gerhardsson, "Sower," 185).

The parable is made up of a fourfold series of scenes in which the seeds which fall on the path are eaten by the birds (v. 4), those which fall on the rocky ground are scorched and wither (vv. 5-6), those which fall among thorn are choked (v. 7), and those which fall on good soil produce fruit (v. 8). These four scenes fall into two groups: the seeds which do not produce fruit (scenes 1-3) and the scene which does (scene 4).

The parable of the Sower is a parable of contrast (failure and success), which is a feature common to all the parables of Growth. The contrast is between the seeds that perish (vv. 4-7) and the seeds that produce fruit (v. 8), between the Word as proclaimed to the Jews, who have not responded to it, and the Word proclaimed to the disciples, or Church, who have.

> **3b** Listen! A sower went out to sow. **4** And as he sowed, some seeds fell on the path, and the birds came and ate them up. **5** Other seeds fell on rocky ground, where they did not have much soil, and they sprang up quickly, since they had no depth of soil. **6** But when the sun rose, they were scorched; and since they had no root, they withered away. **7** Other seeds fell among thorns, and the thorns grew up and choked them. **8** Other seeds fell on good soil and brought forth grain, some a hundredfold, some sixty, some thirty. **9** Let anyone with ears listen!"

The sower is Jesus. During his lifetime he delivered his message personally, after Easter, as the exalted Kyrios he speaks through his Church. The act of sowing is the act of preaching; that which has been sown, or preached, is the Word. Just as the waste of seed was great, so the incidence of failure in the preaching of the Word to the Jews has also proved to be great. But just as the seeds that fell on good soil produced a fine crop, so there are the disciples, or Church, who have been receptive to the proclamation of the Word.

According to B. Gerhardsson, the seven parables of Matthew 13 form a pattern in which the first governs the order and arrangement of the other six ("The Seven Parables in Matthew xiii," *NTS* 19 [1, '72] 16–37). The abstract written by G. MacRae, S.J., reads as follows:

> The Parable of the Sower was the object of meditation which gave rise to specific questions about each of the four categories in the explanation. The six parables answer these questions in such fashion that the second deals with those falling by the wayside, the third and fourth with those falling on stony ground, the fifth and sixth with those falling among thorns, and the seventh with those falling on the good ground. The seven parables thus once formed a "tract" into which Markan material and two secondary explanations, of the tares and of the fishnet, were inserted in the composition of Matthew. The background of the first parable and its (genuine) explanation is the creed of Israel, the *shema*, and the choice of the other six parables was made in light of this understanding. Though the authenticity of all the parables as coming from Jesus is a delicate matter to determine, it seems unlikely that the pattern of the seven comes from him. But these parables do reveal the presuppositions of his teaching, which concerns the kingdom of heaven as already in existence and as already proclaimed in the central creed of Israel. *NTA* 17 (3, '73) #913.

The first three instances (the seed on the path, rocky ground, and on the thorns) are the three cases of unsuccessful sowing. These particular instances have not been selected at random. We would most expect to find *rain*, without which a Palestinian harvest would fail absolutely. The Biblical texts frequently emphasize the importance of rain, and the pious Jew was daily reminded of this in the *Shema*, where it is said that there can be no growth unless God gives the former and the latter rain (Deut 11:14, 17). The three examples cited are not imaginative pictures of the obstacles and difficulties that can face the sower. The factors in the parable which affect the fate of the seed have been chosen in accordance with a certain system. In all four cases the type of ground is the primary factor, and in the first three instances it has only a destructive effect. It is also to be noted that it is not common for Palestinian field to contain so many different types of ground. The parable, one must conclude, does not offer a purely natural and unforced agricultural illustration. The construction was consciously and intentionally made.

Among the factors pointing in that direction is the fact that the unsuccessful sowings come first. That failures should precede successes is a common idea and a frequently employed device in folk tales (the "law of the final climax"). The unsuccessful sowings could have been given a different order, and we note that the actual parable is built, to a large extent, upon certain inherited metaphors.

The Parable (13:3b-9) and the Interpretation (13:18-23) fit each other as hand to glove. Here the scribal pattern, evident in the Interpretation, is the key. The order in which the four moments are placed is determined by the underlying theme of the Interpretation. This demands that each stage in the Parable be taken in a certain order because it is based on the Shema, in its scribal interpretation. *"The parable is constructed for the interpretation it receives in the Gospels.* The primary here is not the *parable* but the fourfold theme which is developed in the Interpretation"* (B. Gerhardsson, "Sower," 187).

Verse 4: "Some seeds fell on the path." We do not have to speculate about the meaning of this unsuccessful sowing; it is clearly indicated in the interpretation. "When anyone hears the word of the kingdom and does not understand it, the evil one comes and snatches away what is sown in his heart; this is what was sown on the path" (v. 19). Only here in the Interpretation does Matthew mention "the heart (*hē kardia*)." The fate of the seed in this instance depends on whether "the heart" is fulfilling its spiritual role or not. It is with those who hear the word and "do not understand (*me synientes*)" that the evil one is successful. In the Purpose of the Parables passage, which came just before the Interpretation, Matthew has just depicted the ignorant crowds with a "formula quotation" as a people whose "heart has grown dull (*epachynthē gar hē kardia*)," *a people who do not "understand with the heart (tē kardia synosin*)," a people who see and hear without seeing or hearing or understanding (v. 15). In this first instance, the listeners' deficiency is closely associated with the "heart." The sowing is unsuccessful because the listener does not fulfill the divine demand which the scribes found implied in one of the phrases of the Shema, "You shall love the Lord your God *with all your heart.*"

This scene is illustrated by the parable of the weeds.

Verse 5-6: "Other seeds fell on rocky ground." Again, the meaning is indicated in the Interpretation. "This is the one who hears the word and immediately receives it with joy; yet such a person has no root in himself, but endures for a while, and when tribulation or persecution arises on account of the word, immediately he falls away" (vv. 20-21). This last sentence places the person in a well-known category: those who are not prepared to undergo suffering or martyrdom for the sake of God's word (*dia ton logon*) (v. 21). In times of persecution the people of God had to choose between "things of this world" and "things of the world to come." Not having any roots, or having only dried up roots, was a traditional image of instability and transitoriness. The type of hearer depicted in verses 20-21 is, in other words, the one who denies God and falls away in order to save his soul (life).

This scene is illustrated by two parables of the tract (Mustard Seed and Leaven) which, in turn, are connected with the second phase of the *Shema*, Love of God with all one's soul.

Verse 7: "Other seeds fell upon thorns." Turning to the interpretation we read: "This is the one who hears the word, but the cares of the world and the lure of riches choke the word, and it proves unfruitful" (v. 22). The things which choke the word in this situation are amply and briefly denoted as wealth (*tou ploutou*), i.e., mammon. The "cares of the world (this age) (*he merimna tou aiōnos*) is the subjective aspect, human spiritual bondage to this world.

The proper attitude to wealth and property was found by the scribes to be enshrined in the formula of the Shema: "You shall love the Lord your God *with all your might*"; for them "might" denoted mammon: riches and property.

This scene is illustrated by the parables of the Treasure and the Pearl, and is connected with the third phase of the Shema, Love of God with all one's Might.

Verse 8: "Other seeds fell on good soil." "This," we read in the Interpretation (v. 23), "is the one who hears the word and understands it (*ho ton logon akouōn kai synieis*): who indeed bears fruit and yields (*poiei*), in one case a hundredfold, in another, sixty, and in another thirty" (v. 23). Once again, we note the significance that Matthew attaches to "understanding (*syneis*)." The somewhat vague expression in Mark "and accept (the word)," has been sharpened in Matthew: "understand."

"And brought forth (*karpophorei kai poiei*) grain"—which is the decisive point: the hearing and the understanding become an event. "To bear fruit" is a traditional image for an active loyalty to the covenant, a righteousness that was shown in life and in *deed*. This manner of speech is found in the words of Jesus, especially well preserved in Matthew ("to make (do) fruit, *poiein karpon*): of trees, 3:10; 7:17-19; 12:33; of seed, 13:26; of men, 3:8; 13:23; 21:43; "fruit" in the sense of "works," 7:16,

20). We find there also the expression *to do* (the heavenly) Father's will, do the word, do the words of Jesus. In verse 23, the double significance of the term *poiein* is utilized felicitously, associations being made with both the image and the abstract—to do (form) fruit and to do (effect) what the word says.

"Hundredfold, sixty, thirty." The significance of these numbers is, strangely, not made clear in the Interpretation. But the overall structure of the tract suggests a solution. Those who bear fruit a hundredfold are those whose obedient heart determines that they sacrifice not only their property (might, mammon) but even the most precious things of all— their life (soul). These are the martyrs. Those who bear fruit sixtyfold have an obedient heart and give up their goods, but are not compelled to give their life for the sake of the Word. Those who bear fruit thirtyfold also have an obedient and undivided heart, but are not compelled to offer either their life or all their property for God's sake.

Verse 9: "He who has ears, let him hear." Those of the good ground are here depicted as those who fulfill the covenant obligations, living wholly according to the words of the first and greatest command of the Law, "Hear, O Israel: the Lord our God is one Lord; and you shall love the Lord your God with all your heart, and with all your soul, and with all your might (riches, property)." The divine word they are to hear this time is the Word of the Kingdom, the teaching of Jesus and early Christianity about the Kingdom of God. When this word now sounds in Israel, it is given to those who "have" and not to those who "have not." Blinded eyes cannot see it, nor can it be heard by deafened ears.

The Purpose of the Parables, 13:10-17

In this passage, which is Matthew's composition, the theme that he has been developing is forcefully underlined: the disciples, or Church, are placed in stark contrast to the Jews. Making use of catchwords, Matthew establishes a series of statements that are antithetically parallel: verse 10 "to them," verse 11 "to you"; verse 12 "whoever has," "whoever has not"; verse 13b, "they do not see," verse 16 "because you see." The quotation from Isaiah (vv. 14-15) is probably a later interpolation.

> **10** Then the disciples came and asked him, "Why do you speak to them in parables?" **11** He answered, "To you it has been given to know the secrets of the kingdom of heaven, but to them it has not been given. **12** For to those who have, more will be given, and they will have an abundance; but from those who have nothing, even what they have will be taken away. **13** The reason I speak to them in parables is that seeing they

do not perceive, and hearing they do not listen, nor do they understand."
14 With them indeed is fulfilled the prophecy of Isaiah that says:
"You will indeed listen, but not understand,
and you will indeed look, but never perceive.
15 For this people's heart has grown dull,
and their ears are hard of hearing,
and they have shut their eyes;
so that they might not look with their eyes,
and listen with their ears,
and understand with their heart and turn—and I would heal them."
16 But blessed are your eyes, for they see, and your ears, for they hear.
17 Truly I tell you, many prophets and righteous people longed to see
what you see, but did not see it, and to hear what you hear, but did not
hear it.

Verse 10: "The disciples came." D. Bauer sees this as an instance of
discourse/narrative integration (p. 131). "The disciples came
(*proselthontes*) and said." *Proserchomai* is overwhelmingly peculiar to
Matthew. Combined with *lego* it serves as a more or less stereotyped formula by which to introduce direct discourse. But *proserchomai* also has
a more profound meaning, which lies in the cultic overtones it can acquire.
In Hellenistic Greek literature, it is often used in the sense of coming
before a deity; in the LXX, it frequently denotes the act of approaching
God or of coming for sacrifice or worship; and in the writings of Josephus,
it appears in connection with stepping before a king. *Proserchomai* occurs 52 times in Matthew, and in no less than 49 it signals the approach
of others to Jesus. On three occasions, those who approach Jesus address
him directly as Kyrios. In two of these three occasions the salutation is
followed by a prayer for deliverance. Finally, Matthew often couples
proserchomai with verbs that themselves have a cultic coloring ("to fall
down and worship, to serve, beseech, kneel down before").
All this suggest that for Matthew *proserchomai* has acquired a cultic
connotation. It ascribes a lordly dignity to Jesus, portraying him as a person of royal dignity whom the disciples approach in full awareness of his
majestic status.

Verse 11: "To you it has been given (*hoti hymin dedotai*)." The use
of the verb *dedotai* in the passive was originally dictated by Jewish reluc-
tance to pronounce the divine name. Consequently, the expression "it has
been given to you" is a circumlocution for "God has given to you." "To
know"—"knowledge" is a distinctive mark of the disciples of Jesus.
Moreover, by standing in juxtaposition to *dedotai*, *gnonai* characterizes
the knowledge of the disciples as a gift of God.

"To you (*hymin*) . . . to them (*ekeinois*)." By his use of antithetic parallelism, Matthew starkly contrasts the disciples with the Jews. As he talks with his disciples in private, he tells them not only of their own privileged status but also of the judgment befalling the Jews. In contrast to the blessing that he pronounces upon the disciples stand the oft-repeated references to the Jewish crowds as "them (*autois*)." In this way Matthew effectively makes of *autois* a technical term designating the Jews, with the connotation of "apartness" or "alienation." By means of it, Matthew pictures the Jews as a people who stand outside the circle of those who participate in the joy and salvation of the Messianic Age.

"The secrets of the kingdom of heaven (*ta mystēria tēs basilaias tōn ouranōn*)." These are "those insights (knowledge) concerning God's kingly rule which God reveals to the disciples, or Church, in and through Jesus" (*Parables*, 44). Matthew uses the plural of *mysterion* while Mark uses the singular (4:1). Thereby Matthew indicates that the secrets of the Kingdom must be defined comprehensively. Mark's *mysterion* is eschatological and Christological in a very strict sense, proclaiming that the kingdom of God has come in the person and words and works of Jesus. Matthew, for his part, is thinking in broader categories. He envisages not only eschatology, but ethics as well, and he expresses this with the plural number, *mysteria*. Matthew designates some of his parables "parables of the Kingdom" and in these parables the accent is squarely on matters of ethics (Hidden Treasure, Pearl, Unforgiving Servant).

Why is Matthew so keen upon a dual emphasis incorporating ethics and eschatology? This can be traced back to Matthew's view of history. As a Christian, Matthew is firmly convinced that the eschatological rule of God has already come in Jesus. However, this rule has not brought about an end of history, as Jewish expectation would have it. In taking account of these two factors, Matthew then affirms that the secrets of the Kingdom, knowledge about the kingly rule of God, have to do with those matters of both faith (eschatology) and life (ethics), which together constitute the Christian existence between the Resurrection and the *parousia* as it is governed by the rule of God. The disciples and the Church are privileged as regards the quality of revelation they have received. This revelation comes to them as a gift of God through Jesus. It consists of knowledge of the secrets of the kingdom of heaven, which embraces the whole of ethics and eschatology, the faith and life of the disciple living under God's kingly rule.

"But to them it has not been given (*ekeinois de ou dedotai*)." "To you . . . to them" establishes the antithetic parallel. In compliance with Israel's tradition, Matthew refers both the granting of knowledge and the withholding of knowledge to the divine resolve of God. In this way, Matthew introduces the twin categories of grace and judgment, applying the former to the disciples and the latter to the Jews.

Verse 12: "More will be given." The "more" the disciples will receive and the "abundance" they will then have is the kingdom itself. Here Jesus declares to the disciples that inherent in the capacity granted them by God to comprehend divine revelation is the promise of inheriting God's latter-day kingdom. The message of Jesus as it concerns the disciples is one that emphasizes their privileged status. This status results from the unique time they live in, the divine revelation imparted to them, and the glorious promise they are given. This is the joyful side of the message of Jesus in this pericope. The other, somber side concerns the Jews.

Verse 13: "Why I speak to them in parables." According to the tradition Matthew has incorporated here, the Jews cannot comprehend the parables (cf. *supra,* p. 217).

Verse 14-15: There are good reasons to believe that the quotation from Isaiah is a later interpolation. On pages 27-28 of his *Parables*, J. Kingsbury lists eight such reasons.

Verse 16: "Blessed (*makarioi*) are your eyes." In calling the disciples "blessed," Jesus imputes to them the joy that is distinctive of the person who participates in the salvation associated with God's eschatological rule.

Verse 17: "Prophets and righteous people longed." In their original form, the force of verses 16-17 lay in the recognition that he who spoke these words, the earthly Jesus, was in truth Israel's long-awaited Messiah. Matthew not only transmits this idea, but stresses it still more by placing the particle "Truly" at the head of verse 17, the purpose of which is to underline the messianic authority of this saying of Jesus.

The corollary in verses 16f of the fact that Jesus is the Messiah is the thought that the disciples have been given to understand this, and thereby to share in the joyous events of salvation which he has inaugurated. The disciples are furthermore said to "see" and "hear," that is, they are the intelligent eye- and ear-witnesses to the words and work of Jesus which comprise the dawn of the Messianic Age. Indeed, the disciples are even declared to be more honored than "prophets and righteous men", all those in the history of Israel, namely, who longed in vain to experience the breaking in of the Messianic Age. Accordingly, throughout this pericope the disciples are described as of privileged status because their age is the Age of the Messiah.

In the parables Jesus imparts the "secrets of the kingdom of heaven" to the disciples. These secrets are: (1) In the person of Jesus the Kingdom of Heaven, or the end-time rule of God confronts people as a present, though hidden reality tending toward its consummation in the final judgment Jesus will conduct at the end of the age (13:31-32, 33). (2) Through hearing the proclamation of the Gospel of the kingdom, people are called to decision for or against it. Wholehearted allegiance is asked of those who accept, and they are led by it to love God with heart, soul, and mind and their neighbor as themselves (13:8, 29). (3) Until the consummation of the age all persons live under the influence of one of two opposing powers: that of God's end-time rule in allegiance to the earthly and exalted Jesus, or in the kingdom of evil under the aegis of Satan (13:24-30), (3642). (4) Disciples of Jesus living in the sphere of God's end-time rule are summoned to be single-mindedly dedicated to doing the "greater righteousness," God's will as taught by Jesus (13:44-45).

The Interpretation of the Parable of the Sower, 13:18-23

> **18** "Hear then the parable of the sower. **19** When anyone hears the word of the kingdom and does not understand it, the evil one comes and snatches away what is sown in the heart; this is what was sown on the path. **20** As for what was sown on rocky ground, this is the one who hears the word and immediately receives it with joy; **21** yet such a person has no root, but endures only for a while, and when trouble or persecution arises on account of the word, that person immediately falls away. **22** As for what was sown among thorns, this is the one who hears the word, but the cares of the world and the lure of wealth choke the word, and it yields nothing. **23** But as for what was sown on good soil, this is the one who hears the word and understands it, who indeed bears fruit and yields, in one case a hundredfold, in another sixty, and in another thirty."

Verse 18: "Hear, then (*Hymeis oun akousate*)."—the emphatic "you" once more distinguishes the disciples, who "understand," while the "hear" is a vivid reminder that the Interpretation is based on the Shema, which in turn establishes the pattern of the Sower (cf. Parable of the Sower, pp. 211-12). The first three sowings are those that are unsuccessful.

Verse 19: "Sown on the path"—(cf. v. 4) "Some seeds fell on the path." We do not have to speculate about the meaning of this unsuccessful sowing; it is clearly indicated in the interpretation. "When anyone hears the word of the kingdom and does not understand it, the evil one comes and snatches away what is sown in the heart; this is what was sown on the path" (v. 19). Only here in the Interpretation does Matthew mention "the heart (*he kardia*)." The fate of the seed in this instance depends on whether "the heart" is fulfilling its spiritual role or not. It is with those who hear the word and "do not understand (*pantos akouontos . . . kai me syn-ientos*") that the evil one is successful. In the Purpose of the Parables passage, which came just before the Interpretation, Matthew has just depicted the ignorant crowds with a "formula quotation" as a people "whose heart has grown dull," a people who "do not understand with the heart (*mepote . . . tē kardia synōsin*"), a people who see and hear without seeing or hearing or understanding (*synienai*, vv. 14, 15). In this first instance, the listeners' deficiency is closely associated with the "heart." The sowing is unsuccessful because the listener does not fulfill the divine demand which the scribes found implied in one of the phrases of the Shema, "You shall love the Lord your God *with all your heart*."

Verse 20: "Sown on rocky ground" (cf. v. 5): "Other seeds fall on rocky ground." Again the meaning is indicated in the Interpretation. "This is he who hears the word and immediately receives it with joy; yet such a person has no root, but endures only for a while, and when trouble or persecution arises on account of the word, immediately he falls away" (vv. 20-21). This last sentence places the person in a well-known category: those who are not prepared to undergo suffering or martyrdom for the sake of God's word. In times of persecution, the people of God had to choose between "things of this world (*ta proskaira*) and "things of the world to come (*ta aiōnia*)." Not having any roots, or having only dried up roots, was a traditional image of instability and transitoriness. The type of hearer depicted in verses 20-21 is, in other words, the one who denies God and falls away in order to save his soul (life).

Along with the "salvation-historical" and the "cosmic" dimensions of the kingdom of heaven, Matthew also stresses the "existential," or the personal, dimension. This has been apparent from the beginning of Jesus' ministry to Israel. New life can result from an encounter with the Rule of God. The occasion for such encounters is the presence of the kingdom in the person and words and deeds of Jesus Messiah, the Son of God. Encounter with Jesus places a person in a crisis of decision. The choice is between "repenting" and "entering" the Kingdom and rejecting Jesus as the Messiah (cf. Matthew 11-12). In Matthew's own time following the resurrection, encounter with the Church's proclamation of the Gospel of the kingdom precipitates the same crisis of decision. One either "under-stands" the word (v. 23) and is "baptized" and observes all that Jesus has commanded (28:19-20), or one does "not understand" the word and consequently falls under the power of Satan (v. 19).

Verse 21: "When trouble or persecution arises"—the social and reli-gious climate in which Matthew's readers found themselves was one of intense conflict (cf. Introduction, Sectarian Language, p. 10). On the one hand, Christians were living in close proximity to hostile pagans. They were being hauled into court by gentile authorities, hated "by all," and even put to death (10:18, 22; 13:21; 24:9). On the other hand, they were also living in close proximity to a vigorous Jewish community. The parable of the Weeds (13:24-30) may refer to this directly, while the story of the payment of the temple tax (17:24-27) can be interpreted to mean that the Jewish Christians in Matthew's community were being encouraged, despite their "freedom," not to offend Jews by refusing to participate in the collection of contributions throughout Jewry in support of the Patriarchy at Jamnia. This speaks for close contact between Jews and Matthew's readers.

Verse 22: "Sown among thorns"—(cf. v. 7). "Other seeds fell among thorns." Turning to the interpretation we read: "This is the one who hears the word, but the cares of the world and the lure of wealth choke the word, and it yields nothing." The things which choke the word in this situation are amply and briefly denoted as wealth, i.e., mammon (*ploutos*). The "cares of the world [this age] (*hē merimna tou aiōnos*)" is the subjective aspect, humanity's spiritual bondage to this world.

The proper attitude to wealth and property was found by the scribes to be enshrined in the formula of the Shema: "You shall love the Lord your God *with all your might*"; for them "might" denoted mammon: riches and property.

"Cares of the world and lure of wealth." There are indications that Matthew's community was rather well-off and lived near an urban center. Matthew's readers were accustomed to dealing in a wide range of money. While Matthew makes no reference whatever to the *lepton*, the smallest unit of money cited in the Gospels, he refers to six other coins varying in value between 1/4 cent (*kodrantes*) and $1,088 (*talanton*). If the three terms silver, gold, and talent, are taken into account, they occur in Matthew's Gospel no fewer than twenty-eight times, as compared with a single use of the word silver by Mark and a fourfold use of it by Luke.

Verse 23: "What was sown on good soil"—(cf. v. 7). "This," we read in the Interpretation, "is the one who hears the word and understands it; who indeed bears fruit, and yields, in one case a hundredfold, in another sixty, and in another thirty. Once again, we note the significance that Matthew attaches to *understanding* (*synieis*). The somewhat vague expression in Mark, "and accept (the word)," has been sharpened in Matthew: "understand."

The decisive point is this: the hearing and the understanding become an event. "To bear fruit" is a traditional image for an active loyalty to the covenant, a righteousness that was shown in life and in *deed*. This manner of speech is found in the words of Jesus, especially well preserved in Matthew. We find there also the expression *to do* (the heavenly) Father's will, do the word, do the words of Jesus. In verse 23, the double significance of the term *poiein* is utilized felicitously, associations being made with both the image and the abstract—to do (form) fruit and to do (effect) what the word says.

"Hundredfold, sixty, thirty." The significance of these numbers is, strangely, not made clear in the Interpretation. But the overall structure of the "tract of seven parables" suggests a solution. Those who bear fruit a hundredfold are those whose obedient heart determines that they sacrifice not only their property (might, mammon) but even the most precious things of all—their life (soul). These are the martyrs. Those who bear fruit sixtyfold have an obedient heart and give up their goods, but are not compelled to give their life for the sake of the Word. Those who bear fruit thirtyfold also have an obedient and undivided heart, but are not compelled to offer either their life or all their property for God's sake. Whoever receives Jesus may be likened to a "good tree" that produces "good fruit" or to a "good man" who brings forth "good things" out of a "good treasure" (12:35)—that is to say, this person, like Jesus Son of God himself, does the will of the heavenly Father and so abounds in rightousness more than the scribes and Pharisees (5:20). At Jesus' coming, this disciple will be identified by Jesus as one of the "righteous" who will "inherit eternal life" (25:46).

The Parable of the Wheat and the Weeds, 13:24-30

The parable of the Sower was the product of Jesus' long, prayerful meditation on the Shema, the creed of his people. It seems likely that Jesus also spoke the other six parables that make up the "tract of seven parables" (tares, mustard seed, leaven, treasure, pearl of great price, fish in the net). Then, in the course of long, prayerful meditation on his Master's parable of the Sower, some unknown disciple of Jesus discovered that the other six parables could be arranged in such a way as to expand and illustrate the parable of the Sower in its different parts.

We do not know who this person was, but we do know what kind of a person he was. He was a "scribe who had become a learner in the kingdom of heaven"; he had understood his Master's directions on what to do if one thirsts "to know the secrets of the kingdom"; and he had made use of his authority to "bring out of his treasure what is new and what is old" (v. 52). Traces of this contemplative's elegant work are observable in other parts of Matthew's Gospel; the long temptation narrative seems to have come from his hand.

The parable of the Sower is divided between the inadequate and the adequate hearers. The inadequate hearers are represented by the seed which falls on the path, on the stony ground, and among thorns. The adequate hearers are represented by the seed which falls upon good ground.

Each division of the parable of the Sower raises questions—questions which are answered by one or more of the other six parables of the tract. First, the seed by the wayside and the question it raises. "As he sowed, some seeds fell on the path . . ." (v. 4)—this is the case of the completely hardened person who hears the word but does not understand it, so the Evil One comes and steals away what has been sown in his heart. Anyone who meditates over this finds himself confronted with questions that require answers. How can there be such utterly hopeless parts of God's field, such hopeless cases among his people? Where have they come from: why does God not sweep them away: what will be the end of them? It is precisely these questions that are answered by the parable that comes first after the Interpretation, the weeds among the wheat.

> **24** He put before them another parable: The kingdom of heaven may be compared to someone who sowed good seed in his field; **25** but while everybody was asleep, an enemy came and sowed weeds among the wheat, and then went away. **26** So when the plants came up and bore grain, then the weeds appeared as well. **27** And the slaves of the householder came and said to him, 'Master, did you not sow good seed in your field? Where, then, did these weeds come from?' **28** He answered, 'An enemy has done this.' The slaves said to him, 'Then do you want us to go and gather them?' **29** But he replied, 'No; for in gathering the weeds you would uproot the wheat along with them. **30** Let both of them grow together until the harvest, and at harvest time I will tell the reapers, Collect the weeds first and bind them in bundles to be burned, but gather the wheat into my barn.' "

Verse 24: "Put before them (*autois*)"—i.e., the crowds. The setting of the parable is the lake (13:1-3a) where Jesus is addressing the Jewish crowds apologetically.

"The kingdom of heaven." The "kingdom of heaven" refers to God's Kingdom, or kingly rule, as a present and future reality. God has always been the ruler of the world and, in a special sense, of Israel. In Jesus, however, God has manifested his rule eschatologically, and, through Jesus, also in the Twelve. God continues to exercise his rule in the Church through Jesus, the Kyrios. Finally, at the Parousia of Jesus, the Son of Man, God will manifest his rule in all its fullness and glory before the whole human race. The "kingdom of heaven" is no less than God's total salvation for mankind as revealed in Jesus. As a result, the term "kingdom of heaven" can denote the message Matthew's Church proclaims, the doctrine it teaches, the hope it cherishes, and the life it is to lead.

"May be compared (*homoiōthē*)." This aorist passive form of the verb *homoioo* is peculiar to Matthew (cf. 18:23; 22:2). Some translate it in the same manner as the other Matthean idiom, "is like *homoios estin*" on the grounds that both forms are derived from the Aramaic. But since Matthew wrote in Greek and was a careful editor, it is doubtful whether he regarded the matter so simply. Elsewhere, the future passive form (*homoiōthesetai*, 25:1; 7:24, 26) clearly points to the future . By the same token *homoiothe* clearly points to the past. It follows that for Matthew the "kingdom of heaven" is a present reality and already has a history behind it. This has an important bearing on the interpretation of the parable of the weeds.

"Compared to someone (*anthropo*)." This "someone" who supervises the sowing is identified in verse 27 as the "householder (*oikodespotes*)." This term is genuinely Matthean; it is applied to Jesus (10:25), God (20:1, 11; 21:33), and even Christians (13:52; 24:43). Here the context shows that the "man" is a transparent symbol for Jesus, who in Matthew's time is the exalted Kyrios: the man is addressed as "sir (*Kyrie*)" in verse 27. This "master of the house" is authoritative and governs both the direction and the climax of the parable (vv. 29-30), through his slaves (disciples) and reapers (angels of judgment).

"Good seed in his field"—in view of the setting (Jesus addressing the Jewish crowds beside the lake) the field is "Israel" (i.e., the people of Israel), not a geographical area. We take Matthew's opening statement at face value: Jesus spoke another parable to "them," (i.e., the Jews).

Good seed in his field. As in the parable of the Sower, the seed alludes to the Word. The relationship between the good seed that is sown and the stalks of wheat that bud and produce fruit (v. 26) is the relationship that exists between the Word of proclamation and the person in whom the Word has taken hold and exercises its influence. Matthew has described this for us already in 13:23.

"The man, the master of the house, is Jesus, the field is Israel, and the seed is the Word, which, moreover, is good in the sense that it is intended to beget a people who will live under God's kingly rule, conforming to his will in works of obedience and love. With these actors in mind, it is evident that behind the statement in verse 24b that the man sowed good seed in his field is the idea that Jesus has come, and, through the vehicle of his own message (as Jesus Messiah) and the Kerygma of his Church (as Jesus Kyrios), he has preached the 'Word' in Israel, a Word designed to produce a nation living under and doing the will of God" (*Parables*, 71).

Verse 25: "An enemy (*ho echthros*)." The opposing forces are Jesus, the master of the house, with his slaves and reapers, on the one hand,

and his "enemy," i.e., the personal adversary of the master of the house, on the other. The "enemy" is an allusion to the Devil or Satan (cf. 13:39). That the Greek reads *echthros* and not, as we might expect, *poneros*, simply attests to the fact that *echthros* was already firmly anchored in this parable by the time Matthew adopted it.

At 10:36 Matthew reveals how he understands *echthros*: "and a man's enemies will be the members of his own household." The passage deals with the nature of discipleship and the high price of commitment. There Jesus points out that the disciple's salvation hinges upon his professed allegiance to Jesus (10:32f). But as a direct result of such allegiance, the disciple may well find himself at odds with his own relatives (10:34). Hence, according to 10:36, an enemy is that person in whom the disciple comes into conflict because of his allegiance to Jesus.

The devil is the enemy, indeed, the arch-enemy of both Jesus and his Church (13:25, 28, 39). He is the personification of a will that is inimical to all for which Jesus stands. We also note here that the object of the enemy's attack is what belongs to the master rather than the master himself—the devil is enemy more in the ecclesiological sphere then in the Christological sphere. Just as Jesus came to raise up a people who would do the will of God (v. 24b), so Satan, too has been at work in Israel, to raise up a people that is unfaithful to God and to the doing of his will (v. 25).

"Sowed weeds (*zizania*) among the wheat." Darnel (*Lolium temulentum*) is a poisonous Palestinian weed that is botanically related to wheat and all but indistinguishable from it until the individual plants begin to mature. The Rabbis looked upon darnel as a degenerate form of wheat, the product of the sexual excesses that took place even in the plant world before the flood (cf. Gen 6:12). In haggadic etymology the Aramaic word for darnel, *zunim* (plural of *zun*), is derived from the verb *zanah*, which means to "commit fornication." Matthew has inserted the word "adulterous" into his Markan text in two places (12:39; 16:4). In both instances, Jesus is entangled in debate with the leaders of the Jews ("scribes and Pharisees," 12:38; "Pharisees and Sadducees," 16:1). These interpolations are thinly veiled allusions to Old Testament prophets (Hosea, Jeremiah, and Ezekiel), who openly denounced the Israel of their time for being religiously unfaithful to God. Matthew makes the same charge against the contemporary Judaism with which he is involved (cf. 8:11; 21:43).

Verse 26: "The weeds appeared also." This brings us to the key situation in the parable of the Tares—the presence of wheat and darnel side by side in the same field. In terms of the circumstances of Matthew's Church, this becomes an apt description for the presence of two quite different bodies of "Israelites" existing side by side but in opposition to each other—the Church, or "true Israel," and Pharisaic Judaism, or "unbelieving Israel."

Verse 27: "The servants (*hoi douloi*, lit. "slaves") of the householder." In the New Testament a slave is one who possesses no personal autonomy and is totally subject to the will of another, be it that of God, man, or other forces. Matthew, in harmony with other New Testament writers, applies a religious connotation to the word "slave." The apostles and other leaders are "slaves," yet the entire body of Matthew's Church is expected to identify itself with the slave. In Matthew the term "slave" is undergoing a process of "Christianization." Matthew never designates contemporary Jews as slaves. Where the word slave refers to a body of Jews as such, it signifies the prophets of the Old Testament. Otherwise, it is reserved for the apostles, martyrs, missionaries, and member of the Church. In our parable, it is the Church that is speaking through the mouth of the slaves (vv. 27f).

"Master, did you not sow." The two questions asked by the slaves reflect disquietitude over the fact that in spite of the coming of the Messiah and the missionary efforts of the Church, there was such a large segment of the chosen nation that had not responded to the Word in obedience and faith, and a genuine desire that the whole of Jewry should be won to the Way that finds its center in Jesus (cf. v.29; 10:6; 15:24).

Verse 28: "An enemy has done this." The failure to convert the Jews did not lack an explanation in the eyes of Matthew and his Church. Satan had been at work among this people. Because of this, a chasm existed between the two camps of "Israelites." The one community, described as wheat and represented by the slaves, was living under the dominion of God. The other, described as darnel, was living under the dominion of Satan (cf. 12:22-37). "To go and gather them?"—this question is at once both an inquiry and a proposal. The Church, or at least an element within it, advocated forcing a formal and irrevocable separation between itself and the rest of Judaism.

Verse 29: "No; lest . . . you root up (*ekrizosete*) the wheat." The Church is not to effect a final withdrawal from unbelieving Israel, thus invoking judgment upon it. However, the specific reason given for making this decision (lest the wheat be uprooted) betrays concern for the Church's missionary outreach. Jesus Kyrios calls upon his followers to undertake further missionary endeavor. It is his will that none of those in reprobate Israel should be lost who might be brought to acknowledge him as Lord.

Verse 30: "Grow together until the harvest." This injunction contains several emphases. To begin with, it presupposes the passage of time; hence, it documents the delay of the Parousia as experienced by Matthew's Church. Further, the words "Let both of them grow together" are a declaration to Matthew's Church to the effect that, again it is the resolve of Jesus Kyrios that for the time being the wheat and the darnel (true Israel and unbelieving Israel) are not to be irrevocably cut off from each other.

The parable of the weeds gives at least an indication that Matthew's Church was very much in contact with Pharisaic Judaism. Regardless of the large measure of internal autonomy it had attained, it was at least outwardly affiliated with Judaism and perhaps even maintained some sort of relationship with its league of synagogues.

A Pair of Parables: The Mustard Seed, The Leaven, 13:31-33

The parable of the Sower is divided into three classes of inadequate hearers and one class of adequate hearers. The inadequate hearers are represented by the seed which falls on the path, on the stony ground, and among thorns. The adequate hearers are represented by the seed which falls upon good ground.

Each division of the parable of the Sower raises questions—questions which are answered by one or more of the other six parables of the "tract of seven parables." We have just seen how the questions raised by the seed on the path are answered by the parable of the weeds among the wheat. Questions raised by the second group of inadequate hearers are answered by two parables, a pair—the parables of the mustard seed and of the leaven.

The note of universalism, the broader appeal of the Gospel is present also in the parables of the kingdom in chapter 13. Subtle indications of universalism are expressed in the reference to the extensive growth of the mustard plant, and in the likeness of the kingdom to a net 'that was thrown into the sea and caught fish of every kind' (13:47). A much clearer indication of universalism appears, however, in the interpretation of the parable of the weeds where the field in which the servants of the household sow good seed is "the world" (13:38).

> 31 He put before them another parable: "The kingdom of heaven is like a mustard seed that someone took and sowed in his field; 32 it is the smallest of all the seeds, but when it has grown it is the greatest of shrubs and becomes a tree, so that the birds of the air come and make nests in its branches." 33 He told them another parable: "The kingdom

of heaven is like yeast that a woman took and mixed in with three measures of flour until all of it was leavened."

Verse 31: "Which someone (*anthrōpos*) took." In the preceding parable (Weeds), "someone (*anthrōpos*) who sowed (aor. part.) good seed in his field." Here, a "someone" (*anthrōpos*) sowed (aor. ind.) in his field. Matthew evidently wanted to establish a parallel between the two. And again, "someone" is Jesus (cf. v. 24). "And sowed (*espeiren*)"—(aor. indic), while the action in the rest of the parable is described in the present tense. It is also worth noting that Matthew has changed Mark's text in this instance (cf. Mark 4:31b). Matthew is making a statement about a past event. "In his field;" a comparison with Mark and Luke reveals that only the Matthean rescension of the Mustard Seed contains this phrase. On the other hand, it also appears in Weeds (cf. 13:24b). Now it is true that the mustard plant was not generally known as either a garden herb (Luke) or a wild bush (Mark), but as Matthew states, as a cultivated shrub that the farmer normally placed in his field. Still, the possibility is strong that Matthew employs this phrase, not so much to display a superior knowledge of agricultural practice, but to assimilate the parable of the mustard seed to the parable of the Weeds. If this is the case, Matthew makes mention of the "field" in the parable of the mustard seed, just as in the parable of the weeds, because it alludes to "Israel."

Matthew has used the aorist indicative of the verb "sow" in order that the parable might contain a statement about a past event; the man stands for Jesus and the field for Israel. When taken together, these facts divulge that Matthew has drafted this clause so that the parable will affirm that Jesus brought the Kingdom of Heaven to Israel.

Verse 32: "Smallest of all the seeds . . . greatest of shrubs." The usual interpretation of Weeds centers upon this contrast, which is interpreted as depicting the meager beginning of the Kingdom and its mighty conclusion. Although technically speaking, the mustard seed is not "the smallest of all the seeds" (v. 32a), it was nonetheless proverbial among the Jews as the most minute of quantities (cf. 17:20 = Lk 17:6). Then, of no other small seed did the fully grown plant attain the size of the mustard herb. Hence, it can be said that the mustard seed depicts perfectly both the insignificant manner in which the kingdom first appeared, namely, in the person Jesus, and the glorious form it would assume at the End of the Age. Matthew prepares for Jesus, the exalted Kyrios, to assert that the "kingdom of heaven" has already come to Israel, but, contrary to Jewish expectations, in an insignificant manner, in the historical person Jesus, and, through him, also in his Church.

"When it has grown . . ." The "kingdom of heaven" is like the mustard seed also in growth. In association with the growth of the kingdom, Matthew envisages also the growth of the Church. For Matthew, his Church stands squarely within the tradition of the apostles, and God's kingly rule in Jesus Kyrios is a present reality in it. The parable of the mustard seed shows how closely Matthew can relate the Church to the "kingdom of heaven" without, however, identifying the two. Even as the "kingdom of heaven" confronted the Jews in Jesus, so it confronts them at a later time in the Church.

"The birds of the air come." The picture of a tree in which birds nest or beasts find shade is a familiar Old Testamemt image for a mighty empire. Consequently, it is appropriate as an allusion to God's fully established kingdom. "The birds of the air" also represents a veiled reference to the Gentiles. J. Jeremias points out that *kataskenoō* is an "eschatological technical term for the incorporation of the Gentiles into the people of God" (*Parables*, p. 147). Matthew often expresses the idea that the kingdom of God will comprise both Jews and Gentiles.

Matthew utilizes this parable to give expression to the conviction that the Church, and not the Jews, is the eschatological community of God, because the Church is the place where God is even now gathering together Jews and Gentiles into one body in anticipation of his magnificent kingdom.

As noted above, this, the usual interpretation, centers upon the contrast between the meager beginning of the Kingdom and its mighty conclusion. B. Gerhaardson's awareness of the "tract of seven parables" turns his attention in another direction. In that tract, the Mustard Seed is the expansion upon the "seed on rocky ground." And in the Interpretation it was explained that these hearers fall away "when trouble or persecution arises on account of the word" (v. 21). Gerhaardson emphasizes that we must pay attention to the story itself and what happens in it. "There can be an enormous growth, a whole tree, because the mustard seed is taken and sown in the field. The mystery lies not in the contrast between the beginning and the end, but in fact that a powerful process, with immense consequences, is set in motion when a little seed is placed, hidden, buried, in the ground. The verb *speirein* (v. 31) is a key word in this parable. The mustard seed is the smallest of all seeds, *but when it is sown in the field* it shows its miraculous power and reaches its fulfillment. This is where the emphasis is" (*Seven Parables*, 21–22). The blood of martyrs is not spilt in vain. One of the secrets of the kingdom is that when a sacrifice is made, when a life is offered, then God's field becomes fruitful, its plants luxuriant and its harvest plenteous.

Verse 33: "Took and mixed in with ("hid," *enekrypsen*) in three measures of flour." A large amount of flour—it would produce enough bread to feed one hundred persons at a single meal. Again, the usual interpretation concentrates on the contrast. "The contrast between the small lump of leaven and the great mass of bread is essentially the same as that between the tiny mustard seed and the 'tree' resulting from it" (*Parables*, 86). Although leaven is a traditional Jewish metaphor for "bad things" having great effects, the stress in this parable does not lie on the "bad things" but on the "great effects," and sometimes the power of leaven could be used positively, as of the leavening influence of the Torah.

Again Gerhaardson's awareness of the "tract of seven parables" turns his attention elsewhere. A woman takes the leaven, "hides, mixes in with" three measures of flour, and then come the results. Note the use of the somewhat strange word "hide." Because this happens the leaven has its miraculous effect. So long as it is in its own bowl, it is alone and is as unfruitful as the seed in its bin. It is not said in this parable that the leaven is little: what is said is that the leaven penetrates a huge lump of dough; it fills the whole measure.

Again we need to keep in mind the Interpretation, with its emphasis on falling away in time of tribulation and persecution. The leaven can leaven the lump, (influence it, change its character) under one condition only—it must, to use drastic language, "die" in the dough. When this happens, the dough is changed into its likeness and becomes large and powerful. The Leaven illuminates why some disciples have to give their lives for the sake of the "kingdom of heaven."

Matthew's "Purpose of the Parables" Passage, 13:34-35

Matthew's attitudes and positions appear in the changes he makes in Mark's "Purpose of the Parables" passage, and in the formula quotation he has attached. This is another point where discourse and narrative are integrated. The discourses are integrated into the narrative framework, and there is no alternation between narrative and discourse material. There is much "discourse" in the narrative section and there are narrative elements within the discourses.

In the same way as the Sermon on the Mount and the Missionary Discourse, the parables of the kingdom (ch. 13) are related to the surrounding context. Chapter 13 stands in the midst of the rejection of Jesus by Israel as a whole. The repudiation by all segments of Israel, except the disciples, explains why Jesus turns away from the crowds and turns toward his disciples in chapter 13. "The following material (chs. 14–16) gives concrete examples of this dual turning: Jesus has less to do with the crowds and repeatedly withdraws from his opponents, while at the same time Jesus reveals himself to his disciples, finally drawing from them the confession that he is the Christ, the Son of God" (Bauer, 130).

> **34** Jesus told the crowds all these things in parables: without a parable he told them nothing. **35** This was to fulfill what had been spoken through the prophet:
> "I will open my mouth to speak in
>   parables;
>   I will proclaim what has been hidden
>   from the foundation of the world."

Verse 34: "To the crowds in parables"—in the addition to Mark's text, Matthew explicitly restates his position regarding the crowds and parables. "Nothing (*ouden*) without a parable"—by substituting *ouden* for Mark's *ouk*, Matthew turns Mark's matter of fact statement "he did not speak to them except in parables" (4:34) into an emphatic assertion. Matthew drops completely Mark's concluding remark, "but privately he explained everything to his disciples," thus eliminating any vestige of what appears in Mark to be a double tradition.

Matthew's elimination of Mark's reference to the need of the disciples for explanation is motivated by his insistence that by virtue of their call, the disciples are already enlightened and therefore do comprehend the person and message of Jesus. His other editorial changes all tend to place Jesus (and the disciples) opposite the crowds and to accentuate the fact that intercourse between the two groups is characterized by the speaking in parables, i.e., what for the crowds is incomprehensible speech. Verse 34, therefore, recapitulates the first part of Matthew's parable chapter by depicting the impasse that exists between Jesus (and the Church) and the Jews.

Verse 35: "Spoken by the prophet"—Matthew adds a formula quotation, which with his interest in prophecy, he assigned to "the prophet," even though it comes from the Psalm 78:2" (*Matthew*, 149). In common with all formula quotations, verse 35 is intended to document the fulfillment of Scripture: Jesus is acting according to the prophesied resolve of God when he speaks in parables. Such fulfillment of Scripture is important for Matthew because the validity of Jesus' speech in parables is directly dependent upon its having been authorized by God himself. The quotation also testifies to the Messiahship of Jesus. Because it is in and through Jesus that the hidden revelation of God is disclosed, the revelation that the prophets and righteous of old desired in vain to see and hear (cf. v. 16), Jesus must necessarily be the Messiah.

"What has been hidden" (*kekrymmena*). The quotation is also a recapitulation of Jesus' apology in parables. "What has been hidden" comprises the content of the parables of Jesus. Yet the parable, according to the context (13:10b), can only be understood by the person to whom God has given the necessary insight. Hence, there is a perfect correlation in the quotation between parable and revelation, between form and content. Both possess the quality of "hiddenness"; in both the intent is comprehensible only to the eye of faith. This quotation tersely captures the hallmark of 13:1-4: the deep division between the Church and unbelieving Judaism. Finally, this quotation attests to the eschatological consciousness of Matthew's Church. Since Matthew's Church regards itself as the recipient of the divine revelation that has been hidden from the foundation of the world but now made known through the parables of Jesus, it gives testimony to its conviction that it is the true people of God.

Homily on the Parable of the Tares, 13:36-43

Verse 36 begins the second half of Matthew's parable chapter, which consists of parable material imparted to the disciples in private. At the beginning of the parable chapter, "Jesus went out of the house" (v. 1), sat beside the sea, and great crowds gathered. The return of Jesus to the house (v. 36) signals his break with the crowds and symbolically, his break with Israel. It is not an accident that this rupture occurs halfway through the Gospel. Henceforth Israel will show greater and greater hostility, and Jesus will turn more and more to his disciples, to devote himself to their formation.

> 36 Then he left the crowds and went into the house. And his disciples approached him, saying, "Explain to us the parable of the weeds of the field." 37 He answered, "The one who sows the good seed is the Son of Man; 38 the field is the world, and the good seed are the children of the kingdom; the weeds are the children of the evil one, 39 and the enemy who sowed them is the devil; the harvest is the end of the age, and the reapers are angels. 40 Just as the weeds are collected and burned up with fire, so will it be at the end of the age. 41 The Son of Man will send his angels, and they will collect out of his kingdom all causes of sin and all evildoers, 42 and they will throw them into the furnace of fire, where there will be weeping and gnashing of teeth. 43 Then the righteous will shine like the sun in the kingdom of their father. Let anyone with ears listen!"

Verse 36: "Left the crowds and went into the house." This is a major change of setting—Matthew now pictures Jesus and his disciples in the house alone. The teaching of the second half of the parable chapter is directed exclusively to the disciples. In Mark *oikia—oikos* not only designates a dwelling, but is often also a veiled reference to Mark's Church. In the activity of Jesus "in the house" Mark grounds the kerygmatic, didactic, cultic, and apologetic practices that took place in the assembly of the Christian community to which he belonged. In Matthew, on the other hand, the "house" is a specific dwelling in Capernaum but nothing more.

Verse 36: "Disciples approached (*proselthon*) to him, saying" (Cf. 13:10). When Matthew invokes the idiom "And his disciples came to him and said" he is attributing a divine dignity to Jesus, i.e., the disciples "approach" Jesus with the same reverent demeanor that would be due to a king or deity. Hence, Matthew is once again portraying the earthly Jesus in the stature of the exalted Kyrios in order that he may speak to a situation that has become acute in the Church.

"Explain (*Diasapheson*) to us"—not to be understood as part of the ongoing efforts of Jesus to overcome the spiritual blindness of his followers, but as a homiletic expansion upon truths that were already part of the disciples' belief.

The parable of the Weeds and the so-called Explanation should really be regarded as quite separate pieces. The parable is located in the fist half of the chapter, the Explanation in the second; the parable is spoken to the crowds but the Explanation to the disciples; the setting of the parable is the lake, while that of the Explanation is the house. Despite an external similarity of language, the dissimilarity between Weeds and its alleged interpretation is so great as to require that the two pericopes be treated separately.

Verse 37: "Sows the good seed . . . the Son of Man." The function of the catalogue of terms (vv. 37–39) is simply to make the following description of the Last Judgment intelligible. Its sober style contrasts sharply with the description of the Judgment itself. From Matthew's vantage point in history, Jesus' public ministry was already a thing of the past. The "present" he has in mind here is the post-Easter situation of his own day. Here Matthew is thinking of Jesus as the "exalted Christ," the enthroned Kyrios who even now exercises his lordship. Matthew can ascribe to Jesus the present task of sowing the good seed, for it is he who, as the exalted Christ, stands behind the proclamatory activity of his Church (28:18). And as the exalted Christ, Jesus can also be expected to return at the End of the Age (24:42). Matthew's concept of Jesus as the exalted Christ, the ruling Kyrios, encompasses both his present work in the post-Easter era and his future return as Judge.

Verse 38: "The field is the world (*kosmos*)." The "world" here is synonymous with the Kingdom of the Son of Man mentioned in verse 41. It is the earthly realm over which the Son of Man rules in the "present" and comes to judge in the "future." But it is not coterminous with the Church—if Matthew had desired to identify the world with the Church we should expect to find *ekklesia* in place of "his Kingdom" in verse 41. Also, when we consider the way in which Matthew otherwise uses *kosmos* in his Gospel, he is not likely to have used it to signify the Church. "The world, the flesh, and the devil" came to sum up all that is in opposition to the kingdom. Also to be noted: "In the Danielic passage the kingdom is eternal, whereas the kingdom of the Son of man in Matthew is not eternal, but will, at the eschaton, become the kingdom of the Father (13.41-43)," (Bauer, 111).

"Children of the kingdom"—The "good seed" are the "children of the Kingdom." These, along with the angels (v. 39) stand under the banner of the Son of Man. They are of one spirit with God and consequently "akin" to God. In verse 43 this group is redefined as the "righteous" (*dikaioi*). "Sons of the evil one"—"the Evil One" is further defined as "the enemy" and "the devil" in the next verse. These emulate the Evil One and therefore are "akin" to him. In verse 41 they are described as "those who give offense" (*ta skandala*) and "evildoers" (*tous poiountas tēn anomian*).

Verse 39: "The enemy (*ho echthros*) . . . is the devil (*ho diabolos*)." Opposed to the Son of Man and his forces is, above all, the "Devil", who is also described as the "Evil One (*ho poneros*, v. 38)" and the "Enemy." In Matthew when the Devil is designated as the Evil One, he is viewed as the transcendent personification of all lawlessness; when he is designated as the Enemy, he is seen principally as the inimical will who is bent on destroying the allegiance that is due to Jesus alone.

Devil is the LXX translation of the Hebrew word *satan*. Of the two, only "satan" is a proper noun (4:10; 16:23). Theologically, there is no difference in meaning between *diabolos and satanas*. The striking thing is that in portraying the malevolent will as the Devil, or Satan, Matthew goes into surprisingly great detail. His description is such that the Devil becomes the cosmic antagonist of Jesus, the servant, and Jesus, the Son of Man.

The Devil made his debut in the Temptation story (4:13-17), where he is identified as "the Tempter (*ho peirazōn*)." His peculiar function or office is to "tempt"—to endeavor to set a person at variance with the will of God. In establishing the Devil as the counterpart of the Son of Man, Matthew ascribes to him a universal field of operations. The Devil lays claim to the whole "world" even though his authority to do so is exposed as a lie (4:8). Moreover, he has a "kingdom" where he exercises rulership (1:38). In this respect, Matthew sees the Devil at work both within the Church and beyond the Church. Testimony to the Devil's influence within the Church is Jesus' rebuke to Peter, "Get behind me, Satan!" (16:23). Testimony to the Devil's influence beyond the Church is Matthew's characterization of the leaders of the Jews as the "agents" of the Devil, for they, too. 'tempt" Jesus (22:35; 16:1).

But for all his power, the Devil is by no means a sovereign personality. He is subordinate to God (4:1) and to the Son of Man (25:31-46), and his rule is restricted to the era of the Church, since at the Latter Day he, his angels, and his "sons," i.e. those who are placed at the "left hand" of the Son of Man (25:33, 41), will be cast into the eternal fire (13:42; 25:41).

Here, in verse 39, Matthew tells us that it is none other than the Devil who has sown the "weeds," or "sons of the Evil one." The Devil, the arch-enemy of the Son of Man, is, like the latter, exercising his ruling power in the world during the present age. His ambition is to raise up for himself his own followers even (and particularly) within the Church, people whose allegiance he can claim in that he leads them to live apart from the Law of God in disobedience.

"The harvest (*ho therismos*) is the close of the age (*synteleia aiōnos*)." This "harvest at the end of the Age" is the central message of the Explanation of the Weeds. The Son of Man will send out his angels to begin the great judicial assembly which will lead into the Final Judgment. The outcome of this will be that the sons of the Evil One will experience the condemnation of fire, but the righteous will experience the splendor of the Father's Kingdom—a message that is set forth in rich apocalyptic imagery. "The close of the age" is a formula found only in Matthew. "It denotes the termination of the existing world order when present history has run its course (24.3; 28.20), after which there will be a transformation of all things and God will reign supreme (13.43; 25 34, 41; 26.29). The immediate arrival of the End of the Age will be signalled by the return of Jesus Son of Man and the beginning of the Last Judgement" (*Parables,* 107). It bears the character of promise and threat, and should motivate the Christian to reexamine his life. "Reapers are angels"—angels are a standard feature in apocalyptic scenes dealing with judgment (cf. v. 30).

An indication of universalism appears as well in the interpretation of the parable of the weeds. "The field where the servants of the household sow good seed is 'the world' (13.38)" (Bauer, 123).

Verse 41: "All causes of sin (*ta skandala*) and all evildoers (*tous poiountas tēn anomian*)." A *skandalon* is a person or thing potentially capable of causing another's spiritual ruination. Here, Matthew is thinking of people both within and without the Church who make themselves responsible for the spiritual ruination of others, either by preventing them from coming to faith in Jesus (e.g., the leaders of the Jews), or by causing those who already believe to lose their faith by persecution (e.g., Jews and Gentiles) or by the advocacy of heresy or of a way of life that conflicts with the will of God (e.g., false Christians). At 16:21 Jesus addresses Peter as "Satan," because Peter, by rejecting the idea that Jesus should suffer and die, becomes a *skandalon* for Jesus—tempting him not to do the prescribed will of God.

"All evildoers"—those both within and without the Church who strike at the heart of God's Law because they neither advocate nor keep the commandments as Jesus has promulgated them. Here the stress is on the individual's own offense—on his own disobedience towards the Law of God with its center in the works of love demanded by Jesus.

Verse 42: "The furnace of fire (*tēn kaminon tou pyros*)"—the stark alternative to the bliss of God's end-time kingdom or eternal life. "Weep and gnash"—an expression of anguish and remorse.

Verse 43: "The righteous (*hoi dikaioi*)"—the true disciples are designated by the great Old Testament and Jewish title of honor, "the righteous." "Shine like the sun"—a theme typical of Jewish apocalyptic. God himself is the source of all light. Therefore to shine like the sun, or to be made like the light of the stars, or to become like angels is to partake of God's glory (*doxa*). This means to be cleansed from all imperfection and invested with physical impeccability, moral purity, and a religious kinship to God.

A Second Pair of Parables, The Treasure, The Pearl, 13:44-46

For the relationship between the Sower and the Tract of Seven Parables, cf. Introduction to the first pair of parables (vv. 31-33). Questions raised by the third group of inadequate hearers, those among the thorns, are answered by the second pair of parables—the parables of the Treasure and of the Pearl.

> **44** "The Kingdom of heaven is like treasure hidden in a field, which someone found and hid; then in his joy he goes and sells all that he has and buys that field.
> **45** "Again, the kingdom of heaven is like a merchant in search of the fine pearls; **46** on finding one pearl of great value, he went and sold all that he had and bought it.

Verse 44: "Treasure hidden (*thēsaurō* kekrymmenō) in a field." In the Old Testament we see again and again how God and what he gives (himself, his word, his law, his ordinances, heavenly wisdom, saving knowledge) is compared to (hidden) treasure (Job, Prov, Sir, Wis), or to something that is more precious and difficult to obtain than pearls, jewels, gold, silver and other valuables (Job, Ps, Prov, Wis, Baruch). A wealth of imagery was available to the author of the parable: treasure, pearl, precious, more precious than, seek, find, obtain, buy, etc., and idea of hiddenness as well.

As the parable develops, it becomes clear that the man did not own the field when he found the treasure. "Found and his (*ekrypsen*)"—the double use of *kryptō* results in a strong emphasis on the idea of "hiddenness"—the treasure is hidden in the field and the man, when he has found it, hides it again. What is depicted here is not a simple, open transaction; there is something mysterious in the sale, for it is only afterwards that it can be seen that the man has made a good bargain. "Sells all that he has (*pōlei hosa echei*)"—reappears in the following parable.

J. Derrett has shed extraordinary light on this parable. We moderns find the parable especially perplexing. When we look at it according to our legal concepts, we conclude that the finder has apparently taken a mean or even dishonest advantage of the owner of the field. But Derrett affirms: "The finder was perfectly entitled in morals and law to do what he did. His behavior was proper, and indeed inevitable. He would have been an idiot if he had acted otherwise" (*Law in the New Testament*; cf. J. Kingsbury, *Parables*, 112–13).

The treasure, a hoard of coins, had been buried in a field during a time of war. One did not become owner of the treasure by becoming owner of the field. Movables could be acquired only by a formal taking of possession, which was indicated by a lifting or drawing; the object had to be moved. A buried treasure could be acquired only by being lifted or dragged. Treasure could not be transferred to the owner of the field by those who never owned it. The owner of the field had never acquired the treasure at all, and so he did not own it.

The finder was a day-laborer who came upon the treasure in the course of, and as a normal part of, the undertaking assigned him. Under these circumstances, if he moved the treasure, ownership would pass to his employer. But the finder had no obligation to do this. Since the owner of the field had no rights to the treasure, there was no reason why he should be told of it. No sooner had the finder found the treasure than he covered it up again. Anyone who went to the spot could lift the treasure and acquire it, and would owe nothing to anyone. The finder said nothing about the treasure and managed to buy the field.

Verse 46: "Sold all that he had (*pepraken panta hosa eichen*)." The situation of the merchant who found one pearl of great values is similar in one respect: he went and sold all that he had and bought it. But this was in the merchant's ordinary line of work. Here then is no explicit mention of the idea of "hiddenness," but it is there if we look more closely. With our fixed prices and quick sales, we westerners miss many things that would be self-evident to an easterner, for whom the art of buying and selling is to hide one's cards until the transaction is over. "An oriental merchant who has made the discovery of his life is not so foolish as to reveal it by leaping for joy. He keeps a straight face; if he says anything it is to complain that he will now be ruined, and that his wife and children will have to beg in the streets; the joy is kept for later" (B. Gerhardsson, "Seven Parables," pp. 23–24). It is important to note that it is a *merchant* who finds the pearl of great value and the phrase in the previous parable about the man going away and *in his joy* selling what he owns, is omitted here.

The situation of the finder of the treasure was decidedly different. What he did was not in his ordinary line of work. He was not skilled in finding treasures, nor did he expect to find one. His find could not be acquired with the same effort as would be used in the ordinary course of the acquirer's daily life. "Our finder could not enjoy his treasure without altering his way of life and becoming, perhaps quite incongruously, a landowner. His effort was undoubtedly greater. His joy would have been impossible without intelligent and proper exploitation of his opportunity: and evidently that meant more effort for him than the commercial speculation of the merchant" (J. Derrett, 14).

The point of Jesus' parable comes home to us. His disciples must act with the same decisiveness when they find their treasure, the "kingdom of God." This kingdom is both present and future—it has not yet been fully manifested. At present it too is hidden in part, its secret covered up, except to the eyes of faith. But the disciple knows what it is and where it is. And he is willing to sell all that he has to buy the field where the treasure lies. Common to the two parables is the "value" of the discovered objects, and the "sacrifice," or "total investment," the men make. Even as the laborer and the merchant responded by selling all they possessed in order to obtain, respectively, the field with its treasure and the pearl, so the disciple responds to God's kingly rule by committing himself without reserve to the doing of God's will.

Concluding Parable (The Net), and Conclusion, 13:47-53

After listing three classes of inadequate hearers, the parable of the Sower cites one class of adequate hearers: the seed that "fell on good soil and brought forth grain, some a hundredfold, some sixty, some thirty" (v. 8). This is the mystery of those who hear the word and understand it. But this class of hearers also raises questions. Anyone thinking over this comes face to face with new questions: why is it that the people of God ("the children of the kingdom," v. 38) does not consist entirely of "men of the good soil," i.e. those who come up to the requirements which God has made? When will it become clear who are those who do come up to the required standard?

In the final parable, that of the good and bad fish in the net (7), the kingdom is compared with another strange situation. It is like what happens when you go fishing with a net. Out at sea, the net floats away, hidden under the surface of the water, enclosing all kinds of fish. But when the net is full, and you pull it up in the daylight on the beach, you put the good ones into the pots and throw the bad ones away. Fishing—such is life—consists of two moments: first, a huge, general ingathering under the surface and secondly, a final selection on the beach, when the required fish are kept and the useless thrown away. "A small but significant difference between this parable and the parable of the tares (2) should be pointed out once again. There, the main interest lies in the bad ones and their fate, whereas in the parable of the fish-net (7) the interest is primarily in the selection of the good" (Seven Parables, 24-25).

> **47** "Again, the kingdom of heaven is like a net which was thrown into the sea and caught fish of every kind; **48** when it was full, they drew it ashore, sat down, and put the good into baskets but threw out the bad. **49** So it will be at the end of the age. The angels will come out and separate the evil from the righteous, **50** and throw them into the furnace of fire, where there will be weeping and gnashing of teeth.
>
> **51** "Have you understood all this?" They said to him, "Yes." **52** And he said to them, "Therefore every scribe who has been trained for the kingdom of heaven is like a master of a household who brings out of his treasure what is new and what is old."
>
> **53** When Jesus had finished these parables, he left that place.

Verse 47: "A net (*sagēnē*)"—a dragnet. "Today in the Sea of Galilee large seines 300 feet long, requiring 16–20 men, are in use. These are spread from the bank and from boats" (J. Mckenzie, p. 612). "Thrown into the sea (*blētheisē*)—the aor. passive makes it easy to interpret it of divine activity, to be paired with the *eplērothē* in the next verse. "Fish of every kind"—while the net can gather fish "of every kind," it does not gather all the fish in the entire sea—an indication already that the focal point is the Church and not the nations.

Verse 48: "When it was full (*eplērōthē*)." If the act of throwing alludes to the present activity of Jesus who, as the exalted Kyrios, even now sends out his earthly ambassadors to call men into God's kingdom, it follows that eplērōthē alludes to the fact that this same Jesus (the Son of Man, v. 37), will return at the End of the Age. Then he will send out his agents, the angels, to carry out the final judicial process; "sorted the good . . . the bad"—redefined as the righteous and the evil in the next verse.

Verse 49: "The close of the age"—(cf. v. 39). "The evil (ponērous) from (*ek mesou*) the righteous"—throughout the parable of the net, Matthew consistently presses affirmation that the Church, too, will experience the Final Judgment. The parable of the Tares reaches its climax in the admonition to "let both grow together until the harvest" (v. 30), but the parable of the net does so in the declaration that "the evil" will be separated "from the righteous." The parable of the weeds deals essentially with the problem of "believing Israel" (Church) as opposed to "unbelieving Israel" (Pharisaic Judaism), while the parable of the Net deals with the problem of "bad and good" in the same institution, the Church. In Weeds the major issue is believing Israel as opposed to unbelieving Israel within a regional framework; in the explanation of Weeds, it is the sons of the kingdom as opposed to the sons of the Evil One within a universal framework; and in the parable of the net it is the righteous as opposed to the evil within the framework of the Church. The relationship between Weeds, its Explanation, and the Net is not one of identity, but of progression.

Verse 50: "Furnace of fire"—(cf. v. 42)

Verse 51: "Have you understood (*Synēkate*)"—reinforces Matthew's picture of the disciples as the enlightened followers of Jesus. The disciples, i.e., the Church, are indeed capable of understanding the message of Jesus. Verse 51 is directly related to verse 36, where the disciples are depicted as requesting Jesus to "explain" to them the parable of the darnel of the field, whereupon Jesus begins with the second half of his parable discourse, delivered solely to the disciples. With the discourse at an end, Matthew now has Jesus ask the disciples if they were able to "understand" all these things, and they answer in the affirmative.

Verse 52: "He said to them, 'Therefore (*Dia touto*).' "—because the disciples have understood the secrets delivered to them in parables, they *therefore* qualify as scribes. "Every scribe"—in the ancient Near East the designation "scribe" covered a variety of offices, from that of the local scribe who copied documents and contracts for the people, to government officials invested with serious responsibilities. Like the modern secretary, the scribe was generally concerned with written records, bureaucracy, and administration. Jeremiah's associate, Baruch, who recorded his words, was also a scribe (Jer 36:32). In postexilic times (sixth century B.C.), Ezra the scribe was sent by the Persian king to instruct and guide the inhabitants of Judea. He was both an official of the Persian Empire and learned in the laws and customs of Israel (Ezra 7). In the Maccabean period (167–63 B.C.), the learned Hasideans are called scribes, with the probable implication that they were learned in the Mosaic law. The term does not seem to denote a group with particular beliefs or a set political program, but rather learned men of whatever party or persuasion.

In Matthew the scribes are paired with the Pharisees in questioning Jesus. "Scribal traditions continued on into rabbinic Judaism, where the emphasis on study, knowledge of the law, and learned argument probably derived from the earlier learned class. Our sources tell us little about scribal training but literacy and knowledge of the law demanded education, active teaching, the ability to interpret Scripture, and experience in judging individual cases" (P. Achtemeier, *Harper's Bible Dictionary*, 914).

Since it is the disciples, i.e., the entire Church, who are being addressed (cf. v. 51), Matthew identifies "every scribe" with those members of his Church who have understood all things. "Have been trained (*matheteutheis*)—(from the transitive *mahēteuo*), with the meaning of "has been instructed." Some see it as derived from the deponent *mathēteuomai* ("to be or to become a disciple"), and suggest that Matthew intended it as an allusion to his name and as a self-portrait. But "being or becoming a disciple" does not get to the heart of the issue under discussion here.

"*For* the kingdom of heaven (*tē basileia tōn ouranōn*)"—dative of respect ("*concerning* the kingdom of heaven"). The "kingdom of heaven" is the object about which the scribe in question has been instructed, a concept that complies with Matthew's position that the parables of Jesus reveal truths, or secrets, concerning God's kingly rule to those to whom God has given the eyes of faith (v. 11). "A householder (*oikodespotes*)"— (cf. v. 27). Matthew employs this term variously to refer to God, Jesus, or even Christians. Here, it is plainly the Christian who is the master of the house.

"Out of his treasure (*thesaurou*)"—(cf. v. 44). The word means: 1) a store laid up, treasure; 2) a store or treasure-house. Here it has the latter sense—a place where the master would keep provisions of every kind in order to meet the assorted needs of his household. But Matthew often invests the word with a second dimension. A person's treasure—that to which he gives his undivided allegiance—exercises such a controlling influence over his life that such a one may be identified by his treasure: "For where your treasure is, there your heart will be also" (6:21). Now the Christian who is a true disciple of Jesus has his treasure "in heaven" (19:21)—his heart, i.e., he himself, is devoted to God alone. As the householder draws from his storeroom, so the Christian lives out of a heart that is devoted to God: "For out of the abundance of the heart the mouth speaks. The good person brings good things out of a good treasure" (12:34-35).

"What is new and what is old (*kaina kai palaia*)." Which is to say that "every person learned in the Law and the prophets (i.e., a scribe) who also understands Jesus' announcement of the coming of the kingdom is like a householder who brings forth from his storeroom things new (the proclamation of Jesus the Fulfiller) and old (the Law and the prophets)" (Meier, 154). The order of the words is significant: contrary to natural expectations, the "new" is placed before the "old." The two shed light on each other; but the definitive norm is the new, the fulfillment. The reference to "new and old" sends us back to 5:17 and 9:17.

Verse 53: "And when Jesus had finished"—signals the end of the third discourse (cf. Introduction, Fivefold Division, p. 6).

Rejection at Nazareth, 13:54-58

The response to both Jesus' teaching and mighty works is unbelief. Jesus is even repudiated in his home town of Nazareth and will continue to meet with rejection by all segments of Israel through the following subsection, chapters 14–16.

> 54 He came to his hometown and began to teach the people in their synagogue, so that they were astounded and said, "Where did this man get this wisdom and these deeds of power? 55 Is not this the carpenter's son? Is not his mother called Mary? And are not his brothers James and Joseph and Simon and Judas? 56 And are not all his sisters with us? Where then did this man get all this?" 57 And they took offense at him. But Jesus said to them. "Prophets are not without honor except in their own country and in their own house." 58 And he did not do many deeds of power there, because of their unbelief.

Verse 54: "His hometown (*eis tēn patrida autou*)." Nazareth becomes the first stop on Jesus' itinerant ministry around Galilee. But the name of "his hometown" is not mentioned; the reference may be precisely vague and so paradigmatic of all Israel. The Markan story is abbreviated: the sabbath is not mentioned, and the disciples are omitted. Thus Matthew focuses the narrative entirely on Jesus.

"They were astounded (*ekplēssesthai*)." While the crowds hearing the Sermon on the Mount were "astounded" in a positive way, the astonishment of Nazareth turns out to be negative. By an inclusion, the first and last questions of the Nazarenes (vv. 54 and 56), Matthew emphasizes the basic question of the origin of Jesus' wise teaching and powerful miracles (a perfect summary of chs. 5–9).

Verse 55: "The carpenter's son (*tou tektonos hyios*)." (Cf. LN 45.9). In Biblical times one who was regarded as a *tekton* would be skilled in the use of wood and stone and possibly even metal. In between the first and last questions are the questions which explain why Jesus' wisdom and power do not generate faith at Nazareth: the Nazarenes know him too well. Familiarity breeds contempt, even for the Messiah. The contempt can be felt in the "this man (*touto*)" of verses 54 and 56, which might be translated "this fellow." The Nazarenes think they know all about Jesus because they think they know his earthly origins and his true family. He is the son of a "carpenter" (or "craftsman," "artisan"); they can name his mother and brothers; and his sisters still live in the town. There is an irony in these objections which reminds one of John's Gospel: everything the Nazarenes affirm is in one sense true and in another, deeper sense false.

"His mother called Mary." Matthew separates the question about Jesus' father from the question about his mother and brothers. His infancy narrative made it known that the unnamed Joseph is not the real father of Jesus the Son of God. Actually, the true family of Jesus is composed not of blood relatives but of obedient disciples (12:46-50). Jesus, the final prophet of God, experiences the definitive rejection of Israel; thus does he recapitulate the rejection of all of the persecuted prophets before him.

Verse 58: "Did not do many deeds of power." Matthew was probably shocked by Mark's saying that Jesus *could* do no mighty work there. Impotence is changed to refusal, and the reference to Jesus' marveling at their unbelief is dropped. Similarly, the reverent Matthew changes the Markan designation of Jesus as a "carpenter" to "the son of the carpenter." "Neither impotence nor ignorance nor emotions nor social status must impugn Jesus' dignity. Matthew also omits a reference to finding no acceptance among 'his relatives' (cf. Mk 6:4); this may be an attempt to soften Mark's hostility towards Jesus' family, though the omission could also be explained by Matthew's avoidance of needless repetition" (Meier, *ad loc*).

Murder of John the Baptist, 14:1-12

Throughout the subsection chapters 14–16 Jesus continues to meet with rejection by all segments of Israel. The response to both his teaching and mighty works is unbelief (13.53-58). After Jesus is repudiated in his home town of Nazareth, comes news of Herod's murder of John the Baptist, which underlines the fact that "this generation" has rejected Jesus (14:1-

12). In the material which follows (chs. 14-16), concrete examples of a dual turning become evident. Jesus has less to do with the crowds and repeatedly withdraws from his opponents, while at the same time he reveals himself to his disciples, finally drawing from them the confession that he is the Christ, the Son of God.

> **14:1** At that time Herod the ruler heard reports about Jesus; **2** and he said to his servants, "This is John the Baptist; he has been raised from the dead, and for this reason these powers are at work in him." **3** For Herod had arrested John, bound him, and put him in prison on account of Herodias, his brother Philip's wife, **4** because John had been telling him, "It is not lawful for you to have her." **5** Though Herod wanted to put him to death, he feared the crowd, because they regarded him as a prophet. **6** But when Herod's birthday came, the daughter of Herodias danced before the company, and she pleased Herod **7** so much that he promised on oath to grant her whatever she might ask. **8** Prompted by her mother, she said, "Give me the head of John the Baptist here on a platter." **9** The king was grieved, yet out of regard for his oaths and for the guests, he commanded it to be given; **10** he sent and had John beheaded in the prison. **11** The head was brought on a platter and given to the girl, who brought it to her mother. **12** His disciples came and took the body and buried it; then they went and told Jesus.

In chapter 2 Herod the Great tried to murder the infant Jesus; now his son, Herod Antipas, tetrarch of Galilee and Perea, kills John the prophet. This in turn prefigures the violent death of the final prophet, Jesus. Mark has the narrative of John's death follow immediately upon the rejection at Nazareth; the rejection of both prophets by "this generation" is thus profiled. The murder of John and Herod's concern about Jesus form the occasion for Jesus' withdrawal (14:13).

Verses 1-2: "Herod the ruler." The tetrarch (LN 37.78) Herod (Antipas) had heard the report about Jesus and concluded that Jesus was John raised from the dead. According to his interpretation, the powers of one awakened to new life are active in Jesus, whom Herod believes is John raised from the dead (LN 4.23) (cf. the comparison of John with Elijah Redivivus in 11:14; 17:10-13).

Literary critics have called attention to temporal relations that govern the reporting of events in literature. A distinction is made between *story time* and *discourse time*. "Story time refers to the order in which events are conceived to have occurred by the implied author in creating the world of the story. Discourse time refers to the order in which the events are described for the reader by the narrator" (Powell, 36). Matthew's reader is not told about the murder of John the Baptist until 14:1-2, and then the narrator goes on to explain how Herod had John executed (14:3-12).

Verses 3-5: "For Herod (*ho gar Herodes*) had seized." According to L. Cope, the *gar* of this opening phrase signals the beginning of an insertion (the story of John and Herodias) whose close is signaled by the *de* of verse 13. Verses 3-5 give the reason Herod came to this conclusion. According to Josephus (*Ant* 18,5,2 [116-19] Herod was frightened by John's successful activity and had thrown him into the fortress Machraeus and had him executed.

The synoptic explanation of the arrest, with its legendary embellishments, must stem from the group picture of the Baptist circle; the charge of public immorality according to Leviticus 20:21 was enough for Herod to arrest John. But his intention to kill him as well clashed with the people's positive opinion: they held John to be a prophet (cf. 21:26).

Verses 6-11: How the Baptist's death finally came about is reported via a legend which, as is his custom, Matthew has greatly shortened. The principal agent is the wife of Herod; yet he remains responsible. The account itself is—even in Matthew's edited version—unhistorical. But attempts to discover its historical kernel and its historical value misjudge the real meaning of the tradition. With the help of a narrative drawn from the Acts-of-the-Martyrs genre, the violent death of the Baptist is presented as the capricious act of a despot (in v. 9 Matthew also speaks of a "King"). The macabre details can be marked down to the operetta character.

Verse 12: John's disciples (cf. 9:14) come to fetch the body and bury it, and therewith we are brought back into the realm of stark reality. Finally they go to Jesus and announce John's death to him, i.e., that he has undergone a prophet's fate (cf., 21:33-43; 23:29-36). This information causes Jesus to depart and hide (14:13).

The Baptist's history mirrors Jesus' fate: John is the "typical" prophet of disobedient Israel; and in a special way he suffers a prophet's death. Here, worldly power hostile to God kills John as it will kill Jesus (cf. 26:4). The community recognizes the connection between John and Jesus: both "take a stand" against power hostile to God and for the Kingdom of God. So the two are presented similarly. Matthew informs his community about the Baptist because he anticipated Jesus' fate.

While the ministry of John precedes that of Jesus, the term "forerunner" connotes more than mere temporal precedence. As Jesus' forerunner, John foreshadows in his person and work the person and work of Jesus. The time of fulfillment involves not only the ministry of Jesus, but also that of John the Baptist. John the Baptist and Jesus both come in fulfillment of prophecy (1.23; 3:2). John and Jesus alike suffer at the hands of this "evil generation" (14.1-12; ch. 27); Matthew records that both John and Jesus are "delivered up" (14:12; 27:2).

The Disciples Doubt their Authority, 14:13-21

Jesus turned away from the crowds by speaking to them in parables which they are unable to understand (13:1-35), and thereafter he withdraws time and again from his religious opponents. Yet even during this period, Jesus does not totally abandon his ministry to Israel. Although he no longer teaches or preaches to them, he continues to manifest himself as Israel's Messiah by means of his healings and his feedings of the crowds.

> 13 Now when Jesus heard this, he withdrew from there in a boat to a deserted place by himself. But when the crowds heard it, they followed him on foot from the towns. 14 When he went ashore, he saw a great crowd, and he had compassion for them and cured their sick. 15 When it was evening, the disciples came to him and said, "This is a deserted place, and the hour is now late; send the crowds away so that they may go into the villages and buy food for themselves." 16 Jesus said to them, "They need not go away; you give them something to eat." 17 They replied, "We have nothing here but five loaves and two fish." 18 And he said, "Bring them here to me." 19 Then he ordered the crowds to sit down on the grass. Taking the five loaves and the two fish, he looked up to heaven, and blessed and broke the loaves, and gave them to the disciples, and the disciples gave them to the crowds. 20 And all ate and were filled; and they took up what was left over of the broken pieces, twelve baskets full. 21 And those who ate were about five thousand men, besides women and children.

In verse 13 Matthew establishes the connection with the preceding pericope. In the face of Herod's persecution he flees, but the crowds follow him to his place of refuge.

Verse 13a: "Now when Jesus heard this (*Akousas de ho Iēsous*)." The *de* here signals the close of the insertion (cf. L. Cope, v. 3). The thesis of L. Cope was summarized in *NTA* by D. Harrington as follows:

> The tradition about the reaction of Herod to Jesus (Mt 14:1-2) has been tied to an account of Jesus' activity in and around Nazareth (13:53-58), and Jesus' subsequent withdrawal from the area (14:13) coincides with Josephus' estimate of Herod's reaction to John the Baptist (see *Ant.* 18:116-119). But in 14:3-12 Matthew paused to tell the readers about

John's death (see 4:12) and introduced the story with *gar*, the standard Greek device for noting an explanatory insertion. The conjunction *de* in *akousas de ho Iesous* in 14:13 is merely the usual way of noting the resumption of the original context. Since this reading of the passage is not only possible but also grammatically correct and logically more probable, the so-called Matthean mistake in 14:13 can no longer be cited as one of the sure signs of Matthew's dependence on Mark 21 (2, '77, #381).

"He withdrew (*anechōrēsen*, LN 15.513) . . . to a lonely place apart (*eis erēmon topon, kat' idian*, LN 1.86)." A remarkably complete expression of Jesus' attachment to the wilderness tradition. Historicizing the connecting text introduces the flight motif; Jesus flees not because John is dead, but because Herod falsely regards him as the new head of the Baptist movement (cf. 14:2).

Verses 13b–14: "On foot (*pezē*, LN 8.50) from the towns (*apo tōn poleōn*, LN 1.88)." The crowds follow (cf. 4:25; 8:1; 12:15; 19:2; 20:29) not to become followers, but because they recognize his healing power (14:2, 14). The picture of the helpless multitude (flock without a shepherd), part of the mission theology used in 9:35, is now used soteriologically; Jesus' compassion is not the expression of an emotion, but the messianically qualified reaching out to the suffering (*arrōstos*: weak, helpless, sick, only here in Matthew. LN 23.147).

Verse 15: The disciples intervene with Jesus, saying that, since it was already late (*opsia*, evening), he should send the crowds into the villages to buy food (LN 5.1, fns) for themselves. The disciples' words, indicating that it was a wilderness district and that the hour was already late, is not a request for a miracle but a request to come to the crowds' help.

Verses 16–19: Jesus' refusal is followed by the surprising imperative: "You give them something to eat!" (so word for word also in Mark and Luke). Attention is strongly fixed upon the disciples. The purpose behind the dialogue is to show the disciples to be of "little faith" (cf. v. 17 with 16:8). The disciples have an essential share in the miraculous feeding, but the eucharistic praxis of the community does not shine through, here but only Jesus' efforts to free his disciples from the fault of little faith. The "looking up to heaven" as an act of confidence and trust (in this sense only here in Matthew) and the "Blessing" (the prayer of praise before meals according to Jewish prescription) function as an acknowledgment of the divine power.

Verses 20–21: In Matthew the demonstration of the miracle and the manifestation of the divine power happens in a fourfold fashion: all eat; (all) were satisfied; twelve baskets (LN 6.150) with broken pieces were gathered (Mark: also of the fish); there were 5,000 men, not counting woman and children (in Luke the numbers are lacking; Mark mentions only the men).

At the end of the parable discourse, Jesus asks the disciples whether they have understood "the secrets of the kingdom" he has taught them. Their reply is unequivocally yes! (13:51). Yet, on other occasions the disciples show that they can falter in their understanding, and this engenders conflict between Jesus and them. Twice in wilderness places Jesus expects the disciples to act on their awareness that he has endowed them with authority (10:1) and hence, to feed 5,000 and 4,000 men (14:16; 15:32-33). "In both instances, however, the disciples give no hint of being aware that they have been endowed with such authority. On the contrary, they stand overwhelmed by Jesus' expectations, so that Jesus himself must feed the men and demonstrate that he has not placed demands upon them incapable of fulfillment (14:13-21; 15:32-38)" (*Story*, 138).

Here Jesus is also presented as the lord of the community who makes his disciples, so the community members, co-workers of his saving service and transmitters of his salvation gifts. But the disciples are members of "little faith," who through hesitation, vacillation, and doubt bring into question the manifestation of the divine power. Matthew's community is also marked by this "little faith." Having the miracle accounts, they should learn that in the light of God's power demonstration there is no place for little faith.

Disciples' Little Faith in a Storm, 14:22-33

Jesus' hiding of divine revelation and making it known corresponds to the fact that whereas all Israel turns away from Jesus (11:16-19; 12:14, 24), the disciples continue to adhere to him (12:4-50). While hiding his divine revelation from Israel, God imparts it to the disciples. And what is the nature and substance of this revelation? It concerns in greatest measure two matters. One matter is the mysteries of the kingdom of heaven (13:11). And the other is insight into Jesus' identity as the Son of God (14:33; 16:16). Narrative material frequently contains *paraenetic* value for the post-Easter church. This is especially true of the narrative material in the boat scenes at 8:23-27 and 14:22-33.

> 22 Immediately he made the disciples get into the boat and go on ahead to the other side, while he dismissed the crowds. 23 And after he had dismissed the crowds, he went up the mountain by himself to pray. When evening came, he was there alone, 24 but by this time the boat, battered

by the waves, was far from the land, for the wind was against them. **25** And early in the morning he came walking toward them on the sea. **26** But when the disciples saw him walking on the sea, they were terrified, saying, "It is a ghost!" And they cried out in fear. **27** But immediately Jesus spoke to them and said, "Take heart, it is I; do not be afraid."

28 Peter answered him, "Lord, if it is you, command me to come to you on the water. **29** He said, "Come." So Peter got out of the boat, started walking on the water, and came toward Jesus. **30** But when he noticed the strong wind, he became frightened, and beginning to sink, he cried out, "Lord, save me!" **31** Jesus immediately reached out his hand and caught him, saying to him, "You of little faith, why did you doubt?" **32** When they got into the boat, the wind ceased. **33** And those in the boat, worshipped him saying, "Truly you are the son of God."

Verses 22-23: "Then he made the disciples." "Then" connects the pericope with the preceding miracle account. A ground for the requiring ("made," *anagkazō* = require, force) is not given. That the euphoric mood of the people could have a negative effect on the disciples is a worthwhile consideration. The boat was mentioned already in 14:13; otherwise Matthew's geographic knowledge is shaky or was of little concern to him. While his disciples travel to the other shore, Jesus leaves the crowds and betakes himself to a mountain (5:1; 15:29), to be alone (cf. 14:13) and to pray (cf. 26:36-44, LN 33.178). Critical situations are faced in being alone and in prayer.

Verses 24-25: "Many furlongs (*stadious*, LN 81.27) distant from the land (*apo tēs gēs*, LN 1.60)." The disciples on the water run into trouble; they are threatened by the high waves (literally: forced; *basanizō* here has a transferred sense: the contrary wind threatens the boat; cf. 8:24). In this situation, late at night (between three and six a.m.), Jesus approaches the disciples; his approach has the appearance of a wandering progression (*peripateō* = go, go about, wander) and is described in theophany style. Already in Exodus 19:16 and Ezekiel 1:4 (cf. Ps 107:28, 29) the storm belongs to a theophany narrative.

Verses 26-27: The disciples are terrified and say that it is a ghost (literally an "appearance" LN 12.42) (cf. Job 20:8; Wis 17:14). They cry out for fear. Immediately they hear Jesus' (threefold) reassuring word: "Take heart, it is I; do not be afraid"—he whom you know (and no ghost). "It is I" ("everyday self-identification," so Gundry 299) is found only here in the synoptic tradition. At the same time, in the context of walking on water, etc., "the everyday self-identification *ego eimi* may carry overtones of the divine title I AM" (Gundry, *ad loc*).

Verses 28-29: Matthew adds a scene taken from his "Peter tradition" (cf. the redactional turns of phrase "he answered," "Peter," "Lord") which were of meaning to the community. Peter is presented as one in whom the emotions of courage and doubt lie close together (cf. 26:33, 35; 26:69-75). The hesitant expression "If it is you," does not spring from lack of recognition, but makes explicit the "little faith" with which Jesus reproaches Peter in verse 31. The initiative, to be allowed to walk on the water (LN 15.107), must be sanctioned ("command me!" with following infinitive); only then Peter hears the imperative "Come!" A typical disciple, Peter wants to have an order to follow.

Verses 30-31: In the Peter scene (as already in v. 28) "the water" is mentioned explicitly (no longer "the sea" as earlier), which perhaps underlines Peter's fear and helplessness. Peter's "noticing" ("feeling") the strong wind suffices to revive the first fear (v. 27); cosmic power shakes the hard-won trust in Jesus, who can save him from going under (*katapontizomai*). Peter's outcry "Lord, save me!" (LN 21.18, cf. 8:25) is the culmination of Matthew's insertion. Ultimately the certainty wins out in Peter that Jesus alone can help. Immediately (cf. v. 22) Jesus reaches out his hand to save (cf. 8:3; cf. Ps 144:7; Ps 18:17-18). But the reproach continues: Peter's "little faith" (not his unbelief) is upbraided (cf. 6:30; 8:26; 16:8 [17:20]; in temptation situations "little faith" manifests itself in doubt.

Verses 32-33: After the insertion (vv. 28-31), verse 32a again connects with the sea-danger pericope, and the passage ends with a chorus closure. The wind dies down (LN 68.40), the (disciples in the boat) worship Jesus and say: "Truly you are the Son of God." The purpose of the (double) narrative is to reveal Jesus as the Son of God; the theophany miracle makes possible Jesus' epiphany. Unlike Matthew 16:16b, "Son" here does not have the article, but the meaning of the difference is difficult to assess.

The two sea-epiphanies—that of the storm-stilling (8:23-27) and that of the sea-walking (14:22-23)—work together to reveal a new and unique aspect of the significance of Jesus' person. The importance and uniqueness of these epiphanies becomes evident from the viewpoint of its various theological dimensions. (1) *Christologically*, the two epiphanies enrich and further specify the content of Matthew's presentation of Jesus' *divine sonship* by showing that Jesus is the Son of God in the sense of the one equipped by God with absolute divine power for the salvation of his people. 2) The *soteriological* dimension is evident in the function of the sea-walking motif itself, which has a double aspect. "By walking on the stormy sea Jesus not only divinely dominates it but also crosses it, and thus rescues the disciples by making the sea crossable for them. Hence, at the same time that Jesus is manifesting his possession of unique divine power, he is also exercising it in order to rescue the disciples" (J. Heil, *Jesus Walking on the Sea,* 171). (3) The *ecclesiological* dimension (cf. 16:16).

Summarizing Passage, 14:34-36

In addition to the three main Summary Statements strung along Part II, Matthew also includes a number of others that somewhat resemble these, which brings the total up to six.

> **34** When they had crossed over, they came to land at Gennesaret. **35** After the people of that place recognized him, they sent word throughout the region and brought all who were sick, **36** and begged him that they might touch even the fringe of his cloak; and all who touched it were healed.

Here Matthew brings together generalizing elements of the Jesus tradition. While Matthew sometimes inserts new elements, these passages remain basically similar. This passage corresponds in content to Mark 6:53-56, but here too, Matthew has a shorter version with different terminology. Typical for him are the concepts "send," "bring to," and "heal."

Verses 34-35: After the return to the west bank of the Sea of Gennesaret, Jesus is immediately recognized; the men (*hoi andres*) of that place (LN 80.1) allow the sick from all that region (LN 1.80) to be brought to Jesus (Matthew uses *aner* "man" only eight times and almost exclusively to designate the human species; 1:16 is an exception ["husband of Mary"]).

Verse 36: As in 9:20, the sick manifest simple faith, believing that to touch the fringe of Jesus' garment would work a cure (cf. Num 15:38-39; Deut 22:12), and in fact their faith was heard. *Diasozo* is seldom used in the New Testament (Matthew once; Luke six times; 1 Pet 3:20). In the LXX (about 70 times) it has the meaning: save, gain security, escape. Here the prefix *dia-* has a perfective sense: to heal fully, permanently (LN 23.136). Gundry has "were completely delivered" (302).

For Matthew's community the summarizing passage was not simply a repetition of Jesus' healing activity reported earlier. The evangelist's catechetical objective comes to the fore by the frequent mention that in Jesus the eschatological salvation time has opened. The verb "heal" in the sense of "save" especially evokes this eschatological aspect.

Jesus' Disciples and the Tradition of the Elders, 15:1-20

In Matthew's story Jesus' teaching occasions less conflict than one might expect. The reason is that the religious leaders are the recipients of none of the great discourses of Jesus; even Jesus' speech of woes (ch. 23) is not delivered to the scribes and Pharisees but to the disciples and the crowds. It is in certain of the debates Jesus has with the religious leaders that his teaching generates conflict.

At issue in these debates is the correct interpretation of, or the proper adherence to, the Mosaic law or the Pharisaic tradition of the elders. We have already encountered a number of these cases: the practice of having table fellowship with toll-collectors and sinners (9:10-13); the nonobservance of the custom of fasting (9:14-15); alleged violations of the sabbath law (12:1-8, 9-14). And now, Jesus is charged with noncompliance with the ritual obligation of washing the hands before eating (15:1-20).

> 15:1 Then Pharisees and scribes came to Jesus from Jerusalem and said, 2 "Why do your disciples break the tradition of the elders? For they do not wash their hands before they eat." 3 He answered them, "And why do you break the commandment of God for the sake of your tradition? 4 For God said, 'Honor your father and your mother,' and, 'Whoever speaks evil of father or mother must surely die.' 5 But you say that whoever tells father or mother, 'Whatever support you might have had from me is given to God,' then that person need not honor the father. 6 So, for the sake of your tradition, you make void the word of God. 7 You hypocrites! Isaiah prophesied rightly about you when he said:
> 8 'This people honors me with their lips,
>   but their hearts are far from me;
> 9 in vain do they worship me,
>   teaching human precepts as doctrines.' "
> 10 Then he called the crowd to him and said to them. "Listen and understand. 11 It is not what goes into the mouth that defiles a person, but it is what comes out of the mouth that defiles." 12 Then the disciples approached and said to him, "Do you know that the Pharisees took offense when they heard what you said?" 13 He answered, "Every plant that my heavenly Father has not planted will be uprooted. 14 Let them alone; they are blind guides of the blind. And if one blind person guides another, both will fall into a pit." 15 But Peter said to him, "Explain this parable to us." 16 Then he said, "Are you also still without understanding? 17 Do you not see that whatever goes into the mouth enters the stomach, and goes out into the sewer? 18 But what comes out of the mouth proceeds from the heart, and this is what defiles. 19 For out of the heart come evil intentions, murder, adultery, fornication, theft, false witness, slander. 20 These are what defile a person, but to eat with unwashed hands does not defile."

Verses 1-2: "The tradition (*paradosis*, LN 33.239) of the elders." An unstressed "Then" serves as introduction to the controversy. The mention of Jerusalem underlines the authority of the discussion partners (only here in Matthew are the Pharisees mentioned before the scribes, and this in dependence on the source [cf. Mark 7:1]). Their question concerns the grounds (for *dia ti* cf. 13:10), which justifies the transgression of a tradition of the elders. Already in the question Matthew uses *parabaino* (transgress, depart from, disregard LN 36.28) to present an equivalence between the conduct of the disciples and that of the opponents (cf. v. 2 with v. 3): the criticism of the disciples serves as the basis for a charge against the religious leaders. So Jesus is made responsible for the religious/ethical conduct of the disciples, i.e., for the observance of the halacah. Not washing of hands before meals is presented as an offense against the Jewish tradition.

Verse 3: In the counter-question a much more serious charge is raised against the questioners: they violate God's command. Thereby the contrast "human enactment—divine command" is delineated as the decisive point of controversy.

Verse 4: In antithetic form ("God commanded—but you say") the theme is clarified through the Fourth Commandment (cf. Exod 20:12; Deut 5:16 in connection with Exod 21:17; Lev 20:9), on the one hand, and the ethical-religious practice of the Jews on the other (cf. 4:11, affinity of the religious leaders with Satan). That God's name stands instead of Moses sharpens the contrast still more. "In substance, Jesus' teaching is the exposition of the will of God in terms of its original intention" (19:4, 8). So here, "in debate with the Pharisees and scribes from Jerusalem, Jesus introduces his quotation of the law not with the words 'For Moses said. . . .,' but with the words 'For God said . . .'" (15:4) (*Story*, 64).

Verse 5: "He need not." There is no explicit reference to the Corban Practice (cf. Lev 1:2; Num 7:3) in Matthew. "Matthew uses *doron* so often that he regards the Aramaic 'Corban' and the formula of translation as unnecessary" (Gundry, *ad loc*). The Greek term (*doron* is the sacrificial gift) expresses Matthew's polemic against sacrifice and cult (cf. 5:23-24; also 12:7 and 9:13). The Jews replaced the social commandment of higher rank with a halacic cult ordinance (on Corban practice, cf. J.D.M. Derrett, "Korban, ho estin doron," in NTS 16 [1969/70] 364–368). Over a commandment of God they placed a cult ordinance, and indeed high-handedly (cf. the repetition of the "for the sake of your tradition" in v. 6b). "In effect, Matthew makes the Pharisees and scribes issue a commandment ('. . . shall not honor . . .') contrary to God's commandment ('Honor . . .')" Gundry, *ad loc*.

Verses 7-9: The epithet "hypocrite" (LN 88.288) does not characterize the pious, outer appearance(s) and the actual inner unrighteousness of the opponents, but has reference to their responsibility toward the Torah, of which they claimed to be the legitimate protectors. They imparted a false accent in the presentation and interpretation of the Torah. The citation of Isaiah 29:13 (LXX) speaks in the first part of the contrast "lips (mouth)—heart," which can refer to hypocrisy in the usual sense; but the weight rests upon the second part of the citation, where the teaching activity of the religious leaders is characterized as the teaching of human ordinances (*entalma* [elsewhere only in Mark 7:7 and Col 2:22]: command in the sense of ordinance); to one command of God (v. 3 singular) many human ordinances are contrasted (the Pharisaic tradition alone had 613).

Verses 10-11: The "controversy" is over, but the theme sketched therein is expanded for the instruction of the people. While in verses 3-9 it was said that God's command cannot be sacrificed for human ordinances, in verses 10-20 it is affirmed that the demand for genuine purity in accordance with God's command is identical with the demand for genuine recognition of God's will. The double imperative ('Listen and understand') points the hearers to the importance of the saying in verse 11. In Matthew the teaching saying has a smoother form than it has in Mark; he applies the saying almost concretely to eating ("mouth" [twice]), to establish the relation to the opening question (which is then confirmed in v. 20). Only now does Matthew address the question of defilement directly (*koinoō,* to make common, to defile, LN 53.33); man is not made common (before God) because he has not followed human ordinances (e.g., eaten unclean food), but because he has not followed God's commandment. How this teaching is to be more precisely understood will emerge from the commentary in verses 12-19.

Verse 12: Again ("Then") there follows a change of scene which leads into a disciple instruction; it opens with the disciples' observation that the Pharisees (the scribes are not mentioned) took offense (LN 25.180) at Jesus' teaching.

Verses 13-14: Jesus answers with a saying which expresses the thought of judgment on the Pharisees (cf. Luke 6:39). The metaphor of the "plant" (LN 3.1) is anticipated in various forms in the Old Testament Jewish tradition (Isa 5:1-7; 60:21; Jer 45:4; Jub 1:16; 7:34; 21:24). Jesus forgoes speaking a judgment on the Pharisees; this is not matter for the disciples ("Let them alone!"). But it is important for them to know that the opponents, standing under God's judgment, are "blind guides" (LN 32.42, in the synoptics only here and 23:16, 24). The profane proverb characterizes as such those who, not seeing, would show the right (law) way, but are themselves blind and so lose the way (for fall into a pit, Is 24:18; Jer 48:44; Ps 7:15; Prov 26:27).

Verses 15-19: After the small insertion and Peter's request for an explanation of the parable (LN 33.15), Jesus gives the requested explanation in a reference to the second table of the Decalogue, but not without prefixing a reference to the disciples' non-understanding. In verse 19 Matthew does not make use of a "catalog of vices" (so Mark; many exegetes uncritically transfer this sketch to Matthew), but points to violations of the fifth, sixth, seventh, and eighth commandments (and precisely in this order). So the Decalogue background determines the order in Matthew. Stressed at the beginning stand "evil thoughts," which have their basis and origin in a "(stony) heart" (cf. Gen 6:5; Exod 35:21). The next five transgressions then exemplify the first. The *blasphemai* (LN 33.400) are a summing up, because Matthew concretizes his argument on the "mouths" of man, and so, "the profaning speech of the mouth" stands in contrast to the meal which does not defile.

Verse 20: "These," (*tauta*) refers to the transgressions mentioned in verse 19 since these are an interpretation of the proverb (v. 11). "To eat with unwashed hands"—connects back to verse 2b, where the same phrase is used. "With this inclusio the passage returns to the question about the tradition of the elders and ends with a denial of that tradition" (Grundy, *ad hoc*).

Many of the objectives and aims that were present in the Sabbath controversy in (12:1-8) can also be seen in this dispute about purity and unwashed hands. Matthew has taken this story over from Mark 7 and transformed it so that it does not conflict with his view of the role and meaning of the law in his community . A story which Mark uses to set aside the laws and traditions of the Jewish leaders in his setting is applied by Matthew in a manner that articulates and defends the interpretation of these purity laws within his setting.

Matthew shows Jesus setting the traditions which the Pharisees and scribes follow against the commands of God. In following their tradition they have neglected the law of God. The Pharisees and scribes have focused on external matters, failing to realize that it is really internal matters, issues relating to one's thoughts, attitudes, and desires which cause defilement (*koinoi*) in a person.

"According to Matthew, Jesus and the disciples do not play fast and loose with the law or the Pharisaic *paradosis*. Matthew and his community are very sensitive to this charge" (Overman, 83). Responding to any accusation that his community has set aside the law, Matthew offers a subtle and reasoned explanation for the disciples of Jesus asserting that they have neither broken this law nor violated the traditions.

In the eyes of the religious leaders Jesus is a threat to the continued existence of Jewish society, for he places himself above law and tradition. "In Jesus' perspective, the debates concerning law and tradition are all to be resolved by the proper application of one basic principle, or better, of a single attitude of the heart, namely, utter devotion to God and radical love of the neighbor (5:48; 22:37-40)" (*Story*, 63).

Jesus, Son of David, and the Canaanite Woman, 15:21-28

In the genealogy (1:1-16) Matthew asserts that God has guided the whole of Israel's history so that it might culminate in the birth of "Jesus," the protagonist of his story, who is "Son of Abraham," "Son of David," and "Messiah." Jesus, born of Mary but not fathered by Joseph, is legitimately Son of David because Joseph son of David adopts him into his line.

Later in his story, Matthew portrays Jesus as acting in his capacity as the Son of David and hence, fulfilling in his ministry the end-time expectations associated with David (21:9, 15). This means especially that "Jesus performs acts of healing as the Son of David. Those directly or indirectly linked with these acts are people who count for nothing in Israel's society: the 'blind' and such 'disenfranchised persons' as a Gentile woman (15:21-28) and children (21:15). Just as the title 'Son of Abraham' characterizes Jesus as the one in whom the Gentiles will find blessing, so the title 'Son of David' characterizes Jesus as the one in whom Israel will find blessing" (*Story*, 47-48). Finally, as the Son of David, Jesus enters Jerusalem and "takes possession" of it, yet shows himself in so doing to be not a warrior king, but the humble King of peace (21:4-5).

> 21 Jesus left that place and went away to the district of Tyre and Sidon.
> 22 Just then a Canaanite woman from that region came out and started shouting, "Have mercy on me Lord, Son of David; my daughter is tormented by a demon. 23 But he did not answer her at all. And his disciples came and urged him, saying, "Send her away, for she keeps shouting after us." 24 He answered, "I was sent only to the lost sheep of the house of Israel." 25 But she came and knelt before him, saying, "Lord, help me." 26 He answered, "It is not fair to take the children's food and throw it to the dogs." 27 She said, "Yes, Lord, yet even the dogs eat the crumbs that fall from their masters' table." 28 Then Jesus answered her, "Woman, great is your faith! Let it be done for you as you wish." And her daughter was healed instantly.

At the heart of the account is Jesus' dialogue with the woman which closes with a healing word.

Verse 21: The incident happened in Phoenicia (northwest of Galilee), so on Gentile territory (regarding the two city names, cf. 11:21, 22 and the Old Testament tradition, LN 1.79, fn. 13).

Verse 22: The pro forma "Just then, *kai idou*," introduces the account proper and awakens the hearers' attention. The woman is called a "Canaanite" (only here in the New Testament; but cf. Matt 10:4), and the phrase "that region" indicates that the woman is a Gentile. With the cry typical for Matthew (cf.9:27; 20:30, 31; cf. also 17:15), the woman begs for help, but first for herself; only in conclusion does she speak of her daughter's need, of the possession (LN 78.17, fn1). The principal person is the Gentile woman. The title that the woman chooses for Jesus, "Son of David," presupposes the limitation of his ministry to Israel (cf. 24, 26) and the woman's acquiescence in this limitation. But the address "Lord," expresses the firm conviction that the limitation is not definitive "The prefixing of 'Lord' . . . shows that she hopes to win from Jesus an exceptional benefit in view of his universal dominion" (Gundry 311). In the ordering of the two titles the scope of the pericope is already indicated: turning to Israel does not exclude a mission to the Gentiles; for faith is no national privilege.

Verses 23-24: At first Jesus refuses to be drawn into a dialogue with the Gentile woman; indeed his disciples intervene and ask him to put an end to the bother; chase her off. Jesus' answer is in fact an answer to the controverted question whether the Gentile mission can be justified; he knows that he has been sent to Israel (for the shepherd theme, cf. 9:36; "House of Israel"), as he had first sent the disciples only to Israel (10:6). Thereby the strongly particularized character of Jesus' mission is clearly seen. But the role of faith stands at the center of the pericope and determines the insertion and the entire pericope. Neither belonging to Israel nor Jesus' mission to it guarantees salvation, but only faith (v. 28). The particularized saying does take Israel's leading role into consideration, but at the same time breaks through the schematized "thinking" of a nation-bound faith.

Verses 25-27: "Even the dogs (*kynaria*, LN 4.35) eat the crumbs (*apo tōn psichiōn* LN 5.5)." The woman's request meets with success. Her request ("Help "me!") moves the dialogue in the direction intended by Matthew: it concerns a salvation opportunity also for Gentiles. Yet the woman recognizes Israel's precedence ("Yes, Lord"; now deliberately without "Son of David"), but in verse 27b the turning point is announced: the turning point, indicated in the image of the dogs, is faith.

Verse 28: "Woman"(*gyne*, 9.34). Great, even mighty is the woman's faith, who only now is deemed worthy of a response. Involved here is a faith that is capable of anything, that can even move mountains (cf. 17:20; 21:21-22; 8:10, 13; 9:2, 22, 29 likewise 18:1-14). The tacked-on confirmation of the healing is really a manifestation (cf. at 9:5) of the essential element—faith.

Faith is the theme of this pericope. It indicates to the community what faith means and what "scope" it has. Thereby the theme "Church and Israel," which was being discussed in the community, is addressed, culminating in the theme "Israel's Election—Salvation for all." The real addressees of the teaching is Matthew's community, which is separating itself from contemporary Judaism. It now has the duty to proclaim salvation to all, without exception. The presupposition is always faith. Israel's prerogative is not taken away, but critically measured against hope of salvation for all. Old Testament promise and Christian message are united, in that the Church breaks out of the time-conditioned framework of Jewish salvation expectation.

The note of universalism found already in parables (ch. 13) is picked up again in chapter 15. As the particularism of chapter 10 gives way to the witness the disciples will bear to the Gentiles, so Jesus' initial refusal to heal the daughter of the Canaanite women is followed by an acquiescence to her plea. Because these blind and disenfranchised persons "see" and "confess" that Jesus is Israel's Davidic Messiah, they play a significant role in the conflict Jesus has with Israel. "Son of David" constitutes for them their evaluative point of view concerning Jesus' identity. This calls attention to the guilt that is Israel's for not receiving Jesus as its Davidic Messiah.

Many Cured on the Mountain, 15:29-31

While Mark, in 7:31-37 (as a conclusion to the pericope of the Syro-Phoenician woman) reports the healing of a deaf-mute (marked by manipulative gestures), Matthew in a summarizing statement, mentions the healing of many sick. Matthew is interested in the broad statement that Jesus is the helper of all (cf. 12:15; 14:13, 14; 10:1), rather than the great number of spectacular miracles. The reference to "and many other (sick)" is found elsewhere in the New Testament only at Luke (8:3; 22:65) and Acts (15:35). The phraseology of 31b is also Lukan (cf. 2:20; 5:25-26; 7:16; 13:13; 17:15; 18:43; 23:47; Acts 11:18; 21:20) rather than Matthean, but the addition of "Israel" comes from Matthew.

> 29 After Jesus had left that place, he passed along the Sea of Galilee, and he went up the mountain, where he sat down. 30 Great crowds came

to him, bringing with them the lame, the maimed, the blind, the mute, and many others. They put them at his feet, and he cured them, **31** so that the crowd was amazed when they saw the mute speaking, the maimed whole, the lame walking, and the blind seeing. And they praised the God of Israel.

Verse 29: "Up the mountain." "Mountain" here has the nature of a "setting." The story of a narrative is made up not only of "characters" and "events," but also of "settings." A "setting" is the place or time or social circumstances in which a character acts. In some instances, a setting simply makes action possible. In other instances, the setting may be highly charged with meaning.

Within the context of Matthew's story, particular times and places can be important. The so-called "formula-quotations" highlight some ten occurrences associated with the life of Jesus as being special example of the fulfillment of prophecy. As for place, a number of place-names are charged with meaning (Bethlehem, Egypt, Nazareth, Capernaum, Chorazin, Bethsaida, Galilee. Jerusalem, cf. *Story*, 28-29). Other locations, too, are of significance (desert, synagogue, sea, temple).

The "mountain" is a site of end-time revelation. Here Jesus Son of God, unlike Israel son of God of old, resists temptation and keeps faith with God (4:8-10). Here God declares Jesus to be his unique son (transfiguration, 9:7), here Jesus also performs such end-time acts as teaching the will of God (Sermon on the Mount, 5:1-2), and here, cures the people. On the mountain Jesus will also foretell the events that will lead up to the close of the age (24:3); and, following his resurrection, commission his disciples to their end-time ministry (28:16). So, the reference to "the mountain" is not a place indication, but pertains to the summary statement that "great crowds" came to him. In order to express that Jesus manifested himself to many, Matthew inserts the mountain motif.

Verse 30: The crowds bring sick of all kinds to Jesus. "Put (*rhipteo*: throw, throw off) at his feet" is unusual and points to an act of submission and humble recognition.

Verse 31: The reaction of the crowd (cf. at 4:24) is amazement (cf. at 8:27; 9:33), which finds expression in reverent glorification of the God of Israel. In Jesus, the God of Israel (cf. Isa 29:23; Ps 41:14; 106:48), is at work. In the healings of the sick God's power is made visible.

This summary passage about Jesus' healing activity has a twofold function: on the one hand it was meant to inculcate subjection to the healer; on the other, it was meant to show that in Jesus God is ultimately the real healer. The final acclamation in the pericope must also be directed to the God of Israel, who through all ages showers good things on humans and who does this "at the end of the ages" in a special way, in Jesus.

Feeding the Crowd of Four Thousand, 15:32-39

For a second time Jesus feeds a crowd in a wilderness spot. Like the first feeding, this is a nontherapeutic miracle (cf. 8:23). In these miracles the focus is on Jesus and the disciples, and the characteristic feature is that Jesus reveals, in the midst of situations in which the disciples exhibit "little faith," his awesome authority by exercising power over the forces of nature. These startling revelations are meant to bring the disciples to realize that such authority as he exercises, he makes available to them through the avenue of faith.

> **32** Then Jesus called his disciples to him and said, "I have compassion for the crowd, because they have been with me now for three days and have nothing to eat; and I do not want to send them away hungry, for they might faint on the way." **33** The disciples said to him, "Where are we to get enough bread in the desert to feed so great a crowd?" **34** Jesus asked them, "How many loaves have you?" They said, "Seven, and a few small fish." **35** Then ordering the crowd to sit down on the ground, **36** he took the seven loaves and the fish; and after giving thanks he broke them and gave them to the disciples, and the disciples gave them to the crowds. **37** And all of them ate and were filled; and they took up the broken pieces left over, seven baskets full. **38** Those who had eaten were four thousand men, besides women and children. **39** After sending away the crowds, he got into the boat and went to the region of Magadan.

In response to the strident opposition of the religious leaders, Jesus continually withdraws from them (14.13; 15.21; 16.4). And Jesus is no longer said to preach or teach in any positive sense; yet he graciously continues to present himself as the Messiah of Israel through healing (14.34-36; 15.29-31) and feedings (14:13-21; 15.32-39).

Verse 32: "To send them away hungry (*nēsteis*, LN 23.31)." In Matthew both the presence and the need of the crowds is motivated by what is said in the preceding summary (they have been with him for three days). As distinct from 14:13-21, the initiative comes from Jesus alone: they must not faint on the way (*eklyomai*, LN 23.16).

Verses 33-34: The disciples object, citing the "desert," the "great crowd," and to the amount of bread necessary to fill (*kortazō*, LN 23.16) the need. Yet the seven loaves will not only prove sufficient, but even provide a surplus (seven baskets).

Verses 35-36: The preparation of the food happens as in 14:19, but is described more briefly; Jesus pronounces a blessing (re *eucharisteō*, cf. 26:27) and leaves the waiting to the disciples.

Verses 37-38: Instead of the twelve of the first feeding narrative, only seven baskets (*spyris*, LN 6.149) are filled with broken pieces (but it is no longer women's baskets but panniers [for food stuffs]). The number of diners is smaller; a reason for this change is not obvious.

Verse 39: The framing verse closes the pericope: Jesus sends the crowds away, and he himself goes to a historically unverifiable place. The change to "Magdala" is superfluous.

Jesus gives the disciples this startling revelation to make them realize that the authority he exercises in the miracle, he also makes available to them through the avenue of faith. In the later situation of their worldwide mission, failure on the part of the disciples to avail themselves of the authority Jesus would impart to them will be to run the risk of failing at their tasks (28:18-20).

Second Request for a Sign, 16:1-4

Anticipated in the first half of Part II, conflict with the religious leaders breaks into the open in the latter half of Part II, starting at chapter 11. Throughout the rest of Part II, Jesus and the religious leaders clash in fierce debate. The leaders accuse Jesus for a second time of acting on the authority of the prince of demons, and he assails them for being evil, like a "brood of vipers" (12:24-37). They demand of him a sign to prove that he acts on the authority of God and not of Satan (12:38-45); they attack his disciples for transgressing the tradition of the elders by eating with unwashed hands. And they once more insist, likewise for a second time, that he give them a sign, and he reiterates his charge that they are both evil and faithless to God (16:1-4).

As the religious leaders see it, Jesus is not the Son of God who speaks and acts on the authority of God so as to call Israel to repentance and to life in the sphere of God's end-time Rule. Instead, they understand him to be a "deceiver" (false messiah) who acts in collusion with Satan and who threatens both to usurp their authority as Israel's rightful leaders and to subvert the nation through the overthrow of law, tradition, and temple cult.

> **16:1** The Pharisees and Sadducees came, and to test Jesus they asked him to show them a sign from heaven. **2** He answered them, "When it is evening they say, 'It will be fair weather for the sky is red.' **3** And in the morning, 'It will be stormy today, for the sky is red and threaten-

ing.' You know how to interpret the appearance of the sky, but you cannot interpret the signs of the times.' **4** An evil and adulterous generation asks for a sign, but no sign will be given to it except the sign of Jonah.' Then he left them and went away.

Verse 1: "And the Pharisees and the Sadducees came (*proselthontes*)." Matthew establishes a frame for the scene with two participles, "came" verse 1 and "left" verse 4. Pharisees and Sadducees are named together only by Matthew and in Acts (23:6, 7, 8): the two groups are the chief representatives of contemporary Judaism. The request is made with the intention of "tempting" Jesus, i.e. to call his authority into question (LN 27.31, 46). The tempting objective of the devil at the beginning of Jesus' ministry (4:13) continues in the request of his earthly opponents: 16:1; 19:3; 22:18, 35. By a "sign (LN 33.477) from heaven" is not meant a "mighty work" (a healing) nor a nontherapeutic miracle (such as walking on the sea or rescue from the storm at sea), but—according to 24:3, 24, 30—a visible, spectacular nature event that transpires on command and legitimates the claim of a person to exalted status and to power (the verb means literally: to show, display). Since it comes from heaven, it is to be regarded as a certification by God, as a demonstration worked by God.

"They ask him (*epērōtēsan* [LN 33.16] . . . to show them (*epideixai*)"—Matthew gains a parallel between the two occurrences of the prefix *ep-*. "The prefix escalates the meaning of the *epērōtēsan* from a simple asking to an insistent demand" (Gundry, *ad loc*).

Verses 2a–4: "Evil and adulterous generation." The epithets that appear in Jesus' answer, which are drawn from tradition, express, first, that those who ask represent an entire generation, that in them the Jews in general speak. Involved is the mentality of those who, because they belong to the covenant people, claim the right to challenge everyone they come across who makes a religious claim. In itself, this is a justifiable claim, but a risky one because, in the light of of their tempting tendency, it expresses a false outlook. This people, characterized as the contemporary generation now addressed, is likened to Israel, which the prophets likened to adulterous persons because of its infidelity and defection from Yahweh (cf. Jer 3:8-9 5:7; Hos 2:4; Ezek 16:15-34). Because this generation is hardened in its infidelity, a sign must be refused it.

The exception conceded in verse 4b does not abrogate the original and absolute "No!" For "Sign of Jonah" does not mean one of the five miracles mentioned in the book of the prophet Jonah. It consists rather in his prophetic activity (see at 12:39). For Matthew, Jonah is a sign in the sense that in his preaching of penance, he leads the inhabitants of Ninevah to conversion. So Jesus' answer affirms: If a sign should be given them it could only be that of the prophet Jonah, and this only in so far as he provoked conversion and penance among the Ninivites. So ends—without further discussion—the short speech: verse 4c only reports Jesus' abrupt departure. The brittle harshness of this notice underlines, once again, the absoluteness of Jesus' refusal.

"When the prediction is made that false messiahs and false prophets will arise and perform miracles, their acts are not termed deeds of power but 'signs and wonders' (24:24). Jesus and the disciples, in turn, are never reported as doing 'wonders' (*terata*) and the 'sign' (*semeion*) is characterized as a miraculous feat that the religious leaders demand of Jesus as they tempt him to prove he is not in collusion with Satan (12:24, 38; 16:1). The sign Jesus does give them, a word prophesying his death and resurrection (12:39-40; 27:63), is not what they have in mind. When the death and resurrection occur, the leaders refuse to acknowledge them (27:62-64)" (*Story*, 68–69).

Only two positions are possible. "The right, which is the way of God; and the wrong, which is the way of the devil. There is ultimately no middle ground. Throughout the Gospel, [Jesus'] opponents are related to Satan even as Jesus is related to God. Like the devil (4:1-11), they ask for a sign (12.38; 16.1-5)" (Bauer, 69).

The request for a faith spectacle is an expression of unfaith. It is to be found not just in Israel and its Jewish representatives, but also in Matthew's community doubt about Jesus breaks through again and again, doubt about his claim, and his mission. The opinion that the doubt (as manifestation of an open or latent "little faith" could be dispelled by a spectacular event, is condemned. The doubt itself would not be dispelled, and the attempt to dispel the doubt through a marvelous manifestation is itself an expression of incipient non-faith.

The Yeast of the Pharisees, 16:5-12

In addition to his conflict with the religious leaders, Jesus also had a conflict with the disciples. Although it was of a different nature, it was real enough and arose from the disciples' "little faith." On two occasions the disciples, faced with a challenging situation, were badly shaken: although Jesus has given them to share in his authority, they do not undertake to feed the crowds, but despair of their resources (14:16-17; 15:33). Out on the water, the disciples lose the courage of faith and become "terrified"when confronted with what they think is an apparition they cry out in terror (14:26), and Peter, having received permission to walk on the water, is suddenly overcome by doubt (14:30-31). Now their worry about not having bread shows that they had forgotten the five loaves and the seven.

> 5 When the disciples reached the other side, they had forgotten to bring any bread. 6 Jesus said to them, "Watch out and beware of the yeast of the Pharisees and Sadducees." 7 They said to one another, "It is because we have brought no bread." 8 And becoming aware of it, Jesus said, "You of little faith, why are you talking about having no bread? 9 Do you still not perceive? Do you not remember the five loaves for the five thousand, and how many baskets you gathered? 10 Or the seven loaves for the four thousand, and how many baskets you gathered? 11 How could you fail to perceive that I was not speaking about bread? Beware of the yeast of the Pharisees and Sadducees!" 12 Then they understood that he had not told them to beware of the yeast of bread, but of the teaching of the Pharisees and Sadducees.

This disciple instruction, which has a strongly parenetic tone, has a counterpart in Mark 8:14-21. Both versions reveal that here two episodes, stemming from different sources, were fused: the episode of the forgotten bread and the warning against the leaven of the Pharisees. In Matthew the anecdote embraces verses 5, 7-10, and the parenesis verses 6, 11, 12.

Verse 5: Jesus and his disciples meet again; the reference to forgetfulness (*epilanthanomai*: forget, LN 29.114) serves as an opportunity to insert a vigorous parenesis.

Verse 6: "Take heed and beware." Caution is demanded, in the sense that the disciples must keep themselves far removed from the leaven of the religious leaders. Here "the *zymē* of the Pharisees and the Sadducees is equated with their teaching, but the context would indicate clearly that this was a type of hypocritical teaching, since the religious leaders said one thing but did something quite different" (LN 88.237). The metaphor stands for the teaching of the two leading religious groups of contemporary Judaism (cf. v. 12): Jesus warns against a teaching that shows itself above all in a defective relationship to right understanding of law. The parenesis means: forgetfulness regarding food shows itself in the much more serious carelessness regarding false law teaching (Luke refers to the hypocrisy of the Pharisees).

Verses 7-10: The joining of two originally separate pericopes can give rise to misunderstanding and was intended to do so. It leads to the rebuke: "O men of little faith!" The "little faith" consists of "not yet perceiving" (cf. at 6:30); as compared with Mark 8:17-18, the reproach is toned down and weakened. Jesus' reproaches not for the hardness of heart but "only" little faith (cf. 6:30; 8:26; 14:31; 17:20). The reference to the first and second great feeding scenes in Matthew serves to show that the condition for "not yet perceiving" is fully unjustified.

Verses 11-12: Verse 9 is repeated: If you witnessed the twofold feeding, how can you not know? Only now is the contrast, with its strong literary tone, shown to be theological: it is not a question of earthly bread, but (cf. v. 6) of the harmful teaching of the Jewish leaders. In verse 12 then it is said that the non-understanding of the disciples is finally removed. (*Syniemi* [originally, "bring together"] means here: to understand the connection rightly).

The discipleship of the community is based on Jesus' call, to which the disciples understanding must correspond. Insight into Jesus' claim is endangered through the teaching of the Jewish leaders, which is operative and penetrating as contaminating leaven (Exod 23:18; Lev 2:11).

According to 16:12 the nonperception of the disciples is overcome, for upon an initial "still-not-perceiving," there finally follows: "Then they understood." Therein, the members Matthew's community are distinguished from the Jews, from whom the Kingdom of God is taken (8:10-13: because of their unbelief; 21:43: because they bear no fruit).

So in Matthew's community the danger of nonunderstanding still remains, and precisely because of the enduring presence of "little faith." The community is warned not to allow the tension between faith and nonfaith to become a full scale test of strength by which finally it will be destroyed. Watchfulness and caution must characterize the life of the disciples of Christ.

Jesus' conflict with the disciples is as fully embedded in the plot of Matthew's story as is Jesus' conflict with Israel. At places in the story, the disciples, too, "are setting their minds not on divine things but on human things" (16:21-23). Nevertheless, the conflict Jesus has with them is of a fundamentally different order from that between Jesus and Israel or between Jesus and the nations. The disciples, after all, are not enemies of Jesus, but his followers. The source of their conflict with Jesus is their periodic failure to comport themselves in a manner that befits children of God and disciples of Jesus (10:1), who live in the sphere of God's endtime Rule. Jesus calls the disciples to come after him, entrusts them with a mission to Israel, and makes them the recipients of divine revelation. For these very reasons he must also engage them in conflict as they show themselves to be persons of "little faith," and so do not avail themselves of the authority he has imparted to them.

Caesarea Philippi: Peter's Confession, 16:13-20

This is the climax of Part II. According to D. Bauer, Kingsbury's three-fold division of Matthew's Gospel is a Topical Outline based upon "Superscriptions." The "superscriptions" are the repeated formulaic statements at 4:17 and 6:21: "From that time Jesus began." Part II (4:17–16:20) and Part III (16:21–28:20) demonstrate the same continuity with their respective "superscriptions" and the same unity as obtained for Part I (1:1–4:16). Part II, "The Proclamation of Jesus" is tied together by three summary passages (4:23-21; 9:35; 11:1) and by a logical progression leading up to the climax of Peter's confession.

Climax is produced by the causal movement within the part. The contrasting responses to Jesus by the people and by the disciples come to a high point of intensity and clarification when Jesus asks his disciples the questions that stand behind all the material in these chapters: Who do people say the Son of Man is?" and "Who do you say that I am?"

The contrasting responses to Jesus by the people and by the disciples come to a climax with the confession from the disciples that Jesus is "the Christ, the Son of the living God." This confession from Peter, who speaks for all the disciples, is correct, since it comes not from humans (cf. 16:13), but is revealed by God (16:17), since it meets with a blessing from Jesus (16.7), and since it agrees with God's point of view expressed in 3:17.

> **13** Now when Jesus came into the district of Caesarea Philippi, he asked his disciples, "Who do people say that the Son of Man is?" **14** And they said, "Some say John the Baptist, but others Elijah, and still others Jeremiah or one of the prophets." **15** He said to them, "But who do you say that I am?" **16** Simon Peter answered, "You are the Messiah, the Son of the living God." **17** And Jesus answered him, "Blessed are you, Simon son of Jonah! For flesh and blood has not revealed this to you, but my Father in heaven. **18** And I tell you, you are Peter, and on this rock I will build my church, and the gates of Hades will not prevail against it. **19** I will give you the keys of the kingdom of heaven, and whatever you bind on earth will be bound in heaven, and whatever you loose on earth will be loosed in heaven." **20** Then he sternly ordered the disciples not to tell anyone that he was the Messiah.

Verses 13-15: "Who do people say . . . who do you say." The contrasting responses to Jesus by the people and by the disciples come to a high point of intensity and clarification when Jesus asks his disciples the question that stands behind all the material in Part II.

Verse 16: You are . . . the Son of the living God." Matthew applied to Jesus a number of Christological titles, including "Christ," "Son of

David," "Son of Abraham," and "king," yet the primary Christological title in Matthew is that of "Son of God." "This conclusion is supported by the centrality of this category in the first main division of the Gospel, which presents the person of Jesus, by its connection to the recurring climaxes in the Gospel (3.17; 16.13-20, 26-28), and by its connection to the inclusio having to do with the presence of God, or Jesus, with the eschatological community (1.23; 28.20). Jesus is the Son of God in the sense that he has his origin in God (1.21), in the sense that he perfectly obeys the will of his Father (4.1-11) (ch. 27), and in the sense that he enjoys a unique filial relationship with the Father (11.25-30). The role of Jesus as Son of God is understood in terms of the presence of God with his end-time people: in the person of his Son, God has drawn near to dwell among his people (1.23, 28.20)" (Bauer, 145).

Verse 18: "You are Peter." Jesus' promise to Peter has been carefully prepared for in Matthew's Gospel, especially by the two sea-rescue epiphanics, that of the storm-stilling (8:23-27) and that of the sea-walking (14:22-33). The rescue of Peter from sinking into the waters (14:28-31) prepares for, and gives further content to, the meaning of the climactic confession of Jesus as "the Christ, the Son of the living God" by Peter in 16:16. In addition, the manifestation of Jesus' absolute divine power in rescuing the disciples and Peter by walking on the sea substantiates the further revelation of Jesus' character as the one who can build and protect his Church on the "rock" of Peter (16:18-29), (Heil, 170).

The *ecclesiological* dimension of the Matthean account is seen in the roles played by the disciples and Peter. The readers of Matthew can identify, through their own experiences of distressful situations, with the extreme distress of the disciples in crossing the stormy sea, and, even more graphically, with the situation of Peter in need of immediate assistance from sinking in the waters. The disciples' and Peter's experience of rescue by the exercise of Jesus' power to walk on the sea, and their consequent confession of Jesus as the Son of God, calls the readers of Matthew not only to a faith in Jesus as the one who can rescue them from their worst situations of distress, but also to a realization that Jesus is the Son of God in the sense that he is the one divinely empowered to save the community of those who believe in him. This ecclesiological dimension of the Matthean sea-walking power of Jesus substantiates his promise of building his Church on the "rock" of Peter, and of its protection "from the gates of Hades" (16:18). This manifestation of Jesus' power gives Matthew's readers the assurance that the Church of those who believe and follow Jesus is divinely protected.

Verse 18: "On this rock," as E. Schillebeeckx and B. van Iersel have pointed out, the members of Matthew's community could hardly have suppressed an ironic, affectionate smile when they connected Peter, the "rock," with the conduct he had displayed in the sea-walking incident, and, indeed, throughout his life (cf. *BTB* 17 (2, 1987), 64–69. The Church was built on the authority Jesus entrusted to Peter, not on Peter's character.

Verse 19: "Bind on earth . . . bound in heaven" (Cf. Introduction, Sacred Canopy, pp. ₆₆; cf. also J. Overman, *Bind and Loose,* pp. 105, 106, 138, 152).

Verse 19: "Not to tell anyone." Peter's confession meets with a command from Jesus that the disciples tell no one that he is the Messiah, that is, the Messiah Son of God (cf. 16:20 with 16:16). Although the disciples correctly understand who Jesus is, they do not as yet know that central to Jesus' divine sonship is death on the cross.

From the conflicting thoughts about Jesus' identity (v. 14), Matthew fashions two evaluative points of view with which he brings the entire second part of his story to its culmination, in Peter's confession near Caesarea Philippi (16:13-20). The one evaluative point of view is that of the various segments making up the Jewish public. "Some say John the Baptist, others say Elijah, and others Jeremiah or one of the prophets." The evaluative point of view concerning Jesus' identity, which the Jewish public takes, is that he is a prophet of some stature or other. This evaluative point of view is false. To think of Jesus as a prophet does not tally with God's "thinking" about Jesus (3:17, 16:23e).

The second, contrasting, evaluative point of view is that of Peter, who speaks on behalf of the disciples: "You are the Messiah, the Son of the living God!" (16:16). This evaluative point of view is correct. It elicits from Jesus a "blessing" (v. 17), and it tallies with the way God "thinks" about Jesus. "Accordingly, to bring the second part of his story to its culmination, Matthew shows that whereas the public in Israel does not receive Jesus and wrongly conceives of him as being a prophet, Peter, as spokesman for the disciples, confesses Jesus aright to be the Son of God and so reveals that the disciples' evaluative point of view concerning Jesus' identity is in alignment with that of God" (*Story,* 75).

Part III:
The Journey of Jesus Messiah to Jerusalem and His Suffering, Death, and Resurrection (16:21–28:20)

In Part III of his story (16:21–28:20), Matthew tells of Jesus' journey to Jerusalem and of his suffering, death, and resurrection. As for the disciples, Jesus must enter into intense conflict with them because they reject the notion that he must suffer and that his suffering is a summons to them to servanthood. Matthew shows how the disciples are led to appropriate Jesus' evaluative point of view, according to which suffering sonship summons to suffering discipleship, that servanthood constitutes the essence of discipleship.

The superscription for Part III is found in 16:21, where Matthew declares: "From that time on, Jesus began to show his disciples that he must go to Jerusalem and undergo great suffering at the hands of the elders and chief priests and scribes, and be killed, and on the third day be raised." The two basic elements are the journey and the presentation Jesus makes to his disciples of the necessity for such an undertaking. The journey is expanded or particularized throughout Part III by means of climax; the necessity for the journey is expanded or particularized by means of the flow of the story, which involves repetition of comparison and the repetition of contrast (cf. D. Bauer, p. 96). Only in 16:21 does Matthew directly and explicitly introduce the theme of the passion and resurrection, and it is here, for the first time, that Jesus instructs his disciples regarding his passion and resurrection.

To lend cohesion to Part III of his story Matthew employs two literary devices: the journey and the passion prediction. Prior to 16:21, Jesus' travels have the character of "withdrawal in the face of danger," from conspiracy on the part of the religious leaders to kill him (12:14-15). From

16:21 on, Jesus' travels assume the character of a "divinely ordained journey to Jerusalem," even though he does not actually leave Galilee and head for Jerusalem until 19:1.

There are three passion predictions in Part III (16:21; 17:22; 20:17-19), which are the counterpart to the major summary passages found in the second part of Matthew's story (4:23; 9:35; 11:1). These passion predictions invite the reader to view the whole of Jesus' life story following 16:21 from the single over-riding perspective of his passion and resurrection. At the same time, they invite the reader to construe the interaction of Jesus with the disciples throughout this part as controlled by Jesus' concern to inculcate in them his understanding of discipleship as servanthood.

Second Superscription, First Passion Prediction, 16:21-23

> **21** From that time on, Jesus began to show his disciples that he must go to Jerusalem and undergo great suffering at the hands of the elders and chief priests and scribes, and be killed, and on the third day be raised. **22** And Peter took him aside and began to rebuke him, saying, "God forbid it, Lord! This must never happen to you." **23** But he turned and said to Peter, "Get behind me, Satan! You are a stumbling block to me; for you are setting your mind not on divine things but on human things."

Verse 21: "From that time on, Jesus began." Verse 1:1 serves as the general heading (superscription) for Part I (1:1-4:16). This implies that the succeeding division or divisions of Matthew's Gospel will also begin with a superscription; and that is what one finds in 4:17 and 16:21.

Verse 4:17 is parallel in form to 16:21. "Both passages contain the preposition 'from' plus the phrase 'Jesus began,' plus the infinitive ('to preach and to say' in 4.17; 'to show' in 16.21), plus a summary of content of the message (direct discourse in 4.17; object clause introduced by 'that' in 16.21)" (D. Bauer, 85). In addition to this, parallelisms are distinguished by their asyndetic character (lack of connective). The asyndeton is all the more remarkable when one examines the liberal use of connectives in the material surrounding each of these verses. The asyndetic character of the phrase "from that time" in 4:17 and 16:21, then, underscores the formulaic character of this phase.

"Jesus began to *show*." Matthew begins this (III) part of his story with a narrative comment: "From that time Jesus began to show. . . ." And the word Jesus speaks is this: "If any want to become my followers, let them deny themselves and take up their cross and follow me" (16:24). "The emphasis in the narrative comment on 'showing' (*deiknyein*) is significant, for its use here is such that it necessarily encompasses both words and deeds, both speaking and doing. Combine these two passages while keeping this latter observation in mind, and the following Matthean axiom regarding discipleship emerges: Jesus reveals to his disciples, in all he says and in all he does beginning with 16:21, that God has ordained that he should go to Jerusalem to suffer, and that his way of suffering is a summons to them also to go the way of suffering (i.e., the way of servanthood (cf. 20:28 and 16:24) that suffering defined as servanthood, is the essence of discipleship and that Jesus will show the disciples in what he says and does that this is in fact the case" (*"Akolouthein,"* 139).

"He must go to Jerusalem." Jesus' first act is to tell his disciples that God has ordained he should go to Jerusalem and there be made by the religious leaders to suffer and die.

Verse 22: "God forbid it, Lord!" On hearing this, Peter rejects out of hand the idea that such a fate should ever befall Jesus, and Jesus reprimands him for "setting his mind not on divine things but on human things." Peter's inability to comprehend that death is the essence of Jesus' ministry is only part of the malady afflicting the disciples: they are also incapable of perceiving that servanthood is the essence of discipleship (16:24).

Verse 23: "Get behind me, Satan!" God rules in "the kingdom of heaven" and has his angels to do his bidding. Satan also has a kingdom. In this sphere of power Satan himself rules, and he has at his command both angels and demons. The religious leaders, especially, have affinity with Satan. Nor do the disciples escape the machinations of Satan. Peter "stands in" for Satan as he rejects the notion that Jesus should submit, in obedience to God, to suffering and death. In addition, those who follow Jesus are continually in danger of becoming servants of "lawlessness" and "evil," of which Satan is the root source. To meet this danger, Jesus instructs the disciples in the Lord's Prayer to petition God, ". . . but deliver us from the Evil One."

Following God's baptismal declaration, Jesus Son of God proves, in conflict with Satan, that he is perfect in obedience to God and superior in strength to Satan. Although Satan, the transcendent fountainhead of evil, continues to vie with Jesus Son of God in this age for the allegiance of humans, at the consummation he, his angels, and all those who give him their fealty will be consigned by Jesus to perdition.

Peter's immediate reaction to Jesus' prediction of his passion is: "God forbid it, Lord!' This must never happen to you!" (v.22). In reply, Jesus reproves Peter, warning him that in taking exception to the notion that Jesus must suffer and die he is functioning as the mouthpiece not of God, but of Satan (v.23). Then, addressing all the disciples, Jesus tells them that the corollary to suffering sonship is suffering discipleship (v. 24). "These words Jesus has with the disciples here at the outset of the third part of the story adumbrate the conflict he will henceforth have with them: Jesus' struggle will be to wean the disciples from an evaluative point of view which can make them more akin to Satan than to God and to bring them to realize that suffering, or servanthood, is indeed the essence of discipleship" (*"Akolouthein,"* 139).

Cross-bearing for Jesus and the disciples, 16:24-28

Matthew's Gospel is essentially a story about Jesus, and within this story the great discourses point to Jesus' activity of instructing and commanding the community of his disciples, with particular reference to issues relevant to the post-Easter existence of the Church. The existence of the five discourses underscores a major aspect of Jesus' presence with his community throughout history, that of speaking words of instruction and commandment.

But there are also some commands that could be understood as having to do primarily with the post-Easter church that are found outside the great discourses, and our passage is one of them. The position of these cases reflects other concerns of Matthew. "16.24, for instance, reflects Matthew's desire to place this paradigmatic call to cross-bearing at the beginning of the division 16.21-28.20" (Bauer, 133).

> **24** Then Jesus told his disciples, "If any want to become my followers, let them deny themselves and take up their cross and follow me. **25** For those who want to save their life will lose it, and those who lose their life for my sake will find it. **26** For what will it profit them if they gain the whole world but forfeit their life? Or what will they give in return for their life? **27** "For the Son of Man is to come with his angels in the glory of his Father, and then he will repay everyone for what has been done. **28** Truly I tell you there are some standing here who will not taste death before they see the Son of Man coming in his kingdom."

Verse 24: Matthew inserted the discipleship saying already in the Mission Address (10:38-39); while there discipleship as precondition is stressed, here it is demanded both as precondition and still more, as consequence. The logion is strengthened through "deny himself" (so also Mark and Luke); *arnēomai* ("say no, deny, reject") interprets the cross carrying as self-sacrifice; both are preconditions for following on Jesus' way. For "follow" in the literal and metaphorical senses, cf. 10:38.

Verses 25-26: "Save their life . . . lose it." In rejecting Jesus' prediction of his sufferings (v. 21), Peter betrays his illusions about his own future. Not only must the believer accept the Messiah's shattering prediction of verse 21; he must accept it as a prophecy of his own destiny, as well as the destiny of his Lord. For, as verse 25 drives home, "The paradox of temporal loss for eternal gain is the law of Christian existence. A truly fulfilled life eludes the grasp of the person who selfishly seeks self-fulfillment. Only those who cease to grasp at life, only those who give up their little projects of a tailored-to-order existence and who surrender their lives to God in imitation of and for the sake of the crucified Jesus will receive the fullness of life as a gift, from God" (Meier, *ad loc*). All human conceptions of loss and gain have been turned upside down (v. 26). Winning the whole world is not success but failure, because this world is passing away, along with anyone who pins all his hope on a universe under judgment. On the last day, not all the treasures a person has gained on earth will buy the one thing he has lost, his own salvation, his own true, eternal life. Jesus is going to the cross to give the only acceptable ransom or exchange for man's life (20:28). If a disciple will not accept and imitate Christ's ransom, he will find no other on the last day.

Verse 27: "The Son of Man is to come." The idea of final judgment, which stands behind verses 25-26, here becomes explicit. An apocalyptic scene presents a quasi-Jewish "Trinity" (the Son of Man, his Father, and his angels). The angels are pointedly said to be the angels of the transcendent "Son of Man" in Matthew 16:27. And, most importantly for a full appreciation of Matthew's "Son"-Christology, God the Father is called the Father of the Son of Man ("his *father*"). It is this Son of Man, coming in and surrounded by "glory," the light proper to and radiating from the divinity, who will hold the last judgment. Being the judge of the whole cosmos, he will reward and punish each person, disciple and unbeliever alike, according to his concrete way of acting.

Verse 28: "Some standing here." Under the influence of verse 27, verse 28 was reformulated to introduce the Son of Man. With the solemn Amen-formula of the apocalyptic seer, the earthly Son of Man assures his disciples that some of them will not die until they see the "Son of Man" coming in his kingdom. 'While the original saying standing behind Mark 9:1 may have expressed the early Christians' longing for an imminent parousia, such can hardly be the meaning of 16:28 in the mind of Matthew, who is writing ca. A.D. 90. Matthew's own theology has come to grips with the phenomenon of a second and even a third generation of Christians" (J. Meier, *ad loc*). The stringency of judgment, not its imminence, is the main motive in Matthew's moral exhortation. Matthew makes a distinction between the Son of Man's coming in apocalyptic glory to judge on the last day and his coming to his Church in an anticipated "Parousia" at the end of the Gospel (cf. 28:6-20). At that moment, after the turning point of the ages (the death-resurrection), Jesus the Son of Man can proclaim for the first time that he has received all power over the cosmos (28:18). Then, for the first time, do the disciples see him coming "in his kingdom."

Pointing to the repetition of comparison between the cross of Jesus and the cross of the disciples, D. Bauer writes:

> The expectations of discipleship in 16.21-28.20 are presented in the same terms as this portrait of Jesus. The paradigmatic statement regarding discipleship comes almost immediately after the general statement of 16.21. In 16.24 Jesus tells his disciples, 'If anyone would come after me, let him deny himself, take up his cross, and follow me'. 'To deny oneself', as Heinrich Schlier (TDNT, I 459) has put it, means to say no to the self or to reject a claim upon the self. It thus involves the element of self-surrender. 'To take up one's cross', in the context of 16.21- 28.20 means to emulate Jesus in the way of the cross; this emulation, as we have just seen, involves faithfulness to the will of God, especially in terms of endurance of suffering for the sake of the kingdom and an attitude of humility and of selfless service for others. 106.

According to U. Luz, this pericope belongs to the most important of the Gospel. Matthew 16:13-28 is not a summary of Christological sayings—Matthew does not develop a Christological "teaching." Rather he brings Peter's Christological confession into the life-realm. To that extent, it is also a parallel to 7:21-23, where Matthew for the first time makes it clear that "confession without praxis is useless (*das Beklenntnis ohne Praxis nichs nützt*"), II. p. 496.

The Transfiguration, 17:1-9

Jesus' first passion prediction and words to the disciples about suffering for himself, and his disciples words, are followed by his transfiguration in the sight of Peter, James, and John (vv. 1-9), and by his ensuing conversation with them about the suffering of John the Baptist as foreshadowing the suffering he must soon endure (vv. 10-13).

> **17:1** Six days later, Jesus took with him Peter and James and his brother John and led them up a high mountain, by themselves. **2** And he was transfigured before them, and his face shone like the sun, and his clothes became dazzling white. **3** Suddenly there appeared to them Moses and

Elijah, talking with him. 4 Then Peter said to Jesus, "Lord, it is good for us to be here; if you wish, I will make three dwellings here, one for you, one for Moses, and one for Elijah." 5 While he was still speaking, suddenly a bright cloud overshadowed them, and from the cloud a voice said, "This is my Son, the Beloved, with him I am well pleased, listen to him!" 6 When the disciples heard this, they fell to the ground and were overcome by fear. 7 But Jesus came and touched them, saying, "Get up and do not be afraid." 8 And when they looked up, they saw no one except Jesus himself alone. 9 As they were coming down the mountain, Jesus ordered them, "Tell no one about the vision until after the Son of Man has been raised from the dead."

Verse 1: Taking the three disciples with him, Jesus ascends a high mountain. Atop this mountain he is suddenly transfigured before them.

Verse 2: "Face shone like the sun." The transfiguration (the metamorphosis; cf. the Greek term *metamorphoō*: transform, change) happens suddenly. To strengthen the emphasis on the (terrifying) event (cf. v. 6), Matthew mentions (like Luke, but not Mark), that the face of the transfigured Jesus shone (*lampros*, LN 14.50) like the sun; this sign of divine glorification (Ps 104:2; Exod 34:29; Dan 10:6; Apoc 1:16; 10:1) blends with the apocalyptic symbolism, according to which the faces of the just in the resurrection will shine like the sun (4 Ezra 7:97; Dan 12:3). According to 13:43, Matthew understands the event as a reference to Jesus' eschatological glory. To this corresponds the note that his garments became white as light; (*leukos*: shining, bright, white). *Hemation* (in the plural) expresses as symbol the true nature of the wearer.

Verse 3: The appearances of Moses and Elijah is introduced by Matthew's stressing particle *kai idou* ("And behold," "Suddenly"). The sequence "Moses and Elijah" corresponds to Jewish tradition, which accords a higher value to the Torah (Law) than the Nebiim (Prophets): the mediation of divine wisdom takes precedence over its interpretation. Both speak with Jesus; the "wordless dialogue" underlines the character of the vision (the *ophte* [like Acts 7:26] has a general meaning and mirrors the speech usage of the LXX, where it is often the technical term in theophanies and angelophanies).

Verse 4: Peter reacts by addressing Jesus with the title: "Lord," which is typical for disciples in Matthew. He declares the appearance to be "good," i.e., fitting. The purpose of the "booths" is to make this assembly lasting. Analogous to the tabernacle ("tent of meeting" between Yahweh and Israel) (Exod 33:9; Num 12:5), the booth is the sign of the presence of divine glory (John 1:14; Apoc 21:3) (cf. W. Michaelis: *skene* in TWNT VII 379–80). Peter's request is unrealistically unperceptive: a resting place for Jesus is not yet, for Moses and Elijah no more, in question (the Markan parallel refers expressly to this misunderstanding).

Verse 5: While Peter was still speaking the cloud vision takes place (note the repeated "suddenly"). *Episkiazo* means "overshadow," "hide" (LN 14.62), and expresses the complete covering of the disciples (Exod 40:34-35 LXX). From a bright cloud they hear a voice exclaim, "This is my Son, the Beloved; with him I am well pleased; listen to him!" (17:5). The voice is that of God, and for the second time, God bursts into the world of Matthew's story as "actor" and expresses his evaluative point of view concerning Jesus' identity. Whereas the announcement ("This is my Son, the Beloved, with whom I am well pleased") repeats the baptismal declaration (3:17), the injunction ("listen to him!") is new. Within the context of Matthew's story, the purpose of the announcement is to confirm to the three the truth of the confession Peter had made on behalf of all the disciples near Caesarea Philippi that Jesus is God's Son (cf. 17:5 with 16:16; 14:33). The purpose of the injunction is to exhort the three to receive and not to reject, as Peter had done, the new word Jesus had delivered to the disciples: that he, whom they rightly perceive to be the Messiah Son of God, has been ordained by God to submit to suffering and death in Jerusalem (cf. 17:5 with 16:21-23).

Verses 6-7: This scene, fashioned by Matthew (cf. Dan 10; Apoc 1:9-20; Acts 26:13-18) describes the effect of the hearing: mortals cannot bear the presence of the divine (Gen 17:3; Jos 5:14; Ez 1:28). The disciples' fear (LN 25.252) is banished only by the approach, the touch, the comforting and encouraging words (cf. Ez 2:1-3). The theological meaning is that Matthew sees the whole scene as an instruction concerning what the disciples will experience at their resurrection ("Rise"): the "Lord," arrived at splendor through suffering and death, will "come" to all who have "heard him" (cf. 28:18) and raise them up (*egeiro*: technical term for resurrection).

Verse 8: The vision and the audition come suddenly to an end; regarding "lift up their eyes" (Gen 18:2; 22:13; Josh 5:13. LN 24.34). The disciples see only Jesus, alone, and in his earthly form.

Verse 9: Again Jesus is named explicitly (cf. v. 8), which points to a new thought, but one which is connected with the epiphany ("as they were coming down the mountain"): the disciples must be silent about "the vision" until after the resurrection of the Son of Man. *Horama* (vision) appears only twelve times in the New Testament, of which eleven are in Acts; by the use of the term, Matthew intends the whole incident to be interpreted as a vision of the future splendor of the exalted Son of Man. Its effect on the witnesses, filling out the Old Testament view, is grace-filled, and encouraging.

As Jesus and the three descend from the mountain, Jesus commands them to silence concerning their experience (17:9). The importance of this command is dual: With respect to the plot of Matthew's story, Jesus' command informs the implied reader that not until the resurrection will the disciples comprehend that death is the essence of the ministry of Jesus Son of God. And with respect to the truth of the divine sonship of Jesus, Jesus' command serves, like the one following Peter's confession as well, to suppress knowledge of this truth so that the experience of the three disciples atop the mountain does not result in its public disclosure.

1. In the context of Jesus' way to Jerusalem (and thereby to death) the transfiguration takes on a special meaning. Going to death is not Jesus' end, but the transition into the exaltation of the Son of Man. To the disciples accompanying their Lord, who represents the community, the declaration is made that exaltation and glorification of the Son of Man will come at the end. Whoever listens to him, viz. the Messiah for all and the prophet of the end-time, will himself have a share in this resurrection. But what it means for the community "to hear," they know already from 7:21, 24; 16:18, 24, 28. The time "between" (between promise and fulfillment) cannot be shortened, but must be understood as the time for practical action and so, of watchfulness.

2. By the command to silence, the community is enjoined not to become absorbed in the imparted vision or to try to shorten the time of waiting. The instruction given Peter, who thought to make the future present by booth-building, applies to the entire community. So here too, misunderstanding characterizes Matthew's community when it is confronted with the Suffering Messiah. The future in glory already specifies the present. But the present is the time when it is fitting to live always in the light of the hoped for future, but at the same time in the awareness that in the already fulfilled time, "to hear" and "to do" are the precondition for participation in the promised future.

Elijah's Return, 17:10-13

After his first passion prediction, Jesus warns the disciples that they would have their own share of suffering (16:24-28). And after his transfiguration, Jesus speaks to them about the suffering of John the Baptist as foreshadowing the suffering he must soon endure.

10 And the disciples asked him, "Why, then, do the scribes say that Elijah must come first?" **11** He replied, "Elijah is indeed coming and will restore all things; **12** but I tell you that Elijah has already come, and they did not recognize him, but they did to him whatever they pleased. So also the Son of Man is about to suffer at their hands.'' **13** Then the disciples understood that he was speaking to them about John the Baptist.

Verses 10-11: "Why do the scribes say." The disciples' question is grounded on the opinion of the scribes current in Judaism, which was based on the combined texts of 1 Kings 17–2 Kings 2 and Malachi 3:1, 4:4-6 (cf. Sir 48:1-12). Among other things, Elijah was understood as precursor. Jesus both approves and corrects the disciples' question: Elijah does indeed come and will restore all things (for the Old Testament and Jewish scripture basis cf. J. Jeremias, *Hel(e)ias*" in *TWNT* II 931-934; the Elijah Redivivus brings the restitution of the People of God as is promised in Isa 11:1-12; Jer 12:14-17; Amos 9:11).

Verse 12: In antithetic form ("but") Jesus now gives his first answer. Elijah has already,unknown and unnoticed, come (cf. 11:14) and he suffered the typical prophet's fate—no recognition, rather arbitrary treatment (for "whatever they pleased" (cf. Dan 8:4 and Sir 8:15). But this was also the Baptist's fate, 11:12; 14:3-12; 21:32; personal identity is based on the suffering identity. In the third part of the answer, the fate of the Son of Man (cf. at 17:22-23) is likened to that of the returning Elijah. The time of Elijah is past, but not that of the Elijah-fate, so now the time has come for the Son of Man (*mello*, future sense LN 71.36) to suffer a prophet's fate.

"So also the Son of Man is about to suffer." Jesus drives home the point he tried to impress on the disciples in 16:21, the same point he will inculcate again and again through the rest of the Gospel: the Son of Man, the final prophet, must suffer a prophet's fate. Triumphant Son of God, yet martyred Son of Man—the paradox revealed at Caesarea Philippi has been graphically repeated and confirmed by God on the mount of transfiguration.

Verse 13: "Then the disciples understood." The Matthean disciples of course understand—at least about the Baptist. The part of the mystery of suffering that touches them more directly will again give rise to little faith.

The prophet Malachi had prophesied that before the terrible day of the Lord came, Elijah would be sent to ready Israel for the judgment this day would bring (4:5-6). In John's ministry, this prophecy becomes reality, but in altered fashion: John is the forerunner not of God, but of Jesus Messiah; and he prepares the way not for the final judgment as such, but for the ministry of Jesus.

An Epileptic Boy and the Disciples' Little Faith, 17:14-20

On the mountain of transfiguration Jesus predicts his passion, tells the disciples that they will have their share of suffering, and speaks of the sufferings of John the Baptist as foreshadowing his own. Jesus and the three disciples then descend the mountain to the crowd and the other disciples and Jesus teaches the disciples of the power of faith.

> **14** When they came to the crowd, a man came to him, knelt before him, **15** and said, "Lord, have mercy on my son, for he is an epileptic and he suffers terribly; he often falls into the fire and often into the water. **16** And I brought him to your disciples, but they could not cure him." **17** Jesus answered, "You faithless and perverse generation, how much longer must I be with you? How much longer must I put up with you? Bring him here to me." **18** And Jesus rebuked the demon, and it came out of him, and the boy was cured instantly. **19** Then the disciples came to Jesus privately and said, "Why could we not cast it out?" **20** He said to them, "Because of your little faith. For truly I tell you, if you have faith the size of a mustard seed, you will say to this mountain. 'Move from here to there,' and it will move, and nothing will be impossible for you."

This healing account, in all three synoptics (cf. Mk 9:14-29; Lk 9:37-43a), has received a special form through the hand of the redactors. Mark's expanded narrative (sixteen verses) is very short in Luke; that of Matthew is even shorter and tighter. Each evangelist connects a personal intention to the pericope. Especially important for Matthew is the contrast between Jesus and the disciples as brought out by the miracle and Jesus' words spoken in connection with it. That the sick boy is possessed Matthew mentions only in passing and not until verse 18; this manifests his tendency to allow belief in demons and fear of demons to pass into the background. The concluding word in Matthew (cf. Lk 17:6) is to be understood as his personal commentary on this healing pericope.

Verses 14-15: Jesus, his disciples, and the crowd form the scene into which "a man" enters as representative petitioner. Approaching Jesus, he manifests his trust with a genuflection (LN 17.19) and a respectful address ("Lord"). Thus the theme "Faith" dominates right from the start.

The request concerns his sick son who suffers from epilepsy (from an illness, which—according to primitive medical opinion—is connected with the phases of the moon (*seleniazetai*) and leads to uncontrollable seizures (LN 23.169). The health condition is serious (*kakos*, LN 20.18); in the seizures the youth often falls into the fire or into the water (so into "life threatening elements").

Verse 16: The petitioner refers to the inability of Jesus' disciples to "cure" (the therapeutic motif is stressed again). This report bespeaks a general disbelieving attitude on the part of the disciples.

Verse 17a, b: This generation—and the disciples are included here—is "faithless"; it does not believe that God was acting to save in Jesus of Nazareth. But it is also "perverse" (*diastrepho:* misguided, LN 88.264); it runs in the wrong direction (cf. Luke 9:41 and the rebuke in Deut 32:5, 20). This generation is hard to bear for one who has come for its salvation. How much longer must he "Put up with (*anechomai*)" them?

Verses 17c-18: The second "scene" ("Bring him here to me.") stands in strong contrast to the powerless disciples. The healing—only now is there mention of a demon—follows a curt order; without resistance, without injuring the sick boy, without a demonstration, the demon obeys. So it is not a question of an exorcism, but of a healing (*therapeuō:* serve, care for sick person, make healthy).

Verses 19-20: The third "scene" provides a stern lesson for the disciples, who are shaken by their powerlessness. The inability of verse 16 is taken up: *dia ti* why were we not able to help.

The historical present (NRSV "he said") introduces the decisive statement (v. 20): "Because of your little faith!" So among the disciples too, the question arises: What possibilities does faith open up? It is very hard to set the limit—to say that faith will carry you this far, and no further.

When Jesus comes down from the mountain and encounters the inability of the disciples to cast out the demon, Jesus again alludes to his imminent end when he asks, "How much longer must I be with you? How much longer must I put up with you?" This pericope is a stern warning to Matthew's community, always in danger of falling back into "little faith."

The Second Passion Prediction, 17:22-23

Still in Galilee, Jesus predicts his passion to the disciples for a second time. This prediction reminds the reader of the leitmotif of Part III of Matthew's story and conveys a sense of heightened tension. His prediction "distresses" the disciples; what he has said they understand, but why he does not turn aside from the events he has foretold escapes them.

22 As they were gathering in Galilee, Jesus said to them. "The Son of Man is going to be betrayed into human hands, **23** and they will kill him, and on the third day he will be raised." And they were greatly distressed.

A second passion prediction is introduced to stress the suffering and resurrection prophecy. Although there was already a reference in 16:13-22 to orientation toward Jerusalem, it is important for Matthew to place the three passion sayings before the Jerusalem events (first and second predictions in Galilee; the third prediction on the way to Jerusalem), so as to link Jesus' message and work with Jesus' passion, death, and resurrection.

Verses 22-23: The unspecified "they" are the disciples. As in the first passion prediction, Jesus stood before them and "said" (so also Luke, while Mark speaks of a "teaching"). Jesus' words contain a word play: the "Son of Man" will be delivered into the "hands of men" (the same word order is found in Luke). The second prediction refers to the intention to kill, the third to the fact of the resurrection (as in 16:21, Matthew speaks of resurrection on the third day). Matthew (unlike Mark and Luke) does not mention the disciples non-understanding and fear; yet the reference to the disciples' distress reveals that they find it hard to accept Jesus' passion fate.

Part II and Part III demonstrate the same continuity with their respective "superscriptions" and the same unity as obtained in Part I. Part II is tied together by three summary passages (4:23-25; 9:35; 11:1), and by a logical progression leading up to the climax of Peter's confession at Caesarea Philippi. Part III is also bound together by predictions of Jesus' death and resurrection (16:21; 17:22-23; 20:17-29). "Jerusalem" is explicitly mentioned at 16:21, and this geographical-theological reference to the passion and resurrection of Jesus establishes the overall theme which pervades these chapters. The climax to this section comes with the death and resurrection of Jesus and especially his final commissioning in 28:16-20.

This repetition of summary predictions is closely related to the geographical framework, since each of these predictions includes a reference to the journey to Jerusalem. "The journey motif is expressed in the first two passion predictions by Matthew (16.21; 17.22), but in the third passion prediction both Matthew and Jesus draw attention to the relationship between the journey of Jesus to Jerusalem and his passion and resurrection (20.17-18). Matthew has therefore constructed a pattern of prediction and fulfillment which undergirds the motif of the journey of Jesus to Jerusalem and provides that journey with its theological meaning" (Bauer, 97).

Avoiding Offense: The Temple Tax, 17:24-27

There are abundant signs that the members of Matthew's community were living in close proximity to hostile pagans. They were seemingly being hauled into court by Gentile authorities, judicially harassed, hated by all, and even put to death. On the other hand, it likewise seems that they were living in close proximity to a vigorous Jewish community. And Matthew is concerned that members of his community should not give needless offense to the Jews. It is with a view to the Church's relationship to Israel that Matthew reports the story of the payment of the temple tax.

> **24** When they reached Capernaum, the collectors of the temple tax came to Peter and said, "Does your teacher not pay the temple tax?" **25** He said, "Yes, he does." And when he came home, Jesus spoke of it first, asking, "What do you think, Simon? From whom do kings of the earth take toll or tribute? From their children or from others?" **26** When Peter said, "From others," Jesus said to him, "Then the children are free. **27** However, so that we do not give offense to them, go to the sea and cast a hook; take the first fish that comes up; and when you open its mouth, you will find a coin; take that and give it to them for you and me."

Verse 24: "When they reached Capernaum" (cf. at 4:13 8:5; 11:23). Jesus returns to Capernaum for the last time, an important stage on his momentous journey to Jerusalem. The idea of the coming visit to Jerusalem is hinted at by the motif of the temple and the possible clash which is avoided. The collectors of the temple tax naturally seek to collect it from Jesus in his hometown. The annual tax was to be paid by all male Jews over nineteen (cf. Exod 30:13-15), but priests and sometimes rabbis claimed exemption. Since even the enemies of Jesus considered him a "teacher," the collectors ask whether Jesus will pay the tax; the form of their question indicates that they expect that he will. Without reflecting, Peter answers yes. Peter obviously does not understand the full implications of eschatological fulfillment.

Verse 25: "But when he came home." Jesus needs to correct Peter. The "kings of the earth" are worldly rulers (cf. Ps 2:2; 89:27) who have the right to have taxes ("toll and tribute") collected through agents (LN 57.179): "*telos* [toll] probably refers primarily to custom duties, while *kēnsos* [tribute] refers to a direct tax upon all adult males." It is a question of civil taxes (so also Rom 14:7) which the *telones*, the tax farmers, exacted as tribute [*tributum capitis*]. The "kings of the earth" exacted this tribute from strangers (not from family, from their own people), therefore, not from their own sons. But because Jesus and Peter are "sons" (LN 11.69), they enjoy freedom from the tax. Jesus here claims the "father/son" relationship in a special degree, on another, higher level. God's (house)community stands high above the subjects of a worldly ruler.

Verse 26: "Then the children are free." This filial language is another way of establishing a comparison between Jesus and the disciples. In addition to the elements of mission and ethical behavior, this language also points to the essential comparison between Jesus and the role of the disciples. "Matthew indicates that both Jesus and the disciples are 'sons' of God and 'know' God as Father. Jesus' unique filial relationship to God as his son is maintained by the care Matthew exercises in having Jesus consistently differentiate between 'my father' and 'your father'; the Matthean Jesus never speaks of 'our Father' " (Bauer, 62). Yet the fact remains that both Jesus and the disciples are identified, respectively, as "Son" and "sons" of the Father. Here, Jesus indicates explicitly that the privileges of sonship which he enjoys belong, in certain cases, also to the disciples.

Verse 27: "So that we do not give offense (*me skandalizomen*)" LN 25.179. The tax farmers (and those they work for) should be given no cause for complaint. But the nature and the manner of providing the money (underlined with the help of an exaggerated nature miracle) should demonstrate that Jesus did not regard the payment of these taxes to be obligatory. The miraculous provision of the money (*statēr*, LN 6.80) underlines the theological message, that earthly legal structures receive their validity from the heavenly level.

"Take the first fish." "In addition to the expression of Jesus' authority within his ministry and in his relation to the Church, this authority is also indicated by references to Jesus' transcendent knowledge" (Bauer, 120). The predictions that Jesus makes are fulfilled. This transcendent knowledge is demonstrated also by the ability of Jesus to discern the thoughts of others (8:4) and to know of events at which he was not present, as here. Moreover, Jesus has the ability to declare the eschatological future (19:28; chs. 24-25).

The story of the payment of the temple tax seems to indicate that the Jewish Christians in Matthew's community were being encouraged, despite their "freedom," not to offend Jews by refusing to participate in the collection of contributions throughout Jewry in support of the Patriarchy at Jamnia. The destruction of Jerusalem created a religious vacuum in Judaism. But Johanan ben Zakkai received permission from Vespasian to found a school for the study of the law in Jamnia (Jabneh). The

Jewish Christians wondered whether they should support this new religious institution.

The dialogue between Jesus and Peter supplies the answer. The parable about "the kings of the earth" reaffirmed the Christians' fundamental freedom and made them aware of their union with Jesus and their special relation to the Father. "But since an external expression of independence might run the risk of offending their fellow-Jews, the further instructions to Peter (v. 27) suggested that the Jewish Christians donate to the High Council. Thus, Matthew understood Jesus' teaching about the freedom of sons and his instructions for paying the half-shekel as a norm which he applied to a new situation after the destruction of the temple" (W. Thompson, *Divided Community*, 68).

ECCLESIOLOGICAL DISCOURSE, CHAPTER 18

In the house at Capernaum a final time, Jesus first engages Peter in dialogue about the payment of the temple tax (17:24-27), and then delivers his ecclesiological discourse to all the disciples (18:1-35). In this discourse, Jesus instructs the disciples regarding their life together as a community. The characteristic mark of this life is "true greatness" (v. 1), that is, showing infinite concern for one another and forgiving one another.

Toward those on the outside, the disciples, as sons of God and his followers, are in principle free and responsible only to God. At the same time, they must not lead lives in society that are less than exemplary, or employ their freedom to give needless offense to others and hence, foreclose the possibility that others may become his followers. Toward one another, the disciples should lead lives that comport themselves with a community presided over by Jesus: in recognition of their total dependence on God, they deal with one another in the spirit of loving concern, of circumspection, of mutuality, and of forgiveness.

Jesus' message to the disciples is that loving concern for the neighbor and the spirit of forgiveness are to be the hallmarks of the community of believers in whose midst he, the Son of God, will ever be present.

As the parable discourse dealt with the mystery of the Kingdom growing like a hidden seed in an unfriendly world, so chapter 18 deals with the relations within the Church, the conditions necessary for healthy interaction among disciples. The problems of living together are apparent from the key-words; the Church must come to terms with scandal, members who go astray, sinful brothers who resist correction, and the tendency of righteous members to set limits on forgiveness. "In other words, the basic problem in Church life is sin, and the basic solution is the mercy of the Father" (J. Meier, 200).

Greatness in the Kingdom, 18:1-5

In the house at Capernaum a final time, Jesus first engages Peter in dialogue about the temple tax (17:24-27) and then delivers his ecclesiological discourse to all the disciples (18:1-35). The theme that underlies the ecclesiological discourse is "life within the community of the Church." The two broad sections that make up this discourse are: 1) On true greatness as consisting in humbling oneself so as to serve the neighbor (18:1-14); and 2) On gaining and forgiving the errant disciple (18:15-35). In this passage Matthew borrows from the "household code" genre (cf. *NJBC* 54.26).

> **1** At that time the disciples came to Jesus and asked, "Who is the greatest in the kingdom of heaven?" **2** He called a child, whom he put among them, **3** and said, "Truly I tell you, unless you change and become like children, you will never enter the kingdom of heaven. **4** Whoever becomes humble like this child is the greatest in the kingdom of heaven. **5** Whoever welcomes one such child in my name welcomes me.

Verse 1: "At that time"—a new (literary) beginning, which at the same time signals the crucial meaning of what follows. The objective of a comprehensive community rule is clear; it is a question of true greatness in the Kingdom of God. *"The disciples came"*—the addresees are the implied readers in their position bctwccn rcsurrcction and parousia. They overhear words Jesus addresses to the disciples of Jesus' time; the message is for them. *In the kingdom of heaven"*—taken in conjunction with verse 3 ("enter the kingdom of heaven"), the disciples' question does not mean, who now in the disciples' circle is the greatest, but who in the final fulfilled Kingdom of God will be the greatest. "The question may primarily refer to the final stage of the kingdom after the last judgment; but, granted Matthew's idea of a number of stages in the coming of the kingdom . . . the question also envisages greatness in the Church, the main instrument of the kingdom in this present age" (J.Meier, *ad loc.*).

The disciples recognize, in contrast to Israel's leaders, Jesus as the herald of the Kingdom of God, even if they are often of "little faith," but never without faith and confession.

Verse 2: "He called a child." The answer to the disciples' question, which is not oriented to the historical situation but given as a fundamental theological consideration, comes in a twofold form: in word and sign. The sign is a child, viewed as an exemplar and contrast to the body of adults chosen by God. That the child is placed obtrusively in the midst of the men underlines the sign character still further.

Verse 3: The explanation of the sign (in direct address) is not embodied in a teaching, but in an address to the disciples. Matthew's "Truly, I tell you" emphasizes the basic character of the pronouncement. "Become like children"—in the kingdom of God, which is being realized in the community, the only acceptable attitude involves turning and becoming like children (cf. 3:2; 4:17). This interrelation of picture and word is in the prophetic tradition; the sign that Jesus uses here so skillfully is a prophetic sign. The greatest is the one humbling himself; the type of the greatest is the small, ignored, often overlooked child. "Change" (*strepho* here indicates a mental and character change in the sense of *metanoia*, moral reorientation (LN 31.60, 41.50).

We must forget our contemporary views of childhood and realize that, at the time of Jesus, children were pieces of property without any rights. Powerless to defend themselves, they had to rely totally on others. Jesus is recommending not childishness but a child-like trust in a loving Father. Jesus has declared that one of the characteristics of members in the eschatological community is "meekness" (5:5), a term which Matthew connects with "gentleness" or "humility" (1:29). Apparently, these terms are at least generally synonymous for Matthew. Jesus demands humility of his followers in 18:3-4 and 23:12. But Matthew presents Jesus as the prime model of humility.

Verse 4: From this condition for entrance Jesus then draws a conclusion about greatness in the kingdom: greatness belongs to the one who maintains this childlike sense of littleness, and so proves he or she belongs to the free children of God (cf. 17:26). The sense of verse 3 climaxes in the verb "humble one's self" *tapeinoo* (LN 88.56) in verse 4, which expresses the correct attitude before God. But this involves not just the experience of humility before God, but the voluntary act of self-abasement. Only those will receive the end-time reward of exaltation who have made themselves small, humble, patient. The demanded refashioning of heart and the change of mentality demanded reveal the ethical character of Jesus' demands.

Verse 5: "One such child." Such a humble person is a brother of Jesus, and therefore whoever receives such a humble person—be that person a child or a child-like Christian—because of Jesus will receive the Son himself. If that happens "in Jesus' name," i.e., in the spirit of discipleship and fraternity, then one really receives Jesus himself. "*Epi to onomati*" has, as already in the LXX, the meaning of "in relation to (the authority of)."

Matthew fashioned this scene around the contrasts great/small, high/low, honored/despised. At the beginning of the community discourse he points out the only attitude valid before God. Who counts as great before God? Not the important, the honored, cultivated, those who are regarded as great "in the world"; but the small, unmentioned, those standing in the background and the shadows of the mighty, count as great before him, This important message is placed up front, at the beginning of the community discourse because the community must not ignore this urgent message. The "poor in spirit" are identical with the humble who expect nothing from human powers and everything from heavenly help. Greatest in the Kingdom of Heaven is one like that child that Jesus places in the midst of the disciples.

Called through baptism to follow Jesus, the risen and exalted Son of God who presides over and resides in his Church, the intended readers of Matthew's Gospel know themselves to be "children of God" and "brothers and sisters" of Jesus and of one another. As children of God, they are also "little ones," for they understand themselves to be totally dependent on their heavenly Father (18:3, 6, 10). As the brothers and sisters of Jesus and of one another, they were at the same time the "servants" and the "slaves" of one another (20:25-28).

Stumbling Blocks before Little Ones, 18:6-9

6 "If any of you put a stumbling block before one of these little ones who believe in me, it would be better for you if a great millstone were fastened around your neck and you were drowned in the depth of the sea. 7 Woe to the world because of stumbling blocks! Occasions for stumbling are bound to come, but woe to the one by whom the stumbling block comes! 8 If your hand or your foot causes you to stumble, cut it off and throw it away; it is better for you to enter life maimed or lame than to have two hands or two feet and to be thrown into the eternal fire. 9 And if your eye causes you to stumble, tear it out and throw it away; it is better for you to enter life with one eye than to have two eyes and to be thrown into the hell of fire.

Here Matthew has worked two traditions together. First he takes up the pericope also handed on by Luke (17:1-2) of offenses against the little ones. To this he adds the saying that temptations must come (v. 7b); they are grounded in the condition of this world. Then Matthew adds a tradition also witnessed by Mark (9:43-48), but which he again shortens. The warning against scandal reflects an actual discussion in the community between the progressive and conservative groups as we see them also (e.g., in 1 Cor 16 or in Rom 14).

Verse 6: Matthew speaks of "cause to sin (*skandalise*)," a word he uses frequently (13:41; 16:23; 18:7 [three times]. It is not found in Mark,; Luke uses it only once. Matthew uses it for leading astray, cause the downfall of a community brother. The *mikroi* (the little ones) are those who believe in Christ. They do believe but are shaky in the faith and are easily led astray. Whoever gives a shove to these helpless and wavering ones, should be destroyed. A millstone (*mylos onikos*, LH 4.32; 7.69, i.e., upper stone moved by an ass, much larger than that of a handmill), so a very great weight, should be placed around his neck, to banish him to the depth of the sea, the dwelling place of demons. This punishment, exceeding all measures, is thought of as a fitting warning. Yet this possibility gives a glimpse into the horrible depths of the mystery. With a millstone about his neck the scandalizer is sunk to the bottom "of the sea"—a destruction forever and always.

Verse 7: The "woe" exclamation is directed to the whole world, a prophetic word of warning to all. Regarding offense there remains for all only a choice between two possibilities, the horrifying torture of hell fire and heavenly lot in the Father's Kingdom. The "necessity" expressed by *anagkē*, i.e., force (LN 71.38), with which the evil must happen, is that of the self-destructive power of evil: "For evil ripens, even as God's seed ripens."

Verses 8-9: Jesus knows what fearsome scandals this selfish power-crazed world will experience as it hurtles towards its end. Jesus warns his disciples not to give into the drive for power. Better to suffer physical loss than eternal damnation. Matthew used a similar exhortation to spiritual rather than physical integrity when he forbade sexual lust in the individual (5:29-30); here it forbids lust for power in the Church.

The "little ones" must be treated with kindness and respect. In verse 6 we have a warning of the unspeakable fate that is in store at the judgment for anyone who causes trouble for them. The verb "put a stumbling block before" verges on the meaning "lead into apostasy." "It is probably, at least in the understanding of Matthew, aimed at false teachers who lead simple Christians into error or unbelief, rather than at vicious people who lead children into criminal conduct." (E. Beare, *ad loc*).

The Care of Sheep Going Astray, 18:10-14

After the severe warnings about the evil of scandal (18:5-9), the tone of the discourse becomes doctrinal, as Jesus presents the parable of the sheep going astray. Matthew's repetition of the key-phrase "one of these little ones" (vv. 10a, 14) recalls "one of these little ones who believe in me" (v. 6) and the question about its meaning. In the previous context, it described a disciple whose faith in Jesus can be weakened. The phrase "these little ones" frames the parable and marks a literary unit in the discourse (vv. 10, 14).

> **10** "Take care that you do not despise one of these little ones; for, I tell you, in heaven their angels continually see the face of my Father in heaven. **12** What do you think? If a shepherd has a hundred sheep, and one of them has gone astray, does he not leave the ninety-nine on the mountains and go in search of the one that went astray? **13** And if he finds it, truly I tell you, he rejoices over it more than over the ninety-nine that never went astray. **14** So it is not the will of your Father in heaven that one of these little ones should be lost."

In Matthew's version, this pericope consists of three parts: a) a demand that "little ones" not be despised (v. 10); b) the parable of the Lost Sheep (vv. 12-13); c) the explanation of the parable (v. 14). The repetition of the number ninety-nine in verse 13 makes it clear that in Matthew, the contrast between the one and the ninety-nine stands in the foreground; for the care of the "one" is the Father's will (cf. EvThom 107: "I love you more than the ninety-nine)." Verse 11 ("For the Son of Man comes [to seek and] to save the lost") is inserted here incorrectly; it is lacking in the oldest witnesses of the various text groups. Clearly it is taken over from Luke 19:10, to provide a (closer) connection between verse 10 and verses 1-3.

Verse 10: "See that you do not despise" (*Kataphroneō* = despise, count for little), is found in the New Testament only nine times, elsewhere in Matthew only at 6:24; the verb expresses the absolute opposite of "love," and "honor" (LN 88.192). Three times in chapter 18 Matthew speaks of "one of these little ones" (v. 6, 10, 14; cf. already 10:42). Verse 6 is concerned with those whose faith in Jesus can be endangered by offenses; here it is a question of a community member who is ignored or even despised by others. The previous warning (v. 6) "one of these little ones who believe in me" described the disciple whose faith in Jesus can be weakened through scandal. Another disciple can cause him to stumble and fall. The present prohibition goes beyond that warning to forbid all forms of contempt. It is addressed to all the disciples (second person plural), but the concrete situation which might cause their disdain is not described. The general expression "one of these little ones" refers to a member of the community whom the disciples may be apt to disregard or even condemn.

"Their angels always behold." Jewish theology had developed the idea of the guardian angel, but the rabbis also held that only the highest of angels could have direst access to the divine presence, "see the face of my father." Jesus thus declares that it is the highest types of angels who watch over the little ones and who plead their cause before God—who, Jesus pointedly adds, is "my Father."

Verses 12: "Leave the ninety-nine on the mountain." The disciples must paradoxically care more for these weak Christians, like the shepherd who acts against all human calculations by leaving the ninety-nine safe sheep and seeking the one sheep which has strayed.

Verse 13: "He rejoices over it." The disciples, like the shepherd should experience more joy in actively saving the endangered sheep than in passively tending the sheep who are safe.

Verse 14: As is typical in Matthew, even the exhortation to rejoice is traced back to the will of "your Father" that not one of the little ones be lost. Doing the will of the Father, the essence of the Matthean ethic, is not some dreadfully dour duty; it is sharing the redemptive joy of Jesus. The mention of the "little ones" in verse 14 provides an inclusion with the beginning of the subsection (v. 6).

The prohibition in verse 10a goes beyond the previous warnings against scandal (vv. 5-9) to forbid any form of contempt. It is addressed to all the disciples, and the more general tone suggests that "one of these little ones" refers to any disciple whom the others may be inclined to disregard or condemn. The reason for such contempt (lack of faith, youth, poverty, moral weakness, etc.) is not indicated.

A close association between "one of these little ones" (vv. 10a, 14) and the one sheep going astray is suggested. "This association," W. Thompson writes in his *Divided Community*, explains Matthew's interpretation of the parable (vv. 12-13) and the final doctrinal statement (v. 14).

> First of all, he distinguishes between *planan* ["go astray"] (vv. 12-13) and *apollumai* ["be lost"] (v. 14). This distinction is unimportant at the level of imagery, but becomes decisive in the application to the community. For even though "one of these little ones" has begun to go astray from the community of disciples, it is the will of the Father in heaven that he not be lost. Secondly, Matthew emphasizes the contrast between the one sheep going astray and the ninety-nine that never went astray. Applied to the community, this contrast affirms the value and importance of "one of these little ones" whose angel looks upon the face of the Father in heaven. Thirdly, Matthew indicates that the shepherd may not always find the one sheep (*ean genetai heurein auto*). This means that the disciple who has begun to go astray may not always be found and brought back to the community. Finally, Matthew presents the par-

able as the basis in human experience for understanding the Father's will with regard to "one of these little ones" (v. 14). He has emphasized the shepherd's zeal because it resembles the Father's concern that not one of the disciples be lost. Therefore, "one of these little ones" is the disciple toward whom others may be inclined to show disregard or even contempt because he has begun to go astray from the community. But he actually enjoys a special position of honor before the Father in heaven who wills that he not be lost. The implications of this teaching for the other disciples will be made more specific in the following instructions about reconciliation (vv. 15-20) (p. 164).

Reconciling a Community Member, 18:15-20

Indications are that by A.D. 85 or 90 the Matthean community had already developed a structure for governing its communal life. The outlines of this structure can be discerned in Matthew's portrait of the disciples. We have already seen how Peter is depicted as receiving from Jesus the promise of the power of the "keys of the kingdom of heaven." Now this is further specified by the power of "binding and loosing," which pertains to the regulation of Church doctrine and Church discipline.

> **15** "If another member of the church sins against you, go and point out the fault when the two of you are alone. If the member listens to you, you have regained that one. **16** But if you are not listened to, take one or two others along with you, so that every word may be confirmed by the evidence of two or three witnesses. **17** If the member refuses to listen to them, tell it to the church; and if the offender refuses to listen even to the church, let such a one be to you as a Gentile and a tax collector. **18** Truly I tell you, whatever you bind on earth will be bound in heaven, and whatever you loose on earth will be loosed in heaven. **19** Again, truly I tell you, if two of you agree on earth about anything you ask, it will be done for you by my Father in heaven. **20** For where two or three are gathered in my name, I am there among them."

This pericope is special to Matthew; only verse 15 has a short parallel in Luke 17:3. The latter warns the erring member to correct his behavior and urges that he be forgiven if he reforms. Matthew, for his part, gives a three-step ordered procedure to be followed: correction with no one else present (v. 15); in case of refusal, addition of two community members (v. 16); in the case of further stubborn refusal, public correction before the community (v. 17). This reflects Jewish legal practices.

Verse 15: "The two of you are alone." "Sin" in the community is handled here under the aspect of fraternal correction. "Sin" (*hamartanō*) is an offense of a community member against a fellow member. The offense endangers the unity of the community, which is guaranteed only through mutual love. The one who notices the failings of another, must take the first step toward overcoming them: to go and correct him privately. According to Leviticus 19:17b "you shall reason with your neighbor." The observed failing should be openly named, yet first in private speech, whereby the guilty one is spared, a scandal avoided, and a reputation saved. If the dialogue is successful, then the one who took the initiative can chalk up a success (*kerdainō*, means to mark up a win).

·Verse 16: "One or two others." If the erring brother does not listen, according to Deuteronomy 19:15, a new effort should be made and this time before witnesses. These are not thought of as criminal witnesses; the verdicts of the Jewish trial proceedings (Deut 19:15) were aimed more at establishing the full truth and avoiding a serious misjudgment.

Verse 17: "Tell it to the Church." If this attempt also fails, the case must be laid before the Ekklesia. Here the word Ekklesia designates the community of believers gathered in the place. The Jewish expulsion from the synagogue is not involved here (or a similar procedure); rather the whole community with the weight of its authority should repeat the warning and give correction. If the culprit will not listen to the community then let the judgment be (according to a proverbial expression): "Let him be as a Gentile and a tax collector." Through his refusal to use prudence and to repent, the sinner already stands outside the community and should be regarded as such.

Verse 18: "Bind and loose" (cf. 16:19. Cf. also Introduction, Sacred Canopy, p. 9). The redactional, "Truly I say to you," underlines the connection and stresses verse 18 as summation of verses 15-17. "Bind" and "loose" are technical terms from rabbinical theological vocabulary, by which is designated either the exercise of teaching power (what is permitted or forbidden), or of the disciplinary power (reception and exclusion of a member from the community). So the logion verse 18 transfers authority to the community to decide concerning the exclusion and readmittance of one of its members. The parallel to 16:19 is not to be overlooked; there, the normal authority was given to a single person (Peter), now here to the Ekklesia. And both transfers are sanctioned by Jesus. Here it is sufficient to establish that the Church, the community gathered on the spot, possesses the full and unrestricted power to decide concerning the membership of its members.

Matthew is unique among the Synoptic evangelists in the amount of authority he invests in the disciples. Here the power of binding and loosing is granted to the community in 18:18 and to Peter particularly in 16:19. Here the decisions of the community and its leaders are depicted as possessing the authority and sanction of heaven. The decisions that are made in the community are at the same time also made in heaven. Here J. Meier speaks of an anti-hierarchical tendency in chapter 18 (p. 206), but J. Gnilka sees no contradiction between 16:19 and this text. "The Petrine authority extends to the whole Church in 16:19 while here it is a question of authority exercised in a local community" (II, p. 139).

Verse 19: "On earth . . . in heaven." (cf. Introduction, Sacred Canopy, p. 9).

Verse 20: "I am there among them." "What such close association with Jesus means is explained by Matthew in the key passages 1:23 ('Emmanuel . . . God [is] *with us*'), 18:20 ('there am I *in the midst of them*'), and 28:20 ('I am *with you* always'). It means that through his presence Jesus Messiah, the earthly and exalted Son of God, mediates to his disciples or church the gracious, saving presence of God and his Rule" (J. Kingsbury, *Story*, 131–32). These references to the presence of Jesus in the midst of his community (1:23; 18:20; 26:29) lead up to the climactic declaration of 28:20. As the disciples confront their universal mission, Jesus promises to be with them always. In other words, the post-Easter existence of the Church is characterized above all by the continual presence of Jesus.

Forgiveness in the Kingdom of Heaven, 18:21-35

Acceptance of suffering and service by the disciples in analogy to Jesus stands behind the instructions which Jesus gives to his disciples throughout the section on community life. His followers are not to insist on their own prerogatives when these prerogatives cause offense to others (17:24-27; 18:5-14); rather, they are to humble themselves like little children (18:1-4; 19:13-15). The disciples are not to orient their lives around response to personal hurt, but they are to forgive others freely (18.21-35).

> **21** Then Peter came and said to him, "Lord, if another member of the church sins against me, how often should I forgive? As many as seven times?" **22** Jesus said to him, "Not seven times, but, I tell you, seventy-seven times.
> **23** "For this reason the kingdom of heaven may be compared to a king who wished to settle accounts with his slaves. **24** When he began

the reckoning, one who owed him ten thousand talents was brought to him, **25** and, as he could not pay, his lord ordered him to be sold, together with his wife and children and all his possessions, and payment to be made. **26** So the slave fell on his knees before him, saying, "Have patience with me, and I will pay you everything." **27** And out of pity for him, the lord of that slave released him and forgave him the debt. **28** But that same slave, as he went out, came upon one of his fellow slaves who owed him a hundred denarii; and seizing him by the throat, he said, "Pay what you owe." **29** Then his fellow slave fell down and pleaded with him, "Have patience with me, and I will pay you." **30** But he refused; then he went and threw him into prison until he would pay the debt. **31** When his fellow slaves saw what had happened, they were greatly disturbed, and they went and reported to their lord all that had taken place. **32** Then his lord summoned him and said to him, "You wicked slave! I forgave you all that debt because you pleaded with me. **33** Should you not have had mercy on your fellow slave, as I had mercy on you? **34** And in anger his lord handed him over to be tortured until he would pay his entire debt. **35** So my heavenly Father will also do to every one of you, if you do not forgive your brother or sister from your heart."

In this pericope the focus shifts again, this time to the brother who is not recalcitrant, but who sins often and therefore needs forgiveness often. Since guilt is readily admitted, forgiveness remains on a one-to-one level. The parable is handed on only by Matthew. In the context of chapter 18 and as the closure of the chapter which dealt with the relations of community members with one another, it serves as a vivid illustration of the preceding sayings, above all of the one about unrestricted forgiveness 18:21-22, In verse 35, outside the parable, Matthew limits it to the Christian fellow member (in the community), while originally it was applied to all.

The two debtors find themselves in an extreme situation (cf. v. 26 with v. 29); yet the greatness of their debts is unequal. The reaction of the first, to whom an enormous debt is forgiven, against his fellow servant, who owes him a small debt, is monstrous, but therein lies the meaning of the parable: it shows that the severe punishment of the first servant is correct.

Verse 21: Again Peter acts as spokesman (14:28; 15:15; 16:16, 22; 17:4; 19:27). The short dialogue begins with a direct question; the address "lord" is meaningful. The one standing before Peter is not the teacher and master, but the *Kyrios* endowed with authority and filled with God's splendor, who imparts his authorative teaching. The theme of sin is continued; but now it is said clearly that a sin against one's own brother is involved (*hamarano* means the violation of the love of neighbor). The theme is the measure of forgiveness; more exactly, the question about "how often" (LN 67.14). Behind it stands the thought that an "excess" of forgiveness cannot be expected of a person (something like: "enough is enough!"). The number named in the question is a common round number. The questioners understand "seven times" (LN 60.73; fn8) as the maximum; if this maximum is used up, then—so the intended meaning is—so also is the duty of forgiveness.

Verse 22: In Jesus' answer (which is a historical present), after the question which sets a limit, a number is cited that expresses an utterly unlimited readiness for forgiveness (LN 60.74). This unexpected answer has the sound of a proverb, but by its form and succinctness, it carries conviction (possibly Jesus reverses Lamech vindication song of Gen 4:24).

The community, versed in the Old Testament scriptures knew the song that Lamech, one of Cain's descendants, sang before his wives:

> "Adah and Zillah: hear my voice;
>   you wives of Lamech, hearken to what I say:
> I have slain a man for wounding me,
>   a young man for striking me.
> If Cain is avenged sevenfold,
>   truly Lamech seventy-sevenfold."

Cain had rejoiced in Yahweh's protection, no one dare kill him (Gen 4:15); but if it happened, Cain would be revenged sevenfold: In his pride, Lamech would outdo Cain: he will receive a revenge out of all proportion, unlimited.

Against the example of unlimited revenge, Jesus sets unlimited reconciliation. Since sin is so rife in the world, it can only be balked where an equally great amount of good is set against it. To the "natural insistence on right," Matthew's community must make its own the "totally opposed" command ("I tell you") and form its community life according to it. Natural sensibilities have no place there, where mercy becomes the highest norm of fraternal behavior (cf. the fifth beatitude 5:7).

Verse 23: "The kingdom of heaven may be compared to." The parable makes a statement about the kingdom of heaven, or more precisely, about the behavior of persons under the claim of "the kingdom of heaven." It is the story of a king who one day settled accounts (*synairo logon* is a business term, LN 57.228); the servants are not slaves but administrators. "Therefore (*dia tanto*)" establishes a connection with the preceding in both form and content: the theme of forgiveness and reconciliation is continued.

Verses 24-25: First one is brought in who owes an enormous sum (*talanton*, LN 6.82). The administrator is unable to pay the debt; the king, now designated as "lord" orders (LN 33.323) the debtor and his family and his goods to be sold to save what could be saved (here Hellenistic legal arrangements are involved).

Verses 26-27: The debtor throws himself down before his master and appeals to his generosity (LN 25.168). He is ready to repay everything; so he asks for a debt deferment. The master has pity, cancels the order that he be sold, and forgives him the debt (*daneion* = loan, then debt, a technical term of the loan trade of antiquity, LN 57.210G). The master's pity (forgiveness) goes far beyond the administrator's request.

Verses 28-30: The narrative continues with a contrast. The one who had just experienced mercy and forgiveness of debt in superabundant measure, meets a fellow servant (LN 87.81), who owes him a comparatively minimal sum (*dēnarion*, LN 6.75). On the demand, "Pay what you owe" (which is lacking in vv. 24-25), the first administrator's actions are repeated ("fell down," "besought," appeal for "patience"). But "he refused," remains hard, and does to his fellow servant what he himself had been spared: He has his debtor imprisoned.

Verse 31: His fellow servants are incensed (*lypeo* literally means "to be sad"), and they report the affair to their master (*diasapheō* = make clear LN 33.260). They do this in the hope that their master will take steps against the first servant to help the second.

Verses 32-34: The parable culminates in the master's speech (the present historical refers to the high point of the parable and narrative); the administrator is wicked because he drew no corresponding consequence out of the magnanimity that his master had shown him. The words ("should not you have had") make the point clearly, that mercy must be answered by mercy. The burden of debt is restored, and the servant is delivered to the jailers (LN 37.126). This again reveals a non-Jewish background. There is no hope: "Till he should pay all his debt" can only mean, "that there will be no end to the punishment" (Jeremias, *Parables*, 210).

Verse 35: The application comes from Matthew (cf. "So also,""my heavenly Father," "do," "brother" etc.). It has the community situation reflected in chapter 18 in mind; every member must forgive every other "from his heart." The king (viz., lord), is now presented as the Heavenly Father, who makes his own forgiveness of debt dependent upon the member's readiness for reconciliation.

As a whole, the narrative treats of God and of his behavior toward humans. Two meanings above all are brought home to the community:

a) The warning against hardness of heart: if community members do not forgive one another, their eternal salvation is in danger. Only those will receive forgiveness on judgment day who have done the same for other members.

b) The proportion of God's forgiveness: the king's debt forgiveness in the parable exceeds all human dimensions. But community members must know that they are dependent upon this superabundant mercy. Everyone heaps sin upon sin, guilt upon guilt, just like the first servant. Thereby, the relationship of the brothers among themselves is raised to a entirely new level. They are related as persons who live by the mercy of the same Lord.

Once again, Matthew not only presents an earlier tradition, but also re-interprets it to meet the needs of his community. He transformed an earlier saying into a more dramatic dialogue about unlimited forgiveness (vv. 21-22). He introduced the story of the unforgiving servant (vv. 23-24) to illustrate the Father's attitude toward a disciple who fails to forgive a personal offense (v. 35). "This evidence reveals Matthew's interpretation and provides an insight into the concrete situation which influenced his arrangement and composition. The members of his community needed a forceful reminder that they should always forgive a personal offense. Matthew concludes the discourse with this important lesson" (W. Thompson, *Divided Community*, 237).

Close of Fourth Discourse, Journey to Jerusalem, 19:1-2

Leaving Galilee at last, Jesus moves toward Jerusalem, traveling first into the regions of Judea across the Jordan. From 16:21 on, the narrative of Matthew's Gospel is unified by means of the journey to Jerusalem. Matthew alerts the reader to this journey already in 16:21, where he tells us that Jesus shows his disciples that he must go to Jerusalem. The reference to "go" is significant, for by it Matthew gives notice that Jesus will continue his travels through Galilee (17:22) to Capernaum (17:24), then away from Galilee to Judea beyond the Jordan (19:1), on to Jericho (20:29), until he and his disciples reach the environs of Jerusalem in 21:1, and Jerusalem itself in 21:10.

> **19:1** When Jesus had finished saying these things, he left Galilee and went to the region of Judea beyond the Jordan. **2** Large crowds followed him, and he cured them there.

Verse 1: For the closure formula of the fourth speech, see what is said at 7:28. With the first half of the verse, Matthew closes out the foregoing discourse, with the second half he introduces the following literary unit. "He left Galilee"—at this point it is well to note that Matthew is at pains to show that this ministry takes place almost exclusively within the confines of Israel. Galilee is the place of Jesus' activity, and he traverses the whole of it. It is from Galilee that news of him spreads throughout all Syria (4:24), and it is to Galilee that the crowds from the Decapolis, Jerusalem, Judea, and across the Jordan come to be with him (4:25). When Jesus leaves Galilee, it is only briefly. When he withdraws into the regions of Tyre and Sodom, he merely crosses the border, for it is said of the Canaanite woman that she "came out" toward him (15:21-28). Only once does Jesus undertake a journey during his public ministry that is actually regarded as taking him away from the environs of Galilee, and this is his fateful trip to Jerusalem (19:2).

Verse 2: "Large crowds follow him." *Akoloutheō* here has the literal, not the metaphorical meaning of full discipleship which involves cost and commitment (cf. 8:1). Instead of a teaching of the people (so Mark 10:1), Matthew speaks of Jesus' healing the sick (cf. 4:23; 14:14). "Curiously, at this point Mark stresses Jesus' teaching, which Matthew changes to healing. Perhaps Matthew has in mind that since the parable chapter (chap. 13), Jesus has withdrawn from any extensive teaching of the crowds— though this teaching ministry will resume in Jerusalem" (Meier, 214).

Marriage in the Light of the Kingdom, 19:3-9

As Jesus makes his way to Jerusalem, he teaches the disciples and heals the sick. Only once does he clash with the religious leaders (19:3-9), over the question of divorce. Married couples and celibates are the first groups in the Church considered in this section of the Gospel. Jesus first excludes divorce by presenting the positive teaching on marriage from Genesis, then explains the reason for the Mosaic permission of divorce in Deuteronomy, and concludes with a statement of casuistic law equating divorce with adultery.

> **3** Some Pharisees came to him, and to test him they asked, "Is it lawful for a man to divorce his wife for any cause?" **4** He answered, "Have you not read that the one who made them at the beginning 'made them male and female,' **5** and said, 'For this reason a man shall leave his father and mother and be joined to his wife, and the two shall become one flesh? **6** So they are no longer two, but one flesh. Therefore what

God has joined together, let no one separate." **7** They said to him, "Why then did Moses command us to give a certificate of dismissal and to divorce her?" **8** He said to them, "It was because you were so hard-hearted that Moses allowed you to divorce your wives, but from the beginning it was not so. **9** And I say to you, whoever divorces his wife, except for unchastity, and marries another commits adultery."

Verse 3: "To test him." Matthew emphasizes from the start that the Pharisees come with malicious intent to put Jesus to the test (cf. 22:18, 35). They ask about the grounds for divorce. Many commentators presume that "for any cause" refers to the dispute between the schools of Hillel and Shammai. But asking Jesus to side with one of the two famous and revered schools hardly constitutes the type of malicious and dangerous test we see elsewhere in Matthew's presentation of the Jewish leaders The Pharisees already know about Jesus' teaching on divorce (5:31-32), and now seek to force Jesus into an open break with the Torah.

Verses 4-5: "Made them male (*arsen*, LN 79.102) and female (*thēlos*, LN 72.103)." The scripture proof from Genesis (1:17; 2:24) stands up front. Matthew understands this text, which he quotes according to the LXX, as a word of God. Matthew uses the creation commandment and adapts it for the point he is making. Through the explicit naming of the creation (*ho ktisas* "the one who made them") and through the stressing of the second citation ("and said"), he adapts the text for his scripture argumentation. The relation of man and woman and their joining into one (single) flesh (*kollaō*—"glueing together") is the meaning of the scripture proof. Jesus appeals to the original will of the Creator, as expressed in Genesis. God made human beings male and female for the precise purpose of lasting union. At Qumran, Genesis 1:27 was used to reject at least polygamy or marriage after one's partner's death, and perhaps even divorce.

Verse 6: "One flesh"—the unity of two humans, joined together (LN 34.73) by God (*synzeugnymi:* "place together under a yoke"). This indicates the closest personal union possible; Jesus draws the conclusion that no mere human can undo the bond which the Creator himself has cemented.

Verses 7-8: "Certificate (*apostasion*, LN 33fn8) of dismissal." The Pharisees see that Jesus' exegesis of Genesis does away with divorce, and so they counter with the specific rule for drawing up a document of divorce in Deuteronomy 24:1. The main point is the reason for Moses' command/concession: the Israelites' "hardness of heart" (*sklēroklardia* LN 88.224). This phrase refers not to lack of feelings or a low cultural level, but to Israel's unwillingness to be taught and guided by God's word, a sin exonerated by the prophets. The divorce provisions of the Torah thus reflect the rebellious will of fallen man, not the gracious will of the Creator.

Verse 9: "Marries another commits adultery." Since Jesus is bringing in the kingdom, which is paradise regained, he also reestablishes the original will of the Creator for marriage in paradise. Jesus then adds a casuistic rule ("if-then"); if any man (notice the male perspective) transgresses Jesus' apodictic rule, he commits adultery, which is what his divorce and remarriage amount to. "As in 5:32 Matthew has added the provision 'except for unchastity (*porneia*).' *Porneia* refers here to incestuous unions contracted by Christians before baptism; Matthew's point is that one cannot appeal to the Lord's prohibition of divorce to justify the maintenance of such unions. Thus, the 'exceptive clause' does not really weaken Jesus' absolute prohibition of divorce" (Meier, 215-16).

At every turn, Jesus' teaching is the exposition of the will of God in terms of its original intention. Thus in debate with the Pharisees and scribes from Jerusalem, Jesus introduces his quotation of the law not with the words "For Moses said . . .," but with the words "For God said . . ." (15:4). Here, in debate with the Pharisees on divorce, Jesus flatly declares that the will of Moses is to be looked upon as having been transcended by the will of God (19:4, 7-9). Later, in debate with the Sadducees over the question of the resurrection, Jesus refutes their argument with the telling question, "Have you not read what was said to you by God. . . .?" (22:31). "Plainly, Jesus advances the claim in his teaching that he is the supreme arbiter of the will of God" (*Story*, 64).

Celibacy in the Light of the Kingdom, 19:10-12

Married couples and celibates are the two groups that Jesus addresses first on the way to Jerusalem.

> **10** His disciples said to him, "If such is the case of a man with his wife, it is better not to marry. **11** But he said to them, "Not everyone can accept this teaching, but only those to whom it is given. **12** For there are eunuchs who have been so from birth, and there are eunuchs who have been made eunuchs by others and there are eunuchs who have made themselves eunuchs for the sake of the kingdom of heaven. Let anyone accept this who can."

This exchange is special to Matthew. It is separated from the preceding controversy by the fact that this is a disciple instruction. On the other hand, the content connection is very close; the disciples' question in verse 10 takes up the theme of verses 3-9; in both instances, relations between man and woman, or marital relations between husband and wife.

Verse 10: "Better not to marry." In the disciples' question the problem treated in the foregoing is taken up again. That Matthew understands the prohibition to be absolute is clear from the disciples' astonishment. If Jesus had simply championed the position of Shammai over that of Hillel, there would hardly be cause for such a shocked exclamation that the unmarried state is preferable. The disciples' opinion ("it is better") is directed to the statement about marriage made in verses 3-9, but especially in verse 9; a certain resignation and helplessness ("if such is the case") is evident "The case *aitia*" (cf. LN 89.1).

Verse 11: "Can accept this teaching." Jesus' answer underlines the importance of the question. Jesus takes up the disciples' hardly serious judgment about the unmarried state and takes it seriously. Remaining unmarried is better—but only for some people, who have received a special gift from God (divine passive). "Accept *chorein*" means literally: "to make room;" (LN 31.57): "to be able to accept a message and respond accordingly."

Verse 12: The threefold speech is connected to verse 11 by "For" (indicating reason). Eunuchs are mentioned three times (the verb *eunouchizō* comes only here in the New Testament (LN 9:25-2). The first group of eunuchs are men destined to remain unmarried from birth, the second are men who are condemned to non-marriage by enemy intervention. The third group are, finally, those who, for the sake of the kingdom of God, remain unmarried voluntarily. As there are those of the first and second kind, so there are also those of the third kind. Legal thinking is not the heart of the matter, but prophetic conviction and resolution.

The third kind are not those who are eunuchs by birth or castration; rather, they are the voluntary "eunuchs" who embrace celibacy because of the kingdom. While the New Testament never explicitly states that Jesus was celibate, the veiled invitation to and praise of celibacy because of the kingdom makes sense only if a celibate Jesus is speaking it. But it is not meant for all disciples, only those who can "accept it" because God has given it to them (v. 11; cf. the similar teaching in 1 Cor 7).

As the lone teaching concerning voluntary celibacy, this pericope has a unique position in Matthew and reflects a concrete situation. Voluntary celebacy may have been an offence in the (Jewish oriented) community; and the readiness for tolerance and accepance may have been realized in the community only with difficulty, and not without resistance. But the demand of the community leaders prevails: voluntary celibates are to be honored in the community; for their special nearness to the kingdom of

God is a sign with an eschatological character. The approbation frees this group from hatred for having chosen a way of life, which according to Jewish tradition, does not correspond to God's creation plan. So the reason is advanced; "for the sake of the kingdom of heaven" is the new motif that legitimates this way of life. The Matthean community was divided. The strong denunciation of causing scandal to "little ones" (18:5-9) indicates that scandal was a concrete threat (vv. 5-9), and the prominenece given to reconciliation implies that the need for fraternal correction was urgent (vv. 15-20) (cf. W. Thompson, *Divided Community*, 266).

Children in the Kingdom, 19:13-15

Along with married couples and celibates, children receive special attention in Jesus' teaching on the way to Jerusalem. The disciples reflect in their behavior that they have still not made Jesus' way of the cross their own. They are still bent on saving their lives and avoiding suffering and death. To their credit, they do understand Jesus' predictions of his passion (26:2), and it is said, following the second one, that they are "distressed" by it (17:22-23). Nevertheless, they also show that they are "status-conscious" (19:13-15), "enamoured of wealth" (19:23-26), "anxious about their future" (19:27), and "desirous of power and position" (20:20-24).

> **13** Then little children were being brought to him in order that he might lay his hands on them and pray. The disciples spoke sternly to those who brought them; **14** but Jesus said, "Let the little children come to me, and do not stop them; for it is to such as these that the kingdom of heaven belongs." **15** And he laid his hands on them and went on his way.

Verse 13: A direct connection with the preceding is not visible; the "Then" connection is only loose. The choice of the verb "bring to" must be Matthew's; the addressees are the "large crowds" mentioned in 19:1. Yet the real addressees of the teaching are the disciples who wish to prevent Jesus from laying hands on the children and praying for them. Instead of the original "touch" (cf. in Mark and Luke), Matthew draws from verse 15 the more expressive "laying on of hands." The disciples object to this "bother"—they rebuke the crowds (*epitamaō*, correct by a strong word); so the addressees of the correction are not the children but the crowds. They do not understand that to precisely "such" (v. 14) the kingdom of God belongs.

Verses 14-15: Jesus' answer to the disciples is sharp and authoritative: "Let the little children come to me and do not stop them" (LN 13.146).

Access to God must not be closed to the small and helpless. Neither directly nor indirectly is the saying an argument for the baptism of children; much more, it is an intervention for the humble and unimportant who might be hindered from coming to Jesus. Demonstratively, Jesus lays his hands on the children brought to him as an unmistakable sign how his words are to be understood. Yet the disciples still do not understand.

The recurring contrast between Jesus and the disciples appears already at the beginning of Part III. Immediately after the first passion prediction (16:21), Peter strongly censures Jesus for declaring that the Christ must suffer and die. "In the light of Peter's rejection of this prediction and the slowness of the disciples to accept Jesus' teaching of the cross, the heavenly voice in 17.5 declares not only 'This is my beloved son, with whom I am well pleased', as in 3.17, but adds the words 'listen to him'. Yet the disciples still do not understand that the kingdom belongs to children (19.13-15)" (Bauer, 107).

The Rich in the Kingdom of God, 19:16-22

The next "state of life" which is confronted with the cross is that of the rich person. Matthew does not tell us at the beginning that the eager inquirer is a rich *young* man. His youth (which can range between 24 and 40 years) is mentioned in verses 20 and 22, and his riches are disclosed only at the end of the story.

> **16** Then someone came to him and said, "Teacher, what good deed must I do to have eternal life?" **17** And he said to him, "Why do you ask me about what is good? There is only one who is good. If you wish to enter into life, keep the commandments." **18** He said to him, "Which ones?" And Jesus said, "You shall not murder; You shall not commit adultery; You shall not steal; you shall not bear false witness; **19** Honor your father and mother; also, You shall love your neighbor as yourself." **20** The young man said to him, "I have kept all these; what do I still lack?" **21** Jesus said to him, "If you wish to be perfect, go, sell your possessions, and give the money to the poor, and you will have treasure in heaven; then come, follow me." **22** When the young man heard this word, he went away grieving, for he had many possessions.

Verse 18: The inquirer addresses Jesus as "teacher," the title used by unbelievers. He asks about doing a "good deed," reflecting Jewish piety, which sought to do good deeds beyond the strict demands of the Law to ensure entrance into heaven. The man speaks in very Johannine terms of "eternal life (*Zoe aionios*)"—according to apocalyptic thought patterns (cf. Dan 12:2)—life after the resurrection of the dead in a coming aeon, in which a person can win a share only through right conduct. As the subsequent verses show, having eternal life is equivalent to entering into life (v. 17), being perfect (v. 21), entering the kingdom (v. 23), and being saved (v. 25).

Verse 17: In Mark, Jesus answers gruffly: "Why do you call me good?" Matthew removes such a scandalous statement from his version, making "good" the object of the inquiry. Reverently, Matthew avoids naming God in the allusion to the great Jewish prayer, the *Shema'* ("One who is good" alludes to Deut 6:4). Jesus' rebuke aims at deflecting the idle flattery of a superficial admirer and raising the young man's mind to more serious issues. The good God has expressed his will of goodness in the commandments. Here "commandments *entolai*" are—as elsewhere always in Matthew—the commandments of the Decalogue.

Verses 18-19: That the inquirer has to ask *which* commandments does not argue well, though the relative importance of various commandments was a subject of debate among the rabbis. Jesus cites the second table of the Decalogue, in the order of fifth, sixth, seventh, eighth, and fourth. Matthew then adds the command of love of neighbor from Leviticus 19:18 (cf. Matt 22:39), which acts as the criterion for interpreting all other commands in the Mosaic Law. And yet, as we shall see, it is still part of the Mosaic Law; it is not the last word on how one enters life. Matthew understood the Decalogue commandments as the summa of the social obligations and as expression of his concept of righteousness, even as in 22:40 and 7:12. The love commandment added by Matthew is for him, on account of its complex content message, the most important summation of all social norms of behavior.

Verse 20: The questioner, designated in verse 16 as "someone," is now presented as *neaniskos*, "young man" (up to forty years) (so also in v. 22). Possibly this more precise description was influenced by the saying in Mark and Luke, according to which the young man stresses that he observed (*phylasso*, LN 36.19) all these from his youth. Now he wants to know: What do I still lack? We have no reason to suppose that the young man is lying when he says this. He has observed all, *including* the law of love. Yet he senses that he still lacks something. Jesus' "maieutic" method has brought him to ask the question himself.

Verse 21: "if you wish to be perfect (*teleios*)." The word appears nineteen times in the New Testament; in the Gospels it appears only three times, and only in Matthew (LN 88.36). With his Old Testament background, Matthew understands *teleios* in terms of whole-hearted, complete dedication to God (cf. 5:48). "If you wish to be perfect" is parallel to "if you wish to enter into life" (v. 17), and means the same thing. We are dealing with the basic requirements for salvation (v. 25), requirements incumbent on all. Matthew is not teaching a two-tier morality of commandments for the masses and counsels for the elite. "On this 'perfection,' this whole-hearted dedication to doing *justice* (5:20), to doing God's will completely, hangs every disciple's salvation" (J. Meier, p. 220). For this particular young man it means the way of renunciation and poverty. The ultimate demand of God's will, even above love of neighbor, is a sacrificial following of Christ on the way to his cross.

Verse 22: "He had many possessions." The young man's reaction is one of shock; for he is very rich (*ktema* in the plural: possessions LN 57.15). He cannot divest himself of his possessions; the demand for complete renunciation of goods is beyond him. Possibly his sorrow expresses the admission that he cannot measure up to the demand. The young man possesses great riches, or rather, they possess him. Sadly realizing he cannot serve God and mammon (6:24), he decides to maintain his loyalty to the latter.

The Rich and the Kingdom, 19:23-30

On the way to Jerusalem, Jesus takes a radical stand against divorce, counters the status-consciousness of the disciples by blessing the children (19:13-15), and, now, warns the disciples against the perils of wealth while also giving them a vision of the end-time rewards of discipleship.

> **23** Then Jesus said to his disciples, "Truly I tell you, it will be hard for a rich person to enter the kingdom of heaven. **24** Again I tell you, it is easier for a camel to go through the eye of a needle than for someone who is rich to enter the kingdom of God." **25** When the disciples heard this, they were greatly astounded and said, "Then who can be saved?" **26** But Jesus looked at them and said, "For mortals it is impossible, but for God all things are possible." **27** Then Peter said in reply, "Look, we have left everything and followed you. What then will we have?" **28** Jesus said to them, "Truly I tell you, at the renewal of all things, when the Son of Man is seated on the throne of his glory, you who have followed me will also sit on twelve thrones, judging the twelve tribes of Israel. **29** And everyone who has left houses or brothers or sisters or father or mother or children or fields, for my name's sake, will receive a hundredfold, and will inherit eternal life. **30** But many who are first will be last, and the last will be first.

The pericope about the danger of riches that follows immediately (also in Mark and Luke) is seen by many exegetes as forming a unit with the pericope of the rich young man. Yet, despite the fact that the themes are generally the same, it may be more correct to expound 19:23-30 separately, because here it is no longer a question of instructing the people, but the disciples. Matthew's redactional addition ("Truly I tell you" v. 23) applies the teaching of the following saying concretely to the call to discipleship. The "proverbial saying" in verse 24 interprets the warning directed to the rich with an almost exaggerated sharpness.

Verse 23: With "Then," Matthew detaches the disciple instruction now beginning from the preceding instruction. The expletive "Truly" (fifty-eight times in Matthew, of which thirty-four are redactional) introduces Jesus' reference to the extreme difficulty of admission to the kingdom of heaven. For a rich person arrives in the Kingdom only with difficulty (*dyskolo* [adverb] not found elsewhere in the New Testament, LN 22.32).

Verse 24: Here the statement of principle is taken up and clarified by an image, but at the same time sharpened, as is shown also by the repetition of "I tell you." Behind the image, knowingly conceived as a paradox, lies the idea of a narrow door, which leads to eternal life (cf. 7:13-14). The image is drawn from echatological imagery (cf. J. Jeremias, *pyle*, TWNTII 920-927). All attempts to weaken the hardness of the hyperbole are misguided; it was also known to rabbinic Judaism, (LN 6.215, 216). This is a paradoxical way of referring to an *adynatos*, an impossibility (v. 26 and the adjective *adynatos*).

Those who try to mitigate the hyperbole miss the point, which is precisely the impossibility, and not just the difficulty, of the rich person's salvation. The astonished disciples understand all too clearly. They had entertained the popular notion that riches were a sign of God's favor; if God's favorites cannot be saved, who can?

Verse 25: Jesus' assertion that it is practically impossible for a rich person to enter the kingdom of God sets off a vigorous reaction from the disciples (cf. Matthew's insertion of adverb *sphodra*: "greatly"; of eleven New Testament appearances of the adverb, seven are found in Matthew). Their question is understandable: Who then can still be saved? "Be saved" corresponds to "enter the kingdom of God" of verse 24.

Verse 26: In Jesus' answer, which is introduced by the indication that Jesus looked at the disciples (sharply), (i.e., made eye contact with them), the real theme comes to expression: What is impossible for humans is possible for God; for with Him "all things" are possible (Mark 14:36; Acts 20:16). With allusion to the Old Testament (Gen 18:14; cf. Job 42:2; Zach

8:6), God's power is unlimited, and so what is impossible for humans is included as well. This sentence then takes on a general meaning: "Clearly Jesus declares that no person of himself can enter the kingdom of God and so be saved, it is God's work. Salvation *is* impossible, if it must be achieved by human beings, no matter how rich. The good news of Jesus is that salvation is the free gift of the omnipotent God" (Meier, 221).

Verse 27: "What then will we have?" Against the rich human, who would not give up his possessions, are set the disciples, who have forsaken all for Christ. As the spokesman for the disciples, Peter asks the blunt question: What then will we have? The Matthean Jesus does not hesitate to speak of heavenly reward (5:19; 6:1-8, 20), provided it is not understood as a legal claim on God. Jesus' initial answer actually concerns only the twelve apostles (cf. the twelve thrones and tribes), but Matthew shows a tendency to equate "the Twelve" with "all the disciples." Here he sees the Twelve as the prime example of what every disciple should be.

Verse 28: "At the renewal of all things" (*palinggenesis,* LN 67.147). The reward saying is introduced by another Amen-word, making it a solemn declaration. Since the disciples have entered unreservedly into the following of Jesus, to them is promised the judgment of the twelve tribes of Israel. Old Testament tradition lies behind this grounding of the eschatological judge function of the twelve, according to which the just will have a share in the Basileia of the Son of David, who is at the same time the judging Son of Man. The concept of a re-creation (*paliggenesia*) (in the New Testament elsewhere only in Tit 3:5) is striking; it stems from Hellenism and is met in (Hellenistically oriented) Judaism in the first instance in Philo of Alexandria (Cher 114). In Jewish apocalyptic thought, the conception of the "new world" comes closest to the idea; Matthew must have taken over the conception from this apocalyptic tradition and the imagery connected with it. Matthew does not mean the end of the cosmos, but a fulfillment (cf. 13:39, 40, 49; 24:3; 28:20) in the sense that all creation experiences the lordship of the Son of Man. The re-creation is the revelation of the Easter gift achieved through Christ: eternal life (for all), and the judgment for Israel through the Twelve.

With an Amen-word which reveals the conditions of the final judgment, Jesus assures the Twelve that on the last day they will have the status of the twelve founding patriarchs of Israel, and indeed will "judge" Israel. The apostles, poor and persecuted by their own people in this age, will see the tables reversed in the age to come (cf. v. 30). Instead of being condemned (cf. 10:17-23), they will judge and condemn an unbelieving Israel (cf. 23:29-39), and thus share in the power and glory of the victorious Son of Man.

Verse 29: "Inherit eternal life." With the phrase "And everyone who
. . ." the circle of the Twelve is exceeded: the theme of "renunciation
of goods" again wins universal meaning. The fulfillment of the command
about interpersonal behavior brings the same reward as the leaving of
earthly goods and the subordination of family ties (cf. 10:37). The promise touches all those who willingly suffer loss of family or goods for the
"name" of Jesus (i.e., for the person of Jesus), especially as known
through missionary preaching. While the reward of a "hundredfold" could
be in this life, Matthew's omission of Mark's phrase, "in this time," suggests that he places the entire reward in the "new world." The phrase "to
inherit eternal life" forms a neat inclusion with the question of the young
man in verse 16. By relinquishing their goods, the disciples will inherit
what the young man sought in vain to possess. Thus all human standards
and plans are inverted.

Verse 30: This verse is the introduction to the following parable, the
laborers in the vineyard; in content it has only a loose connection with
19:23-29, apparently on the basis of the thought of reward on judgment
day. All human standards and plans are inverted. Many who are first in
this world will be last in the world to come, while the last, will be first
(i.e., admitted to the kingdom). Verse 30 also appears as the last verse
of the following parable (v. 16). But there, the two halves of the verse
are reversed, thus acting out verbally the reversal it speaks of. The two
verses (19:30 and 20:16) are examples of both inclusion and chiasm.

Laborers in the Vineyard, 20:1-16

On the way to Jerusalem, Jesus takes a radical stand against divorce,
counters the status-consciousness of the disciples by blessing the children
(19:13-15), and warns the disciples against the perils of wealth. Now
through his narration of the parable of the laborers in the vineyard, he
challenges the disciples to be as unsistingly generous in their behavior toward one another as God is toward them.

> 1 For the kingdom of heaven is like a landowner who went out early
> in the morning to hire laborers for his vineyard. 2 After agreeing with
> the laborers for the usual daily wage, he sent them into his vineyard.
> 3 When he went out about nine o'clock, he saw others standing idle in
> the marketplace; 4 and he said to them, "You also go into the vineyard,
> and I will pay you whatever is right." So they went. 5 When he went
> out again about noon and about three o'clock, he did the same. 6 And
> about five o'clock he went out and found others standing around; and
> he said to them, "Why are you standing here idle all day?" 7 They said

to him, "Because no one has hired us." He said to them, "You also go into the vineyard." **8** When evening came, the owner of the vineyard said to his manager, "Call the laborers and give them their pay, beginning with the last and then going to the first." **9** When those hired about five o'clock came, each of them received the usual daily wage. **10** Now when the first came, they thought they would receive more; but each of them also received the usual daily wage. **11** And when they received it, they grumbled against the landowner, **12** saying, "These last worked only one hour, and you have made them equal to us who have borne the burden of the day and the scorching heat." **13** But he replied to one of them, "Friend, I am doing you no wrong; did you not agree with me for the usual daily wage? **14** Take what belongs to you and go; I choose to give to this last the same as I give to you. **15** Am I not allowed to do what I choose with what belongs to me? Or are you envious because I am generous? **16** So the last will be first, and the first will be last."

This parable is special to Matthew. Its meaning and explanation had already been fixed before the final redaction of Matthew (cf. Jeremias, *Parables*, 29–35). In this interpretative process, allegorical elements were introduced at a relatively early stage. The insertion of the parable into his Gospel at this point must have been determined by the intention to illustrate the saying of 19:30 about the first last and the last first, as the redactional insertion of verse 16 shows. This verse hardly corresponds to the narrative objective of the parable, but Matthew seems unconcerned about this, as long as his main point comes across, as it does.

Narrative framework gives not only the structure, but also points the way to the proper understanding of the parable. Verses 1-7: The householder takes the initiative and hires laborers, in stages, to send them into his vineyard; verses 8-15: payment is made (vv. 8-10), a critical situation arises (vv. 11-15); a third element, that would bring a solution to the crisis (cf. 18:31-34) is lacking in the present parable. The narrator has deliberately omitted that element and the omission is part of the parable.

Verses 1-2: "Laborers for his vineyard (*ampelōn*, LN 5:28)." According to Matthew's understanding, the parable presents a picture of "the kingdom of heaven" in which the behavior of a householder is narrated. Early in the morning he hires (*misthoomai*, LN 57.172) laborers for his vineyard. As wage, a denarius (a day's wage, cf. Tob 5:14) is agreed upon.

Verses 3-5a: With workers of the third hour (about nine o'clock) a specified, agreed-upon wage is not mentioned; the householder mentions "whatever is right" (v. 4). We would be inclined to think of a wage adjusted to the shorter work period, but it is just here that the parable cuts across our expectations. "Right" is to be explained from verse 13.

Verse 5b: At the sixth and ninth hours (twelve noon and three p.m.) the procedure is repeated. There is no explicit reference to the wage, no definitive expectation is awakened ("he did the same").

Verses 6-7: With the laborers of the eleventh hour the wage question is not even mentioned; actually only one hour of work is involved, for which no wage is specified.

Verses 8-9: With these expectations, the laborers go to receive their wages, only to have their expectation turned upside down. That evening, on the same day (cf. Lev 19:13; Deut 24:14-15) the steward (LN 37.86) is told to pay the workers their wage, "beginning with the last, up to the first"; the payment takes place in reverse order—those hired first must observe how the last hired receive the same wage.

Verses 10-11: Since finally the first hired receive the same wage, they see their expectations dashed; their reaction was loud grumbling against the householder (*goggyzo* [six times—of a total of seven—in Matthew] as expression of murmuring dissatisfaction after dashed expectations).

Verses 12-16: The decisive relationship "Householder—Laborer" reaches the critical phase in the dialogue. Only one laborer, one of the first hired, now dissatisfied (vv. 13-15), is spokesman. He objects to an unjust leveling (*isous poiein*: to make equal [with regard to wages]). The householder rejects in a friendly way (the address "Friend" is found only in Matthew, LN 34.16) the allegation that he has committed an injustice against the first hired. There can be no question of this, since they received the wage agreed upon in the morning. So the real theme of the parable does not lie in a criticism of Jewish hiring practices, nor does it concentrate on the problem of social relations. The real message comes to expression, in question form, in the threefold structured reply of the householder: a) I have kept the agreed-upon arrangement; b) I am permitted to do what I wish; c) I have done no wrong but shown generosity (LN 57.108, 110). Generosity toward those who need generosity—that is the real theme of the parable. Jewish reward thought is radically transformed: not earthly-human standards and norms determine the end-time reward but only God's merciful behavior, according to divine right, which insures to the last the same chance as the first. The addition of verse 16 fits—like all proverbs—the meaning of the parable only partially.

The parable rejects purely earthly–worldly norms. Protest and indignation against the good-natured generosity of others (God's) is rejected. This generosity of God was visible in Jesus' behavior, for which reason he was exposed to a multitude of misunderstandings. He was aware of these misinterpretations, and justifies his behavior in the parable of equal reward for all. The charge that he is a despiser of the Torah on account of his all-embracing generosity Jesus counters with the image of the good shepherd. But the critical question (v. 15) also contains a severe warning: the grumblers must not grow hardened in their grumbling, but must earnestly consider that a "no" to God's (and Jesus') generosity and mercy conceals the danger of shutting off entrance to the Kingdom of God.

2. To be called into discipleship by Jesus means to break with earthly standards with all trust. In the call into discipleship, first is not always first and last not always last. God's standard is not identical with the earthly standard, even when this often makes use of colorful proverbs.

3. "The Matthean Jesus does not hesitate to speak of heavenly reward (5:19; 6:1-18, 20) provided it is not understood as a legal claim on God" (J. Meier, p. 222). Matthew keeps the reward theme closely connected with Jesus' preaching about God and God's lordship. The ethics of Matthew's Gospel cannot be unmotivated, without promise of reward, since it stands under the demand of obedience. It is strongly eschatologically oriented and always bound up with the coming of the Basileia. Above all, it is Christologically based: the disciples are not related to their Lord as partners with equal rights, but as servants, subjects, whose freedom consists in the hope for a just reward from their Lord, but which they can in no way demand. The disciples are enjoined always to view the promise of reward in connection with the all-embracing promise of salvation to all.

Third Passion Prediction, 20:17-19

Three summary statements are spaced out in Part II and three passion predictions in Part III. The repetition of the latter is closely related to the geographical framework, since each of these predictions includes a reference to the journey to Jerusalem. The journey motif is expressed in the first two passion predictions by Matthew (16:21; 17:22), while in the third passion prediction, both Matthew and Jesus draw attention to the relationship between the journey of Jesus to Jerusalem and his passion and resurrection (20:17-19). "Matthew has therefore constructed a pattern of prediction and fulfillment which undergirds the motif of the journey of Jesus to Jerusalem and provides that journey with its theological meaning" (Bauer, 97).

> 17 While Jesus was going up to Jerusalem, he took the twelve disciples aside by themselves, and said to them on the way, 18 "See, we are going up to Jerusalem, and the Son of Man will be handed over to the chief priests and scribes, and they will condemn him to death; 19 then they will hand him over to the Gentiles to be mocked and flogged and crucified; and on the third day he will be raised."

The third (and last) passion prediction is in all three synoptics. The nearness of Jerusalem, the place of Jesus' passion, prompts Matthew to give more precise details about the passion event; in a catchword sequence, the most important facts of the Jerusalem events are narrated. The designation of Jesus' death as crucifixion (v. 19) underlines the passion prediction as a call to followership even to death on a cross.

Verse 17: "While Jesus was going up (*anabainon*)," (LN 15.101. 15.19). Jesus' *anabasis* to Jerusalem (it was mentioned already in the first passion prediction) is an evocative description of Jesus' way of the cross. It is an opportunity once more to prepare the disciples underway *kai en tē hodō*) for the coming event by special instruction.

Verses 18-19: With the introductory particle "see" (found also in the parallel accounts), Matthew introduces direct address into which the twelve are explicitly drawn—"we are going up." In four sayings, of which the third is further clarified by three detailed elements (mocking, flogging, and crucifixion following on deliverance to the Gentiles), the central passion events are listed. As was the case in earlier sayings, the explicit reference to the resurrection on the third day in the context of the passion account is to be understood as a Christological and Soteriological interpretation of the whole passion event.

As in the first two passion predictions, the text should remind the community of Isaiah 50. Above all, Isaiah 50:6 should convince the community that the passion happens in conformity with Scripture and was necessary from the point of view of salvation history: "I gave my back to those who struck me . . . I hid not my face from shame and spitting." The Suffering Servant of God, who although he was sent as a messenger of good news to the captives in Babylon (cf. Isa 41:27 with 42:1), was rejected as an agent of God's justice, is a type of Jesus and his fate. In the degrading actions, reference is made to the humiliation and powerlessness of the suffering Just One. But the resurrection on the third day means the victory over ignominy and abandonment.

A Mother's Ambition and Servanthood, 20:20-28

On the way to Jerusalem Jesus has been trying to teach the disciples what the way of servanthood and suffering entails. He has warned them against status consciousness by blessing the children, warned them against the perils of wealth, and challenged them to be unstintingly generous in their behavior toward one another as God is toward them (parable of the laborers), Yet, even after Jesus gives his most comprehensive passion prediction, James and John now seek the highest seats in the kingdom, and the other ten are indignant because they themselves wanted a fair shake at these positions of honor 20:24.

> **20** Then the mother of the sons of Zebedee came to him with her sons, and kneeling before him, she asked a favor of him. **21** And he said to her, "What do you want?" She said to him, "Declare that these two sons of mine will sit, one at your right hand and one on your left, in your kingdom." **22** But Jesus answered, "You do not know what you are asking. Are you able to drink the cup that I am about to drink?" They said to him, "We are able." **23** He said to them, "You will indeed drink my cup, but to sit at my right hand and at my left, this is not mine to grant, but it is for those for whom it has been prepared by my Father." **24** When the ten heard it, they were angry with the two brothers. **25** But Jesus called them to him and said, "You know that the rulers of the Gentiles lord it over them, and their great ones are tyrants over them. **26** It will not be so among you; but whoever wishes to be great among you must be your servant, **27** and whoever wishes to be first among you must be your slave **28** just as the Son of Man came not to be served but to serve, and to give his life a ransom for many."

This pericope consists of two parts: 1) verses 20-23: the request of the mother of the sons of Zebedee and Jesus' negative response; 2) verses 24-28, the instruction of the disciples about the right attitude toward rank. Both parts are also found in Mark (10:35-45); Luke (22:24-27) contains a parallel to the second part. As in Mark, this passage follows directly upon the third passion prediction; thereby it is brought into connection with the suffering Son of Man.

Verse 20: The unstressed "Then" serves as connection with the foregoing; "come to (prosēlthen)," one of Matthew's favorite words, and prepares for the dialogue (cf. at 4:3, 11). The sons of the petitioning ("kneeling") mother are not introduced by their names, but corresponding to Jewish custom, by their father's name (cf. at 4:21; 10:2). By the fact that Matthew (unlike Mark) lets the mother present the petitions, the sons are somewhat exonerated. And by omitting the title "teacher" (found in Mark), Matthew stresses that in question is not the teacher/pupil relationship, but the theme of the suffering Son of Man, who subjects himself to the Father's will (cf. v. 28).

Verse 21: To Jesus' question, "What do you want?" (LN 25.1), the mother utters her petition (historical present); the imperative "Command" expresses the recognition of Jesus' authority. For her "two sons" (cf. 26:37), Jesus should provide two places of prominence in his kingdom: a throne for each, one to his right and one to his left (cf. 19:28; Apoc

20:4). The kingdom, which elsewhere is the kingdom of heaven or of the Father, is here ascribed to the Son (yet compare also 13:41; 16:28: "his kingdom"). "Sitting" implied glorification, and the idea judgment seats.

Verse 22: "You do not know." In the first answer, which is now directed to the two disciples, it is not their non-understanding that is stressed, but the consequences of the petition—what would follow from it. They must not overlook that the way into the kingdom leads through suffering. The second answer is put in the form of a question; it asks about (LN 67.62) the ability, the strength, to share in Jesus' passion. According to *Ascensio Isaiae* 5:13, the "cup," which God has mixed, refers to martyrdom, which will come only to prophets, but not to the the disciples of the prophets. "We are able"—the unqualified assurance of readiness for suffering given by the sons of Zebedee should have been followed by a positive answer on Jesus' part.

Verse 23: "You will indeed drink." Jesus answers (historical present) with a double saying: he accepts the suffering readiness of the sons of Zebedee, this is not called into question; but the privilege of sitting on a throne is not Jesus' affair; "not mine to grant" (*ouk estin emon*), does not lie within my competence (LN 92.2). It is the "affair" of him who decided this (expressed by the divine passive (LN 77.3) by predetermination.

Verse 24: "When the ten heard it." The rest of the twelve are drawn into the scene by the introduction of a new theme; they have heard the dialogue and been "angry" (*aganakteō*), seldom used in the New Testament, means: to be unwilling.

Verse 25: The ten disciples are drawn into the teaching; thereby their objection will be shown to be unjustified. A picture out of everyday life, what they know, opens the instruction: among the Gentiles, the magnates rule over the people (LN 37.48, 50) and the great men oppress them. Jesus calls to mind the everyday experience of the powerless, who suffer under the might (arbitrarily used) of the mighty.

Verses 26-27: "It will not be." This worldliness disorder must not penetrate the disciple circle: so the first, negative, and absolutely formulated imperative. Instead (*alla*) among the disciples, another, opposite, fully reversed order must prevail: whoever would be great, must be servant (LN 35. 20) who would be first, must be subordinate. Three times "among you" appears prominently to make clear the contrast of disciple behavior to worldly behavior. A "humility rule" (cf. Mk 9:35; Mt 5:19; 23:11) is transformed into a binding community rule. Disciples "are not to insist on exercising authority over others, but are rather to act as servants and slaves to others (20.25-28). Even as Jesus was faithful to the will and calling of God for him, so they are to obey faithfully the will of God as Jesus has interpreted it for them" (Bauer, 106).

Verse 28: "His life a ransom for many." Closely related to lowliness and meekness is the notion of servanthood. The principle of servanthood related to many instructions in Matthew, especially those in chapters 18 and 24-25. In 20:26-28, this comparison between Jesus and the expectations for the disciples is brought out explicitly: "Whoever wishes to be first among you must be your slave; just as the Son of Man came not to be served but to serve, and to give his life a ransom for many" (vv. 27-28).

The "just as" of verse 28 has both a comparative ("just as") and causal ("just because") sense. The Church must be the servant for others "just as" and "just because" Jesus the Son of Man, the future judge, has entered this world not with royal pomp and splendor, but as a lowly servant. Having fulfilled his ministry with the lowliness and care of a servant, he will now consummate this service by the death of the suffering servant, an atoning sacrifice for the sake of and in the place of "many"—(a Semitic way of designating "all"). Precisely because Jesus is the Messiah, the transcendent Son of God, and the Son of Man coming to judge, the image of the Son of Man as suffering servant is all the more striking. "His power is the power of service; he exalts himself and his authority over others by lowering himself to death. He becomes Son of Man with all power and authority (28:18) by first becoming Son of Man sacrificed on the cross. His death above all is a sacrifice 'for the remission of sins' (cf. 26:28), a 'ransom' (*lytron*) which buys back, redeems, frees captive mankind from the grip of evil" (Meier, 229).

Although Jesus cannot promise James and John the favors they ask for, he does assure them that they will drink of his "cup," an obvious reference, in light of the following material, to his suffering and death. These references to the approaching death and resurrection of Jesus reach their high point in the declaration Jesus makes just before entering Jerusalem regarding the purpose of his coming: "To give his life as a ransom for many" (v. 28).

When the principle of causation is applied to Matthew, the events of the passion narrative become significant in a way that the great speeches do not. Jesus came not to give speeches, but to give his life. Numerous statements in Matthew establish causal links between events, and a great many of these ultimately link events to Jesus' death on the cross. Indeed, Part II (the entire section of Matthew that deals with Jesus' ministry to Israel, 4:17–16:20) is related to Part III (that section which deals with his passion and resurrection, 16:21-28:20) through the principle of causation.

Matthew tells the story of Jesus' ministry, preaching, and healing in a way that explains why Israel rejected and crucified its Messiah.

"The passion narrative is not simply an epilogue attached to the end of Matthew's Gospel, but is the goal of the entire narrative. Matthew's reader comes to realize that this is in fact the purpose of Jesus' life and ministry: he has come to give his life as a ransom for many (20:28). This affirmation recalls the angel's proleptic announcement at the narrative's beginning that Jesus would 'save his people from their sin' (1:21)" (Powell, 46).

Son of David Outcries in Jericho, 20:29-34

Repeated outcries of "Lord, Son of David, have mercy!" at a stage between Jericho and Jerusalem on the journey to Jerusalem underline how close Jesus and his party have come to Jerusalem. Having passed through Jericho in the company of the disciples and a great crowd, Jesus heals two blind men who appeal to him in faith as Israel's Davidic Messiah. The "sight" of these blind men discloses the "blindness" of Israel's sight.

> 29 As they were leaving Jericho, a large crowd followed him. 30 There were two blind men sitting by the roadside. When they heard that Jesus was passing by, they shouted, "Lord, have mercy on us, Son of David!" 31 The crowd sternly ordered them to be quiet, but they shouted even more loudly, "Have mercy on us, Lord, Son of David!" 32 Jesus stood still and called them, saying, "What do you want me to do for you?" 33 They said to him, "Lord, let our eyes be opened." 34 Moved with compassion, Jesus touched their eyes. Immediately they regained their sight and followed him.

This healing account is also found in the other two synoptics; Matthew used it already in the miracle cycle, chapters 8-9. Striking in Matthew is the healing by touch alone and not through an accompanying word of power (as is the case in 9:29). Twice, he replaces the name "Jesus" with "Lord."

Verse 29: "Large crowd followed"—in the literal, not the metaphorical sense (cf. 4:25; 8:1). The crowd following Jesus (*akoloutheō* here has a neutral, not specific sense) constitutes the public before which the miracle takes place.

Verse 30: The Matthean "There were" introduces the two blind men who are sitting at the side of the road: from there they hear (aorist participle) that Jesus was passing by (*parago*, in New Testament is most often intransitive: pass by; cf. 9:9, 27). They begin to cry out and to beg for mercy (for *eleeo*, cf. 5:7, 9-27). The address "Lord" expresses respect; the addition of "Son of David" is not just a genealogical indicator of origin, but a messianic confession: Jesus, the son of David, in his earthly working serves as a visible sign of the coming salvation; with the title is bound up a reference to Jesus' messianic quality, yet it is striking that a merciful act of the Son of David is spoken of in only three miracle accounts (9:27; 15:22; 20:30-31). (For Son of David, cf. 9:27).

Verse 31: "Crowd sternly ordered." The negative reaction of the crowd serves both to heighten the tension and also affords an opportunity for the blind men to cry out all the louder and to repeat their request in the same words. Hereby, the merciful action of the Son of David is brought to the fore in a way that cannot be ignored.

Verse 32: Jesus stops (aorist participle from the intransitive *histemi*) and calls the blind men. Jesus' question about their request is not a superfluous delay in the narrative flow, but a device to emphasize the leading character in the action: Jesus and the two blind men are closely joined in faith dialogue.

Verses 33-34: The two petitioners ask in their answer (historical present) that "their eyes be opened"; Matthew chooses this term in dependence on Isaiah 35:5; 42:7, to display Jesus' salvation action as the fulfillment of prophetic sayings. It is striking that Matthew here mentions the touching, although he otherwise takes just the opposite tack and lays all the emphasis on the faith address and omits corporal manipulation. Also striking is the use of *omma*: "eye" (only here and Mark 8:23, LN 9.23). The healing takes place immediately; and the two blind men straightway "follow" Jesus.

Associated with Matthew's use of "to follow (*akolouthein*)" in verse 34 is no word to the effect that Jesus has summoned the blind men to be with him or that they have embraced the cost of discipleship. The function of *akolouthein* in verse 34 is to extend the scene described in verse 29, the opening verse of the pericope. Matthew has written in verse 29 that as Jesus and his disciples were going away from Jericho, "a large crowd followed him." Then, at the end of the pericope in verse 34, Matthew writes that the two blind men healed, "followed him." "The line of thought, therefore, is that these two men, once Jesus has given them their sight, join the great crowd that is walking with him from Jericho to Jerusalem (20:29; 21:8-11). Still, neither the crowd nor they are to be understood as being disciples of Jesus. Consequently, of all the commentators noted above with respect to their opinion on *akolouthein* in 20:34,

Benoit and Filson prove to have captured best the intention of the text" ("*Akolouthein*," 62).

1. On the way to Jerusalem the healing of the blind men is the last healing episode presented in a narrative form (yet to come is only 21:14, a very short summary about healings); therefore it made a deep impression on the community. In this last manifestation of God's power in Jesus, the community is once more drawn into the great connection between the prophetic salvation hope and promises, and present fulfillment in Jesus' actions. The word of Isaiah, that the eyes of the blind would be opened, is fulfilled—literally before the eyes of the community. Yet the opening of eyes is not only a signal, that the salvation time is opening, but it also has a recruiting aspect: it calls to followership.

2. The community's knowledge that Jesus (the Lord) is David's descendent and thereby gifted with all the assets of this Davidic descent, is rounded out with the reference: as David's son Jesus is the herald of divine mercy. In healing action David's Son is manifested to the community as the Messiah, whose messianic actions consist in the showing of mercy. Precisely against the background of the impending death fate this message has decisive eschatological meaning for the community: in Jesus' death God's mercy toward men reaches its high point even if this death at first sight seems to be a defeat.

The first part of Part III of Matthew's story (16:21–20:34) has been organized around Jesus' journey to Jerusalem, in the course of which he instructs the disciples about the way of suffering and servanthood. Only once do the religious leaders engage Jesus in controversy during the journey. Once he is in Jerusalem, however, Jesus spends the bulk of his time in the temple (21:1–23:39), which becomes the site of a climactic, two-day clash between him and the religious leaders (21:12–23:39).

The controversies are acutely confrontational in tone, for Jesus himself is directly attacked in each instance. The questions put to Jesus are all of the weightiest kind. The atmosphere in which these controversies take place is one of intense hostility. One after another, the various groups of Jewish officialdom become involved. The chief priests and the scribes (21:15), the chief priests and the elders of the people (21:23), the disciples of the Pharisees with the Herodians (22:16), the Sadducees (22:23), a lawyer of the Pharisees (22:35), and the Pharisees (22:41).

The disciples continue to follow Jesus and to function as eye- and ear-witnesses to his activity, to be instructed by him, and to carry out assignments he gives them (cf. 21:1-7; 26:17-19). But it becomes ever more apparent that they have not made Jesus' way their own. Jesus' way is devotion to God and love of the neighbor, which lead him to suffering and death. The basis of the disciples' way is still self-concern, which is the opposite of servanthood. "It counts as important having status in the eyes of others, possessing wealth, exercising authority over others, overcoming might with might, and 'saving one's life' no matter what the cost. The end to which the disciples' evaluative point of view leads them is apostasy" (*Story,* 141).

Once Jesus reaches Jerusalem events move steadily toward the cross. Although the crowds hail him as "Son of David" (21:9), as far as they are concerned he is only the "prophet Jesus" (21:11), showing that they still do not recognize his true identity. Jesus is, in fact, much more than Son of David. At the end of the section 21:1–22:45, Jesus asks the Pharisees the question regarding the Son of David: If the Messiah is the Son of David, how is it that David calls him Lord? (22:43). Although Jesus leaves the question unanswered, the reader knows the answer; Jesus is Son of David insofar as he stands in the lineage of David, but he is also David's lord since he is the Son of God and, therefore, superior to David. "Therefore, the true identity of Jesus remains lost to Israel as a whole. This ignorance regarding Jesus' identity points ahead to his condemnation by Israel as a whole in chapter 27" (Bauer, 99).

Davidic King Mounted on an Ass, 21:1-11

From the outskirts of Jericho, Jesus journeys up to Jerusalem, arriving at the Mount of Olives (v. 1). He dispatches two disciples to obtain the "messianic mounts," and enters Jerusalem with great ceremony. He "takes possession" of the city as Israel's Davidic Messiah-King, but in humility and peace and without display of military might.

> **21:1** When they had come near Jerusalem and had reached Bethphage, at the Mount of Olives, Jesus sent two disciples, **2** saying to them, "Go into the village ahead of you, and immediately you will find a donkey tied, and a colt with her; untie them and bring them to me. **3** If any one says anything to you, just say this, 'The Lord needs them.' And he will send them immediately." **4** This took place to fulfill what had been spoken through the prophet, saying,
> **5** "Tell the daughter of Zion
> Look, your king is coming to you,
>   humble, and mounted on a donkey,
>   and on a colt, the foal of a donkey."
> **6** The disciples went and did as Jesus had directed them; **7** they brought the donkey and the colt, and put their cloaks on them, and he sat on them. **8** A very large crowd spread their cloaks on the road, and others cut branches from the trees and spread them on the road. **9** The crowds

that went ahead of him and that followed were shouting,
"Hosanna to the son of David!
  Blessed is the one who comes in the name of the Lord!
Hosanna in the highest heaven!"
10 When he entered Jerusalem, the whole city was in turmoil, asking,
"Who is this?" **11** The crowds were saying, "This is the prophet Jesus
from Nazareth in Galilee."

Verse 1: The Mount of Olives (cf. also 24:3; 26:30), a ridge lying to
the northeast of Jerusalem; for old Jerusalem it was important because
of the olive groves found there (LN 3. 9).

Verse 2: "A donkey tied . . . and a colt." The LXX is the first to speak
clearly, possibly through the addition of "and," of two animals. While
in Matthew's quotation only one animal is involved (which by reason of
the parallelismus membrorum is mentioned twice), Matthew had read two
animals because in the Greek version, two different words were used. This
interpretation he then adapted to the entire pericope of the entry. He
doesn't do it out of a historicizing motive, but because for Matthew, Scripture contains a promise given by God, whose exact fulfillment manifests
God's fidelity.

Verse 3: "The Lord needs them." "Jesus' self-designation as 'The Lord'
is unique in the Markan-Matthean narrative of the pre-Easter Jesus; the
paschal glory is already shining through the narrative" (Meier, *ad loc*).

Verses 4-5: In Matthew's quotation, the opening words of Zechariah's
text ("Rejoice greatly, O daughter Zion! Shout aloud, O daughter of
Jerusalem!" 9:9) are replaced with Isaiah 62:11. Since according to Matthew's understanding, Jerusalem is no setting for joy, but occasion for
lamenting and penance, he mentions, by way of introduction, the injunction to "daughter of Zion" to take note of what is happening. The
Zechariah citation also explains the event in a messianic sense, while for
Matthew the weight of the quote does not lie on the royal title; only the
contrast is important for him, the king coming on a humble mount instead of upon a mighty steed (LN 15.97). Jesus makes his appearance on
the "humble one" ("triumphant" and "victorious" of the Zech text are
deliberately omitted) on a "peaceable" mount (cf. Gen 49:11; Judg 10:4;
12:14). The Messiah does not rely on warlike power, and this is especially
true of the peaceable king of Isaiah 11:1-10. This gentleness of the king
corresponds to an important trait in Matthew's picture of Jesus.

Verse 9: "Were shouting." The imperfect tense of repetition stresses
that they set up "a great cry." Alone among the synoptics, Matthew has
the Hosanna cry addressed directly to Jesus personally, as the Son of

David. "Hosanna"—"The acclamation Hosanna comes from the Hebrew of Psalms 118:25. *Hoshianna*, i.e.,'Save [us], we beseech [thee]!' The addition 'to the Son of David' indicates that by Matthew's time, and probably by Jesus' time, the cry had lost its literal meaning and had become a general shout of jubilation and welcome" (Meier, *ad loc*). "To the Son of David" is—"To affirm that Jesus is the Son of Abraham seems to pose no problem in Matthew's story. But the same cannot be said as regards the title 'Son of David.'. . . . Jesus can legitimately be designated the Son of David because Joseph son of David obeys the instructions he receives from the angel of the Lord and gives Jesus his name (1:20-21, 25). In other words, Jesus, born of Mary but not fathered by Joseph, is legitimately Son of David because Joseph son of David adopts him into his line" (*Story*, 43). In the course of his narrative, Matthew portrays Jesus as acting in his capacity as the Son of David and hence, fulfilling in his ministry the end-time expectations associated with David (cf. 9:27-31).

Verse 10: "Who is this?" After hailing Jesus as "the Son of David," the crowds still ask "who is this?"

Verse 11: "The prophet Jesus." Once the crowds raised the question of whether Jesus was the Son of David (12:23), but the grammatical form in which they put their question anticipates a negative answer (12:23). And when asked who this Jesus is whom they had hailed as the Son of David upon his entry into Jerusalem (v. 9), they reply that he is the prophet from Nazareth (v. 11). "Prophet" is exactly what the crowds take Jesus to be, and this is in Matthew's story a misguided conception, for Jesus is in reality the Messiah Son of God (3:17; 16:16).

While Jesus' entry into Jerusalem is enshrouded in the fulfillment of Old Testament prophecy, it is at the same time ironic. The Jewish crowds do receive Jesus into Jerusalem as the Son of David (21:9), but when they are asked by the inhabitants of Jerusalem who this Jesus is, they reply that he is "the prophet from Nazareth of Galilee." "Exactly as the disciples had said when questioned by Jesus near Caesarea Philippi, the evaluative point of view of the Jewish public concerning Jesus' identity is that he is no more than a prophet (16:13-14; 21:46). In hailing Jesus as the Son of David, the Jewish crowds have spoken the truth, but they have done so unwittingly, seeing in him but a prophet" (*Story*, 80-81).

The Son of David claims his Temple, 21:12-17

Jesus spends his first two days in Jerusalem in the temple, in ever sharper conflict with the religious leaders. The circle of the religious leaders who approach Jesus in the temple to debate him widens to the point where it includes representatives of all the groups. First he engages "the chief priests and the scribes (v. 15) and they dispute his right to accept the acclaim of the children who were hailing him as Son of David.

> **12** Then Jesus entered the temple and drove out all who were selling and buying in the temple, and he overturned the tables of the money changers and the seats of those who sold doves. **13** He said to them, "It is written,
>
> > "My house shall be called a house of prayer;
> > but you are making it a den of robbers."
>
> **14** The blind and the lame came to him in the temple, and he cured them. **15** But when the chief priests and the scribes saw the amazing things that he did, and heard the children crying out in the temple, "Hosanna to the Son of David," they became angry **16** and said to him, "Do you hear what these are saying?" Jesus said to them, "Yes; have you never read,
>
> > 'Out of the mouths of infants and nursing babies
> > you have prepared praise for yourself?"
>
> **17** He left them, went out of the city to Bethany where he spent the night.

Verse 12: "Then Jesus entered the temple (*ieron*, LN 7.16)." Jesus' name is explicitly mentioned to distinguish the principal actor from the prophets mentioned in verse 11. Verse 12b creates the event in narrative form; by the addition of "all" (sellers and buyers), verse 12b takes on the character of a saying of universal application, which in verse 12c is again narrowed down. Striking is the phrase "seats of those who sold doves." *Kathedra* means chair, stool: chair in the sense of teaching chair. Even if the idea of teaching chair is most commonly connected with *kathedra* one can hardly make out that the pigeon sellers should be presented as rabbis or jurists. An authoritative action is indicated already by the "overturning."

Verse 13: Jesus' word accompanying the action is a quotation of Isaiah 56:7, which promises to the outsider and the outcast under specific conditions, that they can be present in the temple "for my house shall be called a house of prayer for all peoples." Matthew omits the "all peoples" of the citation (cf. also Luke); Jesus' action is directed solely against the Jews, who have rendered inoperative the prophetic saying about the temple. It was the presence of businessmen, operating in the courtyard, that upset Jesus. In the present tense the "result" of the misguided behavior is represented again with a citation (Jer 7:11): Jesus criticizes the prevailing situation. He intervenes for the holiness of the whole temple complex, to make the true worship of God possible.

Verse 14: Matthew demonstrates Jesus' power by noting that straightway blind and lame come to him in the temple, who otherwise were excluded from visiting the temple on account of their blemishes (cf. 2 Sam 5:8 [LXX]). By restoring the temple again to its proper purpose, Jesus makes entrance possible precisely for those for whose sake the temple was built.

Verse 15: "Chief priests and scribes." The second half of the pericope opens with a mention that the chief priests and scribes saw "the amazing things." *Thaumasia* is found only here in the New Testament: substative adjective refers to the healings mentioned in verse 14. At the same time, the temple authorities take note of the joyful outcry directed to Jesus by the children (LN 9.41) present, who take up the cry with which Jesus was greeted when he entered Jerusalem. The "amazing things" are expressly interpreted as messianic revelation ("Son of David"). Jesus' action and the worship of the children underlines the malice of the chief priests and the scribes.

Verse 16: The question of the Jewish leaders is rhetorical (even if it is answered by Jesus with an emphatic Yes), but it makes an important explanation, which makes use of a scripture quote (Ps 8:3) possible. In the New Testament tradition, Psalm 8 is applied to the Messiah also in 1 Corinthians 15:27; Ephesians 1:22; Hebrews 2:12. Already in 11:25, the knowledge of God is promised to the unworldly. With an unmistakable reproach Jesus rejects the questioners' implication. To forbid the children (*nepion*, LN 9.43) the necessary consequence of a known psalm text touching on mighty works, is to resist God. The cry "Hosanna" is just as much in place here as it was at the entry into Jerusalem.

Verse 17: Without waiting for a retort, Jesus leaves the the temple and the city and goes to Bethany to stay over night.

The temple scene reminds the community of the history of Israel which was closely bound up with the temple. Although in the Old Testament and the LXX, the temple was almost never called *hieron*, the community knows that the Holy Place of Jerusalem is meant. But they also know that the history of the Holy Place was by no means always "holy history." The prophets had complained that crimes against justice and lack of love of neighbor had led the exaggerated temple cult to become a great scandal. The wisdom literature never tired of repeating the prophetic contrast of Proverbs 15:8: "The sacrifice of the wicked is an abomination to the Lord, but the prayer of the upright is his delight." Standing in this tradition the community immediately grasps the meaning of the scene; with prophetic authority. Jesus proclaims by an act that cannot be ignored that the place of prayer has become a den of robbers through profaning commercial activity.

Yet the instruction of the community does not stop there. The saying that the temple is open to all who need the help of God, provokes the anger of those responsible; but this cannot stop the Hosanna outcry of the children, who now acknowledge Jesus the prophet as Messiah, who restored the holy place to its original meaning. Through the reproach and complaining question: "Have you never read?," it is stressed that the right explanation of the history of Israel makes possible the correct understanding of what has happened in Jesus and is still happening.

The temple, which is both the place of God's presence and the seat of the religious leaders' authority, becomes the site for the last great confrontation between Jesus and the religious leaders prior to the passion (21:12–22:46). Extreme tension suffuses the several controversies that take place there. The tone of all these controversies is acutely confrontational, and it is consistently Jesus who is directly challenged over issues that pertain to what he teaches or does.

The Fig Tree: "Little Faith" leads to Amazement, 21:18-22

In Part III of Matthew's story (16:21–28:20), the characterization of the disciples develops principally through a direct comparison of their values with the values of Jesus The disciples remain susceptible to bouts of "little faith." Here they are unwarrantedly "amazed" when the fig tree Jesus curses suddenly withers.

> **18** In the morning, when he returned to the city, he was hungry. **19** And seeing a fig tree by the side of the road, he went to it and found nothing at all on it but leaves. Then he said to it. "May no fruit ever come from you again! And the fig tree withered at once. **20** When the disciples saw it, they were amazed, saying, "How did the fig tree wither at once?" **21** Jesus answered them, "Truly I tell you, if you have faith and do not doubt, not only will you do what has been done to the fig tree, but even if you say to this mountain, 'Be lifted up and thrown into the sea,' it will be done. **22** Whatever you ask for in prayer with faith, you will receive."

The cursing of the fig tree is a nontherapeutic miracle (cf. 23-27). In these Jesus reveals, in the midst of situations in which the disciples exhibit "little faith," his awesome authority. He does this by exercising power over the forces of nature: he calms wind and wave (8:23-27), twice feeds the multitudes (14:13-21; 15:32-39), walks on water and rescues Peter from drowning (14:22-33). Now he curses a fig tree. Jesus' purpose is to bring them to realize that such authority as he exercises, he makes available to them through the avenue of faith.

Verse 18: According to Matthew's time scheme the event takes place early on the second day in Jerusalem; from Bethany (v. 14) Jesus returns to Jerusalem. Matthew places the cursing and the withering of the fig tree on the same day, uniting what Mark divides over two days. Matthew thus heightens the miracle by making it instantaneous.

Verse 19: "Ever come from you." On the way, Jesus sees a fig tree; he approaches it to pick some figs (which was permitted according to Deut 23:25-26), but finds none. The tree has only leaves (*phyllon* in the NT appears only in the plural; leaves, foliage). "A tree is a symbol of life; the fig as the sweetest fruit of the Levant a Biblical symbol of beatitude. Thus a barren fig tree s a symbol of blighted promise, failure. Perhaps it here represents the failure of the Pharisees and Sadducees to renew the life of the people (21:43)" (*NJBC, ad loc*). The event is a reference to the impending crisis, and Jesus' curse is followed immediately (*parachrēma* [adverb] by the drying up and withering; so the tree dies suddenly on the spot. The miracle is a prophetic parable-in-action, such as Isaiah, Jeremiah, and Ezekiel performed. Judaism, especially Pharisaic Judaism, is covered with the ostentatious foliage of external piety, but truly obedient deeds, the fruit of religion, are lacking. Jesus therefore rejects the old people of God and creates a new one, which will produce the kingdom's fruits (so 21:43). This parable-in-action foreshadows the parables of judgment on Israel.

Verse 20: The disciples' question broadens Jesus' answer.

Verse 21: "Even if you say to this mountain." If disciples fulfill the required condition (doubt-free faith), they will be able to perform not only what happened to the fig tree, but much greater things. Matthew makes Jesus' action a paradigm of the disciples' faith. Doubt-free faith suffices to remove a mountain of obstructions. The phrases "mountain moving faith" has an apocalyptic-eschatological meaning: where there is true faith, obstacles are pushed aside which stand in the way of the coming of God (cf. 3:3 [Is 40:3]: Prepare the way of the Lord. . .). A faith free of doubt guarantees ("Truly I tell you") that a prayer takes on eschatological dynamic.

Verse 22: "Faith with prayer." "Thus Jesus tells his disciples that they can share his miraculous power and do still greater things, provided they have faith, and express their faith in prayer" (Meier, *ad loc*).

The theme of Jesus' mighty works is continued through a word of cursing—the community knew about the power of the curse from Jewish tradition. But Jesus actualizes what the curse intended. And now, the disciples share in this action; indeed, they are promised that they will work greater, even more unlikely things. Yet the requirement cannot be ignored: they must have faith that is free of doubt. The community, which has entered into the followership of Jesus' disciples, must be convinced. They must know that Jesus stands by his promise, provided that the faith expressing itself in prayer is not compromised by doubt. Matthew takes doubt very seriously as a persistent danger for faith (cf. 6:30; 8:26; 14:31; 16:8; 17:20).

Conflict in the Temple: Chief Priests and Elders, 21:23-27

During the two days of conflict with Jesus in the temple, representatives of all the groups in Judaism join in. The "chief priests and the elders" ask "by what authority" he is doing "these things: "cleansing" the temple, curing the sick, accepting messianic acclamations. When Jesus, in response to this question, links his authority to that of John the Baptist, the reader recalls that Jesus is aligned to John not only in terms of authority, but also in terms of rejection and suffering.

> **23** When he entered the temple, the chief priests and the elders of the people came to him as he was teaching, and said, "By what authority are you doing these things, and who gave you this authority?" **24** Jesus said to them, "I will also ask you one question; if you tell me the answer, then I will also tell you by what authority I do these things. **25** Did the baptism of John come from heaven, or was it of human origin?" And they argued with one another, "If we say, 'From heaven,' he will say to us, 'Why then did you not believe him?' **26** But if we say, 'Of human origin,' we are afraid of the crowd; for all regard John as a prophet." **27** So they answered Jesus, "We do not know." And he said to them, "Neither will I tell you by what authority I am doing these things.

Verse 23: A genitive absolute establishes the connection with the fig tree pericope. The expression that Jesus "was teaching," may indicate the precise direction of their discussion. The representatives of Israel approach Jesus and, in a double question, indicate that that they view his entrance into the temple as unfitting and presumptuous. Earlier, some "scribes" had asked Jesus indirectly about the *exousia* (freedom, ability, power, authority) to forgive sins (9:1-8), Now the "chief priests and the elders" ask him about the right to teach publicly in the temple. 'These things" in the first question is possibly connected with the cleansing of the temple, yet the question about Jesus' authority is principally motivated by his teaching activity in the temple. The authorities inquire about the content and the origin of this power, of what kind it is, and who gave it to him.

The religious leaders attempt to impugn the authority of Jesus in two ways. On the one hand, they dispute his right to act as he does, "by what authority he does "these things": forgiving sins, having table fellowship with toll-collectors and sinners, suspending the fasting law, interpreting the law, "cleansing" the temple, accepting messianic acclamations. "On the other hand, the religious leaders also attack Jesus personally: they charge him with having allied himself with the prince of demons (9:32-34; 12:24), they cast aspersions on his integrity by demanding that he prove by means of a 'sign' that he acts on the authority of God and not of Satan; they treat as a lie the claims he makes about himself, say, in his parables (21:33-46); or, following his death, they brand him as a 'deceiver,' or false messiah (27:63)" (*Story,* 126).

Verse 24: "I also will ask you one question (*logon hena*)." LN 33.98: "*logos* may be rendered as 'question' in view of the preceding *erotaō*." Jesus' answer comes in the form of counter question (which is expressly underlined as such) and through the personal pronoun (first person singular), Jesus' person is strongly emphasized. *Logos* (literally: the saying, the speech) has here—like *dabar* in Hebrew—the meaning of the thing, the fact that Jesus makes his own answer dependent on the (proper) answer to the question.

Verse 25: Jesus questions his "opponents" about the origin of John's baptism, placing it under the alternative origins: divine (*ex ouranou*) or earthly-human (*ex anthrōpou*). Did the Baptist act by the power of a divine mission as a prophet, or on the basis of only a human authority? The questioners, at first inquisitorial, become unsure of themselves. The possibility first raised, to recognize John's baptism as coming from God, is rejected. The reason is obvious; then Jesus would ask about the refusal of their belief in the eschatological meaning of John's baptism.

"And they argued." A notable example of "narrative comment." From time to time "Matthew as narrator directs comments to the reader that provide him or her with inside information most often not available to the characters in the story. By means of such commentary, Matthew explains certain matters or, more significantly, interprets characters and events and renders judgment on them. By making the reader the recipient of inside information, Matthew places him or her in the privileged position of being better informed than the characters in the story" (*Story,* 32-33). Included among "narrative comments" are the many statements that apprise the reader of the thoughts (21:25-27), feelings (2:10, 22), perceptions (21:45; 22:18), and intentions (21:46) of characters. Through these comments, Matthew also urges the reader to appropriate as "true" his understanding of Jesus.

Verse 26: "Of human origin." The second possibility places the two alternatives in antithetic parallelism. To say that John's baptism is "of human origin" (commensurate with, and therefore against God's will) would expose them to the anger of the crowds. "We are afraid of the crowd," for all regard John as a prophet.

Verse 27: Jesus' opponents try to extract themselves from the affair. "We do not know." Since Jesus' counter question has not been answered, he in turn refuses an answer. The condition he laid down was not fulfilled (cf. again the stressed "I"). In Jesus' answer, verse 24d is repeated word for word. Jesus' authority is not called into question by his refusal to answer; rather it is directly established because Jesus authoritatively refuses any further discussion with his antagonists.

Matthew, who passed on this account, evaluates the question about authority just as Jesus himself evaluates it; the representatives of Israel have, with all deliberation, rejected the reality of Jesus' claim to authority. Their behavior is all the more reprehensible because in fear they take "refuge in flight," in the flight of feigned ignorance. Their refusal means that they knowingly bring into question their claim to be God's Israel.

This makes the theological dimension clear to the community. Only those who accept the authority of Jesus' claim can retain a personal relationship with God. The community as People of God lives up to this calling if it recognizes Jesus' actions and words as "from heaven," as certified by God and endowed with divine power.

Parable of the Two Sons, 21:28-32

Mark has one parable at this point in the narrative, that of the evil tenants. Matthew has three parables of judgment that hammer away at some of his basic themes. By rejecting and killing the Son, Israel itself has been rejected, and the Gentiles (another "nation") have received the kingdom (the vineyard, the marriage feast) instead. The Church, like Israel of old, is now God's son, worker, and table-guest. But, warns Matthew, its call likewise stands under judgment. Only obedience can transform initial call into final election.

In the parable of the two sons, Jesus condemns the religious leaders for failing to repent at the preaching of John the Baptist. Like disobedient children, they fail to do the will of the Father who has called them.

Although the kingdom has been theirs, they have failed to deliver its fruit, and as a consequence the kingdom will be taken away from them (21:43).

> **28** "What do you think? A man had two sons; he went to the first and said, 'Son, go and work in the vineyard today.' **29** He answered, 'I will not'; but later he changed his mind and went. **30** The father went to the second and said the same; and he answered, 'I go, sir,' but he did not go. **31** Which of the two did the will of his father?" They said, "The first." Jesus said to them, "Truly I tell you, the tax collectors and the prostitutes are going into the kingdom of God ahead of you. **32** For John came to you in the way of righteousness and you did not believe him, but the tax collectors and the prostitutes believed him; and even after you saw it, you did not change your minds and believe him.

Verse 28: "What do you think?" After the redactional introduction the active characters are presented; a man and his two sons. (*Teknon* in the literal sense is a "child," but this context demands the understanding of "son"). The two sons are contrasted; and the broader narrative context involves a contrast of two opposing patterns of behavior. The two are ordered successively to work "today" in the vineyard; the order requires an immediate response.

Verse 29-30: The first son initially says No, but "later" (*hysteron*, LN 67.50) goes to work; the second initially says Yes, but then does not go. The first son's words, "I will not," touch on the intention of the parable. Soon after his refusal he repents (in the synoptic tradition the verb *metamelomai* is met only in Matthew; in application it becomes equivalent to the common New Testament term *metanoeō*, signifying a change of mind and heart vis-a-vis God). Striking and unusual is the address "Sir," where one would expect "Father." Possibly this can be seen as an indication that the parable originally concerned a master and his two servants.

Verse 31: "Which of the two." The question, which of the two sons did the father's will, finds an obvious answer: only the first corresponds to the father's will. Taking into consideration that the narrative constellation Father/Son/Work in the Vineyard metaphorically refers to the relation of God to his creature, the conclusion necessarily follows that our parable is concerned with God's claim and the human's response. Man can—which question and answer express—through insight and repentance take back his No to God and speak a Yes, on which everything depends. Concretely the tax collectors and the harlots have already spoken their yes, and as a consequence go into the kingdom before you. This promise of verse 31b does not contrast these two groups of sinners with another concrete group (such as Pharisees or the just). Strictly speaking the theme concerns only this conversion of an initial No into a Yes, led on by Jesus' word, in which the Father's will is more visible.

Verse 32: In conclusion, Matthew first lends the parable a definite heilsgeschichlich dimension. By re-establishing the connection with the Baptist (cf. 21:25), he insures the soteriological understanding, John proclaimed the way of justice; but the so-called just rejected the preaching. On the other hand, the (so-called unjust) tax collectors and harlots did believe. While these express their belief in repentance and penance, the "just," although they were eyewitnesses, did not repent and so did not find their way to faith.

The parable is directed to the community: a No to the Father is not irreparable; by repentance it can be turned into a Yes. The example for this is not the just, but the sinners. Precisely because they are sinners, they know the need for repentance. So the Baptist's call for repentance, which had paved the way for Jesus' repentance preaching, also applies to the community, for the proper accomplishment of the Father's will presupposes that the community be aware of the never ceasing need for active repentance.

It is important that in this connection Matthew speak of a "believing of faith." This theme, which he seldom treats, serves as the link between the three parables of this section. To believe is the Yes of the community to the way of righteousness, joining and adhesion to God, as was demanded in the Baptist's preaching and in Jesus' proclamation. The degree to which this must be of concern to the community Matthew expresses by the use of the present tense: (If not), sinners "are going into the Kingdom of God ahead of you."

The note of universalism is found also in the parables against Israel. The notion that the Gentiles will receive the invitation of the Gospel in consequence of the rejection of Israel is made explicit in the parables of the two sons, the vineyard, and the marriage feast. Although the first of these parables (21:28-32) relates more to moral and religious outcasts than to Gentiles, the latter two parables indicate clearly that a change in those who possess the kingdom is about to occur. In connection with the parable of the vineyard, Jesus expressly states that "the kingdom of God will be taken away from you and given to a people (*ethnos*) that produces the fruits of the kingdom" (21:43). In the parable of the marriage feast, those who were originally invited are found unworthy, with the result that the servants are instructed to search along the main streets for those who would take their places (22:9).

Parable of the Wicked Tenants, 21:33-46

During his stay in the temple, Jesus speaks in parables. The three parables he narrates bespeak judgment on Israel because of its repudiation of John the Baptist (21:28-32), of himself (21:33-46), and of his messengers (22:1-10). Of particular importance to the plot of Matthew's story is the second of these parables, that of the wicked husbandmen (21:33-46).

In terms of such matters as "plot" and "evaluative point of view," Jesus' telling of the parable of the wicked husbandmen constitutes a key event in the sense that it has direct bearing on another event to come, namely, the trial of Jesus before the Sanhedrin. "With this parable, Jesus for the first time pointedly confronts the Jewish public in the persons of its leaders with the claim that he is the Son of God. What is more, Jesus advances this claim in striking fashion: he draws on the phraseology that the heavenly voice had employed both at the baptism and the transfiguration so as to appropriate for himself the evaluative point of view concerning his identity of God" (J. Kingsbury, "The Wicked Husbandmen," *JBL* 105 [1986] 652).

> **33** "Listen to another parable. There was a landowner who planted a vineyard, put a fence around it, dug a wine press in it, and built a watchtower. Then he leased it to tenants and went to another country. **34** When the harvest time had come, he sent his slaves to the tenants to collect his produce. **35** But the tenants seized his slaves and beat one, killed another, and stoned another. **36** Again he sent other slaves more than the first; and they treated them in the same way. **37** Finally he sent his son to them, saying, "They will respect my son." **38** But when the tenants saw the son, they said to themselves. "This is the heir; come let us kill him and get his inheritance." **39** So they seized him, threw him out of the vineyard, and killed him. **40** Now when the owner of the vineyard comes, what will he do to those tenants?" **41** They said to him, "He will put those wretches to a miserable death, and lease the vineyard to other tenants who will give him the produce at the harvest time." **42** Jesus said to them, "Have you never read in the scriptures:
> 'The stone that the builders rejected
>   has become the cornerstone;
> This was the Lord's doing,
>   and it is amazing in our eyes'?
> **43** Therefore I tell you, the kingdom of God will be taken away from you and given to a people that produces the fruits of the kingdom. **44** The one who falls on this stone will be broken to pieces; and it will crush anyone on whom it falls." **45** When the chief priests and the Pharisees

heard his parables, they realized that he was speaking about them. **46** They wanted to arrest him, but they feared the crowds, because they regarded him as a prophet.

Verse 33: Mark's "man" becomes a "landowner," emphasizing ownership and rights to the produce ("*his* produce" in v. 34). The motif of the vineyard comes from Isaiah 5:1-7. The householder becomes an absentee landlord, which helps explain the tension between him and his tenants.

Verse 34: At harvest time, the owner wants the entire produce (contrast Mark's "some of the fruit"); the total and exclusive claim of God is clear. The fruits are the good works which God demands of his creatures, the doing of God's will, *justice.*

Verse 35-36: Matthew divides the servants into two groups, representing the pre- and post-exilic prophets (cf. the division of Israelite history in 1:1-17 and the Jewish division of prophetic books into "former" and "latter"). The violent fate of the prophets is a common theme in Jewish literature and Matthew's theology (cf. 23:37).

Verse 37: The periodization of salvation history is highlighted; Matthew adds "Finally": the eschatological hour of the son has struck.

Verse 38: "This is the heir." The plotting of the tenants is not so outlandish; if a Jewish proselyte died without heir, the tenants would have first claim on the land they worked. The motif of the connection between the Son, the inheritance, and those who wish to share the inheritance, is a common theme throughout the New Testament (cf. Rom 8:17).

Verse 39: Matthew changes Mark's order to mirror the events of Christ's passion. The tenants first throw the son outside the vineyard (the image shifts to symbolize Jerusalem), and then they kill him (cf. Heb 13:12).

Verse 40: Jesus' question tears away the veil of symbols: the *Lord* of the vineyard will *come* to pass judgment.

Verses 41-42: "Put those wretches to a [wretched] death (*kakous kakōs apolesei*)." The answer quotes a classical Greek play on words, seen in Sophocles' *Ajax* and repeated by Josephus.

Verse 43: "The kingdom of God will be taken away." Right after the text referring to the resurrection, Matthew has Jesus announce that after the death-resurrection, God will take the kingdom from Israel and give it to a people which will produce the harvest of justice, the good works, that God wills. The vineyard no longer symbolizes Israel (v. 33) or Jerusalem (v. 39), but the kingdom of God, already present and given to Israel in the Old Testament, but now transferred to the New People made up of both Jews and Gentiles, the Church.

Verses 45-46: "Wanted to arrest him." For the moment, the leaders fear to seize Jesus because of the crowd (cf. 26:5). Following in the steps of the martyred Old Testament prophets and the Baptist, Jesus approaches his passion. But he does so with full knowledge of what will happen and in full command, because he is totally obedient to the Father's will (cf. 26:2, 42).

In the parable of the wicked tenants, Jesus sketches God's dealings with Israel in the history of salvation. His death and resurrection are the decisive events in the whole of salvation history. As Jesus speaks of the son, or of himself, he presents the owner of the vineyard (God), as referring to him as "my son" ("They will respect my son," v. 37). This reference to "my son" calls to mind the words the heavenly voice uttered at the baptism and the transfiguration ("This is my Son, the Beloved," 3:17; 17:5). Accordingly, it is with phraseology attributable to God himself that Jesus asserts in this parable that God looks upon him as his Son.

At his trial, the high priest abruptly puts Jesus' own claim to him in the form of a question, and when Jesus replies in the affirmative, the high priest and the Sanhedrin condemn him to death for having committed blasphemy against God (26:57-68).

Parable of the Wedding Banquet, 22:1-14

After three days of sharp conflict, Matthew shows Jesus speaking three parables, which bespeak judgment on Israel owing to its repudiation of John the Baptist (the two sons), of himself (the wicked husbandmen), and now, of his messengers (the wedding banquet). The parable of the Wedding Banquet is like a somewhat disjointed homily in which Matthew reminds his community successively: (1) that the first invited did not come (vv. 1-6); (2) for which they were punished (v. 7); (3) that exclusion and substitution have taken place (vv. 8-10); (4) that the newly invited had better look to their behavior in the banquet hall. Matthew treats first of the failure of the Jews and then views the community as a mixture of weeds and wheat before the judgment.

> 22:1 Once more Jesus spoke to them in parables, saying: 2 "The kingdom of heaven may be compared to a king who gave a wedding banquet for his son. 3 He sent his slaves to call those who had been invited to the wedding banquet, but they would not come. 4 Again he sent other slaves, saying, 'Tell those who have been invited: Look, I have prepared my dinner, my oxen and my fat calves have been slaughtered, and everything is ready; come to the wedding banquet.' 5 But they made light of it and went away, one to his farm, another to his business, 6 while the

rest seized his slaves, mistreated them, and killed them. **7** The king was enraged. He sent his troops, destroyed those murderers, and burned their city. **8** Then he said to his slaves, 'The wedding is ready, but those invited were not worthy. **9** Go therefore into the main streets, and invite everyone you find to the wedding banquet.' **10** Those slaves went out into the streets and gathered all whom they found, both good and bad; so the wedding hall was filled with guests. **11** But when the king came in to see the guests, he noticed a man there who was not wearing a wedding robe, **12** and he said to him, 'Friend, how did you get in here without a wedding robe?' And he was speechless. **13** Then the king said to the attendants, 'Bind him hand and foot, and throw him into the outer darkness, where there will be weeping and gnashing of teeth.' **14** For many are called, but few are chosen.''

Verses 1-2: "A king gave . . . for his son." Matthew has changed an ordinary meal given by "a man" (in Luke) into a royal wedding feast. The motifs of father and son, the sending of two groups of servants, the murder of the servants, the punishment of the murderers, and the transfer of some privileges to a new group all tie this parable to the preceding parable of the tenants, which Matthew may have used as a model when he reformulated the parable of the feast. In the process, the periodization of salvation history and the situation of the Church come to the fore.

The marriage feast was a well-known Jewish image for the joy of the last days; the New Testament taking up the practice of Jesus, often uses table-fellowship with humanity in heaven (cf. Matt 25:10; Rev 19:7-9). Matthew has made the meal a royal one; Matthew is especially fond of the images of king and kingdom. By this change an ordinary meal is changed into a wedding banquet of eschatological fulfillment.

Verses 3-4: "Sent his slaves . . . sent other slaves." The two groups of servants are probably not the former and latter prophets (as in 21:34-36), but rather the prophets of the Old Testament and the apostles of the New Testament (J. Gnilka wants to keep the text open to both interpretations, II. p. 238). The unity of the two covenants is the sad history of God's gracious call to the banquet and Israel's violent rejection of the messengers conveying the invitation. God's patience with Israel is underscored by the second invitation, which has become all the more pressing because "everything is ready." The last days have come. "The second invitation brings us into the Christian dispensation. That is why in this parable the son himself is not sent or killed; he is thought of as already with his father in glory" (Meier, *ad loc*).

Verses 5-6: It is the second group of servants, the apostles, who undergo the violent fate of the prophets at the hands of Israel. At best, some

Israelites ignore the messengers, while the rest (especially the leaders) kill them.

Verses 7: "Burned their city." "To ascertain the date of the Gospel," J. Kingsbury writes, "a glance at the parable of the great supper may prove helpful. At 22:7, one finds what many scholars consider to be a clear allusion to the destruction of Jerusalem (A.D. 66–70). From the first evangelist's own vantage point in history, this event apparently already lies in the past (cf. 21:41). Add to this the datum that Ignatius, writing shortly after the turn of the century (cf. A.D. 100 or 115), seemingly has knowledge of the Gospel of Matthew, and one arrives rather quickly at A.D. 85 or 90 as the date of writing" (*Story,* 148).

The intrusive nature of verse 7 is obvious. This seems to indicate that Matthew is referring to the destruction of Jerusalem as a past event. Yet one does not get the impression from the whole of Matthew's Gospel that Jerusalem's destruction is an urgent problem from the recent past. Consequently, the Gospel should be dated a good while after A.D. 70.

Verse 8: "Those invited were not worthy." The king enunciates the theme of the whole parable: who is *worthy* to partake in the (eschatological) banquet?

Verses 9-10: "Invite everyone." Now the wedding (and the meal) are ready and it must be celebrated. So the parable narrative uses the opportunity to introduce a new motif: (Lk 14:21), the uncalled are called. These uninvited are clearly distinguished from the invited of the first half of the parable; they are people who not only were not invited, but they do not even belong to the city dwellers (the city indeed has been destroyed). They are people from the district immediately before the gates of the city (*diexodos,* LN 1.102: "go to where the main streets leave the city"), so where the city streets give way to country paths. Strangers, nameless unknowns— the phrase "as many as you find" expresses the "unelectedness" of the the new group. The servants carry out their assignment: They go to those roads and gather all whom they find (*synagō* is Matthew's favorite word in this sense: "to assemble," gather men). The echoing "both bad and good" does not fit too well in the context: apparently with this insertion Matthew wishes to prepare the way for the incident of the wedding garment, verses 11-13(14). Now finally the celebration can take place: the "wedding" has its guests, the banquet can begin.

Verse 11: "Not wearing a wedding robe." The successful but hasty gathering in of the Gentiles raises a new problem. The world is a mixed bag of good and evil. Not everyone admitted to the hall (called) will remain as a guest (chosen). The separation will come at the final judgment, when the king (God) will enter the hall to examine (judge) who has been admitted. Oriental courtesy demanded that any guest at a wedding banquet have the proper wedding garment, which in the parable, symbolizes a life lived in keeping with God's call, a life of justice, of doing God's will. The king finds one in attendance without a wedding garment—a life that has undergone no basic change, a life that has not produced fruits worthy of repentance (3:8).

Verse 12: "Friend (*hetaire*." LN 34:16: "A person who is associated with someone else, though not necessarily involving personal affection (as in the case of *philos*)." The king addresses the insensitive person as "friend" (cf. 20:13; 26:50), indicating a cool distance between the gracious benefactor and the recipient who fails to correspond to the kindness shown. The latter's silence shows he has no excuse.

Verse 13: "Bind him hand and foot." "In the description of his punishment, the reality signified shines clearly through the parable. Those in the Church who have presumed on God's gracious invitation after the rejection of the Jews and who have not corresponded to the demands of the invitation by producing fruit (cf. 21:41, 43) will face the same fate. They too will suffer eternal rejection (cf. 8:12, of the Jews; 25:3, of the unproductive servant; also 13:42, 50). The Church, like Israel, is subject to judgment; and, if the Church is not vigilant, it can be rejected just as Israel was" (Meier, 249).

Verse 14; "Many called . . . few chosen." Like many proverbial summations to parables, this one does not fit exactly, yet it fits well enough to express Matthew's general intention. Church members are warned to take their call to the kingdom seriously. Only this can make them "worthy." "For the invited (*klētoi*, the called) are many, but the chosen (*eklektoi*) are few."

Conflict about Taxes: Pharisees and Herodians, 22:15-22

After the cycle of three parables (all of which touch on Israel's exclusion), conflict with another group of religious leaders begins. The secret intent of the disciples of the Pharisees and the Herodians is to "entrap" Jesus in his speech.

> **15** Then the Pharisees went and plotted to entrap him in what he said. **16** So they sent their disciples to him, along with the Herodians, saying, "Teacher, we know that you are sincere, and teach the way of God in accordance with truth, and show deference to no one for you do not regard people with partiality. **17** Tell us, then, what you think. Is it law-

ful to pay taxes to the emperor, or not?" **18** But Jesus, aware of their malice, said, "Why are you putting me to the test, you hypocrites? **19** Show me the coin used for the tax." And they brought him a denarius. **20** Then he said to them, "Whose head is this, and whose title?" **21** They answered, "The emperor's." Then he said to them, "Give therefore to the emperor the things that are the emperor's and to God the things that are God's." **22** When they heard this, they were amazed; and they left him and went away.

Verse 15: "Plotted to entrap" The Pharisees come together and form a plot (*symboulion elabon*; Latinism [*concilium capere*] "to resolve") to entrap (*pagideuō*) Jesus in a saying. "Entrap" reflects a rare Greek word for snaring animals during a hunt).

Verse 16: "Sent their disciples." The reference to the "disciples" of the Pharisees reflects Matthew's time, when the Pharisaic rabbis became the undisputed teachers of Judaism. The Pharisees remain in the background; they send their disciples "with the Herodians." The Herodians, supporters of the dynasty of Herod, are mentioned only obliquely; having disappeared from the Jewish scene by the time Matthew is writing, they are of no concern to the evangelist. The Jerusalem authorities make use of Galilean opponents of Jesus.

The unbelief of the questioners is apparent from the first word out of their mouths; "teacher" is always used in Matthew by people who are not true disciples. The adversaries speak the truth without meaning it. Jesus does indeed speak the blunt truth and refuses to tailor his message to fit the desires of his audience; that is what will lead him to the cross.

"Regard people with partiality" (*blepo eis prosōpon*, LN 30.10). The snare consists in the answer to the question about God's command regarding the head tax introduced by Caesar (LN 37.74) in the year A.D. 7; (*kēnsos* is a loan word, cf. the Latin *census*). The Zealots violently reject payment of a tax and called upon Jews to refuse to pay taxes; on the other hand the Pharisees (appealing to Dan 2:21, 37-39; 4:17, 25) supported an irenic approach that men must bear foreign rule with its claims. If Jesus had spoken out for a tax boycott, he would have given the word for a political disturbance; if he had declared for a payment of the tax, he could have been charged with recognizing the Caesar cult.

"Is it lawful." The trap the Pharisees lay is a dilemma: either Jesus accepts taxation from Rome, and so loses the esteem of the people and the support of almost all Jewish factions except the Sadducees; or he rejects Rome's taxation, and so makes himself liable to arrest and trial for fomenting rebellion like the Zealots. While the Herodians, in principle, would want an answer favoring taxation, and the Pharisees, in principle, would want an answer rejecting it, their common, malicious desire is to discredit Jesus, whatever answer he gives.

Verse 18: Jesus sees through the malicious intention (*poneria* is here the hidden, hostile intention . . . with which they wish to test him). The addition "(you hypocrites)" "doubles the wickedness of the Pharisees" (Gundry 443).

"You hypocrites." Since the questioners are insincere, Jesus feels no obligation to give a direct, detailed answer to guide troubled consciences. Jesus calls his adversaries hypocrites to their face and later he will excoriate their hypocrisy at greater length in chapter 23.

Verse 19: "Show me the coin." Jesus asks that he be brought a tax coin (*nomisma*, LN 6.70). They fetch a denarius, a silver coin, which on the obverse side had a picture of Emperor Tiberius.

Verses 20: "Whose head . . . whose title?" By this apparently simple action, Jesus says; "I do not possess the coin used to pay the tribute; *you, who seem so troubled about it, do carry and use the coin.*" And that willingness to use Caesar's money in their business transactions is a tacit acceptance of Caesar's imperial system and the healthy business climate he guarantees.

Verse 21: "Give to the emperor." If they are so ready to acknowledge Caesar's sovereignty when it is to their advantage, then they should pay up when Caesar demands his tribute. Jesus does not give a detailed theory of political obligations or church-state relations; his answer is a witty *ad hominem* argument. You willingly carry the coin which bears the image and inscription of Caesar (here, Tiberius); therefore, give back to Caesar what is his.

"And to God." This rule, of course, stands under and is judged by a still greater obligation: to recognize the sovereignty of the supreme sovereign. How the two obligations are reconciled is not explained by the axiom; this was not the time or place for such an explanation.

There is, however, a final barb in Jesus' words. It has been Jesus' constant accusation since he entered Jerusalem that the Jewish leaders have not "given" God the fruits, the just works, due him (cf. 22:41, 43). They should worry less about what is due Caesar and pay more attention to giving God his due!

Summing up, J. Gnilka writes that Jesus takes the fact that the coin bears Caesar's image as an *ad hominem* argument that taxation is Caesar's right. But the point of the saying lies in the juxtaposition of Caesar and God. Along with the recognition of imperial taxation, God is to be regarded under all circumstances as the one to whom the greater obedience is due (II. pp. 248-49).

Verse 22: The reaction of the "tempters" is astonishment, they are taken aback and confused; they leave Jesus and depart.

In the first place, the pericope has a negative message for the community. The community, embedded in the pagan Roman environment, is reminded that Zealotlike zeal (even to war with the Roman legions) hinders a faith-filled existence. For a Church at risk and being tested, worldly things are to be handled according to worldly-legal norms; this realistic approach need not disturb anyone's conscience. Yet the exchange (even today often cited inappropriately) must not be understood in the sense of a divinely willed loyalty to the state under any and all circumstances. Most important for the community is the positive message on which the real emphasis lies. The connecting "and" in "to emperor and to God" must be understood by the community in an adverse sense: "but" the only important thing is all-embracing obedience to God, the complete fulfillment of God's will. For when God's Lordship prevails and his "will is done," then every earthly power is relativized. For the community it is no longer worldly power—no matter how powerful it is—that is the decisive thing, but only God with his claim to possession over the entire person.

The problem of the legality of paying taxes to Caesar, along with table fellowship, fasting, sabbath law, washing of hands, and divorce, are issues that "constitute an index of the 'flash points' that motivate the religious leaders not only to oppose Jesus but also to conspire to take his life (12:14; 26:3-4). In their eyes, Jesus is a threat to the continued existence of Jewish society, for he places himself above law and tradition. In Jesus' perspective, the debates concerning law and tradition are all to be resolved by the proper application of one basic principle, or better, of a single attitude of the heart, namely, utter devotion to God and radical love of the neighbor (5:48; 22:37-40)" (*Story,* 63).

Conflict with Sadducees: Resurrection, 22:23-33

The Pharisees having failed, the Sadducees, whom Matthew sees as the other great party in the united Jewish magisterium (cf. 16:12), attempt to make Jesus look ridiculous.

> 23 The same day Sadducees came to him, who say that there is no resurrection; and they asked him a question, 24 saying, "Teacher, Moses said, 'If a man dies, having no children, his brother must marry the widow, and raise up children for his brother.' 25 Now there were seven brothers among us; the first married, and died, and having no children left his wife to his brother. 26 So to the second and third, down to the seventh.

27 After them all, the woman died. 28 In the resurrection, therefore, to which of the seven will she be wife? For they all had her.''

29 Jesus answered them, ''You are wrong, because you know neither the scriptures nor the power of God. 30 For in the resurrection they neither marry nor are given in marriage, but are like angels in heaven. 31 And as for the resurrection of the dead, have you not read what was said to you by God, 32 'I am the God of Abraham, the God of Isaac and the God of Jacob? He is God not of the dead, but of the living.'' 33 And when the crowd heard it, they were astounded at his teaching.

Verse 23: After the Pharisees, or their disciples, with the Herodians, now the Sadducees are the dialogue partners; they approach Jesus with the conviction that there is no resurrection (*anastasin,* LN 23.93). A very conservative group in religious conviction and behavior in the Judaism of Jesus' time, they had not taken over the opinion which developed in early Judaism and was widespread in the apocalyptic, that the dead will be wakened from the dead.

Verse 24: ''Raise up children'' (*anastēsei sperma,* LN 23.59). They address Jesus as ''Teacher,'' the title used by unbelievers. They recall a word of Moses (''Moses said''), quoting loosely a combination of Deuteronomy 25:5-6 and Genesis 38:8, the basis of the ''law of levirate'' (from the Latin *levir,* ''brother-in-law''; in Luke, ''Moses wrote''), to refer to levirate marriage in a Scripture passage quoted freely.

Verses 25-27: The three verses sketch a ''model case,'' in which a specific consequence of the Mosaic prescription is tested and through which an answer of Jesus should be provoked. Mathew places the ''seven brothers'' emphatically at the end of the example introduction (the number, of itself, a ''round'' number thereby takes on a certain emphasis in the sense of a deliberate exaggeration). Matthew inserts ''among us'' to actualize the otherwise theoretical question. The oldest brother dies childless; in like manner all the other brothers, who one after the other—as the levirate law prescribed—marry the wife of the eldest brother. Matthew now uses *teleutao,* to end, to come to an end; cf. 2:19; 9:18 and better 15:4: ''let him surely die.'' The use of *sperma* (seed) in the sense of offspring is in conformity with the citation Genesis 38:8 LXX. For the rest, Matthew shortens the reading of the example; his interest extends only to Jesus' answer to this problem.

Verse 28: ''To which of the seven.'' The Sadducees' question is motivated by a number of presuppositions of Sadducean theology The Sadducees accepted only the written Scriptures and only the Pentateuch. On this basis they rejected the resurrection of the dead, claiming that it was not to be found in the Pentateuch. On the basis of their Pentateuch-only approach, they also saw in the law of levirate a clear negation of resurrection. Without any developed idea of an after-life, early Israelites sought immortality in their off-spring; it was vital that a man's name continue in his descendants. The law of levirate stipulated that the children begotten of the new union between in-laws would bear the name of the dead man and continue his life. The Sadducees also believed that resurrection from the dead would mean a miraculous return to the conditions and relationships of this earthly life. Accordingly, the Sadducees' question presupposes that the resurrected woman will have to resume her marriage relationship—but with whom? The Sadducees choose the number seven, the symbol of fullness and perfection, to underscore the absurdity of the situation.

Verses 29-30: "You are wrong." Jesus' answer first establishes the error of the questioners. Their error is twofold: they do not understand how to read the Scriptures; nor do they know the extent of God's power. In the resurrection, the distinction between man and woman will be removed (cf. also Gal 3:27-28). A new creation produces a situation comparable to that of the angels. This reference contains another polemical thorn, since the Sadducees also deny the existence of angels. Angels do not know any reproduction (LN 34.723) since in Judaism they were regarded as immortal.

Verse 30: "Like angels in heaven." Jesus than proceeds to treat these two points in reverse order (creating a chiasm). Resurrection is not a "coming back" to earthly life; it is a going forward into a totally new type of life in God's presence. ("In heaven" may be a reverent periphrasis for "before God"). Like the angels, they are not married; the physical and sexual relationships of this world are transcended. Jesus does not mean that the saved have no bodies, The comparison with angels is meant to suggest the idea of a new kind of bodily existence (cf. Paul's idea of the "spiritual body" in 1 Cor 15:35-50.

Verse 31: "As for the resurrection of the dead"—Jesus then corrects the Sadducees' interpretation of Scripture. His argumentation is rabbinic, and may not strike a modern western mind as cogent.

Verse 32: "Not God of the dead." Jesus answers by citing Exodus 3:6 and building an argument on it, which contends that the patriarchs are immortal. In Exodus 3:6, God identifies himself in terms of his relationship with the deceased patriarchs Abraham, Isaac, and Jacob. How can the immortal God, the fullness of life and the source of life, be defined in terms of corpses which have long since crumbled into dust? Matthew sharpens this point by stressing that God has spoken this definition *to you* and that in doing so, he has used the present tense: "I *am* the God of Abraham." When the words of the Pentateuch are read today in the hearing of the Sadducees, God continues to define himself in the present by his relationship with the patriarchs. The only conclusion possible is that this relationship continues even today. Death has not broken the living bond, the deep covenant relationship which bound these men to the living God. God has the power to make all things live in union with himself.

Verse 33: "They were astonished." The reaction of the crowd points to Jesus as a teacher (cf. v. 23), who imparts his teaching, his *didache*, to hearers with power and authority (cf. 7:28). Having been defeated on their own terms, the Sadducees feel astonishment, just as the Pharisees marveled (v. 22). An unspoken irony of this whole pericope is that the Sadducees, the aristocratic priestly class, will soon precipitate Jesus' own death and resurrection.

The community knows that the Old Testament and the Jewish tradition, Ezekiel 37 and Isaiah 26:19 (cf. 26:14) speak only tentatively of an awakening of the dead, but was perhaps later understood in this Jesus' sense, and which definitively found its concrete expression in the second century B.C. (Dan 12:1-2; 2 Macc 7:9-11, 14, 23, 29, 36; 12:41-46). In Jesus' time the concept was a firm article of faith for Pharisees. Jesus makes this conviction his own, and demands that the disciples live in this conviction.

A warning to the community is contained in Jesus' answer. The question regarding a possible resurrection is not to be discussed under a purely human, earthly-worldly aspect, as was the case in the example cited by the Sadducees. He who denies the resurrection is lacking in true knowledge of who God really is: a God in power as we also read in scripture. The believer must know that he will not go into the "shadows of Sheol," but into everlasting life.

Conflict: About the Greatest Commandment, 22:34-40

Once again the Pharisees return to the fray, this time sending one of their members (a lawyer) to argue their case. Jesus not only answers his question about the "greatest commandment," but also indicates (v. 40) the core value by which the rest of the law is to be understood.

> **34** When the Pharisees heard that he had silenced the Sadducees they gathered together, **35** and one of them, a lawyer, asked him a question to test him. **36** "Teacher, which commandment in the law is the greatest?" **37** He said to him, " 'You shall love the Lord God with all your heart,

and with all your soul, and with all our mind.' **38** This is the greatest and first commandment. **39** And a second is like it: "You shall love your neighbor as yourself." **40** On these two commandments hang all the law and the prophets."

Matthew has changed this pericope from a friendly discussion to a conflict. In the parallel passages in Mark and Luke, the person asking the question comes off in a rather positive light and is praised by Jesus (Mark 12:34; Luke 1:28). In Matthew's version the lawyer comes "to test Jesus." This antagonistic attitude is clearly contrasted with the response of the crowd at the end of the previous pericope (the discussion about resurrection), where it is said that the crowd was "astounded" at Jesus' teaching. Matthew often significantly alters the material in the conflict stories he takes over from the tradition. This redactional work aims at offering a response to, and a defense against, the accusations of the Jewish opponents in this setting who take issue with the his view and use of the law. The preponderance of the Matthean conflict stories seek to legitimate the *halacha* of the first Gospel over against the claims of Pharisaism.

Verses 34-35: Jesus had silenced (*phioō,* LN 33.123) the Sadducean opponents. Thereupon, the Pharisees gather about him and one of them (a lawyer) asks him the tempting question (cf. 16:1; 19:3; 22:18) about the great (*protē entolē*) commandment in the law, i.e., in the Torah.

"Lawyer" means the same thing as Matthew's frequent "scribe"; a professionally trained theologian, whose main source book was the Law of Moses, The lawyer "tests" or "tempts" Jesus, a word which in the Synoptic Gospels always has a negative connotation. The lawyer's unbelief is clear from the tell-tale address, "teacher." Matthew replaces Mark's "first commandment" with "great commandment"; especially in Greek with a Semitic background, "great" can equal "greatest." In theory, all the commandments were to be observed with equal diligence. But practical necessity forced distinctions to be made within the 613 commandments of the Law between "light" and "heavy." Knowing Jesus' claim to sovereignty over the Law, the lawyer may hope to trap him in a damaging statement.

Verse 2: "Heart, soul, mind." In his reply Jesus first cites the heart of the *Shema'*. The confession "Hear, Israel" is supposedly known in Matthew's "Jewish/Christian" community; Matthew may have been warned off the address "Israel," because in his opponents he did not see true children of Israel. Love of God entails one's whole being: heart (center of knowing and willing as well as feeling), mind, and soul (one's whole life and energies). Love is not so much a matter of feeling as a matter of doing. The individual members (LN 26.3, 4) serve to underline the necessary operation of all human powers or the whole person in the realization of the commandment of the love of God.

Verse 38: The "great" commandment (v. 35) is now also interpreted by Matthew as the "first," in the sense that the importance of this first commandment is elevated above all other commandments.

Verse 39: "And a second." But there is a *second* which is *like* to the first: love of neighbor (Lev 19:18) (cf. Matt 5:43; 19:19). Notice the careful balance; God must come first, but there is no true love of him which is not incarnated in love of neighbor. The love of neighbor is put on the same level as the commandment of the love of God: the *homoios* (*estin*) expresses equal worth, equal rank.

Verse 40: "Hang all the law and the prophets." This addition, found only in Matthew, emphasizes his belief that the law, while still valid, must be understood and applied in light of the so-called love command, which is a combination of Deuteronomy 6:5 and Leviticus 19:18. The Law and the Prophets depend (*krematai*) on this one command. This command to love is the community's "authoritative, interpretative principle." This in no way dismisses the law for the community. Matthew does mean, however, that one's understanding and application of the law must now be shaped in light of the love command. In Matthew's view, Jesus did not break the law. Instead, he offered a particular interpretation of it which the Matthean community practices and which Matthew is at obvious pains to show is superior to that of the Pharisees.

In contrast, the Markan community revels a clear attitude of freedom from the law. This is not Jesus' view of the law as seen through the Matthean community.

> According to Matthew, neither Jesus nor those who follow him are lawbreakers. In response to this charge Matthew, through his reshaping of the conflict stories, offers a reasoned argument aimed at demonstrating that the actions of his community are consonant with the Law and the Prophets. Those who would undo the law—and those who accuse the Matthean community of doing so—do not correctly understand and interpret the law. The conflict stories in Matthew's Gospel offer examples of that correct interpretation, which came to them through Jesus. This interpretation is repeatedly placed over against that of the Pharisees, whom Matthew regularly imports as Jesus' partners in debate. The Matthean understanding of the law, informed by love and compassion (5:44; 8:13; 12:7; 22:39), is depicted as the true interpretation.
>
> Matthew is contending with and responding to claims from his Jewish opponents that his community fails to follow the law. Matthew has en-

gaged his opponents, claiming that they, not the Matthean community, fail to understand the law. What has shaped the Matthean conflict stories is a struggle with a Jewish group that claims Matthew's community is not law-abiding. Matthew has used these stories to defend his community's view of the law and to assert the truth of their interpretation over that of his opponents (Overman, 86).

In 5:17-20, Jesus affirms that the law will retain its validity. "Exactly how one is to construe all the things of the law as being done comes to light, as will soon be seen, in Jesus' teaching of love as that which lies at the heart of the whole of the law (and the prophets) (22:37-40)" (J. Kingsbury, *Story*, 65). The righteousness the disciples are to evince in their lives is a conduct that shows itself to be superior to ("greater" than) that which typifies the scribes and Pharisees (5:20).

Conflict: Son of David/Son of God, 22:41-46

At the end of this long series of conflicts, Jesus turns the table and puts a qustion to the Pharisees, his inveterate opponents. Whose son is Jesus?

> **41** Now while the Pharisees were gathered together, Jesus asked them this question: **42** "What do you think of the Messiah? Whose son is he?" They said to him, "The son of David." **43** He said to them, "How is it then that David by the Spirit calls him Lord, saying,
> **44** "The Lord said to my Lord,
>   'Sit at my right hand,
>   until I put your enemies
>   under your feet'' "?
> **45** If David thus calls him Lord, how can he be his son?" **46** No one was able to give him an answer, nor from that day did anyone dare to ask him any more questions.

Verses 41: Jesus asks the assembled Pharisees whose son Christ is (an initially harmless sounding question). This form of the question presupposes that more than one sonship could be involved, in other words, that the contrast to David's son would be the Son of God. The Pharisees' answer (in the historical present) is: The Christ is the son of David. The answer remains uncontested and so is acknowledged by Jesus; for Matthew, Jesus' David-sonship is "clearly scriptural," a firm part of his Christology.

Verse 42: "The son of David." The Pharisees answer Jesus' question with the opinion common to their party: the Messiah would be David's son (cf. Isa 9:2-7; 11:1-9; Jer 23:5; Ezek 34:23; Zech 3:8; 13:1). Jesus' question was not an idle one, since conceptions of the Messiah varied. Qumran expected two Messiahs, a royal Davidic Messiah and a priestly Messiah of the house of Aaron."

Verse 43: "David by the Spirit." Jesus replies to the Pharisees with another question, or rather with two questions (vv. 43-45), framing a citation of Psalm 110:1, the Old Testament text most frequently cited in the New Testament. Jesus second question takes off from the Pharisees' answer. If the answer is correct then the problem arises, how David in the Spirit can call Christ "Lord." Jesus' question does not have a polemic character, but points out a "Christological problem," to which the opponents know no answer. Matthew speaks only of *pneuma* (Mk: in the "Holy Spirit"); he means the spirit of God, filling and moving humans, in the abbreviated diction of the Apoclypse (Apoc 1:10; 4:2; 17:3; 21:10), which emphasizes the "being" more than the "speaking" in spirit.

Verses 44: The rabbis considered Psalm 110 to have been written by King David under divine inspiration, and possibly at the time of Jesus it was already considered messianic. If David, prompted by the Spirit, refers to the Messiah as "my Lord" when he says that the Lord (Yahweh) soke to "my Lord" (the Messiah), how could this messiah whom David treats so reverently be David's descendant?

In Matthew, the citation serves not only to state the problem, how a son can be the lord of his father, but also to point out the Kyrios-saying as the core of the confrontation. For Matthew the saying, Jesus is God's son, is relevant for his Christological conception (cf. 14:33; 16:16); yet here the primary purpose is to to bring Jesus' Lord-ship to the fore.

Verse 45: The conclusion to be drawn from the confrontation is placed in question form: If David calls the Christ Lord, how can this Christ be his son (cf. the parallel drawn between v. 45 and v. 43b), *Pōs* here has the meaning: "in what way"; Matthew wants to express that the Christ "in a certain respect" is at one and the same time David's Lord and David's son, and David's son is at the same time Kyrios and Son of God.

Verse 46: The imposing conclusion is at the same time closure of the entire chapter. There follows the Woes against the scribes and Pharisees, which lead over to the fifth great discourse of the Gospel, the apocalyptic. This composition underlines one last time the outlook of the evangelist: Jesus' appearance as the son of David enkindles the resistance of the Pharisees, which seals their fate.

In the course of the conflict stories, Jesus' opponents have proposed several questions to him and he had always produced a striking answer. He asks one question of them, and they are reduced to silence.

THE CHAPTER OF WOES, CHAPTER 23

The two days of intense conflict in the temple have come to a halt. Jesus first reduced the Sadducees to silence in the discourse about the resurrection from the dead. Then Jesus put a question to the Pharisees, still gathered in the temple, about Jesus Son of David/Son of God. "But no one was able to give him an answer, nor from that day did anyone dare to ask him any more questions" (22:46). Jesus establishes relations with the various groups of religious leaders and later discontinues these relations in the reverse order (cf. 24:1-3).

Unable to best Jesus in debate, the religious leaders leave the scene of the temple at the end of chapter 22. But Jesus still has words for them. Alone with the crowds and the disciples, Jesus seizes the offensive and attacks the scribes and Pharisees in his scathing speech of woes (ch. 23). In a series of seven woes, Jesus charges the scribes and Pharisees with hypocrisy of the highest order. This chapter sets forth the character and motives which stand behind the opponents of Jesus and have caused them to condemn the innocent (cf. 12.7) and murder the prophets (23.31). Following this speech, verbal exchanges between Jesus and the religious leaders are no more possible, and the leaders concentrate on destroying Jesus, not through debate, but through death on the cross.

The conflicts between Jesus and the religious leaders, which point to the death of Jesus at the hands of these opponents, come to a climax in this litany regarding the guilt of Israel. Here the sinfulness of Israel, which stands behind the attacks of the religious leaders against Jesus and explains their plots to kill the Son of God, is clearly set forth, as are the dire consequences of their murderous actions.

Here it comes out clearly that this important discourse was not addressed to the religious leaders. This helps to explain why "Surprisingly, Jesus' teaching occasions less conflict in Matthew's story than one would expect. The reason is that the religious leaders are the recipients of none of the great discourses of Jesus, and even Jesus' speech of woes is not delivered to the scribes and Pharisees but to the disciples and the crowds (chap. 23). It is in certain of the debates Jesus has with the religious leaders that his teaching generates conflict" (*Story*, 63).

Ostensively the discourse of woes is addressed to the disciples and crowds of chapter 23, but they are not the audience Matthew is really addressing. He is "speaking past" that audience and addressing the implied readers, the members of his own Church and Christians of all ages. The "insight" that "the implied reader not only is present throughout Matthew to hear the entire story but also has a position of his or her own that lies between the resurrection and the Parousia, is of no little significance, especially for understanding the great discourses of Jesus (chaps. 5-7,; 10; 13; 18; [23]; 24-25)'' (*Story*, 38).

Matthew's presentation of Jesus, of the disciples, and of the religious leaders indicates that these intended readers were living in close proximity to Jews. With an eye to the Jews about him, Matthew portrays Jesus Son of God as the ideal Israelite and elevates him above Moses as the supreme teacher of the will of God (cf. the Sermon on the Mount). Matthew's description of Christian piety as the righteousness "greater" than that of the scribes and Pharisees may also have the Jews "next door" in mind (5:20). This also helps to explain the many invectives that are hurled at the religious leaders throughout the Gospel (cf. ch. 23).

Chapter 23 is not counted among the five great discourses because it does not have the stereotyped conclusion, nor does it have the unified audience of the discourses (the disciples). Chapter 23 begins as an address to the crowds and the disciples (vv. 1-12), turns to address the scribes and Pharisees (vv. 13-36) and concludes with an apostrophe to Jerusalem (vv. 37-39).

The Pharisees in Moses' Seat, 23:1-12

Matthew was in a difficult position. He had to denounce the wrong-doings of the religious leaders and insist on the "greater righteousness" of the Christian way. At the same time he felt obligated to repulse charges that the members of his community were non-observers of the Law. He wrestled with this problem already in the pericope on the "great commandment" (22:34-40). There, he insisted that all the law and the prophets "hang" on the two commandments of love. The Law is not done away with, but observed in a new spirit. Now he comes back to the problem again.

> **23:1** Then Jesus said to the crowds and to his disciples, **2** "The scribes and the Pharisees sit on Moses' seat; **3** therefore, do whatever they teach you and follow it; but do not do as they do, for they do not practice what they teach. **4** They tie up heavy burdens, hard to bear, and lay them on the shoulders of others; but they themselves are unwilling to lift a finger to move them. **5** They do all their deeds to be seen by others; for they make their phylacteries broad and their fringes long. **6** They love to have the place of honor at banquets and the best seats in the synagogues, **7** and to be greeted with respect in the marketplaces, and to have people call them rabbi. **8** But you are not to be called rabbi, for you have one teacher, and you are all students. **9** And call no one your father on earth, for you have one father—the one in heaven. **10** Nor are

you to be called instructors, for you have one instructor, the Messiah. **11** The greatest among you will be your servant. **12** All who exalt themselves will be humbled, and all who humble themselves will be exalted.''

Verse 1: "To the crowds and to his disciples." When he began his account of Jesus' ministry at 4:17, Matthew depicted Jesus as becoming successively involved with three major groups: the disciples, the crowds, and the religious leaders. Matthew now depicts Jesus' involvement with each of these same three groups as being successively terminated in a reverse order to the initial one, establishing a chiasm. By reducing the religious *leaders* in open debate to silence, Jesus forces their withdrawal from the scene (22:46). Jesus then publicly addresses the *crowds* in the temple, together with the disciples (23:1). Then leaving the temple, Jesus delivers his eschatological discourse to the *disciples* alone (24:1-3). This chiastic pattern indicates that the culmination of the story is at hand; only the passion of Jesus still remains to be narrated.

Verses 2: "Sit on Moses' seat." With Moses there began a valid and binding teaching tradition that manifested itself symbolically in a "Moses' " seat. The valid incumbents of this seat are—according to Matthew—the scribes and Pharisees, whatever their doctrinal difference may have been, for Matthew the scribes and Pharisee present a united front of opposition. The scribes and the Pharisees are the "legitimate" heirs of the tradition established by Moses (LN 37.44).

Verse 3: "Therefore do." Therefore, there follows the demand to practice and observe (two imperatives) everything that is taught by the successors of Moses. The all-embracing "whatever," indicates the extent to which Matthew remains bound to Jewish tradition. The stress is on "But do not do" verse 3bc, which marks a decisive limitation (cf. the contrasting "but"). The holders of the teachers' chair do not show themselves to the people and to Jesus' disciples as completely reliable interpreters, but as teachers who do not "practice" the teaching that is handed on. Their practice stands in conflict with the teaching, the practice does not correspond to the words, which constitutes hypocrisy.

Two things follow therefrom: the disciples must learn to equate word and doing, teaching and practice, speech and behavior, and the disciples must recall that hypocrisy, behavior that clashes with the teaching, is not to be practiced. For the teaching of Moses can only be followed in a true form when human action stands in conformity with it.

While Jesus' conflicts with the religious leaders may suggest a wholesale rejection on his part of the tradition of the elders, it cannot be denied that at verses 2-3, he gives the crowds and the disciples to understand that "the scribes and the Pharisees sit on Moses' seat; therefore, do whatever they teach you." This is Matthew's supreme effort in showing respect for the Law. But it must be understood within the parameter he has already established: all must be judged by the law of love of God and neighbor. "One thing is certain: in the world of Matthew's story, the norm for judging whether the observance of any aspect of the tradition of the elders fosters the doing of the will of God is whether such observance expresses wholehearted devotion to God or radical love of the neighbor" (*Story*, 67).

To be perfect is to be wholehearted, or single-hearted, in the devotion with which one serves God (5:48; Deut. 18:13). To be hypocritical is to be "divided"—a form of inner incongruity. Hypocrisy is paying honor to God with the lips while the heart is far from him (15:7-8), making pronouncements about what is right while not practicing them (v. 3c); and appearing outwardly to be righteous while being inwardly full of lawlessness (v. 28).

Verse 4: "Lay them on the shoulders of others"—a first form of hypocrisy. The "yoke of Torah," or "of the kingdom of Heaven," which the rabbis placed upon the faithful was a heavy burden. With their legal knowledge, the scribes and Pharisees could find ways to escape the full rigor of the Law. The Qumran name for the Pharisees was "the expounders of smooth things;" but their injunctions were difficult for people in other trades and walks of life.

Verse 5: "Phylacteries and fringes." Verse 5 begins the second form of hypocrisy: what they do, they do mostly for the sake of ostentation. Three examples are given, First, phylacteries (LN 6.195) and fringes (LN 6.180).

Verses 6: "Places of honor." The second example of ostentatiousness is the love of guest-of-honor seating at feasts (e. g., next to the host and the seats on the raised podium in the synagogue, facing the people and in front of the ark in which the scrolls were reserved).

Verse 7: "Have people call them rabbi" (LN 33.246); a third form of hypocrisy. The use of titles in a community is inevitable. Matthew seems to be alarmed by a type of hierarchy and nomenclature that would break down the distinction between his community and that of the Jews.

Verse 8: "Not to be called rabbi." The reason is both Christological and eschatological. For the addressees, and concretely that is the community of Matthew, only one is the Teacher (with article!). While here the "one" is not specified more closely, he is already recognizable, and in verse 10 he is designated as "The Messiah." Among the disciples there is no longer rabbi, teacher, or master. For—and therewith the more ecclesiological reason—the community is a community of brothers (for the earlier use of "brother" to designate members of the Matthew's community, cf. 5:22, 23, 24). There are no exceptions to this [cf. "all" as one of Matthew's favorite terms, used seven times in ch. 23 [vv. 3, 5, 8, 20, 27, 35, 36]). Such was Matthew's ideal. Inevitably, as the "time of the Church" grew longer, conditions changed, and the organization of the Church developed, adjustment had to be made. But the ideal must always stand before us.

"You have one teacher." De facto, already in Matthew's time there were various functionaries in the Church, and they had to have labels and be ordered one to another. One or possibly two groups within the Matthean community have been identified such as the "prophets," and "teachers." They were designated variously ("righteous," "rabbi," "scribe" and the "wise." They were expert in matters pertaining to the scripture and the law. The verses 10:41 and 23:34 show that Christian teachers also served as missionaries to the Jews, perhaps conversing or debating with them about the meaning of the scriptures, the law, and the traditions in light of the coming of Jesus Messiah.

Verses 9: "Call no one your father." "The title 'Abba' was used in ordinary conversation with old men, but was not given to rabbis. . . . The disciples, however, are not to address any man as 'my father' because the honor of the name Father ('abba') is appropriate to God only, and was probably Jesus' own unique way of addressing God" (D. Hill, *ad loc*). Since the form of "Father" in Aramaic would be *Abba*, the sacred cry of early Christians, one could understand Matthew's objection to the practice.

Verse 11-12: Two commonly held teachings for the disciples close the section. The question, who is greatest in the kingdom of heaven, was already the opening theme of the Community Discourse (18:1-5; cf. too 20:26-27). There Jesus' answer had been given through a reference to the behavior of children. Now the community receives an answer in the form of a double saying put together by Matthew. He is the greater who is the servant of the community (cf. the second person plural pronoun) (cf. Matt 20:26, 27). This rule of conduct is (v. 12) legitimated through an authentically formulated rule of faith: God, the almighty agent acting (theological passive), reverses the earthly order and establishes his "heavenly" order. Old Testament thought (cf. Job 22:29; Prov 29:23; Ez 21:26) is taken up but is now grounded on Jesus' authority.

Seven Woes against the Scribes and Pharisees, 23:13-33

With his love of numerical pattern, Matthew composed a series of seven *woes*, well known in prophetic and apocalyptic literature. The word "woe," which expresses both the seer's dismay and his threat of punishment, originated as a cry of lament over the dead. Here Jesus, the eschatological prophet, weeps over those who do not know that they are already dead within (vv. 27-28) and are destined for a swift death without (vv. 35-38). Jesus had begun his first discourse with the beatitudes (5:12), proclaiming final happiness to those who suffer now. In the chapter of woes, the transition to the final discourse, Jesus proclaims eternal woe to those who pride themselves on their own righteousness.

13 "But woe to you, scribes and Pharisees, hypocrites! For you lock people out of the kingdom of heaven. For you do not go in yourselves, and when others are going in, you stop them. 15 Woe to you, scribes and Pharisees, hypocrites! For you cross sea and land to make a single convert, and you make the new convert twice as much a child of hell as yourselves.

16 "Woe to you, blind guides, who say, 'Whoever swears by the sanctuary is bound by nothing, but whoever swears by the gold of the sanctuary is bound by the oath.' 17 You blind fools! For which is greater, the gold or the sanctuary that has made the gold sacred? 18 And you say, 'Whoever swears by the altar is bound by nothing, but whoever swears by the gift that is on the alter is bound by the oath.' 19 How blind you are! For which is greater, the gift or the altar that makes the gift sacred? 20 So whoever swears by the altar, swears by it and by everything on it; 21 and whoever swears by the sanctuary, swears by it and the one who dwells in it; 22 and whoever swears by heaven, swears by the throne of God and by the one who is seated upon it.

23 "Woe to you, scribes and Pharisees, hypocrites! For you tithe mint, dill, and cummin, and have neglected the weightier matters of the law, justice and mercy and faith. It is these you ought to have practiced without neglecting the others. 24 You blind guides! You strain out a gnat but swallow a camel!

25 "Woe to you, scribes and Pharisees, hypocrites! For you clean the outside of the cup and of the plate, but inside they are full of greed and self-indulgence. 26 You blind Pharisees! First clean the inside of the cup, so that the outside also may become clean.

27 "Woe to you, scribes and Pharisees, hypocrites! For you are like whitewashed tombs, which on the outside look beautiful, but inside they are full of the bones of the dead and of all kinds of filth. 28 So you also on the outside look righteous to others, but inside you are full of hypocrisy and lawlessness.

29 "Woe to you, scribes and Pharisees, hypocrites! For you build the tombs of the prophets and decorate the graves of the righteous, 30 and you say, 'If we had lived in the days of our ancestors, we would not have

taken part with them in shedding the blood of the prophets.' **31** Thus you testify against yourselves that you are descendants of those who murdered the prophets. **32** Fill up, then, the measure of your ancestors. **33** You snakes, you brood of vipers! How can you escape being sentenced to hell?''

Matthew not only analyzes the nature and severity of the disobedience and guilt of Jesus' opponents, but he also indicates the basis of their wrongdoing. He links the failure of the opponents to fulfill to will of God with their inability to determine what that will is. This confusion regarding the will of God is connected with a dependence upon the tradition of the elders, which in many ways contradicts the will of God expressed in the Old Testament (vv. 16-22).

Verse 13a: "But woe to you *ouai hymen*!'' LN 22.9: "A state of intense hardship or distress—'disaster, horror'. . . . In some languages there may not be a noun for 'disaster,' but one can express the meaning of the Greek term *ouai* as 'how greatly one will suffer' or 'what terrible pain will come to one.' '' The "woe" expresses a strong and branding judgment, similar to a curse (Garland, *Intention*, 87): the judgment is the judgment of God. "Hypocrites!''—LN 88.227: "*hypokrinomai,* to give an impression of having certain purposes or motivations, while in reality having quite different ones—to pretend, to act hypocritically, pretense, hypocrisy.''

In six of the seven woes the addressees are characterized as "hypocrites.'' In the third this reproach is lacking because the characterization "blind guides'' has replaced the expression "scribes and Pharisees.'' Matthew uses hypocrite thirteen times (Mark once, Luke three times). The redactional insertion of "hypocrite'' (v. 28 as summary of the first six woes) confirms that for Matthew, all the charges against the Jewish leaders are summed up and the term *hypokrinomai* goes beyond the meaning of "pretense,'' or "hypocrisy'' in ordinary use. It is an expression of full reversal of God's will through false interpretation of the Torah, or its replacement through human tradition. "This connection of hypocrisy with distortion of God's commandments by the authorized, legitimate leaders of Israel can explain the connection of *hypocrisis* and *anomia* in 23:28'' (Garland, *Intention*, 116).

The First Woe condemns the dishonesty of those who have the power to either open or close the entrance to the kingdom, who understand themselves to be the trustees of the Old Testament revelation. But in reality, their teaching perverts the simple and central truths of the law through casuistry, so not only they themselves, but also those trusting in them do not gain admittance to the kingdom.

Second Woe, verse 15: "Cross sea and land." This woe condemns the proselytism of the Jewish leaders; they strive tirelessly to win just one. If he is finally won, he submits entirely to the Torah, but by reason of the false interpretation of the Torah by the recruiters he becomes "twice as much a child of hell" as themselves. By their fiery zeal they bind the convert to their false interpretation of the Law.

Third Woe, verses 16-20: "Blind guides." The teaching activity of the scribes and Pharisees is again the subject matter. Matthew makes the point that in drawing punctilious distinctions between oaths that are binding and oaths that are not, they succeed only in showing themselves to be false teachers. Matthew uses cultic terms, but he is not interested in the cult itself. The message of 5:21-26 is taken up again: humility before God is more important than cultic hair-splitting. Nor is it the purpose of verses 16-22 to show the oath as binding before God, but to eliminate false swearing. Verses 20b and 21 repeat the conclusion already expressed in question form and in reverse order (Schweizer, 83). So the context shows that "it is matter of condemnation, not of confirmation" (Garland, *Intention*, 133). The leaders of the people are false leaders (v. 16: "blind guides"; v. 17; "blind fools" v. 19: "blind men"), and the charge is directed against their activity as Torah interpreters.

Fourth Woe, verses 23-24: "Strain out a gnat." Again the "Teachers of the People" are condemned on account of their interpretation of the Law (cf. Luke 11:42). Matthew's list (mint, dill [LN 3.22], cummin) has rigorists in view who subject every kind of growth to the tithe (Deut 14:22-23 speaks only of corn, wine, and oil). By the broadening of the essential requirements of the Torah (the "weightier" parts of the Law), the interpreters involved themselves in bagatelles. The blind guides forget what is great (important) and small (unimportant) in the law (cf. O. Michel, *kamelos* in *TWNT* III 598). While they go beyond what the law requires and tithe the most insignificant of the garden herbs, they neglect in the process those matters that constitute the very essence of the law.

Fifth Woe, verses 25-26: "The outside of the cup." The fifth and sixth woes are alike in content, dealing with the cleansing of cups and bowls (LN 6.135) and with the contact with (polluting) graves (vv. 27-28). What form the two logia had originally is hard to determine, for both Matthew and Luke have reworked their source redactionally. The meaning expressed by the first image is: utensils must be cleansed where the food is. The proper order of values should determine the interpretation of the Torah. Whoever presents the secondary as primary is a "blind Pharisee." Although they scrupulously concern themselves with minor things, such as the cleansing of the outside of vessels, they overlook the circumstance that they ought to be concerned with major things, like the moral integrity of the inner person.

Sixth Woe, verses 27-28: "Whitewashed tombs." Again Matthew holds the contrast between "inner" and "outer" before the leaders of the people. According to Luke, the Pharisees are like unmarked tombs, which people don't recognize as such; so they are the undoing for the unwary. In Matthew the graves are indeed marked, but only by camouflage to cover up what is really inside. The contrast is that the addressees present themselves to others as outwardly "righteous" (*dikaioi*—those who wish to be regarded as just by all), yet are "full of hypocrisy and iniquity." Here too, responsibility toward the Torah is involved. "On the outside they look beautiful"—this underlines the contrast between outward pleasing appearance and inner "ugliness." "The scribes and Pharisees in a similar way are a father of uncleanness like graves, which they mark out so carefully, that people might avoid them" (Garland, 157). Outwardly they appear to people to be righteous, that is, those who know and do God's will; but inwardly they are full of pretension and lawlessness, for they are blind to the will of God.

Seventh Woe, verses 29-31; "You are descendants." This woe concerns itself with the leaders of the people, insofar as they are concerned about the graves of the prophets (LN 7.75, 76). Recalling their reverence toward the murdered prophets, they boast "if we had lived," and claim to be more just than their fathers. The emphasis of Matthew's judgment lies on the words: "You are descendants," i.e., the leaders of the people smugly hold themselves as justified in distancing themselves from the complaint against their fathers, they are in fact the direct descendants and "of the same kind." They are in truth murderers.

Verse 32: "Fill up the measure of your ancestors." *Plerosate* (aorist imperative) expresses a demand directed to the addressees in the sense of a word of the prophets (cf. Amos 4:4; Isa 6:9; 8:9-10; Jer 7:21 and Apoc 22:11). Now, in this generation, the measure (of guilt) shall overflow (cf. 1 Thess 2:15-16).

Verse 33 is Matthew's conclusion (cf. 3:7; 12:34), and expresses the thought that God will soon bring in the end-judgment (*krisis*, LN 38.1); after that conversion will no longer be possible.

"As hypocrites who are both lawless and false teachers, the religious leaders are furthermore depicted as being 'spiritually blind' ('blind guides'; 15:14). In their blindness, they can be observed either to give no leadership to the people (9:36), or ineluctably to lead them into a 'pit' (15:13-14). It is in Jesus' speech of woes that illustrations abound as to what it means for the leaders to be blind guides" (*Story*, 21).

What the Future Holds for Disciples, 23:34-36

Here Jesus speaks in the apocalyptic vein as the personified Wisdom of God, directing the course of salvation history. The persecutions spoken of are the culmination of the whole fearful history of Israel's apostasy. By the sending of prophets and others, opportunity will be given to the Jews to complete the measure of their crimes as they again reject the messengers. These persecutions reflect the persecutions the early Christians suffered at the hands of over-zealous Pharisees and also of the Romans.

> **34** "Therefore I send you prophets, sages, and scribes, some of whom you will kill and crucify, and some you will flog in your synagogues and pursue from town to town, **35** so that upon you may come all the righteous blood shed on earth, from the blood of righteous Abel to the blood of Zechariah son of Barachiah, whom you murdered between the sanctuary and the altar. **36** Truly I tell you, all this will come upon this generation.

Verse 34: "I will send you." Those addressed by Jesus (*pros hymas*) are the whole people (Israel), more especially the generation of Jesus and the early Church. *Apostellō* has a concrete meaning in Matthew: "send, send forth (with a specific assignment)." Jesus sends messengers, missionaries. The three groups that Matthew names are Christian missionaries (Garland, *Intention* 175): prophets, sages (*sophoi*), and scribes (*grammateis*; 23:34). These people were expert in matters pertaining to the scripture and the law. The verses 10:41 and 23:34, in which three of these four terms occur, show that Christian teachers, too, served as missionaries to the Jews, perhaps conversing or debating with them about the meaning of the scriptures, the law, and the traditions in light of the coming of Jesus Messiah.

These missionaries suffer Jesus' fate, but not all ("some of whom"). Some of them will be killed, and even crucified, some will be scourged and persecuted (*diokō*, LN 15.158) from town to town (cf. 10:17b, 23; 16:21; 17:23; 20:19; 26:2). Jesus' messengers suffer a fate similar to the one Jesus suffered.

Verse 35: "Come all the righteous blood." In doing such things to the messengers, the Jews fill up "the measure of their ancestors" (23:32: all just blood that was ever poured out, "comes upon" the Jews [cf. Lev 20:9, 11, 12, 13, 16; Ez 18:13]). "Blood" is an expression of judgment, which established the guilt of a breaker of the Law (cf. 27:25). The two examples (Abel and Zechariah) illustrate what the Jews have done with Jesus; they are the "murders" of the just, from the beginning down to the present (cf. Acts 7:52). Unjustly spilled blood (LN 20.84) cries out for retribution (cf. Gen 4:10; 9:6; Job 16:18; Isa 26:21; Ez 24:7-8; Joel 4:19). "All the righteous blood" applies not only to all Christian missionaries, but above all to the Messiah Jesus.

Verse 36: "All this will come." "This blanket condemnation of the Jewish leaders must be read in the light both of the Church's experience of persecution and of Jerusalem's destruction in A.D. 70. The Church saw the latter as an apocalyptic event, a judgment exacted for the death of Christ and his faithful, and also as an anticipation of the final judgment. The veiled reference leads neatly into the final section of chapter 23, the address to Jerusalem" (Meier, 273).

The concluding word, an Amen-word ("Truly I tell you"), which speaks of a judgment event that the end-time will bring upon Israel, forces the community to reflect on the history of Israel from the beginning down to the present, and to recognize that this history presents a way that is marked out by the blood of the just. From the blood of the just Abel to that of Zechariah down to the blood of the crucified Jesus, who likewise is a just one (27:19, 24), the guilt piles up until it is brought to full measure.

But the community is not without its share in this event; it cannot act toward it as an uninvolved observer. What happens there involves it also. The community is closely bound up with the history of Israel. And the history of the community (heilsgeschichte) is not *ipso facto* "holy history"; that from call and election an Unheilsgeschichte follow. This is what the community should reflect upon as it hears these charges.

Judgment on Jerusalem, 23:37-39

Now the terrible theme of prophet-killing is centered upon Jerusalem. The "holy city" has proven throughout its unholy history to be an evil city, *the* place in Israel where the prophets have been rejected and murdered. As in the past, so now Jerusalem has rejected the prophet of God. The difference is that this time she has rejected the eschatological prophet, and so she has no future.

> 37 "Jerusalem, Jerusalem, the city that kills the prophets and stones those who are sent to it! How often have I desired to gather your children together as a hen gathers her brood under her wings, and you were not willing! 38 See, your house is left to you, desolate. 39 For I tell you, you will not see me again until you say, 'Blessed is the one who comes in the name of the Lord.' "

Verse 37: "City that kills the prophets." The prophets are indeed the prophets of the past, but are above all Jesus of Nazareth and the Christian messengers of Matthew's community. "To stone" (cf. Acts 7:58, 59; Heb 11:37) interprets "to kill" in the sense of Leviticus 24:10-16; Deutereonomy 17:5, 7. In the Old Testament and in Judaism, stoning was the sacral death punishment. So although not crucifixion but stoning is mentioned, Jesus is also included among the prophets.

"Her brood under her wings" (LN 8.29). Noteworthy about Jesus' conflicts "is the fact that whereas he freely employs his imcomparable authority to vanquish Satan, demons, and the forces of nature and illness, he chooses not to compel humans to do his bidding (23:37; 26:37-45, 53). On the contrary, he calls humans to repentance in view of the gracious nearness of God's kingly rule (4:17). The upshot is that the conflict on which the plot of Matthew's story turns is that between Jesus and Israel" (*Story*, 3-4).

Verse 38: "Your house is left to you, desolate." "House" can stand for Jerusalem (Jer 22:1-9; 23:8), for the temple, or for the entire land of Israel. Here, Israel in a comprehensive sense is represented by Jerusalem. This Israel will be left desolate (*eremos*, LN 85.84).

While "house" could signify Jerusalem or even the whole of Israel, the fact that Jesus is speaking in the temple favors the common Old Testament image of the temple as the house of God. As in Ezekiel 10:1-22; 11:22-25, the Lord will leave his temple. While the full acting out of this threat was accomplished in A.D. 70, the prophecy already begins to be fulfilled in 24:1, when Jesus leaves the temple, and more fully in 27:51, when the curtain of the temple is rent at the death of Christ. "The 'temple' is the house of God (21:13) which is under the control of the religious leaders, especially the chief priests, and which is not serving its intended purpose as a place of worship (21:13). For the brief time Jesus teaches and heals there, he imparts God's benefactions to the people; but once he leaves it, it is deserted (23:38) and ripe for destruction (24:1-2). In point of fact, Jesus himself supplants the temple as the 'place' where God mediates salvation to people" (*Story*, 30).

Verse 39: "You will not see me again." This is the first allusion to the Passion in Matthew. While individual Jews may continue to enter the Church, Israel as a whole is abandoned to its fate. On this sober note, Matthew moves to the eschatological discourse. Since he wishes as direct a connection as possible, he drops Mark's story of the widow's mite (12:41-44).

Chapter 23 ends with the assertion that God will forsake Israel as a punishment for the murder of the prophets, which finds its climax in the death of Jesus and in the persecution of his messengers (cf. 21:37-39, 41;

22:5-7). The repeated invitations to insight and conversion were rejected; Israel was unwilling. Thereby Israel's fate was "chosen, not imposed."

This fate comes to Israel at the time of the gathering through Jesus. Toward Jesus' call, Israel has closed her ears (and her hert), so that in her the Lord's curse has been fulfilled: "This house shall become a desolation" (Jer 22:5).

The community finds itself involved in this tragic turn of events, inasmuch as they are still under way to judgment day and to the day of the manifestation of God's Lordship. But whoever is underway is also always under the burden to confront God's action in history. So Chapter 23 is not an attack exclusively on Israel, but an attempt, in dialogue with Israel, to find a solution to the grave problem of Matthew's community, why Israel had not acknowledged the Messiah and why now in overwhelming mass, the kingdom of God passes over to the Gentiles.

"Five times throughout Matthew's story, the reader encounters the sterco-typed formula: 'Now when Jesus had finished saying these things [these parables; instructing his twelve disciples] . . .' (7:28; 11:1; 13:53; 19:1; 26:1). Each time this formula occurs, it calls attention to the termination of a speech Jesus has delivered. This formula clearly marks out the five great speeches, or discourses, of Jesus. They are: the Sermon on the Mount (chaps. 5-7); the missionary discourse (9:35--10:42); the discourse in parables (13:1—52); the ecclesiological discourse (17:24—18:35); and the eschatological discourse (chaps. 24-25)" (*Story,* 105).

Jesus presents none of his great speeches to the religious leaders (their ears are closed to him). The audiences are the crowds and especially the disciples. In the Sermon on the Mount, Jesus speaks to both the crowds and the disciples, and it is primarily to the crowds that he also delivers the first half of his discourse in parables. Otherwise, the recipients of Jesus' great speeches are exclusively the disciples.

De facto, Jesus' discourses are for the most part "spoken past" the stipulated audience and addressed to the implied reader, who not only is present throughout Matthew to hear the entire story, but also has a position of his or her own that lies between the Resurrection and the Parousia.

Jesus' great speeches contain sayings that seemingly are without relevance for the characters in the story to whom they are addressed. Time and again, Jesus touches on matters that are alien to the immediate situation of the crowds or the disciples; Jesus speaks past his stipulated audience at places in his speeches, and addresses some person(s) other than simply the crowds or the disciples in the story. These persons are the implied readers.

Sayings of Jesus that appear to address a situation other than the one in the story in which the crowds or the disciples find themselves can readily be detected in all the speeches. "Indeed, in one case, Jesus' eschatological discourse (chaps. 24-25), the whole of the speech envisages a different situation owing to the fact that it is prophetic in character and foretells the future (24:3)'' (*Story*, 107).

The eschatological discourse describes for Christian readers what they can expect as they carry out their Great Commission and look forward to the final phases of the coming of the kingdom. The disciples receive from the resurrected and crucified Son of God the commission to go and make all nations his disciples (28:18-20). Having then received this commission, they make their way from the mountain in Galilee to the world that Jesus has described for them in his end-time discourse of chapters 24-25. The disciples receive from Jesus the Great Commission, and embark on a mission to all the nations (28:18-20; chs. 24-25), having been warned what to expect.

As D. Bauer writes: "The future missionary activity of the disciples among the Gentiles is even more clearly presented in the eschatological discourse of chapters 24-25 than in the missionary discourse of chapter 10. Jesus predicts that they will be hated by 'all nations' (*panton ton ethnon*, 24.9), that 'the Gospel of the kingdom will be preached throughout the whole world, as a testimony to all nations before the end (24.14), and that at the end he will gather his elect 'from the four winds, from one end of heaven to the other' (24.41). The sheep and the goats assembled before Jesus at the judgment are identified as 'all the nations' (25.31-46)" (123).

As the Church carries out its great commission it must also read the signs of the times. The theme addressed in the eschatological discourse is also that of the 'last times' (24:34). Here, three larger sections comprise the discourse: (I) On Understanding Aright the Signs of the End (24:4-35); (II) On Being on the Alert for Jesus' Coming at the Consummation of the Age (24:36—25:30); and (III) On the Second Coming of Jesus and the Final Judgment (25:31-46).

Jesus Comes Out of the Temple, 24:1-3

Chapter 23 is closely connected with chapter 24. The seven Woes of chapter 23 treat of the "scribes and Pharisees, hypocrites!" (v. 13), but they are addressed to the disciples. This terrifying indictment makes it clear to the disciples that these words apply to them as well: they are not immune to the conduct for which the scribes and Pharisees are reproached.

The Woes end with Jesus' apostrophe on Jerusalem (vv. 37-39), announcing that the city has been abandoned by God, because it has refused to respond to Jesus' efforts on its behalf. This passage ends with the first allusion to the parousia: "You will not see me again until you say, 'Blessed is the one who comes in the name of the Lord' " (v. 39). This is clearly a transition passage anticipating the themes of chapter 24.

The addition of the address to Jerusalem goes hand in hand with the omission, singular at first sight, of the episode of the poor widow reported by Mark at this point: by placing her two copper coins into the treasure of the temple, she gave more than all the others (12:41-44). This omission has a plausible explanation only in Matthew's desire to avoid an interruption between the finale of chapter 23 and the beginning of chapter 24.

> **24:1** As Jesus came out of the temple and was going away, his disciples came to point out to him the buildings of the temple. **2** Then he asked them, "You see all these, do you not? Truly I tell you, not one stone will be left here upon another; all will be thrown down." **3** When he was sitting on the Mount of Olives, the disciples came to him privately, saying, "Tell us, when will this be, and what will be the sign of your coming and of the end of the age?"

In some instances there is uncertainty about where the discourses begin. So here it is suggested that the eschatological discourse begins at 23:1; 24:1; or 24:3. "These observations imply that the discourses are closely related in each case to the preceding material and that the preceding material flows naturally into the discourse" (Bauer, 130).

Verse 1: "Jesus came out of the temple and was going away." The apostrophe on Jerusalem at the end of chapter 23 directs attention to the way Matthew has edited the first three verses of chapter 24. According to Mark 13:1, it was at the moment when Jesus left the temple ("as he came out of the temple") that one of his disciples addressed him directly: "Look, Teacher, what large stones and what large buildings!" According to Matthew, Jesus had already left the temple ("Jesus came out of the temple and was going away.") when "his disciples came to point out to him the buildings of the temple." The distance between Jesus and the temple is increased, and at the same time the element of admiration which Mark attributes to a disciple is eliminated. This appears even more clearly in verse 3. There, where Mark shows Jesus, sitting "on the Mount of Olives opposite the temple," Matthew notes simply that Jesus "sat on the Mount of Olives." The placement "opposite the temple" constitutes a hermeneutic key to the discourse. It seems likely that if Matthew suppresses it, this is not simply for the sake of brevity. This suppression is situated in the same line as the addition which makes it clear that Jesus had left the temple (v. 1).

The "temple," under the control of the religious leaders, is not serving its intended purpose as a place of worship (21:13). For the brief time Jesus teaches and heals there, he imparts God's benefactions to people; but once he leaves it, it is deserted (23:38) and ripe for destruction (24:1-2). Jesus himself supplants the temple as the "place" where God mediates salvation to people.

Jesus reduces the religious *leaders* in open debate to silence and forces their withdrawal from the scene (22:46). Jesus then publicly addresses the *crowds* in the temple, together with the disciples (23:1). Now leaving the temple, Jesus delivers his eschatological discourse to the *disciples* alone (24:1-3). Through the use of this chiastic pattern, Matthew signals the reader that the culmination of his story is at hand.

Verse 2: "Not one stone will be left here upon another." Verse 2 reports Jesus' declaration after the intervention of the disciple (Mark), or disciples (Matthew). In both versions Jesus begins with a question. Mark: "Do you see these great buildings?"; Matthew: "You see all these, do you not?" The prediction follows, shorter in Mark ("There will not be left here one stone upon another"); in Matthew ("Truly, I tell you, not one stone will be left here upon another; all will be thrown down"). In Matthew, as in Mark, the prediction refers directly to the temple; but Matthew's vague "all these" in the initial question leaves room for doubt; does it not apply to Jerusalem as a whole to which Jesus had addressed the apostrophe reported in the preceding verses?

A change of audience is also to be noted. In Mark, the introduction of verse 1 is attributed to "one of his disciples;" that of verse 4 to four disciples designated by name: "Peter, James, John, and Andrew." In Matthew it is a group of disciples which is involved in both instances: "his disciples came" (v. 1), "the disciples came to him" (v. 3). The great discourse just beginning is addressed not to some disciples only, but to the entire group of disciples, contrary to the discourse of chapter 23 pronounced before the crowd and the disciples (23:1).

Verse 3: "Sign of your coming." It is the question put by the disciples that especially deserves our attention, for it is this that determines the theme of the discourse. This question is double in both cases. In Mark the question is double: the disciples wished to know especially "when will this be," then, "what will be the sign that all these things are about to be accomplished" (13:4). In Matthew, the question remains double. But we note immediately that the second part is much more precise: the "sign" about which Jesus is asked is that of "your coming and the end of the age." Unified in Greek under one article, the two events are not distinct: the glorious return of Jesus must coincide with the end of the present world and the inauguration of the world to come. So the question arises whether the first part of the question ("Tell us, when will this be") bears upon a different object than that which the second part is at such pains to make explicit. To attribute to it another object, the destruction of the temple, seems possible only by neglecting the application with which Matthew turns the attention from the temple. Indeed it is not evident with him that the prediction of verse 2 concerns only the temple (dealt with in v. 1), rather than Jerusalem (of which the preceding verses speak (23:37-39) and "the present generation" when "all these things must happen" (23:36). Moreover, at the beginning of verse 3, Matthew has eliminated the indication according to which Jesus was "opposite the temple" (Mark 13:3), keeping only the localization on the Mount of Olives. Thus, no more than in Mark, do the two parts of the question of the disciples seem to refer to two objects that are really different: the second part only explains the first.

One therefore has the impression that the introduction to the eschatological discourse places it in the immediate prolongation of the oracle in which Jesus announces the abandonment of the temple (23:38) and his own disappearance until the moment when, at the parousia, those who see him coming will cry out: "Blessed is he who comes in the name of the Lord" (23:39). The eschatological event par excellence is no longer in Matthew's thought, the destruction of the temple, but the return of Jesus. The new formulation given to the question of verse reorients the entire discourse: it will have for its object the glorious coming of Jesus and that which will be its sign.

(I) On Understanding Aright the Signs of the End (24:4-35)

(I)A Birthpangs and Suffering, 4-14

4 Jesus answered them, "Beware that no one leads you astray. 5 For many will come in my name, saying, 'I am the Messiah!' and they will lead many astray. 6 And you will hear of wars and rumors of wars; see that you are not alarmed; for this must take place, but the end is not yet. 7 For nation will rise against nation, and kingdom against kingdom, and there will be famines and earthquakes in various places; 8 all this is but the beginning of the birthpangs.

9 "Then they will hand you over to be tortured and will put you to death, and you will be hated by all nations because of my name. 10 Then many will fall away, and they will betray one another and hate one another. 11 And many false prophets will arise and lead many astray. 12 And because of the increase of lawlessness, the love of man will grow cold. 13 But the one who endures to the end will be saved. 14 And this

good news of the kingdom will be proclaimed throughout the world, as a testimony to all the nations; and then the end will come."

Verse 4: "Beware that." The disciples are to guard against being deceived by messianic pretenders, with their apocalyptic assurances. Such pretenders seem to have been known in the first century (Acts 5:36; 21:38), and again in the time of the second Jewish war.

Verse 5: "Lead many astray." This initial warning against impostors has the appearance of something preliminary. The danger of being misled is not different from that of becoming alarmed by improperly attributing to wars and other calamities the significance of signs of the immediate end. In denying such significance to calamities, Matthew at the same time rejects the pretensions of the impostors who try to pass themselves off as "the Christ." The way in which he explains this pretension (v. 5) again manifests his Christological comprehension of the "end." "But the end (*ho telos*) is not yet," v. 6. In Matthew's thought, the end can only be a Christological event: "for Matthew the great danger of error is in christology" (*NJBC, ad hoc*). To say that one has not yet arrived at the end (v. 6c) is also to affirm that Christ has not yet come and that those who present themselves as the Christ are only imposters (v. 5).

Verses 6-7: "Wars and rumors of wars." These were regarded as signs of the approaching end in Jewish apocalyptic. In order to curb excited anticipations, Matthew makes two important points: first, these disquieting events must happen according to the purpose of God (cf. Dan; 2:28) and, since history is under the control of God, believers can and should remain calm; and, secondly, these events will be only the *beginning of the sufferings*, (literally, "birthpangs", almost a technical term for the tribulations leading up to the end of the age, which are to be endured by the community of the elect). The disasters experienced are but a prelude, and feverish apocalypticism is out of place.

Verse 8: "All this is but the beginning." Verse 15, which bursts the bonds of story-world of Matthew, works together with this verse to fix the time of the implied reader in the time of the birthpangs. The place that Matthew, the implied author, assigns himself already lies at some distance from the event of the resurrection (28:1-15), and is situated in the time of the messianic woes and the Church's mission to the nations (24:8, 14-15) (cf. v. 15).

Verses 9-12: "Then they will hand you over." The "then" of verse 9 marks the next stage in the process. The strife among nations and natural disasters is matched by the tribulation of the Church. The suffering comes from both without (v. 9) and within (vv. 10-12). Here the persecution is, from the beginning, "by all nations"; here the Jews are understood to be included among "all the nations." The hostile world *hands over* (v. 9) the disciples to death, just as John the Baptist (4:12) and Jesus (26:45) are *handed over*; the Christian community, the successors to the prophets of the end-time, share in their violent fate. Indeed, the Christians are hated precisely because of the "name"—the person and teaching—of Jesus.

Verse 14: "This good news of the kingdom." Jesus presented himself to Israel by "proclaiming" (4:17), and the message he proclaimed was the "good news of the kingdom" (4:23; 9:35). In the time following Easter, the disciples too, will proclaim "the Gospel of the kingdom" (24:14). "By drawing this parallel between Jesus and the post-Easter disciples, Matthew shows that throughout the entire 'time of Jesus,' from his life on earth to his Parousia in splendor, the Gospel of the kingdom has been, is being, and will be proclaimed" (*Story*, 61).

"Will be proclaimed." At 12:21, Matthew quotes from the Old Testament in order to proclaim Jesus as the one in whom the "Gentiles will hope," and at 13:38 he writes that it is in the "world" that "the children of the kingdom" will be raised up. In the parables of the wicked husbandmen (21:33-46) and of the great supper (22:1-14), Matthew employs figurative speech to depict the influx of the Gentiles into the Church (21:41; 22:9-10), Now, "in 24:14 and 26:13 he has Jesus announce that it is throughout the entire world that the Gospel of the kingdom will be proclaimed" (*Story*, 151).

"As a testimony to all nations." The focus of Matthew's story is on the life of Jesus between conception and resurrection. Jesus' conflict with the nations is not part of the story's plot. "This conflict, not narrated in story form, is instead sketched by Jesus in prophetic utterances about the future (cf. chaps. 24-25). This means that as Jesus tells of this conflict, he no longer sees himself as the earthly Son of God but as the exalted Son of God whom God will invest with all authority in heaven and on earth (28:18-20). As the exalted One, Jesus will dispatch his missionary Church to make all nations, including Israel, his disciples (23:34; 24:14)" (*Story*, 8).

(I)B The Great Final Tribulation, 24:15-22

In reading these eschatological passages, an important thing to keep in mind is that the implied reader is the one who is silently and invisibly present throughout Matthew's story to attend to every word. Like the implied author, the implied reader has a place of his or her own within the world of Matthew's story. This position lies, as verse 15 reveals, at some distance from the resurrection but short of the Parousia. This insight is especially significant for understanding the great discourses of Jesus (chs. 5-7; 10; 13; 18; [23]; 24-25).

> 15 "So when you see the desolating sacrilege standing in the holy place, as was spoken of by the prophet Daniel (let the reader understand) 16 then those in Judea must flee to the mountains; 17 the one on the housetop must not go down to take what is in the house; 18 the one in the field must not turn back to get a coat. 19 Woe to those who are pregnant and to those who are nursing infants in those days! 20 Pray that your flight may not be in winter or on a sabbath. 21 For at that time there will be great suffering, such as has not been from the beginning of the world until now, no, and never will be. 22 And if those days had not been cut short, no one would be saved; but for the sake of the elect those days will be cut short."

Verse 15: "The desolating sacrilege" (LN 53.38). The phrase is taken from Daniel 9:27 in the Septuagent (cf. Dan 11:31; 12:11), where it refers to the setting up of an altar to Zeus Olympios in the temple in 168 B.C. by the king of Syria, Antiochus IV Epiphanes. Matthew makes clear that he, too, is thinking of the temple by changing Mark's vague "standing where it should not" to "standing in the holy place." The intended vagueness of this apocalyptic manner of speaking allows the past historical event to act as a model and forewarning of the greater sacrilege still to come; hence, the admonition to read with understanding.

"(Let the reader understand!)." On the basis of this and two other passages, "it is obvious that the place that Matthew, the implied author, assigns himself already lies at some distance from the event of the resurrection (28:1-15) and is situated in the time of the messianic woes and the Church's mission to the nations (24:8, 14-15). From this particular place, Matthew as implied author looks back upon the whole of the story of the life and ministry of Jesus of Nazareth and also involves himself, through his voice as narrator, in every aspect of this story" (*Story*, 33).

This represents Matthew's spatial and temporal "point of view"—the position in time and space from which he observes and describes characters or events. In such passages as 24:15 ("Let the reader understand"), 27:8 ("Until this day"), and 28:15 ("until this day"), Matthew bursts the bounds of the story he is telling of the life and ministry of Jesus in order to address the implied reader directly.

Verse 16-21: The "great tribulation" of the destruction of Jerusalem foreshadows the great tribulation of the end. In the face of such a crisis, one should act decisively and speedily. Those in Judea must flee to the uninhabited mountains of the wasteland near the Dead Sea (v. 6). Those on the flat roofs of Palestinian houses must flee by the outside staircase, without going back to the house to rescue anything (v. 17). Those working in the fields must flee without running back to the edge of the field to pick up their outer garments, laid aside for work (v. 18). Matthew recounts circumstances that would increase the suffering of flight. Being pregnant, having to care for new-born infants (v. 19), trying to flee amid the chilling rains and flooded roads of a Palestinian winter, flight on sabbath, when Christians could easily be spotted by Jews, who restricted their movements to 2,000 paces.

Verse 22: "For the sake of the elect." A word of comfort at the end. The unprecedented tribulations are shortened. "For the sake of the elect" is taken from Jewish eschatology, and could mean either "because there is an elect, faithful people in the world," or, "in order that the elect (i.e. the remnant, those whom God has chosen for his Kingdom, the Christians) may be saved." "It should be noted that these verses and those which follow have the effect of denying the imminence of the End; certain things must happen first" (D. Hill, *ad loc*).

(I)C False Christians and False Prophets, 24:23-28

Matthew takes seriously the subject to which these verses refer. While continuing to follow Mark (13:21-22) he inserts a fragment coming from elsewhere (cf. Luke 17:23-24, 37). This accounts for the fact that verse 26 is only a variant of verse 23. We are given two warnings not to believe the impostors who will pretend to furnish information on the place where Christ is already present. To the negative warnings of verses 23-25 and 26, verses 27-28 add a positive statement on the evidence which must characterize the coming of the Son of Man. This doublet is all the more in place because it offers an excellent transition to the description of the the coming of the Son of Man in the following pericope (24:29-31).

> **23** "Then if anyone says to you, 'Look! Here is the Messiah!' or 'There he is!'—do not believe it. **24** For false messiahs and false prophets will appear and produce great signs and omens, to lead astray, if possible, even the elect. **25** Take note, I have told you beforehand. **26** So, if they say to you, 'Look! He is in the wilderness,' do not go out. If they say, 'Look! He is in the inner rooms,' do not believe it. **27** For as the lightning comes from the east and flashes as far as the west, so will be the coming of the Son of Man. **28** Wherever the corpse is, there the vultures will gather."

Verse 23: "Look! Here is the Messiah!" "Then" of verse 23 introduces a further stage, and a deepening of the affliction, on the Church's journey towards the end.

Verse 24: "Lead astray, if possible." The horror of the last days will reach such a fever pitch that it will seem as though God's set plan for salvation is being undone and even those confirmed in grace are being wrenched from his hand. The false christs and false prophets will offer signs and wonders (perhaps the same signs as his authentic ones, 7:21-23), but their mission is "to lead astray."

Verse 25: "I have told you beforehand." But God is not being taken by surprise; Jesus has predicted these events beforehand for the comfort of the elect. Even the frightening catastrophes preceding the end are directed by God's providence. No doubt Matthew sees these false messiahs and prophets as coming at least in part from within the Church (cf. the evil wonder-working prophets in 7:21-23).

Verse 26: "In the wilderness . . . in the inner rooms." "There is no point in looking for the Messiah in the wilderness (as John the Baptist or the Qumran community), nor in hidden place, as e.g., the Jews could think of Messiah as hidden in the slums of Rome" (D. Hill, *ad loc*). The "inner rooms" could also refer, however, to the Jewish theory of the hidden Messiah, to be revealed at the proper moment.

Verse 27: "As the lightning comes." Matthew tells how Christians can recognize the falsehood of these claimants. The final coming of the Son of Man will be a brilliant, public, cosmic event, as clear and obvious as the lightning bolt which traverses the whole vault of heaven. The manifestation of the Messiah will not be reserved for a small company of initiates. The parousia of the Son of Man (who is clearly identified with Messiah) will be clear to all; no doubt will be possible.

Verse 28: "There the vultures will gather." It is unlikely that *ptoma* ("corpse") includes a reference to the crucified body of Jesus or to the city of Jerusalem sacked by Roman legions. The point here is again the public and certain nature of the parousia, as visible as vultures circling around a carcass. The parousia is mentioned in this pericope dealing with the horrors preceding the end only to point out that the false messiahs and prophets can be detected by their non-public nature. The real discussion of the parousia belongs to the next pericope.

The influence of the impostors, which already disturbed Matthew greatly for the time of the Church, will become even more dangerous when the final stages of the end of time will be unleashed. Verses 27-28 are meant to cut short illusions, so redoubtable in Matthew's eyes. They take the form of two images, both designed to illustrate concretely the idea that, at the parousia, the presence of the Son of Man will be immediately and evidently recognizable. Thus, Matthew gives the impression of opposing certain Jewish conceptions according to which the Messiah, at the end of time, will first remain hidden and unknown, to subsequently reveal his full glory. No! When he will again descend from the sky, the Christ will be as visible for all as lightning which "comes from the east, and shines as far as the west" (v. 27). Thus it will be as recognizable to all as the presence of a corpse is evident everywhere by reason of the gathering of vultures which it provokes, as the proverb has it: "Wherever the corpse is, there the vultures will gather."

Two images furnish Matthew with two key terms of the following section. There it will be a question of the sign of the Son of Man "appearing" (*phanēsetai*) (v. 30), comparable to the "flashing" (*phainetai*) of lightning (v. 27), and to the "gathering" (*synaxaousin*) of the elect by the angels (v. 31), which may echo the proverb about the "gathering" (*synachtēsontai*) of the vultures (v. 28). This is another example of the care with which Matthew arranges transitions.

Verses 23-28 echo the warnings of the preceding section, which warns Christians not to be led astray by impostors (vv. 4b-5 and 11). This is also the situation of the Christian community in verses 23-28. Matthew is concerned above all with the danger to which the Church will be exposed at the time of the great final crisis. And this danger is seen in the light of the analogous danger presented to it at the time by the presence of impostors who threaten to lead the faithful astray. The difficulties that Christians must face in the present color those that they must expect at the great final tribulation. The warnings given in view of a future situation are just those which are of immediate application. Matthew speaks of the future in function of the present and the pastoral preoccupations of concern in the actual situation. It is right now that Christians must not allow themselves to be led astray by imposters.

(I)D The Coming of the Son of Man, 24:29-31

The plot of Matthew's story centers upon the conflict between Jesus and Israel, especially the religious leaders. Jesus is also in conflict with the nations not part of the story's plot, and so not narrated in story form. Instead, this conflict is sketched by Jesus in prophetic utterances about the future, especially in the eschatological discourse (25). Jesus tells of this conflict as the exalted Son of God, whom God will invest with all authority in heaven and on earth (28:18-20). As the exalted One, Jesus will dispatch his missionary Church to make all nations, including Israel, his disciples (21:34; 24:14). The exalted Jesus will return in power and splendor to preside over the final judgment for the salvation or condemnation of all (16:27; 25:31-46).

> **29** "Immediately after the suffering of those days
> the sun will be darkened,
>   and the moon will not give its light;
> the stars will fall from heaven,
>   and the powers of heaven will be shaken.
> **30** Then the sign of the Son of Man will appear in heaven, and then all the tribes of the earth will mourn and they will see the Son of Man coming on the clouds of heaven with power and great glory. **31** And he will send out his angels with a loud trumpet call, and they will gather his elect from the four winds, from one end of heaven to the other.''

A glance at a Synopsis reveals that these three verses of Matthew are notably longer than the four verses which correspond to them in Mark (13:24-27). Matthew's expansion comes most noticeably in verse 30, which describes the coming of the Son of Man (thirty-six words to Mark's fifteen). This indicates the importance that Matthew attached to this scene, toward which the discourse has been directed since the disciples' question to Jesus about "the sign of his coming" (v. 3), and which will dominate it all the way up to the great final description of the judgment in 25:31-46.

Verse 29: "Sun will be darkened." The disciples' question in 24:3 about "the *sign* of your coming" now receives a direct answer. "Immediately after" the horror of the last days reaches its fever pitch (vv. 23-28), the "end of the age" (24:3; 28:20) will come. The spiritual disasters are now matched by cosmic disasters (cf. Isa 13:10; 34:4). The old world passes away completely. The appearance of the Son of Man after the tribulation will be accompanied by cosmic portents described in terms of traditional Jewish apocalyptic. There can be no mistaking the event.

"The powers of heaven." Both Jews and Gentiles thought that the celestial bodies were controlled by angelic or divine beings ("the powers of heaven") who governed the destinies of men. All such powers are swept away as the true cosmocrator, the Son of Man, comes to claim the universe as his own.

Verse 30a: "The sign of the Son of Man." "Then," when the fabric of the old creation is rent, the Son of Man will appear, riding the clouds of heaven like a chariot, as Daniel 7:13 had predicted.

"The sign of the Son of Man" can be understood in two ways. First, one can understand that it is a sign which appertains to the Son of Man, the sign by which the Son of Man will make himself known, that which must announce his coming. Then we would have to do with an object which precedes the Son of Man and is necessarily distinct from him. It is in this direction that the question placed by the disciples in verse 3 naturally points: "What will be the sign of your coming." But it could also be a question of an appositive or expegetic genitive: the sign is none other than the Son of Man himself, identifying himself with it. This is the meaning recommended by the structure of the sentence. Its two parts are parallel. There is a correspondence between the first affirmation: "Then will appear the sign of the Son of Man," and the second: "Then all the tribes of the earth . . . will see the Son of Man coming." What one sees corresponds naturally to what "appears" and "is manifested." Now there is no question of seeing anything other than the Son of Man. The same situation arises in connection with "the sign of Jonah" (Matt 12:39 and 16:4). This "sign of Jonah" is not something that is distinct from Jonah, it is Jonah himself in so far as he was personally a sign. This is how Luke understands it: "For just as Jonah became a sign to the people of Ninevah, so will the Son of Man be to this generation" (11:30). This is also how Matthew understands it: "For as Jonah was three days and three nights in the belly of the whale, so will the Son of Man be three days and three nights in the heart of the earth" (12:40).

In questioning Jesus about "the sign of his parousia" (24:3), the disciples evidently concern themselves with a preliminary event, preceding the glorious return of Jesus and revealing in advance the nearness of his return. In the two cases where Matthew mentions Jesus' word on "the sign of Jonah," it is in a response that Jesus makes to the scribes and Pharisees who ask a sign of him (12:38), or to the Pharisees and Sadducees who ask him to show them a sign from heaven (16:1). In both cases, Jesus becomes indignant with this "evil and adulterous generation which seeks for a sign" (12:39; 16:4). From every indication, Jesus himself in person, is the sign which God offers to his contemporaries. And if the sign given by the exercise of his earthly mission can remain unsatisfactory, Matthew is at pains to explain that the events of Easter will suffice to make Jesus the sign that none can reject without rejecting God himself.

Thus, one can better judge the relationship between Matthew 24:30, the "sign of the Son of Man," and the questions in verse 3 about "the sign of the parousia" of Jesus. The parousia will have no other sign than the apparition of the Son of Man. The end of the world will not be simply the culmination of a series of discernible events enchained one after the other: it will be realized by the personal coming of the Son of Man. It will be the fruit not of a blind mechanism, but of a free decision. As it had been put in verse 3 the question of the "sign" was a poorly stated question. The Christian expectation was not based on the observation of earthly or heavenly phenomena; it rested entirely on faith in the person of Jesus and in his word.

Verse 30b: "All the tribes of the earth." The latter half of verse 30 contains a combination of Daniel 7:13-14 with Zechariah 12:10–14; "when they look upon him whom they have pierced, they shall mourn for him, as one mourns for an only child . . . and the earth shall mourn by tribes" [*NRSV*: "The land shall mourn, each family by itself"]. The same combination is seen in Revelations 1:7. The Son of Man who was pierced (i.e., put to death by crucifixion), will be the same Son of Man who comes in glory to judge. All the tribes of the earth who have refused to become disciples (cf. 28:19)—and not just the Jews—will bewail their imminent condemnation. Compared with 16:27, the total absence of God the Father is striking.

Verse 31: "With a loud trumpet." The Son of Man acts completely on his own authority, sending out *his* angels to gather from all the earth *his* elect. The trumpet is a traditional symbol of the last judgment (cf. Isa 27:13; 1 Thess 4:16). Matthew raises the divine majesty of the Son of Man to great heights.

(I)E Imminence of the End (24:32-35)

After reaching the high point, one must descend. Now we are led back to the time before the "coming of the Son of Man." For the parable of the fig tree the discourse reverts to the second person plural, abandoned since verse 27, in favor of a purely descriptive style. The first, doctrinal part of the discourse ends with an affirmation that the end is certain and near, yet sudden and incalculable. This creates a bridge to the more parenetic or exhortatory half of the discourse. Matthew balances stress on the nearness of the parousia (prominent in Mark) with his own stress on the delay, in the three great parables of the second part pf the discourse.

> **32** "From the fig tree learn its lesson: as soon as its branch becomes tender and puts forth its leaves, you know that summer is near. **33** So also, when you see all these things, you know that he is near, at the very gates. **34** Truly I tell you, this generation will not pass away until all these things have taken place. **35** Heaven and earth will pass away, but my words will not pass away.

Verse 32: "Summer is near." To the disciples' initial question of "when" (v. 3), Jesus replies indirectly, with a parable. The little parable of the

Fig Tree teaches again the lesson of patience; the budding fig tree is a sure sign of summer, and the unmistakable signs mentioned herald the arrival of the Son of Man. During the rainy winter season in Palestine, most trees do not lose their leaves; but the fig tree does. Hence, the reappearance of leaves on the fig tree signals the approach of the dry summer season. Since a good part of the Palestinian harvest takes place during the summer, it is a very apt sign for the final judgment (cf. 13:39).

Verse 33: "When you see (*hotan idēte*?)." This is an exact repetition of verse 15: "when you see the desolating sacrilege." This repetition is also a reminder: the heavens have been led back to the situation which preceded "the coming of the Son of Man" described in the preceding pericope. And it is to the situation that we must limit the scope of "when you see all these things (*panta tauta*)." It is then that you will know "that he is near."

Verse 34: "This generation will not pass away till all these things have taken place." Once again we find the vague expression "all these things (*panta tauta*)," which here takes on a broader meaning than in the preceding verse: it is no longer a question of the terrible preliminaries, but also of the glorious coming of the Son of Man of which the great crisis announces the nearness.

In transcribing such declarations at the end of the first century, Matthew imparts to them a meaning in accordance with his Christian faith. He places them in relation with the destruction of Jerusalem which, for him, already belongs to the past (cf. 22:7). Matthew is fearful that a slackening in the expectation of the Lord's return contributes to the degradation for which he reproaches the Church of his time (cf. v. 12). While Matthew is not content to reproduce Mark's text (13:28-31) unchanged, he imparts only small stylistic changes. Matthew lets the Markan statement stand for the sake of conveying a sense of urgency; in what follows, Matthew will correct any misconceptions by his stress on *delay*. He does not indicate how his readers are to interpret these verses. He shows the same passive attitude he showed in repeating the description of the great tribulation in verses 15-22. The theme does not interest him to the extent that he judges his personal intervention to be opportune. He awaits the favorable occasion to stress what he considers most important, and he finds it in the saying of verse 36 (Mark 13:32). He will make it the starting point of the longest section of his discourse on the parousia.

Verse 35: "My words will not pass away." The vital part of those "words" is the "greater righteousness," love of God and neighbor. It is on that that the members of his community should fix their attention.

(II) On Being on the Alert for Jesus' Coming at the Consummation of the Age, 24:36–25:30

(II)A 24:36-44

Up to this point chapter 24 has tried to calm excessive eschatological fervor and calculation. Now the rest of the discourse tries to stir up a proper eschatological watchfulness in those who have become too immersed in the flow of this world's events. Three parables (the generation of Noah, the two pairs of workers, and the thief in the night) announce the major theme of the second part of the discourse: vigilance and preparedness for the "coming [*parousia*] of the Son of Man" (a motif which forms an inclusion in vv. 37 and 39 and harks back to v. 3).

> 36 "But about that day and hour no one knows, neither the angels of heaven, nor the Son, but only the Father. 37 For as the days of Noah were, so will be the coming of the Son of Man. 38 For as in those days before the flood they were eating and drinking, marrying and giving in marriage, until the day Noah entered the ark, 39 and they knew nothing until the flood came and swept them all away, so too will be the coming of the Son of Man. 40 Then two will be in the field; one will be taken and one will be left. 41 Two women will be grinding meal together; one will be taken and one will be left. 42 Keep awake therefore, for you do not know on what day your Lord is coming. 43 But understand this: if the owner of the house had known what part of the night the thief was coming, he would have stayed awake and would not have let his house be broken into. 44 Therefore you also must be ready, for the Son of Man is coming at an unexpected hour."

Verse 36: "That day and hour." Verse 36 acts as something of a counterbalance to verse 34. The nearness of the parousia must not tempt Christians to indulge in speculation and calculation about precise dates. The motifs of "day" and "hour" will be repeated in verses 42, 44, 50 and in 25:13, along with the theme of uncertainty. The Father alone knows the precise time of the parousia; neither the angelic servants nor even the Son of Man know that. The verse restores the Father to the picture of the consummation, thus balancing verses 29-31. It is in the glory of the Incarnation that Christ accepted those limitations of knowledge which are inseparable from a true humanity. Sharing our human condition, the Son shared also our partial ignorance.

Verses 37-39: "As the days of Noah were." Although Jewish and Christian tradition emphasized the wickedness of the contemporaries of Noah, that is not the point here. Rather, the problem with the flood-generation was that it was so immersed in ordinary, everyday pursuits that it was blind to the imminent disaster of the flood. The people of Noah's day drew the wrong conclusion from their ignorance of the time of the flood and were careless in the things that pertained to God.

Verses 40-42: "Two will be in the field." The final judgment will bring to light distinctions between persons which are hidden in this age. The two men working in the field or the two women grinding meal with a hand-mill look alike to the human eye. But at the parousia (the "then" of v. 40), one will be "taken" into the kingdom while the other will be "left" to reprobation. The pattern of twinning parables of men and women continues here. Vigilance, or lack thereof, is the reason for the separation.

Verses 43-44: "The thief was coming." Another little parable makes explicit the connection with watchfulness. A thief does not publish his timetable, and so the only protection against theft is watching throughout the night (i.e., this present age). The symbol of the thief expresses the sudden, unexpected "break-in" of the parousia. The emphasis on the uncertainty of the time of the parousia (repeated in each of the three subsequent parables) corrects and stands in tension with the listing of signs and the affirmations of the parousia's imminence in the rest of chapter 24. In his conclusion of the unit, Matthew employs a new term, "ready (*hetoimoi*," LN 77.2) to vary the terminology of vigilance.

If Matthew devotes such a large development to this section (46 verses), it is because in his eyes, it immediately concerns not a future situation, even if this future can pertain to a near future (vv. 32-35), but the actual situation of the Church, that to which he had already devoted a special treatment in verses 9-14.

The occasion for turning to the consideration of the present conditions of the Christian life is offered him by the declaration of verse 36: "But of that day and hour no one knows, not even the angels of heaven, nor the Son but the Father only." The new theme that introduces this verse is characterized first by the double expression "the day and the hour" (Mark 13:32). The two terms reappear associated by the parallel of verses 42 and 44, by that of 50, and joined also in 25:13. In these three cases, the mention of the day and the hour is joined, as in 24:36, to the idea of ignorance. This is especially supported in the parable of verses 42-44: ". . . you do not know on what day your Lord is coming. But know this, that if the householder had known in what part of the night the thief is coming . . . the Son of Man is coming at an hour you do not expect." And in 25:13: ". . . you know neither the day nor the hour."

The note of watchfulness is what interests Mastthew in the declaration of verse 36, and he connects to it the units that constitute 24:42-44, 45-

51, and 25:1-13. These three parabolic units are framed by the repetition of the same sentences, which thus form an inclusion and manifest an intention identical to that of the parables. To begin, verse 24:42 reads: "Watch [*NRSV,* "keep awake"] therefore, for you do not know on what day your Lord is coming"; at the end, 25:13: "Watch therefore, for you know neither the day nor the hour." The affirmation according to which "that day and hour no one knows" (24:36) has become the starting point of a long development applying the general affirmation to the disciples: "You know neither the day nor the hour" and underlining the practical consequence that this ignorance entails for them: "watch therefore."

Between the declaration of 24:36 and the paraenetic commentary on it which takes place in the parables of 24:42–25:13, a place must be found for the small unit, 24:37-41. Spontaneously, attention is concentrated on the two uses found there of the expression "the coming of the Son of Man" (vv. 37 and v. 39), an expression used already in verse 27, which prepares the disciples' initial question of Jesus about "the sign of the parousia" (v. 31). Outside of these four cases, the New Testament uses this word "parousia" only in the epistles. Indeed, Matthew has recourse to the technical term of Christian language to explain the meaning of the event to which the discourse as a whole refers: it is not just a question of an anonymous "end" (cf. 24:6, 13, 14), but the glorious coming of the Lord of history.

This expression cannot assure the joining of verses 37-41 to verse 36 and to what verse 36 says about the ignorance of the "Son." In verse 36, the word "Son," used absolutely, is understood in relation to God, called "the Father," and has a different resonance from that which it receives in the expression "Son of Man." Verse 36 is connected with what verses 38-39 say about the contemporaries of Noah who "until the day when Noah entered the ark, and they did not know until the flood came and swept them all away." The precision: "they did not know (*ouk egnosan*)", which is notably lacking in the parallel text of Luke (17:27), is manifestly destined to assure the evocation of the "day" of the deluge into the theme announced by the beginning of verse 36: "But of that day and hour, no one knows."

Once again we note that in the reading of verse 36, Matthew places himself in a perspective that differs from that of later theologians. While the attention of the latter concentrate on what the verse affirms about the ignorance of the "Son," Matthew is so little interested in this particular case that he immediately designates by the title of "Son of Man," he who has been called just "Son," i.e., the Son of God. His attention for his part is concentrated on the initial affirmation in a general sense: no one knows the day or the hour. This is precisely what he underlines in his own way in the finale of the verse by adding to the exception indicated by his source: "but only the Father" (Mark 13:32), Matthew's insistent precision: "but the Father *only* (*monos*)." In opposition to all those who do not know, God alone knows the day and the hour.

Verses 37-41, therefore, call attention to the affirmation of verse 36 regarding the ignorance in which all find themselves on the subject of the day (and the hour). Thus, they contribute to the conclusion that the three parables which follow (24:42-44, 45-51 and 25:1-13) will draw from this ignorance: Jesus' disciples must give proof of their vigilance.

A fourth parable, that of the talents (25:14:30), has been added to the triad of parables which explicitly establish the duty of vigilance on the fact that one does not know the day and the hour. It would have been easy, apparently, to insert in this last parable the key terms which unify the preceding development. Matthew did not consider it necessary, any more than he added explicit paraenetic applications. Perhaps he saw in the passage a transition piece between the explicit paraenctic, to the service of which the three preceding parables had been placed, and the evocation of the last judgment with which the discourse ends (25:31-46), the style of which remains purely descriptive. We observe that if the note of "ignorance" is not absent from the parable of the talents and especially the judgment scene, it is no longer a question of an ignorance concerning the day and the hour. We must speak rather of an ignorance concerning the person of the sovereign judge, he whom the wicked servant knows only as a hard and demanding man (25:24-26), him whom the damned had not been able to recognize and serve in the person of the unfortunate (25:44-45).

(II)B Vigilance 1: Good or Bad Servant, 24:45-51

Matthew ties together three parables of vigilance (prudent or profligate servant, prudent or thoughtless virgins, talents) by underlining in each the theme of delay (24:48; 25:5, 19). This emphasis on delay gives us Matthew's modification of the Markan stress on imminence (24:34). Other themes also connect the three parables: being faithful or prudent, the reward of greater responsibility, the punishment of the wicked who do not watch, eating and drinking, ignorance of the day or hour, weeping and gnashing of teeth.

> **45** "Who then is the faithful and wise slave, whom his master has put in charge of his household, to give the other slaves their allowance of food at the proper time? **46** Blessed is that slave whom his master will find at work when he arrives. **47** Truly I tell you, he will put that one

in charge of all his possessions. **48** But if that wicked slave says to himself, 'My master is delayed.' **49** and he begins to beat his fellow slaves, and eats and drinks with drunkards, **50** the master of that slave will come on a day when he does not expect him and at an hour that he does not know. **51** He will cut him in pieces and put him with the hypocrites, where there will be weeping and gnashing of teeth.''

Verse 45: ''In charge of his household.'' In this parable Matthew contrasts two ways of being a servant of the Lord during the time of waiting for his return. We can think of them as two different persons, or, better, as one person who can react to his situation in different ways. Here Matthew addresses the call to vigilance especially to Church leaders. The reference to the servant's being ''set over his household'' to take care of his fellow servants' needs makes the allusion to Church leaders quite clear. Watchfulness is thus interpreted concretely as prudence and dependability in fulfilling one's obligations towards the community of believers ''at the proper time, and not at one's own convenience.''

Verses 46-47: ''In charge of all his possessions.'' The servant who proves faithful is declared truly happy; his reward on the last day will be still greater responsibility. Church leaders must never forget that all their power is derivative and is conferred only for a time and for the good of others.

Verse 48: ''But the wicked slave.'' Matthew cannot wait to moralize. He calls the slave wicked before he has shown him misbehaving. The delay of the parousia becomes his great temptation (cf. 2 Pet 3:4). He begins to give himself airs as though he were the master and to abuse the authority entrusted to him.

Verse 49: The wicked slave tyrannizes his *fellow* slaves. Throwing caution to the wind, he lapses into excessive eating and drinking with the worst of companions.

Verse 50: The wicked slave is in for a surprise. He has forgotten that he is subject to recall, and his recall is precisely the sudden, unpredictable return of his ''master'' (*kyrios*), the Son of Man after the delay.

Verse 51: ''Put him with the hypocrites.'' Although the original dramatic form of the parable may have spoken simply of a severe beating as punishment, Matthew depicts the gruesome Persian punishment of dismemberment. At first glance, the next phrase, ''put him with the hypocrites,'' seems hopelessly out of place, until we remember that for Matthew the hypocrites are primarily the Jewish leaders, the scribes and the pharisees (cf. chap. 23). The unfaithful Christian leader is no better than the Jewish leaders, and he will receive the same punishment: eternal damnation, symbolized by weeping and gnashing. If the language in verse 51 echoes the terminology of Church discipline in the Matthean Church, then that discipline may have been influenced (in its vocabulary at least) by the practice of excommunication in the Qumran community.

(II)C Vigilance 2: Wise and Foolish Maidens, 25:1-13

This is the second of three parables of vigilance in which Matthew underlines the theme of delay (24:48; 25:5, 19). This emphasis on delay serves as a counterbalance to the stress on imminence found in earlier units (24:34). The parousia will be unexpected, therefore vigilance is required. Vigilance can become something active, a faithfulness to responsibilities given and undertaken (24:45-51). The next two parables will further elucidate the meaning of watchfulness.

> **25:1** "Then the kingdom of heaven will be like this. Ten bridesmaids took their lamps and went to meet the bridegroom. **2** Five of them were foolish, and five were wise. **3** When the foolish took their lamps, they took no oil with them; **4** but the wise took flasks of oil with their lamps. **5** As the bridegroom was delayed, all of them became drowsy and slept. **6** But at midnight there was a shout, 'Look! Here is the bridegroom! Come out to meet him.' **7** Then all those bridesmaids got up and trimmed their lamps. **8** The foolish said to the wise, 'Give us some of your oil, for our lamps are going out.' **9** But the wise replied, 'No! there will not be enough for you and for us; you had better go to the dealers and buy some for yourselves.' **10** And while they went to buy it, the bridegroom came, and those who were ready went with him into the wedding banquet; and the door was shut. **11** Later the other bridesmaids came also, saying, 'Lord, lord, open to us.' **12** But he replied, 'Truly I tell you, I do not know you.' **13** Keep awake therefore, for you know neither the day nor the hour.' "

By his use of parables, Matthew turns Jesus' great speeches into a direct word of address to the implied reader. Through the vehicle of the parable, Jesus, the bearer of God's kingly rule, conveys to the implied reader a vision of human existence as it is lived in the sphere of God's rule: "The Kingdom of Heaven is like" (v. 1). The upshot of Matthew's use of this and other rhetorical devices (imperative mood, the pronoun "you," timeless expressions) is that "the implied reader, in hearing Jesus deliver his great speeches, is made to sense that he or she, along with the crowds or the disciples in the story, is being directly addressed by him" (*Story*, 111).

Verse 1: "Then the kingdom of heaven." The introductory "Then" (*tote*) here is not (as so often in Matthew) a transition particle, but refers back the "coming" (Parousia) mentioned in 24:39, 44, 50. Despite the verbal form in verse 1 "the Kingdom of heaven" is not likened to ten maidens, but to their behavior before a wedding. All the maidens set out to welcome (*eis hypantesin*, LN 15.78) the bridegroom who is on the way, their lamps in hand.

Verse 2: The ten maidens divide into two groups: five foolish and five wise. This division is important for the working of the parable; the idea of "half-and-half" less so. *Moros* ("foolish") is found in the Synoptics only in Matthew (six times); *phronimos* ("wise" is also one of Matthew's favorite words (seven times).

Verses 3-4: The foolish and wise are more accurately described: the foolish ones take only their lamps, while the others take a supply of oil. This relationship of the two groups determines the action of the story, The prudent thing was to take a possible delay into account.

Verse 5: "The bridegroom was delayed (*chronizo*, 67.122)." Since the arrival of the bridegroom is delayed, "all" the waiting girls fell asleep. Neither the long delay of the bridegroom nor the girl's consequent falling asleep are important for the meaning of the parable, nor is an allegorical application to the Pharisees convincing. The information that all fell asleep prepares for the arrival of the bridegroom.

Verse 6: Finally (note the "But") the bridegroom arrives. There follows a loud outcry (*kraugē*, LN 33.84), which is literally a shrieking [so Acts 23:9; Eph 4:31]), a scream of terror [Rev 21:4]. Here, a tumultuous, loud, outcry is meant. With the imperative, "Come out," the maidens are ordered to come and meet the bridegroom.

Verses 7-8: The trimming of the lamps refers to the original' situation in verse 1. The foolish vs. wise behavior now works itself out. The foolish maidens take note of their omission; at the hour they can only turn to the wise. But their oil supply will not suffice to help the five foolish, whose lamps are on the point of going out.

Verse 9: The refusal of the wise maidens is not to be interpreted as egotism, and their referring the foolish to the dealers is not meant ironically. The foolish maidens follow the advice given them. Both elements are constitutive for the course of the narrative: the foolish maidens must go away and therefore come too late to greet the bridegroom.

Verse 10: The wise maidens are ready, for there is plenty of oil on hand for their lamps; they can accompany the bridegroom to the wedding celebration (*eis tous gamous*). After their entrance into the banquet hall, the door is closed behind them. *Gamos* in the singular is the marriage ceremony, the wedding; the plural means the wedding festivities and readily gives over to the meaning "wedding banquet."

Verses 11-12: The (grieving) cry of those left behind is in vain; they have not been equal to their task, now it is too late. The bridegroom's answer with its solemn introduction (cf. 7:23) does not mean: "You are unknown to me," but: "I have nothing to do with you." Even the double "Lord, Lord," does not change this.

Verse 13: Matthew ends with an application of the narrative (cf. 24:42,; 44). "Keep awake" (*gregoreō*, LN 23.72). The grounds for the demand, to be continually watchful, lie in the fact that the day and hour is not known. The demand applies to the whole parable, whose climax is not to leave things to others, but to act oneself. The foolish bridesmaids too superficially supposed that someone else would pay the bill.

The on-hand/not-on-hand oil supply determines the working of the parable. From this point of view the bridegroom's behavior is also understandable. Those he "knows," i.e., with whom he stands in a personal relationship, he admits to the wedding ceremony and to the wedding banquet; those whom he does "not know," with whom there is no community relationship, he excludes. Here Matthew does not dwell, as he usually does, on what is to be done during the delay (good works). Only a reasonable preparedness for the Lord's coming is mentioned. All, even now, must have a personal relationship with the Lord which will be fully realized in the kingdom of heaven.

The parable contains an urgent message for the community. That the wedding is picture for the eschatological time, the community knows from Jewish tradition. All (maidens) have the same starting position for the kingdom's coming; all the same chance. But this will not be used by all. The bridegroom's judgment message is therefore the consequence of unreasonable behavior, for which the foolish are responsible. The community is also enjoined to identify itself with the wise maidens and warned, not to set at risk the decisive meeting with the bridegroom through inadequate readiness, as the foolish maidens had done—because they had carelessly trusted to the help of others.

(II)D Vigilance 3: The Talents, 25:14-30

As a counterbalance to the stress on imminence in the preceding units, Matthew inserts three parables of vigilance (the wicked slave, wise and foolish maidens, the talents), in which he underlines the theme of delay. The parable of the talents is not introduced by words such as "The kingdom is like . . ." but is linked closely with the preceding words: "You know neither the day nor the hour. For it is as . . .'' i.e., like what happens in the unexpected consequences of evildoing.

> **14** For it is as if a man, going on a journey, summoned his slaves and entrusted his property to them; **15** to one he gave five talents, to another two, to another one, to each according to his ability. Then he went away. **16** The one who had received the five talents went off at once and traded with them, and made five more talents. **17** In the same way, the one who had the two talents made two more talents. **18** But the one who had received the one talent went off and dug a hole in the ground and hid his master's money. **19** After a long time the master of those slaves came and settled accounts with them. **20** Then the one who had received the five talents came forward, bringing five more talents, saying, 'Master, you handed over to me five talents; see, I have made five more talents.'
> **21** His master said to him, 'Well done, good and trustworthy slave; you have been trustworthy in a few things, I will put you in charge of many things; enter into the joy of your master.' **22** And the one with the two tlents also came forward, saying, 'Master, you handed over to me twso talents; see, I have made two more talents.' **23** His master said to him, 'Well done, good and trustworthy slave, you have been trustworthy in a few things, I will put you in charge of many things; enter into the joy of your master.' **24** Then the one who had received the one talent also came forward, saying, 'Master, I knew that you were a harsh man, reaping where you did not sow, and gathering where you did not scatter seed; **25** so I was afraid, and I went and hid your talent in the ground. Here you have what is yours.' **26** But his master replied, 'You wicked and lazy slave! You knew, did you, that I reap where I did not sow, and gather where I did not scatter? **27** Then you ought to have invested my money with the bankers, and on my return I would have received what was my own with interest. **28** So he took the talent from him, and gave it to the one with the ten talents. **29** For to all those who have, more will be given, and they will have an abundance; but from those who have nothing, even what they have will be taken away. **30** As for this worthless slave, throw him into the outer darkness, where there will be weeping and gnashing of teeth.' ''

Verse 14: "For it is as if"—With the connecting "For" (v. 14), Matthew makes it known that he understands the parable as the interpretation of the demand for watchfulness in 25:13; also pointing in this direction are verse 30 and the attachment of the judgment parables in 25:31-46.

Verse 15: "To one he gave five talents"—The Lukan Jesus tells a parable about "minas" (Luke 19:11-27), but the Matthean Jesus about "talents," one of the latter being worth approximately fifty times one of the former. This is another indication that Matthew's community was rather wealthy. The man entrusts his property to three servants, not to try them (so Luke) but that they should increase it during his absence. This objective comes out in the phrase "to each according to his ability."

Verses 16-17: The first two servants live up to the trust placed in them: they double the sum entrusted to them by trading (*ergazomai*, LN 57.198).

Verse 18: The third (pointedly set off by *de*) conducts himself differently: he avoids every risk. His only thought is to keep the entrusted sum intact. Instead of trading to earn a profit he buries his master's money: at least it could not be lost. Burying affords a chance of relative security; and it is not any bother to him.

Verse 19: "After a long time (*meta polyn chronon*)." In an addition of his own, Matthew refers to the time "in between," i.e., between the master's departure and his return. The accounting takes place immediately after the master's return. This addition embodies Matthew's principal concerns: vigilance, delay, and judgment.

Verses 20-22: Matthew sketches the course of the accounting in terms similar to those just used. The servants are indicated by the sum that they have received, which prepares the form of the answer of the servants: Five (viz. two) talents you have delivered to me, I have made five (viz. two) more. It is important that in Matthew's version it was the servant who made the profit (in Luke the money earned the profit). The praise with promise of reward aims at a multiple.

Verse 23: "Enter into the joy of your master." In his addition Matthew reaches out from the narrative level already in the parable itself to a thrological level: "joy," and "enter" are technical terms for entering the kingdom of God (cf. J. Schneider *eiserchomai*: TWNT II 671). This makes it clear that the speaker already here in the judgment-accounting is the Son of Man.

Verses 24-25: "I knew that you were a harsh man." The real fault of the third servant is his inaction, which amounted to sheer laziness. He is condemned as evil and inactive—indeed, evil precisely because he is inactive. Out of fear of failure he has refused even to try to succeed.

Verse 26: "You knew, did you." In his reply the master does not contradict the character sketch, save to omit the word "harsh." He is a demanding person. All the parables of Matthew's eschatological discourse stress the fierce demands of Jesus, demands which we must meet if we are to pass the stringent judgment on the last day. The stringency of judgment replaces the imminence of judgment as the main motive in Matthew's moral exhortation.

Verse 28: "Take the talent from him." The lazy servant loses the little he had received.

Verse 29: "To all those who have, more will be given." In content it fits the parable well and forms the credal high point of the parable, which from the beginning was parenthetically designed: whoever comes to the judgment with nothing to show, goes away empty-handed.

In the content of the parable "to those who have, more will be given" refers to a basic law of the interaction between God's free gift and the human response. A disciple who responds generously to the gift of God will receive greater grace still; the stingy will receive nothing further and will lose what he or she does. As with our physical limbs and intellectual talents: exercise brings greater strength; neglect brings atrophy. The "atrophied" disciple will be punished exactly like the dissolute and the thoughtless—with eternal damnation (v. 30; cf. 13:42, 50; 22:13; 24:51). "The parable has a special bite if Matthew intends a particular reference here, as in 24:45-51, to Church leaders. A Christian leader who does not lead is damned" (Meier, 300).

Verse 30: An additional threat of punishment forms redactional closure of the pericope. Even more clearly than has happened already in verse 29, Matthew underlines the rejection of the unfaithful servant through the stereotyped threat of punishment.

(III)A Works of Mercy done to Jesus, 25:31-46

The Last Judgment scene belongs to Matthew's special material. With foresight he has made it the "closure" of his fifth great discourse, the eschatological discourse, and placed it immediately before the beginning of his passion account. Vocabulary and imagery use the apocalyptic tradition and are clearly stamped by the context of the synoptic apocalypse. Not only Israel is brought to judgment, but with her all the nations (v. 32): while in 24:31 only the assembly of the elect was involved, now the judgment extends to all.

The passage reflects Jesus' own concern for preparing oneself to enter the kingdom. It presents a practical religion of deeds of loving-kindness, love of neighbor, addressed to Christian disciples. Discipleship is understood in a very bold way as identical with care of the needy. This is not a denial of faith; it is faith in action.

31 "When the Son of Man comes in his glory, and all the angels with him, then he will sit on the throne of his glory. **32** All the nations will be gathered before him, and he will separate people one from another as a shepherd separates the sheep from the goats, **33** and he will put the sheep at at his right hand and the goats at the left. **34** Then the king will say to those at his right hand, 'Come, you that are blessed by my Father, inherit the kingdom prepared for you from the foundation of the world; **35** for I was hungry and you gave me food, I was thirsty and you gave me something to drink, I was a stranger and you welcomed me, **36** I was naked and you gave me clothing, I was sick and you took care of me, I was in prison and you visited me.' **37** Then the righteous will answer him, 'Lord, when was it that we saw you hungry and gave you food, or thirsty and gave you something to drink? **38** And when was it that we saw you a stranger and welcomed you, or naked and gave you clothing? **39** And when was it that we saw you sick or in prison and visited you?' **40** And the king will answer them, 'Truly I tell you, just as you did it to one of the least of these who are members of my family, you did it to me.' **41** Then he will say to those at his left hand, 'You that are accursed, depart from me into the eternal fire prepared for the devil and his angels; **42** for I was hungry and you gave me no food, I was thirsty and you gave me nothing to drink, **43** I was a stranger and you did not welcome me, naked and you did not give me clothing, sick and in prison and you did not visit me.' **44** Then they also will answer, 'Lord, when was it that we saw you hungry or thirsty or a stranger or naked or sick or in prison, and did not take care of you? **45** Then he will answer them, 'Truly I tell you, just as you did not do it to one of the least of these, you did not do it to me.' **46** And these will go away to eternal punishment, but the righteous into eternal life."

The Last Judgment scene in its present form is structured in antithetic parallelism. After the reference to the coming of the Son of Man and his enthronement on the judgment seat in verse 31b, an extensive exposition follows:

Verses 32-33: all the peoples are gathered and separated into sheep and goats; then there follows the reason for the separation in the form of a parable:

A. verses 34-36: the Kings's praise for those at the right;
    verses 37-39: their astonished question;
        verse 40: the clarifying answer;
B. verses 41-43: the King's rejection of those at the left;
    verse 44: their astonished question;
    verse 45: the clarifying answer.
    verse 46: concluding definitive judgment.

Verse 31: "When the Son of Man comes." God's Kingdom is a reality that will be consummated only in the future. Not until the end of the age, when the exalted Jesus returns with his angels in power and great glory to preside over the final judgment, will the rule of God encompass the world and be acknowledged by all people everywhere.

The end time judge is the coming Son of Man (cf. 13:41; 16:27). The Son of Man will appear with all his angels (cf. Zech 14:5). The glorious throne (cf. 19:38) is the manifestation of judicial authority; the task of the angels is to bring forward all the nations (cf. 13:1; 24:30, 31).

Verses 32-33: "All the nations will be gathered." In addition to his conflict with Israel (and his own disciples) Jesus has a conflict with the nations. But Jesus' conflict with the nations is not part of his story's plot and so is not narrated in story form but sketched by Jesus in prophetic utterances about the future (cf. chaps. 24-25). Jesus dispatched his missionary Church to make all nations, including Israel, his disciples (23:34; 24:14). Jesus' conflict with the nations will finally be resolved at the consummation of the age (24:3), when the exalted Jesus will return in power and splendor to preside over the final judgment.

The "world" judgment is carried out in an act of separation or division (*aphorizō*), a saying which draws on Palestinian shepherd life. The Son of Man acts like a shepherd caring for his flock (cf. Ezek 34:17-22), separating the sheep from the goats. Being more valuable animals, the sheep naturally symbolize the good, and are placed on the right hand, the side of favor. The goats are placed on the left, a sign of disfavor.

Verses 34-35: "Then the king will say." The surprising introduction of a "king" shows that behind the existing text there lies a "king-parable" which was transformed into a Son of Man narrative.

"You that are blessed by my father." The "to the right" are called the "blessed of my father," because from the foundation (*katabolē*, the creation of the world), by power of divine decision, the kingdom has been promised them. Just as Israel inherited an earthly promised land, the new people of God inherit the heavenly kingdom, ruled by the King who is Son of Man.

Verse 36: "For I was hungry." The King welcomes the blessed and then explains the reason for the blessing: they took care of him when he was hungry, thirsty, a foreigner, naked, sick, and imprisoned. Here we have a list of the traditional "corporal works of mercy" as known to Judaism, Christianity, and other religions.

Verse 37: "Lord, when was it." The "blessed" respond to the "Lord" (the King) with a surprised counter-question, in which the named six "works of mercy" are repeated word for word. Their amazement arises from non-understanding. They had never imagined a plan of salvation such as he describes. What astounds them is that the King claims that they did all this "to me." When? How? The King replies by revealing a mystery not even the just comprehended—Jesus has fully identified himself with the poor and outcast and oppressed. Jesus is indeed Emmanuel, God-with-us. "He is with his people, his Church, but he is most especially with the no-accounts of this world, all those in desperate need of the basic necessities of life. The Son of Man, the crucified King who judges all men, is encountered in every one who suffers. His association with the poor in the beatitudes and in his healing activity is broadened here to cosmic scope" (Meier, 304).

Verse 40: "Truly I tell you." The King's answer, introduced with the affirmation formula so typical for Matthew (it is repeated in v. 45 in a negative sense) forms the climax of the dialogue. "One of the least of these who are members of my family"—whoever does a work of mercy to the least member of the family, does it—without knowing it—to the King now judging. A work of mercy toward a member of the King's family is evaluated as a good action toward the King, even if ostensibly "only" a fellow member is helped. The needy are the true "brothers and sisters" of the King.

Verses 41-45: In the antithesis to the salvation message, fashioned in exact parallel, eternal damnation is pronounced on those on the left as punishment for the refused love service. The "Depart from me" stands in exact contrast to 11:28: "Come to me, all you that are weary and are carrying heavy burdens." By their attitude to "the least" they have condemned themselves. The "Father" is no longer mentioned; and it is not said: "[into the eternal fire] prepared for you "from the foundation of the world." The description of the end judgment speaks of a promise or assurance of the riches from the foundation, but not that the damned are assigned to damnation *ab initio*. Those addressed have brought the curse on themselves, which consists in the assignment to eternal fire.

Verse 46: The concluding verse of the end-time description expresses the certainty and the definitiveness of the judgment message. Matthew chose the concept to make clear the definitiveness of "eternal life" and "eternal" punishment. The execution of the King's judgments is described in reverse (chiastic) order, so that the joyful element comes last: irrevocable punishment and incorruptible life. Thus the eschatological discourse ends on a somber as well as a triumphant note. Jesus has spoken this message and the Son of Man who is judge has identified himself fully with the suffering in his teaching. Nothing remains except for him to act out his teaching by becoming the crucified Son of Man in the passion.

THE PASSION, CHAPTERS 26–28

In line with the other major discourses the last, eschatological discourse (chs 24-25) is closely related to its context. In contrast to the Jewish leaders (chs 21-23), the disciples are admonished to be faithful to their calling, lest they too fall under judgment. The positive example of faithfulness to the will of God, even in the midst of suffering and persecution, is found in the majestic obedience of Jesus, which he displays during his passion in chapters 26-28.

Matthew devotes Part III of his story to Jesus' journey to Jerusalem and to his suffering, death, and resurrection (16:21-28:20). The conflict between Jesus and Israel foreshadowed in Part I of the story, which burst into the open in Part II (ch 9) then runs its course to resolution in the passion and resurrection of Jesus (chs 26-28). As the culmination of Matthew's story, the passion account also constitutes the decisive stage in Jesus' conflict with Israel (chs. 26-28). Here, the resolution of this conflict works itself out in dramatic detail.

The reader learns of the resolution of Jesus' conflict with the religious leaders from the passion account itself (chs 26-28). Both the leaders act to achieve Jesus' death, but for different reasons. From the leaders' standpoint, they believe that by bringing Jesus to the cross, they are doing the will of God and purging Israel of a false messiah, or "deceiver" (26:65-66; 27:63). Jesus embraces the cross, because he understands himself to be God's royal Son sent to shed his blood for the forgiveness of sins (21:37-38; 26:28). God is the one who ultimately decides the conflict between them. By raising Jesus from the dead and investing him with all authority, God vindicates Jesus and thus decides the conflict in his favor (28:5-6). The cross of Jesus in Matthew's story serves not as the symbol of his destruction, but as the means whereby God accomplishes the salvation of all humankind.

The climactic movement of the Gospel is towards the suffering, death, and resurrection of Jesus in Jerusalem and ultimately the missionary commissioning by Jesus in 28:15-20. The flow of the narrative moves steadily toward the climactic events in chapters 26-28. In the climax of the cross, the passers-by tempt Jesus as the Son of God, and the Roman soldiers confess that Jesus is the Son of God (26:54). Thus, in accord with the climaxes to the preceding divisions (3:17; 15:16), this last major division also culminates with the declaration that Jesus is the Son of God. Moreover, in the climax of the missionary commissioning, Jesus refers to himself as the Son [of God] (28.19).

These structural features that point to Jesus as the Son of God also indicate that Christology is the central concern of Matthew's Gospel. The climax to each major division of the Gospel (3:17; 16:13-20; 26-28) as well as the climax to the Gospel as a whole (chs 26-28) all deal with the person of Jesus, and affirm that he is the Son of God.

Discourse Finale (and Passion Prediction), 26:1-2

For the fifth and last time Matthew's formal discourse closure appears (v. 1). Five times throughout Matthew's story the reader encounters the stereo-typed formla: "When Jesus had finished. . ." (saying these words, speaking these parables, instructing his twelve disciples), (7:28; 11:1; 13:53; 19:1; 26:1). Each time this formula occurs, it calls attention to the termination of a speech Jesus has delivered. In preparation for the following theme, the disciples are cited as the addressees. Verse 2 is in direct address and there follows an abbreviated passion prediction in these concluding words of the fifth discourse.

> **26:1** When Jesus had finished saying all these things, he said to his disciples, **2** "You know that after two days the Passover is coming, and the Son of Man will be handed over to be crucified."

At the begining of the passion account, Jesus reminds the disciples of the approaching Passover when the Son of Man will be "handed over" to be crucified. These words remind both the disciples and the reader of the three passion-predictions Jesus has already given (16:21; 17:22-23; 20:18-19). Jesus' conflict with Israel is to the death (16:21). Whereas the religious leaders conspire to have Jesus killed so as to destroy him (12:14; 26:2-3), God and Jesus desire Jesus' death because it will constitute the decisive, saving event in the history of salvation.

Verse 1: "Finished saying all these things." To "these things" (cf. 7:28; 19:1), Matthew adds the characteristic and emphatic "all." Only here is "all" added to the otherwise uniform forumulae. "All" here refers not only to chapters 24-25, but to all the discourses.

The discourses are integrated into the flow of the narrative, and Matthew does not load the fact that there are *five* discourses with theological weight. Yet the five great discourses are explicitly noted by Matthew in the transitional statements, which are attention drawing devices. 'This conclusion is supported by (1) their similarity in form; (2) the content of the statements, that is, the fact that on two occasions they indicate the character of the discourse (11.1 = Jesus instructing his twelve disciples; 13.53 = Jesus finishes these parables); (3) the last statement speaks of Jesus finishing 'all' these teachings (26.1), thus indicating that the discourses have come to an end" (Bauer, 132).

The end of the discourses of Jesus works hand in hand with the gradual cessaton of Jesus' ministry in light of his coming passion. Thus, Matthew records in 22:46 that from that time on no one dared ask Jesus any questions; the Jewish leaders leave the scene of Jesus' ministry at the end of chapter 22, and the crowds no longer follow him after chapter 23. Now the discourses cease.

Verse 2: "Your know." Jesus reminds the disciples of his three earlier passion predictions. In Part III (16:21-28:20), Matthew employed the device of the "journey" (16:21-21:11) and the setting of Jerusalem and environs, including the temple (21:12-28:15 [16-20]), in order to forge a cohesive narrative from disparate materials. To keep the reader informed of the tenor of the narrative, Matthew employed three passion-predictions that tell of Jesus' coming suffering, death and resurrection (16:21; 17:22-23; 20:18-19). Now, at the outset of the passion account itself, he calls to mind these three predictions (26:2).

Immediately before the Passion Account, Jesus' passion is proclaimed to the community one final time. To be sure, the disciples "know it" already, but Matthew repeats it once again to strengthen the disciples' knowledge and to remind them of the defection bound up with the knowledge. Defection can be withstood if the community knows that the death fate of their Messiah is not a tragic disaster, but an act of salvation willed by God, to which Jesus willingly submits himself (yet with fear and trembling).

As the narrative moves on to the events of the passion (26:1-2), one can observe that the disciples stray still further from Jesus' evaluative point of view. The result is that they are unable to cope with these events. What Jesus says of Peter in Gethsemane, with an eye to James and John as well, is true of all of the disciples during the passion: "The spirit indeed is willing, but the flesh is weak" (26:41). The disciples are divided in their intentions and loyalties. To be undivided, to be wholehearted, is to be "perfect" (5:48). Jesus, therefore, is perfect; the disciples are not.

To pick up the flow of Matthew's passion account following Jesus' recapitulation of his passion-predictions (v. 2), the initial scenes are calculated to establish, respectively, the culpability of the religious leaders for Jesus' death, the unreadiness of the disciples to master the events that lie before them, and the inability of Judas to foresee the true nature of the act he is committing in agreeing to betray Jesus for gain.

The Religious Leaders Conspire, 26:3-5

After Jesus' recapitulation of his passion-predictions (26:2), the following scenes establish the culpability of the religious leaders for Jesus' death, the disciples' inability to comprehend the events they see unfolding, and Judas' failure to foresee the consequences of his betrayal. In the next scene, then, the chief priests and the elders stand out as the ones most immediately responsible for the death of Jesus (vv. 3-5).

> 3 Then the chief priests and the elders of the people gathered in the palace of the high priest, who was called Caiaphas, 4 and they conspired to arrest Jesus by stealth and kill him. 5 But they said, "Not during the festival, or there may be a riot among the people."

Verse 3: "Then the chief priest and the elders." Having exhausted all options but one, the leaders meet and conspire about how to bring about the arrest and death of Jesus (vv. 3-5). Except for Jesus himself, the religious leaders are the ones who influence the development of the plot of Matthew's story most. In fact, their characterization is shaped by their conflict with Jesus. While Jesus is a "round" character, the religious leaders are "flat" characters. The traits ascribed to them are manifestations of a single "root trait," and they undergo no change in the course of the story. The attitudes that John the Baptist, Jesus, and Matthew as narrator adopt toward them distance the reader from them.

The various groups of leaders are depicted as a *united front,* and not as the diverse or even conflicting parties or classes history knows them to have been. This applies especially to the Pharisees and Sadducees. Yet a few historical distinctions are retained. The stereotyped phrase by which reference is made to the High Council, or Sanhedrin (26:59), is "The chief priests and the elders (of the people)." The "scribes" are also members of the Sanhedrin and the high priest, who is the presiding officer, is Caiaphas (26:3, 57). Until the fall of Jerusalem in A.D. 70 the Sanhedrin exercised broad powers in Palestine of a religious, political, and judicial nature.

Verse 4: "Conspired to arrest Jesus by stealth." "Matthew's description of the secretive session of the leaders and their anxious plotting, as well as their intention not to carry out their plan during the feast, rings with irony and is obviously intended to be a foil to the majesty of Jesus" (D. Senior, *Passion*, 52). While Jesus speaks openly to his disciples, the religious leaders huddle in secret. The Greek word *tote* ("then") and the tense of the verb Matthew uses here suggest that the two scenes happen virtually at the same time. The two formulas "by stealth" and "kill him" correspond to the expressions "deliver up" and "crucify" in verse 2, and at the same time, as contrast expressions, underline the thinking and intention of the opponents.

Verse 5: "Riot among the people." Proceeding "by stealth" is motivated by fear of the people ("not during the festival," literally: "in the feast gathering"), for which great crowds would be coming. An uproar "among the people" (*thorybos*, noise tumult) could easily get started. The crowds are still regarded by the religious leaders as a threat to their guileful plans to capture Jesus and kill him.

The "cast" of the passion is presented: it consists of the leaders of the people. They are shown in their common responsibility, in their isolation from the people, and above all in their craftiness. Because they deliberately separated themselves from the Jewish people, what follows is ultimately only a "drama" between Jesus and the responsible leaders. The people are still undecided, but have no direct part in the "proceeding" against Jesus. The spokesmen decide the outcome, in which the power of God seems to be powerless.

In Jesus' debates with the religious leaders, the correct interpretation of or the proper adherence to, the Mosaic law or the Pharisaic tradition of the elders was almost always at issue. These issues constitute an index of the "flash points" that motivated the religious leaders not only to oppose Jesus, but now also to conspire to take his life. "In their eyes, Jesus is a threat to the continued existence of Jewish society, for he places himself above law and tradition. In Jesus' perspective, the debates concerning law and tradition are all to be resolved by the proper application of one basic principle, or better, of a single attitude of the heart, namely, utter devotion to God and radical love of the neighbor (5:48; 22:37-40)" (*Story*, 63).

Jesus is Prepared for Burial, 26:6-13

As the disciples face the events of the passion with Jesus, they show themselves to be enmeshed in circumstances manifestly beyond either their comprehension or their control. In the next scene, the disciples, who are with Jesus in the house of Simon the leper at Bethany, show themselves unable to comprehend the true significance of events taking place. They misinterpret as a waste of money the woman's anointing Jesus with expensive anointment. They do not perceive that she is, in reality, preparing him for burial.

> 6 Now while Jesus was at Bethany in the house of Simon the leper,
> 7 a woman came to him with an alabaster jar of very costly ointment,

and she poured it on his head as he sat at the table. **8** But when the disciples saw it, they were angry and said, "Why this waste? **9** For this ointment could have been sold for a large sum, and the money given to the poor." **10** But Jesus, aware of this, said to them, "Why do you trouble the woman? She has performed a good service for me. **11** For you always have the poor with you, but you will not always have me. **12** By pouring this ointment on my body she has prepared me for burial. **13** Truly I tell you, wherever this good news is proclaimed in the whole world, what she has done will be told in remembrance of her."

Verse 6: "Simon the leper." There are persons in Matthew's story who seem to meld completely with the setting of which they are a part. Examples of such are the brothers of Jesus ("James," "Joseph," "Simon," and "Judas"; 13:55), "[Jesus'] sisters" (13:56), and, here, "Simon the leper."

Verses 6: "An alabaster jar." An (anonymous) woman approaches Jesus and anoints his head (as a sign of respect for the guest of honor), with a precious oil (*barytimos*, "very expensive"). To prevent the evaporation of the expensive perfume, an amount sufficient for one application would be sealed in a jar, which had to be broken to release the ointment.

Verse 8: When Jesus actually enters upon his passion, the disciples, although they want to stand by him (26:41), are totally unable to cope with events and end up by failing him. Here they show that they are "imperceptive" to the true meaning of what is taking place: when the woman pours ointment on Jesus' head, they indignantly label as wasteful what is in reality the preparation of his body for burial.

Verse 10: "But Jesus, aware of this." "Point of view," another facet of the "discourse" of Matthew, of the way in which Matthew has chosen to put his story across is the "psychological" point of view. This refers to knowledge on the part of Matthew as narrator or of a character about what some (other) character thinks, intends, feels, sees, or otherwise experiences. Omniscience of this kind is predicated both to Matthew and to Jesus. They provide the reader with inside views into the inner workings of others. Here Jesus knows or sees that the disciples have become "angry" at the woman who has poured expensive ointment on his head. The reason the reader is provided with inside views of characters is to shape his or her attitude toward them.

Verses 11-12: "She has prepared me for burial." Indirectly, Jesus speaks a death prediction once again. His death lies just ahead, therefore the "now" of the love service to him is more important than service to the poor, to whom good can be done at any time. So what we have here is not a declaration about the care of the poor, but an expression about what Jesus' imminent death now demands without delay (cf. the antithetic parallelism). Verse 12 gives the definitive justification for the woman's deed: it is an anticipated death anointing; at burial (*entaphizō*, to bury, only here and John 19:40) the corpse was anointed (hence Matthew now uses "body" (*sōma*). There is no mention of anointing at Jesus' death; anticipated now is what could not be done later.

Verse 13: "Wherever this good news." The "Truly I tell you" characterizes the anointing as an integral element of "this good news" (viz. Matthew's). With the future proclamation of the Matthew's Good News, the woman's act of love will be recalled as an exemplary act (*mnēmosynon*: remembrance, commemoration: the objective genitive characterizes the woman's action as an example worthy of imitation for later Christians).

What the phrase "the Gospel of the kingdom" means comes to light in Matthew's use of the terms "Gospel" and "kingdom." To get at the meaning of the term "Gospel," a glance at the passage 26:6-13 is helpful. It reveals that the Gospel is "news" that is inextricably bound up with Jesus—what he has said or done or what has happened to him—and that it begs to be proclaimed to the world. "On balance, then, the term 'Gospel' in the phrase 'the Gospel of the Kingdom' may be defined as the news about the kingdom (which saves or condemns) which is revealed in and through Jesus Messiah, the Son of God, and is announced first to Israel and then to the Gentiles" (*Story*, 61).

Since it is the disciples who object to the woman's action, in Matthew's thought the account is a discipleship rule. The community must learn that while the service of the poor is right, necessary, and obligatory, its place in the scale of value changes when other concerns (here: the death of the Messiah) are involved. Good works are in place any time, but the service of Jesus has its unique Kairos, never to be repeated. And not only the woman's deed is raised to the level of a guiding norm; the woman herself enters New Testament tradition because she merited by her act of love to be offered to later Christians as an example and proposed for imitation.

Thirty Pieces of Silver, 26:14-16

When Jesus actually enters upon his passion, the disciples, although they want to stand by him (26:41), are totally unable to cope with events and end up failing him. They show that they are "imperceptive" to the true meaning of what is taking place when the woman pours ointment on Jesus' head, anointing him for burial. For their part, the religious leaders show that they are "guileful" and "callous." The first move the religious leaders make against Jesus is to obtain custody of him, and they accomplish this only through deceit: they enlist Judas, one of the Twelve, to betray him.

> **14** Then one of the twelve, who was called Judas Iscariot, went to the chief priests **15** and said, "What will you give me if I betray him to you?" They paid him thirty pieces of silver. **16** And from that moment he began to look for an opportunity to betray him.

Verses 14: "One of the twelve." In anticipation of Matthew's special tradition 27:3-10, it is reported that Judas himself—in direct address—takes the initiative; he is willing to deliver Jesus up if enough money is offered him. Judas, who hands Jesus over, becomes the traitor.

Verse 15: "Thirty pieces of silver." This detail, unique to Matthew's Gospel, reinforces the mercenary nature of Judas' betrayal. It also brings into the scene an allusion to the Old Testament, the first of many in the passion story. The text referred to is Zechariah 11:12, which in turn alludes to Exodus 21:32, where the price of thirty shekels of silver is laid down as the payment given in reparation to the master of a slave who is gored by an ox. In Zechariah the amount is meant to be demeaning: it is a paltry sum. "Allusion to this Biblical text indicates a basic conviction of the evangelist: Jesus' betrayal and ultimate death, while seeming to be the triumph of evil, are mysteriously part of God's great drama of salvation" (*Passion*, 56-57).

Verse 16: "And from that moment," in Matthew, always marks a turning point (cf. 4:17; 16:21). Applied to Jesus' life, it also represents a structural element. *Eukairia* ("moment") is here the natural, favorable opportunity, the chance adapted to the undertaking. The delivering up has been set in motion, only the favorable moment need be awaited.

Matthew introduces the Scripture allusion with skill. What the Scriptures had announced—even if in another connection—is fulfilled in Judas' act. And whoever knows the Scriptures and reads them carefully, can perceive the connection between the shepherd's fate in Zechariah and Jesus' fate. If there it is the owner of the flock who pays a paltry sum to the righteous shepherds, so here it is Judas, to whom a paltry sum is paid for the betrayal of Jesus.

Here Judas reveals that he is totally oblivious to the deeper significance of his act of betraying Jesus. In hiring himself out to the chief priests, he places himself in the service of their desire to kill Jesus. In so doing, he has no idea that, ironically, he is thereby also fulfilling scripture and facilitating with his deceit God's plan of salvation. "More tragically, Judas, in selling his services to the chief priests to betray Jesus, unwittingly acts in a manner that is the exact opposite of 'servanthood': Jesus is the servant par excellence, for he delivers himself to death in order that others might gain life; by contrast, Judas delivers Jesus to death in order that he might gain advantage for himself (24:14-16)" (*Story*, 143).

Disciples Prepare the Passover Meal, 26:17-19

The extent to which Jesus moves closer to Jerusalem is also the extent to which his conflict with the disciples becomes increasingly intense. On a positive note, the disciples continue to follow him and to function as eye- and ear-witnesses to his activity, to be instructed by him, and, as here, to carry out obediently assignments he gives them. The disciples continue to be "learners," and they are "obedient" as well, as when they carry out Jesus' instructions for obtaining the donkey and the colt (21:2-7) or in making preparations for the celebration of the Passover (26:18-19).

> 17 On the first day of Unleavened Bread the disciples came to Jesus, saying, "Where do you want us to make the preparations for you to eat the Passover?" 18 He said, "Go into the city to a certain man, and say to him, 'The Teacher says, My time is near; I will keep the Passover at your house with my disciples.' " 19 So the disciples did as Jesus had directed them, and they prepared the Passover meal.

By guiding and predicting events, Jesus manifests that he is aware that in him God is bringing to fulfillment the divine plan of salvation. Thus Jesus tells the disciples, as he sends them to make arrangements for eating the Passover meal, exactly where to go and with whom to speak.

Verse 17: "First day of Unleavened Bread." Matthew speaks only of the feast of Unleavened Bread, yet there is an allusion to the eating of the paschal lamb in the question of the disciples; in direct address they ask where Jesus wished to eat the Passover. On Thursday Jewish households threw out all leavened bread so that they could properly celebrate the Passover (for which the bread was to be unleavened; cf. Exod 12:15). The fast itself would not actually begin until sundown of Thursday.

Verse 18: "The teacher says." The disciples called Jesus "Lord." On this one occasion Jesus instructs the disciples to refer to him as teacher, but this is in regard to a conversation they are to have with a stranger. "Teacher" expresses the way this man will view Jesus.

Jesus' message is: "My time (*Kairos*) is near." Here Kairos has—as a Christological expression—a salvation history meaning: Jesus' passion, his death, is near and makes Jesus manifest as the true Messiah. It brings the Scriptures to ultimate fulfillment and completes God's salvation plan (cf. "Kairos," *Passion*, 57-62). Because the time specified by God is at hand, Jesus will keep the Passover which introduces the Kairos to his disciples (literally: "do;" *poiein to pascha*, a LXX stereotype, cf. Exod 12:48; Num 9:4, 6, 10, 13). The observance of the Passover duty belongs to the divine salvation order. The commemoration of the Exodus happening becomes eschatological actuality in Jesus' death.

Verse 19: "So the disciples did." There is a sense of strong authority here, much like the scene preparing for the great entry into the city of Jerusalem and its temple in 21:1-6.

Matthew's main objective is to convince the community (in the comprehensive sense, all disciples, all Christians) that it is right to carry out the Lord's sayings. If Yahweh was Lord in the Old Testament, so now Jesus is the Teacher as well as Lord. Only by obedient fulfillment of his commands and ordinances, can the history of salvation come to its completion, to its real fulfillment. Jesus' obedience toward the Kairos brought on by the Father is, on the other hand, an example and an obligation for the community. "The theme of the obedience—Jesus' obedience to his Kairos and the obedience of the disciples to their commanding Lord— bound together the Christological and ecclesiological dimensions of Matthew's theology" (*Passion*, 65). Through Jesus' complete obedience the paradigmatic Passover becomes an eschatological event.

"Surely not I, Rabbi," 26:20-25

In contrast to the religious leaders, the disciples, and Judas, Jesus demonstrates, by guiding and predicting events, that he is aware that God is bringing to fulfillment the divine plan of salvation in him and his destiny. Thus, Jesus told the disciples, as he sent them to make arrangements for eating the Passover meal, exactly where to go and with whom to speak (26:17-18). Now, at the Last Supper Jesus shares with the disciples, he predicts that one of them will betray him.

> **20** When it was evening, he took his place with the twelve; **21** and while they were eating, he said, "Truly I tell you, one of you will betray me." **22** And they became greatly distressed and began to say to him one after another, Surely not I, Lord?" **23** He answered, "The one who has dipped his hand into the bowl with me will betray me. **24** The Son of Man goes as it is written of him, but woe to that one by whom the Son of Man is betrayed! It would have been better for that one not to have been born." **25** Judas, who betrayed him, said, "Surely not I, Rabbi?" He replied, "You have said so."

Verse 20: "When it was evening." It was after sundown and the feast of Passover had begun. Jesus and his twelve disciples come into the city to celebrate the Passover meal as planned.

Verse 21: "One of you will betray." But the passion story immediately introduces a poignant note into the celebration. "While they were eating" Jesus makes his dire prediction.

Verse 22: Hearing this, each of the disciples, with a great display of grief, asks Jesus, "Surely not I, Lord?" In its Greek wording, this question assumes that, were Jesus to reply to each disciple, his answer would be, "No [it is not you]." Seen for what they are, the disciples' grief and question are in reality massive expressions of false confidence: none of the disciples actually believes that he could ever do such a thing as betray Jesus. The addition of the title "Lord," which, according to Matthew's vocabulary code, indicates the speech of believers, stands in sharp contrast to the words of Judas in verse 25.

Verse 23: Jesus indicates the betrayer. Later Judas himself attests to both his own guilt and the innocence of Jesus when, in returning the pieces of silver to the chief priests and the elders in the temple, he declares, "I have sinned by betraying innocent blood" (27:4). And by going out and hanging himself, Judas brings to fulfillment the woe Jesus here pronounces.

Verse 24: "The Son of Man goes as it is written." Judas has violated the bond of friendship and trust that Jesus celebrates with his disciples. Judas "dipped his hand with Jesus." "Two currents of the passion tradition and Matthew's own theology merge here. On the one hand, the death of Jesus is not an accident nor an absurd tragedy resulting from Judas' sin. From the first moment of Jesus' existence God's providence has directed him to carry out the work of salvation entrusted to God's Son.

"But neither is Judas a helpless marionette. Jesus addresses a prophet's 'woe' to him because Judas, too, is a responsible child of God and must bear the consequence of his choice. Throughout his Gospel Matthew has stressed the theme of 'judgment.' We are responsible for our decisions: to reject the Gospel and to choose silver would lead Judas to a terrible fate." (*Passion*, 63).

Verse 25: "Surely not I, Rabbi." The confrontation between Jesus and his betrayer, Judas, is the climax of the scene. Although he has already sold himself to the chief priests, Judas asks Jesus whether he will be the one to betray him in such manner as to anticipate that Jesus' answer will be no (26:25). Since his name is already connected with the term "betrayer" in Matthew's mind, the question is hypocritical. The title "Rabbi" used by Judas, which Matthew places only in the mouth of Jesus' opponents, places Judas clearly on the side of enemies. Jesus' answer (in the historical present) is clear and emphatic.

In Matthew the pericope rises steadily to a high point in verse 25. The meaning also comes across clearly to community: the betrayer's confrontation course can no longer be halted. For what up to now may possibly have happened in secret, is now manifest. Betrayal leads to isolation: the withdrawal of the one from the community of the Twelve is so fearsome, that this can be expressed only with the help of a cry of woe (v. 24). The community knows the threatening character of the cry of woe both from Old Testament tradition, and out of Jesus' own mouth.

Jesus Institutes the Eucharist, 26:26-29

Jesus makes the Passover meal itself the occasion on which he explains the significance of his death to the disciples. In the bread they eat, which is his body, they have fellowship with him; in the cup they drink, which is his blood, they share in the atonement for sins which he will accomplish for all; and in the promise he gives them that he will no more drink wine until he is united with them in the Father's kingdom, they have assurance that they will share future bliss with him.

> **26** While they were eating, Jesus took a loaf of bread and after blessing it he broke it, gave it to the disciples, and said, "Take, eat; this is my body." **27** Then he took a cup, and after giving thanks he gave it to them, saying, "Drink from it, all of you; **28** for this is my blood of the covenant which is poured out for many for the forgiveness of sins. **29** I tell you, I will never again drink of this fruit of the vine until that day when I drink it new with you in my Father's kingdom."

Verse 26a: "This is my body." The "institution" account is a profound statement about the meaning of Jesus' death. Jesus takes bread, blesses it, breaks and distributes it to the disciples, inviting them to eat of it. He also blesses and distributes the cup. These ritual gestures recall the earlier feeding stories, one in Jewish territory and one among Gentiles, where Jesus had taken a small amount of provisions and miraculously fed the multitudes (14:13-21; 15:32-39). These stories are a starting point for understanding the meaning of the last supper.

The successive actions of taking bread, giving thanks or pronouncing a blessing, breaking, and distributing are the common form of Jewish grace-at-table; Jesus recycles them to create two parabolic and prophetic actions. Matthew underlines the fact that Jesus gives this sacred food to the disciples. "This is my body" identifies the bread with the whole person of Jesus, in all its corporeal reality, vulnerability, and mortality.

Verse 27: "Drink from it." Following Mark, Matthew uses *eucharistēsas* ("giving thanks") with the cup, while he used *eulogēsas* ("pronouncing a blessing") with the bread.

Verse 28: "My blood of the covenant." The words over the cup with mention of a covenant are more sacrificial in tone than the words over the bread. "The blood of the covenant" recalls the covenant sacrifice of Exodus 24:8. After the animals had been slain, Moses took half of the blood and threw it against the altar (the symbol of Yahweh). After reading the law to the people and receiving their acceptance of it, Moses threw the other half of the blood upon the people, saying: "See the blood of the covenant." By a solemn sacrifice, a common bond of life (symbolized by the blood, the seat of life) has been forged between God and his people. This bond of life, this covenant, demands a new mode of action from the people who now enjoy a special fellowship with God. "Jesus declares the wine in the cup he shares with his disciples to be his blood, i.e., his life poured out in sacrifice to create a bond of life, a community of life, a covenant between God and his new people, the church" (Meier, 319).

The Passover which Jesus eats with his disciples looks ahead to the cross and interprets it. Jesus interprets the meaning of his imminent death in terms of a covenant established with his blood which will bring about the forgiveness of sins "for many." "In the story Matthew tells . . . Jesus is depicted as the Son of God who, in willing obedience to the Father, goes the way of the cross so as to save humankind by shedding his blood for the atonement of sins (1:21; 20:28; 26:28). Or to put it more simply, Jesus is depicted as the son who, in devotion to the Father, serves humankind" (*Story*, 111).

Verse 29: "That day when I drink it new with you." With the phrase "never again" Matthew lays special emphasis on the "salvation history aspect." The Last Supper with the disciples is the Kairos determined by God, which is mediated in the new salvation community by the definitive realization in the coming of the kingdom of the Father. Jesus is not only present with his disciples in their earthly existence, as in chapter 18; his presence is extended forward in time. Here Jesus indicates that his disciples will experience his presence in the eschatological kingdom.

It was not Matthew's intention (or that of the other New Testament "witnesses") to establish a new liturgy, a new form of the community assembly. The Last Supper account has a theological meaning. At the Last

Supper, Jesus explains to his (i.e., all) disciples the meaning of his death and points out the eschatological relevance of his dying:

a) Jesus establishes a grace community, which makes possible salvation for the many, which consists in forgiveness of sins. Jesus' death is an atonement death.

b) This dying is an atoning death because Jesus is the end-time Messiah. The bread gesture with the interpretative word and the cup word with its soteriological application were understood by the community as Jesus' messianic self-revelation.

c) Jesus' death for the many exceeds the boundaries established by the "old covenant." Jesus' death is a death for all. Because he, as Son of the Merciful Father of all, lays down his life, all can win a share in this saving death.

Jesus Predicts Peter's Denial, 26:30-35

When Jesus predicted his betrayal at the Last Supper, all the disciples boldly express confidence in their ability to remain loyal to Jesus. Following the meal and under way to the Mount of Olives, Jesus makes three further predictions, all of which relate to the disciples: they all will desert him; Peter will deny him. But such failure notwithstanding, he will meet them in Galilee after his resurrection and reconcile them to himself.

> **30** When they had sung the hymn, they went out to the Mount of Olives. **31** Then Jesus said to them, "You will all become deserters because of me this night, for it is written,
>
> > 'I will strike the shepherd,
> > and the sheep of the flock
> > will be scattered.'
>
> **32** But after I am raised up, I will go ahead of you to Galilee." **33** Peter said to him, "Though all become deserters because of you, I will never desert you." **34** Jesus said to him, "Truly I tell you, this very night, before the cock crows, you will deny me three times." **35** Peter said to him, "Even though I must die with you, I will not deny you." And so said all the disciples.

Verse 30: "Sung the hymn." The Passover meal traditionally concludes with the singing of the "Hallel" (Pss 114-118), recalling God's redemption of Israel from Egypt and of the individual from death. As Jesus and his disciples leave the supper room they sing these triumphant psalms that acclaim God's redemptive power and his faithfulness to Israel in its struggle for freedom. Precisely at this moment, Jesus shatters the festive mood by speaking of the disciples' flight. This is the only time that the Gospels record that Jesus sang—on the night before his death.

Verses 31: "Then Jesus said" (in historical present) shows that an important saying concerning the disciples follows: "You will all" (i.e., all the disciples without exception) fall. "This night" (cf. v. 34) points to the fact that Jesus will be given over into the hands of sinners, and above all, that the disciples' defection and Peter's denial are sinister events that belong to darkness. "This night" is the hour of utter darkness (cf. vv. 16:11, 29, 34). The citation of Zachariah 13:7 ("for") sets the disciples' defection in perspective (cf. 2:5; 4:6; 4:10) and points to the fulfillment of an Old Testament prophecy. The picture of the Good Shepherd stands here in clear outline.

Verse 32: "After I am raised up." This is the first time in the passion narrative that explicit resurrection vocabulary has been used "I will go ahead of you"—once the slain shepherd is raised up, he will go like a shepherd before his sheep into Galilee. The angel at the tomb will repeat this message to the women (28:7), and the rehabilitated disciples will go into Galilee to receive from the Son of Man their definitive founding as a Church and their universal mission (28:16-20). Above all, the disciples' defections range Jesus' resurrection and appearance in Galilee. The place of Jesus' earthly ministry will also be the place of the post-Easter new beginning. The disciples' disarray is not the end; it cannot hinder the triumph of good over evil.

Verse 33: "I will never desert." Peter, the disciples' spokesman, in direct address rejects Jesus announcement, if only with regard to him personally. With words similar to Jesus' (cf. v. 31a), he accepts the possibility that all others might fall because of Jesus' fate, but absolutely rejects such a possibility for him (*oudepote* here indicates vehement protest against a definitive pronouncement). The emphatic distancing from the behavior of others, the stressed "never" and the indirectly expressed special relationship to Jesus ("because of you") strengthens the contrast to Peter's actual denial which follows (26:69-75).

Verse 34: "Before the cock crows." Jesus' reply comes in the form of one of those prophetic sayings that sweep away objections, and which is introduced by a declarative formula that makes it even more incisive. Again the Kairos, which involves the disciples also, is alluded to "this very night." And Peter failure will be more than that of the others; he will deny Jesus three times (the combination *aparneomai* means betrayal of trust, a fall into faithlessness), and indeed before the end of this decisive night to be heralded by the cock's crow.

Verse 35: Once more Peter speaks out. Again he swears, even more vehemently, his unqualified faithfulness and readiness to follow even onto death (cf. the *ou mē*: an emphatic denial of a future contingency). All the other disciples join in his assurance.

Gethsemane, 26:36-46

On arrival at the Mount of Olives and the Garden of Gethsemane, Jesus attests in prayer to his perfect obedience to the Father: he goes to his death not as one who desires for himself the glory of martyrdom, but because he would do his Father's will. Jesus has had to struggle with the religious leaders and the disciples. In Gethsemane, Jesus even struggles with himself (v. 45). Jesus demonstrates in all he is subjected to that his love for God is perfect, or single-hearted: what God wills, Jesus wills (v. 42).

> **36** Then Jesus went with them to a place called Gethsemane, and he said to his disciples, "Sit here while I go over there and pray." **37** He took with him Peter and the two sons of Zebedee, and began to be grieved and agitated. **38** Then he said to them, "I am deeply grieved, even to death; remain here, and stay awake with me. **39** And going a little further, he threw himself on the ground and prayed, "My Father, if it is possible, let this cup pass from me; yet not what I want but what you want." **40** Then he came to the disciples and found them sleeping; and he said to Peter, "So, could you not stay awake with me one hour? **41** Stay awake and pray that you may not come into the time of trial; the spirit indeed is willing, but the flesh is weak." **42** Again he went away for the second time and prayed, "My Father, if this cannot pass unless I drink it, your will be done." **43** Again he came and found them sleeping for their eyes were heavy. **44** So leaving them again he went away and prayed for the third time, saying the same words. **45** Then he came to the disciples and said to them. "Are you still sleeping and taking your rest? See, the hour is at hand, and the Son of Man is betrayed into the hands of sinners. **46** Get up, let us be going. See, my betrayer is at hand."

Twice in the foregoing, reference was made to "this night" (26:31, 34), and now the most meaningful events of this night are to be reported. This accounts for the relatively large size of the Gethsemane pericope.

Verse 36: "While I go over there and pray." This may be an allusion to the instruction Abraham gave to his young men when he arrived at the place for the sacrifice of his son Isaac: "Stay here with the donkey; the boy and I will go over there" (Gen 22:5). The sacrifice of Isaac as a spectacular story of Biblical faith was a motif of later Jewish theology, and Matthew may invoke it here as he prepares to demonstrate the extraordinary faith of God's Son. In contrast to the story of Abraham and Isaac, Jesus is both offerer and victim, an example of faith more striking than any Biblical precedent.

Verses 37-38: "He took with him Peter." The inner group of disciples (Peter, James, and John) accompany Jesus deeper into the olive grove. The same trio had been privileged to be with Jesus at the transfiguration (17:18). It is intriguing that these same disciples are singled out as having difficulty accepting Jesus' cross (16:22; 20:2-28). Their presence with Jesus in Gethsemane may imply that the disciples who witnessed Jesus' glory will now experience firsthand what it means to share Jesus' "cup," the only authentic means for entering into glory with him. The anguish of Jesus is forcefully described: "He began to be grieved and agitated." His words to the disciples, "I am deeply grieved, even to death" echo Psalm 42, one of the Old Testament's most eloquent prayers expressing the Psalmist's longing for God in the midst of suffering and fear of death.

Verse 39: "Let this cup pass." In a gesture of distress and supplication, Jesus "threw himself on the ground." Matthew reports the whole of Jesus' prayer in direct address, rendering Mark's Aramaic *Abba* with a touching "My father." The cup is the Old Testament symbol of one's fate as prepared by God, be it reward or punishment. Drinking a cup could, in particular, be a symbol of undergoing suffering or punishment (cf. Ps 11:6; Lam 4:21; Is 51:17, 22).

Matthew as narrator is "omniscient." There is nothing in the world of the story of which he does not have full knowledge. Accordingly he knows the words of the prayer Jesus utters in private in Gethsemane.

Verses 40: "Stay awake with me one hour." The added question comes in reproof of the failure: could you not watch even one hour with me? "With me" stresses Matthew's Christological purpose. While "stay awake" can mean simply "not sleeping," in the context more is meant. The hour is an eschatological one, an hour of crisis determined by God. In this sense, "watch" means to be armed and to defend oneself against the danger of being turned aside from complete dedication to Jesus and the Father and to allow oneself to be ensnared by selfishness.

Verse 41: "Stay awake and pray." The renewed injunctions "stay awake" and "pray" are backed up by a purpose clause, lest you enter into "the time of trial" (*peirasmon*). Defection is the great temptation into which a disciple can be lured and in which he can perish. According to the Old Testament understanding of the human, the weakness of the flesh can gain the upper hand in a time of trial, if the power of the Spirit, given by God, does not prevail. In Gethsemane, too, Peter and the two sons of Zebedee, though confident that they possess the fortitude to face death with Jesus, cannot even muster the strength to watch with him but instead fall asleep.

The disciples had wanted to stand by Jesus in his passion, but they could not. As Jesus puts it: "The spirit indeed is willing, but the flesh is weak." In relation to the passion of Jesus, the disciples exhibit many traits that spring from a system of values that is not that of Jesus.

The upshot is that they are unable to cope with events of the passion. What Jesus says of Peter in Gethsemane, with an eye to James and John as well, is true of all of the disciples. They are divided in their intentions and loyalties. To be undivided, to be wholehearted, is to be "perfect" (5:48). Jesus, therefore, is perfect; the disciples are not. Whereas Jesus freely employs his incomparable authority to vanquish Satan, demons and the forces of nature and illness, he chooses not to compel humans to do his bidding.

Verse 42: "Your will be done." In Matthew's Gospel Jesus is the epitome of obedience to the will of God. Jesus submits to baptism even though he has no need to confess sin; by overcoming the temptations of Satan, Jesus son of God remains obedient to the Father, in contrast to the disobedience of Israel during the desert wanderings. Matthew employs the Old Testament fulfillment quotations in part to demonstrate the conformity of Jesus to the will of God as revealed in the scriptures. In everything he fulfills the demands of the law—with his whole heart and with his whole soul and with all his resources. Matthew most directly portrays Jesus as one who submits to the will of God in his account of the prayer in Gethsemane: "not my will, but thine be done." "Finally, the Matthean Jesus demonstrates that his life springs from love when he declares in 20.28 that 'the Son of man came not to be served but to serve and to give his life as ransom for many'" (Bauer, 61).

Verse 43: "Again he came." What Jesus found already at his first return is repeated: the disciples sleeping. Then almost as an excuse the reason is given: their eyes were heavy. But the disciples' failure is not explained away by the excuse.

Verse 44: Matthew reports the third prayer with narrative shortening; the words spoken in prayer are not given; they are to be taken from the second prayer—"saying the same words."

Verses 45-46: The third return ("Then") and a renewed criticism of the disciples (again in question form) leads into the interpretive statement regarding the whole event which can no longer be delayed; for the betrayer has approached. Now the hour has finally come, which is interpreted as the hour of the Son of Man, of whom it is said that he will be delivered into the hands of sinners. The "handing over (*paradidomi*"), mentioned ten times in chapter 26, unfolds unhaltingly. Night and darkness have conquered. "The hour is at hand"—a key temporal reference. Thus Jesus also announces that God's Rule "has come near" (4:17) or "has come to you" (12:28). So here Jesus speaks of the "hour of his betrayal" (v. 45) and he will also speak of the "hour" or "day" that connotes the end or the final judgment.

After Caesarea Philippi "Jesus began to show his disciples that he must (*hoti dei*) go the Jerusalem" (16:21). "But this 'necessity' does not make the journey of Jesus to the cross automatic. Matthew portrays Jesus as struggling with the will of God over his messianic role" (D. Bauer, 105). Peter assumed the role of Satan when he rebuked Jesus for declaring that he must go to Jerusalem to suffer and die (16:23). Jesus responds with the same words he spoke to the tempter in the wilderness: "Get behind me, Satan;" (4:20). In the Garden of Gethsemane, Jesus struggles with his own desire to avoid the cup of suffering. Despite these struggles and temptations, Jesus remains true to the will of God, which means for him the way of the cross and suffering.

The Arrest, 26:47-56

At 26:4-5, the crowds are still regarded by the religious leaders as a threat to their plans to capture Jesus and kill him. Yet at Jesus' arrest these same crowds suddenly appear with Judas, armed and acting on orders from the chief priests and the elders, in order to take Jesus by force.

> 47 While he was still speaking, Judas, one of the twelve, arrived and with him was a large crowd with swords and clubs, from the chief priests and the elders of the people. 48 Now the betrayer had given them a sign, saying, "The one I will kiss is the man; arrest him." 49 At once he came up to Jesus and said, "Greetings, Rabbi!" and kissed him. 50 Jesus said to him, "Friend, do what you are here to do." Then they came and laid hands on Jesus and arrested him. 51 Suddenly, one of those with Jesus put his hand on his sword, drew it, and struck the slave of the high priest, cutting off his ear. 52 Then Jesus said to him, "Put your sword back into its place; for all who take the sword will perish by the sword. 53 Do you think that I cannot appeal to my Father, and he will at once send me more than twelve legions of angels? 54 But how then would the scriptures be fulfilled, which say it must happen in this way?" 55 At that hour Jesus said to the crowds, "Have you come out with swords and clubs to arrest me as though I were a bandit? Day after day I sat in the

temple teaching, and you did not arrest me. **56** But all this has taken place, so that the scriptures of the prophets may be fulfilled." Then all the disciples deserted him and fled.

Verse 47: "While he was still speaking." These words connect the arrest with the preceding Gethsemane account: Jesus' speech (vv. 45b, 46) is interrupted and the arrest account follows set in the same place. It is underlined that Judas, the betrayer, is one of the Twelve. For the accomplishment of his plan he makes use of the crowd which the high priest and the elders of the temple have placed at his disposal. The imminent crisis indicated by the appearance of Judas and the armed band is now inevitable.

"Large crowd with swords and clubs." The first move the religious leaders make against Jesus is to obtain custody of him, and they accomplish this only through deceit: they enlist Judas, one of the Twelve, to betray him (26:14-16) and they send the crowds, whom Jesus had daily taught in the temple, to arrest him and hand him over.

"If the characterization of the religious leaders is wholly negative, the same cannot be said of the Jewish crowds. Like the leaders, the crowds, too, may be dealt with as a single, 'flat' character. They are not rich in traits, and the ones they possess tend not to change until the end of Matthew's story, when they suddenly appear with Judas to arrest Jesus (26:47, 55)" (*Story*, 24).

Verses 48-49: "Had given them a sign" (*semeion*). The previously arranged sign of recognition is now described. Here *semeion* means a visible sign by which a designated person is known. The "signal" is a kiss, a most unlikely one since at the time the kiss was a commonly used sign of greeting. Since the recipient of the kiss is the one who is to be seized, the sign is the expression of a hostile collusion. Instruction and execution are characterized above all by the word of greeting Judas uses. "Greetings (*Chaire*)" underlines that Matthew wishes the kiss to be understood precisely as the gesture of greeting (cf. also 27:29), with which one was accustomed to greet a rabbi. In Matthew, "Rabbi" as form of address is used only by Judas toward Jesus (26:25, 49). Thereby both the word and gesture of greeting take on a clearly pejorative meaning.

Verse 50: "And he came up to Jesus." The redactional introduction (which mentions Jesus again by name, cf. already vv. 50b, 51, 52, 55) serves not only to identify Jesus, but also brings to the fore Jesus' basically uncompromised sovereignty despite the defeat. The address "Friend" in the New Testament is found only in Matthew (20:13; 22:12; 26:50); it takes on a positive or negative meaning according to the context. The rest of Jesus' remark to Judas indicates that Jesus is the "knowing" one who "knowingly" moves toward death (cf. the Passion-predictions and also 26:2, 11, 18, 25); the expression might be completed with an *oida*, "I know."

Verse 51: "One of those with Jesus." "Except for Mary his *mother* (2:11) and toll-collectors and sinners (9:11), the list of those who are 'with Jesus' or of whom it is said that Jesus is 'with them' includes only Peter (26:69, 71), one of Jesus' followers (26:51), Peter and the two sons of Zebedee, and the twelve or eleven disciples" (*Story*, 131).

"Struck the slave." In the hour of Jesus' arrest one of the disciples, in an act of utter futility, endeavors to meet might with might by drawing his sword and cutting off the ear of the slave of the high priest (26:51). Completely forgotten by this disciple are all the words Jesus has spoken to the Twelve concerning his passion. This is indicative of how "futile" are the thoughts and actions of the disciples relative to Jesus' passion.

Verse 52: "Put your sword back." These verses are found only in Matthew: the analysis of the vocabulary, style, and thought pattern point to the redactor's hand. The logion, which forbids every use of force, has a threefold formulation: a) order to put up the sword and the reason for the order, b) Christological interpretation of the situation, c) reference to fulfillment of Scripture. Verse 52 points back to the Sermon on the Mount (5:39, 44; 7:1-2, 12), in which the theme "renunciation of force" plays a decisive role (cf. also the thought of readiness to forgive in 18:21-22, 33-35). The sayings set forth catechetically in the Sermon will be actualized in the sufferings of persecution.

In the Sermon on the Mount Jesus had clearly declared that the use of violence was not to be the way of those committed to God's rule, and here in Gethsemane Jesus again explicitly rejects the option of violence. Rather than continue the endless chain of retribution, with violence spawning yet more violence ("all who take the sword will perish by the sword"), Jesus prophetically breaks the chain. His power is not that of the sword.

Verse 53: "Twelve legions of angels." The Christological reflection of verse 53 (presented as a question) clearly separates Jesus' position from the disciples' behavior. As Son of Man, Jesus was in a position to ask the Father for help which would have determined the outcome in his favor in a trice (twelve legions would represent half of Caesar Augustus' troop strength); a single word would have ensured the request. But what happens here corresponds to the Father's will. To attempt to prevent Jesus' arrest by the use of force would, here and now, be a rejection of God's will (cf. 6:23). "Although he could, if he wanted, call upon his Father and receive for his defense more than twelve legions of angels, he forgoes this and submits, in order to fulfill the scriptures, to betrayal by Judas, to arrest by his opponents, and to abandonment by the other disciples (26:47-56)'' (*Story*, 86).

Verse 54: "It must happen in this way." This thought is underlined with the reference to Scripture, according to which all this must happen. Again the teaching is imparted in the form of a question; the words of the prophets indicate that the arrest "must be so" (cf. the *houtos*). It must be hindered neither through the use of earthly force nor through heavenly intervention.

Verses 55-56. "At that hour" marks the beginning of a new (third) theme within the arrest scene, but above all it indicates that the situation is a decisive one (cf. 25:45). Because it is spoken in the decisive hour, the reference to a "large crowd" (v. 47) receives its unique weight. Jesus objects in the first place to being treated as a robber and, secondly, to the secret and underhand proceedings against him.

"I sat in the temple teaching" indicates what is for Matthew the typical authoritative teaching position (cf. 5:1; 13:1-2; 15:29; 19:28; 20:21, 23; 23:2); the verb *kathezomai* appears only here in Matthew, but is synonymous with other verbs indicating authoritative sitting and teaching. Only Matthew knows of a teaching activity on Jesus' part after the cleansing of the temple. The affirmation of 21:23 (that he taught in the temple) is repeated to underline that the Jewish leaders did not seize the opportunity presented to them. Fearing the people, they shunned the publicity (cf. 21:46; 26:34-5) and so must have recourse to guile (26:5). The concluding "scripture fulfillment" brings out that everything that has happened is a fulfillment of the prophetic scriptures (cf. 1:22; 21:4). The flight of the disciples is not a scripture fulfillment, for Matthew interprets scripture only about Jesus. The flight of the disciples realizes what Jesus had said about the disciples' conduct. The promise of Peter and "all the disciples" (26:35) not to abandon Jesus shows itself "at that hour" to be empty words.

"By placing the flight of the disciples after Jesus' words and by introducing it with the link word 'then,' Matthew seems to imply that only after Jesus had spoken are these events free to happen (as at the moment of arrest, cf. above 26:50). Once again the Gospel implies that underneath the chaos and failure of the scene pulsates God's mysterious providence" (*Passion*, 89).

The Jewish Trial, 26:57-68

Jesus' appearance before the Sanhedrin is the climactic event in this part of the passion account. In putting Jesus on trial, the religious leaders believe that they will finally achieve the resolution of their conflict with Jesus which they have long desired (12:14). At his trial, the high priest abruptly puts Jesus' own claim to him in the form of a question, and when Jesus replies in the affirmative, the high priest and the Sanhedrin condemn him to death for having committed blasphemy against God (26:57-68).

> **57** Those who had arrested Jesus took him to Caiaphas the high priest, in whose house the scribes and the elders had gathered. **58** But Peter was following him at a distance, as far as the courtyard of the high priest; and going inside, he sat with the guards in order to see how this would end. **59** Now the chief priests and the whole council were looking for false testimony against Jesus so that they might put him to death, **60** but they found none, though many false witnesses came forward. At last two came forward, **61** and said, "This fellow said, 'I am able to destroy the temple of God and to build it in three days.' " **62** The high priest stood up and said, "Have you no answer? What is it that they testify against you.?" **63** But Jesus was silent. Then the high priest said to him, "I put you under oath before the living God, tell us if you are the Messiah, the Son of God." **64** Jesus said to him, "You have said so. But I tell you,
>
> > From now on you will see the Son of Man
> > > seated at the right hand of Power
> > > and coming on the clouds of heaven."
>
> **65** Then the high priest tore his clothes and said, "He has blasphemed! You have now heard his blasphemy. **66** What is your verdict?" They answered, "He deserves death." **67** Then they spat in his face and struck him; and some slapped him, **68** saying, "Prophesy to us, you Messiah! Who is it that struck you?"

With his passion at hand, Jesus Messiah, the Son of God, himself controls events that bring him to the cross (cf. vv. 1-12). When therefore, the high priest asks Jesus, "Are you the Messiah, the Son of God?" (v. 63), he is at once reformulating Jesus' claim in nonallegorical terms and aiming to turn it against him in order to destroy him. Moreover, from his own standpoint the high priest succeeds, for Jesus' reply is affirmative "You have said so" (v. 64; cf. 27:43). In consequence of Jesus' reply, the Sanhedrin, at the instigation of the high priest, condemns Jesus to death for blasphemy (vv. 65-66). "And therein lies the irony of Jesus' fate: Jesus is made to die, but the only 'crime' he has committed is that he has dared to claim to be the one God himself has twice said that he is, namely, the Messiah Son of God. Claiming to 'see,' the Israelite leaders show that they are "blind'" (J. Kingsbury, *Matthew*, 56).

Verse 57: "High priest, scribes, elders." During the proceedings, Jesus once again faces, as constituent groups belonging to the Sanhedrin, the chief priests and the elders (26:57, 59), those to whom he had previously addressed the parable of the wicked husbandmen (21:23).

Verse 58: "To see how this would end." Matthew does not place Peter by a fire, warming himself, as in Mark. Peter simply enters the courtyard and sits with the guards or attendants to see what results the arrest and trial of Jesus would have. Perhaps granted Peter's agitated state, "the end" carries the deeper connotation of death.

Verse 59: "False testimony." The innocence of Jesus, a theme struck also in the trial before Pilate, is made clear from the start of the Jewish trial. Despite the deadly intent of the authorities and their complete unscrupulousness (Matthew emphasizes from the beginning that they seek *false* testimony), no convincing witnesses can be found. All the false witnesses who come forward trip over one another's testimony.

Verse 61: "I am able to destroy." "Matthew does not call the two witnesses "false" or say that their witness did not agree. Though their motives may be evil they are speaking the truth about Jesus.

Verse 63: "But Jesus was silent." As the presiding officer of the Sanhedrin, the high priest is privy to the claim to be the Son of God which Jesus had advanced in allegorical form in his parable of the wicked husbandmen.

As long as the testimony brought against him is false, Jesus remains silent (26:59-62). Abruptly, however, the high priest places Jesus under oath to tell the Sanhedrin whether he is the Messiah, the Son of God (26:63). In terms of the plot of Matthew's story, this unexpected query raises the problem as to the source from which the high priest has even gotten the idea to question Jesus about being the Son of God. This source is Jesus himself and his narration of the parable of the wicked husbandmen. As the presiding officer of the Sanhedrin, the high priest has knowledge of the claim to divine sonship which Jesus made in telling his parable to the chief priests and the elders. At the trial, therefore, the high priest seizes on Jesus' own claim, converts it from allegorical speech into literal speech, and hurls it back at Jesus as a weapon by which to destroy him.

Verse 64: "You have said so." Because from Jesus' standpoint false testimony at the trial has suddenly given way to a query that expresses the truth, he breaks his silence and replies in the affirmative "You have said so!" (cf. 28:43). In consequence of Jesus' reply, the Sanhedrin, at the instigation of the high priest, condemns Jesus to death for having committed blasphemy against God (v. 66).

"You will see the Son of Man." Apparently, the Son of Man reference communicates nothing whatever to the high priest and the Sanhedrin about Jesus' identity. In the scenes in which Matthew depicts the Sanhedrin as mocking Jesus, members of the Sanhedrin make Jesus' identity the object of their ridicule. But regardless of the fact that they have all heard Jesus refer to himself as "the Son of Man, in the first scene they taunt him as "Messiah" (v. 68) and in the second as the "Son of God" (27:43). Jesus' public reference to himself as "the Son of man" at his trial is not presented by Matthew as revealing his identity.

Verse 66: "He deserves death." It is ironic that although Jesus is made to die for committing blasphemy against God, his "crime" has been to dare to think about himself as God, at the baptism and the transfiguration, has revealed He does in truth "think" about him (3:17; 17:5; 21:37). In the case of the high priest and the Sanhedrin, the irony is that even while alleging this, they are effectively disavowing God's "thinking" and demonstrating that they have in no way penetrated the secret that Jesus is indeed the Son of God. In resolving their conflict with Jesus as they have, they have achieved the opposite of what they had intended. They have not only not pleased God, but they have also condemned to death the Son he has sent them and called forth his wrath on themselves and their nation (21:43-44; 22:7).

Peter's Denial, 26:69-75

Because of their unwillingness to accept the fact that suffering sonship is a call to suffering discipleship, the disciples became apostate when confronted by the events of Jesus' passion: Judas betrayed Jesus (26:47-50), the disciples fled from him (v.56), and Peter now denies him.

> **69** Now Peter was sitting outside in the courtyard. A servant-girl came to him and said, "You also were with Jesus the Galilean." **70** But he denied it before all of them, saying, "I do not know what you are talking about." **71** When he went out to the porch, another servant-girl saw him, and she said to the bystanders, "This man was with Jesus of Nazareth." **72** Again he denied it with an oath, "I do not know the man." **73** After a little while the bystanders came up and said to Peter, "Certainly you are also one of them, for your accent betrays you." **74** Then he began to curse, and he swore an oath, "I do not know the man!" At that moment the cock crowed. **75** Then Peter remembered what Jesus

had said: "Before the cock crows, you will deny me three times." And he went out and wept bitterly.

Matthew has preserved a threefold structure: the parts are marked off by a heightening of tension and new accusers are provided in each part: a maid, another (maid), the bystanders. The argument in verse 73 ("your accent betrays you") is clearer than "you are a Galilean" (so Mark and Luke).

Verses 69-70. "You also were with Jesus." Matthew takes up the cue given in verse 58; yet the "now" separates the scene from what goes immediately before. Peter sits outside, while in the inner court (cf. at 26:3, 58) the hearing goes on. A maid approaches. As throughout his Gospel the dialogue is the important thing for Matthew. The maid identifies the man as as having been "with Jesus." The list of those who are "with Jesus" or of whom it is said that Jesus is with them includes the following: Mary his mother (2:11), toll-collectors and sinners (9:11), Peter (26:69, 71), one of Jesus' followers (26:51), Peter and the two sons of Zebedee, and the twelve or eleven disciples. The title "Jesus the Galilean" is singular in the New Testament, although the fact that Jesus and his disciples come from Galilee is clear in Matthew from the start. In fact it is not a question of a title, but an observation about the obscure origin of Jesus and Peter. Peter lies "before all of them" (which underlines the intensity of the first denial). Matthew interprets Peter's denial in the sense of a thoroughgoing rejection (*arneomai*, LN 33.277). As in Luke, Peter's denial is short, concise, and to the point: "I do not know what you are talking about."

Verse 71-72. The second denial is set off by a change of place. The identification of Peter by another, second maid, fulfills the Jewish requirement that at least two witnesses agree about a statement. Here too, the public nature of the event is preserved "to the bystanders"; in content the charge corresponds with the first (now Jesus is designated as "Jesus of Nazareth") (cf. 2:23 [4:13; 13:54]). Again "being with Jesus" is the decisive point. Peter's denial is really a betrayal of his Lord (cf. *Passion*, 202) and its hideousness is underlined by the use of an oath. Since according to 5:33-37 the use of any oath (as calling upon God as guarantor and witness) is forbidden, Peter's use of an oath marks his behavior as an offense against Jesus' injunction to abstain entirely from oaths.

Verse 73-74. Finally in the third scene the bystanders (as witnessing public) come to the fore with complaints against Peter; their charge now is that he belongs to the disciples of Jesus. "You are also" lends the identification a special weight: a denial is out of the question. The Galillean dialect clearly betrays Peter to be a member of Jesus' circle of disciples (*delos*; open, public, stands only here in the synoptic tradition). Peter is betrayed by the facts, but he sets out to save himself by cursing and swearing. Again and again ("he began to") he asserts his ignorance, he makes the distance between himself and "the (this) man" ever larger.

Verse 75: Immediately after the definitive denial there follows the cock's crow (v. 74b). It has a twofold effect: Peter recalls and he regrets. The cock's crow, with which Jesus' prophetic word is bound (v. 34) reminds Peter that he had done precisely what he shortly before had rejected as unthinkable: the three fold betrayal has become a reality. Finally Peter leaves the place of the sad event; he had definitively turned his back on Jesus before all the bystanders (cf. v. 58, 69 , 71, 73). Yet the closing remark shows that Peter's self-consciousness had suffered a shock through the cock's crow; the remembrance of Jesus' word makes clear the reprehensiveness of his deed. Peter's first, perhaps purely human reaction, leaves open the possibility of a (later) penitent reflection.

The denial scene clearly stresses the ecclesiological aspect and serves parenetic goals.

1. The important thing about acknowledgement of Jesus is community "with" Jesus. A disciple is a true disciple only when he is aware of this connection. The acknowledgement of Jesus must express itself in practical life style and as living "being with Jesus," as life community with Jesus.

2. In Matthew's Gospel Peter is the leading figure in the disciple circle. The concept is undisputed in the community. For this very reason the denial scene shows Peter also in his contradictory role: the dark side predominates, the light side passes into the background. Peter is presented asImm a warning example: Peter has denied.

3. The parenetic function of Peter's behavior for the community is quite evident. Peter's fall is an indication of the ever present possibility that even in the community the *perasmos*, the temptation, threatens believers. No one—the parenesis insists—is immune from a fall into the ditch of egotistical estrangement, into the night of denial and unbelief.

Peter's bitter tears as the first reaction to the reflection caused by the cock's crow evoke the thought of consolation. No failure or defection must be so conclusive that a halt and reversal is no longer possible. But this consolation for the community is no ticket to carefreeness and guilelessness; much more the imparted comfort wins its earnestness and weight against the background of the Our Father petition: "And lead us not into temptation!" (6:13).

Jesus Handed Over to Pilate, 27:1-2

Historically, until the fall of Jerusalem in A.D. 70, the Sanhedrin exercised broad powers in Palestine of a religious, political, and judicial nature. Necessarily, however, it was obliged to defer to the authority of the respective prefects (procurators) Rome appointed to Palestine. In Matthew's story, the Roman prefect of note is Pilate, so that it is only with his approval and under the auspices of his office that the sentence of death the Sanhedrin gives Jesus can legally be carried out.

> **27:1** When morning came, all the chief priests and the elders of the people conferred together against Jesus in order to bring about his death. **2** They bound him, led him away, and handed him over to Pilate the governor.

These two verses introduce the next scene, the hearing before Pilate in which Matthew takes up where 26:68 left off. These are connected with the preceding denial scene by redactional strokes (de with a genitive absolute construction). Also, the previously cited meeting of the "chief priests and the elders of the people" is continued (cf. 26:27); according to 26:59 the whole Sanhedrin is represented. Since Pilate is mentioned here for the first time, Matthew introduces him with his title of office.

Verses 1-2: According to 26:59 the chief priests and the whole Sanhedrin had sought a false witness against Jesus to kill him; according to 26:66 the guilty verdict is now confirmed. So one of the predictions of the third passion prediction in 20:18 is fulfilled: "Then they will hand him over to the Gentiles" (20:19).

The responsible officials of the Jewish people hand Jesus over to the pagan authorities. The death sentence that they had fixed upon, which was religiously motivated, will now (due to circumstances) be shifted to the political stage. The Jew, Jesus, may not die at the hands of Jews, his fellow believers. The responsibility will be shifted to a court that had nothing to do with religious questions. But the handing over is not just the consequence of the lack of competence, but also indicates that he is definitively expelled from the Jewish faith community. So the die is cast: with the handing over Jesus' fate is sealed, and the leaders of the Jewish people bear the responsibility.

Judas' Despair and suicide, 27:3-10

Having set the stage for the Roman trial, Matthew digresses in order to relate the death of Judas. Judas himself attests to both his own guilt

and the innocence of Jesus when in returning the pieces silver to the chief
priests and the elders in the temple, he declares, "I have sinned by betraying
innocent blood."

> 3 When Judas, his betrayer, saw that Jesus was condemned, he repented
> and brought back the thirty pieces of silver to the chief priests and the
> elders. 4 He said, "I have sinned by betraying innocent blood." But they
> said, "What is that to us? See to it yourself." 5 Throwing down the pieces
> of silver in the temple, he departed; and he went and hanged himself.
> 6 But the chief priests, taking the pieces of silver, said, "It is not lawful
> to put them into the treasury, since they are blood money." 7 After con-
> ferring together, they used them to buy the potter's field as a place to
> bury foreigners. 8 For this reason that field has been called the Field
> of Blood to this day. 9 Then was fulfilled what had been spoken through
> the prophet Jeremiah, "And they took the thirty pieces of silver, the price
> of the one on whom a price had been set, on whom some of the people
> of Israel had set a price, 10 and they gave them for the potter's field,
> as the Lord commanded me."

This pericope is special to Matthew. Judas' end is also reported by Acts
1:16-20; the two traditions differ on many significant points and so do
not go back to a common tradition. But a similarity is visible at those
points where the two traditions see events as fulfilling Old Testament
prophecies. Yet Matthew's tradition is not understandable out of Old
Testament texts alone. The climax of the narrative passed on by Matthew
lies in the fulfillment formula, which is typical for midrashic exegesis, to
which the entire narrative is ordered and which reveals Matthew's theological intention.

Verse 3: Judas comes to realize that Jesus' death sentence has been confirmed. He experiences remorse (in the Gospel tradition the verb
metamelomai, "rue," is found only in Matthew [cf. 21:30, 32]), i.e., he
regrets his action). The text does not speak of conversion or repentance;
the consequences of his action weigh upon him and drive him to return
the money, agreed upon in 26:15, to the Sanhedrin. The sum is named
not only because of 26:15, but above all because of the fulfillment citation in verse 9.

Verse 4: In direct address Judas acknowledges his crime: he has sinned
(for *hamartanō*, cf. 18:15) by betraying Jesus. Yet Jesus' name is avoided;
instead innocent blood appears (the adjective *athōos* is found in the New
Testament only in Matthew 27:4 and 27:24). Judas' self-incrimination is
expressed according to 23:35; the slaying of the Jewish prophets is the
background for term "innocent blood." But the members of the Sanhe-

drin refuse to assume responsibility. Their cool disdain and open irony makes Judas' despair complete. They are "guileful" and "callous," purchasing the services of Judas to betray Jesus, yet leaving him to his own devices in coming to terms with his burden of guilt.

Verse 5: The thread that runs throughout this scene is the blood money which Judas had received from the leaders (26:14-16) and which he now flings back at them in a vain effort to shed his guilt. Judas throws the money in the temple (Zech 11:12-13 is already having its effect on the narrative) and then hangs himself. The allusion is probably to Ahithophel, who betrayed King David for Absalom and then hanged himself when he lost favor with Absalom (2 Sam 17:23). Judas thus fulfills the command of scripture which the Sanhedrin refuses to observe: a false accuser must suffer the same fate as the falsely accused.

Verse 6: "Put them into the treasury" (*korbana*, LN 7. 33), which contained money that could be used only for cultic purposes. "Blood money" (*time haimatos*, LN 57.161): The hypocritical priests having engineered a major miscarriage of justice, suddenly become very scrupulous about the use of the money (cf. 23:23-24). Although various forms of ill-gotten gain were prohibited from use in the temple (cf. Deut 23:18), nothing in the Old Testament covers this exact case.

With the exception of Judas, Jesus' conflict with the disciples does not end in failure for them. As for the guilt of the religious leaders, the chief priests are made to acknowledge this in the words they themselves utter about the "blood money." "And concerning the irony that God is at work in the passion of Jesus to accomplish his purposes, Matthew notes that the religious leaders, in using the blood money Judas had thrown down in the temple to purchase a potter's field for the burial of strangers, unwittingly fulfill OT prophecy (27:6-10)" (*Story*, 88).

Verses 7: To be on he safe side, they use the money to buy a field as a cemetery for "strangers" (probably Gentiles visiting Jerusalem). "The unclean money is used to bury unclean people in an unclean place" (Meier, 339).

Verse 8: "Field of blood to this day." Matthew then tells us that there is a field called the Field of Blood even at his time. Acts 1:19 supplies the Aramaic name, Hakeldama. Later tradition locates this field to the southeast of Jerusalem, at the eastern end of the valley Hinnom ("Gehemma").

In such passages as 24:15 ("let the reader understand"), 27:8 ("this day"), and 28:1-5 ("to this day"), Matthew "bursts the bounds of the story he is telling of the life and ministry of Jesus in order to address the implied reader directly. Temporarily, these passages locate the implied reader at a point after the resurrection but short of the Parousia (cf. *Story*, 147).

Verse 10: Matthew adds a detailed Scripture citation (from Zach 11:13, yet with echoes of Jer 18:2-3; 32:7-9). Thereby he makes it known how he understands the Field of Blood and the suicide tradition. The quote is intended to "prove" that the high priests' use of blood money—and only they are involved—is the fulfillment of an Old Testament prophecy. Not Judas, but some of the sons of Israel, namely the high priests, take the money and give it as payment for the potter's field.

The message for the community in this passage, special to Matthew, lies not primarily in Judas' death; this is mentioned only in passing. Important for the community is the information about what happened to the betrayal wages. The theme of the purchase underlies the entire pericope. It was blood money that, as exchange price, had been paid out; it was money therefore, that was covered with the blood of a prophet. Judas wanted to give it back to free himself of his guilty conscience, the sanhedrenists refuse to provide the relief. Then Judas throws it into the temple, but the money is unclean, it was suitable only for the purchase of a potter's field. The "fate" of the blood money and of all connected with it makes manifest that—against a background of Old Testament prophecy— the exchange value, the delivered-up Jesus, was in reality "innocent blood."

Jesus is Delivered to Pilate, 27:11-14

Faced with the Jewish conspiracy against Jesus, Pilate makes himself complicit by acceding to their demands. The role Pilate plays in the passion account is thus not unlike that of Judas, for by abetting the Jewish conspiracy, Pilate is at the same time, ironically, facilitating God's plan of salvation. At Jesus' hearing, Pilate makes Jesus' identity the issue. He asks Jesus whether he is the 'King of the Jews,' and Jesus replies in the affirmative (v. 11). To Pilate, Jesus' reply means, based on his evaluative point of view, that Jesus is an insurrectionist (27:37). But in spite of this, Pilate indicates by the way he conducts Jesus' hearing that he believes him to be innocent of this charge.

> 11 Now Jesus stood before the governor; and the governor asked him, "Are you the king of the Jews?" Jesus said, "You say so." 12 But when he was accused by the chief priests and elders, he did not answer. 13 Then Pilate said to him, "Do you not hear how many accusations they make against you?" 14 But he gave him no answer, not even to a single charge, so that the governor was greatly amazed.

Verse 11: The first part of the scene reports the governor's question and Jesus' answer. Because of the interjection of the Judas scene, Matthew must start with a new introduction. The official character of the hearing he underlines through the office title "governor." The governor's question leads straightway to the politically charged kernel of the complaint—the accusers argued that Jesus' king claim had political relevance. "King of the Jews" is met in Matthew only in the mouth of non-Jews (2:2; 27:11, 29, 37), the Jews themselves speak of "King of Israel" (27:42). Jesus' reply corresponds to that which he gave in the hearing before the Sanhedrin: "You have said so," i.e., your are right (cf. 26:25; 26:64). The truth brought to expression in the question is confirmed. "You have answered your own question." Jesus answer is half-confirmatory; the ambiguous "you say so" both affirms Jesus' true messiahship and denies the worldly, political connotations.

"The king of the Jews" (11-14). Pilate deals with Jesus on the presumption that the Messiah, the King of the Jews, is one who lays political claim to the throne of Israel. Since Pilate accedes to the charge that Jesus is the King of the Jews, he permits Jesus to be crucified (27:37). According to Pilate's evaluative point of view, too, Jesus is an insurrectionist.

A tactic Matthew employs effectively is to place titles in formulas of identification ("predication formulas") so as to advise the reader in words (declarations or questions) uttered by characters in the story that Jesus is the Messiah (16:16), or is the King of the Jews (Israel) (27:11, 42), or is the Son of David (12:23), or *is* the Son of God (4:33). Significantly, "the Son of Man" never appears in a formula of identification.

In mocking Jesus as "the King of Israel" and the "Son of God," as he hangs on the cross the religious leaders unwittingly attest to the very truths they earlier repudiated as Jesus stood trial before them ("Son of God"; 26:63-64) and was interrogated by Pilate ("King of the Jews"; 27:11).

Verse 12: In the second part of the scene the chief priests and the elders come forward as complainants (*kategoreo*: accuse, declare guilty, charge); Matthew stresses expressly that Jesus refuses to answer (cf. v. 14).

Verse 13: In the third part of the text Pilate speaks once more. Now his question is concerned not with Jesus' silence, but with his "not hearing." This is the only way the astonished Pilate can explain Jesus' silence for himself. As in the hearing before the Sanhedrin (26:57-68), Matthew speaks of "false" testimony, thus establishing a parallel between the two hearings: apparently Pilate judges the complaint of the Jews as true testimony for the prosecution.

Verse 14: "Not even to a single charge." The interrogation closes with Pilate's amazement at Jesus. Despite the governor's encouragement that he answer the charges made against him, Jesus refuses to respond, "not even to a single charge." Matthew may have in mind a similar passage in Isaiah: "Kings shall shut their mouths because of him; for that which had not been told them they shall see" (52:14-15).

Jesus Barabbas or Jesus the Messiah, 27:15-26

The religious leaders practice deceit once more in the scene in which Pilate grants Barabbas release but delivers Jesus to the Roman solders to be crucified. Although Barabbas is known to be a "notorious prisoner" and their motive for acting against Jesus is jealousy or "malice," they persuade the crowds, who in turn prevail upon Pilate, to choose freedom for Barabbas but crucifixion for Jesus.

> **15** Now at the festival the governor was accustomed to release a prisoner for the crowd, anyone whom they wanted. **16** At that time they had a notorious prisoner, called Jesus Barabbas. **17** So after they had gathered, Pilate said to them, "Whom do you want me to release for you, Jesus Barabbas or Jesus who is called the Messiah?" **18** For he realized that it was out of jealousy that they had handed him over. **19** While he was sitting on the judgment seat, his wife sent word to him, "Have nothing to do with that innocent man, for today I have suffered a great deal because of a dream about him." **20** Now the chief priests and the elders persuaded the crowds to ask for Barabbas and to have Jesus killed. **21** The governor again said to them, "Which of the two do you want me to release for you?" And they said, "Barabbas." **22** Pilate said to them, "Then what should I do with Jesus who is called the Messiah?" All of them said, "Let him be crucified!" **23** Then he asked, "Why, what evil has he done?" But they shouted all the more, "Let him be crucified!" **24** So when Pilate saw that he could do nothing, but rather that a riot was beginning, he took some water and washed his hands before the crowd, saying, "I am innocent of this man's blood; see to it yourselves." **25** Then the people as a whole answered, "His blood be on us and on our children!" **26** So he released Barabbas for them; and after flogging Jesus, he handed him over to be crucified.

The hearing before Pilate had ended with the statement that Pilate was "greatly amazed" at Jesus' behavior; so the outcome of the hearing remained open. But Pilate must act, and he does this with an attempt to save Jesus by making use of an amnesty. Matthew omits details that are unimportant to him, and, as usual, develops the dialogue character of the scene.

Verse 15: Matthew sets off the pericope with a new introduction of the governor. According to Matthew the paschal amnesty was sanctioned by custom (*eiōtha* [per. of *ethō*], "to be accustomed"). For this custom there is some historical background but Matthew is interested not in the historical fact, but in the divine action manifesting itself in Jesus. Matthew expressly mentions the release to the "crowd"; the *ochlos* is usually the nameless public at Jesus' works, but can also—as here—manifest its fickleness. In what follows, the crowd takes a position against Jesus.

Verse 16: "Called Jesus Barabbas." Barabbas is a minor character who is introduced by name, and makes a sudden appearance, only to vanish quickly again: "Joseph" (1:18–2:23) and "Mary" (1:18, 13:55) are two other such characters. "Barabbas" serves as a foil for Jesus: a notorious prisoner is set free, whereas an innocent man is delivered up to be crucified.

Verse 18: "He realized that it was out of jealousy." Pilate knows that Jesus had been handed over because of the jealousy of the crowd and its leaders. *Pithonos* ("envy, resentment," LN 88.160) stands here (as also in Mark) somewhat surprisingly as a motive; yet behind it is the Old Testament Jewish tradition that envy specifies the common mind-set of the wicked. Thus we read in Wisdom that: "Through the devil's envy death entered the world, and those who belong to his party experience it" (2:24) (cf. 6:23; 1 Macc 8:16).

Verse 19: Pilate's "wife" serves as a foil for Pilate himself; her warning to Pilate not to have anything to do with "that innocent man" (Jesus) contrasts with Pilate's decision to accede to the Jewish demand that Jesus be put to death.

Verse 20: "Persuaded the crowds." In their guile they are "manipulative," persuading the crowds to demand of Pilate that Jesus be put to death (26:4; 27:20).

Verb 23: "What evil has he done?" Pilate is satisfied that he can proceed legally against Jesus because of his admission that he is "king of the Jews," yet he senses the evil design of the Jewish leaders. The last attempt to save Jesus from death comes in the form of the question about his guilt: What evil, what crime has he committed? This must be presented as stated charge if a death sentence is to be handed down. The reaction of the crowd, which had made a decision long before, consists in the (now more frenzied) demand for Jesus' crucifixion.

Verses 24: "I am innocent of this man's blood." Once Pilate can be satisfied that he has absolved himself of any guilt associated with Jesus' death and that the Jews have taken full responsibility for it, he consents to the legal plea that Jesus be crucified and delivers him to the soldiers.

Verse 25: "His blood be on us." It is ironic that the people to whom God had sent Jesus as Shepherd and King (2:6), should also shout aloud to Pilate, the Roman governor, "His blood be on us and on our children!" The repudiation of Jesus by the people of Israel is complete. They believe they are acting in a God-pleasing manner in order to put to an end to a movement initiated by one who was a false messiah. But they achieve just the opposite: Israel's demise as God' special people. They bring a curse upon themselves and the people, provoke the destruction of Jerusalem (22:7), and unknowingly make themselves responsible for the transfer of God's Rule to another nation, the Church, which becomes God's end-time people.

Verse 26: Finally ("So") Barabbas is released but Jesus is delivered up to scourging and death (cf. the third passion prediction 20:19).

Mockery of the King, 27:27-31

After the hearing before Pilate the soldiers take Jesus to the governor's headquarters, and there make mockery of him as the King of the Jews. By this act, they unwittingly show in what way Jesus truly is the King of the Jews. He is so, not as one who restores to Israel its national splendor and not as one who foments rebellion against Rome, but as the one who saves others by willingly giving himself over to suffering and death.

> 27 Then the soldiers of the governor took Jesus into the governor's headquarters, and they gathered the whole cohort around him. 28 They stripped him and put a scarlet robe on him, 29 and after twisting some thorns into a crown, they put it on his head. They put a reed in his right hand and knelt before him and mocked him, saying, "Hail, King of the Jews!" 30 They spat on him, and took the reed and struck him on the head. 31 After mocking him, they stripped him of the robe and put his own clothes on him. Then they led him away to crucify him.

Verse 27: "Into the governor's headquarters." The governor normally resided at Caesarea Maritima, on the Mediterranean coast; he took up residence in Jerusalem only during the great feasts, when there would be a danger of riot from the large crowds. Whether Pilate's headquarters was the Palace of Herod in western Jerusalem or the fortress Antonia to the northwest of the temple area, is still disputed. A cohort or battalion at full strength numbered 600 men.

Verse 28: "Put a scarlet robe." Scarlet was the color of the ordinary Roman soldier's outer tunic.

Verse 29: "Hail, King of the Jews." The crown of thorns was intended not so much to cause physical pain as to mock Jesus' royal claim. The thorns were meant to imitate the rays of light which radiated from the head of a divinity, symbolized in the pointed edges of a kings' diadem. Matthew adds a reed in Jesus' right hand as a mock-scepter. They kneel as suppliants and greet him with the same *chaire* ("Hail") that Judas used (26:49).

Verse 31: At the end of the pericope, two facts are mentioned in preparation for the scenes at the cross. The soldiers clothe Jesus in his own garments, thus preparing for the dividing of his garments in verse 35. And, despite the fact that Pilate has handed over Jesus to the Jews, the actual execution is carried out by Gentile soldiers, thus preparing for their confession of faith in verse 54.

When Jesus entered Jerusalem as the Son of David, Matthew refers to him as the "humble King" (21:5). This reference points ahead to chapter 27, which tells of the suffering Jesus endures as King at the hands of Pilate. Matthew provides a detailed sketch of the true nature of Jesus' kingship: as he stands draped in a scarlet robe with a crown of thorns on his head and a reed for a scepter in his right hand, the soldiers abuse him and, kneeling in mock obeisance before him, hail him as "King of the Jews." While "King" characterizes Jesus Messiah as a political throne-pretender in the eyes of his enemies, in the eyes of Matthew, it characterizes him as the one in the line of David who establishes his rule, not by exercising dominance over his people, but by suffering on their behalf.

"In Matthew's perspective, therefore, Jesus as the Messiah is not a prophetic but a royal figure. He comes from the house of David, and the entire history of Israel culminates in him; indeed, he means salvation or damnation for people. As the 'King of the Jews [Israel],' the 'public' conception of him is that he is a political throne-pretender. In reality, however, he is the King of his people in the sense that he suffers on their behalf" (*Matthew*, 36).

Jesus is Led to Golgotha, 27:32-38

Matthew presents Jesus' crucifixion as a testing. At Golgotha and on the cross, Jesus does not permit concern for self to put him at odds with God's appointed plan that he relinquish his life.

> **32** As they went out, they came upon a man from Cyrene named Simon; they compelled this man to carry his cross. **33** And when they came to a place called Golgotha (which means Place of a Skull), **34** they offered

him wine to drink, mixed with gall; but when he tasted it, he would not drink it. **35** And when they had crucified him, they divided his clothes among themselves by casting lots; **36** then they sat down there and kept watch over him. **37** Over his head they put the charge against him, which read, "This is Jesus, the King of the Jews." **38** Then two bandits were crucified with him, one on his right and one on his left.

Verse 32: Simon [of Cyrene], who carries Jesus' cross is a "minor character," one of those who appear briefly in a scene then vanish.

Verse 33: "Which means Place of a Skull." Another striking instance of narrative commentary. "In such passages the implied author disrupts the story to speak directly to the reader. Such comments also indicate the place in time that the implied author would assign himself (*Story*, 33). This is one of the three times Matthew provides a translation of Semitic words (1:23; 27:33, 46). At other times he leaves them untranslated (cf. *hraka*, 5:22).

Verse 34: "They offered him wine." Just as his obedience to God led Jesus to suffer hunger in the desert, so now it leads him to suffer thirst on the cross (cf. 4:3-4).

Verse 35: "They divide his clothes." Out of obedience to God, Jesus endures the total loss of all he possesses (his clothes) and even of the prerogative to have his body disposed of as he would wish.

Verse 37: "The charge against him." Herod the Great and, later, Pilate take "King of the Jews" to mean that Jesus is an insurrectionist (2:6, 12; 27:37). Since Pilate accedes to the charge that Jesus is the King of the Jews, he permits Jesus to be crucified.

Verse 38: "Two bandits were crucified." The two robbers are placed on either side of Jesus, perhaps as mock royal attendants, perhaps to make of Jesus the head robber.

Jesus Mocked on the Cross, 27:39-44

On the cross, Jesus exemplifies his own teaching by resisting the temptation to do as the passersby, the religious leaders, and the two robbers call on him to do, namely, to save himself by using his power to descend from the cross.

39 Those who passed by derided him, shaking their heads and **40** saying, "You who would destroy the temple and build it in three days, save yourself! If you are the Son of God, come down from the cross." **41**

> In the same way the chief priests also, along with the scribes and elders, were mocking him, saying, **42** "He saved others; he cannot save himself. He is the King of Israel; let him come down from the cross now, and we will believe him. **43** He trusts in God; let God deliver him now, if he wants to; for he said, 'I am God's Son.' " **44** The bandits who were crucified with him also taunted him in the same way.

To the anonymous passersby are added the chief priests, the scribes, and elders, so making up the whole hierarchy of the Jewish people (v. 41). Even the robbers who were crucified with Jesus reviled him. The motive is the same in all cases: this fellow did not live up to his claim of dignity. The mocking words are interrelated and all consist of two parts: a citation of a saying of Jesus is followed by a demand that he help himself. In verse 43 this twofold relationship is given a forceful theological expression: "He trusts in God." Jesus Messiah, crucified as "King of the Jews," even now in death, in his last agony, must experience the contemptuous mockery of the world. The mockers refuse to acknowledge him as "Son of God" (v. 40, 43).

Verse 39: "Those who passed by." The introduction to the third mocking scene corresponds to Psalm 22:7: "All who see me mock at me; they make mouths at me, they wag their heads." Matthew has made this "key" psalm of Old Testament tradition an interpretative key to his Christologically oriented passion tradition. In condemning Jesus to death at his trial and in blaspheming and mocking him as he hangs upon he cross, the Sanhedrin in the one instance, and the passersby and the religious leaders in the other, repudiate Jesus' claim to be the Son of God.

The mockeries of the passers-by and the religious leaders around the cross resemble in both phraseology and substance the temptations by Satan in chapter 4; they call upon Jesus to demonstrate his divine Sonship by means of a sign. Jesus refuses to yield to these appeals, and with a loud cry he dies (27:50). "Thus the predictions that Jesus made regarding his death come to fulfillment; moreover, his death culminates the process of handing over to the chief priests and elders, handing over to the Gentiles, being mocked, scourged, and crucified" (Bauer, 102).

Verse 40: "If you are the Son of God." Matthew's understanding of Jesus' passion comes to a climax in this conditional expression of the mockers ("if": if really). The passersby imply that Jesus had claimed the authority to tear down the temple on Zion and in its place to build a messianic temple (cf. at 26:61). But this claim is only legitimate if Jesus is the end-time "Son of God," if he is the Messiah sent by God and the one commissioned by the Father. "This messianic identity, as it is contained in various Christological titles, is the burning point of the Matthean presentation of the suffering Jesus" (*Passion*, 284). "Come down from the cross." The phraseology betrays that the passersby, like Satan previously, are testing Jesus and that they consequently have aligned themselves with Satan.

Verses 41-42: "He is the king of Israel." Finally the Jewish leaders, too, join in the chorus of the mockers. The ability to help others fails in the hour when Jesus himself needs help. In the mocking scenes attending the trial and the crucifixion, members of the Sanhedrin make Jesus' identity the object of their ridicule. Matthew places these titles in formulas of identification ("Predication formulas") so as to advise the reader in words (declarations or questions) uttered by characters in the story that Jesus is the Messiah (cf. 16:16), or *is* the King of the Jews (Israel).

Verse 43: "He trusts in God." This verse consists of two saying elements: first the citation of Psalm 22, then the repetition of the Son of God title. It is striking that the citation of Psalm 22:8 comes from the mouths of mockers. This illustrates the way the religious leaders relate to God's word in scripture. The irony is that while they are indeed instrumental in bringing this word to fulfillment, they do so as ones who falsify it and who appeal to it with perverse intent, who repudiate the Son whom God has promised in it to Israel.

Verse 44: Finally in the mocking scene a third group is named which reviles Jesus: the robbers (cf. v. 38). They mock in the same way; their mockery is on the same level as the foregoing. Indirectly, Matthew reduces the mocking leaders to the same level as the robbers.

The passers-by and the religious leaders call out to Jesus to come down from the cross in order to prove that he is the Son of God (v. 43). Moreover, the Roman soldiers confess that Jesus was the Son of God (v. 54). "Jesus thus dies as the obedient Son of God who demonstrates his divine sonship not by performing supernatural signs, but by suffering and dying in compliance with the will of his Father. The climactic movement towards the cross indicates, further, that by dying as the obedient Son of God, Jesus gives his life as a ransom for many (20.28), thus saving his people from their sins (1.21; 26.28)" (Bauer, 144).

Jesus' Death on the Cross, 27:45-54

Jesus' death is accompanied by signs which come not from Jesus, but from God. By means of the supernatural portents, God himself bears witness that Jesus was his Son. In response to these signs, the Roman soldiers cry out, "Truly this man was God's Son!" (v. 54). Thus, in contrast to the Jewish leaders and passers-by, the soldiers rightly interpret the events surrounding the death of Jesus and vindicate Jesus' claim to be the Son of God (cf. 21:37-38; 26:63-64).

> **45** From noon on, darkness came over the whole land until three in the afternoon. **46** And about three o'clock Jesus cried with a loud voice, "Eli, Eli, lema' sabachthani?" that is, "My God, my God, why have you forsaken me?" **47** When some of the bystanders heard it, they said, "This man is calling for Elijah." **48** At once one of them ran and got a sponge, filled it with sour wine, put it on a stick, and gave it to him to drink. **49** But the others said, "Wait, let us see whether Elijah will come to save him." **50** Then Jesus cried again with a loud voice and breathed his last. **51** At that moment the curtain of the temple was torn in two, from top to bottom. The earth shook, and the rocks were split. **52** The tombs also were opened, and many bodies of the saints who had fallen asleep were raised. **53** After his resurrection they came out of the tombs and entered the holy city and appeared to many. **54** Now when the centurion and those with him, who were keeping watch over Jesus, saw the earthquake and what took place, they were terrified and said, "Truly this man was God's Son!"

Verse 45: "Darkness came over the whole earth." In many instances "setting," the place, time, or social circumstances in which a character acts, is of minimal importance. "By contrast, in other instances the setting may be highly charged with meaning. For example, when Matthew reports as Jesus hangs upon the cross, how 'from the sixth hour there was darkness over all the land until the ninth hour' (27:45), he conveys a strong sense of impending disaster" (*Story*, 28).

Verse 46: "That is, 'My God, my God'—another instance of narrative commentary providing inside information. Other striking examples of narrative commentary in Matthew's story are the genealogy (1:1-17); the formula-quotations; the explanation of terms (1:23; 27:33) or translation of foreign words (v. 46). Bilingualism remains an open question. "If at times he translates Semitic words (1:23; 27:33. 46), at other times he leaves them untranslated" (*Story*, 151).

The quotation from Psalm 22:2 is given first in a Hebrew-Aramaic form, then in a Greek translation. The numerous text variants are understandably more numerous in the Hebrew-Aramaic text than in the Greek text. But despite the considerable text variants there is no substantial difference. Jesus speaks the beginning of Psalm 22; this was intended to make it easier to explain why in the appeal to God in Matthew's Hebrew form, the misunderstanding in connection with "Elijah" (cf. v. 47) could arise. Matthew's interest is concentrated on the second verse of the psalm; that Jesus prayed the whole psalm is only a conjecture. Death cry and psalm verse lie on the same level; they bring to expression (as "outcry" and "prayer in need") the abandonment by God of the Suffering Just One. For Matthew they are an opportunity to present the scriptural fulfillment of the divine plan of salvation and the obedient submission of the Son to the Father's will. The mockery and the abandonment, which have characterized the course of events up to this point, reach their high point in Jesus' loud and dramatic cry of abandonment—the Just One feels the full weight of his undertaking.

Verse 47: "This man is calling for Elijah." Matthew presents the crucifixion as a testing. Jesus does not attempt to appeal to Elijah for miraculous deliverance, as some standing at the foot of the cross mistakenly think he does. On the contrary, as Jesus nears the moment he himself has chosen for his death (v. 50), he faces his sense of abandonment by God by crying out to God in trust. Nor is God to disappoint the "trust unto death" that Jesus places in him; on the third day, he is to raise Jesus from the dead. Some bystanders interpret the cry and the prayer falsely. Here Elijah, corresponding to the popular conception, is represented as a helper (cf. J. Jeremias, *Helias*, in TWNT II 930-943, 937). The stressed "this man" standing at the end in the Greek is a contemptuous *houtos*.

Verses 48-49: One of them fills a sponge with sour wine (vinegar), to mitigate Jesus' death pain. But the others ally themselves with the crowd of mockers and tormentors under the cross and try to hinder the good deed. Don't give him any wine; let's see whether Elijah will come to save him (*aphes* here has the sense of "let it be!"). Also the use of the verb "to save" (cf. v. 40, 42 [twice]) underlines the bystanders' sarcasm.

Verse 50: "Jesus cried again." A second cry of agony, stronger than the first (cf. *krazō*, cry, over against *anaboaō*) comes immediately before Jesus' definitive death. The word "cry, scream" as expression of need in the widest sense stems from the agony psalms (Ps 18:7; 22:3, 6, 25; 69:4). Through the (rare in Matthew) "again" the evangelist connects the death cry with verse 46. Since in verse 46 the cry is immediately interpreted as a cry for help, so too is the second, wordless cry. The phrase, "breathed his last" betrays the intention to represent Jesus' death as a voluntary and knowing act of free self-surrender.

Verses 51: "Torn in two, from top to bottom." On the whole, description of spatial settings in the Gospels seems limited to dramatic and utilitarian effect. Scenery is only important insofar as it affects specified actions of the characters. Yet it may also mean that the narrative assumes certain perceptions on the part of the implied reader that do not come automatically to real readers today. Thus when the Gospels report the rending of the temple curtain at Jesus death, "the implied author may be assuming his reader knows what Josephus tells us outright, namely, that the temple curtain was in fact a tapestry on which the heavens were pictorially displayed" (Powell, 72). This establishes a striking parallel between the rending of the heavens at Jesus baptism and the rending of the temple veil at Jesus' death.

Verse 52-53: "The tombs also were opened." Matthew has added to the picture of the tearing of the temple curtain four additional signs, with which the Jewish apocalyptic (cf. Amos 8:9; Joel 2:10; Dan 12:2; Ez 37:1-14) describes the end of the old and the beginning of the new aeon. Matthew stands in this tradition when he represents Jesus' death as cosmic upheaval and rising of the dead. The old world must release the dead for the new, whom God now raises up. Jesus' death was accompanied by cosmic signs which, among other things, point to the eschatological waking of the dead. The separation between God and his people, as expressed in the temple veil, is removed (cf. Eph 2:11-22; Heb 6:19; 10:19). Jesus' death replaces not only the temple cult; much more, it opens up a new salvation economy.

Verse 54: "This man was God's Son." Upon Jesus' death the Roman soldiers, uttering words that are in alignment with God's understanding of Jesus, affirm Jesus to be God's Son. With this affirmation Matthew has, in terms of narrating his story, guided it to a point where knowledge of the identity of Jesus also embraces, as far as the reader is concerned, a mature knowledge of the purpose of Jesus' earthly ministry. So doing, Matthew places the pagans in community with the disciples, who in 14:33 (cf. 16:16) had made a confession to the Christ using the same words.

The Women as Witnesses, 27:55-56

The cross is not the end. The narrative moves on to its ultimate climax. The predictions of Jesus, which have all been fulfilled, included not only death but also resurrection. Indeed, there was mention of Jesus' resurrection in the middle of the account of the crucifixion (27:53). The women who follow Jesus from Galilee witness his death, and they form the link between the crucifixion and resurrection narratives.

55 Many women were also there, looking on from a distance; they had followed Jesus from Galilee and had provided for him. 56 Among them

were Mary Magdalene, and Mary the mother of James and Joseph, and the mother of the sons of Zebedee.

This short narrative piece has a twofold objective: it names witnesses of Jesus' death and mentions by name some persons who were especially close to Jesus, some of whom will also play an important role in the last scene of the passion account.

Verse 55: "Many women were also there" (Matthew maintains spatial unity with the adverb "there" [*ekei*]), looking on from afar. They had followed Jesus from Galilee to Jerusalem and had helped him in various ways. Their presence at the crucifixion makes them witnesses, comparable to the centurion and his soldiers. Because they "followed after" and were "ready to help," they are presented not only as legitimate but as especially outstanding witnesses. Because both cost and commitment is connected with their "following," theirs is discipleship in the metaphorical sense.

Verse 56: "Mary Magdalene"—a minor character who is also a "stock" character, possessing one trait only. But in contrast to the disciples, the religious leaders, and the crowds, they cannot be treated as though they were all alike. The particular trait of any one or group of these persons is what determines to what extent the reader approves or disapproves of that person or group.

The three women are cited by name. Mary, who comes from Magdala, is found—as in Mark—in all the lists of women. The second Mary was the wife of Clopas (John 19:25), the mother of James and Joseph. Then Salome, whom Mark mentions, Matthew identifies as the mother of the sons of Zebedee. The use of the names shows that these three women were held in special respect in the community tradition.

Although the crucifixion and death scene reached their climax in verse 54, Matthew does not take over our two verses just out of "fidelity to tradition." The women are disciples of Jesus who, through serving followership of Jesus, have displayed exemplary reverence. And although they follow the event only from afar, they are, for Matthew's community, important witnesses of the death (and later after the resurrection) of Jesus. But not least, Matthew mentions them because they—unlike the disciples—beyond suffering and death (cf. 27:61; 28:1, 8, 9-10) perdure in their discipleship and have shown themselves faithful to their commitment. Their witness gives the community an example that renders possible the new beginning of the post-Easter community.

The Tomb is Provided, 27:57-61

Like Mary Magdalene, Joseph of Arimathea is a minor character who is also a "stock" character (cf. 27:56), with one trait only. In Mark (15:43) and Luke (23:50-51), Joseph of Arimathea is a member of the council who is looking for the kingdom of God, but in Matthew he is a "rich man . . . who also was a disciple of Jesus."

> 57 When it was evening there came a rich man from Arimathea, named Joseph, who was also a disciple of Jesus. 58 He went to Pilate and asked for the body of Jesus; then Pilate ordered it to be given to him. 59 So Joseph took the body and wrapped it in a clean linen cloth 60 and laid it in his own new tomb, which he had hewn in the rock. He then rolled a great stone to the door of the tomb and went away. 61 Mary Magdalene and the other Mary were there, sitting opposite the tomb.

Behind this short passage was a burial scene which originally was passed on independently. It is a narrative unit, distinct yet related to the preceding, in which the burial (vv. 57-61), the guarding scene (vv. 62-66; 28:11-15), the scene of the empty grave (28:1-5) and the meeting with the women (28:10), were bound together in a content unit.

Verse 57: "When it was evening." A factual break is indicated. Matthew's first reference to "the day of Preparation" comes only in verse 62, since the persons involved are introduced there. Joseph of Arimathea is a rich man, who could afford a grave site close by Jerusalem (and the temple). Joseph himself had become a disciple of Jesus and so did not belong to closed circle of Jewish opposition.

Verse 58: The rich and influential man obtained from Pilate the surrender of the corpse (*sōma* is here—as throughout Homer—the dead man, cf. 27:52). Pilate, the highest ranking authority in this matter, "ordered" the dead body to be handed over (Matthew manages to avoid using the Greek *nekros*, corpse, of the dead Jesus. He knows this term only in relation to dead men: 8:22; 22:32; 23:27; 28:4). Any doubt about the death of Jesus is out of the question.

Verses 59-60: The rich Joseph of Arimathea shows the dead Jesus the reverence due to him; "clean" shroud, i.e., a linen shroud not previously used, a "new" grave, i.e., not previously used, prepared for his own use. Finally Joseph rolls a great stone across the door of the grave, which is also a security measure.

Verse 66: According to 27:56, the two Marys waiting there are witnesses of the event. And as their final service of love at the grave, they sit in wake, by which the continuation of the narrative is assured, and the motive of security as well.

The person who carries out the burial is a disciple of Jesus and so belongs to the large band of *mathētai*. Thereby Joseph of Arimathea becomes an example for the members of the community. The meaning of this example will be further underlined when it is seen and judged in contrast to the rich young man (cf. 19:16-22, 23-26).

The two women (cf. the number two as witnesses in Jewish judicial proceedings) fit in the context of the "security motif" so important for Matthew (cf. the "great" stone before the "door" of the grave). As watchers up to the onset of the strict Sabbath rest they become witnesses against the suspicion that Jesus' body was stolen, a charge leveled again and again against Matthew's community (cf. at 28:11-15).

The Tomb is Sealed, 27:62-66

The religious leaders thought that Jesus' death and burial meant that Jesus, a false messiah who had infected Israel with perilous error, had, as necessity dictated, been destroyed. Yet they are "apprehensive of the future," as they have been throughout Matthew's story. They are concerned that not even the death of Jesus will succeed in purging Israel of the "deception" he has perpetrated.

> 62 The next day, that is, after the day of Preparation, the chief priests and the Pharisees gathered before Pilate 63 and said, "Sir, we remember what that impostor said while he was still alive, 'After three days I will rise again.' 64 Therefore command the tomb to be made secure until the third day; otherwise his disciples may go and steal him away, and tell the people, 'He has been raised from the dead,' and the last deception would be worse than the first." 65 Pilate said to them, "You have a guard of soldiers; go, make it as secure as you can." 66 So they went with the guard and made the tomb secure by sealing the stone.

"Matthew inserts in verses 62-66 a unique report of the setting of a guard at Jesus' tomb, to prepare for a second insertion in 28:11-13, which tells about the bribed circulation of a false report that the disciples stole Jesus' body. These two insertions contrast the deceitfulness of the Jewish leaders and the truthfulness of Jesus in predicting his resurrection after three days. Such truthfulness gives encouragement to his persecuted followers. They may trust his word and hope for like vindication" (Gundry, 582).

Verse 62: "After the day of preparation." The foregoing account is set off with *de*, whereby the watching women are distinguished from the chief priests and the Pharisees. The activity of this group begins on the following day, so on the Sabbath; but Matthew forgoes any mention of this particular. For him the discussion about a possible violation of the Sabbath is irrelevant; his apologetic purpose is uppermost in his mind. The Pharisees are named for the only time in the passion account. They were the ones who had heard Jesus say that he would rise after three days (12:40).

Verse 63: "Sir, we remember." The flattering address "Sir" (*kyrie*) accorded Pilate is in Matthew's style and underlines Pilate's acknowledged authority. The remark "we remember how" sounds like an apology for coming only now with their request; for in the meantime some time has passed, during which what they are only now laying to the charge of Jesus' disciples could have happened. "That impostor" (*planos* [only here in Matthew], one who leads into error, a seducer) betrays their low opinion of Jesus. The statement made by Jesus in his lifetime about his resurrection "after three days" can only refer to 12:40 (the Jonah sign) because Matthew otherwise always speaks of resurrection "on the third day" (16:21; 17:23; 20:19).

Verse 64: "Tomb to be made secure." For the refutation of Jesus' statement a securing of the grave "until the third day" would suffice. The Jews suspect Jesus and his disciples of a fraud to be staged so that it could be said that the statement about the rising of Jesus from the dead had been realized.

Verse 65: Pilate gives way to the pressure, even if unwillingly: "You have a guard! [i.e., your own temple guard—so use them!" Then you wouldn't need to bother the governor. The statement is not indicative but imperative and is clarified by two further imperatives: "Get out!" and "Guard the grave!" "Make it as secure as you can, *Hōs oidate*" are tinged with contempt and scorn.

Verse 66: The Jewish authorities immediately act on their permission, supplementing the guard with a seal on the grave.

The key words of the pericope are "deception" and "security." The suspicions of fraud are aimed at Jesus and his disciples; the content of the intended fraud is to "prove' the prediction of resurrection by stealing the body. Beyond Jesus' death, they want to reduce his claim to absurdity.

That they themselves with this fraud theory do not recognize the absurdity of their procedures is made clear by the exaggerated security measures. A—even if applied too late—guard (and supplementary sealing) should guarantee that a theft is not possible. The incomprehension of the hierarchy could not be made clearer; and this is the point of the passage: their last deception is worse than their first.

The Discovery of the Empty Tomb, 28:1-8

The *fact* that Jesus was raised from the dead stood at the center of early Christian preaching (1 Cor 15:4-5; Rom 1:3-4; 4:25). The *manner* and *circumstances* of the resurrection and the resurrection appearances (like the infancy narratives) lay outside of the normative pattern of the earliest preaching. Certain basic facts were known, but beyond those facts the evangelists were free to pursue their own theological interests.

As had been the case throughout the passion narrative, Matthew utilizes source material from Mark but stamps it with his own distinctive brand. In the case of the resurrection, Mark provides only the story of the discovery of the empty tomb (16:1-8). Matthew adds to that his own special traditions, reporting an appearance of Jesus to the women at the tomb (28:9-10), the continued efforts of Jesus' opponents to counteract the announcement of resurrection (28:11-16), and the final appearance of Jesus to his disciples on a mountain in Galilee, with its climactic missionary commission (28:16-20).

> **28:1** After the sabbath, as the first day of the week was dawning, Mary Magdalene and the other Mary went to see the tomb. **2** And suddenly there was a great earthquake for an angel of the Lord, descending from heaven, came and rolled back the stone and sat on it. **3** His appearance was like lightning, and his clothing white as snow. **4** For fear of him the guards shook and became like dead men. **5** But the angel said to the women, "Do not be afraid; I know that you are looking for Jesus who was crucified. **6** He is not here; for he has been raised, as he said. Come, see the place where he lay. **7** Then go quickly and tell his disciples, 'He has been raised from the dead, and indeed he is going ahead of you to Galilee; there you will see him.' This is my message for you." **8** So they left the tomb quickly with fear and great joy, and ran to tell his disciples.

Verse 1: When the Sabbath was past, so on the evening after the Sabbath, as twilight fell with which—according to the Jewish day division—the first day after the Sabbath began, two women come to visit the grave; Mary from Magdala, and the other Mary. "To see (*theoreo*)" is an apt expression for a pious grave visit (otherwise in Matthew only at 27:55).

Verse 2: "And suddenly (*idou*)" again marks (as often in Matthew) the beginning of the narrative proper. An Old Testament theophany motif serves to represent the event as the definitive conquest of the reign of death. Earthquake is a topos of the liberation miracles (Exod 19:16-25; Isa 29:5-9; Jer 4:19-31). Both motifs (the appearing of the angel and his rolling the stone away) form a unit. The point is not that the stone was great (cf. 27:60), but that a heavenly "intervention" was required. In Matthew's mind the opening of the grave is a divine act: an angel of God (cf. 1:20, 24; 2:13, 19) opened the grave. The freeing of Jesus is not described but indicated indirectly. The mention that the angel sat upon the stone indicates solemn behavior (cf. 21:7; 23:22), which leads to the following verse.

Verse 3: "Like lightning . . . white as snow" is an expression of the angel's dignity (cf. Dan 10:6). As in the transfiguration pericope (17:1-9), the double expression stresses the "other-worldliness" of the appearance. The "angelophany" displays traits of epiphany stories, which in turn build upon liberation miracles.

Verse 4: "The guards shook." Matthew's delayed description of the reaction of the grave guards (cf. 27:54) underlines the theophany event once again. Fear (caused by the earthquake) shakes them, and the motif of quaking is taken up in the verb *seio* (quake, shake), and they "became like dead men." The thought of "being dead" is mentioned to stress the contrast to the risen Crucified One (vv. 5, 6). The "like dead men," i.e., the guards, frightened to death, had no share in the freeing process.

Verse 5: "Jesus who was crucified." In contrast to the behavior of the grave guards, the women respond by listening to the angel. "I know" again underlines the authority and sovereignty of the heavenly messenger. He characterizes Jesus as the *"estauromenos"* (the *perfect* characterizes Jesus as permanently "the crucified"); Jesus is the resurrected Son of God whose end-time glory God had revealed proleptically to Peter, James, and John on the mountain of the transfiguration (17:2, 5). Yet, even as the resurrected Son of God, he remains the crucified Son of God, leading the disciples to comprehend both that death on the cross was the central purpose of his ministry and that servanthood is the essence of discipleship.

It seems doubtful that here we have a short Christological creed: emphasized rather is the contrast: the Crucified (v. 5)—the Risen (v. 6) That the women have come "looking for" Jesus is a delayed interpretation of the angel; verse 1 had not yet expressed this thought. The seeking of the Crucified led to the discovery of the Risen One.

Verse 6: "He has been raised." The angel's declaration to the women that "he has been raised" is central to Matthew's resurrection narrative. The passive voice here is the "divine passive," so that what the angel affirms is that "God has raised Jesus from the dead" (cf. 16:21). "As he said" is a redactional addition on Matthew's part which manifests his catechetical argumentative interest: Jesus had said it in the sayings 12:40; 16:21; 17:9; 23; 26:32. The order "Come," urges the women to see for themselves that "he is not here." Thus the angel directs the women from their vain search for the body to a resurrection proclamation, to a task that no longer moves in the dimension of the past, but is directed to the future.

Verse 7: "Ahead of you to Galilee." Notwithstanding the apostasy of the disciples, however, the angel of the Lord enjoins the women on Easter day to go and remind the disciples of Jesus' earlier promise that, following his resurrection, he would precede them to Galilee where, the angel adds, they will see him, the resurrected Jesus as the crucified one.

The revelation event ends in an imperative to the women: Jesus' disciples must be told as quickly as possible! The disciples are on the point of leaving Jerusalem; haste is therefore commanded. The message to the disciples is "He has been raised from the dead!" With the addition "from the dead," the message takes on a confessional character. All the vocabulary expresses the urgency with which Matthew conceives the resurrection as a message to be proclaimed: "come," "see," "and behold." The purpose is that the disciples be told that they will see him in Galilee. And behind it all stands the authority of the heavenly messenger.

Verse 8: The women quickly carry out the order. "With fear and great joy;" the event has inspired both—fear on account of the inconceivable, joy on account of the content of the message. The key words "departed" and "tell" point forward to words in 28:10.

Jesus' Appearance to the Women, 28:9-10

Prior to Jesus' baptism and following his death, Matthew tracks a series of less prominent characters, but always in the interest of conveying information to the reader about Jesus. As the women (also minor characters) obey the angel and depart from the tomb, the resurrected Jesus himself meets them, and he likewise commands them to tell the disciples to make their way to Galilee, where they will see him. In making reference to the disciples, Jesus calls them "my brothers."

> 9 Suddenly Jesus met them and said, "Greetings!" And they came to him, took hold of his feet, and worshiped him. 10 Then Jesus said to them, "Do not be afraid; go and tell my brothers to go to Galilee; there they will see me."

Originally, Mark's Gospel ended with 16:8. Possibly the tradition(s) that Matthew was using ended at the same place. In any case, with verse 9 Matthew's special material in the Easter tradition begins. It consists of three self-contained parts: 1) Jesus' meeting with the women; 2) a cover-up attempt on the part of the Sanhedrin; 3) the commissioning of the eleven disciples by the Risen One. In place and time, verses 9 and 10 seem to be connected with the resurrection account (with the message to the two women). This piece lacks any place/time indications, and connects with verse 11 just as well as with verse 10. So the two verses are an insertion of the redactor, who in the joining treated the stylistic and content discordances lightly.

Verses 9-10: The two verses—verse 10 especially—are basically only a repetition of what has already been said: the assignment to announce to the disciples the upcoming meeting in Galilee was given already in verse 7 by the angel. Yet two special elements are to be noted: 1) here it is Jesus who gives the assignment; 2) a meeting of the Risen with the woman takes place. Here the embracing of Jesus' feet is an expression of reverence. "Do not be afraid!"—reverential awe was to be expected. This was all the more the case since the Risen himself is speaking. "My brothers" is indeed "unusual" but it does not go beyond the frame of New Testament theology. By "brothers" Matthew means Jesus' disciples. This is one of the few texts in the New Testament in which the disciples are so named; above all, it is the only place in which this characterization is found in Jesus' mouth. This command also brings into view his portrayal of the Church as a brotherhood.

First the women were witnesses to a situation worked by God's power: the grave is open and empty. Now a meeting of the women with the Risen One himself is described, if very briefly and reservedly. It is important above all that the disciples (also those in Matthew's community) are declared to be the brothers and sisters of the Risen One. So the faith of the disciples is based not on the interpretation of a single circumstance (empty grave), also not on a divine revelation verbally imparted (the angel's message), but on the experience of a personal meeting with the Risen Jesus himself. The disciples' defection in the hour of humiliation is forgiven. The message that the dead one lives frees them from the night and darkness of non-understanding, from the grip of human defection. Ahead lies Galilee, where Jesus had formed them into disciples. There the Risen One will meet them, but now as the one who through death and resurrection has become their brother and as such determines the spirit of the post-Easter community.

The Soldiers are Bribed to Lie, 28:11-15

Even the death of Jesus does not bring a halt to the hostilities of the religious leaders toward the anointed Son of God, nor of their subterfuge, as the bribing of the guards and the spreading of false rumors regarding the empty tomb indicate. Their guilt is compounded by their refusal to repent, even at the greatest revelation in salvation history.

> **11** While they were going some of the guard went into the city and told the chief priests everything that had happened. **12** After the priests had assembled with the elders, they devised a plan to give a large sum of money to the soldiers, **13** telling them, "You must say, 'His disciples came by night and stole him away while we were asleep.' **14** If this comes to the governor's ears, we will satisfy him and keep you out of trouble." **15** So they took the money and did as they were directed. And this story is still told among the Jews to this day.

The account of the cover-up attempt (in continuation of 27:62-66 and 28:4) is special to Matthew and strengthens the apologetic tendency. The attempt is doomed to failure and the result is that the story remained alive longer (v. 15b).

Verse 11: "Some of the guards." "When certain of the soldiers bring the leaders this news, they not only do not change their minds about Jesus (cf. 21:32) but they bribe the soldiers to spread the lie that the disciples did indeed come and, finding the guard asleep, make off with Jesus' body (28:11-15)" (*Story*, 125). Matthew's word for guard is *koustōdia*, a Latin loan word, which he used already in 27:65-66, each time referring to the guardsmen at the grave. They announce to the chief priests "everything that had happened." They avoid speaking of the Resurrected One or of the resurrection itself—according to verse 4 they had not experienced these—but speak only of the accompaning circumstances (the signs). The chief priests learn from unprejudiced witnesses, that the sign of Jonah spoken to the scribes and Pharisees (12:40) has been seen.

Verse 12: "They devised a plan." The members of the high council could not deny this report as a fact. Therefore through lies and deceptions they seek to render the report, so dangerous for them, harmless. They decide (together with the elders, cf. 27:4) to give a sum of *argyria* (seven times in Matthew's passion account), silver pieces, silver coins, as hush money to the Roman soldiers. This is entirely in keeping with the Sanhedrin's objective, not to allow the resurrection to become public.

Verses 13-14: The soldiers are instructed about what they should say (cf. at 27:64). "While we were asleep" brings the absurdity of the attempted cover up to its high point: the soldiers are required to acknowledge themselves as sleeping witnesses of a theft. Finally they are also told that they need not worry about possible charges of neglect of duty. If it comes to the procurator's ears, they would calm him down (*peitho*, satisfy); the Jews would see to it that the soldiers could be "kept out of trouble."

Verse 15: "Story is still told." Here too, Matthew bursts the bounds of the story he is telling of the life and ministry of Jesus in order to address the implied reader directly, whose position lies beyond the resurrection but short of the Parousia. The soldiers did as they were told. This version of the Easter event was in circulation down to Matthew's time.

The religious leaders show their characteristic traits to the last. They are "corrupt" and "mendacious," bribing the soldiers following the resurrection to spread the lie that Jesus' disciples came by night and stole his body. They are "calumnious," concocting the lie following the resurrection that the disciples were guilty of stealing the body of Jesus.

The Great Commission, 28:18-20

The Great Commission constitutes the major climax not only of the third part of Matthew's story but also of his entire Gospel. The disciples of Jesus, having seen Jesus in Galilee as the crucified one whom God has raised, at last comprehend that suffering sonship entails suffering discipleship (servanthood), and receive from Jesus the commission to go and make all nations his disciples. "In narrating in this fashion the story of the life and ministry of Jesus, Matthew advances a bold theological claim. This claim is, as the passages 1:23 and 28:20 reveal (cf. 18:20), that in the person of Jesus Messiah, his Son, God has drawn near to abide to the end of time with his people, the Church, thus inaugurating the end-time age of salvation" (*Story*, 63).

> 16 Now the eleven disciples went to Galilee, to the mountain to which Jesus had directed them. 17 When they saw him, they worshiped him; but some doubted. 18 And Jesus came and said to them, "All authority in heaven and on earth has been given to me. 19 Go therefore and make disciples of all nations, baptizing them in the name of the Father and of the Son and of the Holy Spirit, 20 and teaching them to obey everything that I have commanded you. And remember, I am with you always, to the end of the age."

Verse 16: "Went to Galilee." "Galilee" is the region in which Jesus discharges his ministry to Israel of teaching, preaching, and healing (4:23), and where he returns following his resurrection to commission his disciples to their worldwide missionary task. "To the mountain"—the mountain is a place visible from a distance (5:14), but since it is uninhabited, it is also a place that makes solitude possible: 14:23. As in 5:1 (8:1), so also here the mountain is the place of revelation, where the Risen One appears to the eleven. Now Jesus meets them as the "brother" who has "gathered" them from their 'having been scattered' (26:31; 28:16)."

Verse 17: "They worshiped him." The *proskynēsis* often found in Matthew (thirteen times) is here attributed to the disciples; it is an act of faith, but doubt is bound up with it, and doubt on the part of all the disciples. "But some doubted *hoi de*" does not have a partitive meaning, but applies to all the disciples, whose faith at times proves to be "little faith" (the verb *diotazo*, doubt, appears elsewhere only in Matthew 14:31, and with the same meaning). On the mountain in Galilee, the risen Jesus reconciles them to himself. Although they can still fall victim to "little faith," they nonetheless undertake the worldwide missionary task to which he commissions them. They all see in the person of Jesus that crucifixion, or suffering sonship, was the essence of his ministry.

Verse 18: "All authority has been given to me." The disciples' resistance had even led them to the point where they committed apostasy (26:47-50. 56. 69-75). Nevertheless, Jesus overcomes their failure and reconciles them to himself. As proof of this, he commissions them at the last to their worldwide ministry. In bringing Jesus to the cross, the religious leaders were convinced that they were purging Israel of a false Messiah and the fraud he had perpetrated. The resurrection reveals this outlook to be wrong. Through the resurrection, God vindicates Jesus in his conflict with them.

Even as the resurrected Son of God, Jesus remains the crucified Son of God. He is the rejected "stone-son" whom God has placed "at the head of the corner." "He is, in fact, Emmanuel, or 'God with us,' the Son conceived of the Spirit in whom God will abide with the disciples until the consummation of the age (1:20, 23; 28:20)" (*Story*, 92).

Verse 19: "Go therefore and make disciples of all nations." The religious leaders had envisaged that Jesus' death would be the sign of Jesus' destruction. Instead, it is the means whereby God achieves salvation for the world, Jew and Gentile alike. The resolution of Jesus' chief conflict with the disciples is that they appropriate his evaluative point of view concerning both himself and them, and receive from him the Great Commission. Equipped with this insight, the disciples are not again commanded by Jesus, as previously, to silence concerning him (16:20; 17-19), but are instead commissioned to go and make all nations his disciples.

Verse 20: "I am with you always." The topical outline of Matthew's life of Jesus and the salvation-historical context within which it has been situated raises the question of the fundamental message of Matthew's story. The key passages 1:21 and 28:20 form an all-embracing inclusion, and highlight this message. At 1:23, Matthew quotes Isaiah in saying of Jesus Emmanuel "God is with us." And at 28:20, the risen Jesus himself declares to the disciples: "I am with you always, to the close of the age." "Strategically located at the beginning and the end of Matthew's story, these two passages 'enclose' it. In combination, they reveal the message of Matthew's story: *In the person of Jesus Messiah, his Son, God has drawn near to abide to the end of time with his people, the Church, thus inaugurating the eschatological age of salvation."* (J. Kingsbury, *Story*, 41).

Index